160 730304 3
D0343978

Housing and Society

*

Housing and Society

****

GLENN H. BEYER
Professor of Housing and Design
Director, Center for Housing and
Environmental Studies
Cornell University

THE MACMILLAN COMPANY
NEW YORK
COLLIER-MACMILLAN LIMITED
LONDON

First Printing

Earlier edition, entitled *Housing: A Factual Analysis*, copyright 1958 by The Macmillan Company.

Library of Congress catalog card number: 65-12480

THE MACMILLAN COMPANY, NEW YORK
COLLIER-MACMILLAN CANADA, LTD., TORONTO, ONTARIO

Printed in the United States of America

To VIRGINIA *and*
VICKY, CARVEL, GLENN, JR., ANN

PREFACE

*

This book is based on an earlier one entitled *Housing: A Factual Analysis.* The Preface to that book began with these words:

> The planning of human shelter was a relatively simple matter in the days of the cave man. Not so today. The complexity of our society and the tremendous advances in science, not only permit, but also require, man's shelter to be much more than protection against the elements. It must satisfy his economic, social and psychological needs as well.

In the few years since that book was published, none of the factors discussed has declined in importance. Rather, most of the problems we had then are still with us, and certain of them seem to have taken on even greater importance.

Also, during the period since *Housing: A Factual Analysis* was published, the author has become aware of certain shortcomings that existed in that volume. Little emphasis, for example, was placed on the historical aspects of housing, and history seems to be more and more important for our understanding of where we are today. Similarly, no attention was given to the international area—and we are constantly becoming involved in it. Housing of the rapidly expanding number of individuals and families in our aging population has emerged as one of the major new housing problem areas. Cooperative housing now has become an important type of housing in the United States. And a new word has been added to our housing vocabulary—the "condominium."

Because of these and many other developments, perhaps of lesser importance, it is gratifying to be able to present a major revision of the entire first work. As a result of its alteration in theme this volume is divided into five parts: Part 1 provides a background and the new historical material, not only concerning housing but also families and cities. Part 2 focuses on the housing market, financing, and the provision of new housing. Part 3 describes the acquisition and consumption of housing. In Part 4, "Housing Problems and Progress," the emphasis is first on problems treated on an areal basis—central city, suburbs and rural areas—and then the special problems of the aging are discussed. Attention then turns to the important role played by the government in the solution of those problems. There is a final chapter in Part 4 concerned with future housing need and research. Part 5 is concerned with the international picture—first, housing in Western Europe and then housing in the developing countries.

This is not a book on theory. Important theories and concepts are dealt with, but emphasis is given to their application. On some of the problems discussed, there has been more conjecture than statement of fact in the past. Fortunately, some new data have recently become available for several of the important aspects covered, from the 1960 Federal censuses of population and housing and other sources, and an attempt has been made to incorporate such new data and information wherever it would be helpful. It is hoped that through the use of such data in several particular chapters a more objective treatment of housing, a subject which has suffered from lack of objectivity in the past, may be achieved.

Because of the range of material covered by the book, each of the various aspects cannot be dealt with in great detail. However, what are believed to be the significant factors are always described and, to assist the reader who is interested in more detail on a particular subject, additional readings are listed in connection with the principal subjects in each chapter.

With the approach taken, this book may be recognized as a compendium of the nontechnical aspects of housing—a look at Housing and Society. Actually, the first book had its beginning in a Seminar at Cornell University. The students had different interests—to become future architects, city planners, home economists, sociologists, public administration officials, and management and labor leaders. The heterogeneous character of this group, having a common interest in housing, was responsible in part for the pattern of the Seminar and the first book, as well as for this revision.

Speaking even more broadly, everyone has some interest in housing, whether that interest is motivated by personal, business, or civic reasons. Therefore, it is hoped that this volume will prove useful not only to students and teachers in the field, but also to industry and agencies concerned with housing and community facilities, lending institutions, public officials, and citizen groups interested in housing—in fact, to anyone who desires to have at hand a volume that provides a description of housing as it exists in the United States in the early 1960's.

Many source materials have been used in the book's preparation, and an attempt has been made to document those sources as completely as possible. Gratitude is herewith extended to the authors and the publishers of those publications.

There are many individuals, in addition to the authors of those source materials, who have been helpful to me. I am especially indebted to Professor Lewis L. Bower of the Department of Housing and Design at Cornell who, on the basis of his use of *Housing: A Factual Analysis* in his teaching, greatly assisted me in the reorganization and elaboration of the original text. Margaret E. Woods, research associate in the Cornell Center for Housing and Environmental Studies, undertook much of the additional library research needed for many of the chapters, and assisted on many general matters. Henry D. Sheldon of the U. S. Bureau of the Census was extremely helpful in assisting me in various ways with certain census data. My most sincere appreciation goes to my secretaries, Nina Rollins, who typed the several drafts, and Mrs. Rosalie Veit for her assistance in preparing much of the manuscript for publication. Appreciation also must be expressed for the friendly and efficient cooperation of the staffs of the various Cornell University libraries, especially that of the reference department of Olin Library.

Finally, as I indicated in the Preface to the original book, a book of this type could never have been prepared unless the proper environment existed. Housing is a new field for study and one that is still just becoming established in many college and university curricula. Cornell has been a pioneer in this field, both because of the interest of many of my colleagues and the interest of students who wanted to study the subject. The founder of Cornell said "I would found an institution where any person can find instruction in any study." This inscription appears on the University Seal. It is not difficult to see, I am sure, how that philosophy offers substantial encouragement in establishing teaching curricula and providing an environment conducive to the writing of a book in the field of housing.

GLENN H. BEYER

Ithaca, New York

CONTENTS

*

Part 1

****

BACKGROUND AND INTRODUCTION

INTRODUCTION

*

What is *housing?* Basically, it is a product—a highly complex product. First, it is a bulky, durable, and permanent product. It has a fixed location, being used only in the place where it is built. Once built, it tends to remain in existence for many years—frequently, long after it has served its usefulness. It becomes almost a part of the land.

Housing, unlike many other industrial products, is not highly standardized. Many types of materials are used in both the structure and in the furnishings. Different kinds of parts and facilities are incorporated. The structure encompasses a complexity of pipes, ducts, wiring, and plumbing. There are single-family houses, duplexes, apartments, row-houses, and many other types. There is no "bluebook" that supplies regular price quotations in the used housing market.

But housing is more than a complex product. It is both an economic and a social process. It plays a tremendous role in the economy of this country. Approximately one fourth of our national wealth is in the form of city and village dwellings. Almost one fourth of the personal consumption expenditure of our population is represented in housing expenditures.

Housing is also important for other economic reasons. For a high proportion of the 100,000 builders it represents their livelihood. For the materials manufacturer it represents a vast market for his product. For the banker it represents an outlet for his funds. It has a close relationship to public utilities. A vigorous housing program opens up vast opportunities for employment.

There are certain idiosyncratic economic aspects that must also be recognized. Housing is not only sold but also rented. The purchase of new housing, in contrast to the need for food and clothing, is postponable. Higher income is likely to mean a new automobile and many other consumer goods before it means a new house. This makes the establishment of effective demand at any one time a complicated task.

Finally, and probably most important of all, housing has highly significant social implications because it provides the shelter for our basic unit—the family. Almost every person is affected in his day-to-day living by the kind of house in which he lives. Housing, therefore, is also urban planning.

There are many evidences of this. Those families who are forced, of necessity, to live in our slums are not given social opportunities equal to those who are able to live in decent, safe, and desirable housing. Unfortunately, houses are socially (but not so readily physically) expansible. This means that widespread doubling-up takes place as a result of economic necessity and under pressure of acute housing shortages.

Since each family is different from every other family, the use of housing remains ruggedly individualistic. Yet, there are some common requirements of housing: it should provide comfort, contentment, health, and aesthetic satisfactions. The idea that ''a man's house is his castle'' is more than a 350-year-old adage.

In short, housing is deeply involved in our social order.

CHAPTER 1

*

History of American Housing

Most volumes written on the subject of American housing in recent years have given little attention to its history. Yet some understanding of this history is important because from the beginning our country has been populated by diverse groups who brought with them their own, greatly varying, cultures and patterns of living. Although immigration is not the important factor today that it was up to a few decades ago, nevertheless we still see many direct evidences of the influences of different cultures in the housing we have and are still building.

Although we usually consider our country as dating back to 1492, the first colonies were not established until the early 1600's—Jamestown in 1607 and Plymouth in 1620. It is known that during the 1500's many ships sailed for America and that some of the people coming on them remained here. Little is known of the houses they built, however, since apparently those houses either fell down or were torn down and forgotten by those who followed.

The colonists coming to America arrived in different parts of what was then known as the North American Continent. Because they came from different mother countries and settled in different climatic regions of the new land, their first homes differed from each other in several respects. Even among those arriving from the same country there were differences in occupation, religion, and sometimes nationality—factors having some bearing on the kind of homes they were to build.

If there were differences, there were also similarities. In most of the colonies, the settlers were, for the most part, artisans, skilled laborers, and farmers, with a scattered representation of other groups. Practically all of them planned to remain in America and to duplicate, insofar as they could, the civilization with which they had been familiar in their homelands. They brought with them tools, equipment, and supplies. Most important, perhaps, they brought the skills and training received in their home countries. Though it is hardly likely that all of them were equally skilled in housebuilding or other trades, records of the time indicate that among the early colonists were sawyers, housewrights, and other craftsmen familiar with methods of housebuilding.

HOMES OF THE COLONISTS, 1600–1820

It appears that some of the first colonists continued to live for several months in the vessels that brought them, until they were able to erect shelters for themselves. Others, whose vessels returned immediately, had to provide makeshift shelter relatively quickly. The first shelters appear to have been cellars dug out on high ground, with lean-to roofs covered with the best natural material at hand. Two descriptions of the situation are offered here. One, by Carpenter, is as follows:

> They huddled together in caves when they could find them; or dug holes into the sides of the hills and made shelters there by driving in poles which they supported by crotched sticks sunken into the ground at right angles. Upon these, as a framework, branches and leaves and grass were fastened, making rude walls and a roof, which, added to the earth at the back and sides, formed their first homes.
>
> In many parts of the colonies, and especially in the South, they built wigwams like those of the Indians, using mats, grass, or deerskins to cover the poles. Farther north they had wigwams and houses of bark.[1]

Another is by Edward Johnson, who, writing in 1645, said:

> After they have found out a place of aboad, they burrow themselves in the earth for their first shelter, under some hill side, casting the earth aloft upon timber; they make a smoaky fire against the earth at the highest side, and thus these poor servants of Christ provide shelter for themselves, their wives and little ones, keeping off the short showers from their lodgings, but the long rains penetrate through to their grate disturbance in the night season, yet in these poor wigwams they sing Psalms, pray, and praise their God, till they can provide them homes, which ordinarily was not wont to be with many till the Earth, by the Lord's blessing, brought forth bread to feed them, their wives and little ones.[2]

Only rough estimates are available for the length of time that the colonists lived in dugouts, wigwams, or huts, but the period seems to have been a relatively short one. It undoubtedly varied from a year or two for some families and in some colonies to several years for others and in other colonies. The temporary housing frequently was left standing and was occupied by later settlers, after better houses had been built by those who came earlier.[3] This mixture of pioneer and relatively permanent homes was to be typical of the American scene across the continent, as long as frontier conditions prevailed.

Early Homes in New England

For a long time the first houses of colonists in North America were thought to have been log cabins, but there is considerable documentation to indicate that few, if any, log dwellings, with the logs laid horizontally, were built by the English or Dutch in their earliest colonial settlements. Shurtleff, in his excellent little book, *The Log Cabin Myth,* was the first to

[1] Frank G. Carpenter, *How the World Is Housed.* New York: American Book Company, 1911, p. 56.

[2] Reprinted from Elbert Farwell Bemis and John Burchard, 2nd, *The Evolving House,* Vol. I, *A History of the Home.* Cambridge, Mass.: The Technology Press, Massachusetts Institute of Technology, 1933, p. 261. By permission of the M. I. T. Press.

[3] Edith L. Allen, *American Housing, as Affected by Social and Economic Conditions.* Peoria: The Manual Arts Press, 1930, p. 23.

widely publicize the fact that the technique of building log dwellings was brought to America by the Swedes around 1640 and did not spread beyond the Delaware settlement until the eighteenth century.[4]

The first houses of the New Englanders repeated two types prevalent in the part of England from which these colonists came.[5] One was a one-and-a-half-story cottage; the other, a two-story house with gabled roof. The two-story house usually was half-timbered with spaces filled in by wattle and daub. Its best-known features are the projection of the second story over the first, usually across the front of the house only, and the decorative "dewdrop" customarily hanging from each end of the projection. The reason for this overhang has not been traced. Protection of the lower-story walls against rain is given as one reason, the desire to compensate for high land costs by utilizing air space in medieval European cities is another. From the existence of this type of house in Europe, however, it seems to be clearly established that the design was not devised by the colonists for protection against Indians.

The more typical dwelling of the average New Englander was the one-and-a-half-story cottage. This type, known by its gable roof and low one-story eaves, was particularly in evidence along Cape Cod, where building materials were scarce, but it was built throughout New England. In fact, this cottage, or one identical with it in most essential features, appeared in nearly all the other colonies. In later centuries it became the typical American small house.

House frames were hand hewn—a practice followed in building American houses until the nineteenth century, when the balloon frame was invented—and were usually of oak. Roofs were thatched at first, and consequently steep. Most early houses had wooden chimneys, which were lined with clay, though stone chimneys were built in some better houses. In houses with more than one room, the chimney was in the center of the building rather than at the end.

According to Bemis and Burchard, the first sawmill permit was issued in 1649, which would indicate that, before that time: "There were no mills for the manufacture of lumber and all boards were sawed by two men, one working in a saw pit; every joist was hewn four-square with an axe; every nail, bolt, hinge, and lock hammered out individually."[6] In spite of the labor of timber construction, however, most houses in New England were built of wood. One reason was the scarcity of lime, which hampered the use of either stone, abundant in most of New England, or brick, which was being manufactured by 1634.[7] Another reason, of course, was that wood had advantages—its abundance and the greater ease with

[4] Harold R. Shurtleff, *The Log Cabin Myth.* Cambridge, Mass.: Harvard University Press, 1939, p. 3.

[5] Thomas J. Wertenbaker, *The Puritan Oligarchy: The Founding of American Civilization.* New York: Charles Scribner's Sons, 1947, p. 15.

[6] *Op. cit.*, p. 266.

[7] Allen, *op. cit.*, p. 30.

which it could be shaped into suitable building material, as compared with the large stones available.

The houses were not painted until 1734. Windows—what few there were—were small in the early homes and were placed more in accordance with the need for lighting on the inside than for symmetrical balance on the outside. Glass was costly and had to be imported. Numerous attempts were made in colonial times to manufacture glass, but not until after 1790 was any one of them successful on a continuing basis. In the early houses, sliding shutters were customary and window openings were covered with oiled paper; in some areas this practice continued well into the eighteenth century. According to Weeden, "In 1745 not a house in Kennebec (now Maine) had a square of glass in it."[8] However, in other areas, and particularly in better homes, glass was used even during the seventeenth century and windows also were larger. Windows were of the casement type. Most of them opened, but a number were stationary.[9]

It was not long before the colonists learned that some changes in their houses would be needed to meet the rigors of the American climate. Thatch—a constant fire hazard, from the sun in summer or sparks from the chimney in winter—soon was replaced by wood, and the use of shingles for roof covering became fairly widespread by about 1690. Wattle and daub could not withstand violent rains, and clapboards became standard covering for the outside of the house.

Probably one of the most typical features of colonial housing was the relative ease with which existing houses could be adapted to changing circumstances. There were, of course, numerous variations in the way this adaptation was accomplished. Quite often the changes began by converting the loft to a full-sized room. Another room, with a full-sized room above, was built on the other side of the chimney. A lean-to might be added across the back of the house. This latter method changed the shape of the houses and they came to be called "salt-boxes" from their resemblance to early salt boxes. Curiously enough, larger houses came in for a share of conversion as well. Wertenbaker traces changes made in the house in Salem that later became known as the "House of the Seven Gables." This house had been originally a two-story house, with two bedrooms on the second floor, and an attic. As the owner grew more prosperous ". . . he found need for a store. . . . So he built a lean-to in the rear, to which he transferred the kitchen, and converted the old kitchen into the store. Later, he made an addition in front of the hall, which contained a large parlor, the great chamber over it and the great chamber garret. . . ."[10]

Houses usually were rectangular in shape. Ceilings were low. In the one-room cottage, the room, of course, served as kitchen, dining room, living room, and bedroom. The use of the kitchen–living room did not inter-

[8] William B. Weeden, *Economic and Social History of New England, 1620–1789,* Vol. II. Boston: Houghton, Mifflin Company, 1891, p. 531.

[9] Hugh Morrison, *Early American Architecture from the First Colonial Settlements to the National Period.* New York: Oxford University Press, 1952, p. 35.

[10] *Op. cit.,* p. 121.

fere with daytime activities since, in many houses, the bed was fastened to the wall on one side, hooked up and concealed by curtains during the day, and lowered at night. The loft, reached by a ladder or sometimes by stairs, served as a sleeping place for children and as a storage place for food and household supplies. The fireplace, used for cooking and heating, was large—usually large enough for logs several feet long—and in or near it hung kettles and pots for cooking. Quite often the oven protruded through the outside wall of the house. When lean-tos were added, cooking and some other household activities, such as candle-making, were transferred there.

In two-room houses, one room (called the hall) served for general living purposes. The other room was the parlor; it was used to receive important guests, such as the minister, and for important family gatherings—as on Sundays or at weddings or funerals. The parlor also served as a guest bedroom. Customarily, the family's best furniture was kept there.

Furniture was simple and solid, quite often painted, and usually homemade. A table, backless benches, and high and low stools made up most of the furnishings. Clothing and utensils were stored in chests and dressers. Some families had trestle tables, but more often tables were small, and larger families ate their meals in shifts, rather than together. Gateleg tables that could be folded up and placed against the wall when not in use were common.

Following the development of commerce, particularly in the fishing industry, the New England colonies prospered, and some families became wealthy. This new wealth found expression in some fine architectural dwellings and public buildings, beginning shortly after mid-seventeenth century. From then until approximately the time of the Revolution, an architectural style called Late Colonial, which was in effect an adaptation of the Georgian style then prevalent in England, was adopted by wealthy citizens for their homes.

Basic characteristics of this style were balance and proportion. Though brick was sometimes used in the seaport towns, the Late Colonial house was generally made of wood and was painted on the outside. Roofs were lower, and it was during this period that the well-known "captain's walk" was developed—the roof became nearly flat and was enclosed by a railing. Sometimes a cupola was added. Unfortunately for local pride, rather than having been invented in Salem for the use of sea captains, both these features seem to have been imported.[11] Both windows and window panes became larger, and sliding sash windows replaced the casement ones. The change in appearance from the earlier colonial was most noticeable in the even spacing of windows on either side of the doorway. During the eighteenth century, homes of the middle class and farmhouses in New England took on many of these same characteristic features.

Inside these finer houses, ceilings were plastered and walls paneled or papered (by this time paper was being manufactured in the colonies, though the wealthy continued to import it). The kitchen, dining room, and living room became separate rooms, with the kitchen in the back of the

[11] Morrison, *op. cit.*, p. 307.

house. One of the principal features of the new style was the height of the ceilings. In most of the earlier houses, ceilings had been just high enough to clear the heads of normal people, but by the middle of the eighteenth century they were raised to 11 feet and by about 1770 some were even higher. Obviously, this height was only for elegance and had the drawback of making the homes difficult to heat—one of the reasons homes of this type were more popular in the southern climate.

Furniture in these homes, as might be expected, became more elaborate. A wider variety of pieces came into use—secretaries, wing chairs, side chairs, side tables, and others. Some chairs were upholstered, and nearly all pieces had rich carving and were usually made of walnut or mahogany. Some of the furniture undoubtedly was imported, but colonial craftsmen were able to duplicate the English designs successfully. Banjo clocks were invented in Massachusetts during this period, and colonial contributions to household furnishings in the eighteenth century included the silver work of Paul Revere.[12] A distinctive American contribution to home furniture, the Windsor chair, was designed about 1725 and became popular.

Some changes in the design of houses took place following the Revolution, though the models continued to be European. The period from about 1780 to 1820 is usually called the Federal period. The changes were chiefly in design features, and, particularly in New England, represented a continuation of the "dignity" and "restrained ornamentation" of the Late Colonial style and an accentuation of some of its features. Balustrades were lowered to the eaves and practically concealed the roofs. Doorways became more prominent. Carving and ornamentation became finer and subordinated to the over-all plan.[13] Again, this was not the type of housing occupied by most of the people in New England. It was, rather, one more style added to the growing collection, a collection which ranged from this highly developed architectural product to the simple cabins and small houses along the New England frontier.

Homes in the Middle Atlantic Colonies

In contrast to New England, which was settled primarily by the English, the Middle Atlantic colonies were settled by different national and religious groups. These included the Dutch, Quakers, Germans, Swedes, and others.

Homes of the Dutch

The first Dutch, who arrived in 1624 to found the colony of New Netherland, undoubtedly had to live briefly in the same kind of crude huts and pits dug into the ground as had the New Englanders. They must have soon built houses, however, because, according to Carpenter: "Within six years after the Pilgrims first landed on Plymouth Rock . . . there were . . . thirty

[12] H. P. Osborne, *An Outline of the Home Furnishing Periods.* Long Beach: Outline Publishing Company, 1941, p. 90.

[13] Morrison, *op. cit.*, p. 501.

dwellings on the island of Manhattan, and all but one were of bark."[14] This was only a few years after the Dutch had purchased the island from the Indians for the sum of $24.

The first houses of the Dutch were undoubtedly built of wood. Apparently large windmills were set up early by the West India Company, in an effort to develop an export trade in timber and clapboards, and consequently planks and even small beams for housebuilding were abundant.[15] However, most houses in Holland had been built of brick, and since suitable clay and limestone were available, kilns were soon built (1628) so that those houses could be copied in North America. In the rural areas in upstate New York, stone was too abundant to be ignored and was used as a building material.

Alice Earle provides a description of some of these early houses in New Amsterdam:

> Dutch houses were set close to the sidewalk with the gable-end to the street; and had the roof notched like steps,—corbel-roof was the name; and these ends were often of brick, while the rest of the walls were of wood. The roofs were high in proportion to the side walls, and hence steep; they were surmounted usually in Holland fashion with weather-vanes in the shape of horses, lions, geese, sloops, or fish; a rooster was a favorite Dutch weather-vane. There were metal gutters sticking out from every roof almost to the middle of the street; this was most annoying to passers-by in rainy weather, who were deluged with water from the roofs. The cellar windows had small loop-holes with shutters. The windows were always small; some had only sliding shutters, others had but two panes or quarels of glass, as they were called, which were only six or eight inches square. The front doors were cut across horizontally in the middle into two parts, and in early days were hung on leather hinges instead of iron.
>
> . . . Every house had a porch or "stoep," flanked with benches, which were constantly occupied in the summer time; and every evening, in city and village alike, an incessant visiting was kept up from stoop to stoop.[16]

Actually, there were two kinds of Dutch houses in the early colonies, based upon where the immigrants came from and where they settled. One kind was built primarily in New Amsterdam, Albany, and the area around Albany. The people building these houses came for the most part from Amsterdam and nearby cities in that region of Holland. Although many of the houses built by these people had straight pitched roofs, many other houses had the stepped gable typical of houses in Amsterdam during that period. The other kind was built primarily on Long Island, in northern New Jersey, and in southern New York. The people building these homes were primarily Flemish immigrants (and Walloons) from south Holland, who settled in the farm regions of the new territory. The most typical feature of the houses built by these people was the sweep of the eaves and the pronounced over-

[14] *Op. cit.*, p. 56.

[15] Thomas J. Wertenbaker, *The Founding of American Civilization: The Middle Colonies.* New York: Charles Scribner's Sons, 1938, p. 47.

[16] Alice Morse Earle, *Home Life in Colonial Days.* New York: The Macmillan Company, 1898, pp. 9–10.

hang of the roof. This feature was carried over as a part of the immigrants' European inheritance.

One interesting aspect of the early Dutch houses is that they differed considerably from what we consider "Dutch Colonial" architecture today. That style of architecture is typified by the gambrel roof—a curved roof with the upper slope being flatter than the lower slopes, which are relatively steep. This type of roof was not introduced in the Dutch colonies until the eighteenth century. Bailey gives it high praise by indicating: "It is a distinctive architecture and our only indigenous form until the coming of the modern skyscraper."[17]

Several authors writing in recent times have said that technically "Dutch Colonial" is a misnomer. The reason for this seems to be that this type of architecture came into existence after the fall of the New Netherland government. Nevertheless, it seems that the Dutch should still be given credit for it, as the cutting back of the top of the roof to form an obtuse angle at the ridge, combined with the curve or flare at the bottom of the roof is a distinct characteristic of homes built by the Dutch people during this period.[18]

In their early homes, the Dutch tended to have their living rooms on one floor and to use the attic or loft solely for storage of food and household gear. Later, bedrooms were finished off in the attic. The earliest houses probably were one-room affairs, with the fireplace in the middle of the building. As in New England, numerous examples of enlarging houses can be found in the Dutch colonial area. One plan was to build another room of the same size next to the existing room, on the side away from the chimney. This room usually was called the "best bedroom-parlor"; the other was for general cooking–eating–living activities. A ladder, or sometimes a stairway—enclosed, so that valuable heat would not be wasted—led to the loft. Quite often, also, the kitchen was in another wing or, sometimes, in the basement. A characteristic feature of Dutch houses was the built-in bed, in an alcove, concealed by curtains during the day, ". . . so that you may go thro' all the rooms . . . and never see a bed."[19] Houses were further enlarged by adding two narrow rooms at the rear; these were used as bedrooms and also had built-in beds. At first, entrance to these rear rooms was through the front rooms, but later houses had a central hall that led to them.[20] Walls usually were whitewashed or painted white, though wainscoting also was used. Pictures of Scriptural scenes hung on the walls, as did china, Delft, or earthen plates.[21] The scrubbing and rubbing that produced the cleanliness of the Dutch household are so traditional as scarcely to need elaboration here.

In the cities, some two-story houses were built, and city houses could be

[17] Rosalie F. Bailey, *Pre-Revolutionary Dutch Houses and Families in Northern New Jersey and Southern New York*. New York: William Morrow & Company, 1936, p. 20.

[18] *Ibid.*, p. 21.

[19] Quoted in Wertenbaker, *The Middle Colonies, op. cit.*, p. 53.

[20] Thomas Tileston Waterman, *The Dwellings of Colonial America*. Chapel Hill: The University of North Carolina Press, 1950, pp. 201–202.

[21] Wertenbaker, *The Middle Colonies, op. cit.*, p. 53.

enlarged by adding another story as well as by adding rooms. Wood was used at first, and later was replaced by brick. A Swedish traveler, Peter Kalm, described New York in the mid-eighteenth century:

> Most of the houses are built of bricks and are generally strong and neat, and several stories high. Some had, according to the old architecture, turned the gable-ends toward the streets; but the new houses were altered in this respect. Many of the houses had a balcony on the roof, on which people used to sit in the evenings in the summer season; and from thence they had a pleasant view of a great part of the town and likewise part of the adjacent water, and of the opposite shore. The roofs are commonly covered with tile or shingles; the latter of which are made of the white fir which grows higher up in the country. . . . The walls are white-washed within and I did not see hangings, with which the people of this country seem in general to be but little acquainted. The walls were quite covered with all sorts of drawings and pictures in small frames. On each side of the chimneys they had usually a sort of alcove and the wall under the windows was wainscotted and had benches placed near it. The alcove and all the woodwork were painted with a bluish gray color.[22]

As it had in New England, prosperity soon arrived in the Dutch colonies, especially after the development of the lucrative fur trade. The colony was taken over by the English in 1664 and gradually English influences, in domestic as well as public life, began to prevail. The colony, however, always retained some of its Dutch atmosphere.[23] In housing, the Dutch Colonial style prevailed in the rural areas and the fashionable Georgian manner of building was for most of the eighteenth century confined to homes of the very wealthy or to public buildings. The only exceptions were some Georgian and some Federal type houses built in some of the villages along the Mohawk River and westward by New Englanders who moved into the state in the late eighteenth century.

Homes of the Quakers

The impetus for the colonization of parts of New Jersey, Delaware, and Pennsylvania sprang mainly from William Penn, a young Quaker, who came to America to find both a religious sanctuary and wealth. He had inherited a large tract of land, corresponding roughly to present-day Pennsylvania, upon the death of his father in 1670. In his search for settlers, Penn encouraged immigration not only by those of the Quaker religion, who were, of course, to be the dominating element, but also by people of other nationalities and religions—German Protestants, Scotch-Irish Presbyterians, Welsh Baptists, Irish Catholics, and others.

The early settlers, who began arriving in 1682, had rude shelters; along the Delaware, many lived in caves. Apparently these caves were used longer than the governing officials thought they should have been, since the settlers around Philadelphia were urged to build houses for themselves so that the caves might be destroyed completely by 1687. Wood and brick—the latter

[22] Quoted in Waterman, *op. cit.*, p. 208.

[23] D. M. Ellis, *et al.*, *A Short History of New York State*. Ithaca, N.Y.: Cornell University Press, 1957, p. 28.

taking precedence eventually, especially in Philadelphia—were used in Quaker construction, but stone was used also, in places where it was abundant. Sawmills were in operation by 1683, and brick kilns at about the same time. In this region, wooden houses were painted outside and inside from the beginning.[24]

The most characteristic Quaker houses were built in Philadelphia. These houses were usually two or three stories high, narrow in front and deep, with the roof ridge parallel to the short side. Conspicuous features were the pent roof between the windows of the first and second stories, and, sometimes, a door hood. In Philadelphia, three-story houses with small balconies were characteristic. Houses in rural areas and smaller settlements near Philadelphia were much the same as those in the city, except that they had a larger frontage and were more commonly two stories high. Windows were large and well spaced (generally not casement), an indication of the influence of the style prevalent in London at the time the colony was founded.

Pennsylvania, as Shurtleff points out, ". . . was the first English colony to be established on the site of an earlier one by a different race. There were several hundred people of Swedish and Finnish stock within twenty-five miles of Philadelphia when William Penn's first English contingent arrived in 1682."[25] Penn recommended to his settlers a plan that he most likely derived from the homes of the Swedish settlers ". . . build then, a House of thirty foot long and eighteen broad, with a partition neer the middle, and an other to divide one end of the House into two small Rooms."[26] Innumerable variations of this plan have been found in Quaker homes. The most usual seems to have consisted of one large and one small room, with a corner fireplace in each. Sheathed staircases led to the second floor, the plan of which was like that of the first floor.[27] This type of house became fairly standard in homes of the middle class by the first quarter of the eighteenth century.

Philadelphia became a prosperous and important city within about a decade of its founding. As in the cities of New England, prosperous merchants and other wealthy citizens built their homes in the Georgian style, and, later, other wealthy citizens built homes in the Federal style. The Georgian style penetrated rural areas as well, but pent roofs lingered on in rural houses for a considerable period and rough stone continued to be used as a building material.

Homes of the Swedish Colony

In 1638 the Swedish West India Company founded a fur-trading colony on Delaware Bay. The colony covered parts of Pennsylvania, New Jersey, and Delaware. This colony consisted of a ". . . few fortified posts on the bay

[24] Harold Donaldson Eberlein, *The Architecture of Colonial America.* Boston: Little, Brown, and Company, 1925, p. 250.

[25] *Op. cit.,* p. 123.

[26] Quoted in Waterman, *op. cit.,* p. 125.

[27] *Ibid.,* p. 129.

and river, populated by servants of the Company with only enough agricultural population to raise cattle and grow food for the rest.''[28]

While much less attention is devoted by most historians, including those writing about housing, to the contribution of the Swedes than is given to that of the English and Dutch settlers, the Swedes were responsible for introducing into the American colonies the type of house that, in later years, was to become the most historic—the log cabin.[29]

In building their log cabins, the Swedes used round or squared logs notched at the corners, with the ends protruding. A Dutch settler who made a tour of the colonies in 1679-1680 describes one:

> The house . . . was . . . made according to the Swedish mode, and as they usually build their houses here, which are blockhouses, or houses of hewn logs, being nothing else than entire trees, split through the middle or somewhat squared out of the rough, these trees are laid in the form of a square upon each other as high as they wish to have the house, the ends of these timbers are let into each other, about a foot from the ends of them. So stands the whole building without a nail or a spike, the ceiling and roof do not show much finer work, except among the most particular who also have all the ceiling planked and also a glass window. The doors are wide enough but very low, so that everyone must stoop to enter in, always these houses are very tight and warm, but the chimney stands in a corner.[30]

Though several plans were used for interiors, a typical log cabin in the Delaware area had the three-room plan recommended by William Penn to his colonists, with one large room for living and household activities, one of the smaller rooms used for sleeping, and the other as an entry.

Log cabins as pioneer homes did not spread much beyond the Swedish colony before the end of the seventeenth century. Even within the colony, in fact, English settlers living near the Swedes continued to build and live in frame houses.[31] Though the Swedes exercised considerable influence on American housing in the next two centuries, the colony itself lasted only until 1655, when it was taken over by the Dutch.

Homes of the Pennsylvania Germans

After about 1709, when a series of misfortunes had all but driven them from their land, Germans from the Rhine Palatinate responded to William Penn's appeals and began arriving in the Pennsylvania area. Their number included also Germans from other provinces, Walloons, Dutch, French

[28] Shurtleff, *op. cit.*, p. 164.

[29] The authority for this conclusion is Harold R. Shurtleff, author of *The Log Cabin Myth*, whose interests combined architecture and social history. He first became interested in the subject of log cabins while Director of the Research Department set up in connection with the restoration of Williamsburg, Virginia. Later, he entered the Graduate School at Harvard University, where he attempted to establish by documentary proof the actual nature of the first dwellings in the early English settlements and to discover the origin of the log cabin in the United States.

[30] Shurtleff, *op. cit.*, pp. 169–70, quoting from the *Journal of Jasper Danckaerts*, as published in the Original Narratives series, B. B. James and J. F. Jameson, eds.

[31] Shurtleff, *op. cit.*, p. 170.

Huguenots, and probably other nationalities as well. Though there were artisans and mechanics among them, most of the group had been farmers at home, and most of them looked for homes in the fertile lands beyond Philadelphia.

Log cabins were known in most of the northern European countries, and, as had the Swedes, the Germans built log cabins for their pioneer houses. Their method of construction was different from that of the Swedes, according to Wertenbaker, who states:

> The Germans, unlike the Swedes, usually squared the logs, and fitted them one into the other at the corners with an exact and peculiar notching, which lends strength to the walls, reduces the space between logs, and sheds the water outward. The German log house, unlike the typical American log cabin, was not intended to save labor, and is often a marvel of painstaking and skillful workmanship.[32]

Since they came from different parts of Germany, the Germans brought more than one type of cabin with them. A typical one, however, was rectangular in shape, and was usually one-and-a-half (though sometimes two) stories high, with the chimney in the center of the wall.[33] Quite often, baking was done in an outside oven, as in Germany. This was a roofed stone structure, with shelves provided for the cooking utensils. The interiors of the cabins were plain. Floors usually were made of logs or stone, though some cabins had dirt floors. A ladder led to the loft, and furniture was plain and sturdy.

Usually, the first generation lived in the log cabins throughout their lifetimes. Pennsylvania Dutch (German) architecture, however, is best known from the sturdy stone houses with adjoining barns so plentiful in the valleys east of Lancaster, Pennsylvania, built for the most part by subsequent generations of settlers. On them, tiles or shingles replaced thatch for roofing. The interior floor plan in these houses was much the same as that in some of the Dutch and English colonial houses—living hall on one side of the entrance vestibule, the best room on the other side, and the attic for storage and additional sleeping space. Larger houses, of course, had somewhat more elaborate plans and furnishings. Nearly all houses had decorative hand carving, and German legends and folklore were expressed in paintings on chests and in other decorative handiwork.[34]

Homes in the South Atlantic Colonies

The first colony in the South Atlantic region is known to have been that established by Sir Walter Raleigh on Roanoke Island (now in North Carolina) in 1585. However, that colony was short lived, and there is no information available concerning the nature of the homes in which the colonists lived. The next colonization took place at Jamestown, Virginia, in 1607.

[32] *The Middle Colonies, op. cit.*, p. 300.
[33] *Ibid.*, p. 305.
[34] *Ibid.*, pp. 325–345.

Other important colonization in this region was at St. Mary's (in Maryland) in 1634.

According to Shurtleff, "... Jamestown housing was rough, temporary, and haphazard for a comparatively long space of time."[35] Sawmills were not in operation until about 1625, and other necessary items for housebuilding were scarce. Earle provides an example:

> Nails were costly, as were all articles manufactured of iron. . . . When persons were leaving houses, they sometimes set them on fire to gather up the nails from the ashes. To prevent this destruction of buildings, the government of Virginia gave to each planter who was leaving his house as many nails as the house was estimated to have in its frame, provided the owner would not burn the house down.[36]

Bricks seem to have been made at an early date and were used sometimes for the foundations on which the houses rested, and later for chimneys. However, an all-brick house was not built until 1636,[37] and wood remained the usual construction material for houses during the seventeenth century.

The typical dwelling of the tobacco planters of both Virginia and Maryland was a frame cottage, very similar to that found along the shores of New England—one-and-a-half stories high, about 45 feet by 20 feet, with casement windows (some possibly glazed and others provided with shutters only), and steep roofs. Many early cottages, particularly in Virginia, had a porch which extended up to the roof, with the entry enclosed by arches and a small bedroom overhead.[38] As in New England, most of the small dwellings began as one-room houses. When they were enlarged, the additional room was built "... at the end away from the chimney, and this in turn had a chimney in its end wall."[39] Other additions might be made also, but "... the houses followed the same general plan and where there were many apartments they were apt to be in the nature of ells or extensions clustered in a rambling manner about the central core which was of the type common to the country."[40]

In the two-room house, the second room was the parlor. Sometimes a room for sleeping was partitioned off from the general all-purpose living room. In the early days in the Southern colonies, cooking was done inside the house, over the open fireplace, but well before the end of the century kitchen activities were moved to a building separate from the house, an arrangement made feasible by both climate and the presence of servants. Servants lived in detached quarters away from the house.

In South Carolina, early houses had more of a cosmopolitan tinge than those in Virginia and Maryland, a reflection of the admixture of nationalities of which that early settlement was composed. The first colonists, who arrived in South Carolina in 1670, were mainly English and Barbadians,

[35] *Op. cit.*, p. 135.

[36] *Op. cit.*, p. 11.

[37] Waterman, *op. cit.*, p. 13.

[38] Thomas J. Wertenbaker, *The Old South: The Founding of American Civilization.* New York: Charles Scribner's Sons, 1942, p. 76.

[39] Waterman, *op. cit.*, p. 14.

[40] Eberlein, *op. cit.*, pp. 91-92.

as one purpose of the colony at Charleston was to provide homes for the excess white population of Barbados. Also, whereas the subsequent immigration to the other English colonies had been, for the most part, English, South Carolina had numerous immigrants from the West Indies, and, after 1680, a large contingent of French Huguenots.

Wood was the material used for the first permanent houses, of which there were about a hundred in Charleston by 1682.[41] Wertenbaker describes a Charleston house as follows:

> Typical was the so-called single house, the narrow end fronting directly on the street in the manner of Amsterdam or Delft, the main door in the center of the long side, leading into an entrance hall. Since the house was but one room deep, the apartments of each floor were strung out one behind the other.[42]

With this plan, cross ventilation was possible for each room. Morrison credits it with being the ". . . best achieved anywhere in the entire South for withstanding a hot climate and, together with the town's sea breezes and relative freedom from malaria-bearing mosquitoes, accounts for the fact that most of the plantation folk took refuge here for the summer."[43] These were typical houses of the middle and professional class and working men.

Following a fire in 1740, the use of wood as construction material was officially banned—even wooden shingles were prohibited and were to be replaced by tile, slate, or stone—although there is evidence that many wooden homes continued to be built. Typical features of Charleston houses became the stuccoed brick walls, window balconies, and some Dutch features such as the curved Flemish gable and beam anchors. Most typical of all was the piazza across the long side of the house, a feature adapted from housing in the West Indies.

With increased wealth, houses, of course, became larger, especially those of the merchants, who frequently had their shops on the first floor. The kitchen and other quarters were in a wing at the rear, though some were separate from the main house. Wertenbaker quotes an advertisement of a house for sale in 1734 which described it as being ". . . three stories high, 'with two rooms on a floor,' the 'brick kitchen, chaise-house and stable for three horses' apart from the main structure."[44]

In rural areas, the one-and-a-half-story cottage, with a door in both front and rear and an entrance hall, was common. This, according to Morrison, was destined ". . . to become typical in the next century for plantation houses facing a river prospect on one side and a main approach on the land side. . . ."[45]

Prosperity came to the Southern colonies with the development of trade in the staple crops—tobacco, rice, and indigo. Numerous new homes were built as more families acquired wealth and as the plantations moved farther

[41] Morrison, *op. cit.*, p. 170.
[42] *The Old South, op. cit.*, p. 275.
[43] *Op. cit.*, p. 171.
[44] *The Old South, op. cit.*, p. 275.
[45] *Op. cit.*, p. 172.

inland along the river valleys. These homes incorporated the basic features of the Georgian style as evidenced in New England, in their architecture, in interiors, and also in their furnishings. In the South, the American style resembled the Georgian of England in treatment and materials more closely than did the Late Colonial homes in New England.

Georgian influence was to be seen in the houses in southern towns in the exterior decorative details and in the elaboration of the interior surfaces. However, the Georgian style, as Wertenbaker points out, was at its best "... only when there is space for a main pavilion, square or nearly square, set back from the street, with emphasis upon a central doorway approached by stairs, the whole set off, if possible, by flanking subsidiary buildings."[46] Space in the cities did not always permit the fullest expression of Georgian, and consequently many of the best examples of this style in the South are to be found in the plantation country. In Charleston, especially, the well-developed distinctive style of housing resisted incursions of Georgian and later styles, except for a few characteristic features, as, for example, a Georgian entrance or some decorative trim. Exceptions to this, of course, are cities that were being built, or rebuilt, when a particular style was at its height.

Georgian style houses in the South often consisted of a large central rectangular block, two stories high, flanked by one-story units aligned with the main house in a manner designed to emphasize its dignity and importance. A row of columns was added to some porches, as at Mt. Vernon. Others had porticoed doorways. The interiors retained the characteristic features of earlier Southern colonial houses—some bedrooms on the first floor and a hall large enough to be used as a living room, as it frequently was. Stairways were graceful in design and were ornamented by carved balusters and newel posts.

As some of the first buildings in the Federal style that followed the Revolution were constructed in the South, the influence of this new style was felt there early. The style expressed a classical simplicity that was considered fitting for the new Republic whose leaders apparently sought to demonstrate a kinship with the ancient republics of Greece and Rome. Monticello is a well-known example of this style.[47] The temple form, based on Roman designs, was one basis of the style. Another was the circular Roman temple form (e.g., Monticello), with rooms symmetrically placed around a central unit. Exteriors of some houses had curved projections.

Inside the houses, the designs of the Federal period replaced the ornate decorative carving of the Georgian period. White was used on the interior surfaces, as part of the classical motif. Rooms sometimes were oval, and some had projecting bays. Another change, possibly more important and certainly more permanent, was evident in the organization of the interior. A trend toward privacy in living arrangements had been exhibited in Georgian homes, with separate rooms provided for different functions. In

[46] *The Old South, op. cit.*, pp. 283–284.
[47] Eberlein, *op. cit.*, p. 164.

the typical Federal house, there was even more specialization of rooms for different functions, and the design and furnishings of the room reflected its specific purpose. Library, study, and offices were added, particularly in Southern homes, which were the center of a complex agricultural community and an active social life. In the dining rooms, for instance, a recessed place for the sideboard was part of the design of the room. Dressing rooms were separated from sleeping rooms. Privacy from servants' activities was achieved by the addition of a back stairs. In the main hall, stairs often were placed in an alcove. (In some Northern houses, a serving pantry was added between kitchen and dining room; in others, quite often the kitchen was in the basement.) In Southern houses, sometimes the main living rooms were on a separate floor from the entrance hall, and the kitchen and buildings for most of the household activities remained, of course, apart from the main house.[48]

Features such as these frequently made the houses comfortable as well as impressive. Conveniences, however, such as central heating, cookstoves, or inside toilets, were practically nonexistent even for the wealthy, and bathing with frequency or regularity was not yet considered a necessity.

In the South as in the North, of course, no one style completely accounted for all the houses. Much of the area was still in the colonial phase. Georgia, for example, settled in 1732, did not share the general prosperity of the period preceding the Revolution. A few houses were built in the Georgian style, but it exercised little influence. For the most part, one-and-a-half-story cottages, similar to those in Virginia in the seventeenth century, were the typical permanent houses. Homes of the planters in Georgia were typical of homes of planters in other colonies—rectangular houses of four or five rooms with simple furnishings. Also, many large houses in all parts of the South simply "grew" through the numerous additions that were made to meet the needs of their owners. Some of these might have a few architectural details of a prevalent style.

The cabins of the slaves were usually one-room affairs designed for one family; if there was more than one room, more than one family usually lived in the cabin. The cabins were set out in rows, and interiors varied according to the attitudes of the owner. Some might have wooden floors and brick chimneys; others had wooden chimneys and no floors. Light was provided by the fireplace. Furnishings were simple and confined to the barest necessities.[49]

Along the Piedmont and in the Shenandoah Valley were farming regions peopled by Germans, Scotch-Irish, and other small farmers from the coastal South who, unable to compete with the big plantations, had moved into the Piedmont and beyond. In this section of the Southern states, the log cabin was the typical pioneer dwelling. These usually began as one-room dwellings

[48] Fiske Kimball, *Domestic Architecture of the American Colonies and of the Early Republic*. New York: Charles Scribner's Sons, 1922, pp. 145–261.

[49] Edgar W. Martin, *The Standard of Living in 1860*. Chicago: University of Chicago Press, 1942, p. 133.

about 16 feet by 24 feet, and were later enlarged to two rooms. A common type that developed was made up of two separate cabins, with lofts, connected by a covered passageway. Sometimes the ladder to the lofts was in the passageway. This open area provided a pleasant living space for the family during the hot summers. This type of cabin, also built in other areas where pioneers settled, had various names—in parts of the South it was popularly known as the "dog-trot" cabin. Many of these cabins were replaced eventually by stone houses, with the log cabin retained sometimes as a wing of the later house. Many of the newer houses exhibited characteristics of Late Colonial Georgian, but, in their plain and sturdy style, were completely unlike the homes of the planters.

Colonial Buildings in the Far Southeast and Southwest

Long before the colonization of New England and the Middle Atlantic and South Atlantic regions, Spanish explorers were sailing to and penetrating other parts of what is now the United States. Ponce de Leon landed near St. Augustine in 1513, there was a voyage into Tampa Bay in 1528, another up the Rio Grande to the region of El Paso in 1535, and some exploration of the Pacific Coast beyond what is now San Francisco in 1542. The city of St. Augustine was founded in 1565.

Though the Spanish built missions and forts in the Southeast, fires and intermittent warfare with the Indians, French, and English destroyed nearly all early Spanish buildings in that region. (One of the oldest houses remains in St. Augustine. It is alleged to have been built in 1564, but it was more probably built in 1763.)[50] In 1763, Spain ceded territory east of the Mississippi to England, and architectural influences in the Southeast shifted to one or another of the colonial styles of the English colonies as settlers from them moved in.

Spanish buildings in the Southwest and West, however, have left a deeper impression. The Spaniards adopted the Indian custom of using adobe, and the missions and forts throughout this territory were built of that material. The Indians, who were converted to Christianity at the missions and taught crafts, trades, and agricultural methods, assisted in the construction.

The typical design of the missions (and of most other Spanish building) was a grouping of the houses, church, and other structures around a large open court. Tiles, which were manufactured at the missions, became the standard roofing material. Windows usually were barred and not glazed. Few towns were established—the Spanish were conquerors rather than colonists—but when one was, as, for instance, at present-day Los Angeles, adobe remained the favored building material. The missions served as models for the ranches and haciendas on the small land holdings that later became the usual type of settlement. Adobe and wood (for windows and doors) and tile for roofing remained standard. A typical arrangement was three wings around a patio, which was open on one side. A corridor or veranda, sup-

[50] Morrison, *op. cit.*, p. 183.

ported on wooden posts, faced the patio and served as a lounge; several rooms opened on it.[51] Pickering states:

> The interiors of these Spanish houses were generally as simple as the exteriors. The walls were plastered and whitewashed but the monotony was sometimes relieved by accents of brilliant color in the painted wooden doors, the tile floors, and occasionally in the plain, sturdy furniture. Usually the furnishings corresponded to the character of the house itself. In the more modest homes, a few chairs, benches, tables, and beds constituted the sole furnishings; but in the larger haciendas the appointments were as fine as those in Spain. Here the floors were covered with carpets, and windows were decorated with brocaded curtains. Sofas and chairs were upholstered in velvet, while the chests and tables were often reinforced with wrought iron and decorated with Moorish details.[52]

Colonial Buildings in the Mississippi Valley

Although the colonial empire of France in North America was immense—so immense, in fact, that the land east of the Mississippi River and west of the original thirteen states was known as New France until about 1670—French power and influence declined before the Revolutionary War.

There were French settlements in the Great Lakes and St. Lawrence River areas and down the Mississippi to the Gulf of Mexico. Forts and trading centers were established, one being set up at New Orleans in 1718. A sprinkling of towns was established in the Mississippi Valley, mostly in the eighteenth century—Cahokia, St. Louis, and St. Genevieve, to name a few.

Typical French construction in the Mississippi Valley was the palisade house, with logs set upright, at first in the ground, later on foundations to prevent rotting. Morrison describes the typical French pioneer house as ". . . of one story, containing three or more rooms placed in line, with stone chimney in the center or at the end, the whole surrounded by a *galerie* which gave access to the rooms."[53] Usually outside stairs led to the upper floor. The court house at Cahokia, built around 1737 as a residence, is, except for its larger size, a typical example of French construction in the eighteenth century.

In New Orleans many early houses, especially those in the bottom lands, ". . . were raised 6 or 8 feet above the ground on brick piers as a precaution against floods. Later, when this safety factor was found unnecessary, the 'raised cottage' style, as it came to be called, persisted . . ."[54] and became typical of plantation houses in Louisiana. These houses, too, had galleries and outside stairways. Interiors were plain, with wooden floors and walls plastered and papered. Kitchens were usually in separate buildings. Even though fires destroyed much of the French construction, and many buildings

[51] *Ibid.*, pp. 243–244.

[52] Ernest Pickering, *The Homes of America.* New York: Thomas Y. Crowell Company, 1951, p. 146.

[53] *Op. cit.*, p. 257.

[54] *Ibid.*, p. 259.

in New Orleans are in later styles, the French influence can easily be detected in the older quarters of New Orleans today.

Colonial Buildings in Alaska

Although it is perhaps inappropriate to speak of an Alaskan colonial style of building, it is interesting to note that a Russian style of building was found when Americans took over the territory. Hamlin describes this as follows:

> . . . When Alaska was purchased from Russia, her new masters found and made use of buildings erected by the Russians at Sitka and Nome about 1840—buildings with colonnades and cornices, with cupolas and trim, which were the wooden provincial expression of the classic mania that had created the magnificence of St. Petersburg.[55]

Here again we see the influence of a European country on the architecture of one of our fifty states. However, because of the sparcity of population in this northern territory, many buildings were not necessary. Furthermore, because of the isolated nature of Russian colonization, the influence of this type of architecture did not spread beyond the few small cities.

HOUSING, 1820–1930

During the seventeenth and eighteenth centuries, the emphasis in America had been on colonizing a new land and, after 1776, on establishing the independence of a new country on a firm basis. Pioneering and colonizing new land were major activities throughout the nineteenth century, but this period also marked the beginning of our present-day culture and manner of life. Bemis and Burchard summarize these changes as follows:

> Life in the United States throughout the nineteenth century and indeed well into the twentieth may be considered in two phases: the steady growth of culture and of the physical convenience in the more settled areas; and the more static life on the frontier, which, however, itself was always on the move.[56]

Western Expansion

The expansion to the West was not of a simple, singular character. It differed among the pioneers settling in the South and Southwest, the Middle West, west of the Mississippi River, in the mining regions, and in the Far West.

Settlement of the Deep South and Southwest

Before the end of the eighteenth century, Southern planters had moved westward as their tobacco fields became exhausted or as higher profits made

[55] Talbot Hamlin, *Greek Revival Architecture in America*. New York: Oxford University Press, 1944, pp. 312–313.
[56] *Op. cit.*, p. 292.

cultivation of more land desirable. By 1815, cotton had been established as the principal staple crop in the South. Between 1815 and 1860, cotton plantations ". . . advanced from South Carolina and Georgia across . . . Alabama and Mississippi, occupied the great valley up to Memphis, pushed up the Red River of Louisiana to the Indian Territory, and passed the boundary of Mexico into Texas. . . ."[57] Tobacco plantations in Kentucky and sugar plantations in Louisiana were extensions of much the same type of living conditions. However, this later "planter society" included among its ancestry some of the pioneers of an earlier generation who had moved inland and been brought up in log cabins.

Plantations, of course, needed fairly large houses as headquarters for the economic livelihood of the family and as centers of social activity. Long visits between plantations, with large-scale entertainment, was a general custom. The style of building used in the most elaborate of these new plantation homes was, for the most part, Greek Revival. This had followed the Federal style and is sometimes considered an outgrowth or continuation of that style. The most easily recognized form is the Greek temple with a row of columns across the narrow front of the building (which, in cities, usually was turned toward the street), the roof carried forward to form a pediment, and decorations in Greek style.[58]

In these homes, halls were large, and rooms were arranged so that doors could be thrown back and several rooms made into one. Rooms included a parlor, a library, downstairs bedrooms, and a study; there were, of course, sleeping rooms on another floor. Frequently, a ballroom was part of the plan. Hamlin states: "These later houses are enormous in scale, ceiling height, and room size; lavish in interior trim, at times to the point of lush decadence; palatial rather than domestic. . . ."[59]

Relatively few planters lived on this scale. Somewhat more typical Southern homes were rectangular in shape, with fewer special rooms. They had, however, the row of columns across the two-story porch, or perhaps around the house, or sometimes on the inner side of a wing. On smaller houses and cottages, the columns were more likely to be but one story high.[60]

While we frequently have an image of the people in the Deep South living on plantations, the majority of the Southern whites fell into a different category. Because of their lower status in the social scale, they are frequently referred to as "poor whites." Different groups of them were called by different local terms, such as "Georgia Crackers" or "hillbillies" or "pineywoods people" (for those living in the pine woods areas of the Carolinas), "dirt eaters," "clay eaters," or "sand eaters" (for those who lived on semi-barren land) and "the tallow-faced gentry." These families lived on what they could produce for themselves, from their small farms or from hunting, trapping, or fishing, for the most part near their homes. Their

[57] Samuel Eliot Morison and Henry Steele Commager, *The Growth of the American Republic,* Vol. 1. New York: Oxford University Press, 3d printing, 1943, p. 533.

[58] Pickering, *op. cit.*, pp. 198–200.

[59] *Op. cit.*, p. 208.

[60] *Ibid.*, p. 208.

one-room cabins and the furnishings for those cabins reflected a most primitive stage of pioneer life.

There was still another group that usually is not mentioned—the freed Negroes. It has been estimated that over 12,000 freed Negro families owned their homes at the time of Emancipation,[61] many of them living in such cities as Baltimore and Washington and many others living in small villages. Although a few of the freed Negroes had become prosperous and purchased large and well built homes, the majority "... labored under social handicaps even when they could earn a good living ..." and were nearly as badly housed as the slaves.[62]

Settlement of the Middle West

In the North, before the immigrations of 1848, there were not the sharp distinctions in housing for different groups that were found in the South. Rather, the tendency "... was toward comfortable and often commodious dwellings of relatively comparable dimensions for the general population."[63]

In the 1790's, settlers from New England moved across the Mohawk Valley and into western New York; some went farther inland, into Ohio and Illinois. By this time, the Germans and Scotch-Irish also were moving northward up the Susquehanna and, later, farther north. Housing in the westerly portions of the Middle States was a mixture of the log cabin and framed cottages, with a few dwellings in small towns built in the Georgian or Federal style.

As lands opened in the Middle West and West, pioneers moved into them from all parts of the North and they were joined by many Southerners as well. By successive migrations, the pioneers were into Missouri by 1830—halfway across the continent. Improvements in transportation, such as the completion of the Erie Canal in 1825 and the building of turnpikes between Pennsylvania and Ohio and along other routes to the West, not only assisted the pioneers, who generally were farmers, to reach the western regions but also provided them with a market for agricultural produce once they became established. This was essential to settlement as: "Only the roughest and most primitive subsistence farmers cared to settle in a region whence they could not send a cash crop to market."[64]

A usual pattern was for the pioneering families to build temporary shelters until they received their first returns from the land they were cultivating, to see what their land would support (if anything). Some lived in their covered wagons for a while, until some kind of shelter could be set up. Later settlers often left their families at neighbors' homes until a shelter could be erected, and boarding houses or hotels also were available for those who were settling near established communities.

[61] George E. Haynes, *The Trend of the Races,* quoted in Thomas D. Eliot, ed., *American Standards and Planes of Living.* Boston: Ginn and Co., 1931, pp. 130–131.

[62] Martin, *op. cit.*, p. 126.

[63] Henry Pratt Fairchild, *Main Street—The American Town Past and Present.* New York: The Greystone Press, 1941, p. 10.

[64] Morison and Commager, *op. cit.*, p. 497.

The log cabin was the pioneer home here. Numerous versions were found—some single cabins, some double, and a few larger. Occasionally, there were glass windows, but more often oiled paper was used. Sometimes there was a puncheon floor—split logs laid with the rounded side down—but quite often floors were dirt, perhaps strewn with reeds, over which a carpet, when it could be afforded, was placed. Chimneys were commonly stick and clay, and fireplace fires had to be carefully checked, especially at night. Settlers going westward in the early stages were inclined to travel in groups and to settle near each other, for protection and mutual assistance. One form of group activity was helping each other build homes, and house "raisings" were social events.

A description of the journey and building the cabin for what may well be considered a typical pioneering family during those years is given by Clark:

> December 20, 1825, father and mother started to move to Indiana. Mother rode in a wagon driving the horses with a cow tied to the tail-gate and father walked, driving a small bunch of sheep. Father had saved a little money, with which he bought one hundred and twenty acres of land, of the government, for two dollars per acre, fifty cents per acre cash down and the balance on long time. When they reached their land they were alone in the forest, only one family within ten miles. . . . They slept in the wagon until father could build a little one-room log cabin. . . . To build his cabin father cut logs out of trees the same size, twelve feet long for the ends and fourteen feet long for the sides. He laid the two first end logs at the proper places, trimmed or edged the upper side near the ends, so as to fit perfectly a corresponding notch cut on the under side of the first two logs for the sides. When these four logs were thus placed in position the foundation for the cabin was complete. He then prepared logs enough for the entire house with edges and notches to fit into each other as the cabin went up. . . . After the house was up father split or rived boards three feet long and six inches wide with which to make a roof. There were no shingles nor were there any nails. The first course of boards was laid and a straight pole placed on them and tied and secured in position to firmly hold this course in place. Then the second course was laid lapping six inches over the first and secured in like manner with another pole, and other courses were laid until the house was completely covered. The floor was mother earth. The chimney was built of sticks, but well plastered on the inside with mortar made of yellow clay and water.
>
> The windows were square holes cut in the walls and covered with paper or thin white muslin. The single door-way was an opening cut in the wall, cased with a slab of wood secured by wooden pegs driven into the ends of the logs. The door was made of split boards, which was hung on wooden hinges and swung out. It was fastened by a wooden latch which fell in a notch in the inside, and was raised from the outside by a string which always hung out.
>
> A necessary article of furniture for this cabin was a bedstead. Only one post was required. It was set up four feet from one wall and six feet from another wall. Two large holes were bored into this post two feet from the ground; and two holes opposite these in the walls, and into these holes were inserted two poles, smoothed with a drawing knife, one four feet long and the other six feet long.

This structure constituted a frame upon which were placed split boards for the bed to rest upon.[65]

Another author, Eliza W. Farnham, in a book published in 1846, describes one of the prairie houses as follows:

The entire tenement is sixteen feet by twenty. It has a door and window in each end, and a partition of very thin boards dividing it into two rooms. One of these is nine feet deep, the other eleven. The preponderance in size has been given to the rear apartment, which is finished inside with boards of the same description as those outside, and put on in the same manner; except that, instead of lapping, they do not quite meet, and therefore hold out the most unlimited invitation to winds and vermin, to enter and examine the premises. Nearby opposite the doorway, for as yet there is no door, which leads to the other room, stands a Franklin stove, making every effort to look social, as if it had been an old acquaintance in some of the pleasant sitting-rooms of the east. . . . We pass through into the next room. This is got up in very creditable style. The proportions, to be sure, are not just what one may call elegant, being sixteen feet one way and nine the other. But the walls are plastered.[66]

There is some indication that the actual process of getting the new homes built for these people was not as difficult as might have been expected. One author states, ''I could not but marvel how many carpenters had happened to 'locate' within a few miles of each other in this favored spot; but I have since learned that a plane, a chisel, and two dollars a day make a carpenter in Michigan.''[67]

There were some problems that had to be confronted under the conditions in which many pioneers found themselves. One of those problems is evident from this description:

Young pigs were thus tempted, nay, heartlessly allured into all manner of offenses which grow out of too close an investigation of pails, kettles, boxes, mops, brooms, and other articles that usually consort at the back doors of dwellings which have neither closet, cellar, chamber, or entry. . . .[68]

The problems existed not only at the ''back doors'' but apparently also on the kitchen shelves, as indicated by the following description:

My shelves were the favorite resort of whole troops of mice, to whose obtuse senses the volume of experience was a sealed book. For though they explored every aperture and crevice daily, and found not the slightest morsel to gratify the appetite withal, they returned each day as eager and expectant as before. Nothing but personal inspection satisfied them, and nearly as often as this was repeated, I had to follow it with the application of soap and water.[69]

Although problems of this type were undoubtedly common in many

[65] James Samuel Clark, *Life in the Middle West.* Chicago: Advance Publishing Co., 1916, p. 10.

[66] Eliza W. Farnham, *Life in Prairie Land.* New York: Harper & Bros., 1846, pp. 146–147.

[67] Mary Cleavers, *Our New Home in the West.* New York: James Miller, 1872, p. 75.

[68] Farnham, *op. cit.*, p. 146.

[69] *Ibid.*, p. 150.

frontier homes, the pioneers settling in the West did experience a considerable degree of comfort in those homes. They were provided with at least the minimum furnishings that were required and they were usually maintained with an immaculateness that bespoke the houses of much finer quality, in which many of these families had lived before coming West.

By 1840, the log cabins in the thinly settled area between the Ohio and Mississippi rivers were giving ground steadily to houses of brick, stone, or wood, depending upon the wishes of the owner and the materials and skill at his command. Cities and villages were growing up and moving out of the pioneer stage by the 1830's, and some before then. Houses in general conformed to a style of building known to the pioneer from the East, and in the larger centers, homes of prosperous citizens were quite likely to be designed after the fashion current in the East.

Ohio provides a typical example of a pattern that was general throughout the settling of the West. Pioneers came from different parts of both North and South. The Pennsylvania Germans who moved in eventually built their typical stone houses. The Southerners who came were inclined to build their permanent homes in a manner similar to the plantation houses of the East, with the characteristic wide veranda. Even the Creole influence from Louisiana could be found, in the gallery around some of the log cabins. Ohio cities reflect that state's early settlement in a few Federal style houses —the popular style there in the 1830's, somewhat behind its peak of popularity in the East. This style was overtaken at about mid-century by Greek Revival with local variations and additions. For example, in addition to the temple type, in Ohio the five-bay house was also a typical Greek Revival house.[70]

Homes in the small towns and on farms in the Middle West by mid-century were likely to be one-and-a-half- or two-and-a-half-story, five- or six-room, frame houses, sometimes with a wing at one side, across which was a porch. Many were similar to the frame house described by Nowlin which his father built: ". . . a good, substantial plain, brick farm-house. Not so palatial as some might admire, but a good substantial house; a brick basement under the whole of it, with two stories above. . . ." There was also a double stoop running the length of the front.[71]

Middle-class homes in the Northern and Midwestern areas, by mid-century, usually consisted of parlor or sitting room (sometimes both), kitchen, bedrooms for family and hired help (if any), and a spare room for guests. Parlors where they existed were usually kept closed, and the sitting room or kitchen was where the family gathered. Either the kitchen or sitting room was used as a dining room. Interiors usually were whitewashed, but some were painted, and a few might even be papered.[72]

For most settlers, the ascent from log cabin to house was usually in easy

[70] Hamlin, *op. cit.*, pp. 279–289.

[71] William Nowlin, *The Bark Covered House*. Detroit: Printed for the Author, 1876. Reprinted, Chicago: The Lakeside Press, R. R. Donnelly & Sons Co., 1937, p. 270.

[72] Martin, *op. cit.*, pp. 116–120.

stages and took considerable time. Nowlin's first home, a single-room log cabin, was built in 1834; a second log cabin was put up in 1836, and the frame house described above, in 1854. This progression seems to have been fairly typical; sometimes the early cabin was first enlarged and sometimes a third cabin was built near the first or second. Outbuildings and barns were usually improved before the family's living quarters were. The frame house (or house of stone or brick) was planned over a period of years, while money was being accumulated for its construction. Consequently, though some decorations might be added, in general, conservatism kept the more bizarre stylistic expressions at a minimum.

The log-cabin stage was shorter, of course, in settlements near good transportation facilities. For example, around Chicago, frame houses were built as soon as sawed timber could be made available, usually within the first two or three years. Once the sawmill was operating, all that was necessary were family resources to purchase the lumber and pay for the construction. Family resources were, of course, highly important. Though many settlers eager to reach the lands in the Midwest and West invested all their funds in equipment and supplies for the journey, others came better provided. In Wisconsin, for example, many settlers built fairly large houses almost at once—two stories, two fireplaces, cellars, and sometimes two porches—and enlarged them with wings and lean-tos.

However, it was a long time before the log cabin was completely crowded out by houses. Migration was a continuing process throughout the century. Also, not all land was equally fertile, so a house was not always economically feasible. Or, even when it was, not all families felt that better housing was a crucial need, and thus the log cabin remained in use. There was also in evidence the perpetual pioneer, who continued to look for unsettled areas, to whom elbow-room was more important than a permanent home.

In addition to pioneers from the eastern states, the West, and more particularly the Midwest, received a share of the foreign immigrants who reached the United States around mid-nineteenth century. A typical, but by no means the only, group were the Germans who came to Wisconsin and Missouri, where they built their permanent homes in a style based on models in Germany. These houses were usually half-timbered and filled with a whitewashed plaster, with German double doors at the entrance. Roofs were thatched at first. Later, tile was used, though shingled roofs were also quite frequent. Roofs in general were steep, and the walls heavy. The style sometimes was modified by local influences, as shown by the lower roofs on some houses. These usually were one-and-a-half-story houses, sometimes on high basements, with the central-hall plan followed in the interior. Wood or stone was used, depending upon the availability of stone, and brick was used later. Other groups who settled in the inland regions also added houses typical of their homelands to the growing melange of American varieties.

Housing West of the Mississippi River

While the land comprising the area between the Ohio and the Mississippi was reaching various levels of settlement before mid-century, land farther west remained sparsely settled. One reason was the lack of forests for shelter and for building cabins; another was the scarcity of surface water; and a third, the isolation from markets. Many early pioneers preferred to continue on into the forested Northwest rather than to stop on the prairies. By 1850, however, improved farm machinery made it possible for one man, or one family, to manage a prairie farm, and railroads were being built out of Chicago and other cities into the prairie regions.[73]

In such prairie states as Kansas and Nebraska, the early settlers built sod houses or, where there was a hill or ravine, dugouts, as pioneer dwellings. Fairchild gives a description:

> Over great stretches of the western plains when the pioneers arrived they found neither wood nor stone. Of necessity they adopted the materials at hand. The result was the dugout or the sod house, or a combination of the two. A dugout is simply a little cave excavated from the bank of a ravine or "draw." A sod house is built of tablets cut from the tough surface of the grassgrown land, used in the manner of bricks or stone blocks. Such wood as was available had to be reserved for the rafters of the roof and the lintels and casings of the doors and windows.[74]

A more detailed description of these houses is provided by Martin:

> Typically, the dugout would be an excavation in the side of a hill, perhaps twelve by fourteen feet. In each corner was set a heavy forked timber; poles were laid upon these and across the four sides. Split logs or lumber was then laid upon the poles, upon which thick sods were placed to form a solid roof; sometimes a piece of canvas would be stretched beneath to form a ceiling. The floor might be of puncheons or of dirt pounded hard and covered with cornhusk mats. Sometimes side walls would be built up of sods, and sometimes there would be a log front. In later years the dugout might have an interior of rough, unplastered stone walls. On the level prairie the sod house was more likely to be found than the dugout. This "soddy" had walls of sod piled up around a rectangular floor, frequently sunk below the ground level. The doors were of cloth or hide, and the chimney was only an opening. The soddies were always small, and could be roofed by putting a sod covering over poles stretched across the walls. The furnishings, whether in dugout or soddy, were meager—perhaps a cast-iron cooking stove and a few other articles of metal cooking ware and a few pieces of crockery.
>
> Peculiar to this region was the "hay tent"—two rows of poles were set up, brought together at the top, and the sides thatched with prairie hay. The house was all roof and gable; the windows and doors were in the end. These first houses were replaced in a year or two by "shake" houses—shakes being rude boards split off from a 32-inch section of log. These frame buildings were cold, leaky, and meagerly furnished—sometimes a box for a table, a trunk or chest for wardrobe, and benches for chairs. The bed might be made of rough boards threaded with cords and covered with a mattress stuffed with hay. Quilts and aprons answered the

[73] Morison and Commager, *op. cit.*, pp. 618–619.
[74] *Op. cit.*, p. 12.

purpose of doors and windows. Some of the cabins were papered with newspapers from the East.[75]

The railroads ultimately brought lumber, and eventually ". . . one of the most conspicuous features of these middle western towns is always the lumber yard or lumber yards."[76] Boxlike structures began to appear over the prairie—simple, square or rectangular structures, consisting of one or two rooms, with single slope roofs. Interiors were papered with newspapers. As lumber was raw, cracks developed between the boards, and the spaces often were covered over with strips of cloth.

As noted earlier, building a better house in the farming regions usually lagged well behind providing better barns, stables, or corrals. There was, as might be expected, considerable variety in the permanent homes. In general, the ranch houses were plain and unadorned buildings, with several rooms. In the open country, especially in Kansas, in addition to the regular cellar most of the permanent houses had an additional cavelike cellar, commonly known as a "cyclone cellar," built a few yards from the house. Such a cellar served for storage purposes, and also as protection for the family against the storms that swept across the open prairies. Lightning rods (invented in 1749 by Benjamin Franklin) were standard fixtures. Many of the permanent houses were large; in Oklahoma, for instance, their size ranged from 8 to 15 rooms. Porches, high ceilings, and wide windows also were typical. On many ranches, the development from early shelter to large house could be traced from the cluster of cabin-like buildings around the house. As one boxlike cabin replaced another as a dwelling for the family, the old one was used for farming or ranching activities. Several cabins might mark stages in the progress of the family toward its ultimate shelter in a house.

The pioneers who went farther inland found drier air and arid land. Sometimes there were trees, but they were not always situated where the settlers wanted to build. The Mormons and other settlers built some log cabins, but found adobe also well suited to their needs. These adobe houses were rectangular, with two small rooms and flat roofs (probably covered by thatch or dirt at first, but later shingled). Some had a porch, which seemed to be a necessary adjunct of the American home wherever it might be situated. Floors often were dirt, but occasionally were made of boards. Frequently a lean-to was added to provide additional room. Later houses, of course, were larger—two-storied and with four to six rooms, though many families lived in one-story houses. (It is interesting to note that Brigham Young's residence, with its wide, columned porch across the front of the house, the cupola on the roof, paneled walls and doorways, and carved staircases, copied these features from the New England Late Colonial style.)

Toward the end of the nineteenth century, homesteaders and farmers came to take their chances with dry farming in the arid regions. Houses

[75] *Op. cit.*, pp. 138–139.
[76] Fairchild, *op. cit.*, p. 12.

here most usually were rather small temporary shelters (10 by 14 feet), built of wood and covered with tarpaper. They were, of course, designed for use during warm weather, but many of the cabins were also covered on the inside with tarpaper and made sufficiently comfortable to live in the year around. On the farms that prospered, temporary shelters were replaced by more permanent houses.

Housing in the Mining Regions

Community settlements in the mining regions grew quickly, as prospectors and settlers came in search of wealth from minerals (and sometimes they were abandoned almost as quickly). Many of the early shelters for family living were of flimsy construction. Tents were sometimes used. Some log cabins were built. Most of these had earth floors, though a few had boards for flooring. Roofs were poles covered with grass and dirt. In some of the more isolated regions, door coverings might be buffalo or bear skins, and these also were used as protection in rainy weather from the leaks in the roofs.[77] Furnishings were meager—tables, for instance, were made by placing boards across provision barrels, and boxes were used for chairs.

The fact that many of the early dwellings in these regions were similar to pioneer dwellings in other areas of the frontier is indicated by some descriptions of the first housing built in Denver. The first house there, following the discovery of gold, was built in 1858. As the winter of that year approached, and the first snow fell, most families found it necessary to gain protection from the severity of the weather. Villard describes the situation:

> As a consequence, all set about building rude houses—for the most part of round logs, the cracks stopped with mud, and the roof of earth. There was neither glass nor nails, and many were the expedients resorted to for keeping out cold, providing a means of ingress and egress, and to admit a few rays of light. About one hundred and twenty-five houses were put up during the winter. In their style there was scarce a shade of difference—walls of round or hewed logs, about eight feet high, the cracks chinked with blocks and plastered with mud, a roof frame of rough poles or split timber, covered with dry grass, and that covered with about six inches of earth. They were very dark, very warm, and, in the latter part of the winter, and in spring, when the snows melted and the rains fell, very wet; the rain usually continuing three days in-doors after the weather cleared up out-doors.[78]

This same author also describes his observations as he visited Denver, and other nearby towns in 1859:

> When we first beheld the Cherry Creek towns, early in May last, they consisted of about two hundred log cabins, forming a most curious *ensemble* of wretched architecture, that the emporium of a gold country could hardly be proud of. A few establishments, claiming the denomination "stores," and located in log structures of very modest dimensions, represented the mercantile interest. Of mechanical and industrious pursuits not a trace was perceptible. The aggregate population

[77] Martin, *op. cit.*, p. 147.

[78] Henry Villard, *The Past and Present of the Pike's Peak Gold Regions.* Princeton, N.J.: Princeton University Press, 1932, pp. 13–14.

did not exceed three hundred. But from the moment the existence of gold in paying quantities in the Rocky Mountains became a settled fact, a steady progress characterized every branch of human activity on both banks of Cherry Creek.[79]

In some settlements sawmills were established within a year or two, and frame houses, one or two stories high, painted on the outside and provided with porches, became the rule. Where those materials were available, and resources permitted, brick or stone was used for building homes. Some of these homes were well furnished, since merchants tended to follow successful mining operations. Still, even with prosperity, most homes contained some exhibits of their frontier locale, even if only in the use of skins for rugs.

This same pattern of development occurred in other towns in the mining regions, in other parts of Colorado, and in California, Nevada, Oregon and other Western territories. Many of the towns became permanent and grew into modern cities, but some others were abandoned after the mineral deposits were exhausted. Some of these "ghost" towns can still be seen today.

Housing in the Far West

Early housing in California and the Oregon Territory was, for the most part, built by prospectors. However, the housing in at least two cities, San Francisco and Los Angeles, should be mentioned separately.

San Francisco was a unique city from the start. It was occupied by many different nationalities, including the Spanish, English, French, Italian, and Chinese. As in other areas, the first form of shelter was a crude cabin. Almost from the start, however, some lodging houses existed. Most of the dwellings were of frame constuction (two- or three-story, but some of only one story). Brick dwellings were a rarity because of the fear of earthquakes.

In its early history the city was plagued by several disastrous fires, but each fire was usually followed by hasty rebuilding.

In Southern California, adobe was the principal building material. Martin describes the early houses (about 1859) in Los Angeles as follows:

> . . . most houses were of adobe, with walls three or four feet thick. The ground plan was rectangular, with patios and corridors a characteristic feature. Some had several rooms, but in all houses the architecture was simple; when the house was of two stories, the entrance to the second story was from the outside. Even hearths and chimneys were few, and smoke was carried out not by a chimney but by a pipe leading through the window or wall. Roofs were flat, usually covered with asphalt, but sometimes with tiles. Inner walls were whitewashed, the furniture was scanty and plain; and the glassware and tableware of an inferior grade. Adobes, scantily furnished and usually slovenly in appearance, were the commonest sort of houses throughout that part of the Southwest which had once been Spanish.[80]

Both San Francisco and Los Angeles experienced great booms during the latter half of the nineteenth century, and the construction of houses sometimes fell far short of the demand. The result, as in any areas where

[79] *Ibid.*, p. 130.
[80] *Op. cit.*, p. 143.

there is a serious housing shortage, was extremely high rents for the dwellings available.

Housing in Eastern Cities

While the pioneers were moving westward, the cities in the East were experiencing rapid growth as a result of the Industrial Revolution and the movement of industry out of the home and into the factory. This brought workers into the cities, both from abroad and from rural regions. The result was a heavy demand for new housing.

An indication of the increase in dwelling units during the first half of the nineteenth century is provided by a comparison of a tax list given to Congress in 1798 with the number of dwellings reported by the U. S. Census in 1850. In 1798 there were listed 276,599 dwellings in 16 states; in 1850 there were 3,362,337 in 36 states and territories. The number in each state and territory, and their value, are shown in Table 1–1, p. 43. The three states with the largest number of dwellings in 1850 were New York, Pennsylvania, and Ohio.

There will be other discussions of the growth of cities in following chapters, especially Chapter 3. Therefore, the only purpose here is to mention some of the outstanding historical trends that related to housing.

In order to discuss the history of urban housing during this period, it is necessary to discuss the situation in particular cities, since some were very different from others.

New York

More attention has been given by historians to the housing situation in New York City than to any other city, undoubtedly because of the tremendous growth of the city and because it was unique. The population of New York City was 60,515 in 1800. By 1820 it had increased to 123,706; by 1850, 660,800; and by 1890, to about 2,740,600. This rapid increase in population was caused in part by the horde of immigrants. Many of them ". . . arrived here generally penniless, and . . . brought with them disease and misery."[81]

The homes of the working-class people up to this time had generally been small one- and two-story houses. However, these homes were not adequate to meet the needs of the rapidly expanding population of the city. As a result, there were two developments. The first of these was the overcrowding of those homes, which frequently housed more than one family. The second development was the building of the city's first tenements.

The first house built exclusively for the occupation of tenant families in New York City is believed to have been completed in 1833. It was four

[81] "Tenement House Reform in New York, 1834–1900." Original report prepared for the Tenement House Commission, May 8, 1900, by Lawrence Veiller, Secretary. Report reprinted in slightly revised form in Robert W. DeForest and Lawrence Veiller, eds., *The Tenement House Problem*, Vol. I. New York: The Macmillan Company, 1903, pp. 71–118.

stories high and was designed for occupancy by "many tenants."[82] After that, many structures were built to house families who could afford only cheap rents. A high proportion at first were of the barracks type, built in every possible unoccupied space in the poorer neighborhoods—in sets or rows, one behind the other or side by side, along narrow courts or alleys, or in the backyards of old buildings. The buildings were usually three stories high, with many families on each floor. Many of the rooms lacked both light and ventilation.

In recognition of the evils of the "railroad" type of tenement house which had become prevalent, a competition was organized among architects in New York in 1878 to develop a plan for a better tenement structure on a 25- by 100-foot interior lot. The resulting type of building became known as the "double-decker" or "dumb-bell" (because of its shape) tenement.

The "dumb-bell" tenement was usually five, six, or even seven stories high. The building usually extended the full 25 feet in width, but 90 feet in length, leaving only 10 feet vacant at the rear of the lot. DeForest and Veiller describe it as follows:

> Upon the entrance floor there are generally two stores, one on each side of the building, and these sometimes have two or three living rooms back of them. In the centre is the entrance hallway, a long corridor less than 3 feet wide and extending back 60 feet in length. This hallway is nearly always totally dark, receiving no light except that from the street door and a faint light that comes from the small windows opening upon the stairs, which are placed at one side of the hallway. Each floor above is generally divided into four sets of apartments, there being seven rooms on each side of the hall, extending back from the street to the rear of the building. The front apartments generally consist of four rooms each and the rear apartments of three rooms, making altogether fourteen upon each floor, or in a seven-story house eighty-four rooms exclusive of the stores and rooms back of them. Of these fourteen rooms on each floor, only four receive direct light and air from the street or from the small yard at the back of the building. Generally, along each side of the building is what is termed an "air shaft," being an indentation of the wall to a depth of about 28 inches, and extending in length for a space of from 50 to 60 feet. This shaft is entirely enclosed on four sides, and is, of course, the full height of the building, often from 60 to 72 feet high. The ostensible purpose of the shaft is to provide light and air to the five rooms on each side of the house which get no direct light and air from the street or yard; but as the shafts are narrow and high, being enclosed on all four sides, and without any intake of air at the bottom, these rooms obtain, instead of fresh air and sunshine, foul air and semi-darkness.[83]

These tenements, which were to become the worst type of housing in New York City, were built until 1901. In that year the Tenement House Act of 1901 was passed, under which was set up a Tenement House Department

[82] Charles H. Haswell, *Reminiscences of an Octogenarian,* quoted in James Ford, *Slums and Housing,* Vol. II. Cambridge, Mass.: Harvard University Press, Copyright, 1936, by the President and Fellows of Harvard College, p. 867.

[83] *Op. cit.,* pp. 8–9.

with authority for correcting many of the evils of the "Old-Law" tenements. The new type structures provided more space, light, and ventilation, and were the forerunners of today's better apartment-type structures.

Obviously, there was some better housing built in New York City during this period, for the higher income classes. One of these types was the "brownstone," which received its name from the material of which it was made. Brownstones, many of which were built on Fifth Avenue below Central Park in New York in the 1840's and 1850's, were expensive houses. They were not more than three stories high, and generally were 20 to 30 feet wide. However, the small quantity of that and similarly expensive housing is completely overshadowed by the hundreds of tenement houses that were built to house the majority of the city's rapidly growing population.

Boston

Tenement houses were also built in Boston during this period, but only a few were five stories high; the majority were four stories high. Characteristic of Boston also were the wooden "threedeckers" (the tenements were usually built of brick) which were also found in many other cities during this period, especially in New England. "Threedeckers" were built to house three or more families. Together these two types of housing accommodated half of Boston's population as late as 1930.

Philadelphia

Philadelphia was a city where even the working people generally had individual homes. Occasionally these homes were occupied by as many as three families, but this was the exception rather than the rule. During the early part of this century, many row houses were built, usually two stories in height with brick exteriors. (These were facilitated by the typical lot size—from 14 to 20 feet in width and often 50 feet in depth.)

Baltimore and Washington

Beginning about 1850, two-story row houses were built in Baltimore and Washington in an attempt to utilize all possible space on the narrow lots of the city. This type of building, of brick with white steps, spread into the countryside. Though some of them became poor housing, the row houses prevented the building of the tenements found in cities farther north.

Other Cities

In most of the other principal cities of the country, such as Chicago, Detroit, Cleveland, and St. Louis, most of the working people lived chiefly in small one- and two-story houses. These houses sometimes were designed for occupancy by two families, but seldom by more than three. Tenements of the type known in New York and Boston were practically unknown in these cities. There were some row houses in most of the cities, but they were not as prominent as in Philadelphia, Baltimore, or Washington. The differences in housing that did exist were more with reference to lot size, sanitary conditions, and so on. Overcrowding, the poor condition of many houses, and poor sanitary conditions brought on slum conditions, which will be discussed in Chapter 10.[84]

Improvements in Major Household Facilities and Equipment

During the last half of the eighteenth century, and especially during the nineteenth century, some significant improvements were made in a number of important and basic household facilities and items of equipment. These improvements primarily concerned heating, cooking, and refrigeration facilities, lighting, and sanitation.

Fireplaces were generally used for cooking until about 1840, when they began to be replaced by cast-iron kitchen ranges, heated by coal or wood. (These ranges became standard equipment in homes during the next forty years.) Gas stoves were in use by 1850, but the use of gas for cooking was only slowly accepted in the United States. Also, the kerosene stove came into use about 1880 and remained a means of cooking, particularly in small towns and rural areas, well into the twentieth century. Electricity for cooking was first used in the 1880's but there were some serious drawbacks—both the equipment and the current were expensive and electric power was sporadic. For home use, the electric stove did not become a satisfactory means of cooking until the twentieth century.

Fireplaces were also used for heating colonial and frontier homes. Cast-iron ranges, which replaced fireplaces for cooking, also replaced them for heating. A furnace for central heating was invented in 1815. Even though by 1860, according to Martin, ". . . more or less practical systems had been devised. . . . Furnaces were still in the luxury class, not only because of the expense of installation, but because (at least in the popular opinion) furnaces were inefficient in that they required a tremendous consumption of fuel if they were to affect the more distant rooms."[85] Furnaces were equipped with flues or pipes leading to registers in the rooms above the basement, and usually only the main floor was heated. Hot water and steam heating were in use in commercial buildings, and in some homes. Central heating, like other home equipment, underwent a series of improvements throughout the century and later. Stoves continued to be used for heating, however.

Before 1930 hot air or hot water or steam furnaces were in general use, and oil, gas, and electricity provided fuel. Furnaces were built as "standard" equipment in houses. Heating facilities had been relegated to the

[84] For elaboration of this discussion, and for a discussion of the housing in other cities, the reader is referred to these two sources: Robert W. DeForest and Lawrence Veiller, eds., *The Tenement House Problem,* Vol. I, *op. cit.,* pp. 119–170, and James Ford, *Slums and Housing,* Vol. I, *op. cit.,* pp. 263–278.

[85] *Op. cit.,* p. 93.

basement, or at least out of sight, and were designed to provide space in basements for other activities.

Refrigeration was another early housing problem. Numerous methods were used to keep food from spoiling, such as storing supplies in cellars, near springs, or in wells. Some houses had ice closets built in, and after about 1876 ice boxes were available for home use. Ice was cut from nearby lakes during the winter months and stored in ice houses. Ice houses for storage of ice had developed steadily from colonial times, at first being placed underground, then built above ground and equipped with double walls and doors.

Throughout the nineteenth century, this remained the usual method of obtaining refrigeration. Commercial ice-freezing machines were developed by 1876 and used in such southern cities as Atlanta and New Orleans to manufacture ice artificially. However, these were not suited for household use and they were too expensive.

By 1916 or 1917 the mechanical electric refrigerator was produced. The machinery was complicated and frequently maintenance was a discouraging factor. In the 1920's, however, the electric (or gas) refrigerator became an almost indispensable piece of household equipment.

Rush lights, home-made candles, and light from the fireplace, which were the primary kinds of lighting in colonial homes, began to be replaced by lamps during the nineteenth century.

Numerous lamps were invented early in that century. The first prominent one was invented by the Marquis d'Arlandes in France in 1784. Another important one was the Carcel lamp (about 1800), another was the Moderator lamp (1836), and still another was the camphene lamp (around 1845). These lamps were generally different from each other from the standpoint of type of wick and mechanical features, as well as the kind of fuel used. Until coal oil became available, such products as turpentine, whale oil, train oil, lard oil, tallow, stearine, and other animal and vegetable products were used for lighting. (These frequently varied in odor and in quality of illumination.) When oil wells were brought into production in 1859, and the oil began to be refined the following year, lamps using coal oil (kerosene) came into existence almost immediately. It took only a short time to reduce both the smoke and the odor that made such lamps unpopular at first. The kerosene lamp, with its flat wick and glass chimney, was the means of lighting most widely used for the remainder of the century in cities, and into the twentieth century in rural areas.[86] (Before the 1850's, lamps either did not use chimneys or used imported ones, since they were not manufactured in the United States before that period.) Wealthy householders frequently had hanging lamps, sometimes protected by hurricane shields, and chandeliers were found in the more elaborate homes.

Gas had been used for lighting purposes since early in the nineteenth century, more in the North than in the South: "In the forties and fifties

[86] Martin, *op. cit.*, pp. 94–96.

gas lamps came to be used to some extent in the homes of the upper and middle classes in such cities as Boston, New York, Philadelphia, and Baltimore, and architects were drawing up their plans to include facilities for gaslighting.''[87]

In 1874, Edison patented the electric light. This came into general use and replaced all other types, including gas lights, but not until after the production and transmission of electricity made its use on a large scale possible.

The matter of sanitation has been one of the most serious problems related to American housing throughout its history. Any widespread improvement in sanitation required water supplies and sewers. Boston was the first city to install a sewer system, in 1652, but it was inadequate almost from the start. It took more than two hundred years before municipal sewerage systems were no longer novelties. In fact, when a system was to be designed for Brooklyn, in 1857, there still was little knowledge on which to draw.[88]

The first water closet had been invented in England in the sixteenth century, but it was of an extremely primitive design. Later and more advanced models were patented in that country in the 1770's, one patented in 1778 having a valve at the bottom. Little progress was made during the next half century, but the first American patent for a water closet was entered in 1833.[89]

However, water closets were still relatively scarce by 1860, partly because of the lack of municipal supplies and sewerage and the great burden they placed on already overstrained cesspools. It was 1900 before they were installed in most houses in cities. Rural housing improvement was slower and many farm houses even today still have outdoor privies.

Most cities made little progress in supplying residences with continuous and dependable water supplies until about 1850. Before that time, central pumps and wells were the chief sources of supply. In smaller communities without a municipal water supply, individual householders found it necessary to provide their own wells. In the West, artesian water supplies were developed in some areas. For washing, rain water was collected from the roof and piped into cisterns, which usually were underground but in some instances were on the roof or inside the house, high enough to provide pressure. A small force pump was used to bring the water to the location where it was required.

Water was, of course, unheated at first. Some water was available in reservoirs attached to kitchen ranges, but by the 1840's, boilers had become a chief source of hot water and remained so for many families until central heating had become an established part of the house.

For most people, at least in the nineteenth century, early bathing and

[87] Martin, *op. cit.*, p. 97.

[88] J. J. Cosgrove, *History of Sanitation.* Pittsburgh: Standard Sanitary Manufacturing Company, 1909, p. 87.

[89] *Ibid.*, pp. 119–120.

washing facilities consisted of a pitcher and basin. The weekly bath was becoming an established practice, but since the water frequently had to be carried in from wells, it was sometimes used by several people. In small houses, bathing, having no place of its own, was a disruptive process. It usually took place in front of the fire or near the stove, in the kitchen or sitting room, and the privacy of the bather was protected by a screen; the rest of the family was relegated to whatever other space they might find while the activity was in process.

There is some question concerning when the first bathtub was introduced into this country. Official government records from 1834 indicate that bathtubs with plumbing had been installed in the White House and were in use at the time of Andrew Jackson's administration. It took some time for this facility to gain popular acceptance, as it was initally denounced by the clergy and even claimed by some doctors to be unhealthful. The first bathtubs were wooden boxes (usually oak or pine) lined with copper, lead, or zinc. Even when cast-iron tubs were put on the market in the 1850's, they were encased in wood.[90] There were some shower baths at this early date, but their numbers were apparently limited by both the scarcity of running water and their general unpopularity.

By the end of the nineteenth century, the general availability of running hot and cold water and sewer systems led to the development of the bathroom as a place separate from other rooms in the house.

There were other important related developments in the nineteenth century, but they concerned living and household operations more than housing *per se*. For example, by about 1850 machine-made furniture was beginning to replace the handcraftsmanship of earlier days. Greater standardization of furniture was one of the results. About the same time, some mechanical devices were being brought out to make housekeeping easier. Carpet sweeping was one of the first tasks to which labor-saving methods were applied. The principal of the vacuum cleaner was formulated around 1859, but it was not until 1920 that the resultant product was widely accepted.[91]

The first American washing machine was developed in 1805, but over a hundred years elapsed before the average household had mechanical assistance in this activity. A mechanical dishwashing machine was invented in 1865. It was hand-propelled and never gained popularity. Faraday introduced an electric motor as early as 1831, but it remained outside the realm of any household equipment until 1889, when it was first used to power a small electric fan.[92] Improvements in most of the other household mechanical devices, including making them more fully automatic, were developments of the twentieth century.

[90] *Ibid.*, p. 120.

[91] Siegfried Giedion, *Mechanization Takes Command.* New York: Oxford University Press, 1948, 2d printing, 1955, p. 548.

[92] *Ibid.*, pp. 557–558.

HOUSING SINCE 1930

This brings us up to the modern era of housing and the major facilities and equipment in the home.

The kinds of housing that have been built in the last few decades are discussed in several of the following chapters—for example, the proportion of sales and rental types and the number of one-family, two-family, and multifamily homes are discussed in Chapter 6 on the production of housing; slum conditions are discussed in Chapter 10, concerned with housing problems in central cities; the kinds of homes being built for the mass of Americans is discussed in Chapter 11 on suburbia; and some of the outstanding examples of modern residential architecture are discussed in Chapter 8 on housing design. In those and other chapters will be discussed the trend toward home ownership, and some of the recent styles of houses, such as the "ranch type" and the "split-level." There will also be a discussion of prefabrication and mobile homes. Also to be mentioned will be the common use today of the new kinds of building materials, and new kinds of household appliances and equipment—air conditioning, such new kitchen appliances as the dishwasher and the garbage disposer, and other "modern" equipment.

American housing has come a long way since the days of the colonists and the Western pioneers. Yet today, almost anywhere in this vast land that a person may travel, he will see homes that can be traced back directly to those described in the preceding pages of this chapter.

READING LIST

HOUSING, 1600–1820

Shurtleff, Harold R. *The Log Cabin Myth.* Cambridge, Mass.: Harvard University Press, 1939.

Wertenbaker, Thomas Jefferson. *The Founding of American Civilization: The Middle Colonies.* New York: Charles Scribner's Sons, 1938.

———. *The Old South: The Founding of American Civilization.* New York: Charles Scribner's Sons, 1942.

———. *The Puritan Oligarchy: The Founding of American Civilization.* New York: Charles Scribner's Sons, 1947.

HOUSING, 1820–1930

DeForest, Robert W. and Lawrence Veiller (eds.) *The Tenement House Problem.* Vols. I and II. New York: The Macmillan Co., 1903.

Federal Writers' Project, Works Progress Administration, American Guide Series (various places, publishers, dates).

Lubove, Roy. *The Progressives and the Slums.* Pittsburgh: University of Pittsburgh Press, 1962.

Martin, Edgar W. *The Standard of Living in 1860.* Chicago: The University of Chicago Press, 1942.

Wood, Edith Elmer. *Recent Trends in American Housing.* New York: The Macmillan Co., 1931.

IMPROVEMENTS IN MAJOR HOUSEHOLD FACILITIES AND EQUIPMENT

Giedion, Siegfried. *Mechanization Takes Command.* New York: Oxford University Press, 1948.

GENERAL

Bemis, E. F. and John Burchard, 2nd. *The Evolving House. A History of the Home.* Vol. I. Cambridge, Mass.: The Technology Press, M.I.T., 1933.

Lynes, Russell. *The Domesticated Americans.* New York: Harper & Row, 1963.

Morison, Samuel E. and Henry S. Commager. *The Growth of the American Republic.* New York: Oxford University Press, 1942.

Morrison, Hugh. *Early American Architecture.* New York: Oxford University Press, 1952.

Pickering, Ernest. *The Homes of America.* New York: Thomas Y. Crowell Company, 1951.

Table 1–1

NUMBER AND VALUE OF DWELLINGS IN THE UNITED STATES

	1798		*1850*	
	No. dwellings	*Value*	*No. dwellings*	*Value*
Maine	(part of Massachusetts)		95,802	$ 72,109,000
New Hampshire	11,142	$ 4,146,938.90	57,339	43,004,250
Vermont	5,437	1,558,389.36	56,421	42,315,750
Massachusetts	48,984	24,546,826.46	152,835	114,626,250
Rhode Island	7,037	2,984,002.87	22,379	16,784,250
Connecticut	23,465	8,149,479.28	64,013	48,009,750
New York	33,416	25,495,631.39	473,936	354,452,000
New Jersey	19,624	9,149,918.84	81,064	60,798,000
Pennsylvania	51,772	29,321,048.33	386,216	289,662,000
Delaware	5,094	2,180,165.83	15,290	11,464,500
Maryland	16,933	10,738,286.63	81,708	61,281,000
District of Columbia	—	—	7,917	5,937,750
Virginia	27,693	11,248,267.67	165,815	124,361,270
North Carolina	11,760	2,932,893.09	104,996	78,747,000
South Carolina	6,427	5,008,292.93	52,642	39,481,500
Georgia	3,446	1,797,631.25	91,206	68,404,500
Florida	—	—	9,022	6,766,500
Alabama	—	—	73,070	54,807,500
Mississippi	—		51,681	38,760,750
Louisiana	—	—	49,101	36,825,750
Texas	—	—	27,988	20,991,000
Arkansas	—	—	28,252	21,189,000
Tennessee	1,030	286,446.83	129,419	97,065,750
Kentucky	3,339	1,139,765.13	130,769	98,076,250
Missouri	—	—	96,849	72,344,850
Illinois	—	—	146,544	109,908,000
Indiana		—	170,178	127,629,500
Ohio	—	—	336,098	252,073,530
Michigan	—	—	71,616	53,712,000
Wisconsin	—	—	56,316	42,237,000
Iowa	—	—	32,962	29,971,500
California	—	—	23,742	17,806,500
Minnesota Territory	—	—	1,002	751,500
New Mexico Territory	—	—	13,453	10,089,750
Oregon Territory	—	—	2,374	1,780,500
Utah Territory	—	—	2,322	1,741,500
Total	276,599	$140,683,984.77	3,362,337	$2,520,967,400

SOURCE: Thomas P. Kettell, "Individual Industries: Buildings and Building Materials," in *Eighty Years' Progress of the United States,* Vol. II, New York and Worcester, Mass.: L. Stebbins, 1861, p. 354.

CHAPTER 2

*

The American Family—Yesterday and Today

Many scholarly investigations of the family have been reported in books and journal articles. Many aspects of the technical discussion, for example, those describing parent–child relationships, are not directly pertinent here. Yet we must have an understanding of the family in any discussion of housing, because it does, after all, constitute the *basic unit of residence.*

What is a family? Glick says:

> Perhaps the word "family" is most often used in referring to a married couple with children. Yet, this is only one of the many types of groups in which people live. The question arises at once, therefore, as to how far a group can deviate from the typical cluster of parents and children and still be regarded as a family. What about the young couple with no children? Or the serviceman's wife who makes her home with her parents? Or the old couple in the home of their son and daughter-in-law? Or the couple living in a hotel? Or the husband and wife who live apart because of the nature of the husband's work, the bachelor and his spinster sister who keep house together, the middle-aged divorced woman and her children who live in an apartment, the widower who lives alone, or the aging mother who lives with her daughter and son-in-law?[1]

For purposes of this discussion, all of these groups are generally considered to represent families. In fact, the variety of related individuals that can make up a family unit is so diverse that "family type" becomes one of the important factors, in studying the family.[2]

The discussion in this chapter will be in two basic parts—the American family in history and the American family today. The historical development will attempt to follow somewhat the pattern of the history of housing in the preceding chapter. The description of the American family today will touch on only the characteristics that are most important because of their relationship to our housing. These characteristics include the variety of family and household compositions, educational attainment and occupational levels of heads of households, personal values, and, finally, two

[1] Paul C. Glick, *American Families.* A Volume in the Census Monograph Series. New York: John Wiley & Sons, Inc., 1957, p. 1.

[2] Later, in consideration of U. S. Census data, a differentiation will be made between "family" and "household." Although there is an important technical distinction between the two terms, for purposes here the word "family" is generally used, both because it is more commonly accepted and because the differences between the two terms are not too significant in any broad discussion of social practice or policy.

importantly related subjects—the mobility and the standards of living of American families. (As will be seen, some of the discussion will relate to individuals rather than to families *per se,* but the matters discussed are important from a family point of view.)

HISTORY OF THE AMERICAN FAMILY

The Colonial Family

There are at least three factors that should be recognized as being basic in the description of colonial families in America. First, they generally had their origin in Europe, and many of their characteristics carried over from that culture. Second, many of them left their mother countries because of certain needs and convictions which were not satisfied there. Finally, the frontier conditions which they found when they reached these shores caused some basic changes in family life which even they themselves perhaps had not foreseen.

The New England Puritan Family

While England was the provenience of the majority American family, it should be remembered that the Puritans who settled in New England and the Quakers who established in the Middle Atlantic colonies came from particular groups and classes of Englishmen—the middle class and dissenters against the traditional religion of their mother country.[3]

When the Puritans landed on the American shores, the families undoubtedly were patriarchal in character—a characteristic that stemmed from English common law and traditional sanction. However, the status of husband and wife tended to be changed, after arrival, by the need for a new role to be served by the woman—that of planting gardens and cooking food, making clothing, and generally maintaining the family while the husband was clearing the land, building the home, and providing for the livelihood of the family.

Two other factors had their influence on the role of the women. First, with the decline in authority imposed by both government (the government merely performed those responsibilities which were left over after family control had been exhausted) and the church (in matters ranging from the decision concerning vocation to the practice of having civil rather than religious marriage ceremonies), Puritan society became more family-centered. In fact, the family was undoubtedly the most important institution in Puritan society. Second, there was a growing individualism at this time. This resulted from economic necessity as well as from the change in relationship to the church.

The general self-sufficiency of the New England family is well known.

[3] For a more complete discussion of Puritan, as well as other colonial families, see Manford Hinshaw Kuhn, "American Families Today: Development and Differentiation of Types," in Howard Becker and Reuben Hill, eds., *Family, Marriage and Parenthood.* Boston: D.C. Heath and Co., 1948, pp. 131–147.

All able family members cooperated on many tasks, both economic and recreational. The training of children also was primarily a family affair. Concerning the most usual type of family, MacGill describes it as consisting of ". . . husband, wife, children, and several adult unmarried women, nominally dependents, really earning their bread in the unpaid service of their relatives."[4]

This writer also provides additional detail concerning the nature and size of colonial families, and the distribution of work-load among the various members:

> . . . The large families were borne by at least two mothers, and . . . the number of children decreased with the later wives. That is, the first wife would have six or seven children in quick succession and die, worn out by maternity and hard work. The second wife, a young vigorous woman, would take up the work and bring up the brood, unbroken by travail, and with some of the older ones very likely at an age when they could be of much help in the simple housekeeping of the times. Three or perhaps four children would be added, generally, it would seem, at longer intervals. Sometimes she, too, died in the struggle, in which case a third soon appeared upon the scene, but with this difference, that the band of assistants was by now a numerous and sufficient one, and it was by no means longer a "one woman-power" household. The work of the colonial household was heavy, but much of it was of a kind requiring little skill, and it was easily done by the younger members. The number of women who actually did the labors attributed to all, who bore and reared at the same time many children, was probably not much larger than at present. Many of the children also did not live long enough to make their upbringing a tax upon the mother's vitality.[5]

How typical this picture is we do not know. There is, at least, considerable evidence that these circumstances existed in a sufficient number of instances to justify their having been reported by other writers who had done research on this period.

From this picture it might be considered that the breaking up of marriages would be rare. However, there actually was a broad and liberal policy toward divorce. Kuhn has stated:

> . . . the emergence of civil marriage and divorce reflected the fact that the individual and the family were really held to be above the church, so much so in fact that there was not going to be any acknowledgement that the church had a right to marry people or for that matter that it had a right to keep them married against their wishes.[6]

The English colonists brought with them many traditions which they were to keep, sometimes with only minor alterations. English private law, for example, became the "common law" of the colonies. Under this law married women were controlled, both in person and in property, by their husbands whom they were bound to serve and obey. Only if her husband died before her was his widow granted the management of her property.

[4] Caroline E. MacGill, "The Myth of the Colonial Housewife," *The Independent*, Vol. LXIX, No. 3237, December 15, 1910, pp. 1318–1322.

[5] *Ibid.*, p. 1322.

[6] *Op. cit.*, p. 138.

The husband was required to maintain his wife in accordance with his means, whether or not she brought him property at marriage. In this connection, Goodsell says: "To be sure, the American colonists were as shrewd bargainers with respect to marriage-contracts as were their English forefathers; and they took good care to see that a dowry, big or little, went with the women of their choice."[7] (The situation was apparently different among later frontier families. Calhoun reports: "The father of the frontier bride usually gave her 'a bed, a lean horse, and some good advice: and having thus discharged his duty . . . returned to his work.' "[8])

The New England Puritan family, then, usually was a middle-class family, owning some property, and living in the midst of a social order which was shaped by forces based on both tradition and the necessities of the time and location.

Families in the Middle Atlantic Colonies

It was pointed out in the preceding chapter that several diverse groups settled in the Middle Atlantic region—the Quakers from England, the Dutch, the Germans, the Swedes and Finns, and others.

The Quakers were in many respects similar to the Puritans; they held the same basic values of industry, sobriety, and thrift, and the functions of the family were much the same. However, there were some differences, related in part to their religious philosophy and in part to their somewhat different occupational patterns.

In Quaker families, the paternalistic character was even less conspicuous than in Puritan families. Although parents treated children with firmness, all family members were considered to be on about the same plane of family regard and esteem. Another relatively important distinction was that there did not exist the sharp delineation between family and religion. Another was that Quakers did not acknowledge the right of the government to perform marriages—people married themselves at a "meeting" and marriages were regulated with great care. Divorces were unheard of among the Quakers.

In their occupational pattern, there were many farmers among the Quakers, but there was a greater tendency for them to become tradesmen and business people. This resulted in greater specialization and greater division of labor than among the Puritans and, at the same time, in somewhat less self-sufficiency.

Though on the whole there were many similarities between the Dutch families in New Netherland and the Puritans in New England, there also were important differences that could undoubtedly be traced back to some of the features of Dutch life in Holland. Perhaps the most important of these was the high position of women. Calhoun indicates that: "The women

[7] Willystine Goodsell, *A History of the Family as a Social and Educational Institution.* New York: The Macmillan Co., 1915, p. 347

[8] Arthur W. Calhoun, *A Social History of the American Family,* Vol. II, p. 132. Copyright 1918, 1945 by Arthur W. Calhoun. Reprinted, 1960, by Barnes & Noble, Inc.

of the Dutch Netherlands in the sixteenth and seventeenth centuries were more highly educated, better protected by the laws, and more prominent in station than any of their contemporaries.''[9] Although they ''were strongly influential, active in affairs, and respected by their husbands'' their ''high ambition was to be able housewives.'' In that position they made the apparel for the family, maintained ''the spotless order of the parlor'' and generally served as ''the head of the household, the sovereign of domestic affairs.'' Some women ''were active as shop-keepers, merchants, ship-owners, Indian traders. It was common for a wife to hold her husband's power of attorney in his absence, to help him in business, or to carry on the business after his death.''[10]

It was also a characteristic of the Dutch to provide general education for their children, at least to the extent that it was feasible for them to do so. The establishment of public schools lagged at first, but such schools flourished before the colony came under English rule—at which time ''these non-conformist agencies were suffered to decline.''

The Dutch were less stringent than the New Englanders in exerting paternal authority but, nevertheless, Dutch children were generally respectful and obedient toward their parents. There apparently were exceptions: in Holland, we are told, the ''great licentiousness of youth'' was one of the reasons the Pilgrims continued their migration to America and ''all foreign observers were amazed at the freedom of children and servants. In the New World the Dutch retained the old ways in large measure.''[11]

While pioneering conditions—the emptiness of the country and the shortage of hands—generally placed a premium on large families, there seem to have been fewer children among Dutch families at this time than among those of New England. One explanation is given by Calhoun: ''It may be that the absence of Puritan rigor allowed a larger proportion of children to survive and that accordingly the Dutch had settled to a lower fecundity.''[12] Yet small families were rare, partly as a result of repeated marriages.

In regard to divorce, the Dutch were more conservative than the Puritans, but divorces were granted ''for just and sound reason.''

German families, who settled in hinterlands from Maine to Georgia but concentrated in Pennsylvania, can be classified as generally being middle class and domestic in character. Calhoun has indicated:

> The Germans gave to America a domestic type of woman. To this fact can be attributed much of the vigor of the population and the solid quality that comes from home training. They laid great emphasis on the household arts, excelling in thoroughness and efficiency. . . . The men loved their homes; they were home-makers —industrious and frugal. The children were trained to industry. . . .

[9] Arthur W. Calhoun, *A Social History of the American Family,* Vol. I, p. 48. Copyright 1917, 1945 by Arthur W. Calhoun. Reprinted, 1960, by Barnes & Noble, Inc.

[10] *Ibid.,* pp. 167–169.

[11] *Ibid.,* p. 175.

[12] *Ibid.,* p. 170.

Home discipline was rigid. When necessary the rod was used. . . . Servants ate with the family on ordinary occasions and were well cared for. . . . Part of the home, sometimes a separate dwelling, was provided for aged parents or grandparents. Often an unmarried daughter held it her duty to remain with the aged parents to the end of their days.[13]

The Swedes gave due attention to family welfare. Swedish women held something of the same eminence held by Dutch women. They may have been more hardy than the New England housewives if we can judge from the following item:

Died in peace in 1771, at Wilmington, Delaware, a pious, elderly matron, who had been mother of 16 children, all married and comfortable; 68 grandchildren, 166 great-grandchildren, and 4 great-great-grandchildren—in all 238 living offspring survived her. The generation of the just shall be blessed.[14]

The Southern Aristocratic Family

Many divergent groups settled in the South Atlantic colonies, as in the Middle Atlantic region, but the English were predominant.

The outstanding characteristic of this region was its marked pattern of social stratification. Although this pattern did not exist among all the different nationalities, and the aristocratic family was in no sense typical of the family in general in the South, the discussion here is limited to that type of family because it represented a different type from those already discussed for New England and the Middle Atlantic colonies.

Kuhn cites two chief reasons for this social development in the South.[15] First, at least in Maryland and Virginia, there was the early establishment of both limited and absolute servitude. A considerable number of voluntarily indentured servants from the pauper classes in England came over to spend varying numbers of years working out their freedom. Also, large numbers of convicts were sent there during the latter half of the seventeenth century. Finally, the pattern of Negro slaveholding developed.

The other reason stems from the fact that many of the early English settlers in this region were Cavaliers who subscribed to the pattern of sharp social gradation that had been followed in England. (Calhoun points out, however, that the leading families of Virginia ''had exactly the same origin as those of New England.'')

Existing conditions promoted a family that was extremely patriarchal. As the pattern of large holdings developed, the family assumed large proportions, frequently with more than two generations and one conjugal pair living in the same manor. The head of the family had dominance over men of younger generations and often, in the custom of the English gentleman, became a man of leisure.

His wife, though subordinate to him, fared like contemporary English

[13] *Ibid.*, pp. 202–204.
[14] *Ibid.*, p. 192.
[15] *Op. cit.*, p. 142.

women of the middle class. In general, women of the South were freer from toil than those of the North, but they had no control over property. Writing of the economic status of the Southern matron, Mrs. Putnam says:

> Her life was on its professional side the life of the Greek lady. . . . Each was the wife and steward of a farmer. Each was responsible for the reception in the house of produce of the farm intended for home consumption. Each must keep order regnant among slaves and goods. A surprising amount of what the household used was in each case made under the lady's direction from raw material produced on the estate. . . . And each was responsible for the health of her household; it was her duty to prevent sickness if possible, and when it came to tend it. Each doubtless if not overtaxed derived satisfaction from the performance of important work bearing directly on the welfare and happiness of those she loved best, but neither could be called a free woman.[16]

Calhoun, quoting a nineteenth-century writer, provides this additional description:

> [The colonial ladies were] noted for their personal attractions; and many, in the higher walks of life, for great dignity of character, modesty, and politeness of behavior, as well as for their activity and frugality in the management of their household affairs. These commendable qualities left their impress and beneficial influence upon succeeding generations. . . . Some spun at the wheel or wove at the hand loom! and cultivated kitchen and flower gardens. They studied the Bible, and other books of sound moral and religious instruction; instilled correct, honorable, virtuous, and patriotic principles into the minds of their children, and presided with dignity and grace at the social entertainment. . . .[17]

Although family government was patriarchal, it was not harsh and forbidding. Children were definitely subordinate, but since most of the work was performed by the lower caste and thus taken away from them, they could spend much of their time in leisure. They were reared in the ideals of their fathers and grandfathers before them. Most of the children were taught by tutors in their own homes. At about the age of sixteen, the boys were sent off for higher study. Girls were trained chiefly in domestic matters and ". . . must learn the accomplishments of the day, to play upon the harpsichord or spinet, and to work impossible dragons and roses on canvas."[18]

The Southern aristocratic household was, of course, highly self-sufficient. Cotton spinning was a home industry and there were many artisans among the indentured servants. George Washington's plantation at Mount Vernon was a specimen of the "self-sufficing estate." He employed carpenters, masons, bricklayers, coopers, and shoemakers. He operated a weaving establishment and a flour mill, and had a vessel to carry produce to market.

The owning class in the South, though actually representing a small proportion of the population, tended to intermarry and in this manner

[16] Emily James Putnam, *The Lady*. New York: Sturgis & Walton Co., 1910, p. 300.
[17] *Op. cit.*, Vol. I, pp. 280–281.
[18] A report "from a Virginia lady," reported in Calhoun, Vol. I, *op. cit.*, pp. 297–298.

built up a landed aristocracy. One of the roles of the woman was, in fact, that of marrying off her children to "proper" mates among the kindred aristocracy. Hence, there resulted a fairly close blood relationship in the upper class. But while the owning class was small in numbers, it exercised wide authority over many members of the lower classes.

Summary

One of the common characteristics of colonial society was the fact that it was family-centered. In each instance there was a close relationship between the family, on the one hand, and such factors as social control and individual behavior, on the other. In general, the attitude toward divorce was more tolerant in the colonies than in their mother countries.

Families of necessity were generally self-sufficient, by modern-day standards; the Southern aristocratic family represented the highest degree and the Quakers, perhaps, the lowest degree of this characteristic. There were vast differences in the matter of equality of status in the different colonies, the Southern aristocratic family reflecting the greatest social stratification and the Quakers the least.

The Germans and Swedes tended to be farmers and to locate in the hinterlands, but most of the other groups (excluding the Southern aristocrats, of course) tended to be business- and trade-minded and more urban in character. Most of the families, except those described in the South, were middle class (although at the close of the Revolution there was much poverty everywhere).

These brief descriptions represent the majority families, but many families among the Puritans, Quakers, Dutch, Germans, and Swedes did not fit these prototypes. There were, of course, other families in the colonies, for example, the French Huguenots, the Welsh, the Moravians, the Scotch Presbyterians, and others. Each has had some influence on the American culture of today. There also were the families (from many of the countries already mentioned and others as well) who took part in the movement to the frontier. The patterns of these families were largely dictated by circumstances: they were of necessity highly self-sufficient; they were closely knit, and they showed characteristics of individualism and equalitarianism unknown in the other colonial families.

The American Family from Independence through the Nineteenth Century

Industry was almost wholly organized around the family in the home until after the middle of the eighteenth century. However, the latter part of that century was a period of mechanical inventions and, except for the country districts where household industry lingered much longer, most industry moved into the factory.

Many of the new machines were of English invention, and manufacturing, especially of textiles, grew rapidly in certain districts of England. But

America was also destined to play its part in the revolution of industry and a number of young men—Eli Whitney, to name one—were to invent some much-needed machinery. Cities grew rapidly with the development of the factory system and the nineteenth century witnessed a mass immigration to this country. One consequence ". . . was to increase greatly the already important heterogeneity of patterns of marriage and family life."[19]

The introduction of the factory system in this country proceeded in a different manner from that in England. In America men were loath to leave their land, since agriculture was profitable. Much of the work in the factories, therefore, fell first into the hands of women, and later, of children. Washington, in a letter to Lafayette, said: "Though I would not force the introduction of manufactures by extravagant encouragements, and to the prejudice of agriculture, yet I conceive much might be done in the way of women, children and others, without taking one really necessary hand from tilling the earth."[20] In 1831, women over ten years of age constituted 68 percent of all employees in the cotton industry throughout the country; in Lowell, Massachusetts, one of the most important cotton manufacturing centers, 80 percent of the workers in the mills were women, of whom the greater proportion were under twenty-five years of age.[21] Not only was their labor as effective as that of men, but they could be hired more cheaply.

This change in the role of women and children had a profound effect, of course, on the family and the home. A completely different relationship developed among family members; society became less family-centered and the husband lost much of his authoritarian role.

There were other changes. One of the most important was the beginning of the emancipation of married women from the legal as well as the economic restrictions that had been placed on them up until this time. Maine, in 1844, was the first state to allow married women the absolute ownership and control of their property. (Some other states followed soon thereafter.) Michigan permitted married women to make a will in 1850.

With these developments also came the possibilities of higher education for American women. Efforts in this direction were led by a small band of devoted women, notably Catherine Beecher, Emma Willard, and Mary Lyon. As a result of their campaigns, several academies and seminaries for girls were opened—Mt. Holyoke Seminary in 1837, Elmira College in 1855, Vassar in 1861, Wellesley in 1870, Smith in 1871, and Bryn Mawr in 1880. Meanwhile, certain men's colleges, notably in the Middle West, opened their doors to women. Oberlin admitted women from its foundation in 1833 and Knox, Antioch, Iowa, Wisconsin, and Washington followed its example. Among Eastern universities, Cornell accepted its first woman

[19] Kuhn, *op. cit.*, p. 150.

[20] Quoted in Frank L. McVey, *Modern Industrialism,* 2d ed. New York: D. Appleton and Co., 1923, p. 48.

[21] Goodsell, *op. cit.*, p. 422.

student in 1870. The women's affiliates, such as Barnard College of Columbia University and Radcliffe College, affiliated with Harvard, appeared later.

Greater independence for women was also achieved during this period by an increase in the number of reasons why a marriage could be dissolved. A further development was the greater authority they were given over their children while they were married, and, in the event of divorce, the greater likelihood of receiving custody of minor children (if the woman was the innocent party).

It should be remembered that these developments, which were to continue and grow in both their nature and scope in the twentieth century, were still novel in the middle of the nineteenth century, and for many women the family pattern they had experienced earlier still existed. As an example, one writer states: "Girls still married too young—were cheated out of their youth. As late as 1850 a girl was rather old at twenty, an old maid at twenty-five."[22]

The Civil War, and especially emancipation of the slaves, effected a revolution in family life in the South. The great estates could not be held together and began to vanish. The collapse of the old system encouraged the younger generation to move to the city, and in some instances to the North and West.

With the advent of the Industrial Revolution and the trend toward urbanism following the Civil War, and with the emancipation of women, a number of disrupting effects on the American family were described by observers at that time. The social literature of the last half of the nineteenth century abounded in references to the instability of the family, and practically predicted the extinction of family organization, at least in its present form. Yet there were many homes—undoubtedly still a majority in the nation—in which families remained together in the strongest personal bonds.

What is most important, perhaps, concerning families and family life in the latter part of the nineteenth century and the early part of the twentieth, is that the most striking phases of that period are discernible in the present-day family. Although some changes have taken place during the last fifty years, these changes have not been of such basic importance (especially when considered in relation to the changes of the previous century) that special attention needs to be given to minute chronology. The principal influencing factors are well known. These include the extension of mass education, continued urbanization, the spread of mass production, the further establishment of equal rights for women and, with it, a continued increase of their numbers in the labor force.

We are now at the point of leaving the general discussion of history, valuable for its contributions from the standpoint of showing us where we have been and how we reached where we are, and will move on to the present day.

[22] Elizabeth Blackwell, *The Laws of Life*. New York: G. P. Putnam, 1852, p. 143.

GENERAL POPULATION TRENDS AND CHARACTERISTICS

The discussion in the remainder of this chapter will be divided into four basic parts. First, there will be a discussion of general population trends and characteristics in the United States. There will follow a discussion of the diversity of family characteristics. After that, consideration will be given to one of the most distinguishing traits of American families that has a profound influence on the housing problem—mobility. The chapter will close with analysis of our standard of living.

Over-all National Population Trends

The population of the American Indian tribes at the time of the coming of the white man has been estimated at one million persons. At the time of the first census, in 1790, the states then forming the nation had a population of 3.9 million, somewhat less than the number of children born each year in recent years. Just before World War II, in 1940, the nation passed the 132-million mark. At that time, population authorities were estimating a *peak* of 165 million persons for the nation, that peak probably to be reached before the end of the century.

To the embarrassment of those authorities, the 165-million mark was passed by 1955 and in 1960 the nation contained over 179 million persons (Table 2–1, p. 77). This figure represented a record increase of nearly 28 million during the decade 1950–60. The birth rate during this period averaged 25 per thousand of the population and the death rate had declined to only 8 per thousand. (This "natural increase" in population, at a rate of 1.7 percent per year, constituted 90 percent of the total population increase, the remaining 10 percent being represented by net immigration from abroad.)

Many persons have felt that a rapid increase in population is a characteristic of only the less-developed countries. However, the 18.5 percent gain between 1950 and 1960 represented the largest gain for this nation since the first decade of the twentieth century—and much of the increase during that earlier decade resulted from the heavy tide of immigration rather than from natural increase.

Characteristics of the General Population

Before discussion of the characteristics of households and families, some characteristics of the general population of the nation will be mentioned. These include its regional distribution and urban character, and some detail will be provided concerning age structure, sex, and the proportions of nonwhite and foreign born in our present-day population.

The U.S. Census divides the nation into four regions: the Northeast, which is comprised of 9 states having a population of 45 million persons in 1960; the South, having 16 states and a population of 55 million; the North Central, with 12 states and 52 million persons; and the West, with 13 states and a population of 28 million. It will be shown later, in the discussion of mobility of our population, that the West is the fastest-growing region, largely as a result of the heavy migration to that region from others.

A concomitant change in population over the years has been that from rural to urban areas.[23] At the time of the 1790 census, only 5 percent of the population lived in urban areas, *compared with approximately 70 percent in 1960*. By 1960, the urban population stood at 125 million, compared with 54 million for the rural population. The recent increase in urban population has been caused primarily by internal migration and is discussed in more detail later.

Since foreign immigration is no longer as important a factor in our population as it has been in the past, the age structure is determined largely by the pattern of birth and death rates. During the 1950's, the median age of our population declined somewhat (from 30.0 years in 1950 to 29.2 years in 1960) because of the "baby boom," but, as can be seen from Figure 1,

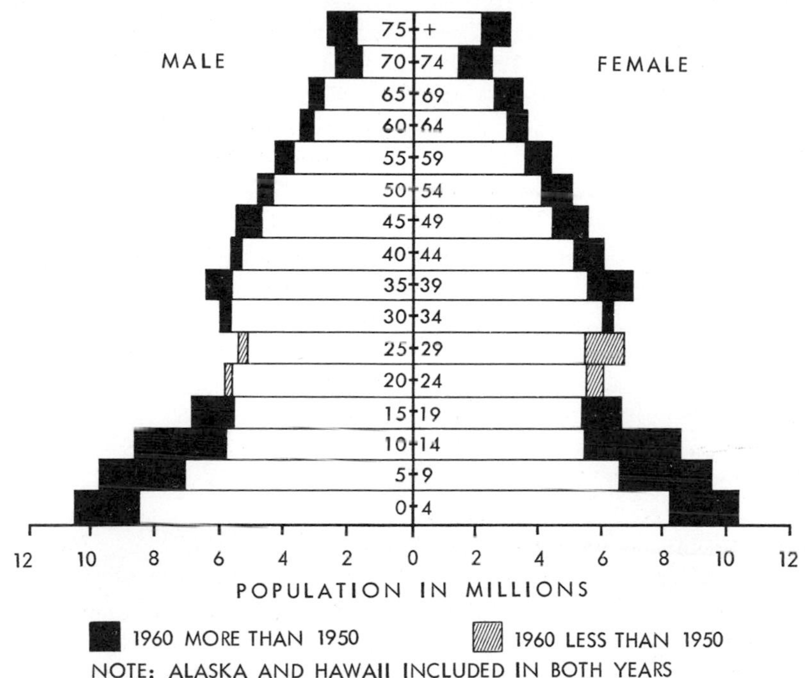

FIGURE 1. *Age and sex distribution of U.S. population 1950 and 1960. (Source of data: U.S. Bureau of the Census,* Census of Population 1960. *General Population Characteristics, PC(1), IB, U.S. Summary, pp. 1–146 and 1–147.)*

[23] The U.S. Census generally defines urban areas as those incorporated or unincorporated places of 2,500 or more inhabitants and the densely settled fringe areas around cities having a density of 1,500 persons per square mile. (See Census volume for exact definition.)

our population during this period grew both younger and older. The Population Reference Bureau, in commenting on this graphic illustration depicting the age profile of the American people, has said: "Its ungainly, full-chested, narrow-waisted, broad-bottomed shape will have profound economic, social and demographic effects on the nation for decades to come."[24] The narrow waistline of the population profile of course reflects the low birth rate during the Depression years of the 1930's.

The greatest increases in population between 1950 and 1960 were in the age groups under twenty years of age. These groups will be moving into marriageable ages and forming new families during the next two decades. (The median age for marriage in 1960 was 20.3 years for women and 22.8 years for men.) Other significant increases were evidenced in the age groups thirty-five and over. One of the most important aspects of this increase is that related to the age groups sixty-five and over, because these groups largely represent retired persons. Numerically, these groups grew from 12.3 million persons in 1950 to 16.6 million in 1960. The problems and implications of this increase are discussed in a later chapter on the aging.

One of the strange phenomena concerning population is that at birth boys outnumber girls about 105 to 100, but at advanced age women outnumber men. As a result of women's outliving men, in 1960 the sex ratio of the total population was 100 to 97 in favor of women. (In the age group seventy-five and over the ratio was 100 to 75 in favor of women.)

Another highly important characteristic of the population is the proportion that is nonwhite. This group has increased at a substantially higher rate than the white population during the past decade—26.8 percent as compared with 17.9 percent. This trend has been developing over several decades, as can be seen from the following percentage distribution:

	Total	*White*	*Nonwhite*
1960	100	88.8	11.2
1950	100	89.5	10.5
1940	100	89.8	10.2
1930	100	89.8	10.2
1920	100	89.7	10.3
1910	100	88.9	11.1
1900	100	87.9	12.1

The nonwhite population has been, of course, predominantly Negro. The increase in their proportion of the population has resulted primarily from their higher birth rate (since the difference in the death rate between Negroes and whites is now very small).

This group represents a significant part of the rural-to-urban migratory movement which has been taking place. Negro migration has been motivated by several factors, generally related to their low socioeconomic status—their desire to find better jobs, better living conditions, and better educational opportunities. In one city, Washington, D.C., Negroes comprised

[24] Population Reference Bureau, Inc., "U.S.A. Population Changes: 1950–60," *Population Bulletin,* Vol. XIX, No. 2, March 1963, p. 30.

approximately half of the total population in 1960. In other cities, the proportion increased significantly over that in 1950.

A last important factor to be mentioned is the declining proportion of foreign born in the United States. This was an important group in our population for many years. However, the last heavy wave of immigrants came to this country in the first two decades of the twentieth century, and those immigrants, if still living, have reached an advanced age. In 1960, in fact, only approximately 5 percent of the population had been born in another country. (This does not include persons of Puerto Rican birth. This group has represented a substantial migration in recent years. Although the largest proportion of the group resided in New York City, Census figures have indicated some diffusion of this population since 1950.)

There are many predictions concerning the population of the nation in the future, with considerable variation in those predictions. However, the estimates have one common characteristic: a prediction of an appreciable increase during the next several decades. This prediction is based on two developments during the last few decades—the heavy rate of post-World War II marriages, and the baby boom of the 1940's and 1950's. Added to this is the fact that, with the continued advances in medical science, people are living longer (see Chapter 13).

At the rate of increase experienced during the last decade, by 1970 the population of the United States should pass the 200-million mark. *By the turn of the century the population of the nation could double the 1960 figure,* or at least come close to doing so. This would mean the equivalent of another New York City, another Los Angeles and Dallas, another Peoria and Seattle—another of all of the cities added together! The continuing growth of urbanism as our standard way of life will be one of the principal results. (This is discussed in the next chapter.) The impact of this growth will, of course, have tremendous economic and social effects on the nation as a whole.

Families and Households

Although the individual constitutes the basic unit in our population, and population statistics regarding individuals therefore remain important, any understanding of housing must primarily center around factors relating to *families* and *households,* since they represent the basic *social* unit whose primacy stems from both biological and social conditions.

At this point, the difference in the terms "household" and "family" should be pointed out, even though the terms are frequently used interchangeably. According to the 1960 U.S. Census:

> A *household* consists of all the persons who occupy a housing unit. A house, an apartment or other group of rooms, or a single room, is regarded as a housing unit when it is occupied or intended for occupancy as separate living quarters, that is, when the occupants do not live and eat with any other persons in the structure and when there is either (1) direct access from the outside or through a common

hall or (2) a kitchen or cooking equipment for the exclusive use of the occupants.

A *family* consists of two or more persons living in the same household who are related to each other by blood, marriage, or adoption; all persons living in one household who are related to each other are regarded as one family.

Not all households contain families, because a household may be composed of a group of unrelated persons, *or one person living alone.* A few households contain more than one family, that is, two family groups in the same household in which none of the members of one family is related to any of the members of the other family. Strangely, therefore, even though households may contain one or more families, Census data indicate that there are more households than families in the United States. This results from one-person units, which are included in household statistics but not in family statistics. This also is the reason why the average family size is larger than the average household size, according to Census statistics.

The number of households in the United States has consistently increased faster than the population. This can be observed by comparing the percent-of-increase columns in Table 2–2 (p. 77). This greater increase in number of households is, of course, reflected in households smaller in size from decade to decade—from an average of 4.8 persons in 1900 to 3.4 persons in 1960.

There is, of course, immense variation in the nature of households. One manner in which households can be described is to indicate the relationship of the members to the head of the household. These relationships, showing differences in the percentage distributions, can be seen from the data in Table 2–3 (p. 78).

Before discussing what the data in that table show, it is desirable to first provide some additional definitions of terms. The *head of the household* is the person considered to be the head by household members. (However, if a married woman is living with her husband, that husband is always classified as the head by the U.S. Census, regardless of what is reported by household members.) The *head of a primary family* is a head of a household living with one or more persons related to him by blood, marriage, or adoption. A *primary individual* is a household head living alone or with persons none of whom is related to him.

It can be seen, from the data in Table 2–3, that a fourth of the population was made up of heads of primary families in 1960, approximately 22 percent was composed of wives of heads, and a third was composed of children under eighteen of heads. The most common types of household, therefore, as would be expected, are those having a husband and wife, with or without children. While that may be common knowledge, what is perhaps not so well known is that one out of every ten families has a relative other than wife or child living in the household and one out of twenty families represents a household head living alone or with persons none of whom are related to him.

There are some differences based upon where families live, the most important of which are reflected in the average size of household and average size of family. Those living in central cities are the smallest and, within urban areas, those living in the urban fringe (suburbia) are the largest. The largest families, in general, however, are those living in rural areas.

Between 1950 and 1960, there was a slight increase in the population per primary family for the nation as a whole (from 3.61 to 3.65), reflecting the increased number of children, but a decline in the population per household (from 3.42 to 3.29), reflecting more persons living alone or in small households of unrelated members.

The last-mentioned trend should not be interpreted, however, as indicating a decline in new family formation. The 1960 Census showed that 67 percent of persons fourteen years old and older were married—approximately the same proportion as in 1950. This figure was 7 percent higher than the percentage in 1940. In 1960, 22 percent of this population group was single, 8 percent widowed, and 3 percent divorced. The proportion of married persons is somewhat smaller among nonwhites than among whites.

Another manner in which households can be described is by indicating the various kinds of units or groups of which they are comprised. For example, in addition to primary families, some households contain secondary families and subfamilies. A secondary family is one living in a household with a primary family, but not related to the head of the household. A subfamily is a married couple with or without children, or one parent with one or more single children under eighteen years of age, related to but not including the head of the household or his wife. (The most common example is a young married couple sharing the home of the husband's or wife's parents. This also makes them members of the primary family.)

In March 1961 there were 53,291,000 households in the United States and 45,435,000 of them contained families. Most of these were primary families (45,278,000 or 99.7 percent) and 1,531,000 of the primary families (or 3.4 percent) contained subfamilies. A total of only 157,000 of the families (or 0.3 percent of all families) were secondary families.[25] It can be seen from these figures that, numerically, secondary families and subfamilies are not highly important in American society today.

Other Household and Family Characteristics

As has been the case during most periods in the history of our nation, Americans are still moving upward in our affluent society. Indicators of this are their educational level, their occupational patterns, and their income levels. After these are touched on, a brief discussion of another characteristic of families, their personal value orientations, will follow.

Educational Attainment

The general level of education has improved appreciably in the nation since 1940. In that year, for example, only 14 percent of Americans twenty-

[25] U.S. Bureau of the Census, *Current Population Reports,* Population Characteristics, "Household and Family Characteristics: March 1961," Series P-20, No. 116, May 1, 1962.

five years old or over had graduated from high school. By 1960 the proportion reached 25 percent. Included in these figures are 5 percent in 1940 who had graduated from college, compared with 8 percent two decades later.

Even more striking were the gains made among the nonwhite population. In 1940 only 4 percent had graduated from high school. By 1950 this proportion had increased to 9 percent and by 1960 to 14 percent.

Measured in terms of median years of education attained, for the total population group aged twenty-five years and over there was an increase from 8.6 years in 1940 to 10.6 years in 1960. The increase for nonwhites was somewhat greater, from a median of 5.8 years in 1940 to 8.2 years in 1960 (Table 2–4, p. 79).

Occupational Levels

In recent years there also has been an important shift in the labor force, fewer persons being employed in unskilled labor and more in skilled labor. Farm employment has been declining significantly, from a point where it had represented well over a third of the labor force in 1900 to only 6 percent in 1960. The proportion of common laborers has declined from 13 percent at the turn of the century to only 5 percent in 1960. Private household service has declined from 5 percent to 3 percent.

On the other hand, there has been an increase in other kinds of manual and service jobs. Operatives have increased from 13 percent to 19 percent over the past sixty years, craftsmen from 11 percent to 14 percent, and service workers other than private household workers from 4 percent to 9 percent.

The most significant increases, however, have been among white-collar workers, which, as a group, have increased from 18 percent in 1900 to 43 percent in 1960. In this group the largest increase has been in the clerical class, from 3 percent in 1900 to 15 percent in 1960. Professional and technical workers have increased from 4 percent to 12 percent. Managers, officials, and proprietors have increased from 6 percent to 9 percent, and sales workers from 5 percent to 8 percent (Table 2–5, p. 80).

Income Levels

Data showing income levels give evidence of the vastly expanding middle class in the United States. This expansion has resulted in a corresponding decline in the lower class. The per capita personal income figures, which are available for years since 1929, confirm this trend. This trend, in current dollars, over recent years has been as follows:

Year	*Per capita Income*
1929	$ 703
1940	595
1950	1,491
1955	1,866
1959	2,160
1960	2,223

SOURCE: U.S. Department of Commerce, Office of Business Economics, *Survey of Current Business,* August 1961.

More important than per capita income, from the standpoint of housing, is family income. In 1947 the median income for families in the United States was $3,033; by 1960 it had increased to $5,625. In other words, family income had nearly doubled in a period of thirteen years. This increase in the median figures results in large part from the higher proportion of families who had incomes in the upper brackets. For example, in 1947, only 9 percent had incomes from $6,000 to $9,999, compared with 31 percent in 1960. Furthermore, in 1947 only 3 percent of the families had incomes of $10,000 and over, compared with 14 percent in 1960 (Table 2–6, p. 81).

These average figures, of course, conceal important differences that exist among different regions and groups in the population. For example, there are important regional differences; the highest median income in 1959 was in the Pacific states ($6,572) and the lowest was in the East South Central states ($3,793). There also are important differences between white and nonwhite families. In the East South Central states, for example, white families had a median income of $4,384 compared with a median of only $1,880 for nonwhite families. Similar differences, though not always so extreme, were found in other regions (Table 2–7, p. 81). Urban families generally have higher incomes than rural families; these differences are discussed in more detail in Chapter 12.

There are other differences based on other factors. Families with male head, married, wife present, had the highest median incomes if the head was between the ages of thirty-five and forty-four years ($6,344). It was next highest among heads aged forty-five to fifty-four years ($6,256), followed by heads aged under thirty-five years ($5,377), and heads aged fifty-five years and over ($4,719). Five-person families were found to have the highest incomes ($5,975), followed by four-person families ($5,932), three-person families ($5,429), six-person families or more ($5,271), and two-person families ($4,754).

Of course, the increases in income over the years, which have been indicated, have not meant equivalent increases in either take-home pay, because of taxes, or in purchasing power, because of inflation.

The influence of taxes is shown in the data in Table 2–8 (p. 82). It can be seen from the data in that table how the taxes paid by families in the highest gross income classes force them down into lower net income classes. The most significant influence of this tax "take" is, naturally, at the highest income level. Approximately 23 percent of the families were in the $15,000 and over class before taxes in 1960, but only 17 percent were in that class after taxes.

Price Fluctuations

The dollar in 1961 purchased less than half in consumer goods what it had purchased in 1940. The monthly average of purchasing power, as measured by consumer prices, stood at only 78.2 in 1961, compared with 166.9 in 1940 (base period 1947–1949 = 100). The drop in purchasing power in between 1940 and 1961 for wholesale prices was from 195.7 to 84.0, and for retail food prices, from 209.2 to 82.6. The year-to-year changes are shown in Table 2–9 (p. 82).

The specific changes in the prices of different commodities are reported in the Federal consumer price index. From this index it can be seen that housing costs—including a composite of costs of home purchase and other homeowner costs, rent, utilities, house furnishings, and household operation—have increased in recent years, from 95.0 in 1947 to 133.6 in 1962. This increase has been exceeded only by increases in the cost of medical care, personal care, and transportation. The increases for apparel, food, and recreation were considerably smaller (Table 2–10, p. 83).

Despite taxes and the increases in costs of living that have been noted, the nation's level of living has continued to rise. More families continue to reach the middle and upper income brackets, and when family income has been adjusted for price increases, Americans have still fared better than ever before.

Yet it should not be forgotten that there is a tremendous range between the bottom and top levels of income, and between these levels, as Williams observes, ". . . are great differences in total life-situation in terms of medical care and health, food, clothing, shelter, education, recreation, and general access to the comforts and amenities of life in our culture."[26] These differences, especially with reference to shelter, will be pointed out in many places in the remainder of this book—in the discussion of standard of living, social structure of cities, and in the descriptions of the populations making up the central cities, suburbia, and rural areas. The constant increase in the cost of housing is discussed further in Chapters 4 and 15.

Personal Values

The characteristics of families discussed thus far—their size and composition, and the educational attainment and occupational and income levels of the head of the families—are easily understood and are generally quite measurable. Each characteristic has a direct or indirect influence on the housing needs of the particular family.

There is still another characteristic, undoubtedly equally important but much more difficult to describe and, at the moment, almost impossible to measure. This characteristic is the family's "personal value" orientation.

Personal values are defined in one study as "the totality of a number of factors, such as an individual's ideals, motives, attitudes, and tastes, which are determined by his cultural background, education, habits, and experiences."[27] Some elaboration, and some indication of how the term "value" differs from closely related terms, will be helpful. A value differs from a *preference,* inasmuch as a preference generally is based on an individual's

[26] Robin M. Williams, Jr., *American Society,* 2d ed., rev. New York: Alfred A. Knopf, 1960 (reprinted 1963), p. 101.

[27] Glenn H. Beyer, Thomas W. Mackesey, James E. Montgomery, *Houses Are for People,* Research Publication No. 3. Ithaca, N.Y.: Cornell University Housing Research Center, 1955, p. 49.

range of experience and may not be justified on the basis of any commonly accepted standards or moral judgments. A value differs from an *attitude,* inasmuch as an attitude may refer only to what is "desired," whereas a value is what is "desirable." Both preferences and attitudes are likely to change more frequently than values; values tend to endure.[28]

So long as individuals continue to have "wishes" and tend to "appraise" what they want, "values" will inevitably enter in. Part of their importance in any study of housing rests in their relationship to *motivations,* because, as indicated, values tend to establish the direction in which action is taken. However, values should not be regarded as motivation *per se.* Motivations are only one of the elements; they comprise the element that is concerned with the individual's standards, but do not include the other factors that make up the total situation. In other words, an individual's action is usually a compromise between values and other aspects of a situation. Although much remains to be learned about the complex linkage between values and motivation, it should be possible to use values in predicting behavior.[29]

Personal values represent the basic qualities of people—their *real* likes and dislikes. These basic qualities are not hastily formed, and therefore will not be hastily changed. Studying housing needs by obtaining a better understanding of people should ultimately permit more satisfactory planning and house design than studying families' preferences (what they *say* they prefer), their buying habits, or even time-and-motion studies or studies of people living and working in the artificial environment of a laboratory.

What are some of the personal values individuals hold? There are many different groupings, depending upon the focus of the subject under discussion. Williams presents an excellent general grouping.[30] A grouping pertinent to a discussion of housing has been provided through research at Cornell University. In that research, nine specific values were identified and studied. The "labels" given to them, and a brief description of each, is as follows:

1. *Economy.* Economy was recognized as a value when a person tends to emphasize the *economical* uses of goods and services. Because, to a degree, all goods are scarce, persons with this value will consciously or unconsciously measure—not always in monetary terms—the worth of one item against the worth of another before making a choice. Is it a good investment and will he get a good return for it? His selections of food, clothing, shelter, recreation and, to some extent, of companions, will be influenced by his economic bias. He will be quick to sense economic pressures because of an instinctive alertness to them.

2. *Family centrism.* A family with this value tends to be self-sufficient and tightly knit. Members of the family have a strong feeling of unity. They will often judge situations to be good or bad, desirable or undesirable, in the light of their

[28] Glenn H. Beyer, *Housing and Personal Values,* Memoir 364. Ithaca, N. Y.: Cornell University Agricultural Experiment Station, July 1959, pp. 4–5.

[29] *Ibid.,* p. 5.

[30] *Op. cit.,* pp. 415–420. See also Talcott Parsons and Edward A. Shils, eds., *Toward A General Theory of Action;* Part 4, Chapter 2, "Values and Value-Orientations in the Theory of Action: An Exploration in Definition and Classification." Cambridge, Mass.: Harvard University Press, 1951.

effect on the family group. Their allegiance and loyalty will be given to their close family and relatives before they will be given to outside individuals or groups.

3. *Physical health.* A person with this value makes his decisions according to what he thinks their effect will be on his physical well-being. He will want to promote, or at least not to impair, his physical health. He will be concerned with sunshine, fresh air, diet, physical exercise, and so on, and will tend to avoid situations that might lead to ill health or accidents.

4. *Aesthetics.* A person evidences an aesthetic value when he evaluates his environment in terms of its orderliness, harmony, and beauty. He will be sensitive to sight, sound, and touch in a way that is highly personal. He will value what he himself sees or experiences, as opposed to what social opinion says he should experience. His reactions will be immediate and spontaneous rather than delayed and analytical.

5. *Leisure.* A person may be said to be influenced primarily by a desire for leisure if he judges situations according to their effect on his freedom to live his life in a way that will bring him greatest personal enjoyment. In other words, he values leisure because he wants to pursue interests and activities of his own choosing. Such a person will want more time than the average person for painting, gardening, reading, relaxing, listening to records or to the radio, indulging in hobbies, and so on. Leisure is to him an end in itself, just as an aesthetic experience is an end in itself to some others.

6. *Equality.* This value comes into play in situations that involve rank, rights, or privileges. A person with this value will be sensitive to the needs of others and will conduct himself as justly as he can. He will consider unchecked authority, dominance, and submission to be out of bounds; he will treat others as equals or as near-equals and his family relationships will be based on mutual respect. If he is driven to behave unjustly, he will suffer guilt and regret.

7. *Freedom.* A person who values freedom places great emphasis on being allowed to make as many of his own decisions as possible. He tends to rebel at handed-down decisions, at assignments, regimentation, and other forms of restriction. He believes that he should be able to act largely as he sees fit. Thus, to a considerable extent, he is an individualist and a nonconformist. He will repudiate the authority of custom as quickly as the authority of his employer.

8. *Mental health.* The person who values mental health is one who wants peace of mind. He will try to achieve this by trying to control his environment or, if he cannot do that, adjusting to it in a way that will reduce frustration, anxiety, and other inner conflicts. An individual of this kind will be relatively conservative in his social relationships, since risk might produce pain or unhappiness. He is likely to have a constant need for psychological security and will want to feel that his environment is ordered and predictable. Such a person, then, will weigh each new situation before deciding what course of action to pursue. Finally, he will be strongly inclined to think of himself before others.

9. *Social prestige.* The power of this drive is observed in our society in the strong urge of many individuals to move upward socially. These social climbers feel they must have the attention and respect of their peers. Often, they attempt to obtain or hold that respect by an extravagant display of automobiles, clothing, and housing. Persons who value social prestige are unlikely to admit its hold on them.[31]

Individuals do not, of course, hold only one personal value; they may be oriented toward many. The characteristics of some values overlap the

[31] Adapted from Beyer, Mackesey, and Montgomery, *op. cit.*, pp. 50–51.

characteristics of others. Both of these factors cause clusters of certain values. The Cornell research, for example, found that the nine values identified above could be incorporated into four groups to which the following labels were attached: "economy" (economy value, sometimes including freedom value); "family centrism" (family centrism, equality, and physical health values); "personal" (aesthetics, leisure, and mental health values, sometimes including freedom value); and "prestige" (social prestige value).[32]

Individuals having their dominant orientations in the different clusters of values give evidence of having different characteristics. Those in the "economy" and "family centrism" groups seem to be primarily extroverts, realistic, insensitive, practical in their demands, and interested more in necessities than in luxuries. They also tend to observe their basic physical needs carefully. A primary difference between the two groups is that those dominantly oriented toward economics are more individual-minded, whereas those oriented toward family centrism are more group- or collective-minded. Those in the "personal" group tend more to be introspective, idealistic, sensitive, personal- or individual-minded, more whimsical in their demands, and they may sometimes disregard basic physical needs in favor of luxuries. The characteristics of the "social prestige" group are difficult to describe, because they can vary over a wide range. The important thing is that this group desperately wants the social approval of the peer group. To gain and hold this approval, individuals will do whatever seems necessary and appropriate. The deceptive aspect about this group, however, is that in the process of gaining prestige they may approximate the characteristics of any of the other groups, especially the "personal" group—but with different motives. Although this group has generally been associated with lavish display and wealth, this need not necessarily be the case. Lack of display may in many instances constitute the hallmark of desirability.

An important question is: How many American families have *dominant* personal value orientations that place them in one or the other of these groups? Because of lack of research, this question cannot be answered. The single study in which an attempt was made at measurement indicated that approximately a third of American families probably fell in the "economy" group, another third in the "family centrism" group, and about 10 percent in the "personal" group.[33] The remaining one fourth could not be classified; this proportion may approximate the group primarily oriented toward social prestige.

Better understanding of the personal value orientations of American families may hold the key to many factors, including more appropriate design of housing for different groups, which could add to greater satisfaction with life in general. Certainly, if value patterns could be adequately identified in individual families, and if it were known what housing characteristics would best satisfy the different value orientations, we could provide more

[32] *Ibid.*, pp. 2–7.
[33] *Ibid.*, p. 56.

satisfactory housing in the future than in the past. This factor is discussed further in Chapter 8.

Mobility—An American Family Characteristic

Another important characteristic of American families is their tendency to be highly mobile. This factor is, of course, important to any consideration of housing needs and desires because when a family moves, it gives up one dwelling unit and occupies another.

The term "mobility" is generally used in this discussion because that term normally applies to persons who move from one dwelling unit to another in the same community—which, as we will see, represents the highest proportion of the total movement of people. Another term, "migration," is sometimes used interchangeably with "mobility," but it usually refers to movement of a relatively large number of persons to another, usually distant area, frequently in quest of better, or at least different, living conditions. For example, "migration" would be the proper term to apply to the three great movements of population in this country (a) to the West from the North and South, (b) to the North from the South (the movement that has especially involved large numbers of Negroes), and (c) the continuous movement from rural to urban areas.

Sometimes the differentiation between these two terms cannot be made in existing statistics; this accounts for what might be considered contradictory use of one or the other of the terms in the discussion that follows.

Nature and Scope of Recent Mobility

It has already been mentioned that mobility has been an important factor from both a regional and an urban-rural point of view.

Although the West is the smallest region in the nation with respect to population, it also is the fastest growing as a result of continuing heavy migration westward. The percentage changes during the last decade, according to the U.S. Census, were as follows:

PERCENTAGE GAINS AND LOSSES IN POPULATION AS A RESULT OF NATURAL INCREASE AND MIGRATION

Region	*Natural Increase*	*Migration*	*Total*
United States	16.7	1.8	18.5
Northeast	12.3	0.9	13.2
North Central	16.4	−0.3	16.1
South	19.5	−3.0	16.5
West	19.9	19.1	38.9

California has experienced the most dramatic and continued growth of any state over the last several decades, but the West as a whole has experienced heavy in-migration during recent years. The South as a whole has experienced high rates of in-migration to its metropolitan areas but equally high rates of out-migration from its nonmetropolitan areas. (Florida, however, attracted migrants to nearly all portions of the state and was the state with the highest in-migration during the 1950's.) The South-to-North migration that built up after World War I and continued until the late 1940's seems to have slackened. The North Central region experienced net migration gains in its industrial complexes on the south and west shores of Lake Michigan and in northeastern Ohio and southern Michigan, but the western portion of the region lost population. In the Northeast, there were gains in the coastal industrial belt but losses in the Appalachian plateau, the ridge and valley area, and in much of New England.

Between 1950 and 1960 the rural population of the nation declined numerically for the first time in history—a loss of 425,000 persons. This loss is attributed primarily to the migration of Negroes into cities in both the South and the North, although there also was similar migration, on a much smaller scale, among the white population. The changes for the 1950–1960 period, according to the U.S. Census, were as follows:

PERCENTAGE GAINS AND LOSSES IN POPULATION, URBAN AND RURAL

Region	*Urban*	*Rural*
United States	29.3	−0.8
Northeast	14.2	9.0
North Central	24.5	1.1
South	40.1	−5.9
West	55.3	1.7

That most of the population increase previously described for the West was urban in nature can be seen from these data. The data also reflect substantial urban growth in the South.

This has been the broad picture of movement between regions and from rural to urban areas over the last decade. Let us now look particularly at the recent two-year period 1958–1959, and examine this movement in more detail. Approximately 13,772,000 households—one out of every five households in the United States—moved during this two-year period.[34]

The proportion of movement was equal between those families who had previously lived inside standard metropolitan statistical areas (SMSA) and those who lived outside such areas—approximately 26 percent in each instance. For those who moved within metropolitan areas the movement also was about the same for those who lived in central cities and those not living in the central cities.

Most of the moves were over a short geographic distance. This is indicated by the fact that half of all the movers who previously lived inside the nation's metropolitan areas moved to a different residence within the same area in which they had been living.

[34] Much of the information in this section is based on U.S. Bureau of the Census, *Census of Housing 1960,* Components of Inventory Change, HC (4), Part 1B–1: Inventory Characteristics, United States and Regions.

The 1960 Census provides some interesting information concerning the movement within metropolitan areas. (For definition of Census "standard metropolitan statistical area," which is referred to here, see p. 88.) It shows, for example, that, of the households who previously lived in central cities but moved to another place in the same metropolitan area, only 23 percent moved outside the central city. This amounted to 823,000 households. (In contrast, 2,781,000, or 77 percent, households moved to another location within the central city.) On the other hand, 436,000 households moved into the central city from some area outside of it in the same metropolitan area. In other words, nearly twice as many people move out of the city into the suburbs as move from the suburbs in.

The Census data also show that during the two-year period 1958–1959 about 13 percent of the movers left a different metropolitan area to move somewhere else. Of these, approximately half went to another metropolitan area (less than a fourth moved into a central city); the other half moved outside of any metropolitan area.

The data also show that about 38 percent had previously been living outside of any metropolitan area. Most of these households remained outside metropolitan areas in their new location.

The percentage figures are given in Table 2–11 (p. 84). These figures show that a great many families, numerically, are moving outside central cities, and many are moving from outside our metropolitan areas into them, thus tending to support the general opinions that have been widely circulated. However, what is perhaps more important is that the *proportions* show that most movers living in the central cities are *not* moving away from them, and most movers living outside metropolitan areas are *not* moving into them. One exception is with reference to the rather low proportion of movers from one state to another (6 percent of all movers). Over half (56 percent) of this group moved into a metropolitan area, the proportions being approximately equal for those moving into central cities and those not moving into central cities.

About 8,830,000, or two thirds of the households that moved, were renters; the remaining 4,942,000 owned their homes. The highest proportion of movers (35.3 percent) were found in the West—over a third of the households in that region had moved during the two-year period. Among renters, nearly 60 percent, and among owners, 20 percent, had moved. Next in rank from the standpoint of mobility was the population of the South. A total of 28 percent of the households in that region had moved—about half of the renters and 16 percent of the owners. The proportions were somewhat lower in the North Central and Northeast regions, as can be seen from the data in Table 2–12 (p. 85).

According to the U.S. Census:

Home ownership among the Nation's recent movers rose from 23 percent in previous units (2,752,000 owner households) to 39 percent in the present units (4,572,000 owner households). Although most of the recent movers who were formerly renters remained renters after their move, about 2,598,000, or three-tenths of the 9 million former renters, shifted to owner occupancy. With respect to the 2.8 million former homeowners, the same proportion (three-tenths) changed to renter occupancy; in terms of absolute numbers, however, only 778,000 became renters. . . .[35]

In other words, although the basic shift, where a shift of tenure is involved, is from renting to owning, a substantial number of families are making changes in reverse of the general trend.

The youngest segment of the population is most mobile, and families become less mobile as they increase in age. For example, among 44 percent of the mover families, the head was under thirty-five years of age. In another 24 percent he was between the ages of thirty-five and forty-four, and in an equal number of instances, he was between forty-five and sixty-four. Only 7 percent of the mover families had heads aged sixty-five years and over.

Household heads who moved from units that were previously renter-occupied were younger than those moving from units that were owner-occupied. For example, about half of the household heads who moved from renter-occupied units were under thirty-five years of age, compared with only 27 percent of the heads of previously owner-occupied units. The data are shown in Table 2–13 (p. 85).

If data concerning rent levels and value can be used as criteria, it can be assumed that renters do not tend to upgrade themselves when they move as much as owners do. Among renter-movers, according to the U.S. Census, 42 percent had an increase in rent, 27 percent reported that their rent went down, and 31 percent reported that they had remained in the same rent class. On the other hand, data on value of owner-occupied units showed marked upward changes from the previous to the present dwelling. A total of 63 percent of those who moved in either 1958 or 1959 reported that the value of their present dwelling was higher than that of their previous one, only 12 percent reported that it went down, and 25 percent reported that it remained in the same class as before. The median contract rent for previously occupied units was $59 and increased to $62 for present units; the median value for previously owned properties was $12,100 and increased to $15,500.

Observing movers who previously owned and who moved to other owned properties, it can be seen that 11 percent of the previously occupied properties were valued at less than $5,000, but only 6 percent of the presently occupied properties fell in that value class. Also, 15 percent of the previously occupied properties fell in the $7,500 to $9,900 class, compared with only 7 percent of the presently occupied units in that price range. On the other hand, 25 percent of the presently occupied units were valued at $20,000 or more, compared with only 11 percent of the previously occupied units (Table 2–14, p. 86).

One difficulty in explaining the reasons for mobility that are important

[35] *Ibid.*, p. 17.

to housing is that many of the studies that have been made relate to *individuals* rather than to *households*.[36] It is known, however, that the basic reasons for mobility fall into two general categories—involuntary moves and those made voluntarily. Involuntary moves may result from eviction, demolition of a building, fire damage, and the like, but they may also result from such factors as loss of income, change in job location, new household formation, and so forth. A voluntary move may arise either from some dissatisfaction with the housing unit or simply a desire for a "better" unit. Rossi found that three fifths of the moves of families he studied were voluntary.[37]

Perhaps the most important reason for voluntary moves is the shortage of space in relation to a family's needs. The probably typical newly married couple occupies a rented apartment. At this stage any moving is likely to grow out of dissatisfactions with that apartment—with regard to amount of space, street noises, heating equipment, cost of the apartment, or its location—rather than the pressure of family size. However, when the first child arrives the family feels the pressure of both space and economics. As soon as the economic problem becomes resolved so that the family can afford more space, a move to a larger unit usually takes place. Today this move is likely to be to an owned home.

A few decades ago most American families only purchased one home in a lifetime. Today, many purchase two or three. A Cornell study investigated some of the improvements recent movers felt they had obtained in their new units.[38] No questions were asked about the interior space and its arrangement, but several questions were asked about neighborhood and location. The items and the percentages of families indicating improvement in their new location over their previous one are as follows:

Improvement Cited	*Percent*
Enough room outside the house for personal enjoyment	60
Free from traffic noises	50
Free from dangerous traffic	46
Free from factory or other fumes or smoke	41
Free from interference of neighboring families	30

Some questions also were asked about improved location from the point of view of social relations. Following are the items and the percentages of families indicating this kind of improvement:

Improvement Cited	*Percent*
Plenty of outdoor play space for children	55
Near right kind of playmates for children	27
Neighbors of good social standing	31
Near houses of good friends	27

Rossi found that few moves resulted because of the journey to work.[39] A

[36] An exception is the excellent study reported in Peter H. Rossi, *Why Families Move.* Glencoe, 111.: The Free Press, 1955.

[37] *Ibid.*, p. 135, Table 8–1.

[38] Glenn H. Beyer, Thomas W. Mackesey, and James E. Montgomery, *op. cit.*, pp. 31–32.

[39] *Op. cit.*, pp. 31, 32.

Cornell study arrived at the same conclusion, indicating that other factors than location of employment were more important to the location of housing.[40]

Much of the change to a second and possibly a third owner-occupied home is undoubtedly a direct result of a desire for "upgrading" or upward social mobility, made possible through increased personal incomes (individuals moving up the occupational ladder) and liberal home financing plans (discussed in Chapter 5). This reason has been cited in much of the literature regarding suburbia.

Finally, some mobility, though perhaps a small proportion of the total, is caused by broken families. Divorce, separation, or widowhood (especially at a young age) is likely to result in a change in housing for reason of economics, space, or location (or some combination of these).

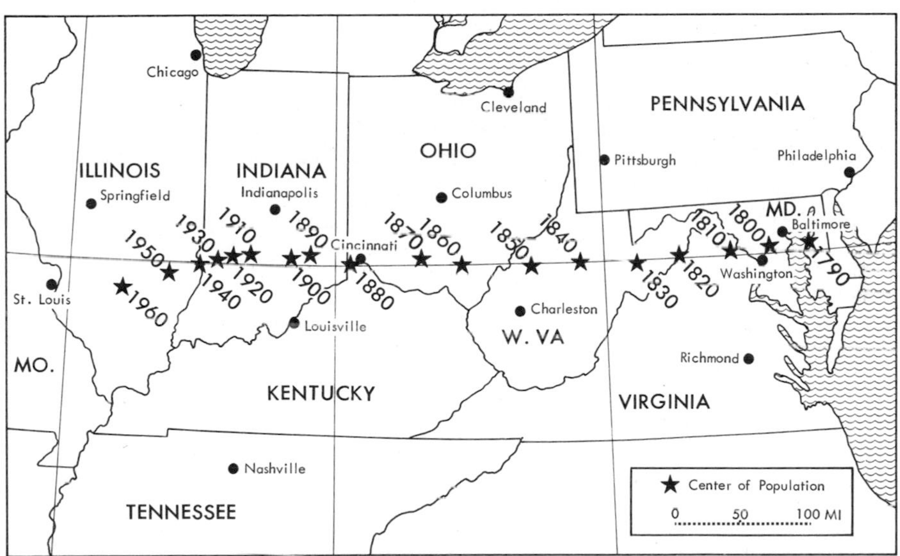

FIGURE 2. *Centers of population for conterminous United States 1790 to 1960. (Source of data: U.S. Bureau of the Census,* Census of Population 1960. *Vol. I, Part A, p. xi.)*

A high rate of mobility, much of it over short distances, has existed in this country from colonial times to the present. There has been a general movement of the population westward throughout our history. This can best be depicted by the constant westward movement, in each decade since the first census, of the centers of population for the nation. In 1790, this center was near Baltimore, Maryland; by 1960, it was in the south-central part of the state of Illinois (Figure 2).

Americans seem to be movers, and the factors that have brought about

[40] Leonard P. Adams and Thomas W. Mackesey, *Commuting Patterns of Industrial Workers,* Research Publication No. 1. Ithaca, N.Y.: Cornell University Housing Research Center, 1955.

mobility in the past are not likely to diminish in importance. A comparably high rate of mobility is, therefore, expected to continue in the future.

STANDARD OF LIVING

Any discussion of the American family would be deficient if it did not include reference to our standard of living. Yet any brief discussion of that subject is made difficult by the general complexity of the term, caused in large part by the many definitions of what is being discussed. As Pipping states: "The definitions of the concept standard of living are innumerable."[41]

"Standard of living" as used here will refer to those things which are "so important to the consumer, that if any one of them is lacking forces to restore it are immediately put into action."[42] Or as stated by Kyrk: "All those things one insists upon having—the essential values to be sought—make up one's standard of living; in other words, they determine the first things to be secured through the expenditure of time and money."[43] The term obviously has certain social connotations when used in reference to "minimum standards" or "raising the standards of living," a general goal set forth in the Charter of the United Nations.[44]

It is implied in these definitions that the *standard* of living may be different from the *manner* of living. A family may not be able to live up to the standard it holds. However, an individual may not be conscious of his standard of living. In fact, more often than not, he has not consciously thought through the process by which he spends his income in return for real goods and services—in the case under discussion, housing. Given a set of values, at a given moment in time, in relationship to a given income, it is the degree of motivation behind the striving to obtain certain goods and services that determines whether or not they are part of an individual's standard of living.

It is also clear that there is no single standard of living. Devine has said: "Each individual has his own standard, determining every choice he makes. Each family has its own, the result of combinations, consolidations, and compromises among the standards of its individual members. Each locality and each nation has its standard, produced by the inter-play of an infinite number of economic, social, and psychic forces. . . ."[45] Pipping has in-

[41] Hugo E. Pipping, *Standard of Living,* Societas Scientiarum Fennica, Commentationes Humanarum Litterarum XVIII, 4. Helsingfors, Finland: Centraltryckeriet, 1953, p. 113.

[42] Edward T. Devine, *The Normal Life,* 2d ed., rev. New York: Douglas C. McMurtrie, 1917, p. 1.

[43] Hazel Kyrk, *The Family in the American Economy.* Chicago: University of Chicago Press, 1953, p. 374.

[44] Report of a Committee of Experts convened by the Secretary-General of the United Nations jointly with the International Labour Office and the United Nations Educational, Scientific and Cultural Organization, *Report on International Definition and Measurement of Standards and Levels of Living.* New York: United Nations, 1954, p. 2.

[45] *Op. cit.,* p. 1.

dicated that: "It [standard of living] relates clearly to social groups (family, class) and to status, and has taken shape via custom."[46]

For example, our ever-expanding middle class usually demands relatively high standards of physical health and comfort in its housing, at least as compared with large groups in the populations in other countries. Thus, in most of our new suburban homes we demand not only central heating systems, but also automatic clothes and dishwashing machines, garbage disposers, and the like. Many families want air conditioning today. We also emphasize leisure, and as a result we subscribe to many magazines, have several radios in a single home, usually at least one television set, and frequently a stereophonic record player. We want our homes to be in locations free from noise and smoke and away from dangerous traffic. We also like to have them free from interference of neighboring families.

The general standards of living of this large group of Americans is relatively easy to describe, at least in general terms. Yet one must be careful about generalizing too far. For example, there undoubtedly are differences in the standards of many college teachers and plumbers who may receive nearly equivalent income. There also seem to be differences between the "newly rich" and those who attained their wealth earlier. Warner and Lunt found, for example, that the highest proportionate expenditures for automobiles and household maintenance occurred in the lower-upper class, among those families just on the margin of acceptance into the upper-upper elite.[47] Frazier makes the same point in reference to middle-class Negroes: ". . . one would only need to read Negro newspapers and magazines to see to what extent conspicuous consumption is still the dominant pattern of this class. . . . School teachers and college professors who earn less than $10,000 a year are building homes that cost $40,000 and $50,000 and entertaining lavishly."[48]

The greatest discrepancy between manner of living and standard of living undoubtedly exists among families of our lowest income class. This class includes a high proportion of nonwhite persons and a significant proportion of rural people—although, of course, many nonwhite and rural persons do not fall in this class and many other persons do.

The industrial progress we have made in this country, which has permitted the great expansion of the middle class, has in actuality worked against the lowest income group. As Harrington has said:

> In the optimistic theory, technology is an undisguised blessing. A general increase in productivity, the argument goes, generates a higher standard of living for the whole people. And indeed, this has been true for the middle and upper thirds of American society, the people who made such striking gains in the last

[46] *Op. cit.*, p. 121.

[47] W. Lloyd Warner and Paul S. Lunt, *The Social Life of a Modern Community.* New Haven: Yale University Press, 1941, p. 299.

[48] E. Franklin Frazier, *Black Bourgeoisie.* New York: Collier Books, 1962, p. 11.

two decades. . . . The other Americans are the victims of the very inventions and machines that have provided a higher living standard for the rest of the society.[49]

The low-income group also has been the subject of a pamphlet published recently by the Conference on Economic Progress. The authors indicate: "The most obvious unmet needs in the United States are concentrated among the more than two-fifths of a nation who still live in poverty or deprivation. They need better education, health services, and housing. . . ." This report mentions the "9½ million seriously deficient dwelling units in the United States, or about one-sixth of the total of 58 million units."[50]

Many of the individuals in the lowest income class still live below a decent and comfortable level of living. Undoubtedly, many of them have set standards for themselves appreciably above what their means will allow. Many others, however, probably have either not thought of higher standards or have given up in despair of attaining them.

As more and more of the lower-income people reach the middle class, they will be creating for themselves higher standards of living. The standards for the middle-income class may also be expected to continue to rise. This has been the history of our nation. Certainly the standards of the early colonists were not as high as those Americans living two hundred years later—when larger dwellings, wood and coal ranges, and oil lamps were among the principal amenities of living sought. And the standards of the late nineteenth century were not as high as the standards which most of our population set for themselves today.

Cross-cultural comparisons are difficult, if not impossible, to make. Yet, there is considerable evidence that nowhere else in the world have such high standards of living been reached as in this nation. To quote Williams again:

The high level of real income in the United States has been copiously documented: if America has not been the Eldorado it was thought to be by countless immigrants to its shores, it has, at any rate, produced a high level of material comfort for the great majority of the population. It is true that the material rewards of the system have often proved to be insecure and that great enclaves of the population still do not share greatly in "the American standard of living," but the tangible rewards are great enough, seen against any standards of comparison accessible to the population, to be a strong force supporting the status quo. At the same time the real possibilities of acquiring greater income and prestige have reinforced efforts to strive within the system rather than to challenge it. These real possibilities—combined with the persistence of the attitudes of an earlier era—have led to the transfer of hope and ambition to the next generation. Belief in the American Dream of upward mobility is resilient and thus far has been sufficiently reinforced by actual rises to stand as a prime support of adjustment to the existing situation.[51]

[49] Michael Harrington, *The Other America.* New York: The Macmillan Company, 1962, p. 12.

[50] *Poverty and Deprivation in the United States,* Washington, D. C.: Conference on Economic Progress, April 1962, pp. 1, 66.

[51] *Op. cit.,* pp. 142–143.

READING LIST

HISTORY OF THE AMERICAN FAMILY

Calhoun, Arthur W. *A Social History of the American Family from Colonial Times to the Present.* Vol. I, Colonial Period; Vol. II, From Independence through the Civil War; Vol. III, Since the Civil War. Cleveland: The Arthur H. Clark Co., 1917, 1918, 1919. Reprinted in 3 vols., New York: Barnes & Noble, Inc., 1960 (paperback).

Goodsell, Willystine. *A History of the Family as a Social and Educational Institution.* New York: The Macmillan Co., 1915.

Kuhn, Manford Hinshaw. "American Families Today: Development and Differentiation of Types," in Howard Becker and Reuben Hill (eds.) *Family, Marriage and Parenthood.* Boston: D. C. Heath and Co., 1948.

THE AMERICAN FAMILY TODAY

Anshen, Ruth Nanda (ed.) *The Family: Its Function and Destiny.* New York: Harper & Bros., 1949.

Becker, Howard and Reuben Hill (eds.) *Family, Marriage and Parenthood.* Boston: D. C. Heath and Co., 1948.

Bossard, James H. S. and Eleanor S. Boll. *Ritual in Family Living,* 2d ed. Philadelphia: University of Pennsylvania Press, 1956.

Burgess, Ernest W. "The Family in a Changing Society," in Paul K. Hatt and Albert J. Reiss, Jr., *Cities and Society.* New York: The Free Press of Glencoe, Inc., 3rd printing August 1961.

Glick, Paul C. *American Families.* A Volume in the Census Monograph Series. New York: John Wiley & Sons, Inc., 1957.

Miller, Herman P. *Income of the American People.* A Volume in the Census Monograph Series. New York: John Wiley & Sons, Inc., 1955.

Parsons, Talcott and Robert F. Bales. *Family, Socialization and Interaction Process.* Glencoe, Ill.: The Free Press, 1955.

Sirjamaki, John. *The American Family in the Twentieth Century.* Cambridge, Mass.: Harvard University Press, 1955.

Taeuber, Conrad and Irene B. Taeuber. *The Changing Population of the United States.* A Volume in the Census Monograph Series. New York: John Wiley & Sons, Inc., 1958.

PERSONAL VALUES

Beyer, Glenn H. *Housing and Personal Values.* Memoir 364. Ithaca, N.Y.: Cornell University Agricultural Experiment Station, July 1959.

———, Thomas W. Mackesey and James E. Montgomery. *Houses Are for People.* Research Publication No. 3. Ithaca, N.Y.: Cornell University Housing Research Center, 1955.

Cutler, Virginia F. *Personal and Family Values in the Choice of a Home.* Ithaca, N.Y.: Cornell University Agricultural Experiment Station, Bulletin 840, November 1947.

Williams, Robin M., Jr. *American Society,* 2d ed. rev. New York: Alfred A. Knopf, 1960, Chapter XI.

MOBILITY

Foote, Nelson N., *et al. Housing Choices and Housing Constraints.* New York: McGraw-Hill Book Co., 1960, Chapter 6.

Lipset, Seymour M. "Social Mobility and Urbanization," in Paul K. Hatt and Albert J. Reiss, Jr., *Cities and Society*. New York: The Free Press of Glencoe, Inc., 3d printing August 1961.

Rossi, Peter H. *Why Families Move*. Glencoe, Ill.: The Free Press, 1955.

STANDARD OF LIVING

Duhl, Leonard J. (ed.) *The Urban Condition—People and Policy in the Metropolis*. New York: Basic Books, Inc., 1963.

Harrington, Michael. *The Other America*. New York: The Macmillan Co., 1962.

Kyrk, Hazel. *The Family in the American Economy*. Chicago: The University of Chicago Press, 1953.

Martin, Edgar W. *The Standard of Living in 1860*. Chicago: The University of Chicago Press, 1942.

Pipping, Hugo E. *Standard of Living*. Societas Scientiarum Fennica, Commentationes Humanarum Litterarum XVIII, 4. Helsingfors, Finland: Centraltryckeriet, 1953.

Streightoff, Frank Hatch. *The Standard of Living Among the Industrial People of America*. Boston: Houghton Mifflin Co., 1911.

Wright, Chester Whitney. *Economic History of the United States,* 2d ed. New York: McGraw-Hill Book Co., 1949, Chapter XLV.

Table 2–1

POPULATION OF THE UNITED STATES,* 1790 to 1960

Census Year	*Population*	*Increase Over Preceding Census*	
		Number	*Percent*
1790	3,929,214	—	—%
1800	5,308,483	1,379,269	35.1
1810	7,239,881	1,931,398	36.4
1820	9,638,453	2,398,572	33.1
1830	12,866,020	3,227,567	33.5
1840	17,069,453	4,203,433	32.7
1850	23,191,876	6,122,423	35.9
1860	31,443,321	8,251,445	35.6
1870	38,558,371	7,115,050	22.6
1880	50,189,209	11,630,838	30.2
1890	62,979,766	12,790,557	25.5
1900	76,212,168	13,232,402	21.0
1910	92,228,496	16,016,328	21.0
1920	106,021,537	13,793,041	15.0
1930	123,202,624	17,181,087	16.2
1940	132,164,569	8,961,945	7.3
1950	151,325,798	19,161,229	14.5
1960	179,323,175	27,997,377	18.5

SOURCE: U.S. Bureau of the Census, "Our Growing Population," Graphic Pamphlets GP60-1, Washington, D.C.: U.S. Government Printing Office, 1961, p. 2.
* Includes Alaska since 1870 and Hawaii since 1900.

Table 2–2

COMPARISON IN GROWTH OF NUMBER OF NONFARM HOUSEHOLDS AND POPULATION

	Occupied Dwelling Units (or Households)		*Population*		
Year	*Number of Households*	*Percent Increase*	*Number of Persons (Millions)*	*Percent Increase*	*Average Household Size*
1900	16.0	—	76.2	— %	4.8
1910	20.3	27.0	92.2	21.0	4.5
1920	24.4	20.2	106.0	15.0	4.3
1930	30.0	22.8	123.2	16.2	4.1
1940	35.0	16.5	132.2	7.3	3.8
1950	43.0	22.9	151.3	14.5	3.5
1960	53.0	23.4	179.3	18.5	3.4

SOURCE: Derived from U.S. Bureau of the Census, *Census of Housing 1960.* States and Small Areas, HC (1), No. 1, U.S. Summary, p. xxvi.

Table 2–3

PERCENTAGE DISTRIBUTION OF HOUSEHOLD CHARACTERISTICS FOR THE UNITED STATES BY SIZE OF PLACE, 1960

	1960							
	Urban					*Rural*		
	Urbanized Areas		*Other Urban*					
Household Characteristics	*Central Cities*	*Urban Fringe*	*10,000 or More*	*2,500 to 10,000*	*Urban Total*	*1,000 to 2,500*	*Other Rural*	*Rural Total*
Total population (number in thousands)	57,975	37,873	16,173	13,247	125,268	6,497	47,558	54,055
Percentage in households	97.2%	98.1%	95.8%	97.5%	97.4%	98.6%	96.8%	97.0%
Head of household	31.9	28.7	30.2	30.5	30.6	31.0	26.7	27.2
Head of primary family	*25.1*	*25.5*	*24.9*	*25.4*	*25.3*	*25.8*	*23.9*	*24.1*
Primary individual	*6.8*	*3.2*	*5.3*	*5.1*	*5.3*	*5.2*	*2.8*	*3.1*
Wife of head	21.1	23.1	21.6	22.3	21.9	22.7	21.6	21.7
Child under 18 of head	29.7	35.5	32.3	33.1	32.1	33.3	36.1	35.8
Other relative of head	12.2	9.4	9.9	10.0	10.8	10.3	11.3	11.2
Nonrelatives of head	2.4	1.4	1.8	1.5	1.9	1.4	1.1	1.1
Percentage in group quarters	2.8	1.9	4.2	2.5	2.6	1.4	3.2	3.0
Population per household	3.05	3.41	3.17	3.19	3.18	3.18	3.63	3.56
Population per primary family	3.50	3.66	3.57	3.57	3.57	3.57	3.89	3.85

SOURCE: U.S. Bureau of the Census, *Census of Population 1960*, General Population Characteristics, PC(1), 1B, U.S. Summary, p. 1–157.

Table 2–4

PERCENTAGE DISTRIBUTION OF YEARS OF SCHOOL COMPLETED BY PERSONS TWENTY-FIVE AND OVER, BY COLOR, 1940, 1950, AND 1960

Years of School Completed	*Total*			*White*			*Nonwhite*		
	1940	*1950*	*1960*	*1940*	*1950*	*1960*	*1940*	*1950*	*1960*
Total of population twenty-five years old and over (number in thousands)	74,776	87,885	99,438	68,000	79,515	89,581	6,776	8,370	9,857
None	3.8%	2.6%	2.3%	3.1%	2.1%	1.9%	10.5%	7.0%	5.6%
Elementary school:									
One to Four	9.9	8.5	6.1	7.8	6.8	4.8	31.3	25.6	17.8
Five and Six	11.5	9.4	7.5	10.6	8.4	6.7	21.5	18.5	14.6
Seven	7.0	7.0	6.4	6.8	6.8	6.1	8.4	9.5	8.8
Eight	28.2	20.8	17.5	29.8	21.7	18.1	11.9	11.9	12.8
High school:									
One to Three	15.2	17.4	19.2	15.8	17.8	19.3	8.7	13.5	18.7
Four	14.3	20.7	24.6	15.3	22.0	25.8	4.5	8.6	13.8
College:									
One to Three	5.5	7.3	8.8	5.9	7.8	9.3	1.9	3.0	4.4
Four or more	4.6	6.2	7.7	4.9	6.6	8.1	1.3	2.3	3.5
Median, years	8.6	9.3	10.6	8.7	9.7	10.9	5.8	6.9	8.2

SOURCE: U.S. Bureau of the Census, *Census of Population 1960*. General Social and Economic Characteristics, PC (1), 1C, U.S. Summary, pp. 1–207, 1–209.

Table 2–5

PERCENTAGE DISTRIBUTION OF OCCUPATIONS OF THE ECONOMICALLY ACTIVE CIVILIAN POPULATION, 1900–1960*

Major Occupation Group	*1960*	*1950*	*1940*	*1930*	*1920*	*1910*	*1900*
Total (number in millions)	61.5	59.0	51.7	48.7	42.2	37.3	29.0
White-collar, except farm	43.3%	36.6%	31.1%	29.4%	24.9%	21.3%	17.6%
Professional, technical, and kindred	11.7	8.6	7.5	6.8	5.4	4.7	4.3
Managers, officials, and proprietors, except farm	8.8	8.7	7.3	7.4	6.6	6.6	5.8
Clerical and kindred	15.1	12.3	9.6	8.9	8.0	5.3	3.0
Sales workers	7.5	7.0	6.7	6.3	4.9	4.7	4.5
Manual and service	50.3	51.6	51.5	49.4	48.1	47.7	44.9
Manual	38.6	41.1	39.8	39.6	40.2	38.2	35.8
Craftsmen, foremen, and kindred	*14.2*	*14.1*	*12.0*	*12.8*	*13.0*	*11.6*	*10.5*
Operatives and kindred	*19.3*	*20.4*	*18.4*	*15.8*	*15.6*	*14.6*	*12.8*
Laborers, except farm and mine	*5.1*	*6.6*	*9.4*	*11.0*	*11.6*	*12.0*	*12.5*
Service	11.7	10.5	11.7	9.8	7.8	9.6	9.0
Private household	*2.8*	*2.6*	*4.7*	*4.1*	*3.3*	*5.0*	*5.4*
Service, except private household	*8.9*	*7.9*	*7.1*	*5.7*	*4.5*	*4.6*	*3.6*
Farm	6.4	11.8	17.4	21.2	27.0	30.9	37.5
Farmers and farm managers	4.1	7.4	10.4	12.4	15.3	16.5	19.9
Farm laborers and foremen	2.3	4.4	7.0	8.8	11.7	14.4	17.7

SOURCE: 1900 to 1950, *The Economic Almanac 1962*, New York: National Industrial Conference Board 1962 (reporting Census data), p. 53; 1960, derived from U. S. Bureau of the Census, *Census of Population 1960*, General Social and Economic Characteristics, PC (1), 1C, U.S. Summary, p. 1–216.

* The universe denoted as "the economically active civilian population" refers for 1940, 1950, and 1960 to persons fourteen years old and over in the experienced civilian labor force; for earlier years, it refers to civilian gainful workers ten years old and over. No attempt was made to revise the 1900–1930 figures to a labor force basis.

Table 2–6

PERCENTAGE DISTRIBUTION OF MONEY INCOME OF FAMILIES, 1947 to 1960

	Income Level								
Year	*Under $1,000*	*$1,000 to $1,999*	*$2,000 to $2,999*	*$3,000 to $3,999*	*$4,000 to $4,999*	*$5,000 to $5,999*	*$6,000 to $9,999*	*$10,000 and Over*	*Median Income*
1947	10.7%	16.6%	22.0%	19.7%	11.7%	7.7%	8.9%	2.7%	$3,033
1948	10.6	14.5	20.5	20.7	13.0	8.1	9.8	2.8	3,190
1949	12.1	14.8	20.6	20.0	12.1	7.8	9.8	2.6	3,107
1950	11.5	13.2	17.9	20.6	13.6	9.0	11.0	3.2	3,319
1951	9.2	11.4	15.4	19.7	15.6	10.8	14.4	3.6	3,714
1952	8.5	10.8	14.2	18.6	15.4	11.9	16.5	4.1	3,889
1953	8.6	9.9	11.7	15.8	15.9	13.2	19.8	5.4	4,233
1954	8.8	11.0	11.9	15.5	15.6	11.9	19.6	5.8	4,167
1955	7.7	9.9	11.0	14.6	15.4	12.7	22.4	6.2	4,420
1956	6.5	8.9	10.2	12.5	14.8	13.7	25.4	7.9	4,787
1957	6.4	8.4	9.6	11.8	14.1	14.5	26.6	8.4	4,978
1958	5.6	8.8	9.8	11.1	13.4	13.7	27.5	10.0	5,095
1959	5.1	8.3	9.3	10.1	11.7	13.2	30.1	12.2	5,417
1960	5.0	8.0	8.7	9.8	10.5	12.8	30.8	14.3	5,625

SOURCE: U.S. Bureau of the Census, *Current Population Reports,* Consumer Income, "Income of Families and Persons in the United States: 1960," Series P–60, No. 37, January 17, 1962, p. 36.

Table 2–7

MEDIAN INCOME IN 1959 OF FAMILIES, BY REGIONS

	Total	*White*	*Nonwhite*
Northeast			
New England	$6,128	$6,168	$4,354
Middle Atlantic	$6,211	$6,367	$4,373
North Central:			
East North Central	$6,215	$6,355	$4,477
West North Central	$5,154	$5,215	$3,552
South:			
South Atlantic	$4,713	$5,280	$2,551
East South Central	$3,793	$4,384	$1,880
West South Central	$4,548	$5,019	$2,294
West:			
Mountain	$5,660	$5,744	$3,202
Pacific	$6,572	$6,677	$5,214

SOURCE: U.S. Bureau of the Census, *Census of Population 1960.* Detailed Characteristics, PC (1), 1D, U.S. Summary, p. 1–766.

Table 2–8

PERCENTAGE DISTRIBUTION OF AGGREGATE FAMILY PERSONAL INCOME BEFORE AND AFTER TAXES, 1960

Income	*Before Taxes*	*After Taxes*
Under $2,000	2.1%	2.5%
$2,000 to $2,999	3.3	4.1
$3,000 to $3,999	5.4	6.7
$4,000 to $4,999	7.4	9.2
$5,000 to $5,999	8.6	10.7
$6,000 to $7,499	14.0	15.3
$7,500 to $9,999	18.4	17.8
$10,000 to $14,999	18.2	17.0
$15,000 and over	22.6	16.7
Total	100.0%	100.0%

SOURCE: U.S. Department of Commerce, *Survey of Current Business*, April 1962, pp. 11 and 16.

Table 2–9

PURCHASING POWER OF THE DOLLAR, 1940 TO 1961
(1947–1949 = 100)

	Monthly Average, as Measured by		
Year	*Wholesale Prices*	*Consumer Prices*	*Retail Food Prices*
1940	195.7	166.9	209.2
1941	176.1	159.0	191.6
1942	155.8	143.5	163.1
1943	149.3	135.1	146.4
1944	147.9	133.0	148.4
1945	145.3	130.0	145.1
1946	127.1	119.9	126.6
1947	103.7	104.7	104.3
1948	95.8	97.3	96.1
1949	100.8	98.2	100.0
1950	97.0	97.3	98.8
1951	87.1	90.1	88.8
1952	89.6	88.1	87.3
1953	90.8	87.4	88.7
1954	90.7	87.1	88.8
1955	90.3	87.3	90.2
1956	87.5	86.1	89.5
1957	85.0	83.2	86.7
1958	83.9	81.0	83.1
1959	83.7	80.3	84.5
1960	83.6	79.1	83.5
1961	84.0	78.2	82.6

SOURCE: U.S. Bureau of the Census, *Statistical Abstract of the United States: 1962*. Washington, D.C.: U.S. Government Printing Office, 1962, p. 343.

Table 2–10

CONSUMER PRICE INDEX, 1947 TO 1962
(1947–1949 = 100)

Year	*All Items*	*Food*	*Housing*	*Apparel*	*Transportation*	*Medical Care*	*Personal Care*	*Reading and Recreation*	*Other Goods and Services*
1947	95.5	95.9	95.0	97.1	90.6	94.9	97.6	95.5	96.1
1948	102.8	104.1	101.7	103.5	100.9	100.9	101.3	100.4	100.5
1949	101.8	100.0	103.3	99.4	108.5	104.1	101.1	104.1	103.4
1950	102.8	101.2	106.1	98.1	111.3	106.0	101.1	103.4	105.2
1951	111.0	112.6	112.4	106.9	118.4	111.1	110.5	106.5	109.7
1952	113.5	114.6	114.6	105.8	126.2	117.2	111.8	107.0	115.4
1953	114.4	112.8	117.7	104.8	129.7	121.3	112.8	108.0	118.2
1954	114.8	112.6	119.1	104.3	128.0	125.2	113.4	107.0	120.1
1955	114.5	110.9	120.0	103.7	126.4	128.0	115.3	106.6	120.2
1956	116.2	111.7	121.7	105.5	128.7	132.6	120.0	108.1	122.0
1957	120.2	115.4	125.6	106.9	136.0	138.0	124.4	112.2	125.5
1958	123.5	120.3	127.7	107.0	140.5	144.6	128.6	116.7	127.2
1959	124.6	118.3	129.2	107.9	146.3	150.8	131.2	118.6	129.7
1960	126.5	119.7	131.5	109.4	146.2	156.2	133.3	121.5	132.2
1961	127.8	121.1	132.5	110.2	147.9	160.9	134.0	124.1	133.2
1962	129.3	122.3	133.6	110.6	151.0	165.1	136.4	126.9	134.2

SOURCE: U.S. Department of Labor, Bureau of Labor Statistics periodic reports on Consumer Price Index.

Table 2–11

PREVIOUS AND PRESENT LOCATIONS OF RECENT MOVERS, 1959

	Total		Location of Present Unit		
			Inside SMSA's		
Location of Previous Unit	*Number*	*Percent*	*In Central Cities*	*Not in Central Cities*	*Outside SMSA's*
Inside same SMSA	5,872,000	49.8%	54.8%	45.2%	—%
In central cities	3,604,000	30.5	77.2	22.8	—
Not in central cities	2,268,000	19.2	19.2	80.8	—
Inside different SMSA	1,496,000	12.7	22.5	29.3	48.2
In central cities	742,000	6.3	26.1	32.1	41.8
Not in central cities	754,000	6.4	18.8	26.5	54.7
Outside SMSA's	4,430,000	37.5	6.9	8.5	84.6
Same state	3,715,000	31.5	3.0	4.6	92.4
Same county	*2,964,000*	*25.1*	—	0.7	99.3
Different county	*751,000*	*6.4*	14.6	20.1	65.3
Different state	715,000	6.1	27.3	28.8	43.9
Total*	11,797,000	100.0	32.7	29.4	37.9

SOURCE: Derived from U.S. Bureau of the Census, *Census of Housing 1960.* Components of Inventory Change. HC(4), Part 1B-1: Inventory Characteristics, United States and Regions, p. 17.

* Based on number of households reporting the same heads during both previous and present occupancy. This represented 86 percent of all households that moved.

Table 2–12

ALL OCCUPIED UNITS AND UNITS OCCUPIED BY RECENT MOVERS, BY REGION AND TENURE, 1959

Region and Tenure	*All Occupied Units*	*Units Occupied by Recent Movers*	
		Number	*Percent of All Occupied Units*
Northeast	13,546,000	2,742,000	20.2%
Owner occupied	7,791,000	989,000	12.7
Renter occupied	5,755,000	1,753,000	30.5
North Central	15,265,000	3,578,000	23.4
Owner occupied	10,411,000	1,425,000	13.7
Renter occupied	4,854,000	2,153,000	44.4
South	15,452,000	4,384,000	28.4
Owner occupied	9,545,000	1,501,000	15.7
Renter occupied	5,907,000	2,883,000	48.8
West	8,692,000	3,068,000	35.3
Owner occupied	5,218,000	1,027,000	19.7
Renter occupied	3,474,000	2,041,000	58.7
Total U.S.	52,955,000	13,772,000	26.0
Owner occupied	32,966,000	4,942,000	15.0
Renter occupied	19,990,000	8,830,000	44.2

SOURCE: U.S. Bureau of the Census, *Census of Housing 1960*. Components of Inventory Change. HC(4), Part 1B-1: Inventory Characteristics, United States and Regions, p. 16.

Table 2–13

AGE OF HEAD OF HOUSEHOLD BY TENURE OF PREVIOUS AND PRESENT UNITS OF RECENT MOVERS, 1959

	Number	*Age of Head*			
		Under 35 Years	*35 to 44 Years*	*45 to 64 Years*	*65 Years and Over*
Previous unit owner-occupied	2,752,000	27.0%	28.4%	33.4%	11.3%
Present unit owner-occupied	1,974,000	23.9	30.2	34.5	11.4
Present unit renter-occupied	778,000	34.7	23.9	30.5	10.9
Previous unit renter-occupied	9,045,000	49.6	22.0	22.2	6.2
Present unit owner-occupied	2,598,000	49.7	26.3	19.7	4.3
Present unit renter-occupied	6,447,000	49.6	20.2	23.1	7.0
Total U.S.*	11,797,000	44.3%	23.5%	24.8%	7.4%

SOURCE: U.S. Bureau of the Census, *Census of Housing 1960*. Components of Inventory Change. HC(4), Part 1B-1: Inventory Characteristics, United States and Regions, p. 17.

* Based on number of households reporting the same heads during previous and present occupancy.

Table 2–14

PREVIOUS AND PRESENT PROPERTY VALUES OF RECENT MOVERS, 1959

Previous Property Value	*Total*		*Present Property Values*									
	Number	*Percent*	*Less than $5,000*	*$5,000 to $7,400*	*$7,500 to $9,900*	*$10,000 to $12,400*	*$12,500 to $14,900*	*$15,000 to $17,400*	*$17,500 to $19,900*	*$20,000 to $24,900*	*$25,000 or More*	*Not Reported*
Less than $5,000	138,447	10.5%	34.7%	19.2%	15.6%	13.5%	8.6%	5.3%	0.9%	0.9%	— %	1.3%
$5,000 to $7,400	117,141	8.9	3.6	19.1	15.7	13.0	24.4	10.8	7.7	1.9	2.4	1.4
$7,500 to $9,900	198,879	15.1	2.0	9.1	9.7	21.2	23.5	15.8	13.4	1.6	2.6	1.1
$10,000 to $12,400	177,363	13.5	1.1	1.1	5.8	27.3	25.0	17.0	8.8	8.9	5.0	—
$12,500 to $14,900	193,520	14.7	1.0	2.8	2.7	8.9	21.8	21.9	15.3	12.0	12.7	0.9
$15,000 to $17,400	150,002	11.4	—	—	1.1	6.1	6.6	13.5	24.9	26.2	20.5	1.1
$17,500 to $19,900	93,233	7.1	—	—	1.2	5.0	8.1	8.2	34.3	26.2	17.0	—
$20,000 to $24,900	69,254	5.3	—	—	—	—	5.1	10.9	8.3	22.9	52.8	—
$25,000 or more	67,704	5.2	—	—	2.3	3.1	1.3	6.5	3.4	5.5	77.9	—
Not reported	108,608	8.3	11.5	4.2	5.3	12.9	11.2	19.3	6.9	13.9	7.1	7.7
Total*	1,314,151	100.0%	5.5%	6.0%	6.5%	13.1%	15.8%	14.0%	12.7%	11.0%	14.1%	1.3%

SOURCE: U.S. Bureau of the Census, *Census of Housing 1960*. Components of Inventory Change. HC(4), Part 1B-1: Inventory Characteristics, United States and Regions, p. 28.

* Based on number of households reporting the same heads during previous and present occupancy, owner-occupied nonfarm units only.

CHAPTER 3

*

American Cities: Perspective of Their Growth

Man first sought shelter as a protection from the elements. Shortly, he discovered that this shelter, if near that of others, would also serve as a protection against his enemies. This discovery gradually led to the establishment of villages. During the Mesopotamian, Greek, and Roman civilizations, cities developed as fortresses. In the Middle Ages, trading centers such as Constantinople developed and grew. With the spread of Christianity in the West, cities tended to form around cathedrals.

The primary force in the development of cities as we know them, however, was the Industrial Revolution. At first, manufacturing towns were established near easy sources of power. As industrialization grew, bringing with it cheaper and quicker transportation and new sources of power, industries and their supporting services tended to move to the most advantageous location, where total costs—procurement, processing, and distribution—would be minimized. Transportation was a primary factor.

HISTORICAL GROWTH OF AMERICAN CITIES

The first cities in the United States were seaports—New York, Philadelphia, Baltimore, Charleston, and Boston. At the time of the first U. S. Census in 1790, these cities were extremely small. Philadelphia, the largest, had a population of only 42,520. New York had a population of only 33,131. The first Census listed only six cities (population more than 8,000)—the five major seaports and another of lesser importance, Salem, Massachusetts. Their combined population was only 131,472, 3 percent of the total population of the nation at that time.

In 1790 there were only 24 incorporated places of 2,500 population or more. They represented 5 percent of the nation's population. Twenty years later, in 1810, the number of places having a population of 2,500 or more had increased to 46, representing 7 percent of the population. (By this time, three new "river cities"—Cincinnati, St. Louis, and New Orleans—were beginning to challenge the domination of the Atlantic seaports.) By 1850 there were 236 places of such size, representing 15 percent of the population; by 1900 there were 1,737, representing 40 percent; by 1950 there were 3,873, representing 57 percent. In 1960 there were 5,022 incorporated places of 2,500 or more, representing 63 percent of the population. Another 7 percent of the population lived in other kinds of urban areas, bringing the total urban population to 70 percent. From these figures it can be seen that, in the period of 170 years, the nation has changed from one made up almost entirely of farmers to one primarily urban.

Most urban areas in the nation today, of course, are no longer confined to the corporate limits of their central cities. A few cities which are exceptions to this rule, such as Phoenix, Arizona, have only been able to keep abreast of the general urban sprawl by pushing their city limits outward through annexation.

The essential *unity* of a central city and the densely built-up surrounding settlement is generally recognized. The term used by the U. S. Census for these areas is "standard metropolitan statistical area." An "SMSA" is defined as a county or group of contiguous counties (except in New England) which contains at least one city of 50,000 inhabitants or more or "twin cities" with a combined population of at least 50,000. In addition to the county, or counties, containing such a city or cities, contiguous counties are included in a standard metropolitan statistical area if, according to certain criteria, they are essentially metropolitan in character and are socially and economically integrated with the central city. In New England, towns and cities are the units used in defining standard metropolitan statistical areas.

In 1960, there were 212 metropolitan areas in the United States. They had a total population of 112,885,178, 63 percent of the nation's population. Twenty-four metropolitan areas had a population of over a million inhabitants.

The areas combined had an increase in population of 26 percent between 1950 and 1960. (The increase for the remainder of the country was only 7 percent.) A total of 138, or about two thirds, had gains of 20 percent or more, and 62 had increases of one third or more. One area, Fort Lauderdale–Hollywood, (Florida), almost quadrupled in population. Six others—Las Vegas, Nevada, Midland, Texas, Orlando, Florida, San José, California, Odessa, Texas, and Phoenix, Arizona,—more than doubled in population. Only eight metropolitan areas lost population. They were Altoona, Pennsylvania, Jersey City, New Jersey, Johnstown, Pennsylvania, St. Joseph, Missouri, Scranton, Pennsylvania, Texarkana, Tex.-Ark., Wheeling, West Virginia, and Wilkes-Barre–Hazleton, Pennsylvania.

The metropolitan–nonmetropolitan pattern of increase varied considerably among regions. In the South, the population inside such areas increased at a rate 13 times as great as the population outside those areas. In the North Central states the rate of increase was over three times that outside such areas. In the West it was more than twice the rate of population growth of nonmetropolitan areas. In the Northeast, the increases were about the same for metropolitan and nonmetropolitan areas.[1]

[1] There exists a great variation in density among these areas, resulting from the fact that whole counties are used as a basis for defining them. For example, 13 areas—Bakersfield, California, Billings, Montana, Duluth–Superior, Minn.-Wis., Eugene, Oregon, Fargo–Moorhead, N. Dak.-Minn., Great Falls, Montana, Laredo, Texas, Las Vegas, Nevada, Pueblo, Colorado, Reno, Nevada, San Angelo, Texas, San Bernardino–Riverside–Ontario, California, and Tucson, Arizona,—had a population density of less than 50 inhabitants per

EARLY STUDIES OF THE CITY

The growth of cities is not, of course, unique to the United States, although the full range of growth from infant hamlets and villages to mature large metropolises has probably occurred more rapidly, and certainly more recently, here than in most European countries. Because of the important nature of this growth, it is not surprising that a number of scholars in many countries have given their attention to it.

Early writings concerning the city fall into two general categories: those dealing with the physical and external aspects and those emphasizing sociological or, more specifically, moral aspects.

Several English economists, during the seventeenth, eighteenth, and nineteenth centuries, gave their attention to the physical and external aspects. One of the first of these was Captain John Graunt. Captain Graunt, writing as early as 1676, was chiefly concerned with estimating the population of the city and recording and analyzing vital statistics. He was followed by Sir William Petty who, in 1682, was trying to find reasons for the congregation of people in cities. Next came Sir James Steuart, who analyzed the distribution of population between farms, villages, hamlets, towns, and cities, in the late 1600's. Adam Smith, in his *Wealth of Nations* (1776) and other writings, attempted to explain why cities existed at all and what determined their sizes, as well as contributing insights into general reasons for their location. Simon Gray, writing in 1819, focused on the differentiation, quantification, and location of human activities in a city, and felt that in this "activity" analysis he had a refutation of Malthus' theory that population tends to multiply faster than its means of subsistence ("survival of the fittest"). Joseph Lowe, writing in 1824, expanded Gray's major points.[2]

These were the major Englishmen who first gave attention to the city. There were others in other countries who also became interested in the subject. Among the Germans may be mentioned Wilhelm G. F. Roscher, Karl Bücher, Frederick Ratzel, Johann Heinrich von Thunen, and Alfred Weber, the last two being classified as "location theorists." Several Frenchmen, most notably Pierre Emile Levasseur, Marie Paul Meuriot, and René Maunier, also made early studies of the city and contributed to the beginnings of urban theory.

---

square mile, whereas two standard metropolitan statistical areas—Jersey City and New York—had more than 3,000 inhabitants per square mile. Geographically, the area of San Bernardino County, California, is greater than that of any of the New England states except Maine. In other words, in those parts of the country where counties are large, the use of counties in the definition of such areas yields only a rough approximation of genuinely metropolitan territory, although most of the population in those counties is contained in territory that can be so defined.

[2]This summary, and some of the material that follows in this section, is generally from Barclay G. Jones, "The Theory of the Urban Economy: Origins and Development with Emphasis on Intraurban Distribution of Population and Economic Activity." Unpublished Ph.D. thesis, University of North Carolina, 1960.

Prominent early American writers who dealt with one aspect or another of urban problems included Henry Charles Carey, Charles Horton Cooley, Edward Alsworth Ross, and Frederick Smith Hall. However, most of their works were concerned with limited treatments of specific phenomena.

The first really comprehensive American study in this area was that of Weber.[3] In his much quoted work Weber not only assembled a statistical picture of the growth of cities throughout the world, but also discussed why cities occur, what determines their sizes, how they are located, and some of the economic, political, and social implications.

Weber attributed the concentration of people in cities primarily to economic forces resulting from the Industrial Revolution: steam and machinery, commerce and transportation, and the increased productivity of agriculture. In addition, he cited several secondary or individual causes: (a) the lure of high wages in cities; (b) certain political causes, including legislation promoting freedom of trade and freedom of migration, and the centralization of administration; and (c) certain social causes, including education, amusements, standard of living, intellectual associations, the "social instinct," and the spread of information, which make cities inviting to rural people.

Weber also dwelt on the physical and moral health of the city; he analyzed economic conditions and the economic, political, and social effects of the concentration of population; and, finally, he described tendencies and remedies such as the importance of rapid transit, the possible advantages of decentralization, and the "rise of the suburbs."

Although Weber touched upon some of the sociological effects of the concentration of cities, it was left primarily to others to explore that field. One of the writers taking up this burden was Josiah Strong.[4] He emphasized the materialistic nature of the city and its moral decline with increase in size from the standpoint of the breaking up of homes, the decline of the influence of the church, and the increase in political corruption. A number of reformers wrote important works which influenced the housing movement. One of the most effective of these was Jacob Riis (see Chapter 14). Another writer, Jane Addams,[5] also emphasized the moral deterioration found in cities. Of a number of Germans writing at this period, Georg Simmel and Karl Mannheim should be mentioned. A monumental coverage of the conditions in a single city is Charles Booth's *Life and Labour of the People of London.*

After World War I a group was formed which emphasized the sociological (or, more specifically, the ecological) aspects of city growth early in the twentieth century. This group included a trio of University of Chicago

[3] Adna Ferrin Weber, *The Growth of Cities in the Nineteenth Century.* Originally published New York: The Macmillan Company, 1899; republished Ithaca, N.Y.: Cornell University Press, 1963.

[4] Josiah Strong, *The Twentieth Century City.* New York: Baker and Taylor Co., 1898.

[5] Jane Addams, *The Spirit of Youth and the City Streets.* New York: The Macmillan Company, 1909.

scholars, Park, Burgess, and McKenzie.[6] Park looked on the city as a "natural habitat of civilized man" and believed it represented an externally organized unit in space produced by laws of its own—laws concerning its physical structure and its moral order. Burgess described the external organization of the city in space (see later section on theories of city growth). McKenzie provided a systematic statement of its inner "laws."

Norman S. B. Gras, an economist, treated economic history as the history of urbanization. He classified economic organization into the following stages of development and discussed history in these terms: collectional economy, cultural nomadic economy, settled village economy, town economy, and metropolitan economy. His classic work remains a rich source of information and reference.[7] Robert Murray Haig, studying the economy of New York City in connection with the development of the regional plan of New York and its environs, brought a fresh approach to the study of cities. Previous economists, especially those in the English tradition, had treated cities almost as aberrations in an essentially rural and primarily extractive economy. Haig developed a model of economic efficiency which took account of locational factors. He felt that in man's quest for efficiency he tended continually to try to minimize the costs of transportation. He cast the entire discussion of this subject in a new light:

> The acceptance of the suggestion developed above changes the character of the explanation of the actual existing pattern of population. Instead of explaining why so large a portion of the population is found in the urban areas, one must give reasons why that portion is not even greater. The question is changed from "Why live in the city?" to "Why not live in the city?"[8]

These writings represent the most important early efforts to understand our cities. In addition to attempting to understand the general phenomena at work, certain scholars more recently have focused attention on theories of why cities grow, physically, as they do.

THEORIES OF GROWTH OF CITIES

Three Basic Theories

Three basic theories have been developed which attempt to explain the general structure and growth of American cities (Figure 3). The first of these is the Concentric Zone theory developed by Burgess. The second is the Sector theory developed by Hoyt. The last is the Multiple Nuclei theory of Ullman and Harris. Although none of these theories is developed fully

[6] Robert E. Park, Ernest W. Burgess, Roderick D. McKenzie, *The City*. Chicago: University of Chicago Press, 1925.

[7] Norman Scott Brien Gras, *An Introduction to Economic History*. New York: Harper & Brothers, 1922.

[8] Reprinted by permission of the publishers from Robert Murray Haig, "Toward an Understanding of the Metropolis, Parts I and II," *The Quarterly Journal of Economics*, Cambridge, Mass.: Harvard University Press, Copyright, 1925, XL, Nos. 2 and 3 (February and May 1926), pp. 179–208, 402–434. The quotation is from p. 188.

enough to be applicable in a specific locality, because every city has unique aspects, they all contribute to an understanding of the structure and growth of cities in general.

Burgess believed: "The typical processes of the expansion of the city can best be illustrated, perhaps, by a series of concentric circles, which may be numbered to designate both the successive zones of urban extension and the types of areas differentiated in the process of expansion."[9]

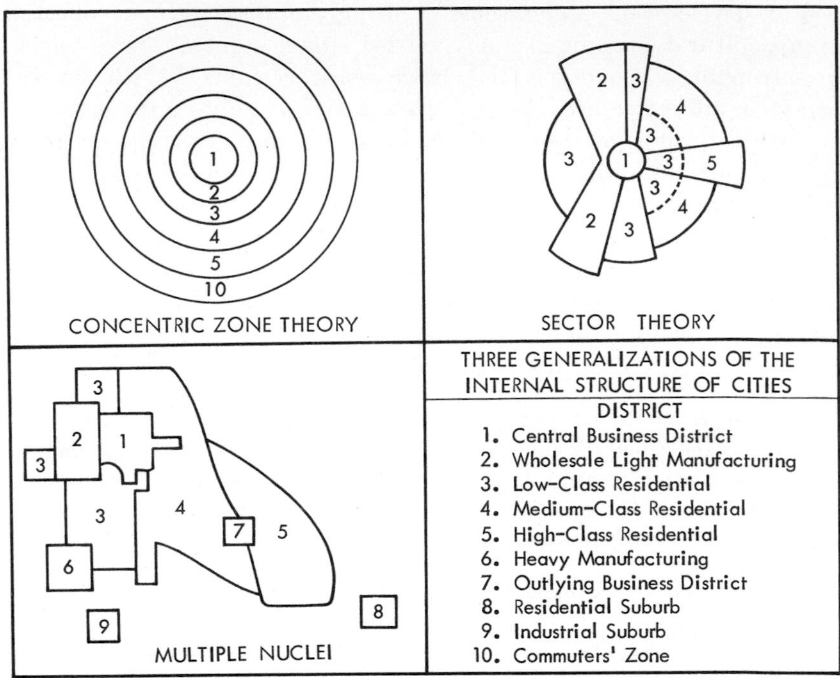

FIGURE 3. *Three theories of the internal structure of cities. (Source: Chauncey D. Harris and Edward L. Ullman, "The Nature of Cities,"* The Annals, *CCXLII, November, 1945, The American Academy of Political and Social Science, Copyright 1945. Used with permission.)*

The composition of the most important concentric zones he identified as follows:

CENTRAL BUSINESS DISTRICT. The core is the downtown retail district with its department stores, specialty shops, office buildings, clubs, banks, theaters, hotels, museums, and so on. These establishments are encircled by the wholesale business district.

ZONE IN TRANSITION. This is the inner ring of housing which clusters close to the business district. Usually it contains most of the poorest housing in the city and, frequently, the oldest. It frequently contains rooming-house districts and other places for the homeless. (It may, however, also contain

[9] Park, Burgess, McKenzie, *op. cit.,* p. 50.

some of the most expensive units; for example, Chicago's Gold Coast, a close-in residential area within easy walking distance of the Loop.) This area is frequently being invaded by business and light manufacturing.

Zone of independent workingmen's houses. This zone is inhabited by the workers in industries who have escaped from the area of deterioration but who desire to live within easy access of their work.

Better residential zone. This is made up of better apartment buildings and single-family dwellings. It is where many small businessmen, professional people, clerks, and salesmen live.

Commuters' zone. This zone, usually beyond the city limits, includes the suburban residential areas or satellite cities, generally within a 30- or 60-minute ride of the central business district.[10]

Hoyt felt that the development of cities is more varied than Burgess' theory suggests, because of important individual topographical and transportation factors.[11]

He observed that heavy industry is more likely to develop along transportation lines than around the central business district. Workingmen's homes tend to be more prevalent near industrial areas. The result is a number of wedges extending from the center of the city to the periphery. (Suburban communities may not be a part of a wedge; nor are they a zone. Rather, they represent isolated developed areas.)

Hoyt went into considerable detail concerning residential areas. He concluded that no strictly geometric pattern could be superimposed on a city to determine the location of low- and high-rent areas because each city is, to a degree, unique. In general, however, he believed that high-rent areas tend to spread along established lines of travel, but that they may also be concentrated on high ground, waterfront areas, open sections of the city, or near the homes of the leaders of the community. The arrangement of the sectors in Hoyt's Sector theory varies from city to city.

Both Burgess and Hoyt, as well as many other writers during the period 1920 to 1940, mentioned the possibility that a city may be developed around several nuclei. However, multinucleation within a city was not formalized as a concept until the writings of Harris and Ullman. These writers believed that: "In many cities the land-use pattern is built not around a single center but around several discrete nuclei."[12]

Harris and Ullman describe their theory as follows:

[10] Ernest W. Burgess, "Urban Areas," in T. V. Smith and Leonard D. White, eds., *Chicago—An Experiment in Social Science Research.* Chicago: University of Chicago Press, 1929, pp. 114–117.

[11] Homer Hoyt, *The Structure and Growth of Residential Neighborhoods in American Cities.* Federal Housing Administration, Washington, D.C.: U.S. Government Printing Office, 1939. It is quite apparent that Hoyt was considerably influenced by Hurd in the development of his basic concepts. See Richard M. Hurd, *Principles of City Land Values.* New York: The Record and Guide, originally printed in 1903 and reprinted in 1905, 1911, and 1924.

[12] Chauncy D. Harris and Edward L. Ullman, "The Nature of Cities," *The Annals of the American Academy of Political and Social Science,* CCXLII, November 1945, p. 14.

The rise of separate nuclei and differentiated districts reflects a combination of the following four factors:

1. Certain activities require specialized facilities. The retail district, for example, is attached to the point of greatest intra-city accessibility, the port district to suitable water front, manufacturing districts to large blocks of land and water or rail connection, and so on.

2. Certain like activities group together because they profit from cohesion. . . . Retail districts benefit from grouping which increases the concentration of potential customers and makes possible comparison shopping. Financial and office-building districts depend on facility of communication among offices within the district. . . .

3. Certain unlike activities are detrimental to each other. The antagonism between factory development and high-class residential development is well known. The heavy concentrations of pedestrians, automobiles, and street cars in the retail district are antagonistic both to the railroad facilities and the street loading required in the wholesale district and to the rail facilities and space needed by large industrial districts, and vice versa.

4. Certain activities are unable to afford the high rents of the most desirable sites. This factor works in conjunction with the foregoing. Examples are bulk wholesaling and storage activities requiring much room, or low-class housing unable to afford the luxury of high land with a view.[13]

These writers recognized a series of distinct districts which have developed around nuclei in most large American cities; the larger the city, the more numerous and specialized are the nuclei. The distinct districts are: the central business district, the wholesale and light-manufacturing district, the heavy industrial district, and the residential district. In addition, minor nuclei may exist in the form of cultural centers (e.g., universities such as Chicago and Harvard), parks and recreational areas, outlying business districts, small industrial centers, and so on. Harris and Ullman also recognized that suburbs, either residential or industrial, and satellite cities (differentiated from suburbs in that they are separated from the central city by greater distance and in general have little daily commuting to and from the central city, despite the fact that their economic activities are closely geared to those of the central city) grow up beyond many cities. It was not claimed by Harris and Ullman that applications of the Concentric Zone or Sector theories do not exist; rather, they believed that the structure and growth of most cities represent a combination of the three theories.

Criticism of the Theories

The principal criticism of the three theories seems to be that they tended to overlook the influence of a large number of variables, e.g., cultural tradition, social organization, power groups, and the like. They tended, rather, to be dominated by the ecological theory of the city.[14]

[13] *Ibid.*, pp. 14–15.

[14] The first formal writings on human ecology, however, did not appear until later, in the works of Hawley and Quinn. See Amos H. Hawley, *Human Ecology: A Theory of Community Structure.* New York: The Ronald Press Company, 1950; and James A. Quinn, *Human Ecology.* Englewood Cliffs, N.J.: Prentice-Hall, Inc., 1950.

Two of the writers who have expressed this criticism are Martindale, in his prefatory remarks to the translation of Max Weber's book, *The City,* and Firey, in reporting the results of an empirical study in Boston. Martindale suggested that basically there are three difficulties with the ecological approach to studying cities:

> First it started analysis off on the wrong track by orienting it to the geo-physical aspects of the city rather than to its social life. . . .
>
> A second fundamental difficulty . . . was the unnecessary "primitivism" of its crucial concepts.
>
> Thirdly, and in part growing out of the first two difficulties, the ecological theory of the city omitted precisely those concepts most traditionally sociological—groups, institutions, social structure.[15]

Firey stressed the importance of cultural and historical values in studying the city, showing ". . . that land use is not a passive deterministic phenomenon but is influenced significantly by volition, tradition and arbitrary planning." His Boston study, he felt, demonstrated "that the economic use of land as manifest in American cities is predicated upon distinct and unique cultural patterns . . ."[16]

Even Louis Wirth, who was a member of the "Chicago school" of ecological theory, with Park, Burgess, and McKenzie, wrote in 1938:

> In the rich literature on the city we look in vain for a theory of urbanism presenting in a systematic fashion the available knowledge concerning the city as a social entity. . . . But despite the multiplication of research . . . we do not as yet have a comprehensive body of compendent hypotheses which may be derived from a set of postulates implicitly contained in a sociological definition of the city . . .[17]

There have been many other writers who have criticized the three basic theories and/or made other contributions to the theory of the growth and structure of cities.[18] It might be concluded, however, that the principal difficulty encountered by students studying particular cities does not lie so much in the lack of a theory or stated hypotheses as in the lack of a

[15] Don Martindale, "Prefatory Remarks: The Theory of the City," in Max Weber, *The City.* Glencoe, Ill.: The Free Press, 1958, pp. 29–30.

[16] Walter Firey, *Land Use in Central Boston.* Cambridge, Mass.: Harvard University Press, 1947. Quotations from the summary of contents on the inside-front cover of the book.

[17] Louis Wirth, "Urbanism as a Way of Life," *American Journal of Sociology,* XLIV, No. 1, July 1938, p. 8.

[18] Some of the well-known writers on this general subject, and examples of pertinent works, are as follows: Maurice R. Davie, "The Pattern of Urban Growth," in *Studies in the Science of Society,* George P. Murdock, ed., New Haven, Conn.: Yale University Press, 1937. William H. Form, "The Place of Social Structure in the Determination of Land Use: Some Implications for a Theory of Urban Ecology," *Social Forces,* 32, May 1954. Walter Isard, *Location and Space-Economy.* Cambridge, Mass.: Technology Press of Massachusetts Institute of Technology, and New York: John Wiley & Sons, 1956. William F. Ogburn, "Inventions of Local Transportation and the Pattern of Cities," *Social Forces,* 24, May 1946. Hans Blumenfeld, "Are Land Use Patterns Predictable?" *Journal of the American Institute of Planners,* XXV, May 1959.

means of applying them. It can be recognized, for example, that most cities have a "center" and different kinds of "zones," but it is often difficult to identify them and, more particularly, to measure their radii.

The foregoing discussion has focused on a background description of our cities—some of the most important early studies of cities in general and the three basic theories of city growth. Let us now examine in greater detail the economic and sociological aspects of urban growth.

ECONOMIC ASPECTS OF OUR CITIES

General Importance of Economic Aspects to Housing

Every city has some characteristic that is basic to its formation and existence. As has been mentioned, most of our early cities were developed at good harbors or on rivers and other routes of transportation. Examples are numerous: New York, Boston, Baltimore, St. Louis, New Orleans, Cincinnati. Others were established near sources of raw materials, such as Scranton (coal) and Hibbing (iron). Still others are growing because of their climate—Miami and Phoenix. In each situation the area had some desirable and commercially exploitable feature.

Since industry and jobs are the important bases for housing, it is worth observing some of the differences that exist among these factors. Some industries pay higher wages than others, and this results in more family income available for housing. In 1961, for example, heads of families who were engaged in finance, insurance, and real estate had a median income of $7,411, the highest of any group; those who were engaged in offering personal services had a median income of only $4,176, the lowest of any group. Incomes of persons engaged in professional services also were high—a median of $7,218 in 1961. For those workers engaged in manufacturing, the median was $6,850; for those in retail trade, it was $5,887.

There also are important differences among persons in the various occupations. Heads of families who were professional or technical workers had a median income of $8,806 in 1961, compared with a median of only $1,694 for those who were private household workers (an extremely small group today). Managers, officials, and proprietors had a median income of $7,904. For craftsmen, the median figure was $6,806; for operatives, $5,826; for sales workers, $7,354; for clerical workers, $6,317.[19]

In industrial cities, such as Pittsburgh and Birmingham, there is a high proportion of operatives and craftsmen in the labor force. Commercial cities, such as Atlanta and Des Moines, also have high proportions of operatives and craftsmen, but an even higher proportion of clerical workers. In Washington, the center of the Federal Government, the proportion of clerks outranks all other groups, followed by professional and technical workers. Resort centers, such as Miami and the Fort Lauderdale–Hollywood

[19] U.S. Bureau of the Census, *Current Population Reports*. Consumer Income. "Income of Families and Persons in the United States: 1961." Series P-60, No. 39, February 28, 1963.

(Florida) areas, show the most even distribution of occupations of any of the different types of areas (Table 3–1, p. 113).

These over-all descriptions of major labor groups, however, are only partially illuminating. Manufacturing, for example, embraces a whole range of products from ships and planes to microscopes and lenses, with an equally wide range in the degree of processing involved.

It also is very significant to a community, from the standpoint of employment and income, and, therefore, of housing, whether the products are finished goods or in partially finished state; whether they require fairly high skills, such as the instrument and photographic industry in Rochester, or only semiskilled and common labor, as in some aspects of the construction industry. It is also important whether substantial value is added to the product in the manufacturing process. Similar differences characterize the various kinds of trade and personal service employment.

Another aspect of the distribution of current employment is the degree of "balance" that may exist among the various industries and occupations. Is a disproportionate percentage of employment concentrated in one line of activity—say, manufacturing—or is it fairly evenly distributed among trade, service industries, manufacturing, transportation, and government? The data for the seven cities shown in Table 3–1 indicate fairly good balance in each instance, even with the variation that exists among the different cities. Single-industry towns, where as much as half of the employment is concentrated in that industry, are not considered as sound economically as communities having diversification.

The economy of a city is also influenced by available transportation facilities. The number of railroads and airlines coming into a city is an important factor. The enlargement of an airport or the building of a throughway is likely to bring about a substantial increase in business. Any change in rates or schedules also, of course, affects the community.

Finally, the economy of a community is influenced, in part, by conditions in the "tributary area" of which it is a part—the area from which it draws the bulk of its raw materials and to which it sells the bulk of the goods and services it produces. The community and its tributary area are in fact inseparable; one cannot be far out of step with the other.

Many individuals and groups—city planners, city administrators, local businessmen, chambers of commerce, and the like—must be able to understand and predict urban growth, and thus they must understand these economic factors in some detail. To date there have been two primary methods of making such studies. The first of these is based on the economic base theory and the second is termed "input-output" analysis.

Economic Base Theory

Economic base analysis is the simpler of the two techniques and the one that has been in use for the longest period of time. Perhaps for those two reasons, it is the one most widely used.

The economic base theory, developed shortly after World War I, was described most clearly by Hoyt in 1939.[20] He suggested that a city grows primarily as a result of the expansion of its basic industries, which he described as those that bring money into the community from the outside. He felt that nonbasic or service industries grow in a certain arithmetic proportion to the basic industries.

The method Hoyt suggested for projecting future total employment and population had five steps:

1. Calculation of employment in each basic industry.

2. Estimation of proportion of basic employment to service employment. (Hoyt originally assumed this ratio would be about 1:1, but later felt that the ratio may increase to 1:2 in some cities.)

3. Estimation of the ratio of population to employment.

4. Estimation of the future trend in basic employment.

5. Calculation of future total employment and population from future basic employment.

Andrews later provided a complete set of ratios as follows:

Basic activities to service activities	1:2
Basic activities to total employment	1:3
Total employment to total population	1:2
Basic activities to total population	1:6[21]

Andrews emphasized that these ratios represent only typical conditions within an urban economy, and that deviations from these averages should be expected from city to city. (This is borne out by the data in Table 3–1.)

One of the advantages of this theory is that it relies on standard sources of data that are usually regularly reported in most communities. Its proponents sometimes relate it to international trade theory: a rising balance of payments for a particular country usually has positive implications for the economy of that country.

In recent years, especially since 1955, considerable criticism has been directed against the theory. Pfouts claims that empirical evidence does not support it.[22] He believes there are other variables just as important as those of the basic industries indicated by Hoyt. Blumenfeld is especially critical of the theory in relation to larger urban areas where, he believes, Hoyt's "nonbasic" activities actually become the basic economic activities—thus, in effect, reversing the theory.[23]

[20] Arthur M. Weimer and Homer Hoyt, *Principles of Urban Real Estate.* New York: The Ronald Press Company, 1939; rev. ed., 1943. Hoyt recently defended the theory in an article "The Utility of The Economic Base Method in Calculating Urban Growth," *Land Economics,* XXXVII, No. 1, February 1961, pp. 51–58. See also Richard B. Andrews, "Mechanics of the Urban Economic Base: Historical Development of the Base Concept," *Land Economics,* XXIX, No. 2, May 1953, pp. 161–167.

[21] Richard B. Andrews, "Mechanics of the Urban Economics Base: The Concept of Base Ratios," *Land Economics,* XXXI, No. 1, February 1955, p. 48.

[22] Ralph W. Pfouts, "An Empirical Testing of the Economic Base Theory," in Ralph W. Pfouts, ed. *The Techniques of Urban Economic Analysis.* West Trenton, N.J.: Chandler-Davis Publishing Co., 1960, pp. 291–306.

[23] Hans Blumenfeld, "The Economic Base of the Metropolis," *Journal of the American Institute of Planners,* XXI, No. 4, Fall 1955, pp. 114–132.

The general consensus concerning the theory is perhaps best summarized by Chapin: ". . . while offering insights into the general make-up of the local economy, this approach has been found lacking in several respects as an entirely satisfactory system for the analysis of the urban economy."[24]

Input–Output Analysis

The input–output method of analysis represents a "technique" for measuring urban growth rather than a "theory," although it is based on recent empirically based theoretical work by Leontief.[25] The statistical emphasis is at a much higher level of refinement than the economic base technique. It is primarily an inductive, empirical method suited to current mathematical techniques utilizing computing machines.

No attempt will be made to describe the technical method here; this is done in other sources.[26] Basically, however, the technique calls for measuring the value of "inputs" of raw materials as against the value of "outputs" of manufactured products, on an inter-industry basis for the metropolitan (or larger) area under consideration. To estimate future growth, reliable predictions of the various economic factors are required.

One of the advantages of the input-output method is that it can better accommodate one of the major characteristics of our urban economies—their dynamism. Even this method, however, has not been developed so that it is possible to have an up-to-date picture of the situation in a community, since data collection, programing, and data processing usually consume several months. However, this system does have advantages over the economic base technique, which is less specific and less up to date when a study is completed.

Chapin, again, has summarized the present status of this technique: ". . . while conceptually a promising approach, the techniques it employs require data in detail not currently obtainable from standard sources, and involve extensive, highly specialized analyses presently outside the competence of the average city planner."[27]

SOCIAL STRUCTURE AND CLASS STRATIFICATION

Our cities, of course, are comprised of individuals and families differing according to social class, ethnic background, race, and the like. Each of

[24] F. Stuart Chapin, Jr., *Urban Land Use Planning*. New York: Harper & Row, 1957, p. 117.

[25] Wassily W. Leontief, *The Structure of American Economy, 1919–1939*, 2d ed. New York: Oxford University Press, 1951, 3rd printing, 1960.

[26] One of the simplest descriptions is provided by Chapin, *op. cit.*, pp. 85–93 and 134–135. A more complete description is provided in Pfouts, *op. cit.*, Part III, "An Alternative Methodology: The Input-Output Approach." In one article in the same source, "Economic Structural Interrelations of Metropolitan Regions," Walter Isard and Robert Kavesh demonstrate the fundamentals of the input-output methods and show how this technique can be used in urban economic studies. In another article, "Regional and Interregional Input-Output Models: An Appraisal," Charles M. Tiebout criticizes the technique.

[27] *Op. cit.*, p. 117.

these factors frequently carries with it different personal traits, different cultural patterns, and different tastes and preferences. Wirth has said:

Considering that age, sex, race, and ethnic origin are associated with other factors such as occupation and interest, it becomes clear that one major characteristic of the urban-dweller is his dissimilarity from his fellows. Never before have such large masses of people of diverse traits as we find in our cities been thrown together into such close physical contact as in the great cities of America. Cities generally, and American cities in particular, comprise a motley of peoples and cultures, of highly differentiated modes of life between which there often is only the faintest communication, the greatest indifference and the broadest tolerance, occasionally bitter strife, but always the sharpest contrast.[28]

Different social groups in society have been recognized through the years. In earlier history, writings concerning the "class struggle" often made reference to such groups as patrician and plebian, lord and serf, guild-master and journeyman, freeman and slave. Marx and Engles used the terms "bourgeoisie" and "proletariat." Generally, these terms referred to an oppressor, on the one hand, and the oppressed, on the other.

Today, we have more of a class-free society than in earlier days, but we still hear and use the terms "lower class," "working class," the "poor," the "upper class," and perhaps most commonly, the "middle class" (in much of the literature about suburbia).

Definition and Examples of Class Stratification

What are the meanings, then, of the terms "social structure" and "class stratification"? Beshers defines social structure as ". . . the over-all pattern or network of social relationships that recur among a designated set of persons." "Social stratification," which is a subclass of social structure, is a ranking system among participants in the social relationships referred to, which has behavioral consequences, whether or not those consequences are recognized by the participants. According to Beshers: "A ranking system exists among any kind of units if a relationship of inequality exists among the units with respect to some characteristic."[29]

What are the factors that cause these differences in level in the ranking system? Centers says: "Social and economic groupings and categories of people distinguished on the basis of occupation, power, income, standard of living, education, function, intelligence or other criteria are easily and properly denoted by the terms stratum or strata."[30]

Kahl says that the terms "class order" and "status order" are composed of six variables, which he lists as follows: (1) prestige, (2) occupation, (3)

[28] *Op. cit.*, pp. 19–20.

[29] James M. Beshers, *Urban Social Structure*. New York: The Free Press of Glencoe, Inc., 1962, pp. 19, 35–36.

[30] Richard Centers, *The Psychology of Social Classes*. Princeton, N.J.: Princeton University Press, 1949, p. 27.

possessions, (4) interaction, (5) class consciousness, and (6) value orientations.[31]

Beshers says: "Direct measures of ranking include the objective indicators of education, income, and occupation, the reputational indicators as developed in a sociometric type of interview, the cultural or style of life symbolic indicators of values such as consumers goods, and subjective psychological identification with classes. . . ."[32]

Studies of Class Stratification in American Communities

Many studies have been made of class stratification in American communities. Unfortunately, even those studies that were best designed and most soundly developed suffered from two serious limitations insofar as their use today is concerned: (a) they were made in relatively small communities, in order that data collection could be kept manageable, and (b) they were made quite a few years ago, and some of the most important ones were made during the Depression years. For these reasons it is doubtful that the specific classes that were defined in them are still appropriate for present-day American society. Certainly the percentage distributions of the population in the different classes reflect a bygone period. Nevertheless, the studies are still important. They point out how an urban society breaks down into various social classes, and they give some general idea of the nature and composition of those classes—both matters of extreme importance to housing. For these reasons, some of the most important of the studies are summarized below.

Yankee City

One of the outstanding studies of class stratification was that undertaken by Warner in Newburyport, Massachusetts, between 1930 and 1935. This was an old, relatively small (17,000 inhabitants) New England community ". . . which maintained a balanced grouping of the members of the society."[33]

Warner classified almost the entire population of this community into six groups based on distinctions that existed in the minds of the people themselves, in combination with information collected by his researchers. Basically, ranking was on the basis of prestige, consumption, and personal interaction. The six classes have been summarized as follows:

[31] Joseph A. Kahl, *The American Class Structure.* New York: Holt, Rinehart, and Winston, rev. ed. 1957, pp. 8–10.

[32] *Op. cit.,* p. 36.

[33] W. Lloyd Warner and Paul S. Lunt, *The Social Life of a Modern Community.* New Haven: Yale University Press, 1941, p. 38. This book represented Volume I of the Yankee City series. Four other volumes also have been published in the series. All five volumes are summarized in *Yankee City,* W. Lloyd Warner, ed., New Haven: Yale University Press, 1963 (paperback).

1. Upper-upper, 1.4 per cent of the total population. This group was the old-family elite, based on sufficient wealth to maintain a large house in the best neighborhood, but the wealth had to have been in the family for more than one generation.

2. Lower-upper, 1.6 per cent. This group was, on the average, slightly richer than the upper-uppers, but their money was newer, their manners thus not quite so polished, their sense of lineage and security less pronounced.

3. Upper-middle, 10.2 per cent. The moderately successful business and professional men and their families, but less affluent than the lower-uppers. Some education and polish were necessary for membership, but lineage was unimportant.

4. Lower-middle, 28.1 per cent. The petty businessmen, the school teachers, the foremen in industry. This group tended to have morals that were close to puritan fundamentalism; they were churchgoers, lodge joiners, and flag wavers.

5. Upper-lower, 32.6 per cent. The solid, respectable laboring people, who kept their houses clean and stayed out of trouble.

6. Lower-lower, 25.2 per cent. The "lulus" or disrespectable and often slovenly people who dug for clams and waited for public relief.[34]

Warner's work was pioneering in this field. Although many students wish he had directed his study to a larger urban area, nonetheless, he not only made important contributions from the standpoint of ranking people on a social basis (prestige, etc.), but he also contributed importantly to methodology for community studies and his work undoubtedly provided a great stimulus for many of the studies that followed.

Middletown

Another important study was the one undertaken by Helen and Robert Lynd in Muncie, Indiana. This study differs from many of the others, in that it covered a time span of 46 years, rather than representing a "photographic still" or "snapshot" study of community life. The Lynds selected Muncie as the location for their study because they considered it typical of American communities, and also because it was believed to be a community "compact and homogeneous enough to be manageable" for this kind of study.

The Lynds first went to Muncie in 1924 to study the effects of industrialization during the period since 1890. During the early decades of the twentieth century the "industrial revolution" in this community had resulted in the building of more factories, the introduction of more machines and assembly-line techniques, and a resulting heavy increase in population. In

[34] Kahl developed these summary descriptions out of "much Warner material." (See W. Lloyd Warner, *Social Class in America.* Chicago: Science Research Associates, 1949, p. 21.) The percentage distributions are from W. Lloyd Warner and Paul S. Lunt, *The Social Life of a Modern Community.* New Haven: Yale University Press, 1941, p. 88. It should be pointed out that the high percentages of population in the lowest classes reflects the Depression years when the study was undertaken.

In later writings, Warner combined the upper-upper and the lower-upper classes, thus suggesting only five classes. See W. Lloyd Warner, *Democracy in Jonesville.* New York: Harper & Bros., 1949. Hollingshead, who was associated with this study but focused his attention on adolescent behavior, also used five classes, but he suggested some differences in class membership. He also changed the pseudonym for the community in which the study was conducted from "Jonesville" to "Elmtown." See August B. Hollingshead, *Elmtown's Youth.* New York: John Wiley & Sons, Inc., 1949.

their first book, *Middletown,* they describe two primary classes, the "working class" and the "business class." They trace the important changes wrought on the craft hierarchy in the working class of that community (as well as less significant changes among the business class). These changes included competition for skilled craftsmen from younger unskilled workers, a greater demand for broader educational opportunities for workers' children, changes in family life as women took jobs in factories, and, from the standpoint of housing, residence frequently outside the traditional "working class" neighborhoods (made possible by higher incomes and the development of new transportation systems).[35]

Robert Lynd returned to Muncie in 1936, during the Depression, and noted many changes. No longer could he define the class system as being comprised primarily of two classes. Rather, he identified these six groups, based on occupation:

1. [A small upper class] . . . consisting of wealthy local manufacturers, bankers, the local head managers of one or two of the national corporations with units in Middletown, and a few well-to-do dependents of all the above, including one or two outstanding lawyers.
2. . . . a larger but still relatively small group, consisting of established smaller manufacturers, merchants, and professional folk . . . and also of most of the better-paid salaried dependents of the city's big-business interests. . . .
3. . . . the minor employed professionals, the very small retailers and entrepreneurs, clerks, clerical workers, small salesmen, civil servants. . . .
4. . . . an aristocracy of local labor: trusted foremen, building trades craftsmen of long standing, and the pick of the city's experienced highly skilled machinists of the sort who send their children to the local college as a matter of course.
5. . . . the numerically overwhelmingly dominant group of the working class; these are the semiskilled or unskilled workers, including machine operatives, truckmen, laborers, the mass of wage earners.
6. . . . the ragged bottom margin, comprising some "poor whites" from the Kentucky, Tennessee, and West Virginia mountains, and in general the type of white worker who lives in the ramshackle, unpainted cottages on the outlying unpaved streets.[36]

It can be seen that there is considerable similarity between the Lynds' ranking and that of Warner.

Plainville

Two studies were undertaken of the class system of Plainville, the first by West during 1939 and 1940 and the second by Gallaher in 1954 and 1955.[37] Plainville was a small village (275 inhabitants) in the Midwest prairie. Although the community looked upon itself as almost without class distinc-

[35] Robert S. Lynd and Helen M. Lynd, *Middletown.* New York: Harcourt, Brace and World, Inc., 1929.

[36] Robert S. Lynd and Helen M. Lynd, *Middletown in Transition.* New York: Harcourt, Brace and World, Inc., 1937, pp. 458–460.

[37] James West, *Plainville, U.S.A.* New York: Columbia University Press, 1945; 4th printing, January 1947. Art Gallaher, Jr., *Plainville Fifteen Years Later.* New York: Columbia University Press, 1961.

tions, West indicated that, on the basis of prestige status, the inhabitants usually fell into either an upper or lower class, the over-all class structure resembling somewhat the shape of a diamond. The criteria on which class distinctions were based included location of residence, technology and methods of farming, family lineage, wealth or property position, degree to which they lived up to local morals, and manners, attitudes, and values. When Gallaher revisited Plainville fifteen years later, he found West's criteria were still valid, but that they had different meanings. There was less emphasis on location of residence and family lineage, but technology and moral values remained as important as before, and style of living based on increased wealth of some families became a new, important criterion.

Studies of Ethnic Background and Race

The studies of Yankee City, Middletown, and Plainville tended to focus on social stratification *per se,* and did not emphasize such other important social factors as ethnic background and race. Most other studies of American communities have tended to have the latter emphasis.

One of the outstanding in this group is a study by Davis of a small (slightly over 10,000 inhabitants) Southern community.[38] Although Davis acknowledged six social classes, he indicated that these classes applied primarily to the whites. The Negro society had an upper and middle class, but most of these residents belonged to the lower class. The Negro classes remained independent, socially and physically, of the parallel classes in white society, though many in the Negro middle class had status equal to that of many of the white individuals in their middle class group.

Davis analyzed the way in which the Negro subcommunity was kept subordinate. Also, one of the most helpful aspects of his study is the clarity with which he describes the attitudes of the members of the different social classes toward members of other classes. For example, he indicated that there was a particular tendency for individuals to minimize differences between their class and the class above them, and to enlarge differences between their own and the classes below them.

A study of another Southern community was undertaken by Dollard.[39] His study was more psychological than anthropological or sociological, relating emotional processes to community structure and functioning. In his analysis of lower-class Negroes, he attributed the lack of motivation for upward mobility (their "carefree" attitude and their so-called "shiftlessness") largely to their depriving environment. Middle-class Negroes were described as having practically the same standards as middle-class whites, but found themselves in a constant struggle, because of the nature of the

[38] Allison Davis, Burleigh B. Gardner, and Mary R. Gardner, *Deep South.* Chicago: University of Chicago Press, 1941.

[39] John Dollard, *Caste and Class in a Southern Town.* New Haven, Conn.: Yale University Press, 1937.

"caste" system, to maintain their position. Hunter[40] examined this matter further and described pressures for change in the caste system from within the Negro community and outside that community (e.g., those pressures emanating from the Federal Government and from Northern groups, both Negro and white).

Lantz studied the differences between two groups in a coal-mining town—the native-born and the foreign-born.[41] Wheeler's study of a community in the Midwest was similar. The ethnic structure was made up primarily of two distinct groups, Yankee settlers and Czech immigrants, both of whom had been in the area for approximately the same length of time.[42] The community studied, called "Valley View," had a population of about 3,300 persons. Wheeler identified seven groups, including three middle classes.

Another study that should be mentioned is Whyte's study of a slum area ("Cornerville") of Chicago.[43] This study focused on the social organization of a slum rather than the particular ethnic population which inhabited it. Whyte described a pattern of several groups operating in slum areas of almost any large city—youthful "gangs," local racketeers, politicians, and the police—and described the interrelationships of these groups.

Finally, mention should be made of the social profile of another large American city, Los Angeles, undertaken by Shevky and Williams.[44] These authors derived three indices: low, middle, and high *social rank* (based on occupation, income levels, and schooling); degree of *urbanization* (as indicated by differences in fertility, differences in age structure, women in paid employment, and physical character of neighborhood); and degree of *isolation* (segregation) of five ethnic groups—Negroes, Mexicans, Orientals, Russians, and Italians. They found that differences in the population, based on these indices, could be graded and measured.

Admittedly, with the advances that have been made in communications and transportation, and with the changes in many of our public laws and regulations, some basic changes are taking place in the social structure of our cities. Social interaction among the various groups tends to break down the barriers that have been holding some of the groups in. Today, many individuals who a few years ago "belonged" to one of the kinds of groups mentioned above, no longer owe their allegiance to that group alone (if at all), but have acquired membership in other social groups.

Although many of the studies mentioned touch on the matter of *social mobility* (as distinct from *physical mobility* discussed in the preceding

40 Floyd Hunter, *Community Power Structure.* Chapel Hill: University of North Carolina Press, 1953, Chapter 5.

41 Herman R. Lantz, *People of Coal Town.* New York: Columbia University Press, 1958.

42 Wayne Wheeler, *Social Stratification in a Plains Community.* Minneapolis: no publisher listed, 1949 (paperback).

43 William Foote Whyte, *Street Corner Society.* Chicago: The University of Chicago Press, 2d ed., 1955.

44 Eshref Shevky and Marilyn Williams, *The Social Areas of Los Angeles.* Berkeley and Los Angeles: University of California Press, 1949.

chapter), perhaps the most careful treatment is by Warner in reporting on his Jonesville study.[45] He listed several indicators of social mobility that differentiated the individual from the level of his family. These included: educational difference (more education); occupational variance (an occupation with somewhat higher prestige); membership transference (belonging to more exclusive clubs or associations); activity deviation (consolidation of position at the new level by changing behavior, such as moving out from family and church activities, possibly joining another church with higher prestige); clique change (joining participation groups with people of higher status or at the newly acquired level); role revision (acceptance by others in the new group); interclass marriage; and residential movement (living in a better area). The indicators are interrelated and interdependent and ". . . change in one is not present without some degree of change in the other factors." Downward mobility follows the same steps.

Because of the scale of the problem, our urban areas probably will remain complex social entities and the problem of social structure will always need to be reckoned with in housing and related matters. More attention is given to this problem in the discussion of neighborhoods in Chapter 9.

Thus far in our discussion of American cities we have seen that they are made up of a complex network of economic and social factors. These factors have been treated in only the broadest terms. Specific problems are treated in more detail later in the book. For example, problems of the central city are considered in Chapter 10; of suburbia, in Chapter 11; and of residential neighborhoods in general, as mentioned above, in Chapter 9.

We have also seen that our cities have experienced rapid growth in recent years and we may expect continued rapid growth in the future. The question then arises: How are we to develop some order in that growth? This is the function of city planning.

CITY PLANNING

History of City Planning

The idea of planning cities has had a long history, undoubtedly beginning when the first settlements became "urban" entities. It has been said that Hippodamus of ancient Greece was the first known city planner. He was noted for using the gridiron pattern in street layouts. Considerable impetus, from the standpoint of civic design, was given to planning during the utopian movement that began with the Renaissance in Europe.[46] In the United States, the housing reform movement of the late nineteenth century, lead by Jacob Riis and Lawrence Veiller, among others, also had its influence.[47] Then followed the "city beautiful" movement which got under way

[45] Lloyd Warner, *Democracy in Jonesville, op. cit.*, Chapter 4.

[46] Christopher Tunnard, *The City of Man.* New York: Charles Scribner's Sons, 1953, pp. 51–144. See also Arthur B. Gallion, *The Urban Pattern: City Planning and Design.* New York: D. Van Nostrand Company, Inc., 1950, pp. 70–172.

[47] Of course, planning in the United States could be considered to have its beginning with the first plat plans for such cities as Pittsburgh, Philadelphia, and Savannah.

at about the turn of the century and continued until the Depression period of the 1930's. Colean describes this movement:

> The Chicago World's Fair of 1893, and the resurrection and reinstitution of the L'Enfant plan for Washington in 1900, were emphatic reassertions of the proposition that the structure of cities could be shaped by the hands of men. The city planning movement thus born was rapidly expanded. . . .
>
> The first emphasis of the new school of planners was on civic pride; its watchword was the city beautiful, and its aim was, through the creation of boulevards, parks and imposing public buildings, to overcome the indifference to environment that too frequently was an outstanding characteristic of the pioneer community.[48]

One of the outstanding accomplishments was Daniel Burnham's plan for Chicago, but many other American cities experienced the results of this movement.

In the meantime, a significant development was taking place in England. In 1898 Ebenezer Howard wrote a book[49] in which he proposed that new towns be built in rural areas which would provide better living conditions for the workers than were provided in London and other large English cities. The first such "garden city" was Letchworth, established in 1903, and the second was Welwyn, founded in 1930.[50] Both were near London. These new towns greatly influenced the planning of certain new communities and other suburban communities in the United States (e.g., Kingsport, Tennessee, a new industrial town; Shaker Heights, a suburb of Cleveland; and the three new towns built by the Farm Security Agency in the Depression years of the 1930's: Greenbelt, Maryland, Green Hills, Ohio, and Greendale, Wisconsin).

Planning Today

City planning, as we know it today, was first developed by a Scotsman, Sir Patrick Geddes.[51] Geddes, a biologist and sociologist, brought scientific methods to the planning of cities. According to one source:

> He insisted that the aim of planning was to provide a healthy and attractive environment. To achieve this aim, all relevant phenomena must be investigated. Geographical, historical, social, industrial, hygienic, and cultural data should all be included in a civic survey. Only after such a survey was completed could a realistic plan be made.
>
> Geddes believed that utility and "human and social uses" must dominate the

[48] Miles L. Colean, *Renewing Our Cities.* New York: The Twentieth Century Fund, 1953, pp. 23–24.

[49] Ebenezer Howard, *To-Morrow: A Peaceful Path to Real Reform.* 1st ed. London: S. Sonnenschein, 1898. Republished under new title, *Garden Cities of To-Morrow,* 1902. New ed. London: Faber & Faber, 1946.

[50] For a history and description of British "New Towns," see Lloyd Rodwin, *The British New Towns Policy.* Cambridge, Mass.: Harvard University Press, 1956.

[51] Patrick Geddes, *Cities in Evolution: An Introduction to the Town Planning Movement and to the Study of Civics.* London: Williams & Norgate, Ltd., 1915. Rev. ed. 1949. London: Oxford University Press, 1950.

planning of projects. He also said that the planner must strive to place himself at "a comprehensive standpoint, the hardest of all to reach—that of the city as a whole." Under a comprehensive view, the city is also recognized as being part of a region.[52]

Chapin has defined city planning as follows:

> City planning may be regarded as a means for systematically anticipating and achieving adjustment in the physical environment of a city consistent with social and economic trends and sound principles of civic design. It involves a continuing process of deriving, organizing, and presenting a broad and comprehensive program for urban development and renewal. It is designed to fulfill local objectives of social, economic, and physical well-being, considering both immediate needs and those of the foreseeable future. It examines the economic basis for an urban center existing in the first place; it investigates its cultural, political, economic, and physical characteristics both as an independent entity and as a component of a whole cluster of urban centers in a given region; and it attempts to design a physical environment which brings these elements into the soundest and most harmonious plan for the development and renewal of the urban area as a whole.[53]

One of the major aspects of planning is the development of what is known as the general plan or the "master plan" for the area. That plan sets forth the relationships among the various areas and various land uses (of which housing is one) that make up the city structure. Actually, the present pattern of land uses in most communities has been shaped by the interaction of these uses upon each other, since few cities in the United States were planned broadly from the outset. The master plan shows this pattern as it has evolved, together with some schematic devices to bring out the means by which the various types of areas are connected with each other (such as by transportation routes) and separated from each other (such as by buffer strips of one sort or another between incompatible uses). It supplies a blueprint for the community's structure and its development.

Considerable impetus has been given to "master planning" by the Federal urban renewal program. Before a community can obtain financial and administrative assistance under that legislation, it must take the initiative and work in the direction of the establishment of a broad "workable program" for its area. (See Chapter 14.)

The master plan and workable program should be guides to future city growth rather than merely an expression of community ego. In other words, they constitute a useful benchmark for those concerned with various phases of the local economy—housing in particular—only if they represent a realistic picture, soundly rooted in facts about the local economy (such as its population potentials), which in turn rest upon the basic potentials of employment and income. These facts are the necessary basis for sound housing plans, and they are no less essential for sound over-all plans into which

[52] Mary McLean, ed., *Local Planning Administration*. Municipal Management Series. Chicago: The International City Managers' Association, 3d ed., 1959, p. 7.

[53] *Op. cit.*, p. xiv.

future housing developments are to fit. The realistic, factual bases of master plans are the standards by which they must be judged, and the criteria of their usefulness to future housing.

One of the major problems in planning our urban areas today results from the many politically individual communities that exist in those areas. Almost every major city has many communities on its borders, with such interaction and dependence between them as to form in essence one community irrespective of political boundaries. The greater New York area, for example, encompasses several hundred separate communities.

Herein is the crux of a serious planning problem: several hundred (or even a dozen) separate entities mean many duplications of essential community services, many separate land and building regulations, and so on. This political separatism often leads to "passing the buck" on such metropolitan-wide problems as water supply, mass transportation, and air pollution. It also involves serious financial inequities, particularly for the central city which generally provides a vast number of specialized services used by the people of the entire area but paid for out of the tax base of the central city alone.

The lack of any over-all governing unit for our metropolitan areas makes any attempt to solve the problems that exist difficult. The small suburbs tend to want to remain independent, and the unincorporated areas often will not agree to incorporation with the central city.

To avoid these obstacles to area-wide government, a few cities have, in recent years, been turning to various types of metropolitan ("metro") governments. The most prominent effort in the United States has been that of Dade County, Florida, which includes the city of Miami and twenty-six other independent municipalities. This particular experiment has run into difficulties, however, because the "metro" government can only exercise those powers turned over to it by the individual cities. Another example is found in the Canadian city, Toronto. Here, in 1954, a new government, known as the "Municipality of Metropolitan Toronto," was established. The components of this new political unit include the city of Toronto and twelve suburbs. The new government takes on many functions for the whole area, but others are retained by the member communities. Many of the problems and many of the benefits of this type of approach to the problems of metropolitanism are already becoming apparent in the Toronto experiment. The most recent effort in this direction has been in Tennessee where city and county governments have been consolidated into what is called the Metropolitan Government of Nashville and Davidson County. This "metro" is the area's sole provider for practically all types of local services, ranging from police and fire protection to the provision of education and recreation. It appears to represent the best example of a streamlined metropolitan government to date.

Another significant recent development in the United States is the tendency toward merging of some of our major population centers into a "megalopolis." One rapidly emerging megalopolis is that which stretches from Boston to Washington, D.C.[54] (Figure 4). Another megalopolis stretches from Milwaukee to Chicago to South Bend. On the West Coast another is emerging from San Francisco and Sacramento to Los Angeles and San Diego. In the Gulf area there is evidence for a future merging of areas from Galveston-Houston to Dallas and Fort Worth, and probably down to San Antonio.[55]

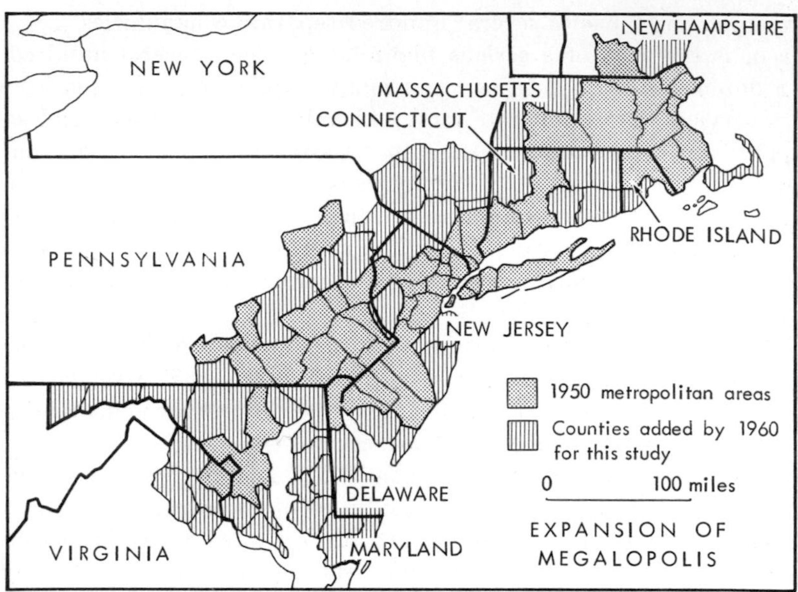

FIGURE 4. *Megalopolis—Northeastern Seaboard of the United States. (Source: Jean Gottmann,* Megalopolis: The Urbanized Northeastern Seaboard of the United States. *New York: The Twentieth Century Fund. Copyright 1961. Used with permission.)*

Gottmann has summarized the causes of this phenomenon by stating: "The human tidal currents within Megalopolis . . . result mainly from the scattering far beyond the 'city walls,' and beyond various limits of local government, of people whose main work, interests, and income are located in urban, built-up districts."[56]

These "tidal currents" will continue, and our cities will keep bursting out of their narrow bounds for as long as our nation continues to grow; and where metropolitan areas are near each other, they will tend to combine. As this occurs, the problems discussed for our metropolitan areas (e.g., the

[54] For a discussion of the development of this region, see Jean Gottmann, *Megalopolis: The Urbanized Northeastern Seaboard of the United States.* New York: The Twentieth Century Fund, 1961.

[55] For a description of these and other metropolitan regions in the United States, see Jerome P. Pickard, *Metropolitanization of the United States.* Research Monograph 2, Washington, D. C.: Urban Land Institute, 1959.

[56] *Op. cit.*, p. 35.

need of area-wide government) will occur on an even larger and more complex scale.

In conclusion, it should be pointed out that few individuals would suggest that unplanned, uncontrolled city growth is superior to planned, controlled growth. However, city planning still has many critics. These critics are sometimes influenced in their opinions because certain private interests have been impinged upon. Sometimes they point out that city planning is still an imperfect instrument and too few people are yet qualified for the leadership required when economic, political, sociological, and aesthetic decisions must be made.[57]

However, it is an objective of planning to encourage orderly development of the community, while constantly maintaining communication with all necessary groups and taking cognizance of the needs and attitudes of the community. The benefits are many and obvious.

More universities are undertaking the training of planners, more communities are establishing planning commissions and adding planners to their staffs, and more funds are becoming available at all levels of government to support planning operations. It may be expected, therefore, that planning in the future will become a firmly established function in all of our cities.

READING LIST

EARLY STUDIES OF THE CITY

Weber, Adna Ferrin. *The Growth of Cities in the Nineteenth Century,* 1st ed. New York: The Macmillan Co., 1899. New ed. Cornell Reprints in Urban Studies. Ithaca, N.Y.: Cornell University Press, 1963.

Weber, Max. *The City.* Glencoe, Ill.: The Free Press, 1958. "Prefatory Remarks: The Theory of the City" by Don Martindale.

THEORIES OF GROWTH OF CITIES

Harris, Chauncy D., and Edward L. Ullman. "The Nature of Cities," Vol. 242, *The Annals of the American Academy of Political and Social Science,* November 1945; reprinted in Paul K. Hatt and Albert J. Reiss, Jr., *Cities and Society.* New York: The Free Press of Glencoe, Inc., 1957, pp. 237–247.

Hoyt, Homer. *The Structure and Growth of Residential Neighborhoods in American Cities.* Federal Housing Administration, Washington, D.C.: U.S. Government Printing Office, 1939.

Park, Robert E., Ernest W. Burgess, Roderick D. McKenzie. *The City.* Chicago: University of Chicago Press, 1925.

[57] One recent writer who has criticized present city planning practices is Jane Jacobs. Mrs. Jacobs suggests, among other things, that a broad diversity of land and property use within each city block is the key to maintaining the cultural vitality, safety, educational function, and economic health of our large cities. She considers that the separation of land uses (commercial, industrial, and residential) into distinct and homogeneous groupings, as advocated by most contemporary city planners, is leading to the "death" of our cities. Although this author bases most of her attitudes on personal experience and observation in a small number of neighborhoods, rather than on any systematic study, many of her ideas are thought-provoking and stimulating. See Jane Jacobs, *The Death and Life of Great American Cities.* New York: Random House, Inc., 1961.

ECONOMIC ASPECTS OF CITIES

Andrews, Richard B. "Urban Economics: An Appraisal of Progress," *Land Economics,* XXXVII, No. 3, August 1961, pp. 219–227. See also 12 articles on the economic base in *Land Economics,* issues from May 1953 to February 1956.

Chapin, F. Stuart, Jr. *Urban Land Use Planning.* New York: Harper & Bros., 1957, Chapter 5.

Isard, Walter. *Methods of Regional Analysis.* Cambridge, Mass.: The Massachusetts Institute of Technology Press, 1960, 2nd printing, 1962.

Pfouts, Ralph W. (ed.) *The Techniques of Urban Economic Analysis.* West Trenton, N.J.: Chandler-Davis Publishing Co., 1960 (paperback).

SOCIAL STRUCTURE AND CLASS STRATIFICATION

Bendix, Reinhard, and Seymour M. Lipset (eds.) *Class, Status and Power.* Glencoe, Ill.: The Free Press, 3rd printing, 1957.

Beshers, James M. *Urban Social Structure.* New York: The Free Press of Glencoe, Inc., 1962.

Centers, Richard. *The Psychology of Social Classes.* Princeton: Princeton University Press, 1949.

Kahl, Joseph A. *The American Class Structure.* New York: Holt, Rinehart, and Winston, 1957.

Stein, Maurice R. *The Eclipse of Community.* Princeton: Princeton University Press, 1960.

See also studies of individual communities referred to in text of chapter.

METROPOLITANISM AND MEGALOPOLISM

Gottmann, Jean. *Megalopolis: The Urbanized Northeastern Seaboard of the United States.* New York: The Twentieth Century Fund, 1961.

McKenzie, R. D. "The Rise of Metropolitan Communities," in Paul K. Hatt and Albert J. Reiss, Jr., *Cities and Society.* New York: The Free Press of Glencoe, 1957.

Pickard, Jerome P. *Metropolitanization of the United States.* Research Monograph 2. Washington, D.C.: Urban Land Institute, 1959.

CITY PLANNING

Chapin, F. Stuart, Jr. *Urban Land Use Planning.* New York: Harper & Bros., 1957.

Gallion, Arthur B. *The Urban Pattern: City Planning and Design.* New York: D. Van Nostrand Co., 1950.

Goodman, Paul and Percival. *Communitas,* 2d ed. New York: Vintage Books, 1960 (paperback).

Jacobs, Jane. *The Death and Life of Great American Cities.* New York: Random House, Inc., 1961.

McLean, Mary (ed.) *Local Planning Administration.* Municipal Management Series. Chicago: The International City Managers' Assn., 3d ed., 1959.

Tunnard, Christopher. *The City of Man.* New York: Charles Scribner's Sons, 1953.

Table 3–1

PERCENTAGE DISTRIBUTION OF OCCUPATIONS OF EMPLOYED PERSONS, SELECTED METROPOLITAN AREAS, 1960

	Industrial		*Commercial*		*Government*	*Resort*	
	Pittsburgh	*Birmingham*	*Atlanta*	*Des Moines*	*Washington*	*Miami*	*Fort Lauderdale-Hollywood*
Total persons (number in thousands)	832,133	217,420	395,190	107,563	791,921	360,097	117,542
Professional, technical	12.1%	10.2%	11.2%	11.6%	19.1%	10.9%	9.0%
Managers, officials, proprietors	7.4	8.8	9.9	11.3	9.1	11.6	14.8
Clerical	15.5	14.8	18.6	21.5	24.6	15.0	12.4
Sales	8.1	8.3	8.7	9.5	6.3	9.2	9.2
Craftsmen	16.5	14.4	12.0	13.0	10.2	13.0	14.8
Operatives	17.5	17.8	15.8	13.8	7.3	11.2	9.9
Private household workers	1.6	5.7	5.0	1.8	3.4	4.1	4.5
Other service workers	8.8	8.9	8.8	8.8	9.1	11.8	12.2
Laborers	8.3	7.1	4.5	4.6	3.7	5.3	8.2
Occupation not reported	4.2	4.0	5.5	4.1	7.2	7.9	5.0

SOURCE: U.S. Bureau of the Census, *Census of Population 1960.* General Social and Economic Characteristics, PC(1), 1C, U.S. Summary, pp. 1–305, 1-306.

Part 2

****

HOUSING MARKET AND HOUSING PRODUCTION

CHAPTER 4

*

The Housing Market

We have seen how our forefathers, after landing on the American shores, provided for their shelter—they first dug out caves or built huts and later built small frame houses. There were no man-made shelters available for them to buy or rent.

Today, there are nearly 60 million houses and apartments in the United States. Sooner or later all of these dwellings come "on the market" for some family.

NATURE OF THE HOUSING MARKET

The housing "market" is more complex than the market for most other commodities. There are, in fact, two different markets, one for the purchase of properties for *sale* and the other for the *rental* of the services of properties, usually for specific periods.

These markets serve several functions.[1] First, the existing stock of dwellings must meet sudden or temporary changes in space requirements of individuals and families. (An extreme example of this occurs during wartime, when there is greatly stepped-up demand in some localities for the currently available supply of houses and apartments.) Second, there must be an increase in the existing supply of dwellings to meet additional permanent demand. This market occurs, of course, on the basis of long-run supply–demand relationships. Finally, the market serves a function relating to land use determination. This function should not be overlooked, because proper land use is important to the proper functioning of a city, both economically and socially.

Markets for many products operate quite efficiently; they frequently are well organized, have central exchange places, and both buyers and sellers usually possess extensive knowledge of many of the forces which are at work. If a person wants to buy a new automobile, for example, he merely needs to visit the various salesrooms that have the general type in which he is interested and make known his preferences concerning well-established characteristics—model, price, seating capacity, color, and the like. Competition, in such instances, can operate easily where the goods are standardized, graded, and bought and sold from samples or models.

For housing, there is no smooth adjustment in supply and demand similar

[1] Arthur M. Weimer and Homer Hoyt, *Principles of Urban Real Estate*, 2d ed. New York: The Ronald Press Company, 1948, pp. 142–165.

to that which exists for automobiles or similar products. Some of the reasons for this condition have been stated by Weimer and Hoyt:

> . . . real properties possess few of the characteristics which make it easy to carry on market dealings in them, and . . . the real estate market is limited in extent, there being no central exchanges to facilitate buying and selling. Furthermore, the real estate market is affected by the seasons, with spring and fall usually representing the active periods of the year. Likewise, the cyclical variations of business activity, the ease or difficulty of financing, and other special factors all have important effects.[2]

As a result of these many and significant factors, the housing market is frequently erratic. Similar to the situation which can occur on Wall Street, a "seller's market" may exist if there is a large number of buyers for a limited number of dwellings and a "buyer's market" may exist if the reverse holds true. Obviously, in a seller's market, prices are likely to rise and in a buyer's market they are likely to decline.

THE NATIONAL HOUSING INVENTORY

Although, as will be pointed out later, housing markets are necessarily *local,* for it is at the community level that competition exists among different dwellings for a single buyer, nevertheless it is important to have an understanding of the total "standing stock" of housing at a particular time. Although all of the dwellings in that standing stock may represent a potential for families seeking different dwellings, certain portions of the inventory are homes "permanently" occupied and, therefore, not available for sale or rent. However, as a result of the long physical and economic life of the dwelling structure, almost all housing units come on the market at one time or another.

In 1960 there were 58,326,357 housing units in the United States.[3] Approximately 36.4 million units, or 62 percent of the total, were located in metropolitan areas (Table 4–1, p. 137). The East North Central Division (Ohio, Indiana, Illinois, Michigan, and Wisconsin) had the largest number of any division—one fifth of all the housing units in the nation. The Middle Atlantic Division (New York, New Jersey, and Pennsylvania) had almost the same proportion. The Mountain Division (Montana, Idaho, Wyoming, Colorado, New Mexico, Arizona, Utah, and Nevada) continued to be the most sparsely settled area of the nation, with less than 4 percent of the housing units in the nation (Table 4–2, p. 137).

Occupancy Characteristics

Of the 58,326,357 housing units in the nation in 1960, 53,023,875, 91 percent, were occupied.

[2] *Ibid.*, pp. 154–155. Used with permission of the publisher.

[3] The basic source of the data in this chapter is U.S. Bureau of the Census, *Census of Housing 1960.* States and Small Areas, HC (1), No. 1, U.S. Summary.

Occupied Units and Population

It is interesting to note that the number of occupied units, over the years, has increased more rapidly than our population. For example, the number of occupied units increased 23 percent between 1950 and 1960, and population increased only 19 percent. During the preceding decade the respective figures were 23 percent and 15 percent. Between 1930 and 1940 they were 17 percent and 7 percent (Table 4–3, p. 138).

What does this mean? The differences are attributable to a number of factors. Undoubtedly the most important factor recently has been the number of individuals (as against families) who maintain their own households. Concomitantly, there are fewer married couples who share their living quarters with others. Before 1940 the decline in the death rate was another reason.

Occupancy by Color

In 1960, 9.7 percent of the occupied units (a total of 5.1 million units) were occupied by a household with a nonwhite head. (Most of these households, of course, were Negro.) This compared with 9.0 percent (3.9 million) in 1950.

Between 1950 and 1960 the number of nonwhite households increased at a faster rate than white households—33 percent as compared with 22 percent. Most of this increase for nonwhite households was within central cities; for white households it was within metropolitan areas, but outside of the central cities.

Over half (54 percent) of the nonwhite households lived in the South. However, the ratio of nonwhites to the total population of the South declined from 20 percent in 1950 to 18 percent in 1960 and the proportions increased in each of the other three regions—from 4 to 6 percent in the North Central region and 5 to 7 percent in the Northeast and Western regions.

Tenure

When information on tenure was first collected by the Bureau of the Census in 1890, 48 percent of the occupied units were occupied by owners. The proportion declined slightly to 46 percent in 1920. The rate then increased during the next ten years, and by 1930 it had regained its 1890 level. As a result of the Depression during the 1930's, however, it had dropped to a low of 44 percent by 1940. After that, the rise in the level of income and liberalized home-financing terms contributed to a sharp rise, to 55 percent home ownership in 1950.

Home ownership in 1960 was at the highest level of any Census year since information on tenure was first collected. Approximately 32.8 million housing units were occupied by their owners in that year, 62 percent of all occupied units. The numerical gain, 9.2 million more than the 23.6 million owner-occupied units in 1950, was the largest of any decade. (The relative gain, however, was second to the gain between 1940 and 1950.)

Home ownership was more prevalent outside metropolitan areas (67 percent) than inside them (59 percent) in 1960. Inside metropolitan areas the rate was substantially higher outside central cities (73 percent) than inside them (47 percent). In rural areas it was slightly higher for farms (74 percent) than in nonfarm areas (70 percent) Table 4–4, p. 138).

The West North Central Division of the United States had the highest rate of owner-occupancy in 1960, 68 percent; the Middle Atlantic Division, with 55 percent, had the lowest (Table 4–5, p. 139). (In only three states—Hawaii, New York, and Alaska—and in the District of Columbia were there more renters than homeowners.)

Home ownership is most common among white households; renting is most common among nonwhite households (Table 4–6, p. 139). In 1960, approximately five out of every eight white households, as compared with three out of every eight nonwhite households, were owners. The rate of increase in home ownership between 1950 and 1960, however, was greater for nonwhites than for whites. During that decade the number of units occupied by nonwhite owners increased from 1.4 million to 2.0 million, 46 percent. The increase among white owners was from 22.3 million to 30.8 million, 38 percent. The increase of nearly 50 percent among nonwhite households may be attributed primarily to a combination of two factors: the lower proportion owning in 1950 and their generally improved economic position by 1960.

Because of the significance of home ownership, Chapter 7 will be devoted to that subject.

Persons-per-Room Ratio

An important index of the general adequacy of a nation's housing supply is provided by the number of occupants per dwelling unit. If the number is large, the unit is considered to be overcrowded. This is an important criterion of substandard housing conditions.

The factor of overcrowding is frequently closely related to family income. There was excessive doubling-up during the Depression of the 1930's, but "undoubling" occurred during the period of wartime prosperity and has continued to do so as family incomes have risen. An increase in the amount of doubling-up usually is accompanied by an increase in vacancy. In periods of prosperity when employment and incomes are at a high level, a decrease in the vacancy rate, accompanied by a decrease in the doubling-up of families, reflects an over-all housing shortage. Such a shortage sometimes leads to overcrowding, as families have to double because the housing supply is inadequate. In summary, then, some families double up through choice, while others double up because of the lack of an adequate supply of housing.

The "overcrowding" factor has not been as important during the recent period when the volume of construction has been high. However, there are some exceptions. For example, the housing needs of minority groups have not been met and there is still considerable overcrowding among these families. Of course, part of this is a reflection of the lack of adequate provision of low-cost housing for all groups.

Two factors in the last two decades (a) the great supply of new houses that were built and (b) the reduced family size, resulted in houses being less crowded in 1960 than they had been in 1950 or 1940.

The best measure available of the utilization of space in housing units is the persons-per-room ratio. (This ratio assumes an equal distribution of persons and rooms, without regard for the size and type of rooms or the age, sex, and relationship of the occupants.) In 1960, only 9 percent of the owner-occupied units and 16 percent of the renter-occupied units had 1.01 or more persons per room. Inside metropolitan areas the percentages were even smaller (Table 4–7, p. 140). These extremely low percentages are an indication of one of the luxuries most Americans, in contrast to people in many other countries, enjoy—ample space in their homes.

The Ecology of Housing

Generally, ecology has been defined as "the study of the relations between organisms and their environment." Since the word derives from the Greek *Oikos,* translated as "a house or place to live in," it seems appropriate to relate this term to the characteristics of our housing supply.

Five characteristics are perhaps most important. These are the value of the owned units and the rents paid for those rented, the quality of the housing, and the age, size, and types of housing units and structures.

Value and Rent

The median value of owner-occupied nonfarm homes in the United States was $11,900 in 1960. Two fifths of the homes had a value between $10,000 and $17,500. A total of 12 percent were in the low-value bracket of less than $5,000 and 15 percent were in the high-value brackets of $20,000 or more.

Homes in metropolitan areas have significantly higher values, on the average, than those outside metropolitan areas. In 1960 the medians were $13,500 and $8,600, respectively. Outside metropolitan areas, one out of every four housing units had a value under $5,000, and only 7 percent were valued at $20,000 or more (Table 4–8, p. 140).

The value of housing has been increasing significantly in recent years. In 1930 the median value for all owner-occupied nonfarm units was $4,800. Because of the Depression of the 1930's, it had dropped to $3,000 in 1940. By 1950 it had increased to $7,400. The $11,900 median value in 1960, therefore, was one and one-half times the median in 1950 and approximately four times the median in 1940.

Part of this increase in value has been caused, of course, by the higher cost of the many new units built during the last two decades. There is usually a close relationship between price of housing and cost of construction. The high price of new housing has also encouraged the price of existing units on the market to rise.

The median monthly gross rent (rent plus the average monthly cost of utilities) was $71 in 1960 (Table 4–9, p. 141). Over half the housing units (55 percent) rented for between $50 and $100. Over a fifth were in the low-rental brackets of less than $50, and 17 percent were in the high-rental brackets of $100 or more. The median rents were higher inside metropolitan areas ($75) than outside those areas ($58). Approximately 1.4 million nonfarm renter-occupied units (nearly half of them in the South) were occupied on a "no cash rent" basis. Most of these represented units provided by relatives not living in the unit and units provided in exchange for services rendered (such as for the caretaker or manager of an apartment structure).

As with the value of owner-occupied homes, the rents of renter-occupied units have been increasing significantly in recent years. The median rent of $71 in 1960 was approximately 1.7 times the $42 median in 1950 and 2.6 times the $27 median in 1940.

A better index of the increased cost of housing than the increases in value or rents in current dollars are the housing items in the Bureau of Labor Statistics Consumer Price Index. The trend of this index since 1947, 1947–1949 representing the base years, is shown in Table 4–10 (p. 141). When all housing items are combined, the index has risen from 95.0 in 1947 to 133.6 in 1962. The item that has risen most sharply is rent—from 94.4 to 145.3. House furnishings have shown the greatest stability, rising only from 97.2 to 103.0. (A comparison of housing prices with prices of other items in the Consumer Price Index was shown in Table 2–10, p. 83).

Quality of Housing

One of the most important characteristics of the supply in the total market is the quality of the housing. Obviously of primary concern is poor-quality housing, although, as will be noted in Chapter 10, another concern is to keep good housing from deteriorating prematurely.

The combination of data on presence or absence of plumbing facilities and their condition, as provided by the U. S. Census, is considered one measure of housing quality. It takes account of the physical characteristics of the housing unit—the structural condition and the presence of basic plumbing facilities (water supply, toilet facilities, and bathing facilities). Although such factors as light, ventilation, and neighborhood also reflect quality, particularly in urban areas, it is not feasible to measure them in a large-scale enumeration of the type undertaken by the U. S. Bureau of the Census. These elements, however, often are associated with high or low rating of plumbing facilities.

In 1960, the U. S. Census of Housing used a three-way classification ("sound," "deteriorating," and "dilapidated") to measure condition, compared with a two-way classification ("not dilapidated" and "dilapidated") in 1950. (Deteriorating housing units are units not dilapidated but needing more repair than would be provided in the course of regular maintenance.)

Three fourths of the housing units in the nation (approximately 43.1 million units) were reported in sound condition and as having all plumbing facilities—piped hot water, private flush toilet, and bathtub or shower—in 1960. An additional 8 percent (approximately 4.6 million units) had all plumbing facilities, but were in deteriorating condition. The remaining 17 percent (approximately 10.6 million units) were dilapidated or lacked one or more plumbing facilities (Table 4–11, p. 142). When some plumbing facility was lacking, it usually was a toilet and/or bathtub.

Measured by condition and presence of plumbing facilities, the quality of housing in the United States improved between 1950 and 1960. The most direct evidence of this is the decrease in the number of units considered dilapidated, from 10 percent to 5 percent. The decrease does not mean that a high proportion of the 1950 dilapidated units had been improved. Rather, the percentage was brought down in part by the larger amount of new construction during the 1950's. Also, many units existing in 1950 were removed from the nation's housing supply through slum clearance, urban renewal, and highway construction. Some were, of course, upgraded through the installation of plumbing facilities and repair of the physical structure.

There was a significantly higher proportion of housing units of sound quality in metropolitan areas than outside those areas—86 percent as compared with 73 percent. The difference is accounted for, in large part, by the substantially higher proportion of units outside metropolitan areas that lacked a toilet and/or bathtub. (Even among units rated in sound condition, the lack of these facilities was much higher outside metropolitan areas than inside them.)

Housing units that were dilapidated or lacked plumbing facilities were distributed unevenly among the various regions of the nation. The South, which included the South Atlantic, East South Central, and West South Central Divisions, with only about three tenths of all the housing units in the United States, had close to half (5.0 million) of all the units that were dilapidated or lacked plumbing facilities in 1960. The housing in the best condition was found in the Northeast (the New England and Middle Atlantic Divisions) and in the Pacific Division of the Western region (Table 4–12, p. 143).

Rental housing is generally of poorer quality than owner-occupied housing. This is most clearly shown by the fact that in 1960 only 66 percent of all the rental units were in sound condition and had all of the necessary plumbing facilities, as compared with 83 percent of the owner-occupied units. Also, 7 percent of the rental units, as compared with less than 3 percent of the owner-occupied units, were dilapidated. Outside metropolitan areas, only half of the rental units were in sound condition and had all plumbing facilities. A total of 12 percent of the rental units outside these areas were dilapidated (Table 4–13, p. 144).

There has been an improvement, since World War II, in the quality of housing occupied by nonwhite families. However, that housing is still well below the standards of the housing occupied by the total population. In

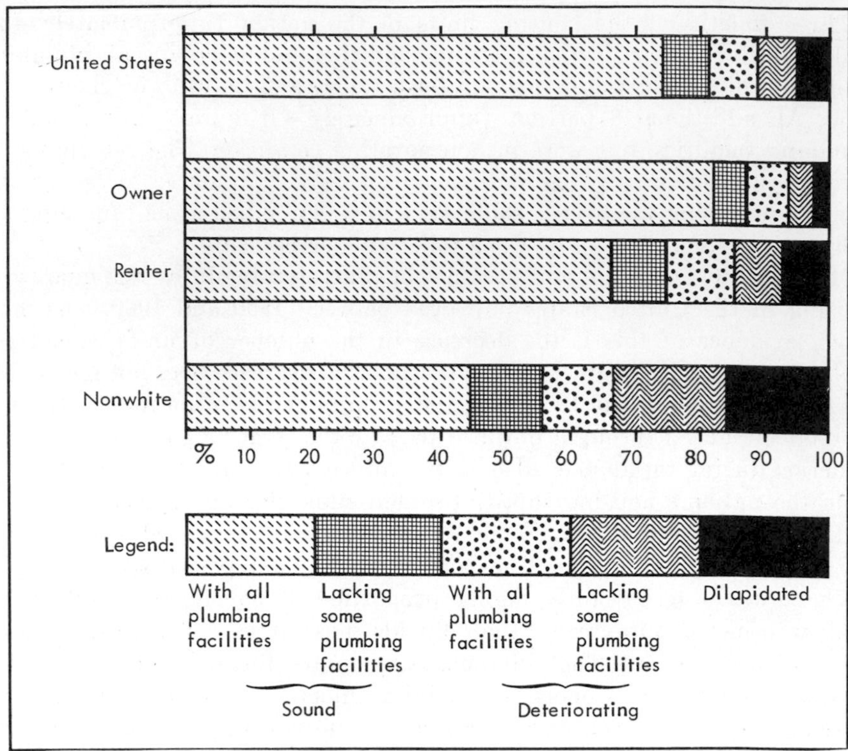

FIGURE 5. *Condition and plumbing facilities of housing units, total, owner and renter, and nonwhite, for the United States, 1960. (Source of data: Derived from U.S. Bureau of the Census,* Census of Housing 1960. *States and Small Areas, HC(1), No. 1, U.S. Summary, pp. 1–4 and 1–225.)*

1960, only 53 percent of the owner units and 39 percent of the renter units occupied by nonwhites were of sound quality and had all plumbing facilities. Furthermore, 12 percent of the owner units and one out of every five of the renter units were dilapidated. These percentages are even greater in housing outside of metropolitan areas. Only one out of every four owner-occupied units occupied by nonwhite families living outside metropolitan areas was sound in quality and had all plumbing facilities. For renter-occupied units, the comparable figure was only one out of ten. Furthermore, for nonwhite families living outside metropolitan areas, one out of every five families who owned their homes and one out of every three who rented, lived in a structure considered dilapidated (Table 4–14, p. 145). The extremely poor condition of much of this housing will be discussed again in the chapter on rural housing.

The foregoing discussion has been limited to a discussion of condition of structures and plumbing facilities. There are, as mentioned earlier, many other things that constitute quality. To a degree, household equipment might be considered one of them.

The decade of the 1950's saw families adding much more household equipment than they had in previous decades. In 1960, for example, 92 percent of the households had one or more radios. A total of 87 percent had one or more television sets. Four out of every five had a telephone. Approximately 6.5 million households, or one out of every eight, had air conditioning (usually one or more room units, rather than a central air conditioning system). Some of the other trends regarding household equipment will be discussed in Chapter 6.

Age of Houses

The age of housing units is significant only as it is related to other characteristics of the housing supply, especially the quality of the units. For example, it is of questionable value to know the number of units over thirty years old without also knowing their condition, size, location, type, and other factors. The age of an existing house may be a rough index of its condition, but age alone will not measure the adequacy of the dwelling or its structural soundness.

Even for dwellings of identical age and construction, the usual life spans of the structures may vary widely, because careful maintenance would materially extend the period of usefulness. A generally accepted rule of thumb for calculating deductions for depreciation and obsolescence on income tax returns has put the life span of a single-family frame dwelling at 33⅓ years. However, this figure is of little use. It is not at all difficult to find many frame dwellings, still completely adequate, that have been in continuous use for well over 100 years and, at the same time, to find houses that are run down and inadequate at a quarter of that age. Sheer youth in housing is no guarantee that a house is good.

The neighborhood also is an important factor with regard to the age of a house. Houses are commonly judged by "the company they keep" rather than by their age. Consider two houses of approximately the same age and original quality. If one is in an area where high standards have been maintained and the other is in an area that has become run down, the former will have a higher value.

The effect of environmental or neighborhood characteristics on the age of dwelling units will vary from community to community. Two important factors in this variation are the extent and effectiveness of local controls, particularly zoning, city planning, and subdivision regulations. Dwelling units in areas that have well-developed and well-administered ordinances will be less adversely affected by their advancing years than those in areas not so "protected." The former are not as likely to be influenced by the forces of blight and depreciation or of obsolescence.

The importance attached to the age of houses also varies from community to community. For example, it nets little to compare the average age of dwelling units in Mobile, Alabama with those in Springfield, Illinois; or those in Springfield, Massachusetts with those in Tulsa, Oklahoma. Rather, the general state of preservation is a far more important criterion.

Within a given community, however, a classification of houses by age is useful for correlation with other characteristics of the housing supply. For example, an age comparison within the Washington, D.C. metropolitan area will indicate that housing units in the Arlington County portion of that area are much newer than those in the District of Columbia proper. Generally speaking, the Arlington County housing might be expected to be of better quality because it is newer. However, here as in many instances, there is a well-known exception—the area of Georgetown where age has been capitalized upon instead of being considered a detriment.

Generally, for the community as a whole a basis is provided for evaluating the need and prospect for rehabilitation, as against the need for outright replacement, when age is analyzed carefully in its relation to such factors as the condition of housing and neighborhood stability. Rehabilitation is usually feasible only where structures are basically sound. Since many older residential buildings were more soundly built than many of the newer ones, plans for rehabilitation may well focus on areas containing structures of the newer type.

Another positive aspect of the age factor is that it is more likely to exert a direct, independent, market influence through *design* than through adequacy or other factors mentioned above. The highly ornate and exaggerated architectural styles that were immensely popular at certain periods in our history have become outmoded, because of their inappropriateness to modern living. In consequence, dwellings built during those periods have fallen low in consumer preference. At the same time, some dwellings, constructed very early in our history but of simple, straightforward design, have proved their adaptability to modern usages and have retained public favor. In some cases they have even increased in popularity, as in Georgetown.

Because of the building boom that has been taking place in the United States during the last ten years, the proportion of new housing in the nation's inventory is substantial. Approximately 16.0 million housing units, amounting to over one fourth (28 percent) of all housing in the nation in 1960, were in structures built in the last ten years (Table 4–15, p. 146). In 1950, only 21 percent of the units were in structures built during the preceding ten years, and in 1940, the comparable figure was 16 percent. These figures show that a higher proportion of the population is constantly living in newer housing.

Despite the large number of new units in 1960, almost half of the housing units (47 percent) were more than 30 years old. The proportion was slightly higher outside metropolitan areas than inside them.

Housing Sizes

The importance of size of houses or apartments lies primarily in its use as a measurement of the adequacy of dwelling units to satisfy the requirements of families of various sizes and composition.

The size of dwelling units in a community has relatively little significance by itself. For example, in Florida, the average size of each unit is small. This might appear to be explainable in terms of the tourist demand and the fact that many of these units house elderly couples. However, a casual glance at the size averages shows that many other Southern cities, not necessarily of the resort type, have a high percentage of small units. (When housing in various European countries is discussed in Chapter 16, the particular case of Sweden will be noted.) Hence, size may be particularly important as an indicator of several factors.

In addition to the importance of the size differential, there is also a difference with relation to the type of structure. Generally, multifamily structures contain smaller units than single-family units. However, this rule is subject to some exceptions, notably the low-cost, small, single-family units built during and immediately after World War II.

Converted units also frequently tend to be small. The extent of conversion varies widely from city to city. The size of units in a community is important in the matter of conversion, since large units, obviously, lend themselves better to being converted into a number of small units than do units that were originally small. This becomes an important factor in urban renewal, since the conversion and rehabilitation of small units is often uneconomical, and thus favors the replacement of those units.

Of course, income is one of the most important elements in determining the size of dwellings families will select, since, under average conditions, the square-foot area that can be rented or purchased increases in a more or less direct relationship with increases in family income. Although certain families in high-income groups may, for reasons of convenience or location or other reasons, choose to live in relatively small apartments, it is obvious that the more spacious, luxury-class apartments will demand a higher rent and will therefore attract families of higher income. Thus, it is safe to assume that, even in multifamily dwellings, the average number of rooms will increase in proportion to the increase in the size of income of the occupant family.

What are today considered large units were built in most communities during earlier periods, when both labor and material were cheaper than they are today. In recent decades, there has been a constant decline in the size of the unit in almost all communities. One- and two-bedroom houses were most commonly built during and just after World War II, when there was a restriction on building materials.

In discussions of the high cost of home building today, the fact is often overlooked that the demands of living have changed and that the house of today is hardly comparable with the house of fifty years ago. *Almost one third of the cost of today's house is attributable to "necessities" in the form of mechanical equipment, much of which was unheard of fifty years ago.* This equipment includes such commonly accepted items as central heating, indoor plumbing, sewage disposal, automatic laundry facilities, dishwashers, electrical wiring for lighting and appliances, and in some instances, air conditioning. It is small wonder then that the average house of today is smaller and more expensive than its predecessor, which, judged by today's standards, was merely *an unequipped shell.*

The median number of rooms for all units in the United States was 4.9 in 1960. However, 20 percent of the units had 3 rooms or less, and 16 percent had 7 rooms or more (Table 4–16, p. 146). There was little difference in the size of units inside and outside metropolitan areas, but there was, of course, a significant difference between owner-occupied and renter units. Owner-occupied units had a median of 5.5 rooms and renter units, a median of 3.9 rooms. Most of the units having 3 rooms or less were renter units, and only a low proportion of the renter units had 7 rooms or more (Table 4–17, p. 147).

Number of Units in Structure

Even a casual survey of houses and apartments in any community will reveal that the housing supply is made up of a variety of significant housing types. This is, of course, a reflection of the fact that housing has in a general way been developed to meet the desires and needs of families of varying composition and with diversified social and economic characteristics. The large family with several small children often will demand a different type of home from the childless employed couple or the elderly family. Similarly, families at different income levels and engaged in different economic pursuits will require housing of different types. Again, housing styles have changed over a period of years, as have urban habits of living. These changes have left their mark in varying degree on the local housing needs the country over.

The large city, with a population of a million or more, usually has a much higher proportion of multifamily units than other areas. Over a third of the housing units in New York and Chicago are of this type. Large cities also have a higher than average proportion of duplexes and row houses. Philadelphia and Baltimore have been especially noted for their long-established patterns of the latter type. On the other hand, smaller communities usually tend to have a high proportion of single-family units.

However, the trend in recent years, in almost all areas, has been toward single-family houses. Whereas the total inventory of housing units in the nation increased 26 percent between 1950 and 1960, the number of single-family, detached units increased 39 percent. In 1960, as a result, there were 40.9 million single-family, detached units in the nation's inventory, representing 70 percent of the total number of housing units. An additional 6 percent were one-family *attached* structures—the row houses and semi-detached houses found in some communities. The aggregate of single-family structures, therefore, represented three fourths of the total housing inventory in 1960. About 8 percent of the units were in structures with two units (duplexes), 5 percent in structures with three or four units, and the remaining 11 percent were in structures with five or more units (Table 4–18, p. 147). The proportion of five-or-more-unit structures was about the same in 1960 as in 1950 and 1940. (During the last few years there has been some upsurge in the building of apartment buildings. This is discussed in Chapter 6.)

LOCAL CHARACTER OF MARKETS

The vast differences among families dictate differences in the houses provided to meet their needs. Various factors of the type described in Chapter 2 influence many of the characteristics of the housing supply, e.g., the size and location of the houses, their condition and facilities, whether they are owned or rented, and the like.

Other factors, as well, have an influence on housing characteristics and trends. The availability of land for large-scale subdivisions may have an important influence on the direction of the city's growth. Certain social attributes of families determine whether or not these locations are acceptable. Construction costs, in addition to influencing location of housing, also influence type of structure, size, and nature of construction. Other important factors include financing, the rising standard of living, and any existing backlog of demand for housing.

When all of these factors are brought together, they involve a market. Rapkin says a market exists ". . . whenever buyers and sellers are in such free communication that the same commodity or service commands the same price, or prices tend toward equality easily and quickly."

He goes on to say:

> However, this definition needs to be further developed to be useful for housing market analysis. . . . How can "sameness" of a commodity be determined? At this point, the concept of substitutability of goods and services becomes a key to understanding the nature of a market.
>
> Given any degree of competition, that is, the ability of a buyer to substitute one thing for another, it becomes possible to view the market as a chain of substitutes bidding through a price mechanism for a purchaser.[4]

Housing markets are necessarily *local,* for it is at the community level that competition exists among different houses for a single buyer. This simple concept defines the extent and limits of the housing market area. This area usually includes a central city, some incorporated and/or unincorporated suburbs, and fringe and ribbon developments extending out from these suburbs. Frequently, topographical characteristics and transportation routes and facilities are important factors in the delineation of the market area. On the basis of this definition, many housing market areas closely approximate the labor market areas, omitting only far-out, isolated houses in which some urban workers live.

The so-called national market, then, is in actuality a mosaic of many very different local markets. Generally speaking, however, even the "com-

[4] Chester Rapkin, Louis Winnick, and David M. Blank, *Housing Market Analysis—A Study of Theory and Methods.* Washington, D.C.: U.S. Government Printing Office, December 1953, p. 8.

munity'' represents too broad an area for all dwellings to be in competition with all others. For this reason, it is desirable sometimes to focus particular attention on what might be termed ''submarkets.''

Within the particular housing market area, in other words, certain dwelling units are likely to combine into clusters, either because of their particular characteristics or because of certain characteristics and requirements of consumers. For example, there may be submarkets based on type of structure—particular families are likely to have a preference for single-family dwellings, whereas others may have a preference for apartments or row houses. Closely related to type of structure is the matter of tenure; many families prefer to own, whereas others want to rent. Another group of submarkets is represented by value level and rental rates, with a continuum existing from the lowest to the highest price or rent. A final classification might be locational. Frequently, families have strong feelings with regard to the kind of neighborhood or area in which they will and will not live (see Chapter 9).

In reality, all of these factors are likely to be linked, which is one of the reasons why the various kinds of submarkets described cannot be neatly shown on a map.

Housing Market Analysis

The evaluation and interpretation of the various demand and supply forces at work in the local housing market has become known as ''housing market analysis.'' The purpose of such analysis is to reduce general impressions concerning the local housing market to quantitative terms.

Nature and Purpose

Housing market analyses are undertaken for different purposes, and those purposes usually determine the nature of the analysis. For example, the Federal Housing Administration, which undertook the first major program of this type and still carries on a market analysis program, has as its primary purpose the determination of the economic soundness of the mortgage market in various localities. It usually wants to know how many single-family units can be safely built in an area, without danger of foreclosure. Sometimes the FHA conducts only partial analyses—if, for example, it wants to determine the economic soundness of a mortgage for a proposed large-scale rental housing project. The Public Housing Administration and local housing authorities conduct local housing market analyses to determine the need for low-rent public housing. FHA studies obviously focus on middle-income families and PHA on those having low incomes. City planning commissions sometimes conduct housing market analyses in connection with their studies of future city growth. Sometimes lending institutions, such as life insurance companies, undertake market studies to determine the soundness of their financial investment in housing in a particular community. Marketing consultants, some builders, and many other groups frequently need to anticipate the future housing market of a community.

The structure of housing market reports has crystallized into a general form over the years, although individual reports made by the types of agencies and groups mentioned above vary widely in form of presentation and degree of sophistication, as well as in areas of emphasis and detail. Rapkin describes, in essence, how market estimates are usually constructed:

> Estimates of housing demand are built up by examining the economy of the area and its employment and income potentialities. To this is added an analysis of probable population growth translated into number of households. These two factors in demand are then combined to yield a probable income distribution of the anticipated number of households and the corresponding rents or prices that households in each income bracket pay on the average.
>
> The estimates of housing supply that may be in existence at a future date are based upon the current inventory (or latest census) of the housing stock detailed as to quality, occupancy, and rent-value distribution. Estimates are then made of the changes in the current stock that many be anticipated by virtue of demolitions, conversions, and rehabilitation, as well as the shift in rent-value distribution due to depreciation and obsolescence. In estimates of housing need which attempt to measure the amount of housing required to accommodate each family adequately, further adjustments are made in the supply data for the elimination of substandard units.
>
> The concluding step consists of matching the two sets of derived estimates: (1) The number of households that will be in existence at a chosen future date, distributed by the rents or prices that they are assumed to be able to afford or are willing to pay for housing, and (2) the rent-value distribution of the existing supply as it is estimated to appear at that time. The difference between these two distributions is taken to represent the housing demand (or surplus) in each rent or value bracket.[5]

The outline below could provide the form for a rather complete local housing market analysis:

1. Definition of housing market area.
2. Analysis of economic base of the area.
   a. Regional setting and historical development.
   b. Relative size and importance of different types of business.
   c. Business trends.
      (1) Capital investment
      (2) Employment and payrolls.
   d. Business outlook.
3. Basic factors in housing demand.
   a. Population trends.
      (1) Total population, family size, household formation.
      (2) Migration.
   b. Family income.

[5] *Ibid.*, pp. 3–4.

c. Cost of living.

4. Basic factors in housing supply.
   a. Present inventory, by characteristics.
   b. Trends in supply (new construction, conversions, and demolitions).
   c. Capacity of local home building industry.
5. Other market factors.
   a. Vacancies.
   b. Price.
   c. Doubling-up and overcrowding.
   d. Construction costs.
   e. Local taxes.
   f. Availability of lots and raw land.
   g. Community controls.
   h. Real estate overhang.
   i. Market activity reflected on deeds recorded, mortgages made, and foreclosures.
   j. Sources and availability of mortgage funds and local mortgage practices.
6. Effective market demand and consumer preferences.
   a. Volume.
   b. Size of units (and lots).
   c. Type and style of units.
   d. Neighborhood or other locational preferences.
   e. Price level.
   f. Financing required.
   g. Special features desired (e.g., air conditioning, type of heating, garages).
   h. Rental market.

All of the items included in this outline are important for understanding a local housing market. The demand factors indicated under points 2 and 3 interact with the supply factors indicated under point 4 in a complex manner, and they influence one another in many ways.

Most of these factors cannot be measured precisely. (An exception is new construction, item 4b. A good indicator of this factor is available on a month-to-month basis for most cities.)[6] In general, certain base information must be used (such as that provided by Federal agencies in Census and other reports), but frequently that information is not available on a city-by-city basis.

No formula accurately describes the relationships between the supply and demand factors, but the results of their interaction is generally depicted in some of the items listed under point 5 of the outline above. The two most important factors in this regard are prices and vacancies. For this reason they are discussed in more detail below.

[6] See "New Housing Units Authorized by Local Building Permits," U.S. Bureau of the Census, *Construction Reports*, issued monthly.

Prices

Although there is usually a close relationship between price of housing and costs of construction, price in the local market is a direct reflection of the relationship between supply and demand. As stated earlier, if the supply is large, relative to demand, the price of dwelling units (including rents) will tend to be lower; conversely, if the demand is large, relative to supply, house prices will tend to be higher. For older houses, current price levels are more important than cost of construction.

Obviously, not all dwelling units will be equally affected. Different prices will exist for different characteristics of housing units based on the demand for those characteristics. Those differences are important because they constitute one of the peculiarities of housing markets, in contrast to markets for other commodities where standardization and a "one-price" tendency are more common.

The price of housing also is significant because of its relationship to many other elements of a housing market. If housing prices are low, relative to cost, that factor will tend to discourage new construction. If housing prices are high, relative to family income, some families will pay a disproportionate amount of their income for housing and others will reduce their housing standards by accepting less desirable units or doubling up with other families. If housing prices are low relative to the investment in existing housing, that fact will be reflected in a decline in standards of maintenance of housing, and also in lack of interest in investment in additional new housing.

Prices and rents, therefore, do not exist in a vacuum. They are determined by the fluctuations in virtually every other element that influences demand and supply. To appraise their significance, it is necessary to consider them in relation to other market factors such as family income, volume of new construction, construction costs, vacancies, taxes, and many other factors. The influence of these various elements varies from time to time and from community to community. Hence the relationship between prices and rents, and between these and the other market forces, cannot be standardized or reduced to a mathematical formula.

Vacancies

A local housing market may be out of balance, either on the side of an excess of dwelling units over those demanded or on the side of excess of demand for units over those available. Furthermore, a market may be more frequently out of balance with respect to the *quality* and *type* of housing than with respect to the total quantity of housing. The most common measure of the degree of balance between supply and demand, both quantitatively and qualitatively, is the *number* and *type* of dwelling units that are vacant and available.

No single vacancy rate can be considered "normal." Some general conclusions that illustrate that fact appear warranted on the basis of various vacancy rates that were found to exist several years ago:

1. In general, large communities tend to have higher vacancy ratios than small communities.

2. Communities with a high proportion of rental units tend to have higher vacancy ratios than communities with a high proportion of owner-occupied units.

3. Communities with a large proportion of multifamily structures show tendencies toward higher vacancy rates than localities that contain predominantly single-family houses.

4. Vacancy rates tend to be highest in the lowest- and the highest-priced classes, indicating that most stable occupancy is found in the middle-type bracket where shifts in demand upward and downward in price have the least net effect.

5. Vacancy ratios in all price classes are consistently highest in the smaller units, decreasing as the size of the units increases.

6. No consistent relationship has been found between vacancies and the proportion of units overcrowded.[7]

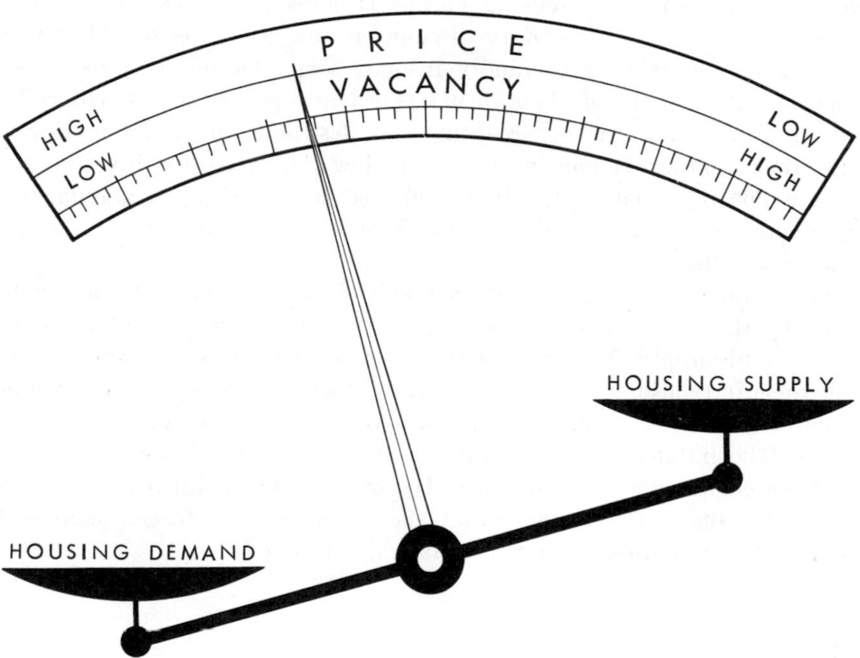

FIGURE 6. *Two factors—price and vacancy—are primarily indicative of the status of the local housing market.*

The above conclusions are not intended to indicate a procedure for developing an "allowable" vacancy ratio. Rather, they serve to guide judgment by pointing out some rather well-established characteristics that are usually found in relation to high and low rates of vacancies.

Several important aspects of the vacancy ratios should be noted. First, it is important to consider "available" units, since there are always many

[7] From an unpublished study in which the author participated in 1946.

units vacant simply because they are not available on the market. This can be seen from 1960 Census data which indicate that while there was a vacancy ratio of 6.1 percent with reference to units that could be used the year round, only 3.4 percent of the units were vacant *and available* (Table 4–19, p. 148). Second, some units are used only seasonally, and therefore would be expected to be vacant out of season. (In 1960, they amounted to 3 percent of the total number of units in the nation.) Finally, it is important to know the price or rental levels of the vacancies; the quality of the structures; their age, type, and location; and the size of the units. Obviously, if there is a surplus of high-priced units, this would have little relationship to the supply of low-priced units. Or, there may be a surplus of two-bedroom units, but this would not necessarily mean that more three-bedroom units were not needed. Again, many expensive, luxurious apartments may be vacant, but this would not mean that there was not a need for more rental housing at low or moderate rents.

A certain number of units in the housing market will and should always be available. The supply of vacant units permits individuals and families some selection in housing. On the other hand, a disproportionate number of vacant dwellings obviously works an economic hardship on owners of the dwellings. The level of vacancy, then, has an extremely important influence not only on the volume, but also on the kind of new construction that is likely to take place.

One of the difficulties concerning the consideration of vacancies in housing market analysis is lack of information concerning them at any given time. Classified advertisements and brokerage listings always offer a clue, but this information is usually limited as an indicator of the total situation. Frequently it is necessary to utilize information available about the recent past as an indication of what to expect in the immediate future.[8]

Of course, local housing markets do not remain static. Therefore, in order to have a current understanding of market conditions, constant or, at least, periodic studies are required.

The type of analysis suggested in the outline given earlier not only would provide an indication of the present local housing situation, but would also permit short-term (and possibly some long-term) predictions.

Because market data of the type required are not generally organized —in fact, are often lacking—only partial analyses are frequently possible. Nonetheless, a local market analysis developed in the most careful and comprehensive manner possible in a specific community becomes an important tool for local interests.

READING LIST

THE HOUSING MARKET

Fisher, Ernest M. *Urban Real Estate Markets: Characteristics and Financing.*

[8] Information on vacancies on a national basis is published quarterly. See U.S. Bureau of the Census, *Current Housing Reports.* "Housing Vacancies," Series H-111.

New York: National Bureau of Economic Research, 1951.

———, and Robert M. Fisher. *Urban Real Estate.* New York: Holt, Rinehart, and Winston, 1954, Chapter 11.

Grebler, Leo. *Housing Market Behavior in a Declining Area.* New York: Columbia University Press, 1952.

Ratcliff, Richard U. *Urban Land Economics.* New York: McGraw-Hill Book Co., Inc., 1949, Chapter 11.

Weimer, Arthur M. and Homer Hoyt. *Principles of Urban Real Estate,* 2d ed. New York: The Ronald Press Co., 1948, Chapter 8.

HOUSING MARKET ANALYSIS

Rapkin, Chester, Louis Winnick, and David M. Blank. *Housing Market Analysis—A Study of Theory and Methods.* Washington, D.C.: U.S. Government Printing Office, December 1953.

GENERAL

Colean, Miles L. *American Housing: Problems and Prospects.* New York: The Twentieth Century Fund, 1947, Part II.

Winnick, Louis. *American Housing and Its Use—The Demand for Shelter Space.* A Volume in the Census Monograph Series. New York: John Wiley & Sons, 1957.

Table 4–1

HOUSING UNITS INSIDE AND OUTSIDE STANDARD METROPOLITAN STATISTICAL AREAS, 1960

	Number	*Percent*
Inside SMSA's	36,386,215	62.4%
In central cities	19,622,145	33.6
Not in central cities	16,764,070	28.7
Outside SMSA's	21,940,142	37.6
Total, United States	58,326,357	100.0%

SOURCE: U.S. Bureau of the Census, *Census of Housing 1960.* States and Small Areas, HC(1), No. 1, U.S. Summary, p. xx.

Table 4–2

PERCENTAGE DISTRIBUTION OF HOUSING UNITS BY DIVISIONS, INSIDE AND OUTSIDE STANDARD METROPOLITAN STATISTICAL AREAS, 1960

			Inside SMSA's		
Division	*Number*	*Total*	*In Central Cities*	*Not in Central Cities*	*Outside SMSA's*
United States	58,326,000	100.0%	33.6%	28.7%	37.6%
New England	3,522,000	6.0	1.9	2.2	2.0
Middle Atlantic	11,277,000	19.3	8.3	7.3	3.8
East North Central	11,658,000	20.0	7.2	5.9	6.9
West North Central	5,140,000	8.8	2.3	1.4	5.1
South Atlantic	8,033,000	13.8	3.5	3.6	6.7
East South Central	3,606,000	6.2	1.3	0.9	3.9
West South Central	5,534,000	9.5	3.6	1.4	4.5
Mountain	2,227,000	3.8	1.2	0.7	2.0
Pacific	7,331,000	12.6	4.5	5.4	2.7

SOURCE: U.S. Bureau of the Census, *Census of Housing 1960.* States and Small Areas, HC(1), No. 1, U.S. Smmary, p. xx.

Table 4–3

OCCUPIED HOUSING UNITS AND POPULATION, 1900 TO 1960

	Occupied Units		*Total Population*		
Census Year and Residence	*Number*	*Increase Over Preceding Census*	*Number*	*Increase Over Preceding Census*	*Population Per Occupied Unit*
Total:					
1960	53,023,875	23.4%	179,323,175	18.5%	3.4
1950	42,968,900	22.9	151,325,798	14.5	3.5
1940	34,963,801	16.5	132,164,569	7.3	3.8
1930	30,001,583	22.8	123,202,624	16.2	4.1
1920	24,435,698	20.2	106,021,537	15.0	4.3
1910	20,325,583	27.0	92,228,496	21.0	4.5
1900	16,005,911	—	76,212,168	—	4.8
Inside SMSA's:					
1960	34,000,044	31.5	112,885,178	26.4	3.3
1950	25,848,079	—	89,316,903	—	3.5
Outside SMSA's:					
1960	19,023,831	11.1	66,437,997	7.1	3.5
1950	17,120,821	—	62,008,895	—	3.6

SOURCE: U.S. Bureau of the Census. *Census of Housing 1960*. States and Small Areas, HC(1), No. 1, U.S. Summary, p. xxvi.

Table 4–4

PERCENTAGE DISTRIBUTION OF TENURE OF OCCUPIED HOUSING UNITS, INSIDE AND OUTSIDE STANDARD METROPOLITAN STATISTICAL AREAS, AND URBAN AND RURAL, 1960

	Number Occupied	*Owner-Occupied*	*Renter-Occupied*
Total, United States	53,023,875	61.9%	38.1%
Inside SMSA's	34,000,044	58.9	41.1
In central cities	18,505,949	47.4	52.6
Not in central cities	15,494,095	72.7	27.3
Outside SMSA's	19,023,831	67.1	32.9
Urban	38,320,370	58.3%	41.7%
Rural	14,703,505	71.2	28.8
Nonfarm	11,137,184	70.3	29.7
Occupied farm	3,566,321	73.8	26.2

SOURCE: Derived from U.S. Bureau of the Census, *Census of Housing 1960*. States and Small Areas, HC(1), No. 1, U.S. Summary, pp. xxvii and xliii.

Table 4–5

TENURE OF OCCUPIED HOUSING UNITS BY DIVISIONS, 1960

Division	*Number Occupied*	*Owner-Occupied*	*Renter-Occupied*
U.S. Total	53,023,875	61.9%	38.1%
New England	3,116,163	59.1	40.9
Middle Atlantic	10,405,988	55.2	44.8
East North Central	10,710,827	66.7	33.3
West North Central	4,667,922	67.8	32.2
South Atlantic	7,266,636	61.0	39.0
East South Central	3,307,354	61.8	38.2
West South Central	4,928,605	63.7	36.3
Mountain	1,975,576	65.2	34.8
Pacific	6,644,804	60.2	39.8

SOURCE: U.S. Bureau of the Census, *Census of Housing 1960.* States and Small Areas, HC(1), No. 1, U.S. Summary, pp. 1-4, 1-5.

Table 4–6

PERCENTAGE DISTRIBUTION OF TENURE AND COLOR OF OCCUPANCY, OCCUPIED HOUSING UNITS, INSIDE AND OUTSIDE STANDARD METROPOLITAN STATISTICAL AREAS, 1960

Tenure and Color	*Total U.S.*	*Inside SMSA's*	*Outside SMSA's*
Total occupied housing units (number in thousands)	53,024	34,000	19,024
Owner-occupied	61.9%	58.9%	67.1%
White	58.2	55.3	63.1
Nonwhite	3.7	3.6	4.0
Renter-occupied	38.1	41.1	32.9
White	32.1	34.4	28.1
Nonwhite	6.0	6.7	4.8

SOURCE: Derived from U.S. Bureau of the Census, *Census of Housing 1960.* States and Small Areas, HC(1), No. 1, U.S. Summary, p. 1-40.

Table 4–7

PERCENTAGE DISTRIBUTION OF PERSONS-PER-ROOM, OCCUPIED-HOUSING UNITS, INSIDE AND OUTSIDE STANDARD METROPOLITAN STATISTICAL AREAS, BY TENURE, 1960

	Total U.S.		*Inside SMSA's*		*Outside SMSA's*	
Persons-Per-Room	*Owner*	*Renter*	*Owner*	*Renter*	*Owner*	*Renter*
Total occupied-housing units (number in thousands)	32,797	20,227	20,036	13,964	12,761	6,263
0.50 or less	46.6%	34.1%	45.1%	35.0%	49.0%	32.0%
0.51 to 0.75	23.5	23.5	24.8	24.2	21.4	22.0
0.76 to 1.00	21.2	26.2	22.3	26.6	19.4	25.4
1.01 to 1.50	6.6	10.1	6.3	9.2	7.2	11.9
1.51 or more	2.1	6.1	1.5	5.0	3.0	8.7

SOURCE: Derived from U.S. Bureau of the Census, *Census of Housing 1960*. States and Small Areas, HC(1), No. 1, U.S. Summary, p. 1–43.

Table 4–8

PERCENTAGE DISTRIBUTION OF VALUE OF OWNER-OCCUPIED HOUSING UNITS, INSIDE AND OUTSIDE STANDARD METROPOLITAN STATISTICAL AREAS, 1960

Value	*Total U.S.*	*Inside SMSA's*	*Outside SMSA's*
Total occupied-housing units (number in thousands)	26,172	17,267	8,904
Less than $5,000	12.2%	5.6%	24.8%
$5,000 to $7,400	12.2	9.0	18.4
$7,500 to $9,900	13.5	12.6	15.4
$10,000 to $12,400	15.6	16.3	14.3
$12,500 to $14,900	13.5	15.7	9.3
$15,000 to $17,400	10.9	12.9	6.8
$17,500 to $19,900	7.2	9.0	3.7
$20,000 to $24,900	7.3	9.1	3.7
$25,000 to $34,900	4.7	5.9	2.3
$35,000 or more	2.9	3.9	1.3
Median dollars	$11,900	$13,500	$8,600

SOURCE: Derived from U.S. Bureau of the Census, *Census of Housing 1960*. States and Small Areas, HC(1), No. 1, U.S. Summary, p. 1–45.

Table 4–9

PERCENTAGE DISTRIBUTION OF GROSS RENT OF RENTER-OCCUPIED HOUSING UNITS, INSIDE AND OUTSIDE STANDARD METROPOLITAN STATISTICAL AREAS, 1960

Rent	*Total U.S.*	*Inside SMSA's*	*Outside SMSA's*
Total renter-occupied units (number in thousands)	19,294	13,860	5,434
Less than $30	5.5%	3.0%	11.9%
$30 to $39	6.3	5.1	9.5
$40 to $49	9.1	8.2	11.2
$50 to $59	11.6	11.4	12.1
$60 to $69	13.2	13.9	11.6
$70 to $79	12.2	13.2	9.6
$80 to $99	18.1	20.5	11.7
$100 to $119	8.8	10.4	4.5
$120 or more	8.0	10.1	3.0
No cash rent	7.2	4.2	14.9
Median dollars	$71	$75	$58

SOURCE: Derived from U.S. Bureau of the Census, *Census of Housing 1960*. States and Small Areas, HC(1), No. 1, U.S. Summary, p. 1–45.

Table 4–10

CONSUMER PRICE INDEX FOR HOUSING ITEMS, 1947 TO 1962 (1947–1949 = 100)

Year	*Total, Housing Items*	*Rent*	*Gas and Electricity*	*Solid Fuels and Fuel Oil*	*House Furnishings*	*Household Operation*
1947	95.0	94.4	97.6	88.8	97.2	97.2
1948	101.7	100.7	100.0	104.4	103.2	102.6
1949	103.3	105.0	102.5	106.8	99.6	100.1
1950	106.1	108.8	102.7	110.5	100.3	101.2
1951	112.4	113.1	103.1	116.4	111.2	109.0
1952	114.6	117.9	104.5	118.7	108.5	111.8
1953	117.7	124.1	106.6	123.9	107.9	115.3
1954	119.1	128.5	107.9	123.5	106.1	117.4
1955	120.0	130.3	110.7	125.2	104.1	119.1
1956	121.7	132.7	111.8	130.7	103.0	122.9
1957	125.6	135.2	113.0	137.4	104.6	127.5
1958	127.7	137.7	117.0	134.9	103.9	131.4
1959	129.2	139.7	119.9	136.6	103.9	134.3
1960	131.5	141.8	124.8	135.6	104.2	137.4
1961	132.5	143.6	125.8	138.5	103.6	138.9
1962	133.6	145.3	125.8	139.2	103.0	140.8

SOURCE: U.S. Department of Labor, Bureau of Labor Statistics periodic reports on Consumer Price Index.

Table 4–11

PERCENTAGE DISTRIBUTION OF PRESENCE AND CONDITION OF PLUMBING FACILITIES, INSIDE AND OUTSIDE STANDARD METROPOLITAN STATISTICAL AREAS, 1960

	1960		
Condition and Plumbing Facilities	*Total U.S.*	*Inside SMSA's*	*Outside SMSA's*
All housing units (number in thousands)	58,318	36,378	21,940
Sound	81.2%	86.1%	73.0%
With all plumbing facilities	74.0	81.8	60.9
Lacking only hot water	0.8	0.6	1.3
Lacking other plumbing facilities	6.4	3.7	10.8
Deteriorating	13.8	10.7	19.2
With all plumbing facilities	7.8	7.6	8.3
Lacking only hot water	0.6	0.5	0.8
Lacking other plumbing facilities	5.4	2.6	10.1
Dilapidated	5.0	3.2	7.8

SOURCE: Derived from U.S. Bureau of the Census, *Census of Housing 1960*. States and Small Areas, HC(1), No. 1, U.S. Summary, p. xxxvi.

Table 4–12

PERCENTAGE DISTRIBUTION OF CONDITION AND PRESENCE OF PLUMBING FACILITIES, BY DIVISIONS, 1960

Condition and Plumbing Facilities	*New England*	*Middle Atlantic*	*East North Central*	*West North Central*	*South Atlantic*	*East South Central*	*West South Central*	*Mountain*	*Pacific*
All housing units (number in thousands)	3,521	11,275	11,656	5,138	8,032	3,606	5,534	2,226	7,330
Sound	85.8%	85.8%	84.0%	79.7%	76.3%	67.0%	72.8%	81.0%	87.2%
With all plumbing facilities	78.7	81.2	77.1	68.6	67.2	53.0	64.8	74.9	83.9
Lacking only hot water	1.8	0.6	0.6	0.8	1.4	1.0	1.5	0.3	0.2
Lacking other plumbing facilities	5.3	4.0	6.3	10.2	7.7	13.0	6.5	5.8	3.1
Deteriorating	11.2	11.2	12.5	15.9	16.0	22.2	18.6	14.1	9.6
With all plumbing facilities	7.6	8.4	7.8	8.0	6.4	6.7	9.3	9.0	7.6
Lacking only hot water	0.8	0.3	0.4	0.5	1.2	0.8	1.2	0.3	0.1
Lacking other plumbing facilities	2.7	2.5	4.3	7.4	8.4	14.7	8.1	4.8	1.9
Dilapidated	3.0	3.0	3.5	4.4	7.7	10.8	8.6	4.9	3.2

SOURCE: Derived from U.S. Bureau of the Census, *Census of Housing 1960*. States and Small Areas, HC(1), No. 1, U.S. Summary, pp. 1–4, 1–5.

Table 4–13

PERCENTAGE DISTRIBUTION OF CONDITION AND PLUMBING FACILITIES, OCCUPIED HOUSING UNITS, INSIDE AND OUTSIDE STANDARD METROPOLITAN STATISTICAL AREAS, BY TENURE, 1960

	Total U.S.		*Inside SMSA's*		*Outside SMSA's*	
Condition and Plumbing Facilities	*Owner*	*Renter*	*Owner*	*Renter*	*Owner*	*Renter*
Total occupied housing units (number in thousands)	32,797	20,227	20,036	13,964	12,761	6,263
Sound	88.0%	73.9%	92.4%	79.2%	81.2%	62.0%
With all plumbing facilities	82.9	65.5	90.5	72.6	70.9	49.7
Lacking some or all facilities	5.1	8.4	1.9	6.6	10.3	12.3
Deteriorating	9.5	19.0	6.2	15.9	14.6	26.0
With all plumbing facilities	5.8	11.0	4.9	11.0	7.1	11.0
Lacking some or all facilities	3.7	8.0	1.3	4.9	7.5	15.0
Dilapidated	2.5	7.1	1.4	4.9	4.2	12.0

SOURCE: Derived from U.S. Bureau of the Census, *Census of Housing 1960.* States and Small Areas, HC(1), No. 1, U.S. Summary, p. 1–40.

Table 4–14

PERCENTAGE DISTRIBUTION OF CONDITION AND PRESENCE OF PLUMBING FACILITIES, OCCUPIED NONWHITE HOUSING UNITS, INSIDE AND OUTSIDE STANDARD METROPOLITAN STATISTICAL AREAS, BY TENURE, 1960

Condition and Plumbing Facilities	*Total U.S.*		*Inside SMSA's*		*Outside SMSA's*	
	Owner	*Renter*	*Owner*	*Renter*	*Owner*	*Renter*
Total occupied units (number in thousands)	1,974	3,171	1,224	2,262	749	909
Sound	64.3%	49.5%	75.2%	58.6%	46.7%	26.9%
With all plumbing facilities	52.6	38.7	69.8	49.8	24.6	11.0
Lacking some or all facilities	11.7	10.8	5.4	8.8	22.1	15.9
Deteriorating	23.8	30.6	18.0	28.0	33.0	37.5
With all plumbing facilities	10.6	12.8	12.4	16.4	7.4	4.0
Lacking some or all facilities	13.2	17.8	5.6	11.6	25.6	33.5
Dilapidated	11.9	19.9	6.8	13.4	20.3	35.6

SOURCE: Derived from U.S. Bureau of the Census, *Census of Housing 1960*. States and Small Areas HC(1), No. 1, U.S. Summary, p. 1-225.

Table 4–15

PERCENTAGE DISTRIBUTION OF YEAR STRUCTURE BUILT, INSIDE AND OUTSIDE STANDARD METROPOLITAN STATISTICAL AREAS, 1960

Year Structure Built	*Total U.S.*	*Inside SMSA's*	*Outside SMSA's*
Total housing units (number in thousands)	58,318	36,378	21,940
1959 to March 1960	3.9%	4.3%	3.3%
1955 to 1958	10.7	11.5	9.3
1950 to 1954	12.9	14.1	11.1
1940 to 1949	14.8	14.5	15.3
1930 to 1939	11.2	10.8	11.7
1929 or earlier	46.5	44.8	49.3

SOURCE: Derived from U.S. Bureau of the Census, *Census of Housing 1960*. States and Small Areas, HC(1), No. 1, U.S. Summary, p. 1–42.

Table 4–16

PERCENTAGE DISTRIBUTION OF NUMBER OF ROOMS, INSIDE AND OUTSIDE STANDARD METROPOLITAN STATISTICAL AREAS, 1960

Rooms	*Total U.S.*	*Inside SMSA's*	*Outside SMSA's*
Total housing units (number in thousands)	58,318	36,378	21,940
One	2.9%	3.3%	2.3%
Two	4.6	4.8	4.4
Three	12.0	12.7	10.7
Four	21.3	20.4	22.8
Five	24.6	25.1	23.7
Six	19.1	19.6	18.3
Seven	8.5	8.1	9.3
Eight or more	7.0	6.0	8.5
Median	4.9	4.8	4.9

SOURCE: Derived from U.S. Bureau of the Census, *Census of Housing 1960*. States and Small Areas, HC(1), No. 1, U.S. Summary, p. 1–41.

Table 4–17

PERCENTAGE DISTRIBUTION OF NUMBER OF ROOMS, OCCUPIED HOUSING UNITS, INSIDE AND OUTSIDE STANDARD METROPOLITAN STATISTICAL AREAS, BY TENURE, 1960

Number of Rooms	*Total U.S.*		*Inside SMSA's*		*Outside SMSA's*	
	Owner	*Renter*	*Owner*	*Renter*	*Owner*	*Renter*
Total occupied housing units (number) in thousands)	32,797	20,227	20,036	13,964	12,761	6,263
One	0.3%	5.5%	0.2%	6.5%	0.5%	3.5%
Two	1.1	8.8	0.8	9.6	1.6	7.0
Three	4.1	23.1	3.4	25.2	5.2	18.4
Four	16.7	28.2	15.0	27.9	19.3	28.6
Five	29.2	18.6	30.6	18.0	26.9	20.0
Six	26.2	9.9	28.1	8.8	23.1	12.3
Seven	12.4	3.4	12.5	2.5	12.3	5.4
Eight or more	10.0	2.5	9.4	1.5	11.1	4.8
Median	5.5	3.9	5.5	3.8	5.4	4.2

SOURCE: Derived from U.S. Bureau of the Census, *Census of Housing 1960*. States and Small Areas, HC(1), No. 1, U.S. Summary, p. 1–41.

Table 4–18

PERCENTAGE DISTRIBUTION OF NUMBER OF UNITS IN STRUCTURE, 1960 COMPARED WITH 1950 AND 1940

Units in Structure	*1960*			*1950*	*1940 Conterminous*
	United States	*Inside SMSA's*	*Outside SMSA's*	*United States*	*United States**
Total housing units (number in thousands)	58,314	36,375	21,940	46,137	37,325
One unit detached	70.1%	60.0%	86.9%	63.9%	64.0%
One unit other and 2 to 4 units	19.2	24.4	10.6	25.0	25.5
1 unit attached	6.3	7.7	3.9	†	†
2 to 4 units	13.0	16.7	6.7	†	†
Five units or more	10.7	15.7	2.5	11.0	10.5

SOURCE: Derived from U.S. Bureau of the Census, *Census of Housing 1960*. States and Small Areas, HC(1), No. 1, U.S. Summary, p. xxxiv.

* Exclusion of Alaska and Hawaii amounts to approximately 113,000 units.

† Category not comparable with 1960 category.

Table 4–19

PERCENTAGES OF VACANT HOUSING UNITS, BY CONDITION AND STATUS, 1960 AND 1950

	1960				
		Inside SMSA's			
Condition and Status	*United States*	*Total*	*In Central Cities*	*Outside SMSA's*	*1950 United States*
Total housing units (number in thousands)	58,326	36,386	19,622	21,940	46,137
Sound or deteriorating	5.2%	4.9%	4.8%	5.8%	3.3%
Available	3.4	3.6	3.9	3.0	1.6
For sale only	*0.9*	*1.0*	*0.7*	*0.8*	*0.5*
For rent	*2.5*	*2.6*	*3.3*	*2.2*	*1.1*
Rented or sold, awaiting occupancy	0.4	0.4	0.3	0.4	
Held for occasional use	0.5	0.3	0.1	0.8	1.7
Held for other reasons	1.0	0.6	0.5	1.6	
Dilapidated	0.9	0.5	0.5	1.5	1.2
Vacant, seasonal	3.0	1.2	0.4	6.0	2.4
Occupied	90.9	93.4	94.3	86.7	93.1
Percentage vacant year round	6.1%	5.4%	5.2%	7.3%	4.5%

SOURCE: Derived from U.S. Bureau of the Census, *Census of Housing 1960*. States and Small Areas, HC(1), No. 1, U.S. Summary, p. xxx.

CHAPTER 5

*

Residential Financing

INTRODUCTION

Credit permits a family to buy a house that otherwise it could not buy for many years. The house may be a new one that the family is building for itself, it may be one built speculatively by a builder, or it may be an existing house owned by someone else.

Because of the expensiveness of homes (the typical American family does not buy any other object as costly), the long-term debt involved in the housing market is enormous—$168.4 billion dollars in 1962 (one-to-four-unit structures) out of a total debt of $250.1 billion dollars outstanding, or 66 percent for all properties in the nation.[1]

The mortgage money market through which this housing is financed will be described in this chapter. However, before discussion of such matters as the volume of mortgages, sources of mortgage credit, types of financing, the secondary market, and the like, it should be pointed out that the market itself is much more complex than may be indicated by a description of these factors as of a particular time. Furthermore, the market is constantly changing. Some of these changes are caused by outside forces, since the housing market must compete with government and with other segments of business and industry for funds (although more than half of all residential mortgage funds come from small deposits and savings, as will be seen later). As a result of this competition, in which housing can be at a comparative disadvantage because of the longer duration of investment it involves, lenders need to make adjustments to market changes by altering terms and conditions of loans.

Because of the importance of housing in our national economy, the Federal Government has found it necessary to intervene through legislation and regulations. As a result, we have not a single mortgage market but, in effect, two—one directly government supported (i.e., FHA, VA, FNMA) and another not directly government supported (i.e., conventional).

There are many aspects of mortgage investment. Some of these will be discussed in the pages to follow; others will be discussed in later chapters. For example, although there is considerable discussion of the Federal Housing Administration and Veterans Administration mortgage programs

[1] Board of Governors of the Federal Reserve System, *Federal Reserve Bulletin*. Figures are published currently.

in this chapter, a detailed description of the operations and programs of those agencies is left for Chapter 14, which will consider broadly the government's role in housing.

VOLUME OF MORTGAGES

In the Residential Finance Survey, taken as a part of the 1960 U. S. Census of Housing, the basic unit of tabulation was the "homeowner property," that is, an owner-occupied property containing one, two, three or four dwelling units.[2] The total number of such properties and the number of one-dwelling-unit properties (which constituted 90 percent of the total), together with the number and percent which had mortgages on them in 1960, are shown below:

	Total Properties	*Mortgaged Properties*	*Percent Mortgaged*
Total one- to four-dwelling unit properties	27,862,000	15,816,000	57
Total one-dwelling unit properties	24,954,000	14,454,000	58

The 57 percent of the homeowner properties that were mortgaged reflected a marked increase over the 44 percent in that status in 1950, and represented a continuation in the upward trend in home mortgage financing since World War II.

Several aspects of these mortgaged properties are worth noting. Regionally, the West, perhaps because of the factors of growth and mobility already mentioned, had the highest proportion of properties with mortgages—approximately two out of every three. The figures for the other regions were as follows: the Northeast region, 57 percent; the South, 55 percent; the North Central region, 53 percent.

The growth of our metropolitan areas undoubtedly was responsible for a higher proportion of the homeowner properties being mortgaged in those areas (63 percent) than outside such areas (45 percent).

As would be expected, such properties included a higher proportion of recently built structures than did nonmortgaged properties. Dwellings built since 1955 included 29 percent mortgaged properties and 7 percent nonmortgaged, of all properties enumerated in 1960.

It is interesting to note that few of the dwelling units in poorest structural condition were mortgaged (perhaps because of their age and low value). The proportion of dwellings that were classified as dilapidated, according to Census terminology, and were mortgaged, was only 1 percent of the total (the proportion dilapidated and not mortgaged was 5 percent).

KINDS OF MORTGAGES

Mortgages are classified in several different ways. First, there are the straight-term and amortized types. There also are "first" mortgages and

[2] U.S. Bureau of the Census, *Census of Housing 1960*, Vol. V, Residential Finance. Part 1, Homeowner Properties.

"second" mortgages (or "junior") mortgages. There are the "open-end" and "package" mortgage types.

Straight-term and Amortized Mortgages

Mortgages are classified from the standpoint of the provision for repayment as *straight-term* and *amortized.* The straight-term mortgage, which was popular in the 1920's, but is quite uncommon today, is one which requires no payment on the principal during the term of the mortgage. The full amount of the mortgage falls due at the end of the period covered by the loan arrangement. When this type of mortgage was popular, the mortgage usually had a maturity period of three to five years, and interest rates commonly ranged up to 10 percent. A down payment of 30 percent to 50 percent was frequently required, but more often than not only interest and taxes were paid during the period of the loan and it would be renewed at maturity date. In periods of depression the lenders found it necessary to "call in" these mortgages. At such times the mortgagors (i.e., the home buyers) usually could not repay the loan, and foreclosures followed. This was the situation of home mortgage financing in the United States in the early 1930's.

An amortized mortgage, which is the prevalent type today, is repaid in specified amounts, frequently on a monthly basis, during the term of the mortgage. The payment includes payment against both principal and interest. In this type of mortgage, because the payments are in equal amounts each month most of the early payments actually go to interest, where as near the end of the amortization period, most of the amount applies against the principal. This results, of course, from the fact that as the principal is reduced, the amount of interest paid necessarily is less.

For the amortized mortgage today the most common arrangement requires the mortgagor to make a cash down payment ranging from 5 to 30 percent, as well as payment of certain other costs incidental to "closing" the mortgage (to be discussed in more detail in Chapter 7). Amortization is usually spread over a period ranging from ten to thirty years (see discussion under different types of lending agencies and different kinds of financing later in this chapter). This planned repayment feature has made amortized mortgages considerably sounder than the earlier straight-term type.

The amortized mortgage has improved the mortgage picture from both the lenders' and borrowers' viewpoints, since the borrower is forced to budget his finances and is building up an equity and the lender probably has changed his operation from a short-term speculative risk to a longer-term investment.

First and Second Mortgages

A "first" mortgage, in another type of classification, is one that establishes for the lender a first claim against the owner's rights in the property. A "second," or junior, mortgage is one that gives a lender a claim against the owner which is subordinate to the rights of the holder of the first mortgage or to other paramount claims.[3]

The junior mortgage is usually involved where the cash payment that the home buyer is able to make is too small to fill the gap between the first mortgage and the price of the house. The seller sometimes accepts the second mortgage as part payment. In other instances, however, the homeowner may need cash to purchase appliances, landscape the yard, or for some other items. In such cases, a second mortgage is sometimes obtained from a household finance or loan agency for the purpose of consolidating the family's debts. During the 1920's, when the straight mortgage was predominant, there often were second and even third and fourth mortgages.

A total of 8 percent of the total number of mortgaged properties were covered by junior mortgages in 1960. This figure has remained stable over the last decade, but there has been some change in the nature of such mortgages. The termination in 1951 of the Veterans Administration's authority to guarantee second mortgages made jointly with FHA first mortgages reduced the proportion of mortgages of that type. In the meantime, homeowner properties with junior mortgages of the conventional type increased enough to offset that decline.

Open-End and Package Mortgages

To overcome the possible problem of changing the mortgage, some home buyers obtain an "open-end" type. This permits the mortgagor to finance his further necessities without rewriting the loan. It has the advantage of a relatively low interest rate, which mortgages carry as compared with general short-term financing, but the disadvantage of incurring almost an indefinite debt obligation.

The "package" mortgage is one that includes household equipment such as ranges, refrigerators, or air conditioning units. These must be included when the mortgage is arranged.

There are no data available to indicate the proportions of open-end or package mortgages, but it is believed their numbers are small, since neither kind has gained broad acceptance in the mortgage market. The package mortgage, of course, sometimes exists without being called by that name, since in some regions it has become a common practice to include certain equipment in the value of the house.

Usually a mortgage is originated when a property is acquired. However, sometimes it is assumed from a former owner of the property, in some instances with a new second mortgage. In other instances there is no property acquisition involved but a mortgage is refinanced, renewed, or extended after the property has been acquired. The mortgages that existed at the time

[3] American Institute of Banking, *Home Mortgage Lending*. New York: American Institute of Banking, 1938, p. 12.

of the 1960 Residential Finance Survey originated in the following proportions:

Status of Mortgage	*Percent*
Made when property acquired	68
Assumed when property acquired	12
Made after property acquired	20

There is some evidence that many mortgages that are made after the property is acquired are used for non-real estate expenses. Such expenses include college education, travel, and various consumer goods such as automobiles and appliances.

Over the period of the loan, the total cost of such mortgages (i.e., payments for interest) is generally far higher than that of a four- or five-year personal loan. However, the smaller monthly payments are usually so attractive to some borrowers that the other considerations are apparently cast aside.

SOURCES OF MORTGAGE CREDIT

The funds for the heavy volume of residential mortgages are provided by several kinds of "primary lenders." These include savings and loan associations, commercial banks, mutual savings banks, life insurance companies, individuals, the Federal Government, mortgage companies, nonprofit organizations, real estate and construction companies, and a few other groups.

The most important, from the standpoint of volume, are the first four listed. Each of these, and their practices, will be described below. It will be noted that there are considerable differences among them. This is a result of two factors: (a) the laws and regulations by which they are governed and (b) managerial policy of the institutions themselves.

Savings and Loan Associations

Savings and loan associations are direct descendants of the British building societies, and have been traditional lenders in the home mortgage field in the United States. They received their start in this country around the middle of the last century, when small groups of individuals pooled their savings for the purpose of accumulating sufficient amounts to make loans to members for the purchase of homes.

Today the investment policies of these associations still reflect their twofold original purpose—savings and mortgage lending—but there is now a greater separation between saver and borrower; they often represent different people.

The level of resources of savings and loan associations—93 billion dollars in 1962—can be seen in Table 5–1 (p. 176). It can also be seen from that table that 84 percent of those resources was in mortgages, a total of 79 billion dollars. On the liability side, 86 percent was in savings capital. Although associations which are members of the Federal Home Loan Bank System may borrow funds from the Federal Home Loan Bank Board, only 4 percent of their liabilities was in this category in 1962, indicating the extent to which they tend to rely almost exclusively on the savings of their depositors for their investment funds.

Strictly speaking, deposits are in the form of shares in the institution. Rather than receiving interest, shareholders are paid dividends. They may withdraw upon giving due notice (but many associations have been paying withdrawal requests upon demand as a matter of course in recent years).

There are variations in the state laws and regulations governing savings and loan associations, but in general they may make conventional loans which are more liberal in several respects than commercial and mutual savings banks. Recent legislation in New York State, the most liberal of any state, permits them to make such loans up to 90 percent of appraised value under certain conditions. The period of loan can be 30 years and mortgages may be in an amount up to $25,000. However, the property must be within 50 miles of the lending institution.

Commercial Banks

Commercial banks (and trust companies) offer many financial services. The most important are commercial and industrial loans, personal loans, checking accounts, savings accounts, and residential mortgage loans.

It can be seen from the data in Table 5–2 (p. 176) that in 1962, 55 percent of their vast aggregate resources—297 billion dollars, an amount appreciably higher than any of the other types of financial institutions being discussed—was in demand deposits and another 33 percent was in time deposits. On the asset side, only 12 percent was in real estate loans, but this still represented 34 billion dollars. (Their principal assets were other loans and securities.)

The legal investment privileges of commercial banks generally are more conservative than those of mutual savings banks and savings and loan associations (although state banks usually have more latitude than do national banks). Although lending policies vary, national banks may invest up to 70 percent of their time deposits or the amount of their capital, whichever is greater, in home mortgages, exclusive of their FHA and VA portfolios. These banks are limited to loaning 75 percent of the appraised value of single-family homes, in conventional loans, for a term up to twenty years. By tradition, the management of many banks has in practice followed more conservative policies than the maximums permitted by law. Most commercial banks are subject to state and Federal laws and regulations which restrict the territory in which they may make conventional loans, usually to an area near their home office.

Although commercial banks play an important role in home mortgages, they play an even more important role in short-term financing, including the financing of building operations through construction loans (discussed in more detail in Chapter 6).

Mutual Savings Banks

Mutual savings banks are found principally in the seventeen Eastern states, that is, in New England and New York and Pennsylvania. They apparently originated in these industrial states in response to a demand for a savings type of institution before networks of commercial banks and savings and loan associations became established, and they have continued to grow since then.

Mutual savings banks, like savings and loan associations, have a dual function—to serve as a depository for savings (as just mentioned) and to grant loans on homes. Like those associations, they are precluded from having checking accounts. Another similarity is that they are nonprofit organizations, and depositors receive dividends rather than interest. Their savings accounts, however, are on a demand basis, requiring a significant degree of liquidity of their assets. Their dividend rate is usually lower than that of savings and loan associations, but higher than the interest rate offered on savings by commercial banks.

The extent to which they can concentrate their mortgage lending in the housing field is limited by state laws. In New York State they may invest up to 65 percent of their assets in home mortgages, excluding their FHA and the guaranteed portion of their VA portfolios. It can be seen, from the data in Table 5–3 (p. 177), that in 1962 they had 70 percent (including FHA and VA mortgages) of their total assets in home loans. This amounted to 32 billion dollars, slightly less than the amount for commercial banks for the nation as a whole. It can also be seen that 90 percent of their liabilities were in deposits.

Terms for conventional mortgages granted by mutual savings banks in most states are generally conservative, although in some states they have been made more liberal in recent years. In New York State, for example, these institutions may loan up to 75 percent of appraised value on single-family properties (in some instances the percentage may be higher on new construction). In that state, they are now permitted to make loans up to 30 years. The area in which they can make loans is usually limited—sometimes as broadly, however, as their own state and contiguous states. They may, of course, purchase FHA and VA loans made by other primary lenders anywhere in the United States.

Life Insurance Companies

The principal characteristic that distinguishes life insurance companies from the other types of institutions discussed is the long-term nature of the funds they acquire. Their principal source of income is the insurance premiums that they collect, usually over the period of the working years of an individual. In most instances the funds are held for many years for the individual having life insurance policies. This is in contrast to the savings and deposits of the other types of lending institutions, many of which can be requested on demand, or at least after a comparatively short interval.

This characteristic has meant that life insurance companies prefer long-term investments for their capital, of which mortgages are one example. It can be seen from the data in Table 5–4 (p. 177) that their combined assets amounted to 133 billion dollars in 1962. Of this amount, 47 billion dollars, 35 percent, was invested in residential and commercial mortgages. In the assets of these companies such mortgages ranked second only to corporate bonds.

Life insurance companies are a most important source of funds for loans on apartment buildings and commercial properties. They are also an important source of funds for the secondary mortgage market (discussed later in this chapter). Where they make loans on single-family units, they are usually extremely selective, favoring quality loans on expensive homes—generally new residences in certain locations in a community. Although a few life insurance companies maintain representatives in different cities, most of them rely on bankers, called "correspondents," to arrange the loans. In some instances, real estate men represent particular companies.

Other Types of Primary Lenders

There are a number of other sources of mortgage funds. One of the most important of these is individuals or individuals' estates. These are not organized or regulated by specific laws in most instances, but some funds from this type of source can be found in many communities.

Another source of mortgage funds is mortgage companies, although in most instances these companies do not invest their own funds but, probably using their own name, invest the funds of others. They "originate" the mortgage, find the ultimate investor, and frequently "service" the loan (i.e., collect monthly payments from the home buyer). While there are some large companies of this type in the nation, usually they are small and operate on little capital. Their income is derived principally from the fees they receive for placing the mortgage and from what they receive for servicing it. In this sense, a more apt term is "mortgage broker." This arrangement has the advantage of balancing out, to a limited degree, mortgage funds in different parts of the country. It permits the flow of funds from areas such as New York to areas of frequent scarcity such as the South and the West.

The last important source of mortgage funds to be mentioned is the Federal Government. The Federal National Mortgage Association is active in the secondary mortgage market. The Federal Housing Administration and the Veterans Administration are holders of some mortgages, but these are limited (with the exception of VA direct lending) to those on which there has been a default and which have been returned to the insuring or guaranteeing agency. Some states have lending agencies, but their volume of mortgages is comparatively small.

Comparative Volume Mortgage Debt Outstanding on One- to Four-Family Homes

The dollar amount of mortgages held by the principal types of lending institutions has been indicated. Loans for types of properties other than one- to four-family homes were included in those figures. It is interesting,

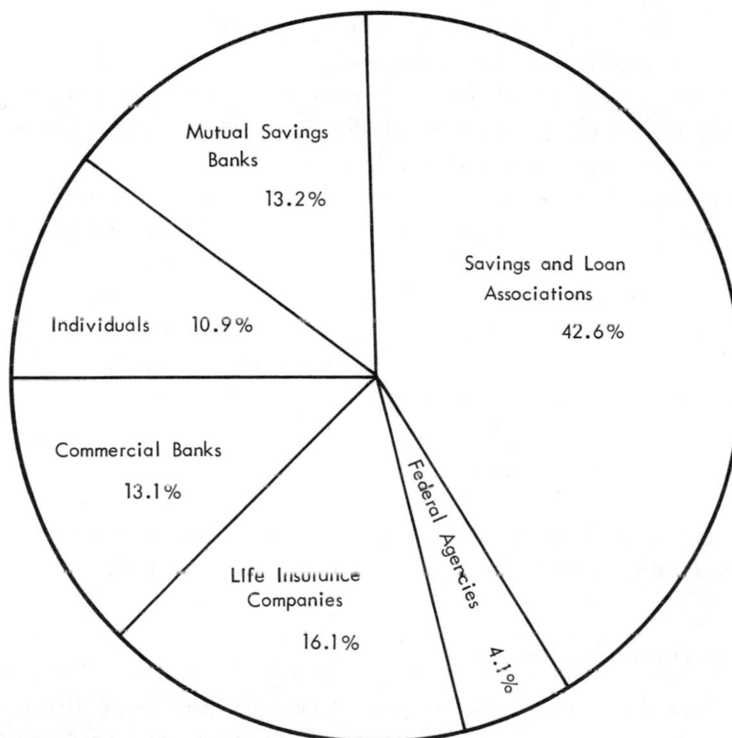

FIGURE 7. *Distribution of estimated mortgage debt outstanding on nonfarm 1- to 4-family homes, 1962. (Source of data: Derived from* Housing Statistics—Annual Data. *Washington, D.C.: Housing and Home Finance Agency, May 1963, p. 37.)*

therefore, to look at more refined figures to see the significance of mortgages on only *homeowner* properties.

It can be seen, from the data in Table 5–5 (p. 178), that savings and loan associations carried 43 percent of the mortgage debt outstanding on such homes in 1962. (Outstanding debt is the unpaid principal balance of the mortgage.) It can also be seen, from the data in the table, that the proportion of the total outstanding mortgage debt held by these associations has been increasing constantly since 1950; in that year it represented only 29 percent of the total.

This increase has been largely at the expense of commercial banks and individuals. In 1962, commercial banks held 13 percent of the mortgage debt on homeowner properties, as compared with 21 percent in 1950; individuals held 11 percent, as compared with 19 percent in 1950.

Over the same period the volume held by mutual savings banks has increased from 10 to 13 percent of the total, and for life insurance companies it has decreased from 19 to 16 percent.

There are several reasons for these trends. Perhaps the most important relates to the increased savings of individuals, most of which are attracted to savings and loan associations because of their aggressive advertising, service competition, and favorable competitive position with regard to dividends paid. Since the deposits of these institutions are invested almost exclusively in real estate and construction loans, their volume and amounts invested in mortgages should continue to increase.

The previous discussion has related to mortgages outstanding. There is additional evidence of the primacy of the position of savings and loan associations in the number and amount of mortgages made in 1962. Their activities constituted nearly two fifths of all nonfarm mortgage recordings of homes valued at $20,000 or less, and 44 percent of the dollar amount of those mortgages. No other type of institution came within 50 percent of those figures, as can be seen from the data in Table 5–6 (p. 178).

TYPES OF FINANCING

Three types of financing are generally available to the various kinds of mortgage lending institutions: conventional, FHA, and VA.

Conventional Financing

Conventional financing is the traditional type. It involves no direct government support of the loans made. This type of financing was used exclusively in this country until the early 1930's, when Depression conditions required government intervention in order to (a) rescue some homeowners against the loss of their properties and (b) increase the level of housing construction.

As was indicated earlier under the discussion of the sources of mortgage credit, the terms and conditions under which conventional loans are made vary among the various types of institutions, and even among states.

Although the history and present operations of the government programs are described in Chapter 14, it is desirable to introduce certain aspects of the Federal Housing Administration and the Veterans Administration programs here, because of their significance in the mortgage market.

Federal Housing Administration

The Federal Housing Administration, probably the best known of the housing agencies, undertakes to insure mortgages to guard against loss on the part of the lending institutions in the event of default by the borrower. This agency was primarily responsible for developing the long-term amortized mortgage at low interest rates in the 1930's. The terms of these loans are regulated, but have been varied over the years in response to economic conditions.

The Housing Act of 1961 authorized the FHA to insure mortgages on single-family homes in amounts up to $25,000. The Act also authorized minimum down payments on such homes of 3 percent of $15,000 value, plus 10 percent of the next $5,000, plus 25 percent of value above $20,000. It also approved terms up to 35 years for proposed construction and up to 30 years for existing homes (with some exceptions, in which longer terms are allowed). More recent housing acts, such as the Act of 1964, have further liberalized some of these terms.

What these terms would mean to a home buyer can be illustrated by the following example: the monthly payment to interest, principal, and mortgage insurance premium on a $25,000, 35-year loan at 5¼ percent interest, which could be used to finance a property valued at $30,000, would be approximately $140.[4]

Veterans Administration

The Veterans Administration, as one phase of its over-all veterans' program, has undertaken a program similar to that of the FHA, except that borrowers under this program must be veterans. The terms and requirements of its loans are very much like those of the FHA. The difference between the two agencies represents primarily the differences in the method of supporting the mortgages: the FHA serves more in the capacity of an insurance agency, promising to redeem the mortgages (by paying government-guaranteed debentures) in the event of foreclosure; the VA "guarantees" to reimburse the lending institution on a certain proportion of the mortgage amount in the event of foreclosure. The FHA program began in 1934, and the Veterans Administration program began ten years later

[4] Every three months the FHA provides a description of the characteristics of the single-family houses on which it has insured the mortgages. This description is available on both a state and metropolitan area or county basis. Data for proposed and for existing homes are kept separate.

Concerning the purchase transaction, data are provided on such items as sales price, mortgage amount, term of mortgage, loan-to-value ratio, and total acquisition cost. Data are also provided on the average amounts of real estate taxes, mortgage payments, and heating and utilities costs. In addition, data are included for certain characteristics of the buyer family, such as the age and income level of the head. (See Federal Housing Administration, "FHA Data for States" and "FHA Data for Selected Housing Areas," *Characteristics of Home Mortgage Transactions Insured by FHA under Section 203*, issued quarterly.)

under the Servicemen's Readjustment Act, better known as the "GI Bill of Rights."

The Veterans Administration guarantees up to 60 percent of the amount of a loan made to an eligible veteran for the purchase, construction, alteration, repair, or improvement of a home or farm dwelling, but the guaranteed portion of the loan cannot exceed $7,500. Since January 1956, loans could be made for a maximum term of 30 years. Since April 1958, no down payment has been required, but the closing costs of loans could not be included in the amount of the loan. Veterans are required to pay these costs in cash unless they are absorbed by the builder or seller.[5]

Distribution of Activity among Different Types

There has been considerable variation in the distribution of the number of mortgages among the three types of financing over the years, conventional mortgages being predominant for most years with the exception of the World War II period. During those years new housing was limited to that needed for war workers, and was "programed" by the Federal Government for each community. Most of the units were built by project builders who could get them up rapidly. Those builders tended to rely on FHA-insured mortgages rather than the conventional type. As a result, in 1943, 80 percent of the total number of home mortgages recorded in the nation were FHA insured.

The VA program also cut into what may have been part of the conventional market, especially since savings and loan associations, which have never looked with favor on the FHA program (probably because that program may have been considered unwarranted competition from the government in their business), did participate in the VA program.

In recent years the proportion of conventional mortgages has been rising again—quite dramatically between 1955 and 1959 and more slowly since that time—and about three fourths of all new mortgages are now of that type. In the meantime, the FHA proportion has been declining slightly and the VA proportion seems to have leveled off at about one mortgage out of every sixteen new ones. The percentage distribution since 1940 is shown in Figure 8 and Table 5–7 (p. 179).

The dollar volume of mortgage recordings better reflects the mortgage picture during any particular year than the number of mortgages on new housing units built, since it also includes mortgages on existing homes. In normal years the percentage distributions may be similar, since the proportion of existing houses to new houses purchased tends to be about two to one. At other times, as during World War II, for example, there is

[5] The Veterans Administration publishes monthly information, on a national basis, for the following items: purchase price distribution of proposed and existing homes, average size of loans, and maturity and down payment characteristics. It also provides summaries of the volume of VA activity, the number of defaults and claims, and a distribution of loans by type of lender. See Veterans Administration, "Loan Guaranty Highlights," issued monthly.

considerable variation between total mortgage recordings and recordings for new housing alone. This can be seen for the year 1943. During that year, when only 20 percent of the new housing was financed with conventional loans, such loans made up 80 percent of the dollar amount of nonfarm residential mortgage recordings. The difference was due, of course, to the fact that a higher proportion of the population had to purchase existing, rather than new, homes during that year, because not enough new homes could be built under wartime restrictions. The percentage distribu-

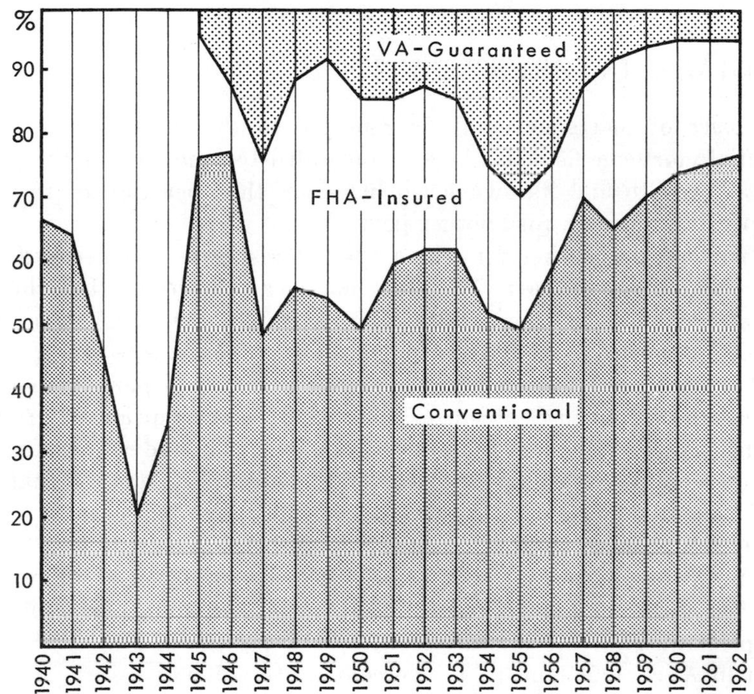

FIGURE 8. *Distribution of nonfarm housing units started, by type of financing, 1940 to 1962. (Period 1959 to 1962 based on new series data. Source of data: 1945 to 1962 derived from* Housing Statistics—Annual Data. *Washington, D.C.: Housing and Home Finance Agency, May 1963, p. 12. 1940 to 1944 data from earlier reports.)*

tion of the amount of nonfarm mortgage recordings of $20,000 or less, by type of financing, for the years 1940 to 1962 is shown in Table 5–8 (p. 180).

As a result of increased activity in conventional loans in recent years, these loans have been representing a constantly increasing proportion of the total outstanding mortgage debt on homeowner properties. The proportion has increased from 56 percent in 1955 to 63 percent in 1962. This increase has been entirely at the cost of outstanding debt in VA mortgages, since there also has been an increase, though smaller, in FHA mortgages (Table 5–9, p. 180).

A final difference that should be mentioned between government-supported mortgages, on the one hand, and conventional mortgages, on the other, is the difference in the proportion of loans made *after* the property is acquired. Almost all FHA and VA mortgages are either made or assumed *when* the property is acquired, but nearly a third of the conventional mortgages are made afterwards. The data in Table 5–10 (p. 181) give an indication of the greater flexibility of conventional as compared with government-supported loans from the standpoint of refinancing, renewing, or extending such mortgages.

MORTGAGE INTEREST RATES

The *price* of mortgage credit is reflected in the interest rate. In the residential mortgage field this rate is controlled for one part of the market, but is allowed to find its own level, based on the operation of the forces of supply and demand, for another part.

The part of the market for which the interest rate is controlled is the government-supported part. This does not mean, however, that there are never any changes in these rates. For example, the FHA rate moved consistently upward from 1951 until early 1961. From a rate of 4¼ percent in 1951 it moved to 5 percent near the end of 1956, to 5¼ percent in August 1957, to 5¾ percent in September 1959. Then, in recognition of gradually declining yields in the money market throughout 1960, the rate was reduced to 5½ percent in February 1961 and 5¼ percent in May of that year. On FHA-insured mortgages, ½ percent insurance premium is always added, bringing the actual costs that much higher to borrowers.

The VA rate also has moved upward since the inception of its program. At the beginning of the program, in 1944, the maximum permissible rate was 4 percent. This rate was increased to 4½ percent in May 1953, to 4¾ percent in April 1958, and to 5¼ percent in July 1959.

During the early 1950's, and before, when there was a considerable supply of mortgage money available, conventional interest rates tended to remain not too far above the FHA and VA rates. From early 1954 until early 1956, the national average was fractionally below 5¼ percent. Thereafter, the rate moved upward until the end of 1957, when it reached 6 percent. With the decline in the business cycle in 1957–1958, it dropped to about 5½ percent, and then moved upward again, to 6¼ percent by early 1960. With another decline in the business cycle in 1960–1961, it declined to 6 percent by mid-1961.

The comparatively high conventional interest rates in recent years reflect many factors. There has been a greater competition for funds, resulting in part from continued general prosperity. At the same time, construction volume has remained at a high level, and property values have continued to rise, requiring higher mortgages per dwelling unit.

Forces such as these are constantly at work, and cause the constant change in interest rates if the necessary supply of mortgage funds is to become available for the residential mortgage market.[6]

MORTGAGE PRACTICES OF DIFFERENT KINDS OF INSTITUTIONS

The mortgage practices of the different kinds of lending institutions can be portrayed most accurately by looking at some of the key characteristics of mortgages they have granted, some of the characteristics of the property on which the loans were made, and some of the owner characteristics. Such information was made available by the 1960 Residential Finance Survey undertaken by the U. S. Bureau of the Census.

Before observing the particular characteristics, it is important to know the extent to which each kind of institution participates in the two government programs, as against the extent to which they concentrate on conventional mortgages.

Savings and loan associations have always favored conventional loans. In 1960, 83 percent of their holdings were of this type. Most of the remainder of their portfolio was in VA-guaranteed loans. (As indicated earlier, they have never participated heavily in the FHA program.) Commercial banks also favor conventional loans, but to a smaller degree. In 1960, 52 percent of their holdings were of this type. These banks, however, have participated in both the FHA and VA programs from the outset of those programs. Mutual savings banks show the most even distribution among the three types of lending. Throughout the history of the VA program, they have participated in it more heavily than have the other types of institutions. They were slow in participating in the FHA program, but today most mutual savings banks carry some loans of this type in their portfolio. The distribution for each primary lender and for each type of financing is shown in Table 5–11 (p. 181).

The conventional loans made by savings and loan associations are usually on a more liberal basis than conventional loans made by other kinds of institutions. For example, the median ratio of purchase price to income was 2.2, a figure higher than for any other type of institution.

On the other hand, savings and loan association loans had a median term somewhat shorter than those of mutual savings banks, and they charged a higher median interest rate.

There is considerable variation in other characteristics relating to conventional loans, insofar as the different kinds of lending institutions are concerned. For example, the median value of all properties on which mortgages were held in 1960 ranged from $9,600 for those on which loans had been made by individuals to $22,200 for those which had been mortgaged by life insurance companies. The median figure for those mortgaged

[6] Interest rates on conventional first-mortgage loans are published each month for the United States and selected metropolitan areas. See Federal Home Loan Bank Board, ''Home Mortgage Interest Rates and Terms.''

by savings and loan associations was about midway between those two points; for commercial banks it was slightly below the mid-point; and for mutual savings banks, slightly above it (Table 5–12, p. 182).

Savings and loan associations, among the various institutional types, were the most liberal in regard to the mortgage amount as a percent of purchase price (66 percent) for their total holdings in 1960. Mutual savings banks and life insurance companies were not far behind, but commercial banks showed their conservative bent, the median percent being only 58.

Life insurance companies and mutual savings banks were most liberal from the standpoint of term of conventional loans—the medians being 20 and 19 years, respectively. The median term for such loans granted by savings and loan associations was 16 years, and among those granted by commercial banks, only 9 years.

Savings and loan associations and commercial banks charged appreciably higher interest rates on their loans than did mutual savings banks and life insurance companies. The difference was approximately 1 percent, the median rate being 6 percent for the first two types of lending institutions and 5 percent for mutual savings banks and life insurance companies.

Apparently the higher interest rate charged by savings and loan associations has not been detrimental to increasing their business, as has been shown by the volume of mortgages they make annually. An explanatory factor may be the kinds of owners to whom a high proportion of their loans are made. These owners apparently are in a somewhat lower income class than owners obtaining mortgages from mutual savings banks and life insurance companies (but not commercial banks) and, therefore, perhaps slightly greater risks. (The median income of owners borrowing from savings and loan associations was only $6,600 in 1960, compared with a median of $7,400 for those borrowing from mutual savings banks and $9,700 for those borrowing from life insurance companies.) Another factor which may make the higher interest rates acceptable is the high median ratio of purchase price to income, which was 2.2 in 1960 (as already indicated). However, this ratio was only slightly lower (2.1) for mutual savings banks, which charged 1 percent less interest.

The mortgages made by individuals are generally made to comparatively low-income purchasers for low-valued properties. In 1960, the median income of these purchasers was only $5,400, the median value of property $9,600, and the median first mortgage $5,700. That mortgage amount represented 85 percent of the median purchase price, an extremely high allowance for conventional mortgages. That higher-than-average risk, which is apparently necessary in order to sell properties to families having incomes at that level, however, is offset by short term of loan (median only 12 years) and high interest rate (6 percent in 1960).

Let us look now briefly at the characteristics of government-supported loans. The first general observation that can be made is that the average purchase prices of houses carrying FHA-insured and VA-guaranteed loans are $2,000 to $3,000 lower than the purchase prices of houses carrying conventional loans (except in the instance of loans made by life insurance companies, where they are over $8,000 lower, and commercial banks, where they are actually slightly higher). On the other hand, the median mortgage amounts are higher, the median terms of loan are longer, and the median interest rates are lower for government-supported loans than for conventional loans. This is due, of course, to the traditionally more liberal terms allowed by the laws and regulations governing these loans.

It can be seen, from the data in Tables 5–13 and 5–14 (pp. 183–184), that the mortgage amount as a percent of purchase price is consistently higher for VA-guaranteed than for FHA-insured loans, for each type of lending institution. About the only other significant difference is in the median age of owners; owners holding VA-guaranteed mortgages are younger, on the average, than owners holding FHA-insured loans.

FORECLOSURES

The economic soundness of the mortgage system that has been in operation in the United States during the last three decades seems to have been proved. After the crisis period of the early 1930's (although foreclosures had actually begun to increase as early as 1926), the long-term amortized mortgage was put into general use in 1934. Other mortgage practices, sounder than those of the earlier years, also were put into practice.

As a result of these new practices, and undoubtedly in part as a result of the continued period of prosperity, the proportion of mortgage delinquencies and defaults had been low. For example, of approximately 21 million mortgaged nonfarm one- to four-family dwelling units mortgaged in 1962, there were only 86,440 foreclosures, a rate of 4.12 per thousand. (In 1933, when the nation had significantly fewer mortgaged homes, 252,400 were foreclosed.) Among the foreclosures that have occurred, the rate is highest among FHA-insured mortgages. Among the 3,477,000 mortgages of this type in existence in 1961, there were 32,248 foreclosures, a rate of 9.27 per thousand. It also was higher among VA-guaranteed mortgages than among conventional mortgages. Of the 3,715,000 VA-guaranteed mortgages in existence in 1961, there were 21,861 foreclosures, a rate of 5.88 per thousand.

Among the defaults and foreclosures that have occurred, the primary causes have been curtailment of income, principally as a result of job layoffs, cuts in work week or wages, and business loss or failure. Death or illness in the family has been the next most important reason, followed by marital difficulties. There also is considerable evidence that many owners had overextended themselves financially. A 1963 government study indicated that the majority of foreclosure cases with FHA or VA loans had involved either no down payments or down payments of no more than 5 percent. It also was found that high expense-to-income ratios for housing, at the time the mortgage loans were originated, characterized an appreciable number of the foreclosures. Also, a significant proportion of the foreclosed owners at the time of foreclosure were transferees, that is, they had purchased the home from the original borrower and assumed the latter's mortgage. Frequently there was a junior mortgage involved.[7]

Although foreclosure rates are still below a critical level, some concern has been expressed because of the increase in their number and rate in recent years.

REGIONAL AND LOCAL MORTGAGE MARKETS

There is considerable variation in the proportion of mortgage lending activity by the different types of lending institutions across the nation, despite what might be considered the leveling-out influences that could be expected to result from the various government programs. This variation results from a combination of historical and traditional factors, some of which have been mentioned, and of variations in demand.

Data from the 1960 Residential Finance Survey indicate that savings and loan associations were carrying the highest proportion of outstanding mortgage debt on one-unit homeowner properties in the North Central and Western regions. In the North Central states they held 41 percent of the total; in the West, 28 percent. (The most nearly equal distribution among the various types of lending institutions was found in the rapidly growing West, where life insurance companies, commercial banks, and individuals all carried a significant proportion of the total debt.)

Savings and loan associations, because they are so numerous in all parts of the nation, also carry a significant proportion of the outstanding debt in the other regions. In the Northeast, their 32 percent was exceeded only by the 38 percent for mutual savings banks; and in the South, their 31 percent was exceeded only by 34 percent for life insurance companies (Table 5–15, p. 185).

There are even greater differences among metropolitan areas. For example, in 1960 savings and loan associations carried over half of the outstanding mortgage debt on one-unit homeowner properties in Baltimore and Chicago; nearly half in Cleveland and St. Louis; but less than a fifth in San Francisco, Buffalo, and Detroit. Commercial banks held over a fourth of the debt in San Francisco and Cleveland, but only 2 percent in Atlanta and Dallas. Mutual savings banks held over half of the debt in Boston and Buffalo, but almost none in Chicago and St. Louis. Life insurance companies held nearly half in Dallas and 38 percent in Atlanta, but less than 2 percent in Boston (Table 5–16, p. 186).

Prosperous communities usually have heavier savings and are attractive to mortgage money from the outside. Depressed communities—those having depressed industries and decreasing population—usually have lower savings and are frequently shunned by lenders, especially those outside the areas.

[7] From news release of the Housing and Home Finance Agency, Washington, D.C., July 19, 1963.

Some special aids have been provided under government programs to assist in the latter type of communities.

DIFFERENCES BETWEEN NEW AND EXISTING HOMES

It has already been mentioned that in a normal year sales of existing homes usually outnumber sales of new homes in approximately a two-to-one ratio. This factor becomes especially important in any study of the mortgage market, because the policies of lending institutions, both those regulated by law and those established voluntarily by management, frequently differ with respect to these two types of housing.

Some differences between new and existing housing can be observed in certain mortgage data provided by the Federal Home Loan Bank Board. One difference is in the median purchase price of dwellings. The median in 1963 was $22,500 for new homes and $17,300 for homes previously occupied. Another difference is in the term of loan. For new houses the median term was 24 years; for existing homes, only 19 years. Interestingly, there seems to be no great difference in the liberalness of the amount of loan. For new houses the median mortgage-to-percent-of-purchase price was 73; for existing homes it was 71 (Table 5–17, p. 187).

SECONDARY MORTGAGE MARKET

Where does the money come from for the mortgage loans that are made each year? It has been mentioned that in 1962 the total outstanding residential nonfarm mortgage debt exceeded 168 billion dollars. It must be obvious that banks and other primary lenders do not carry this entire burden.

Mortgage lenders, in fact, frequently expect to dispose of the mortgages they originate. They often have no desire to retain them as a long-term investment. Also, since the amount they can hold in their mortgage portfolio is limited by law, they must frequently dispose of some in order to obtain liquid funds to assist in the financing of additional new housing. Sometimes, also, they dispose of them in order to obtain liquid funds needed for other purposes. They may be able to obtain higher interest rates on bonds or other investments. Therefore, they sell them in the secondary mortgage market.

How the Secondary Market Operates

In disposing of their mortgages, the primary lending institutions receive varying amounts, despite the fact that a particular mortgage is for a stipulated principal amount, with a stipulated term of years and a stipulated interest rate. The price received depends upon the level of the money market at the time and the "quality" of the mortgage (i.e., the level of risk involved concerning such matters as the type of homeowner and the nature and location of the property). This last-mentioned factor obviously is difficult to determine, especially by a remote buyer, and this is one reason why many secondary mortgage firms rely on FHA and VA loans for purchase, since such loans have government insurance or guarantee. Other mortgage firms may shy away from such loans if they can get higher interest rates on conventional loans.

Discounting works as follows: Suppose a bank has a $10,000 FHA mortgage carrying an interest rate of 5¼ percent. A life insurance company or some other financial institution is willing to put up the money on the property involved, but wants to earn more than 5¼ percent. It may offer the lender $9,700 for the mortgage. That would represent a discount of 3 percent of the face value of the mortgage or, in the terminology of lenders, three points. (The price for such mortgages is quoted like the price for bonds, that is, 100 representing par, meaning the actual outstanding balance, and 97.0 or some other figure meaning that proportion of par.) Since the life insurance company invests only $9,700 but is repaid the full $10,000—plus 5¼ percent interest on $10,000—its actual return on the money invested is higher than 5¼ percent. (Of course, such transactions usually involve more than a single property.)

Builders sometimes also become involved in the secondary mortgage market, but usually only where large subdivisions are built and the builder arranges the mortgage financing for several houses at one time. In disposing of these mortgages they frequently—like primary lending institutions—must sell them at a discount.

Discounting is justified economically on different bases by lending institutions selling mortgages and by builders arranging for their sale. Lenders, on arranging the mortgage in the first place, gain a fee (frequently from 1 to 3 percent of the value of the mortgage) for making the arrangements and, quite commonly, they receive an annual fee of approximately one half of 1 percent on the declining balance for continued servicing of the mortgage, such as making collections, if they sell it to another financier. Builders, on the other hand, can either absorb the discount or pass along all or part of it to the home buyer in the price of the house. (Discounts seldom appear when the home buyer arranges the loan directly with a lending institution—at least until the lender desires to dispose of the mortgage, and then the buyer can no longer be charged with the discounting cost. When home buyers approach a lending institution, the institution will simply refuse to make the loan if it is dissatisfied with the fixed rate of return on it.)

The mortgages purchased in this manner may be for either "immediate" or "future" delivery. Immediate delivery usually means that the lender requires delivery within ninety days. Future delivery indicates a promise to buy a mortgage in the future, generally in three months to a year. Since there is more risk in predicting the future market than knowing the level of the market at the time, future prices are usually discounted more than immediate prices.

Secondary market prices vary from community to community. Prices are likely to be higher in areas where there is a large volume of funds for which an outlet must be found—such as New York City—and lower in areas where there is a shortage of funds.

An example indicating the variation in prices for FHA mortgages having a particular set of terms, for two dates early in 1963, is shown in Table 5–18 (p. 188). It can be seen from the data in that table what variation in prices existed, not only between different FHA zones, but also over a short span of thirty days.

Sources of Funds

The term "secondary market" therefore has come to be used to represent "a congeries of possible buyers who purchase mortgages from the 'primary-market' lenders."[8] According to Wendt and Rathbun, "This critically important link in the home financing process is not a well-organized market in which offers to buy and sell are made known to many participants. Instead, it is a highly segmented market in which there exists no agency to correlate the efforts and activities of the many buyers and sellers."[9]

Federal National Mortgage Association

The Federal Government plays a most active part in the secondary mortgage market through the Federal National Mortgage Association (better known as "Fanny Mae"). This agency has four primary functions:

1. to provide liquidity for FHA-insured and VA-guaranteed mortagages, thus permitting lending institutions to assist in the financing of additional homes by purchasers under the FHA and VA programs;

2. to promote the availability of mortgage financing in those areas around the nation where mortgage investment funds are in short supply, by purchasing eligible mortgages in those areas;

3. to encourage revolving of the FNMA investment authorization, by requiring that the mortgages it purchases meet high credit and other standards, and by aggressive efforts in finding other sources for these mortgages, such as insurance companies, savings banks, savings and loan associations, and trust and pension funds; and

4. by establishing lender confidence in new types of mortgages, such as the GI home loans and special types insured by FHA from time to time.[10]

[8] George B. Hurff, *Residential Mortgage Financing, Jacksonville, Florida, First Six Months of 1950*, Housing Research Paper 23, Housing and Home Finance Agency, Washington, D.C.: U.S. Government Printing Office, December 1952, p. 61.

[9] Paul F. Wendt and Daniel B. Rathbun, *The San Francisco Bay Area Residential Mortgage Market*, Housing Research Paper No. 20, Housing and Home Finance Agency, Washington, D.C.: U.S. Government Printing Office, May 1952, p. 20.

[10] "Background and History of the Federal National Mortgage Association," Washington, D.C.: Federal National Mortgage Association, April 30, 1955 (mimeo.).

The financial transactions of FNMA since its inception in 1938 through 1962 may be summarized as follows: it purchased about 1,180,500 mortgages totaling 12.2 billion dollars. It sold approximately 430,000 mortgages, aggregating 3.5 billion dollars, and liquidated by repayments approximately 123,500 mortgages, totaling 2.0 billion dollars. It had other credits of 51,000 mortgages, totaling 12 million dollars. Thus, its portfolio at the end of 1962 consisted of about 576,000 mortgages having principal balances of approximately 6.1 billion dollars.

FNMA has paid all operating expenses out of earnings, has met its dividend and interest obligations, has had a substantial net income and, since November 1954, has paid a share of its earnings from secondary market operations to the U.S. Treasury as an income tax equivalent, as required by the Housing Act of 1954.

Private Long-Term Investors

It has already been mentioned that life insurance companies are an important source of funds for the secondary mortgage market. Data showing the proportion of their assets held in mortgages was shown in Table 5–4, (p. 177) but it is not known what proportion represented operations in the secondary mortgage market. That proportion is believed to be large.

Certain large savings and commercial banks (generally located in the East), trust companies, and various corporate institutions also participate in this market. Savings and loan associations are not usually active in this market—or, at least, their participation is highly limited.

Corporate Pension Funds

Assets of pension funds of U. S. corporations amounted to 36 million dollars at the end of 1962. These assets have been growing at a rate of about 3.5 million dollars each year in recent years. Only $1,140,000, 3 percent of the total, was invested in mortgages. There has been a steady (though slight) increase in the proportion invested in such assets in recent years (Table 5–19, p. 188).

It has been suggested by many individuals that these funds represent still another substantial potential source of funds for the secondary mortgage market. However, there appears to be little likelihood of any great participation in the mortgage market by this group. There are several important considerations which differentiate the pension fund from other investors. In the first place, holders of these funds prefer extremely long-term investment opportunities, and the security feature generally provided by home mortgages does not appear to represent sufficient appeal. Corporate bonds of good quality and even common stock have had more appeal. The justification for this attitude is that the pension fund—whose investors are not disturbed by market fluctuations and do not have demand liabilities—can find equity investments with favorable return over the long period.

By the same token, the liquidity feature of mortgages, which is attractive to many investors, is not significant to the pension fund. The typical fund is growing rapidly and has no need for liquidity and even less need for the amortization feature, since this only aggravates the problem of the investing officer.

Finally, contributing to the reluctance of many corporations to enter this field is the distaste for having any part in possible foreclosure actions, even though the corporation may be several steps removed from the actual events.

In summary, there is a basic difference between the primary and secondary mortgage markets. The primary market is generally interested in shorter-term turnover (since it operates with limited funds) and a quick profit; the secondary market is more interested in long-term investments. The duality of the system has a number of advantages, for the parties involved and for the general public. It enables the primary market to do a greater volume of business with a resultant increase in profits, since many of the investors would not (or could not) undertake to make loans if they had no ready market, particularly in the case of lenders who are required to keep their assets liquid. In many instances, the lenders in the primary market operate almost as regular agents for the secondary market investors, going so far as actually to service the mortgages. Conversely, the system saves the institutions in the secondary group the expense and trouble of maintaining widespread local offices to negotiate and service all the loans.

The secondary mortgage market, then, is another of the important aspects of housing finance, since it indirectly determines how many families can obtain mortgages in any particular period.

FINANCING RENTAL PROPERTIES

Any type of property may be made available for rental. Although we frequently think of rental properties as being apartments in large multi-family structures, there are many exceptions. In fact, approximately one third of all dwelling units rented are in single-family houses and another one fourth are in two- to four-family structures. This means that less than half (approximately 40 percent) are in structures containing five or more dwelling units. Only about one out of every ten dwelling units are in structures containing fifty or more apartments. Although the detailed numbers concerning individual living units are not available, the above figures can be confirmed through computing the number of units per structure by the number of structures of different sizes, which are shown in Table 5–20 (p. 189.)[11]

[11] The 1960 Residential Finance Survey of the U. S. Bureau of the Census divided properties into two categories—''homeowner'' properties (discussed earlier in this chapter) and all others (discussed in this section). The ''all others'' are called ''rental and vacant'' properties, applying to properties with five dwelling units or more (even

Of the 7.7 million privately owned nonfarm rental properties in the United States in 1960, one third were mortgaged. The total mortgage debt amounted to 27.2 billion dollars. (This figure may be compared with 117.5 billion dollars in mortgage debt outstanding for the 27.9 million owner-occupied, one- to four-dwelling unit properties in the nation in the same year.) Approximately 8 percent of the properties were encumbered with junior as well as first mortgages.

Four out of every five mortgages on rental properties (compared with three out of every five among homeowner properties) were financed conventionally in 1960. Interestingly, Federal insurance or guarantees were limited to properties with either few or many dwelling units—medium-sized properties (structures containing from 5 to 50 units)—were financed almost entirely with conventional mortgages (Table 5–21, p. 190).

The first-mortgage debt outstanding on rental properties is more evenly distributed among the leading types of financial institutions than is the debt on homeowner properties. Savings and loan associations accounted for 26 percent in 1960, compared with a 34 percent share of the outstanding debt on homeowner properties; life insurance companies accounted for 21 percent, the same proportion as for homeowner properties; and mutual savings banks accounted for 19 percent, compared with 14 percent for homeowner properties. Savings and loan associations, however, tended to be the principal holders of mortgages on one- to four-unit properties, whereas mutual savings banks and life insurance companies concentrated on the larger rental properties (Table 5–22, p. 190).

Only half of the mortgages in existence in 1960 had been made when the rental property was acquired by the present owner. Some mortgages were taken over when the property was acquired, but nearly a third of them had been made after the property was acquired. This proportion is appreciably higher than the 20 percent made on homeowner properties after those properties had been acquired (Table 5–23, p. 191). This high proportion probably is the result of the generally shorter terms and presumably greater need for renewal or refinancing on the part of conventional loans on such properties.

The median term, in fact, was only 12 years on conventionally financed first mortgages, as compared with 24 years for FHA-insured and 25 years for VA-guaranteed first mortgages. The shorter terms for conventional mortgages result in part from legal restrictions and in part from conservative management policy on the part of many institutions.

Interest rates for conventional first mortgages tend to be lower on large properties—rates of less than 5 percent are indicated for about half of the properties with 50 units or more, in contrast to one twentieth of the one- to four-unit properties. Two thirds of the small properties had rates

---

though one of the units may be occupied by the owner), and to properties with one to four dwellings units, all of which are either renter-occupied or vacant. See U. S. Bureau of the Census, *Census of Housing 1960*. Vol. V, Residential Finance. Part 2, Rental and Vacant Properties.

of 6 percent or more, compared with one eighth of those with 50 units or more (Table 5–24, p. 192).

Furthermore, interest and principal payments tend to absorb larger shares of the rental receipts in the small mortgaged properties than in the larger properties. The median ratio of these payments (for both first and junior mortgages) to rental receipts was 75 percent for the small properties, 47 percent for 5- to 49-unit properties, and 32 percent for properties with 50 units or more in 1960 (Table 5–25, p. 192).

Newer properties, of course, are more likely to be mortgaged than older properties. In 1960, for example, 35 percent of the mortgaged properties were less than 10 years old, compared with only 14 percent of the nonmortgaged properties. On the other hand, only 47 percent of the mortgaged properties were 20 years old or older, compared with 72 percent of the nonmortgaged properties. Three fourths of the large properties not carrying a mortgage had been built before 1930 (Table 5–26, p. 193).

Because mortgaged properties tend to be newer than nonmortgaged ones, it stands to reason that mortgaged properties would have a higher per-dwelling-unit value. This is clearly confirmed by Census data. For example, the median value per dwelling unit for mortgaged rental properties in 1960 was $8,200, compared with $5,100 for nonmortgaged properties. It might also be assumed that the larger the structure, the lower the value-per-dwelling unit. However, this is confirmed to only a limited extent by estimated 1960 values of such properties. For example, the median value declined from $8,700 on mortgaged properties with one- to four-dwelling units to $5,000 on properties with five to forty-nine dwelling units. It then increased, however, to $6,300 on properties with fifty dwelling units or more (Table 5–27, p. 194). It is not known whether the medium-sized properties contain less space or whether certain building economies over the smaller and larger properties cause these differences. In any event, it can be seen that rental units have a lower value, in general, than homeowner units. (See discussion of the value of homeowner units earlier in this chapter.)

Finally, with regard to rental properties it is important to determine who owns the properties. The majority, whether mortgaged or not, are owned by individuals. The proportion of individual ownership is especially high for small and medium-sized properties. For larger properties, however, ownership is more varied. Of the mortgage-free properties with fifty units or more, two fifths are owned by individuals, and one fifth each by cooperative organizations and real estate corporations. On the other hand, real estate corporations owned the largest proportion—about half—of the mortgaged properties with fifty units or more. Individuals own approximately one fifth; partnerships, 15 percent; and cooperatives, approximately one out of every ten of the large mortgaged properties (Table 5–28, p. 195).

This chapter has described the financing mechanisms for our housing, for both homeowner and rental units. The importance of these mechanisms will become more evident in the next chapter, which describes the production of new housing. In that chapter it will be seen how great a volume of new housing has been produced in recent years, and the types of housing that have been produced. That housing has been made possible in large part because the financial resources have been available. The volume of housing produced in the future, similarly, will depend largely on whether such financial resources continue to be available. Nothing would tend to indicate that the picture in the next few years will be greatly different from the present.

READING LIST

GENERAL

Bryant, Willis R. *Mortgage Lending—Fundamentals and Practices,* 2d ed. New York: McGraw-Hill Book Co., 1962.

Fact Book. Chicago: United States Savings and Loan League. Published annually.

Fisher, Ernest M., and Robert M. Fisher. *Urban Real Estate.* New York: Holt, Rinehart, and Winston, 1954.

Morton, J. E. *Urban Mortgage Lending: Comparative Markets and Experience.* Princeton: Princeton University Press, 1956.

Pease, Robert H., and Homer V. Cherrington. *Mortgage Banking.* New York: McGraw-Hill Book Co., 1953.

Ratcliff, Richard U. *Real Estate Analysis.* New York: McGraw-Hill Book Co., 1961, Chapter VII.

Weimer, Arthur M., and Homer Hoyt. *Principles of Urban Real Estate,* 2d ed. New York: The Ronald Press Co., 1948.

FEDERAL PROGRAMS

Martin, Preston. *Real Estate Principles and Practices.* New York: The Macmillan Co., 1959, Chapters 15 and 16.

Saulnier, R. J., Harold G. Halcrow, and Neil H. Jacoby. *Federal Lending and Loan Insurance.* Princeton: Princeton University Press, 1958, Chapter 8.

TYPES OF LENDING INSTITUTIONS

American Bankers Association. *The Commercial Banking Industry.* Englewood Cliffs, N.J.: Prentice-Hall, Inc., 1962.

Colean, Miles L. *Mortgage Companies.* Englewood Cliffs, N.J.: Prentice-Hall, Inc., 1962.

Kendall, Leon T. *The Savings and Loan Business.* Englewood Cliffs, N.J.: Prentice-Hall, Inc., 1962.

Life Insurance Association of America. *Life Insurance Companies as Financial Institutions.* Englewood Cliffs, N.J.: Prentice-Hall, Inc., 1962.

National Association of Mutual Savings Banks. *Mutual Savings Banking.* Englewood Cliffs, N.J.: Prentice-Hall, Inc., 1962.

SECONDARY MORTGAGE MARKET

Jones, Oliver, and Leo Grebler. *The Secondary Mortgage Market—Its Purpose, Performance and Potential.* Publication of the Real Estate Research Program. Los Angeles: University of California Press, 1961. (Paperback.)

Martin, Preston. *Real Estate Principles and Practices.* New York: The Macmillan Co., 1959, Chapter 17.

RENTAL HOUSING

Martin, Preston. *Real Estate Principles and Practices.* New York: The Macmillan Co., 1959, Chapter 18.

Winnick, Louis. *Rental Housing: Opportunities for Private Investment.* New York: McGraw-Hill Book Co., 1958.

Table 5–1

ASSETS AND LIABILITIES OF SAVINGS AND LOAN ASSOCIATIONS, DECEMBER 1962

	Assets			*Liabilities*	
Mortgages	$78,973,000	84.2%	Savings capital	$80,422,000	85.7%
U.S. Gov't securities	5,549,000	5.9	Reserves and undiv. profits	6,539,000	7.0
Cash	3,946,000	4.2	FHLB and other borrowings	3,633,000	3.9
Other assets	5,348,000	5.7	Other liabilities	3,222,000	3.4
Total	$93,816,000	100.0%	Total	$93,816,000	100.0%

SOURCE: Board of Governors of the Federal Reserve System, *Federal Reserve Bulletin,* May 1963, p. 675. Figures are published currently.

Table 5–2

ASSETS AND LIABILITIES OF COMMERICIAL BANKS, DECEMBER 1962

	Assets			*Liabilities*	
Real estate loans	$ 34,259,000	11.5%	Demand deposits	$163,878,000	55.1%
Other loans	105,847,000	35.6	Time deposits	98,244,000	33.1
Securities	95,732,000	32.2	Borrowings	3,270,000	1.1
Cash assets	54,049,000	18.2	Total capital accounts	28,140,000	9.5
Other assets	7,229,000	2.5	Other liabilities	3,584,000	1.2
Total	$297,116,000	100.0%	Total	$297,116,000	100.0%

SOURCE: Board of Governors of the Federal Reserve System, *Federal Reserve Bulletin,* May 1963, pp. 662, 666. Figures are published currently.

Table 5–3

ASSETS AND LIABILITIES OF MUTUAL SAVINGS BANKS, DECEMBER 1962

	Assets			*Liabilities*	
Mortgages	$32,056,000	69.5%	Deposits	$41,336,000	89.6%
Other loans	602,000	1.3	Other liabilities	828,000	1.8
Government securities	6,634,000	14.4	Surplus accounts	3,957,000	8.6
Corp. & other securities	5,177,000	11.2	Total	$46,121,000	100.0%
Cash & other assets	1,652,000	3.6			
Total	$46,121,000	100.0%			

SOURCE: Board of Governors of the Federal Reserve System, *Federal Reserve Bulletin*, May 1963, p. 674. Figures are published currently.

Table 5–4

ASSETS AND LIABILITIES OF LIFE INSURANCE COMPANIES, 1962

	Assets			*Liabilities, Surplus, and Capital*	
Mortgages	$ 46,902,000	35.2%	Policy reserves	$108,384,000	81.4%
Corporate bonds	51,544,000	38.7	Other liabilities	13,651,000	10.2
Government bonds	12,178,000	9.1	Surplus and capital	11,256,000	8.4
Stocks	6,302,000	4.7	Total	$133,291,000	100.0%
Real estate	4,107,000	3.1			
Other assets	12,258,000	9.2			
Total	$133,291,000	100.0%			

SOURCE: *Life Insurance Fact Book, 1962*. New York: Institute of Life Insurance, pp. 60, 64, 65.

Table 5–5

PERCENTAGE DISTRIBUTION OF ESTIMATED MORTGAGE DEBT OUTSTANDING ON NONFARM ONE- TO FOUR-FAMILY HOUSES, BY TYPE OF HOLDER, SELECTED YEARS

Type of Holder	*1950*	*1955*	*1960*	*1962*
Savings and loan associations	29.0%	34.0%	39.3%	42.6%
Commercial banks	21.0	17.1	13.6	13.1
Mutual savings banks	9.5	12.6	13.0	13.2
Life insurance companies	18.8	20.1	17.6	16.1
Individuals and others	18.6	12.8	11.8	10.9
Federal agencies (FNMA and others)	3.1	3.4	4.7	4.1

SOURCE: Housing and Home Finance Agency, *Housing Statistics—Annual Data*. Washington, D.C.: Housing and Home Finance Agency, May 1963, p. 37.

Table 5–6

PERCENTAGE DISTRIBUTION OF NUMBER AND AMOUNT OF NONFARM MORTGAGE RECORDINGS OF $20,000 OR LESS, BY TYPE OF MORTGAGEE, 1962

Type of Mortgagee	*Number*	*Amount*
Savings and loan associations	39%	44%
Commercial banks	18	17
Mutual savings banks	5	6
Life insurance companies	2	4
Individuals	18	10
Miscellaneous	18	19

SOURCE: *Housing Statistics—Annual Data*. Washington, D.C.: Housing and Home Finance Agency, May 1963, p. 34.

Table 5–7

PERCENTAGE DISTRIBUTION OF NONFARM HOUSING UNITS STARTED, BY TYPE OF FINANCING, 1940–1962

Year	*FHA*	*VA*	*Conventional*
1940	34%	—%	66%
1941	36	—	64
1942	55	—	45
1943	80	—	20
1944	67	—	33
1945	20	4	76
1946	10	13	77
1947	27	25	48
1948	32	12	56
1949	37	9	54
1950	36	15	49
1951	26	15	59
1952	26	13	61
1953	24	15	61
1954	23	26	51
1955	21	30	49
1956	17	25	58
1957	17	13	70
1958	26	9	65
1959	23	7	70
1960	21	6	73
1961	19	6	75
1962	18	6	76

SOURCE: *Housing Statistics—Annual Data.* Washington, D.C.: Housing and Home Finance Agency, May 1963 (years 1940–1944 from earlier reports), p. 12.

Table 5–8

PERCENTAGE DISTRIBUTION OF AMOUNT OF NONFARM MORTGAGE RECORDINGS OF $20,000 OR LESS, BY TYPE OF FINANCING, 1940–1962

Year	*Amount (in millions)*	*FHA*	*VA*	*Conventional*
1940	$ 4,031	19%	—%	81%
1941	4,732	19	—	81
1942	3,943	25	—	75
1943	3,861	20	—	80
1944	4,606	15	—	85
1945	5,650	8	4	88
1946	10,589	4	22	74
1947	11,729	8	28	64
1948	11,882	18	16	66
1949	11,828	19	12	69
1950	16,179	15	19	66
1951	16,405	12	22	66
1952	18,018	11	15	74
1953	19,747	12	16	72
1954	22,974	8	19	73
1955	28,484	11	25	64
1956	27,088	9	22	69
1957	24,244	9	16	75
1958	27,388	17	7	76
1959	32,235	19	9	72
1960	29,341	16	7	77
1961	31,157	15	6	79
1962	34,187	15	8	77

SOURCE: *Housing Statistics—Annual Data.* Washington, D.C.: Housing and Home Finance Agency, May 1963, pp. 34, 35 (years 1940–1944 from earlier reports).

Table 5–9

PERCENTAGE DISTRIBUTION OF ESTIMATED MORTGAGE DEBT OUTSTANDING ON NONFARM ONE- TO FOUR-FAMILY HOUSES, BY TYPE OF FINANCING, SELECTED YEARS

Type of Financing	*1950*	*1955*	*1960*	*1962*
FHA-insured	19.0%	16.2%	19.0%	19.2
VA-guaranteed	22.8	27.9	21.0	17.5
Conventional	58.2	55.9	60.0	63.3

SOURCE: *Housing Statistics—Annual Data.* Washington, D.C.: Housing and Home Finance Agency, May 1963, p. 37.

Table 5–10

PERCENTAGE DISTRIBUTION OF ORIGIN OF FIRST MORTGAGE FOR ONE DWELLING-UNIT HOMEOWNER MORTGAGED PROPERTIES, BY TYPE OF FINANCING

Origin of Mortgage	*FHA*	*VA*	*Conventional*
Made when property acquired	77.3%	74.2%	62.5%
Assumed when property acquired	17.9	23.2	5.9
Made after property acquired	4.8	2.6	31.6

SOURCE: U.S. Bureau of the Census, *Census of Housing 1960*. Vol. V, Residential Finance. Part 1, Homeowner Properties, p. xxv.

Table 5–11

PERCENTAGE DISTRIBUTION OF MORTGAGE DEBT OUTSTANDING ON NONFARM RESIDENTIAL PROPERTIES, BY TYPE OF FINANCING AND TYPE OF HOLDERS, END OF 1960

Type of Holder	*FHA*	*VA*	*Total Government*	*Conventional*
Savings and Loan Associations	5%	12%	17%	83%
Commercial banks	33	15	48	52
Mutual savings banks	28	35	63	37
Life insurance companies	32	24	56	44
Individuals	17	5	22	78
Federal agencies	42	36	78	22
All holders	20%	19%	39%	61%

SOURCE: Federal Housing Administration; Veterans Administration; Federal National Mortgage Association; Federal Home Loan Bank Board; Housing and Home Finance Agency, Office of the Administrator.

Table 5–12

SELECTED PROPERTY, MORTGAGE AND OWNER CHARACTERISTICS, CONVENTIONAL LOANS ON ONE DWELLING-UNIT HOMEOWNER PROPERTIES, BY TYPE OF HOLDER OF FIRST MORTGAGE, 1960

Holder of Mortgage	*Property Value*	*Amount of First Mortgage*	*Mortgage Amount as percent of Purchase Price*	*Outstanding Debt as percent of Value*	*Term of First Mortgage (Years)*	*Interest Rate on First Mortgage*	*Owner's Income*	*Purchase Price-Income Ratio*	*Age of Head of Household*
Savings and loan associations	$15,000	$ 7,800	66%	46%	16	6.0%	$6,600	2.2	44
Commercial banks	13,000	5,600	58	33	9	6.0	6,400	1.9	45
Mutual savings banks	17,200	8,300	63	38	19	5.1	7,400	2.1	45
Life insurance companies	22,200	11,300	62	41	20	5.0	9,700	2.1	44
Individuals	9,600	5,700	85	54	12	6.0	5,400	1.8	43
Total*	13,900	7,300	68	44	15	5.6	6,500	2.0	44

SOURCE: U.S. Bureau of the Census, *Census of Housing 1960*. Vol. V, Residential Finance. Part 1, Homeowner Properties, pp. 26, 27, 28, 29.

* Includes first mortgages held by a few other groups not listed because proportions held were appreciably smaller than those listed. These other groups include mortgage companies, real estate and construction companies, the Federal Government (principally FNMA), state governments, nonprofit organizations, and a few other groups.

Table 5–13

SELECTED PROPERTY, MORTGAGE AND OWNER CHARACTERISTICS, FHA-INSURED LOANS ON ONE DWELLING-UNIT HOMEOWNER PROPERTIES, BY TYPE OF HOLDER OF FIRST MORTGAGE, 1960

Holder of Mortgage	*Property Value*	*Amount of First Mortgage*	*Mortgage Amount as percent of Purchase Price*	*Outstanding Debt as percent of Value*	*Term of First Mortgage (Years)*	*Interest Rate on First Mortgage*	*Owner's Income*	*Purchase Price-Income Ratio*	*Age of Head of Household*
Savings and loan associations	$12,000	$8,800	84%	65%	24	4.6%	$6,200	2.0	40
Commercial banks	14,200	9,100	80	57	23	4.6	7,100	2.0	44
Mutual savings banks	14,300	10,100	86	69	26	4.6	7,100	1.9	39
Life insurance companies	13,900	9,500	82	62	24	4.6	7,300	2.0	41
Individuals	—	—	—	—	—	—	—	—	—
Total*	13,700	9,500	83	64	24	4.6	6,900	2.0	40

SOURCE: U.S. Bureau of the Census, *Census of Housing 1960*. Vol. V, Residential Finance. Part 1, Homeowner Properties, pp. 18, 19, 20, 21.

* Includes first mortgages held by a few other groups not listed because proportions held were appreciably smaller than those listed. These other groups include mortgage companies, real estate and construction companies, the Federal Government (principally FNMA), state governments, nonprofit organizations, and a few other groups.

Table 5–14

SELECTED PROPERTY, MORTGAGE AND OWNER CHARACTERISTICS, VA-GUARANTEED LOANS ON ONE DWELLING-UNIT HOMEOWNER PROPERTIES, BY TYPE OF HOLDER OF FIRST MORTGAGE, 1960

Holder of Mortgage	*Property Value*	*Amount of First Mortgage*	*Mortgage Amount as percent of Purchase Price*	*Outstanding Debt as percent of Value*	*Term of First Mortgage (Years)*	*Interest Rate on First Mortgage*	*Owner's Income*	*Purchase Price-Income Ratio*	*Age of Head of Household*
Savings and loan associations	$13,000	$ 9,900	92%	71%	25	4.5%	$6,800	1.9	37
Commercial banks	14,700	9,100	83	49	22	4.1	6,900	1.8	39
Mutual savings banks	15,000	10,800	91	69	27	4.5	7,000	2.1	38
Life insurance companies	13,900	10,800	91	70	25	4.5	6,900	1.8	38
Individuals	—	—	—	—	—	—	—	—	—
Total*	13,800	10,200	91	67	25	4.5	6,800	2.0	38

SOURCE: U.S. Bureau of the Census, *Census of Housing 1960*. Vol. V, Residential Finance. Part 1, Homeowner Properties, pp. 22, 23, 24, 25.

* Includes first mortgages held by a few other groups not listed because proportions held were appreciably smaller than those listed. These other groups include mortgage companies, real estate and construction companies, the Federal Government (principally FNMA), state governments, nonprofit organizations, and a few other groups.

Table 5–15

PERCENTAGE DISTRIBUTION OF OUTSTANDING FIRST MORTGAGE DEBT ON ONE DWELLING-UNIT HOMEOWNER PROPERTIES, BY TYPE OF HOLDER AND BY REGION, 1960

Type of Holder	*Northeast*	*North Central*	*South*	*West*
Savings and loan associations	32.1%	41.3%	30.9%	28.3%
Commercial banks	15.8	17.4	7.6	19.0
Mutual savings banks	38.0	2.8	10.3	7.3
Life insurance companies	6.3	19.8	33.8	22.3
Individuals	5.6	11.3	6.4	7.0
Other	2.2	7.4	11.0	16.1

SOURCE: U.S. Bureau of the Census, *Census of Housing 1960*. Vol. V, Residential Finance. Part 1, Homeowner Properties, p. xxv.

Table 5–16

OUTSTANDING FIRST MORTGAGE DEBT FOR ONE DWELLING-UNIT HOMEOWNER PROPERTIES, BY TYPE OF HOLDER, FOR SELECTED STANDARD METROPOLITAN STATISTICAL AREAS, 1960

Type of Holder	*Atlanta*	*Baltimore*	*Boston*	*Buffalo*	*Chicago-Northwestern Indiana*	*Cleveland*	*Dallas*	*Detroit*	*St. Louis*	*San Francisco-Oakland*
Savings and loan associations	31.8%	56.4%	34.6%	18.7%	54.7%	46.7%	24.3%	19.6%	46.5%	16.6%
Commercial banks	2.1	4.6	3.0	16.0	14.7	26.5	2.3	15.7	16.9	28.2
Mutual savings banks	18.8	19.7	58.3	50.8	1.3	3.3	8.0	4.2	1.5	13.3
Life insurance companies	38.3	9.5	1.9	7.1	16.1	15.4	47.0	32.4	22.8	24.3
Individuals	3.4	3.0	1.2	6.2	7.1	3.3	4.4	15.2	6.5	4.1
Other	5.6	6.8	1.0	1.2	6.1	4.8	14.0	12.9	5.8	13.5

SOURCE: U.S. Bureau of the Census, *Census of Housing 1960*. Vol. V, Residential Finance. Part 1, Homeowner Properties, p. xxv.

Table 5–17

COMPARISON OF MEDIAN AMOUNT OF PURCHASE PRICE, LOAN TO PERCENT OF PURCHASE PRICE, AND TERM OF LOAN FOR NEW AND EXISTING HOME PURCHASE LOANS, BY TYPE OF MORTGAGE, MARCH 1963

		Median			
	Total	*Savings and Loan Associations*	*Commercial Banks*	*Mutual Savings Banks*	*Life Insurance Companies*
Purchase price					
New	$22,500	$20,700	$22,400	$22,300	$28,100
Existing	$17,300	$16,500	$16,900	$19,900	$26,700
Loan to percent of purchase price					
New	73.4%	76.0%	61.8%	69.2%	70.1%
Existing	71.2	74.1	62.1	66.8	67.4
Term of loan (years)					
New	24.0	23.7	16.6	25.0	26.3
Existing	19.2	20.0	14.1	21.1	24.1

SOURCE: "Home Mortgage Interest Rates and Terms," Federal Home Loan Bank Board, May 1963.

Table 5–18

NET PRICES FOR FHA-INSURED $5\frac{1}{4}$ PERCENT NEW-HOME MORTGAGES (SECTION 203), IMMEDIATE DELIVERY TRANSACTIONS, 30-YEAR MATURITY, MINIMUM DOWN-PAYMENT

FHA Zone	*April 1, 1963*		*March 1, 1963*
	Average	*Range*	*Average*
Northeast	$99.7	$99.00–100.00	$99.3
Middle Atlantic	99.1	97.00–100.00	98.3
Southeast	97.4	96.50–99.00	97.5
North Central	98.0	97.00–99.00	97.9
Southwest	97.9	97.00–98.50	97.6
West	97.7	94.00–98.50	97.4
United States	98.0	94.00–100.00	97.9

SOURCE: U.S. Department of Commerce, "Construction Comments—New Series of Secondary Market Prices, FHA-Insured Mortgages," *Construction Review,* Vol. 2, No. 9, May 1963.

Table 5–19

ASSETS IN CORPORATE PENSION FUNDS, AND AMOUNT AND PERCENT IN MORTGAGES, 1957-1962

Year	*Total Assets (in millions)*	*Assets in Mortgages (in millions)*	*Assets in Mortgages*
1957	$19,319	$313	1.6%
1958	22,094	405	1.8
1959	25,307	576	2.3
1960	28,706	753	2.6
1961	32,368	907	2.8
1962	35,999	1,140	3.2

SOURCE: "Corporate Pension Funds, 1962," Release No. 1902. Washington, D.C.: Securities and Exchange Commission. Release May 24, 1963.

Table 5–20

PERCENTAGE DISTRIBUTION OF NUMBER OF DWELLING UNITS PER PROPERTY FOR RENTAL PROPERTIES,* BY MORTGAGE STATUS, 1960

	All Properties	*Nonmortgaged Properties*	*Mortgaged Properties*
Total rental properties (number in thousands)	7,713	5,162	2,551
One- to-four dwelling-unit properties	92.9%	95.4%	87.8%
One dwelling-unit properties	71.8	75.5	64.4
Two- to-four dwelling-unit properties	21.1	19.9	23.4
Two	*14.5*	*14.1*	*15.3*
Three	*3.8*	*3.4*	*4.6*
Four	*2.7*	*2.4*	*3.4*
Average number	(2.4)	(2.4)	(2.5)
Five- to-forty-nine dwelling-units properties	6.9	4.5	11.7
Five to nine	4.9	3.4	7.6
Ten to fourteen	0.8	0.4	1.6
Fifteen to nineteen	0.6	0.3	1.3
Twenty to twenty-four	0.2	0.1	0.4
Twenty-five to forty-nine	0.4	0.2	0.8
Average number	(9.6)	(8.5)	(10.5)
Fifty- or more dwelling-unit properties	0.2	†	0.5
Fifty to seventy-four	0.1	†	0.3
Seventy-five or more	†	†	0.1
Average number	(120.4)	(116.6)	(120.8)

SOURCE: U.S. Bureau of the Census, *Census of Housing 1960*. Vol. V, Residential Finance. Part 2 Rental and Vacant Properties, p. xxiii.

* Includes vacant units in single-unit properties, in properties with five dwelling units or more, and in properties with one to four dwelling units, unless one of the units in such properties is occupied by the owner.

† Less than one tenth of 1 percent.

Table 5–21

PERCENTAGE DISTRIBUTION OF FIRST AND JUNIOR MORTGAGES AND TYPE OF FINANCING FOR FIRST MORTGAGE, RENTAL PROPERTIES,* BY SIZE OF PROPERTY, 1960

		Properties with		
	All Mortgaged Properties	*One to Four Dwelling Units*	*Five to Forty-nine Dwelling Units*	*Fifty Dwelling Units or More*
Total (number in thousands)	2,551	2,238	299	14
With first mortgage only	91.7%	93.0%	82.3%	83.8%
With junior mortgage	8.3	7.0	17.7	16.2
FHA-insured first mortgage	10.9	12.3	0.8	17.2
VA-guaranteed first mortgage	11.4	12.9		
Conventional first mortgage	77.7	74.8	99.2	82.8

SOURCE: U.S. Bureau of the Census, *Census of Housing 1960*. Vol. V, Residential Finance. Part 2, Rental and Vacant Properties, p. xxiv.

* Includes vacant units in single-unit properties, in properties with five dwelling units or more, and in properties with one to four dwelling units, unless one of the units in such properties is occupied by the owner.

Table 5–22

PERCENTAGE DISTRIBUTION OF FIRST MORTGAGE DEBT ON RENTAL PROPERTIES* BY TYPE OF HOLDER, BY SIZE OF PROPERTY, 1960

		Properties with		
Type of Holder	*All Mortgaged Properties*	*One to Four Dwelling Units*	*Five to Forty-nine Dwelling Units*	*Fifty Dwelling Units or More*
Commercial bank	11.7%	16.1%	10.2%	4.7%
Mutual savings bank	18.5	9.0	15.7	40.0
Savings and loan association	26.2	37.5	28.3	1.7
Life insurance company	20.8	14.0	24.1	30.5
Federal or state agency	5.9	5.2	0.1	13.5
Individual	13.4	15.6	20.3	1.8
Other	3.6	2.7	1.2	7.8

SOURCE: U.S. Bureau of the Census, *Census of Housing 1960*. Vol. V, Residential Finance. Part 2, Rental and Vacant Properties, p. xxvi.

* Includes vacant units in single-unit properties, in properties with five dwelling units or more, and in properties with one to four dwelling units, unless one of the units in such properties is occupied by the owner.

Table 5–23

PERCENTAGE DISTRIBUTION OF ORIGIN OF FIRST MORTGAGE FOR RENTAL PROPERTIES* BY TYPE OF FINANCING, BY SIZE OF PROPERTY, 1960

		Properties with		
Origin of Mortgage	*All Mortgaged Properties*	*One to Four Dwelling Units*	*Five to Forty-nine Dwelling Units*	*Fifty Dwelling Units or More*
All properties:				
Made when property acquired	50.4%	50.2%	52.1%	43.3%
Assumed when property acquired	17.9	18.3	15.4	14.1
Made after property acquired	31.7	31.5	32.5	42.6
Properties with FHA-insured first mortgage:				
Made when property acquired	60.2	60.0	71.8	81.9
Assumed when property acquired	33.5	33.8	28.1	15.4
Made after property acquired	6.2	6.3	0.1	2.7
Properties with VA-guaranteed first mortgage:				
Made when property acquired	45.3	45.3	—	—
Assumed when propetry acquired	52.8	52.8	—	—
Made after property acquired	1.8	1.8	—	—
Properties with conventional first mortgage:				
Made when property acquired	49.7	49.4	51.9	35.3
Assumed when property acquired	10.6	9.8	15.3	13.8
Made after property acquired	39.7	40.8	32.8	50.9

SOURCE: U.S. Bureau of the Census, *Census of Housing 1960*. Vol. V, Residential Finance. Part 2, Rental and Vacant Properties, p. xxvi.

* Includes vacant units in single-unit properties, in properties with five dwelling units or more, and in properties with one to four dwelling units, unless one of the units in such properties is occupied by the owner.

Table 5–24

PERCENTAGE DISTRIBUTION OF INTEREST RATES OF CONVENTIONAL FIRST MORTGAGES FOR RENTAL PROPERTIES,* BY SIZE OF PROPERTY, 1960

		Properties with		
Interest Rate	*All Mortgaged Properties*	*One to Four Dwelling Units*	*Five to Forty-nine Dwelling Units*	*Fifty Dwelling Units or More*
Less than 4.5 percent	3.5%	3.3%	3.4%	23.4%
4.5 to 4.9 percent	3.0	2.0	7.7	25.3
5.0 to 5.4 percent	20.4	19.4	25.7	27.4
5.5 to 5.9 percent	9.7	8.2	18.3	11.0
6.0 to 6.9 percent	56.4	59.4	41.2	12.7
7.0 to 7.9 percent	3.9	4.2	2.4	0.2
8.0 percent or more	3.2	3.5	1.2	—
Median, percent	6.0%	6.0%	5.6%	5.0%

SOURCE: U.S. Bureau of the Census, *Census of Housing 1960*. Vol. V, Residential Finance. Part 2, Rental and Vacant Properties, p. xxvii.

* Includes vacant units in single-unit properties, in properties with five dwelling units or more, and in properties with one to four dwelling units, unless one of the units in such properties is occupied by the owner.

Table 5–25

PERCENTAGE DISTRIBUTION OF INTEREST AND PRINCIPAL PAYMENT AS PERCENT OF RENTAL RECEIPTS FOR RENTAL PROPERTIES,* BY SIZE OF PROPERTY, 1960

		Properties with		
Payments as Percent of Rental Receipts	*All Mortgaged Properties*	*One to Four Dwelling Units*	*Five to Forty-nine Dwelling Units*	*Fifty Dwelling Units or More*
Less than 30 percent	8.1%	4.7%	27.6%	45.4%
30 to 49 percent	17.4	15.7	26.8	41.8
40 to 69 percent	23.4	24.2	18.8	9.6
70 to 89 percent	17.0	18.4	9.3	1.0
90 percent or more	34.1	36.9	17.5	2.2
Median percent				
All properties	71%	75%	47%	32%
With FHA first mortgage	57	57	—	44
With VA first mortgage	69	69	—	—
With conventional first mortgage	77	84	47	28

SOURCE: U.S. Bureau of the Census, *Census of Housing 1960*. Vol. V, Residential Finance. Part 2, Rental and Vacant Properties, p. xxviii.

* Includes vacant units in single-unit properties, in properties with five dwelling units or more, and in properties with one to four dwelling units, unless one of the units in such properties is occupied by the owner.

Table 5–26

PERCENTAGE DISTRIBUTION OF YEAR BUILT FOR RENTAL PROPERTIES* BY MORTGAGE STATUS AND SIZE OF PROPERTY, 1960

			Properties with					
	All Properties		*One to Four Dwelling Units*		*Five to Forty-nine Dwelling Units*		*Fifty Dwelling Units or More*	
Year Built	*Not mortgaged*	*Mortgaged*	*Not mortgaged*	*Mortgaged*	*Not mortgaged*	*Mortgaged*	*Not mortgaged*	*Mortgaged*
1955 to 1959	6.0%	16.2%	6.1%	13.1%	2.6%	16.9%	5.5%	10.8%
1950 to 1954	7.8	18.7	8.1	20.2	2.2	7.3	6.4	16.8
1940 to 1949	14.1	17.7	14.4	13.8	7.5	9.4	8.0	17.0
1930 to 1939	12.6	8.4	12.8	3.7	8.8	6.4	5.3	12.4
1929 or earlier	59.5	39.0	58.6	33.2	78.9	60.0	74.7	43.0

SOURCE: U.S. Bureau of the Census, *Census of Housing 1960*. Vol. V, Residential Finance. Part 2, Rental and Vacant Properties, p. xxix.

* Includes vacant units in single-unit properties, in properties with five dwelling units or more, and in properties with one to four dwelling units, unless one of the units in such properties is occupied by the owner.

Table 5–27

PERCENTAGE DISTRIBUTION OF VALUE PER DWELLING UNIT FOR RENTAL PROPERTIES* BY MORTGAGE STATUS AND SIZE OF PROPERTY, 1960

		Properties with		
Value per Dwelling Unit	*All Properties*	*One to Four Dwelling Units*	*Five to Forty-nine Dwelling Units*	*Fifty Dwelling Units or More*
Nonmortgaged Properties:				
Less than $5,000	49.0%	47.8%	73.4%	49.3%
$5,000 to $7,400	20.7	20.8	18.5	20.8
$7,500 to $9,900	12.0	12.4	3.4	6.4
$10,000 to $14,900	10.9	11.2	4.2	19.4
$15,000 to $19,900	4.2	4.4	0.4	1.7
$20,000 or more	3.2	3.4	0.1	2.3
Median value per dwelling unit	$5,100	$5,300	$5,000–	$5,100
Mortgaged Properties:				
Less than $5,000	22.1%	17.8%	53.7%	35.8%
$5,000 to $7,400	22.1	22.0	22.6	27.5
$7,500 to $9,900	20.5	21.4	14.0	18.8
$10,000 to $14,900	22.1	24.0	7.9	13.9
$15,000 to $19,900	7.1	7.9	1.2	2.3
$20,000 or more	6.1	6.9	0.6	1.7
Median value per dwelling unit	$8,200	$8,700	$5,000–	$6,300
Median value per property	$11,500	$10,700	$42,000	$540,000

SOURCE: U.S. Bureau of the Census, *Census of Housing 1960*. Vol. V, Residential Finance. Part 2, Rental and Vacant Properties, p. xxviii.

* Includes vacant units in single-unit properties, in properties with five dwelling units or more, and in properties with one to four dwelling units, unless one of the units in such properties is occupied by the owner.

Table 5–28

PERCENTAGE DISTRIBUTION OF TYPE OF OWNER OF RENTAL PROPERTIES* BY MORTGAGE STATUS AND SIZE OF PROPERTY, 1960

			Properties with					
	All Properties		*One to Four Dwelling Units*		*Five to Forty-nine dwelling Units*		*Fifty Dwelling Units or More*	
Type of Owner	*Not mortgaged*	*Mortgaged*	*Not mortgaged*	*Mortgaged*	*Not mortgaged*	*Mortgaged*	*Not mortgaged*	*Mortgaged*
Individual	88.8%	89.4%	88.8%	91.0%	88.9%	80.4%	39.8%	19.1%
Partnership	3.4	2.9	3.3	2.1	5.5	8.7	5.7	15.4
Financial institution	0.3	0.2	0.3	0.2	0.3	0.2	2.2	0.7
Cooperative organization	—	0.3	—	0.1	0.1	0.8	20.0	9.2
Real estate corporation	0.7	4.5	0.6	3.6	3.8	8.5	19.8	51.7
Other	6.7	2.7	7.0	2.9	1.4	1.4	12.5	3.9

SOURCE: U.S. Bureau of the Census, *Census of Housing 1960*. Vol. V, Residential Finance. Part 2, Rental and Vacant Properties, p. xxix.

* Includes vacant units in single-unit properties, in properties with five dwelling units or more, and in properties with one to four dwelling units, unless one of the units in such properties is occupied by the owner.

CHAPTER 6

*

Production of Housing

The nation's total "supply" of housing is constantly changing. One of the most significant changes is in the new units continuously being built. New housing production is important for several reasons. It assures a continuing flow of new dwelling units into the total inventory to meet the needs of families who want such units. It is extremely important in the economy of our nation. A vigorous housing program opens up vast employment opportunities; in 1960 housing construction accounted for 4.5 percent of our gross national product.

How many new housing units are being produced annually? What are the principal components involved in building this volume of units? The focus of this chapter is on these questions.

VOLUME AND CHARACTERISTICS OF NEW CONSTRUCTION

The "standing stock" of housing in the United States in 1960, as already indicated, consisted of more than 58 million dwelling units. Although our nation now has a history of several centuries, one fourth of the dwellings in existence in 1960 had been added by new construction since 1950. The numerical gain was close to one and one half times the gain for the preceding decade. (About two thirds were in existence in 1950 and the remaining units—about 6 percent—were formed through conversion, merger, or in some other manner.)[1] (Between 1950 and 1959, 4,530,000 units were lost from the national inventory—slightly over half through demolition and the remainder through other means, such as change to nonresidential use, destruction by fire or flood, being moved from site, or declared uninhabitable for human use.)

The new construction between 1950 and 1959 accounted for 28 percent of the dwellings inside standard metropolitan statistical areas and 22 percent of the total outside these areas in 1959. It accounted for two fifths of the inventory in the "suburban" portions of metropolitan areas, compared with approximately one fifth in central cities.

The volume of new construction over the last decade also varied among

[1] U.S. Bureau of the Census, *Census of Housing 1960,* Components of Inventory Change, HC(4), Part 1A-1, 1950–1959 Components, United States and Regions.

the geographic regions of the nation. The highest proportion of new construction was found in the West—35 percent of the 1959 inventory. It represented 29 percent in the South and 21 percent in the Northeast and North Central regions. (Demolitions also varied by regions, as follows: West, 5 percent; South, 6 percent; Northeast and North Central, 3 percent.)

Almost six times as many new nonfarm dwelling units were built in 1962 as in 1920—a total of 1,458,400 as compared with 247,000. Although there has been a tremendous increase in housing production over the forty-year period, the year-by-year trend has been highly irregular. (Table 6–1, p. 231.)

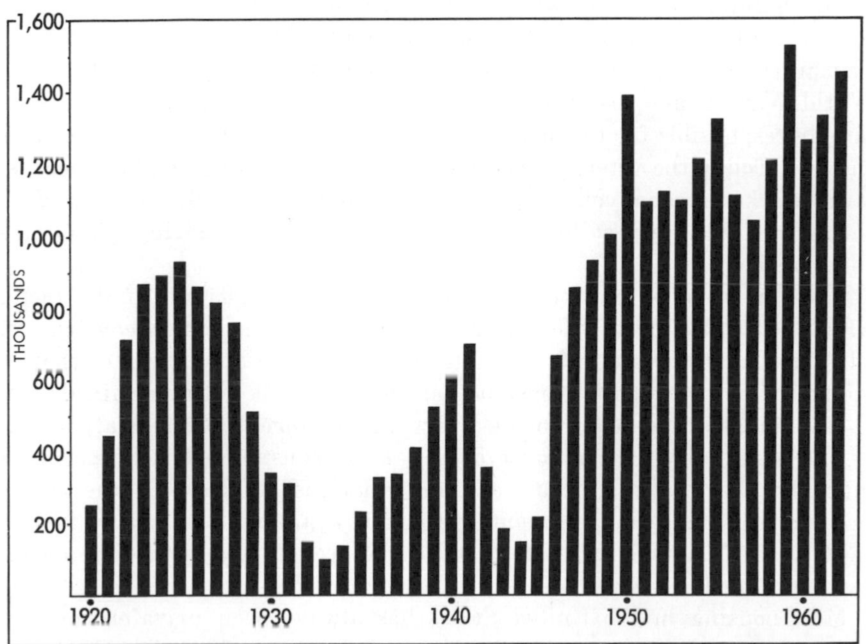

FIGURE 9. *Total nonfarm housing starts, 1920 to 1962. Period 1959 to 1962 based on new series data. (Source of data: U.S. Departments of Commerce and Labor.)*

No one cause accounts for the year-to-year variation in the output of the industry. One explanation is the prospect for reasonable profit on the part of the builders. Private builders undertake the construction of new dwelling units when they expect a profitable market for them. Hence, the annual construction rate is closely related to the "paying" demand for housing, i.e., the number of families in the community desiring shelter who at the same time have the ability to pay for it under the lending terms required.

But even this relationship between new building and demand is not always direct and simple. Because "undoubling" can and does occur, or because housing acquisition is postponable, the demand is never precisely predictable, thus contributing to wide fluctuation from year to year in the volume of new dwelling units built.

Another primary relationship affecting the annual rate of housing production is the cost of construction relative to the existing level of rents and value. If, for example, families have "doubled up" and vacancies are high, rents and values in the community will be depressed. This will affect the rate of return on housing investments and local builders will not be inclined to build new units. This situation has not existed in many communities since World War II, but the principle should not be forgotten. Only when a favorable relationship exists between rents and values on the one hand, and costs of housing on the other (including the land, utilities, the building itself, financing, taxes, maintenance and operation, plus a reasonable profit for the builder) will new dwelling units be added to the supply.

The factor of financing (discussed in detail in Chapter 5) is one of the primary reasons for the record-breaking volume of new construction since World War II, and also for the year-to-year fluctuations. This factor was largely responsible for the many new dwelling units built for veterans after the war. Today the veterans' market is not as large as it was, but there is a large market among young families and families who desire to upgrade themselves with respect to housing. Present liberal financing plans make this possible.

These in broadest outline are some, but by no means all, of the factors which contribute to the wide fluctuations in the volume of new construction. They are mentioned here for the purpose of emphasizing the fact that the volume of new residential construction undertaken is not determined solely by the quantitative requirements (new family formation, migration, etc.) of the community. The number of new units constructed is influenced as much by the financing terms and the relationships between the cost of producing housing and the amount of money available to spend for housing as it is by the number of units that may be needed at a given time by new families entering the market.

Most housing in the United States has always been privately built. A government program of public housing was begun in 1935, but the largest annual number of units ever built under that program was 86,600, in 1941. In only six other years since 1935—1939, 1940, 1942, 1951, 1952, and 1958—were over 50,000 public housing units built.

A generally increasing proportion of new units, over the years, have been built in metropolitan areas, in response to the population growth of those areas (Table 6–1, p. 231). In fact, during the period 1950 to 1959, the proportion of new housing construction in such areas exceeded their proportion of the total population of the United States. The heaviest volume of new construction was built outside the central cities, largely in the suburbs (Table 6–2, p. 232).

An important proportion of the housing built early in the century was of the rental type, usually a third or more of the total from 1900 until World War I.[2] The volume again reached that proportion in 1922, and

[2] For a discussion of the evolution of the statistical series relating to housing units started in the United States and for detailed figures, see U.S. Department of Labor,

continued at that level through 1929. (During five years—1923, 1924, 1926, 1927, and 1928—more than four out of every ten units built were of a rental type.) The 33 percent level was not again reached until 1962 (Table 6–3, p. 233).

Since the Depression years of the 1930's, there has been strong promotion of home ownership (discussed in Chapter 7), aided and abetted by the factor of liberal financing. This has perhaps caused a disproportionate share of building for ownership, but a market "correction" seems to have been begun in 1958, the year in which rental housing construction volume again began to increase. It is interesting to note that of the new rental units built between 1950 and 1959, 40 percent were one-family structures and 23 percent were structures housing two to four families (Table 6–4, p. 234).

Let us also look at some of the other characteristics of recent new construction. The number of rooms in both owner and rental housing units has remained quite stable for some years. The highest proportion of owner homes has five rooms (39 percent), followed by those having six rooms (26 percent). The highest proportion of rental units has four rooms (36 percent), followed by those having three rooms (24 percent). (Table 6–5, p. 235.) A total of 32 percent of the owner-occupied units built between 1950 and 1959 had more than one bathroom.

There was wide variation in the value of the new housing built between 1950 and 1959, the median value of both owner-occupied units ($15,000) and the median gross rent of rental units ($93 per month) being significantly higher than in any previous period in history. The percentage distributions reflecting the averages for the period 1950 to 1959 are shown in Table 6–6, p. 235.

Some of the differences in value result from the quality of the units; others result from size (e.g., the number of rooms and whether or not there is a basement); still others result from differences in cost of construction. There are significant differences in median value from city to city. In Cleveland, for example, the median value of new one-family houses authorized in 1959 was $16,600; in Chicago, $16,000. In contrast, it was only $7,700 in Memphis and $9,300 in Birmingham (Table 6–7, p. 236). These differences reflect different factors; e.g., building costs, building codes, and local customs and needs. The median valuation of apartment units (in five-or-more-family structures) was $10,500 in Providence, Rhode Island, and $8,900 in the New York-Northeastern New Jersey area, compared with only $2,100 in Memphis and $3,700 in Atlanta. Such features as soundproofing, air conditioning, swimming pools, and enclosed parking facilities, as well as the other basic factors (construction costs, building codes, etc.), often accounted for these differences.

Nonfarm Housing Starts 1889–1958, Bulletin No. 1260, Bureau of Labor Statistics (undated). See also U.S. Department of Labor, *Trends in Building Permit Activity*, Bulletin No. 1243, Bureau of Labor Statistics (undated). It should be remembered, however, that both these reports are concerned with the "old series" of building statistics, which was changed in 1959.

There are four principal components to a building operation. There must be land, there must be labor, there must be building materials, and, finally, there must be an entrepreneur (i.e., a manager of the total building operation). Each of these is discussed below.

LAND

One of the ingredients most important to the production of housing is land. Today the shortage of land is one of our most serious problems. Movement to the suburbs has been due primarily to a search for land sufficiently inexpensive so that single-family houses could be built upon it.

The use of land for housing in any community is closely related to other land uses, such as for industry, trade, transportation, and recreation. The concentrations of these separate uses within the housing area and their relation to each other are of prime importance to housing and its development in any community. The location of new housing is decided in terms of these relationships. The same factors are important for determining the extent of rehabilitation for housing in specific areas and for making decisions about the replacement of bad housing with good housing or with some other type of land use.

Similarly, decisions on new factory sites are not made without consideration of where the workers will live, and decisions regarding the location of new shopping centers are not made without first evaluating whether there will be an adequate number of customers with the desired buying power.

An important aspect of the land factor is whether the land is raw or already subdivided. Interest in raw land usually centers around its availability for residential use, which is usually conditioned by a variety of factors. One is its relation to the direction of residential growth. The topography of the land is important, too, for rugged terrain is generally not suitable for anything but higher-priced housing because of the added expense of grading and filling. Low-lying flat lands may also be unusable except for limited purposes. Land that is beyond the reach of city planning, zoning, building codes, and similar controls of the city, presents some risk to the developer.

Vacant subdivided land frequently presents a more serious problem than the development of raw land. Because subdividing commonly has been spasmodic, rather than an orderly process in time, the lots created in one boom may be outmoded or wholly inadequate for use when the next boom comes along. In some communities today there is still a heritage of vacant lots left over from the 1920's. In most instances they are not laid out in conformity with modern subdivision practices, are in arrears for taxes, and possibly have been by-passed by the growth of the city in another direction or for another type of use. For these reasons, the selling of individual building lots *per se* hardly exists as an important factor in most local housing markets. On the other hand, the development of raw land is continuing, syndicates sometimes buying up the land and arranging for the builder to build on it. This becomes costly to the home buyer, because of the profit returned to the syndicate. Lots about 60 by 120 feet in such new subdivisions in the early part of the 1960's commonly sold for $1,800 to $2,000, improved. This increase in cost of an improved lot, together with other factors, has often increased its cost to as much as 15 to 18 percent of the total cost of house and lot (as compared with only 10 percent in the 1940's).

Another important change has taken place in recent years with regard to the development of raw land. Formerly, communities encouraged builders to develop the land and the municipalities would stand an important portion (sometimes up to 80 percent) of the cost of development. By the middle 1950's, this situation had changed to the extent that builders in many localities, developing as much as 100 acres, would be required to give approximately 10 percent of that amount for school facilities, put in the utilities required, and, in some instances, even plant trees. In fact, some communities have reached the point where they have banned any further large-scale development. Some of these cases have been taken to the courts. The community's position is based on its lack of facilities that must follow new housing developments—schools, recreation areas, sewers, water supply, and transportation—and its inability to provide them quickly enough. (The subject of local subdivision controls is discussed in more detail in Chapter 9.)

By and large, too little attention has been paid in the past to the land component of "real estate." Perhaps current interest in rehabilitation and urban renewal will have the salutary effect of highlighting this close relationship, to the ultimate benefit of housing and family living in general.

LABOR

Housebuilding is enmeshed with the construction industry as a whole. Home builders, for example, frequently rely on independent subcontractors to perform part of their construction work. The following work is usually subcontracted:

- Carpentry and cabinet work
- Heating
- Plumbing
- Electrical wiring
- Painting
- Lathing and plastering
- Excavating and grading
- Landscaping
- Masonry
- Linoleum laying
- Tile setting
- Roofing
- Sheet metal work

Number of Employees

There are no data available to indicate the total number of employees engaged by home builders themselves. (The average number of full-time employees per home builder is discussed later.) Data show that general contractors employed 737,000 workers in 1961. However, a high proportion

of those workers were undoubtedly engaged in other than housebuilding.

Plumbing and heating firms employ more workers than any other single type of subcontractor—303,000 in 1961. They are followed by painting and decorating firms, which employed 226,000 in that year. Electrical firms employed 182,000. The number of workers in each of these types of employment has increased significantly in recent years (Table 6–8, p. 237).

Since each of these is an independent group, the home builder retains no direct control over how the work is done, unless he is large enough in size to hire some of these workers on his own work force.

Wages

The proportion of the cost of a house represented in labor, including that provided by subcontractors, varies greatly, depending in part upon the degree of prefabrication. Normally, however, the range is from one third to one half of the total cost.

Generally speaking, housebuilding labor, including that of subcontractors, is more skilled than labor in general and is higher paid. The trend in wages has been upward for many years. The average hourly earnings of electricians, for example, has increased from $2.71 in 1952 to $4.03 in 1961. Plumbing and heating specialists have increased their wages from $2.44 to $3.66 over the same period. For painters and decorators the increase has been from $2.35 to $3.49 (Table 6–9, p. 238).

These hourly wage rates do not mean that the average annual income of these workers is necessarily above others. Because some of the work is still seasonal and dependent on good weather, annual wages are still sometimes low. In recent years, however, the seasonal factor has been less important in building, and with a heavy volume of construction of many types continuing throughout the year in many communities, the losses due to seasonal fluctuations and weather are no longer as serious as they were.

Sequence of Work

One of the problems of the home builder is to arrange the sequence of subcontractors and arrange their services at the particular time he needs them. Each contractor, being independent of the builder, plans his work on the basis of all of the calls for his services. This makes it difficult for the builder to organize his operations efficiently. Obviously small builders are at a greater disadvantage here than medium- and large-scale builders.

It must be remembered that housebuilding labor not only serves the building industry in general—including factory, office building, school, hospital, and other construction—but also serves old as well as new housing. This fact is especially important from the standpoint of painters and decorators, since they probably serve more old than new buildings, including houses.

Restrictive Practices

Building labor has become highly unionized in many parts of the nation and with unionization have come some "restrictive" labor practices that have undoubtedly raised housebuilding costs.

One of the common types of restrictions is the prohibition of use of certain types of equipment, tools, and methods. Criticism of this practice has been especially leveled against the plumbing, painting, and masonry trades. Plumbers, for example, have commonly required that most of their work be done on the site. This has worked especially against prefabrication, discussed later in this chapter. Painters frequently limit the size of brushes used and commonly prohibit the use of spray guns. New mechanized tools, such as mechanical trowels, are seldom used by masons.

A second complaint against the unions is that they allegedly place limitations on output. An example, commonly cited, is the limitation of placing so many bricks a day by bricklayers.

Another common complaint is the method in which unions regulate the number of workers in the trade, allegedly preferring to keep the number of skilled workers low in order to maintain demand and high wages. Sometimes union rolls are closed, and in other situations long apprenticeships and high initiation fees are required.

Related to all of these is the problem generally termed "upgrading of work." This refers to the situation where unskilled or semiskilled labor must be done by journeymen or other more highly skilled workers.

These are probably the most important complaints. Evidence for them has been found in many localities. The extent of these practices nationally, however, has not been determined. Where they are found, they have an obvious influence on raising the cost of housing.

BUILDING MATERIALS

Materials producers have a direct influence on housing, since they determine the types, quality, sizes, and availability of materials. Producers of materials, fixtures, and equipment do not ordinarily design their products for specific types of structures. Manufacturers of plumbing fixtures, for example, sell the same product for use in homes, apartments, hotels, motels, school buildings, hospitals, and office buildings. The same paint, brick, and roofing materials go into buildings of all kinds. This means, of course, that the home builder is purchasing these materials in the same market as contractors who are building other types of buildings. He is not in a strong bargaining position.

Because the home builder generally uses the same materials used in other building construction, and since there are no separate statistics concerning the volume of materials used only for home building, the first parts of this section will discuss building materials generally—their types, their production volume, price trends, and distribution channels. Then there will be a discussion of recent developments in materials. Finally, there will be some discussion concerning recent trends in materials used in home building.

Production

The most important categories of building materials are listed by the U. S. Department of Commerce as follows: lumber and wood products—softwood lumber, hardwood flooring, Douglas fir plywood, insulating boards and hardboard; millwork products—Ponderosa pine doors, hardwood doors, sash and exterior frames; paint, varnish, and lacquer; iron and steel products, ranging from nails to cast-iron soil pipe; heating and plumbing equipment—gas water heaters, cast-iron converters and radiators, warm-air and floor and wall furnaces, and residential oil burners; asphalt products—roofing, siding, insulated brick siding and saturated felts; gypsum board and lath; and structural clay products—brick, structural clay tile, clay sewer pipe, hollow facing tile, and floor and wall tile. The classification is incomplete, inasmuch as it does not include products made from such materials as aluminum and the plastics, and it does not include electrical equipment (e.g., it includes gas but not electric water heaters).

A review of the production volume of the various types of materials indicates how strongly entrenched the traditional materials are. Although many new materials have been offered by manufacturers in recent years, heavy use of both lumber and clay products continues. For example, the production of clay construction products reached an all-time high as recently as 1956 (Table 6–10, p. 239). The fact that production volume of clay construction products has not reached even higher peaks, with the all-time high rate of building in recent years, is perhaps the result of the proliferation of new and improved materials discussed later in this chapter.

Of course, the production figures for the general categories of materials sometimes conceal changes taking place within a particular category. For example, under "lumber and wood products," the production of Douglas fir plywood has increased from 5 billion square feet in 1955 to 9.4 billion square feet in 1962, whereas softwood lumber production, during that same period, declined from 31.6 billion board feet to 26.4 billion board feet. Similarly, under "heating and plumbing equipment," shipment of cast-iron convectors and radiators declined from 28.5 billion square feet in 1955 to 12.4 billion square feet in 1962, but warm-air and floor and wall furnace shipments remained about the same during the two periods. (Data are not available for other types of heating equipment, including electrical.) The U.S. Department of Commerce provides current figures on all of these items in its monthly publication *Construction Review*.

There is a general belief that building material production is concentrated in a few manufacturing firms. A Congressional Committee in 1947 confirmed this for some items.[3] It found, for example, that for six materials as few

[3] "Study of Monopoly Power," Hearings, Subcommittee on Study of Monopoly Power, U.S. House Committee on the Judiciary (81:2), p. 1437 ff.

as eight firms supplied 70 percent or more of the output of each: window glass, 99 percent; linoleum, 95 percent; gypsum products, 94 percent; window shades, 83 percent; vitreous plumbing fixtures, 82 percent; and ceramic tile, 70 percent. Following these, in order of concentration, were asphalt roofing, galvanized steel water pipe, and some hardware items.

On the other hand, there is much competition for such materials as lumber and flooring, millwork, bricks, cast-iron pipe, lighting fixtures, and paint. These particular materials, it should be indicated, represent the largest proportion of the cost of the building materials utilized in residential construction.

Price of Building Materials

It might be assumed that where a few manufacturers supply most of the output of a particular commodity, there would be considerable rigidity of prices. Colean, in fact, in his study of about 15 years ago, said: "It has long been contended that the price of building materials is well sustained in a depression and increases more rapidly with recovery than other commodity prices."[4] He cited figures to show that building materials fell to only 76 points (1929=100), whereas all commodities fell to 62 points during the Depression; building materials increased to 92 points in 1939, whereas all commodities were increasing to only 78.

Although data for use in evaluating recent practices is sparse, there is some evidence that the situation described for the 1930's no longer holds. For example, a few large manufacturers still supply much of the window glass, gypsum products, and plumbing fixtures, and the price indexes for these products increased by 35, 33, and 26 points, respectively, between 1947 and 1962. On the other hand, many smaller firms provide lumber and structural clay products, but the price indexes for these products increased by 19 and 44 points, respectively, during the same period (Table 6–11, p. 240).

In looking at the three principal components making up the cost of housing—land, labor, and materials—one thing seems clear: materials have contributed less to recent cost increases than the other two.

Distribution Channels

Quite commonly, a building material that starts at the manufacturer's must pass through a broker or wholesaler and then through a materials dealer before reaching the builder or the trade contractor. Each level in the distribution process, of course, requires its profit or mark-up. When handling and transportation costs are added to these profits at the different levels, nearly half of the total materials bill is accounted for.

Materials producers have been criticized for not selling directly to builders.

[4] Miles L. Colean, *American Housing: Problems and Prospects.* New York: The Twentieth Century Fund, 1947, p. 111.

Existing practices have worked a hardship on the industry because, even though builders frequently have many alternate sources of supply, the competition among these sources does not usually result in lower prices, because each generally includes a profit mark-up for his own distribution channel.

Recent Developments in Materials

There has been a proliferation of new and improved building materials in the last few years. New applications, in some cases for old materials and in some cases for originally nonbuilding materials, have also been developed.

To a certain extent, the problem of depletion of resources has influenced these developments, since most of our traditional building materials have been found in nature, and many of them are either in short supply or are becoming expensive to obtain. This has resulted in intensive efforts to find the most efficient utilization of these materials through the development of new processing methods, new structural theories, and new applications.

Wood, one of the most traditional of our building materials, affords a striking example of new utilization. Until fairly recently, it was used primarily in the form of heavy timbers or boards. Today we have, in addition, veneers, plywoods, composition boards, and laminates. At present almost all of the short supply of choice hardwoods is turned into veneers, with the exception of the supply used by the furniture industry. (It is obvious that a walnut log turned into a thin sheet of veneer will go immeasurably farther than if it had been cut up into boards.)

Plywood, because of its structural superiority, represents a much more efficient use of the wood than if it is used in the conventional manner. In addition, it has several other advantages over wood in board form: it is available in much larger pieces, is more resistant to warping because of the alternating direction of the wood grain in each layer, and the adhesives used in the bonding process render it more impervious to moisture. In a recent development, plywood is being impregnated under pressure with plastics, rendering it completely water- and rot-proof and suitable for a finished exterior siding material.

Another new form of wood represents an efficient use of what was formerly waste material—wood chips and shavings. These are impregnated with adhesives and molded under heat and pressure into large flat sheets similar to plywood. While possessing none of the structural characteristics of plywood, this material is even more warp-proof than plywood and takes paint better.

New structural theory has permitted the development of laminates—large structural members formed and built up of many small pieces bonded together with adhesives and mechanical fastenings. These built-up members offer a number of striking advantages: extraordinarily large members can be built up from ordinary stock members relatively cheaply; members can be built up from pieces that ordinarily have little structural usefulness; and members can be easily curved or tapered, either for appearance or efficiency, extra material and strength being added where necessary. The use of high-grade material can be limited to places of greatest stress and weaker material be used elsewhere.

The application of new theory to new materials has resulted in still another efficient utilization of wood, namely, stressed-skin construction. In this system, sheets of plywood are combined with solid lumber to form built-up plate girders such as are common in steel construction and large built-up wall and floor panels of great strength.

Similarly, glass, once used almost exclusively for its transparency in the form of window glass, is now found doing many jobs in many different guises. In one form or another, glass is used for its remarkable tensile strength, its insulating properties, its fire retardance, and its weathering resistance.

Plastics, found only in light switches and sockets a few years ago, have increased their usefulness and application in building to the point where it will soon be difficult to find a product that cannot be obtained in plastic or treated with plastic. The most common use in recent years has been in the treatment of other materials, either in the form of paints and sprays or in the coating and impregnation of materials such as plywood or composition boards. These have found wide favor in furniture and in bathroom and kitchen counter tops, where stainproof, mar-resistant and easy-to-clean surfaces are important. Other important uses are flooring materials, plumbing, electrical conduits, lighting baffles, and, increasingly, the development of molded shapes for such things as plumbing fixtures and hardware.

Concrete, a bulky material (once thought of as a kind of artificial stone), has undergone a revolutionary technical metamorphosis. Coupled with advances in the technology of preparing and treating it have come tremendous strides in structural theory. This includes pre-stressing; pre-casting, not only of slabs but also of structural members; and the "lift-slab," a unique system that permits all the floorslabs of a building to be poured one on top of another on the ground and then lifted into proper place and fastened.

Concrete is now regarded as a versatile, plastic material which is fast coming of age. In fact, some of the most exciting structures of this century, built under the direction of such men as Maillart, Nervi, Candella, and Le Corbusier, all use concrete as a medium. The day when their theories and techniques will find application in the housing industry should not be far off.

The various metals, the most recent and still current great materials of building, are finding new applications all the time, mostly, however, for facing and decoration.

The list of the new materials and improved old ones that are finding a place in our building technology can go on endlessly. The same thing can be said of mechanical equipment, the continual development of new and improved heating and air-conditioning equipment, the strides made by the electrical industry in providing new techniques of wiring and lighting, not to mention the ever-growing list of appliances that make life more comfortable and pleasant.

This variety, however, is in some measure a mixed blessing, for it has also increased the problem of material selection to the point where the average builder has difficulty keeping up with what is daily appearing on the market, much less having the necessary technical information to make intelligent decisions. This is particularly true because many of the new materials are highly specialized in their application. Still another consequence of our rapid technological production is the danger of very rapid obsolescence.

The proper selection of a building material is, like the selection of any other product, based upon the weighing of a number of factors: performance, ease of maintenance, life expectancy, availability, ease of working and installing, and cost, as measured in terms of all of the foregoing. In addition, consideration must be given to acceptability under local building codes and regulations, and, in some cases, possible jurisdictional labor disputes over the handling of complex new materials. Finally, in the case of visible materials particular attention must be given to their psychological and aesthetic effect and their suitability.

It should be pointed out, however, that in addition to making the selection process more complex and difficult, this abundance of new materials can also confer new benefits, aside from the obvious ones. One of the most important is the great variety of design solutions that will be possible because of the many alternate ways of solving any given problem.

To a certain degree, materials can be chosen primarily for their aesthetic appeal and be treated in such a way, or used in conjunction with another material to overcome some of their own performance deficiencies.

Paint technology offers some examples of what is in store in the very near future. There are (or soon will be) available, paints that are fire retardant, waterproof, insecticidal, abrasive, and electrically conductive, as well as coatings that may simply be stripped off like a banana peel when a change is desired.

Another recent trend, insofar as the housebuilding industry itself is concerned, has been the borrowing of materials and techniques from industrial and heavy construction, for example, steel frames and the use of metal or plastic sheets as siding material.

Another feature of the building-materials industry today is its increasingly national character. Although there will always be regional differences in design, owing to climate, tradition, and preference, the effect of local production and availability is gradually disappearing. More and more materials are being distributed, if not manufactured, on a national scale.

Trends in Materials Used in Home Building.[5]

The outstanding development in home building during the last two decades, insofar as building materials are concerned, has been the decreasing

[5] This discussion is based on U.S. Department of Labor, *New Housing and its Materials*, Bulletin No. 1231, Bureau of Labor Statistics, August 1958.

use of wood and the substantial increase in the use of aluminum and a variety of composition, synthetic, and other materials.

Structurally, frame houses (i.e., houses constructed with a supporting framework of wooden studs and faced with one or more of a variety of materials) has consistently dominated single-family housing construction in the past twenty-five years, although the proportion of such units declined from 89 percent in 1940 to 83 percent in 1956. (This decrease was due to the increase in masonry construction, from 11 to 16 percent of the total.) However, increasing proportions of the new frame houses were faced with brick veneer or a combination of brick and wood. By 1956, builders reported 33 percent of the exteriors covered with brick or brick and wood facing, as compared with 24 percent wood facing. This was a marked change from the 12 percent brick or brick and wood facing, as compared with 43 percent wood facing, in the earlier period.

The trend toward brick veneer houses accentuated the shift from wood planks to insulation board and other materials for sheathing frame houses between 1940 and 1956. The proportion of wood plank sheathing declined from 49 percent to 31 percent, while the proportion of insulation board increased from 14 percent to 32 percent and the percent of plywood increased from practically none in 1940 to 7 percent in 1956.

The use of various kinds of insulation (applied loose, batts cut to length, rolls, or other forms) increased significantly during this period. In 1940, 10 percent of the walls of both masonry and frame houses were insulated; by 1956, the proportion had increased to a third of the houses. Ceiling insulation was found among only 25 percent of the houses in 1940, but by 1956 four out of every five units had such insulation. (The exceptions generally were stucco and concrete block homes, which were usually built in the South or West.)

There was a marked shift from wood to asphalt for shingles during this period. In 1940, 36 percent of the homes had wooden shingles, compared with only 11 percent in 1956. In the meantime, the proportion of asphalt shingles increased from 47 percent to 66 percent. (Asbestos shingles, not found in any significant proportion in either 1940 or 1950, were used for 7 percent of the homes in 1956.)

There also has been a change in windows. At the beginning of the period, 91 percent of all windows had wooden frames, but the proportion declined to 57 percent by 1956. There were no aluminum window frames in 1940, but by 1956 they made up 29 percent of those in use. Figures are not available for type of window but it is quite obvious that the double-hung type (two sashes, one over the other, both movable) was declining in importance. It constituted 55 percent of the windows used in 1956, compared with 14 percent for the casement type (sash hinged on side to swing like a door), 9 percent for the horizontal slide type, 8 percent picture windows, and 12 percent for other types (awning, projected, jalousie, etc.).

Aluminum increased in importance as a material for screening windows and doors. It was practically unused for these purposes in 1940, but had become the principal type of screening by 1956. Some gutters and downspouts were also being made of this material, but galvanized steel predominated.

The outstanding postwar development in interior wall construction was the extent of the shift from plaster to various types of wallboard materials. In 1940, the walls of 90 percent of the new houses were plastered, but by 1956 this proportion declined to only 44 percent. The change was to dry wall construction, i.e, gypsum board.

In 1956 the walls of the living-dining and bedroom areas of almost three fourths of the house were painted. Several new types of paints that have gained wide acceptance have reduced the proportion of rooms wallpapered. (The kitchen was an exception; walls were papered more often in 1956 than in 1950 but three out of every four new kitchens had painted walls.) Both paint and wallpaper in kitchens were sometimes combined with wainscoting, and such combinations of wall materials were much more common in 1956 than they had been earlier. A similar trend toward wainscoting in bathrooms was also evident. Although ceramic tile maintained a substantial lead over other wainscoting materials—55 percent in bathrooms and 13 percent in kitchens in 1956—plastic tile, not used earlier, was reported to be used in 22 percent of the new bathrooms and 7 percent of the new kitchens in that year.

Hardwood was used in almost 85 percent of the living-room, dining-room, and bedroom areas in 1956. Ceramic tile was used in 38 percent of the bathrooms, a decline from 58 percent in 1940. The use of linoleum declined from 42 percent to 28 percent over the same period. However, in this interval the installation of asphalt and rubber tile and miscellaneous other floor coverings increased. For kitchens, linoleum continued to be preferred (57 percent in 1956) but vinyl tile, a new material since 1940, was being used in 16 percent of the homes.

There has been an important recent change in door styles from the panel type (which has outer frame of full thickness but inner panels of thinner material) to the flush type (which is of uniform thickness over the entire surface dimension of the door). This trend has been especially important with regard to interior doors, where 68 percent were of the flush type on new construction in 1956. However, the trend is similar for exterior doors, 52 percent being of the flush type in that year.

There has been an important change in heating facilities and fuel in homes built since 1940. Almost three fourths of the new houses in 1956 were heated with gas, compared with only 47 percent in 1940. On the other hand, furnaces burning coal and other solid fuels, which were installed in almost two fifths of the houses built in 1940, were not reported in any significant numbers in 1956. Also, the proportion of houses built with furnaces equipped with fans or blowers to force the warm air through ducts to various parts of the house increased from 19 percent in 1940 to 72 percent in 1956. In the same interval the proportion of those built with gravity-type warm-air furnaces declined from 23 percent to an insignificant number, steam systems declined from 9 percent to an insignificant number, hot water systems declined from 13 percent to 8 percent, and floor furnaces without ducts declined from 21 percent to 4 percent.

A total of 6 percent of the homes built in 1956 had a full-home air conditioner, the proportions having been insignificant in earlier years.

Although it was much more common in 1956 for builders to include kitchen appliances and other appliances and equipment as part of the selling price of houses than it had been in earlier years, home buyers usually purchased these items separately if they desired them. The increased proportions of some of the items included by builders, however, can be cited. Electric ranges were installed in 19 percent of the new homes in 1956, compared with only 2 percent in 1940. Dishwashers were installed in 11 percent of the homes in 1956, compared with an insignificant percentage even in 1950. Garbage disposer units were installed in 34 percent of the homes, compared with almost none in 1940 and 5 percent in 1950. Kitchen exhaust fans were installed in 55 percent of the homes in 1956, compared with 17 percent in 1940. Another change was in the type of kitchen sink. In 1956, 67 percent of the kitchens had a double-basin sink, compared with only 23 percent in 1950 and practically none in 1940.

There was a trend from wood to steel kitchen cabinets from 1940 to 1950, but this trend was reversed by 1956, when wood was used for 90 percent of the cabinets. Linoleum, which was used for 57 percent of the kitchen cabinet countertops in 1950, declined in use to 11 percent in 1956. During this same interval, laminated plastic, a postwar innovation as countertop material, increased in use from 15 percent in 1950 to 64 percent in 1956.

Need for Research

Although this picture of the recent development of new building materials would seem to be rather bright, it still leaves much to be desired as regards reducing costs of housing construction and from the standpoint of improving the livability of houses to the extent that should be possible in the middle of the twentieth century. The fact is that building materials producers have not kept up with the advances that have been made in many other industries. The basic reason for this is that most new materials have resulted from efforts at new product development undertaken on a firm-by-firm basis. Most firms have had to spend considerable funds for such product development in order to remain in a favorable competitive position.

On the other hand, most firms have been somewhat short-sighted in being unwilling to spend such funds unless they could expect to obtain dollar-value return from the sales of new products over a very short time. Few have been willing to risk funds for long-term research, including basic research which may not be translatable into a special new product immediately.

Furthermore, firm-by-firm product development and "research" has meant that new, better, and less expensive approaches have not been devised for building the *structure as a whole*. It can be understood why particular groups of firms, such as those manufacturing bricks or lumber, might not want to support research that would show that certain kinds of metals or plastics might be good substitutes for particular uses. Usually research of this type, which cuts across broad areas of industry, must be financed by outside sources (particularly the government), since the results would be in the public interest. However, to date the building products industry has been sufficiently well organized and politically vocal to be able either to effectively stop such a program before it was started (as in the instance of the Civilian Industrial Technology Program proposed by the Department of Commerce in 1963) or to kill such a program shortly after it had been authorized (as in the instance of the research program under the Housing Act of 1949). This whole matter is discussed in more detail in Chapter 15.

THE ENTREPRENEUR

In the early history of our country, a majority of the houses were built by the owner-occupants themselves. They built their residences to be used wholly or in part as the center of their family life. They "produced in order to consume," and built with reference to their personal needs and the needs of their families. Any profit motive usually was secondary. Later, small building firms entered the picture. Their primary motive was to make a profit from their enterprise. Service to the purchaser or community usually was incidental. However, it was recognized that the house (or apartment) had to be built reasonably well or there would be no market. These firms frequently had other businesses, such as commercial or other construction, land development, and the like.

Nature and Size of Building Operations

In 1938, the Bureau of Labor Statistics found that the average builder of single-family houses in 72 cities studied constructed only 3.5 houses a year.[6] At that time, 19 percent of the single-family houses were built by builders producing only one unit per year, 18 percent by those producing two to four units, 15 percent by those producing five to nine units, 18 percent by those producing ten to twenty-four units, and 20 percent by those producing twenty-five to ninety-nine units. Only 10 percent were built by builders producing one hundred units or more per year. Although the proportion is not known, it is generally recognized that many homes were built by families themselves; that is, the owners served as the "contractor" and probably did much of the work themselves.

By 1949, only 7 percent of all new dwellings were built by builders producing only one unit per year, 15 percent by those producing two to four

[6] *Builders of 1-Family Houses in 72 Cities*, Serial No. R-1151, Bureau of Labor Statistics, Washington, D.C., 1940.

units, 10 percent by those producing five to nine units, 14 percent by those producing ten to twenty-four units, 10 percent by those producing twenty-five to forty-nine units, 10 percent by those producing fifty to ninety-nine units, and 34 percent by those producing one hundred units or more (Table 6–12, p. 241). The last-mentioned group most likely included contractors building apartment structures, a group not reflected in the 1939 figures cited above.

In 1959, a survey of members of the home builder's trade association, the National Association of Homebuilders, indicated that the median builder built twenty units. Only 14 percent of the total number of units built by active members of the Association were built by builders producing only one to five units per year, 17 percent by those producing six to ten units, 27 percent by those producing eleven to twenty-five units, 18 percent by those producing twenty-six to fifty units, 12 percent by those producing fifty-one to one hundred units, and 13 percent by those producing over one hundred units (Table 6–13, p. 241).

The figures cited for the years 1938, 1949, and 1959 are not strictly comparable, since those for the first year considered new single-family houses in only 72 cities (excluding the suburbs of those cities); those for 1949 presumably covered sales and rental housing (excluding public housing); and those for 1959 only covered units built by members of the National Association of Homebuilders. Nevertheless, the data provide sufficient evidence of the declining importance of the small-scale home builder, the increasing prominence of the middle-sized builder, and the continued existence of a small percentage of large-scale operators.

Data showing the decline of the owner as entrepreneur are available for only two years—1949 and 1956. During that period, the number of owner-built single-family houses declined from 34 percent to 14 percent (Table 6–14, p. 241).

In an excellent study of the building industry, Maisel classified builders into three groups, on the basis of the size of their operations:

Small builder. This type of firm "builds between one and 24 houses per year, does less than $200,000 in total volume of business, employs fewer than 10 men, has less than $100,000 in total assets, or is owned and managed by a craftsman who spends most of his time actually working on the job."

Medium-sized builder. This type of firm "builds between 25 and 99 units a year, does between $200,000 and $1,000,000 in business, hires between 10 and 99 employees, has $100,000 to $600,000 in total assets, and is owned and managed by an executive who has little or no staff and performs almost all overhead work himself, while also spending a good deal of his time on actual job supervision."

Large builder. This type of firm "completes 100 or more houses a year, has a volume of business of more than $1,000,000, hires 100 or more employees, has more than $600,000 in total assets, and maintains a large overhead staff."[7]

There is much information available concerning the inefficiencies in small

[7] Sherman J. Maisel, *Housebuilding in Transition*. Berkeley and Los Angeles: University of California Press, 1953, p. 21.

building operations.[8] It is evident that when builders construct less than five or ten units a year, they operate on a handicraft basis, supplying many custom details that are costly. Usually such builders engage largely in hand operations, and do not use modern tools and mechanical processes. Little, if any, advantage is taken of the availability of standardized parts and modern technology. This causes excessive wastes of both materials and labor.

In small building operations there also is considerable wastage of labor, owing to many of the conditions at the individual construction site. Idleness of labor is frequently caused by inclement weather, delays in receiving materials, and difficulties in scheduling the sequence of work. Many of these builders are poor managers, and at least until recently, few kept adequate cost records of their operations. Frequently they have not known what profit they were making on individual units until they examined their bank account after their bills had been paid.

These inefficiences applied to practically all builders before World War II (because they generally were small operators) and apply to many of the small builders who are in business today.

On the other hand, large builders of today have gained many efficiencies not heretofore experienced in their operations. For example, they have obtained a better utilization of labor by increasing the use of modern tools and mechanical processes, by having workers perform standardized jobs, and by keeping them at work in the same location for long periods of time. In many instances, large builders also have been able to cut through the complex and costly channels of materials and equipment distribution, thereby reducing the cost of some of the items purchased. Because of the volume of their product they have had improved bargaining power, as compared with the small operator. By utilizing standardized materials wherever possible and having efficient structural designs, they have often reduced the waste of materials. Through large volume, they have been able to take lower profits per unit built.

To some extent they have been able to overcome the problem of seasonal construction by putting in foundations in the fall and building the remainder of the house during the winter. This has permitted them to maintain year round building organizations, with attendant benefits to both builder and labor. (This in itself has not necessarily affected the total annual volume of housebuilding to any great extent. Rather, what it has done is achieve better distribution of construction over the twelve months.) Seasonal building problems, even today, however, are still in evidence, as may be seen from government figures on monthly starts.

Some of the efficiencies gained through large-scale building can be seen from Maisel's composite cost estimates for building operations of different sizes. For a house of the same square-foot area, built in the San Francisco Bay Area in 1949, Maisel computed a composite cost for the small builder

[8] Miles L. Colean, *American Housing: Problems and Prospects*, *op. cit.* On this problem another source is also excellent: Leo Grebler, *Production of New Housing.* New York: Social Science Research Council, 1950.

FIGURE 10. *Some builders are today developing entirely new communities. More than 50,000 people now reside in one of these, Levittown, Pennsylvania. (Photograph courtesy of Levitt and Sons, Inc.)*

of $9,500; for the medium builder, $9,250; and for the large builder, $8,750. The detailed costs are given in Table 6–15 (p. 242).

In addition to the lower cost per house for large builders shown in this table, it is also interesting to note that there are some significant differences in the percentage distribution of the cost items among builders of different size operations. In total expenditures per house, the costs of direct labor, direct materials, and two subcontracting costs—plumbing and painting—are proportionately lower for the large builders. On the other hand, their overhead and profit are appreciably higher than for small builders.

Medium- and large-sized builders frequently have different terms attached to them. Sometimes they are called ''speculative'' builders, ''operative'' builders, ''merchant'' builders, or ''tract'' builders. The 1959 home builders survey found that 37 percent of the builders were primarily individual custom home builders, who built to order, whereas 43 percent were primarily merchant, tract, or speculative builders, and the remaining 20 percent built both to order and in tracts. It also found that 43 percent of the builders built in their own subdivisions, 13 percent built on groups of lots or in someone else's subdivision, 22 percent built on scattered lots, and 22 percent represented some combination of these kinds of buildings.

"Speculative" and "operative" builders usually are defined as builders who build houses in advance of their sale, anticipating a market for them. The 1959 survey found that 33 percent of the builders sold their houses before construction was started, 21 percent sold theirs during construction, 18 percent sold them after the units had been built, and 28 percent represented a combination of these categories.

Firms of this type today are predominantly in the housebuilding business to the exclusion of other businesses, as was not the case some years ago. The 1959 survey found that 40 percent of the builders had no outside business interests and another 34 percent had as their only other business that of land development. A total of 13 percent were also engaged in commercial or other construction, 19 percent were also real estate brokers, 6 percent were also lumber or materials dealers, 4 percent were also involved in the business of financing, and 12 percent had other kinds of outside business interests.

Although it has beeen shown that the median builder in 1959 was one who built twenty homes, this does not mean that builders employ large staffs. In fact, the 1959 survey indicated that 28 percent of the builders had no full-time salaried employees. A total of 37 percent had only one to three employees, 24 percent had four to nine, 8 percent had ten to nineteen, and only 4 percent had over twenty. This is explained by the amount of subcontracting they undertake. The 1959 survey reported that 31 percent of the builders subcontracted 75 to 100 percent of the dollar value of their work. Another 27 percent subcontracted 50 to 74 percent; 23 percent subcontracted 25 to 49 percent; 14 percent subcontracted 10 to 24 percent; 3 percent subcontracted 1 to 9 percent; and only 2 percent used no subcontractors.[9]

Construction Financing

Usually loans are required to finance the *building operation* of a house or apartment project. Probably in most instances, where the family has made a commitment to purchase the house before construction begins, the mortgage financing has been arranged. If the mortgage has been arranged in advance, lenders frequently use the mortgage commitment as a basis for advancing funds needed during construction. In other words, the mortgage on the house serves in lieu of another loan for construction only. The procedure is for the lender (for example, a savings and loan association or commercial bank) to advance funds in installments as they are needed by the builder during the successive stages of construction.

In those instances where houses are built before they are sold, lenders

[9] The source of the above data is the "NAHB Builder Survey," *Journal of Homebuilding*, March 1960.

frequently advance funds if there is an FHA *advance commitment* to insure the mortgage.

If a prospective homeowner owns the land on which the housing is to be built, or if the builder owns the land, credit is frequently provided on the basis of the land's value. Where such an arrangement is made, short-term construction funds are advanced, frequently by a local bank or real estate firm (broker), or by lumber and building supply companies. Some builders prefer to have the loan or credit from lumber and supply firms, believing that, in times of material shortages, they will get preferred treatment. The interest rate on such loans is usually slightly higher than the rates on the mortgage. The amount of the loans will vary, based on the cost of construction. The loan period is a few months, usually not less than four nor more than seven or eight.

Some institutions that are important in mortgage lending have not entered the field of construction financing on a large scale; the outstanding example is insurance companies. One of the reasons undoubtedly is the difficulty involved in supervising this type of loan. Loans required for building multifamily dwellings are an exception.

Financing Tract Developments

Many builders today are engaged in subdivision developments, and the financing of such developments therefore becomes extremely important. Working capital is needed for the down payment on the land, the cost of improvements on the first portion developed, and processing fees and costs. Martin lists the following expenses: "survey and general engineering monumenting; complete street improvements including sanitary sewers with plans and profiles; installation of utilities; general grading and preparation of land for sale; map recording and notarial fees; cost of subdivision guarantee or other title policy; real estate commissioner and brokerage fees; payment of taxes and assessments in full or bonds therefor; surety bonds for improvements and monumenting; map checking fees; street vacation proceedings expense, if any; and selling expense."[10]

Frequently, builders only purchase part of the land in a proposed subdivision, taking options on the remainder until potential demand is determined. Purchase is usually arranged through a down payment, credit being obtained from the seller for the balance. (It is often difficult to borrow funds on the security of vacant land.) Actual construction is usually scheduled, a new group of building sites being prepared while another group is being built on and the houses sold. This minimizes capital requirements.

The extent of other costs depends upon the needs of the subdivision, based in part on local subdivision regulations and on the extent to which

[10] Preston Martin, *Real Estate Principles and Practices.* New York: The Macmillan Co., 1959, p. 69, citing source as The Title Insurance and Trust Company of Los Angeles, California, "When You Subdivide," Los Angeles, 1953, p. 2.

municipalities may use their finances and credit to cover part of the costs. It is sometimes possible, for example, for the municipality to charge the costs of sewer and water mains it may install to the ultimate purchasers of the land, as special assessments repayable over a period of years.

Some developers include shopping centers, and some build apartments in large projects, thus combining income-producing properties with properties for sale.

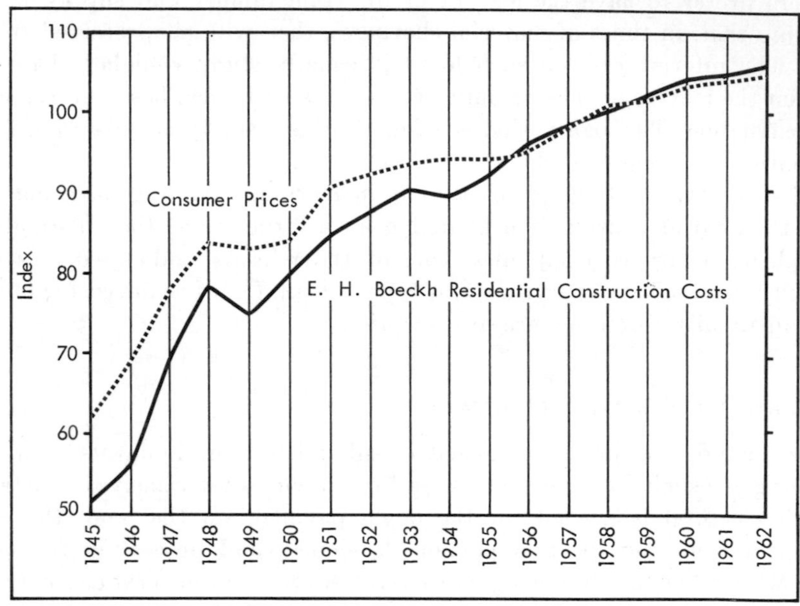

Note: 1957–1959 = 100.

FIGURE 11. *Comparison of residential construction costs and consumer prices, 1945 to 1962. (Source of data: U.S. Departments of Commerce and Labor.)*

The important factor, from the developer's point of view, is to predict as accurately as possible the total costs involved in comparison with the return that may be anticipated. The latter will depend upon a variety of market characteristics and that portion of the market the developer may be able to satisfy.

HOUSING COSTS

In the foregoing discussion, the problem of housing costs was brought up many times. Residential construction costs have been increasing faster than consumer prices for many years.[11]

Using 1957–1959 as a base, construction costs started at 52.3 in 1945,

[11] One method of providing the consumer with low-cost housing has been to build and sell uncompleted, or "shell," houses. Of course, the buyer must complete the house, but he can do this at any pace he sets for himself. The total volume of such houses is small, but they have gained popularity in some areas.

and have risen consistently to 106.3 in 1962. In the meantime, consumer prices rose from 62.7 to 105.4. The year-by-year trends since 1945 are shown in Table 6–16 (p. 243). Earlier data, not shown here because they are available only on different base years than 1957–1959, indicate that this trend has existed since such statistics were first developed early in the century.

It would seem that there should be some reversal of this trend, or at least a leveling out. Mass production in other industries has brought down prices in them, but we have not had the same degree of mass production of housing. The savings gained through large-scale production have been mentioned, but this production to date has not netted savings to the degree that might be desired.

The housebuilding industry tends to place most of the blame for the continued rise in costs on two factors. The first is the restrictive practices of labor (e.g., ''feather-bedding''), already mentioned. The second is the nature of and requirements dictated by local building codes, discussed below.

BUILDING CODES

One of the oldest forms of control over the local housebuilding industry is the building code. These codes govern the types of materials used in construction, the relation of materials to design, sanitary facilities, and the provision of light and air. Building codes normally require buildings to be constructed in such a way as to sustain safely the loads expected from the type of occupancy, and to be reasonably safe against fire hazards and such natural forces as earthquakes and hurricanes.

It can be seen, therefore, that building codes are supposedly written for the protection of public interests. All too often, however, they reflect the interests of certain private groups more interested in private profit than in the public welfare. They have in many cases become frozen by custom, still being of the *specification* type that often prescribes out of date and uneconomical types of materials and methods of construction. In short, they are not based on *performance* required of the material, which would permit taking advantage of technological changes that should be capitalized to the benefit of the housing consumer. This situation results partly from inertia and partly from the influence of vested interests. Under such circumstances, building codes become discriminatory.

Clearly, because of such conditions, building codes have a significant effect upon the cost of housing in the locality—generally the effect of increasing it. Ironically, therefore, building codes may be hindrances rather than helps to sound housing development in the community. Typically, this form of control is not related or coordinated with the other forms of control that affect the local housing scene. In addition, its detrimental effects are often aggravated by lax enforcement.

One of the most common reasons for outdated codes is lack of technical assistance (and/or its cost) to communities. However, today many communities have followed one of four model codes (though most communities have made certain local adaptations):

BUILDING OFFICIALS CONFERENCE OF AMERICA, INC. (CHICAGO, ILL.). This organization has developed what it terms "The Basic Building Code of America." This is the code most generally used throughout the nation. It emphasizes central or national, rather than regional, requirements.

SOUTHERN BUILDING CODE CONGRESS (BIRMINGHAM, ALA.). This organization calls its model code "The Uniform Building Code." It is strongly regional (the Southeastern states) in character.

INTERNATIONAL CONFERENCE OF BUILDING OFFICIALS (LOS ANGELES, CALIF.). This code is called "The Standard Building Code" by its sponsors. Although the name of the sponsoring agency would tend to reflect an international character, it is a regional code, prevailing primarily on the West Coast and particularly in California. (Originally, it had Canadian representation.)

NATIONAL BOARD OF FIRE UNDERWRITERS (NEW YORK CITY). This is the oldest of the model codes, and its sponsors call it "The National Code." It is more national than regional in character.

For some years an informal organization, known as the Joint Committee on Building Codes, has met annually (with subgroups sometimes meeting more frequently), and has carried on discussions concerning the building code problem. Each of the four major code groups is represented on this committee. The committee, however, has no formal organization.

None of the above codes is, in effect, government sponsored at either the Federal or state level. However, several states, such as New York, have established model codes which they encourage communities to adopt.

As long as the different model codes exist, there is a basis for great variation for the different elements in local codes, through reference to one or another of the models mentioned. (Today there are at least 5,000 different local building codes in the nation.) Furthermore, the existing model codes refer to buildings of various types, not simply residences. There has been a tendency in some countries, e.g., Canada, to have special model building codes for homes, and experience in those countries has shown this practice to be relatively successful since housing, quite logically, is different from other building construction. Housing codes in the United States, however, have been limited in their use to the upgrading of existing housing (usually in slum areas) rather than new construction.

Until there is greater uniformity among the four presently recognized model codes, it will, from a technological point of view, remain difficult (if not impossible) to obtain widespread use of any innovations in materials and concepts of home building.

In addition to building codes, there are usually certain other local codes with which home builders must comply. These include codes relating to plumbing, heating, and electrical systems. These codes may be generally considered to be "national" in character; they are based largely on standards established by the National Bureau of Standards in Washington.

PREFABRICATION ("MANUFACTURED HOMES")

One of the ways in which an attempt has been made to reduce housing costs is through prefabrication. Today most home builders use at least some prefabricated parts; for example, window and door assemblies. A smaller proportion use some prefabricated panels in conventional construction. Finally, there is a group of home builders who use a high proportion of prefabricated panels and parts. Because of the importance of this trend in home building today, it is considered in some detail below.

A "prefabricated house" has been defined as follows: "One having walls, partitions, floors, ceilings, and/or roof composed of sections or panels varying in size which have been fabricated in a factory prior to erection on the building foundation. This is in contrast to the conventionally built home which is constructed piece by piece on the site."[12]

From this definition it can be seen that only a part of the prefabricated house is made in a factory. The balance is built or assembled at the site, in a manner similar to conventional housing. The proportion of the house manufactured in a factory is difficult to determine. One study has indicated that 41 percent of the completed unit represented the cost of a house "package" and transportation. The other costs were distributed among preparation of the site and foundation, erection and finishing, subcontracting work, and overhead and profit (see Table 6–17, p. 243).

Prefabrication as a method of home building has only recently come into its own after what Kelly called years of ". . . great expectations and disappointments."[13] According to the Home Manufacturers Association, 186,152 "factory built" homes were produced by an estimated 675 home manufacturers in 1962. This figure represented nearly one out of every five of the single-family houses started in the United States in that year; and this proportion represented the highest proportion of any year to date (Table 6–18, p. 244).

There were many reasons for this long period of development. One was the fact that the pioneers in prefabricated housing developed designs that were highly controversial and revolutionary. The public, including financiers, did not accept Wallis Neff's famed "bubble" house in 1941, or Buck-

[12] *Prefabricated Homes*, Commercial Standard CS-125-47, 2d ed., Prefabricated Home Manufacturers' Institute and U.S. Department of Commerce, Washington, D.C.: U.S. Government Printing Office, 1947, p. 1. It will be noted that this definition excludes so-called pre-cut houses. Sometimes these units also are considered prefabricated because a number of standarized components are involved and because those components are usually produced at a central source. Pre-cutting usually includes the grading, cutting, marking, and packaging of lumber and the preassembly of windows and doors, rather than the production of sections and panels.

[13] Burnham Kelly, *The Prefabrication of Houses*, published jointly by the Technology Press of Massachusetts Institute of Technology and John Wiley & Sons, Inc., New York, 1951, pp. 65–96.

minster Fuller's Dymaxion mast house around 1930.[14] On the other hand, the houses of Robert McLaughlin (American Houses) and Foster Gunnison (Gunnison Homes, now known as U.S. Steel Homes) retained more of a conventional appearance and have gained acceptance.

Experimentation continued up to World War II, aided by such interests as the Farm Security Administration and the Tennessee Valley Authority. The war gave prefabrication one of its greatest stimuli, but also worked a hardship on the industry. For example, government contracts for housing in war-production areas permitted several of the struggling house manufacturers to get established. Factory-made prefabricated panels were used not only for housing (much of it "temporary" in character), but also for dormitories, school buildings, and other war construction. Many a GI had his first experience with prefabricated housing during this period.

On the other hand, prefabricated housing became known as "temporary" housing because of the manner in which it was used during the war. As a result, a stigma became attached to the name which has not yet been completely overcome today.

With the extreme housing shortage that existed after World War II, because there had been so little construction during the war years, and with the new peak in demand because of the returning GI's, it was felt that the prefabricated house would represent at least a partial solution. Under the Veterans Emergency Housing Program of 1946, the government set forth special incentives through which it hoped to have built 250,000 prefabricated houses in 1946 and 600,000 in 1947.[15] Under this program, thirty-two companies were granted government assistance, either in the nature of "guaranteed market contracts" or loan agreements through the Reconstruction Finance Corporation, but only six were able to achieve active production.

Attempts were made to make prefabricated houses out of both steel and aluminum, but these efforts failed. In 1946 only 37,200 prefabricated housing units were produced, and in 1947 this number increased by only 200. Of these totals, however, the majority of the units were being produced by companies outside of the government's "market guarantee" program (some of these companies remaining in production today). To date, only prefabricated houses made of wood have found a wide market. (The Veterans Emergency Housing Program is discussed in more detail in Chapter 14. There is some discussion there of a house that was not made of wood—the famous Lustron steel house.)

Since 1950, prefabricated house manufacturers have made some important strides forward. Not only have they been experimenting with new designs, new materials, and new techniques, but they have improved their marketing methods and stepped up public relations by using mass media in their advertising. (One example of their acceptance of modern marketing

[14] See Alfred Bruce and Harold Sandbank, *A History of Prefabrication*. Raritan, N.J.: John B. Pierce Foundation, Housing Research Division, September 1945, 3d printing.

[15] Wilson W. Wyatt, Housing Expediter, "Veterans Emergency Housing Program; Report to the President," February 7, 1946.

methods is the establishment of "brand" names.) Most firms have sound management and good plant organizations.

Strangely, there has been a concentration of manufactured homes in what one report termed the "prefab belt."[16] This belt is comprised of a group of states in the Midwest, where there has been the heaviest concentration of these homes over the years (especially Ohio, Indiana, and Illinois), and some states to the east of these (principally New York, Pennsylvania, and Maryland). In 1962, over 30 percent of prefabricated house sales were in the three Midwestern states named. One reason given for this concentration has been the limitation placed on manufacturers with respect to the distance from their plant that their product can be shipped. Some companies have attempted to overcome this limitation by establishing more than one plant, in different regions. This expansion, together with the establishment of new firms in different regions, signifies the industry's attempt to break out of, or at least to expand considerably, the "prefab belt." By 1962, some manufactured homes were being erected in every state in the nation (Table 6–19, p. 245).

Several important recent trends in the field of prefabrication are worth noting. Perhaps one of the most important of these, from the standpoint of stability, is the acceptance of the prefabricated house by conventional builders. Recently there has been a distinct trend for builders to become prefabricated house dealers. One of the reasons for this is the shrinking profit of builders in conventional building. Through prefabrication there is a faster turnover of capital. Also, some prefabricated house manufacturers have aided dealers (builders) by providing financing tools in small communities where other sources are not available. An example of this is the National Homes Acceptance Corporation, patterned somewhat after the famous automobile acceptance corporations. (The prefabricated house manufacturers also are the best organized and best promoted segment of the building industry.)

Not only have conventional builders and prefabricated house dealers stopped competing with each other; they have, in effect, joined ranks. It is common practice today for builders to represent a prefabricated house manufacturing firm and also be willing to construct custom-made conventional houses. In a way, this does not represent competition, because prefabricated houses generally have been in a lower price range than

[16] Glenn H. Beyer and Theodore R. Yantis, *Practices and Precepts of Marketing Prefabricated Houses.* Housing and Home Finance Agency, Washington, D.C.: U.S. Government Printing Office, November 1952, p. 8. Prefabricated housing firms have tended to locate there for several reasons. Originally, some of the companies located there because it was the home of their founders (e.g., National Homes at Lafayette, Indiana), and because a good plant site was found there (e.g., U.S. Steel Homes, formerly "Gunnison Homes," at New Albany, Indiana). Another theory is that the cultural background of Midwestern families—their ancestors having been pioneers—makes them more receptive to breaking with tradition and convention than, say, New Englanders or families in the South. Of course, it is generally admitted that prefabricated homes can compete better in small towns, which are characteristic of the Midwest. They are at least competitive with tract builders such as those found on Long Island and in many West Coast cities.

custom-built houses. This lower-price construction, in fact, has been one of the reasons prefabricated housing has sometimes been termed poorer construction than conventional housing.

Another important trend has been that of styling. Prefabricated houses are becoming the leaders in home styling, especially in the low- and middle-price market. This is possible because volume production permits retention of an architect. Some firms have their own architectural staff, whereas others employ "name" architects.

When new materials have become available or new techniques of construction developed, prefabricated house manufacturers have been willing to try them. Usually they have not been willing to move ahead of the financing institutions providing the money for their operation and their mortgages, but often they have been attempting to lead those institutions.

This does not mean that prefabrication has overcome all of its obstacles. On the contrary, some major and basic obstacles still remain in its path. Building codes are one of the problems. Prefabrication is tied to mass production, and mass production to standardization. Yet building codes are established for the purpose of making a house conform to local desires and requirements. The relationship of prefabrication to building codes has two implications. First, a certain amount of the work in building a prefabricated house must remain on the site; second, the number of "models" that any one manufacturer will make is likely always to remain high in order to meet different circumstances in different cities, sections, and regions.

Because of the building code problem, undoubtedly a much higher proportion of prefabricated houses has been erected outside than inside the jurisdiction of cities. For example, although it has been difficult for prefabricated house manufacturers to meet the rigorous controls placed upon them in Chicago, many of the suburbs of Chicago have permitted the erection of prefabricated structures.

Another aspect on which progress has been made, but which still is a problem, is that of financing. For many years, prefabricated house dealers were at a distinct disadvantage in attempting to find mortgage money. Today, this problem has eased in many areas, to the point where the prefabricator is now on a par, so to speak, with the conventional builder, insofar as financing is concerned. In 1962, banks, building and loan associations, and insurance companies were far more sympathetic to the builder of prefabricated houses than at any earlier period.

Two other problems of the prefabricator are manpower and transportation. These problems are inherent in the business. Although, generally speaking, less skilled labor is needed in the plant than on the site, the supply of labor has not been overabundant and it has been difficult to man many of the plants.

Transportation is primarily a problem because it becomes inefficient and uneconomical to carry a house beyond a certain distance (commonly, 300 miles) on a truck. Yet, the panels of many of the houses are of such size that other types of shipment are not practical. Until about 1952, when most of the houses were of the one- or two-bedroom size, it was practical for a truck to carry a whole house. With today's trend toward larger houses, there have been instances where two trucks are required to carry a single house. This doubles the shipping cost.

Finally, perhaps the major obstacle that has retarded the industry is the material out of which most prefabricated houses have been made—wood. Wood is basically a craftsman's material, and does not lend itself readily to the techniques of mass production. As long as prefabricated homes continue to be manufactured from wood in any form (including plywood), the true benefits of mass production cannot be derived. The future with regard to the use of other materials is still cloudy. Unsuccessful efforts at breakthroughs using metals for most of the structure—steel and aluminum—have been cited. In the early 1960's, a number of firms manufacturing plastics were attempting another breakthrough, using their materials. However, to date none has been very successful.

THE HOUSEBUILDING AND AUTOMOBILE INDUSTRIES

Over the years it has been common to draw a comparison between the housebuilding and automobile industries. This comparison was especially prevalent during the period when prefabricated housing was attempting to get its start.

On the surface, there were some reasons for this analogy. The auto "manufacturer," like the home builder, is primarily an *assembler, not a manufacturer*. Both assume responsibility for correlating the many elements that go into their respective products.

A more careful study of the two industries, however, indicates that the general analogy should not be carried too far. Some of the most obvious differences in the products and the industries are as follows:

An automobile is: mobile; land developing and subdividing functions do not exist for the automobile industry.

A house is: attached to a plot of land; not to mention the implications of its location, today it frequently represents more than 15 percent of the total cost of the house and lot.

An automobile is: light, transportable.

A house is: bulky, heavy. A house must be assembled on the lot where it is to be used. This means tens of thousands of "assembly plants" for houses compared with a few for automobiles. Housing, then, is a grass roots operation with no single builder building over 1 percent of all new houses in any single year. There is no housing "Detroit."

An automobile is: impermanent, fragile.

A house is: permanent, durable. Houses are on the market much longer than automobiles, meaning that there is not the high rate of depreciation over a period of years. Filtering down is a common phenomenon among automobiles, which makes low-cost cars readily available to low-income buyers. There is no parallel to the automobile graveyard for housing.

The automobile industry: produces highly standardized products. Standardization permits mass production which in turn permits low cost.

The housing industry: produces a wide variety of custom-made products; even among prefabricated houses, there is only a degree of standardization.

The automobile industry: controls most of its suppliers.

The housing industry: must rely on suppliers it does not control. The housing industry must rely on independent subcontractors in every community. These subcontractors also serve other branches of the construction industry. This creates "sequence of work" problems for home builders that are not experienced by automobile manufacturers. The result, among other things, is less efficiency for home building.

The automobile industry: usually has contracts with labor.

The housing industry: frequently lacks control over its labor market. With regard to labor, the housing industry must "catch as catch can." This frequently lessens efficiency and increases costs. The automobile industry can plan in a more efficient manner because costs are known from labor contracts.

The automobile industry: aids customers in financing purchase through "acceptance corporations."

The housing industry: has few "plans" to assist home buyers. The result is that the home buyer frequently cannot buy when there is a "tight" money situation.

The automobile industry: has complete "servicing" arrangements.

The housing industry: does not service its product.

There are, of course, singular exceptions to several of the points made above in the home building industry, but in general the situation is as has been pictured. It it doubtful whether this industry will ever become as integrated as the automobile industry.

Mobile Homes

The development of the modern mobile home has brought what must be considered to be one segment of the housing industry closer in production methods to those used by the automobile industry. In 1962, it was estimated that 4 million Americans lived in mobile homes. They seem to be preferred by more and more retired couples, newlyweds, married college students, and the like. (They have long been popular for construction workers and certain military personnel.)

The modern mobile home has grown out of the trailer industry. It represents a fully factory-prefabricated home that is mobile in the sense that it can be moved, but which, in more and more instances, becomes permanently attached to a site.

The typical mobile home, in the early 1960's, was 50 feet long and 10 feet wide—the width undoubtedly having been dictated in part by the maximum width allowed by many state highway laws (since they are generally transported from factory to site over the highways). Some manufacturers produce "pull-out" rooms. The walls, floor, and ceiling of such rooms telescope into one side of the trailer when it is being moved, but slide out on rollers to be blocked up at the ends when the home is parked. The average pull-out room adds about 70 square feet to the mobile home's space. Some manufacturers also produce "double-wides," two 10-foot units that are usually shipped by railroad flatcar and joined together on the site, allowing 20-foot wide rooms.

In 1962, 118,000 mobile homes were produced and shipped, in addition to 57,000 trailers. The combined total represents the highest production to date (Table 6–20, p. 246). The 1962 shipments represented 12 percent of all private housing starts in the nation. Most of them were manufactured by relatively small companies.

Most mobile homes are completely equipped at the factory. The more luxurious models have two bathrooms. Many have automatic dishwashers, garbage disposers, and air conditioners, and some include gas or electric fireplaces.

According to the Mobile Home Manufacturers Association, the average price in 1962 was $5,600, compared with $2,400 in 1947. Some models were priced as high as $15,000. The average price per square foot for the typical mobile home was $11, appreciably lower than the price for square footage in an average house in most communities. They are usually financed as automobiles are, rather than through a mortgage.

Mobile homes, however, face several serious problems. Perhaps the most serious is the shortage of "parks." Because of the history of trailer parks, many communities have enacted zoning ordinances prohibiting them. There is a basis for this action: whereas desirable planning would suggest a maximum of 10 mobile homes per acre, allowing area for driveways, parking, recreation, and service areas, many mobile home park operators are crowding 18 or 20 homes on an acre in order to boost their revenue. (Many parks charge monthly rentals of approximately $40 a site, the figure varying according to location, density, facilities, and the like.) To partially correct this situation, the FHA, when it inaugurated its program of insured mortgage loans for mobile home courts in 1955, established a set of minimum property requirements. (A mobile home court was defined as a "parcel of land under single ownership that has been planned and improved for the placement of mobile homes for non-transient use.")

Another problem has been that of financing. The FHA program has the following provisions: (1) the mortgage may be insured up to 75 percent of value, (2) the mortgage limit is $1,500 for each mobile home lot created, (3) the term of loan may not exceed 15 years, (4) the maximum amount of an insured loan on one court is $500,000, (5) the maximum interest rate was 5¼ percent (1960), and (6) the court must not have fewer than 50 units (because it was felt that smaller courts could not be operated profitably).

Although this FHA program offers mortgage insurance to lenders, it had not become popular in the early 1960's probably because most lenders felt that mobile home courts had not yet proved themselves to be sound investments.

Still another problem has been that of finding desirable sites at reasonable costs. Here the mobile home court operator faces the same problems as the ordinary land subdivider.

Approximately a third of the mobile home courts in operation are located in California, Arizona, and Florida. Many of the parks in these states are well planned and well located, and contain many amenities.[17]

CYCLICAL TRENDS IN BUILDING

One of the features of the housebuilding industry has been the violent ups and downs to which it has been subjected. These trends have had a serious impact on the economy of the nation. They result from the natural high levels of construction during periods of prosperity and low levels during periods of depression, and probably represent one of the most important single problems facing the builder.

The cyclical theory, though open to much debate, can be described as follows: (1) The cycle begins on the upswing with a general increase in family incomes. During the period when incomes are low, families double up and the rate of family formation is low. However, when more earnings again occur, marriages increase and families who have lived with relatives or friends begin to demand separate space. (2) Usually these increases in demand precede actual building. Therefore, the price (rent) of existing dwelling units increases. Owners make greater profits, and new construction, in turn, becomes profitable. (3) Speculation and easy credit usually are a part of a ''boom'' economy. As a result of these factors, production outpaces the market and a surplus of housing is built. (4) When more units are available than can be sold, prices begin to decline—and with prices, profits. Soon credit is tightened, and building contracts. Market activity comes to a standstill, with the exception of foreclosures. (5) When the bottom of the trough is reached, refinancing and other factors tend to increase activity again. As incomes again rise, another upswing is underway. The complete cycle from peak to trough and back to peak again, according to economists who support this theory, has in the past taken approximately eighteen or twenty years.

This is an oversimplified explanation of the operations of the building cycle. In refining the description, additional phases would be included, such

[17] J. Ross McKeever, ''The Motionless Mobile Home—The Trailer Problem in Community Development,'' *Urban Land*, Vol. 19, No. 4, April 1960.

as that changes are first reflected in rents, then in prices of existing houses, and then in prices of new houses.

The two sides of the debate concerning the existence of a building cycle are expressed in recent writings of different economists. Pearson, Myers, Paarlberg, and DeGraff have flatly stated: "The volume of building activity can be predicted with reasonable accuracy because of the regularity of the cycle and the unusual similarity in the peaks and troughs."[18] Colean and Newcomb, on the other hand, have stated, ". . . there have been no clear-cut over-all major 18- to 20-year cycles."[19] The two last-mentioned economists tend to relate the up-and-down trends to war and postwar periods.

In either event, whether there are wide cyclical fluctuations or whether there are merely irregular ups and downs in the construction industry on a noncyclical basis, the problem nonetheless remains for the builders. Their fate would seem to rest in hands other their own. Of primary importance here, undoubtedly, would be contra-cyclical programs in the fields of finance and public works. The mortgage guarantee and insurance programs of the Federal Government have been shown to have a most significant influence on construction levels in recent years. There was no evidence in the early 1960's (see Table 6–1, p. 231) that the "regular" 18- to 20-year sharp downturn was appearing when, according to the theory, it was due.

To some extent, builders and/or the materials industry can also help themselves in preventing any drastic downturn. Costs and prices charged for housing have effects on demand, as has been indicated in this chapter. Also, as shown earlier in this chapter, product improvement and innovations in production techniques become a highly important factor. However, none of those factors appears to be as important as financing policies and practices. It is generally assumed that short-term fluctuations in residential construction since World War II (four of which have occurred) were caused mainly by changes in the availability and costs of mortgage funds as a result of the response of the private financial system to changes in monetary policy.[20]

READING LIST

HOUSING PRODUCTION

Abrams, Charles. *The Future of Housing.* New York: Harper & Bros., 1946, Chapters 9, 10, 11, and 12.

Colean, Miles L. *American Housing: Problems and Prospects.* New York: The Twentieth Century Fund, 1947, Part I.

Grebler, Leo. *Production of New Housing.* New York: Social Science Research Council, 1950.

[18] F. A. Pearson, W. I. Myers, Don Paarlberg, and H. DeGraff, "Prices, Building and History," *The Appraisal Journal,* Vol. XX, No. 2, April 1952, p. 168. (Article reprinted from *Farm Economics,* Part I, October 1951.)

[19] Miles L. Colean and Robinson Newcomb, *Stabilizing Construction: The Record and Potential.* New York: McGraw-Hill Book Co., 1952, p. 242.

[20] Eugene A. Brady, "Regional Cycles of Residential Housing Construction and the Interregional Mortgage Market 1954–1959," *Land Economics,* Vol. XXXIX, No. 1, February 1963, pp. 15–30.

Kelly, Burnham. *Design and the Production of Houses.* New York: McGraw-Hill Book Co., Inc., 1959.

Maisel, Sherman J. *Housebuilding in Transition.* Berkeley: University of California Press, 1953.

Meyerson, Martin, Barbara Terrett, and William L. C. Wheaton. *Housing, People, and Cities.* New York: McGraw-Hill Book Co., 1962, Chapters 7, 8, and 9.

Ratcliff, Richard U. *Urban Land Economics.* New York: McGraw-Hill Book Co., Inc., 1949, Chapter 7.

PREFABRICATION

Kelly, Burnham. *The Prefabrication of Houses.* New York: Technology Press of Massachusetts Institute of Technology and John Wiley & Sons, Inc., 1951.

BUILDING CYCLE

Colean, Miles L., and Robinson Newcomb. *Stabilizing Construction: The Record and Potential.* New York: McGraw-Hill Book Co., 1952, Appendix N, "Building Cycles."

Martin, Preston. *Real Estate Principles and Practices.* New York: The Macmillan Co., 1959, Chapter 21.

Pearson, F. A., W. I. Myers, Don Paarlberg, and H. DeGraff. "Prices, Building and History," series of three articles in *Farm Economics,* Part I, October 1951; Part II, December 1951; and Part III, March 1952. Reprinted in *The Appraisal Journal,* April and October 1952 issues.

LAND

New Approaches to Residential Land Development: A Study of Concepts and Innovations, Urban Land Institute, Technical Bulletin No. 40. Washington, D.C.: Urban Land Institute, 1961.

BUILDING CODES

Building Codes. Washington, D.C.: U.S. Chamber of Commerce, 1963.

Table 6–1

TOTAL NONFARM HOUSING STARTS—PRIVATE, PUBLIC, URBAN AND RURAL NONFARM, 1920 TO 1962

Year	*Total*	*Private*	*Public*	*Urban*	*Rural Nonfarm*
1920	247,000	247,000	0	196,000	51,000
1921	449,000	449,000	0	359,000	90,000
1922	716,000	716,000	0	574,000	142,000
1923	871,000	871,000	0	698,000	173,000
1924	893,000	893,000	0	716,000	177,000
1925	937,000	937,000	0	752,000	185,000
1926	849,000	849,000	0	681,000	168,000
1927	810,000	810,000	0	643,000	167,000
1928	753,000	753,000	0	594,000	159,000
1929	509,000	509,000	0	400,000	109,000
1930	330,000	330,000	0	236,000	94,000
1931	254,000	254,000	0	174,000	80,000
1932	134,000	134,000	0	64,000	70,000
1933	93,000	93,000	0	45,000	48,000
1934	126,000	126,000	0	49,000	77,000
1935	221,000	215,700	5,300	117,000	104,000
1936	319,000	304,200	14,800	211,000	108,000
1937	336,000	332,400	3,600	218,000	118,000
1938	406,000	399,300	6,700	262,000	144,000
1939	515,000	458,400	56,600	359,000	156,000
1940	602,600	529,600	73,000	396,600	206,000
1941	706,100	619,500	86,600	434,300	271,800
1942	356,000	301,200	54,800	227,400	128,600
1943	191,000	183,700	7,300	124,400	66,600
1944	141,800	138,700	3,100	96,200	45,600
1945	209,300	208,100	1,200	133,900	75,400
1946	670,500	662,500	8,000	403,700	266,800
1947	849,000	845,600	3,400	479,800	369,200
1948	931,600	913,500	18,100	524,900	406,700
1949	1,025,100	988,800	36,300	588,800	436,300
				*Metropolitan**	*Non-Metropolitan*
1950	1,396,000	1,352,200	43,800	1,021,600	374,400
1951	1,091,300	1,020,100	71,200	776,800	314,500
1952	1,127,000	1,068,500	58,500	794,900	332,100
1953	1,103,800	1,068,300	35,500	803,500	300,300
1954	1,220,400	1,201,700	18,700	896,900	323,500

Table 6–1 *(continued)*

TOTAL NONFARM HOUSING STARTS—PRIVATE, PUBLIC, URBAN AND RURAL NONFARM, 1920 TO 1962

Year	*Total*	*Private*	*Public*	*Urban*	*Rural Nonfarm*
				*Metropolitan**	*Non-Metropolitan*
1955	1,328,900	1,309,500	19,400	975,800	353,100
1956	1,118,100	1,093,900	24,200	779,800	338,300
1957	1,041,900	992,800	49,100	699,700	342,200
1958	1,209,400	1,141,500	67,900	827,000	382,400
1959	1,378,500	1,342,800	35,700	946,100	432,400
New Series†					
1959	1,531,300	1,494,600	36,700	1,076,900	476,600
1960	1,274,000	1,230,100	43,900	889,000	407,000
1961	1,336,800	1,284,800	52,000	947,900	417,100
1962	1,458,400	1,429,000	29,400	1,043,100	439,100

SOURCE: U.S. Department of Labor, except data since 1956. Recent and current data published in *Construction Review.*

Note: For the student interested in earlier trends, reference is made to *The Volume of Residential Construction,* 1889–1950, by David M. Blank, Technical Paper 9, National Bureau of Economic Research, Inc., New York, N.Y., 1954.

* Data for metropolitan and nonmetropolitan areas not strictly comparable because of definitional changes.

† For a description of "new" series, see U.S. Department of Commerce, *Construction Review,* June 1960, pp. 4-10.

Table 6–2

COMPARISON OF 1960 POPULATION DISTRIBUTION AND DISTRIBUTION OF NEW HOUSING CONSTRUCTION, 1950–1959

	Population	*New Housing Construction*
Inside SMSA's	62.9%	65.5%
In central cities	32.3	22.8
Not in central cities	30.6	42.7
Outside SMSA's	37.1	34.5

SOURCES: Derived from U.S. Bureau of the Census, *Census of Population* 1960, Vol. I, Characteristics of the Population, Part A, Number of Inhabitants, and *Census of Housing 1960.* Components of Inventory Change, HC(4), Part 1A-1, 1950–1959 Components, United States and Regions.

Table 6–3

TOTAL NONFARM HOUSING STARTS, SALES AND RENTAL TYPES AND TYPES OF STRUCTURE, 1900 TO 1962

Year	*Total*	*Sales*	*Rental*	*One Family*	*Two Family*	*Three Family or more*
1900	189	65%	35%	65%	16%	19%
1901	275	64	36	64	12	24
1902	240	71	29	71	13	16
1903	253	69	31	69	12	19
1904	315	66	34	66	14	20
1905	507	66	34	66	13	21
1906	487	65	35	65	14	21
1907	432	67	33	67	14	19
1908	416	69	31	69	16	15
1909	492	67	33	67	15	18
1910	387	65	35	65	15	20
1911	395	63	37	63	16	21
1912	426	61	39	61	17	22
1913	421	63	37	63	17	20
1914	421	62	38	62	17	21
1915	433	61	39	61	17	22
1916	437	61	39	61	16	23
1917	240	69	31	69	13	18
1918	124	73	27	74	10	16
1919	315	76	24	76	11	13
1920	247	82	18	82	10	8
1921	449	70	30	70	16	14
1922	716	61	39	61	20	19
1923	871	59	41	59	20	21
1924	893	60	40	60	19	21
1925	937	61	39	61	17	22
1926	849	58	42	58	14	28
1927	810	56	41	56	12	32
1928	753	58	42	58	10	32
1929	509	62	38	62	10	28
1930	330	69	31	69	9	22
1931	254	74	26	74	9	17
1932	134	88	12	88	5	7
1933	93	82	16	82	5	13
1934	126	87	13	87	4	9
1935	221	82	18	83	4	13
1936	319	75	25	77	4	19
1937	336	79	21	79	5	16
1938	406	78	22	78	4	18
1939	515	72	28	78	6	16

Table 6–3 *(continued)*

TOTAL NONFARM HOUSING STARTS, SALES AND RENTAL TYPES AND TYPES OF STRUCTURE, 1900 TO 1962

Year	*Total*	*Sales*	*Rental*	*One Family*	*Two Family*	*Three Family or more*
1940	603	74	26	81	6	13
1941	706	75	25	86	5	9
1942	356	71	29	82	6	12
1943	191	71	29	75	9	16
1944	142	81	19	83	8	9
1945	209	88	12	88	4	8
1946	670	88	12	88	4	8
1947	849	87	13	87	4	9
1948	932	82	18	82	5	13
1949	1,025	77	23	77	4	19
1950	1,396	82	18	83	3	14
1951	1,091	82	18	82	4	14
1952	1,127	83	17	84	4	12
1953	1,104	85	15	85	4	11
1954	1,220	88	12	88	3	9
1955	1,329	90	10	90	2	8
1956	1,118	88	12	89	3	8
1957	1,042	91	9	84	3	13
1958	1,209	77	23	81	3	16
1959	1,378	78	22	79	5	16
New series						
1959	1,531	79	21	80	4	16
1960	1,274	76	24	77	4	19
1961	1,337	71	29	72	4	24
1962	1,458	66	34	66	4	30

SOURCE: Derived from *Housing Statistics—Annual Data.* Washington, D.C.: Housing and Home Finance Agency, April 1962.

Table 6–4

NUMBER OF UNITS IN STRUCTURE, NEW HOUSING CONSTRUCTION 1950–1959, BY TENURE

Number of Units	*Total*	*Owner-Occupied*	*Renter-Occupied*
One	81.0%	94.1%	40.5%
Two to four	7.3	2.1	23.0
Five to nineteen	5.2	} 0.3	20.4
Twenty to forty-nine	} 3.7		4.5
Fifty or more			10.2
Trailer	2.7	3.5	1.4

SOURCE: U.S. Bureau of the Census, *Census of Housing 1960.* Components of Inventory Change, HC(4), Part 1A-1, 1950–1959 Components, United States and Regions, p. 28.

Table 6–5

PERCENTAGES OF NUMBER OF ROOMS IN DWELLING UNITS CONSTRUCTED 1950–1959, BY TENURE

Number of Rooms	*Total*	*Owner-Occupied*	*Renter-Occupied*
One and two	5.7%	1.7%	13.1%
Three	8.8	3.0	24.1
Four	22.8	18.6	35.5
Five	33.2	39.0	18.0
Six	20.5	26.0	7.5
Seven or more	9.0	11.7	1.8
Median	4.9	5.2	3.9

SOURCE: U.S. Bureau of the Census, *Census of Housing 1960.* Components of Inventory Change. HC(4), Part 1A-1, 1950–1959 Components, United States and Regions, pp. 26, 28.

Table 6–6

DISTRIBUTION OF VALUE AND GROSS RENT OF NONFARM DWELLING UNITS CONSTRUCTED 1950–1959

Value	*Percent*	*Gross Rent*	*Percent*
Less than $7,500	5.3%	Less than $40	5.9%
$7,500 to $9,900	7.6	$40 to $59	10.2
$10,000 to $12,400	16.2	$60 to $79	16.0
$12,500 to $14,900	17.7	$80 to $99	27.1
$15,000 to $17,400	14.3	$100 to $119	19.1
$17,500 to $19,900	13.4	$120 to $149	13.4
$20,000 to $24,900	11.7	$150 to $199	5.7
$25,000 to $34,900	9.5	$200 or more	2.6
$35,000 or more	4.5		
Median value	$15,600	Median rent	$93

SOURCE: U.S. Bureau of the Census, *Census of Housing 1960.* Components of Inventory Change. HC(4), Part 1A-1, 1950–1959 Components, United States and Regions, p. 35.

Table 6–7

AVERAGE VALUATION PER UNIT FOR ONE-FAMILY HOUSES AND UNITS IN FIVE-OR-MORE-FAMILY STRUCTURES AUTHORIZED BY BUILDING PERMITS IN SELECTED METROPOLITAN AREAS, 1959

Mertopolitan Area	*One-Family Houses*	*Five-or-More-Family Structures*
Cleveland, Ohio	$16,600	$8,700
Chicago, Ill.	16,000	8,600
Minneapolis-St. Paul, Minn.	15,600	7,200
Los Angeles, Calif.	14,300	6,600
Washington, D.C.	14,200	6,800
New York-Northeastern N.J.	14,000	8,900
San Francisco-Oakland, Calif.	14,000	7,500
Oklahoma City, Okla.	11,800	7,200
Miami, Fla.	10,800	6,200
Atlanta, Ga.	10,700	3,700
Providence, R.I.	10,500	10,500
Phoenix, Ariz.	9,600	6,900
Birmingham, Ala.	9,300	6,600
Memphis, Tenn.	7,700	2,100

SOURCE: U.S. Department of Commerce, *Construction Review,* Vol. 6, No. 9, September 1960.

Table 6–8

EMPLOYEES IN BUILDING CONSTRUCTION INDUSTRY

Year	Total U.S.	General Contractors	Special Trade Contractors: Total	Special Trade Contractors: Plumbing and Heating	Special Trade Contractors: Painting and Decorating	Special Trade Contractors: Electrical Work	Special Trade Contractors: Other Special Trade Contractors
1952	2,119,000	948,300	1,170,800	287,700	156,500	155,700	570,900
1953	2,109,000	934,000	1,175,100	288,900	148,100	159,700	578,400
1954	2,021,000	848,800	1,172,700	283,400	141,400	156,500	591,500
1955	2,279,000	937,700	1,341,600	318,300	165,600	169,100	688,600
1956	2,515,000	1,043,400	1,471,500	334,500	185,600	190,000	761,400
1957	2,183,000	757,900	1,424,700	310,500	201,400	174,200	738,600
1958	2,079,000	750,600	1,328,600	303,600	169,600	173,200	682,200
1959	2,183,000	757,900	1,424,700	310,500	201,400	174,200	738,600
1960	2,219,000	753,700	1,465,200	306,200	216,600	185,900	756,500
1961*	2,187,000	736,800	1,451,000	303,400	226,300	182,400	738,800

SOURCE: Derived from U.S. Bureau of Labor Statistics, *Monthly Labor Review,* various issues.
* Average for first eight months only.

Table 6–9

AVERAGE HOURLY EARNINGS IN BUILDING CONSTRUCTION INDUSTRY

Year	*Total*	*General Contractors*	*Plumbing and Heating*	*Painting and Decorating*	*Electrical Work*	*Other Special Trade Contractors*
1952	$2.31	$2.15	$2.44	$2.35	$2.71	$2.39
1953	2.48	2.34	2.58	2.51	2.84	2.55
1954	2.60	2.47	2.71	2.62	2.92	2.64
1955	2.66	2.52	2.80	2.72	2.98	2.71
1956	2.80	2.64	2.94	2.86	3.18	2.85
1957	2.97	2.77	3.12	3.00	3.37	3.02
1958	3.10	2.88	3.26	3.12	3.55	3.15
1959	3.22	2.98	3.41	3.24	3.70	3.27
1960	3.37	3.11	3.55	3.39	3.89	3.44
1961*	3.48	3.20	3.66	3.49	4.03	3.54

SOURCE: Derived from U.S. Department of Labor, *Monthly Labor Review,* various issues.
* Average for first eight months only.

Table 6–10

INDEXES OF OUTPUT OF SELECTED CONSTRUCTION MATERIALS, 1947–1962
(1947–1949 = 100)

Year	Lumber and Wood Products	Paint, Varnish and Lacquer	Plumbing Fixtures	Heating and Plumbing Equipment	Asphalt Products	Gypsum Products	Structural Clay Products
1947	98.1	102.7	94.5	124.2	114.4	85.8	97.2
1948	105.2	102.1	112.3	91.2	98.2	112.9	103.0
1949	98.0	95.1	93.4	84.7	86.1	101.1	99.7
1950	116.2	113.3	125.2	130.5	105.4	127.5	113.6
1951	114.2	101.5	119.8	105.8	99.0	135.5	122.5
1952	114.5	103.1	94.7	103.8	99.8	129.2	110.3
1953	115.7	108.0	101.0	115.6	100.3	138.9	112.0
1954	117.3	106.7	110.8	122.8	109.9	151.6	128.5
1955	126.6	117.2	139.8	147.0	112.4	178.2	154.2
1956	128.0	117.2	128.5	137.1	101.8	170.4	160.0
1957	116.7	117.4	114.1	120.0	96.5	154.4	133.2
1958	122.0	120.3	117.9	126.6	102.6	172.5	132.3
1959	139.6	129.7	146.1	143.9	105.7	203.4	149.0
1960	127.0	128.9	137.4	126.6	103.4	188.8	140.9
1961	127.4	123.4	126.8	116.2	103.0	186.4	134.9
1962	132.8	126.1	141.8	122.7	110.2	203.3	139.1

SOURCE: *Housing Statistics—Annual Data,* Washington, D.C.: Housing and Home Finance Agency, May 1963.

Table 6–11

INDEXES OF WHOLESALE PRICES OF SELECTED CONSTRUCTION MATERIALS, 1947–1962
(1957–1959 = 100)

Years	*All Materials**	*Lumber*	*Paint*	*Hardware*	*Plumbing Fixtures and Fittings*	*Heating Equipment*	*Window Glass*	*Asphalt Roofing*	*Gypsum Products*	*Structural Clay Products*
1947	71.2	77.5	77.2	61.9	74.0	78.3	65.7	80.3	72.3	59.5
1948	78.9	88.0	78.5	64.3	80.2	83.2	68.9	88.0	78.9	64.6
1949	77.3	80.5	79.3	64.9	80.2	85.1	71.6	87.8	78.2	67.1
1950	83.0	93.9	77.8	70.7	84.5	86.4	75.4	86.5	80.0	71.7
1951	90.7	101.6	85.4	81.4	95.7	94.2	81.1	89.5	89.8	77.4
1952	89.6	99.0	86.5	79.9	91.8	93.5	81.1	87.8	90.0	77.8
1953	90.9	98.1	87.1	83.3	90.6	94.4	86.4	91.6	92.6	81.6
1954	91.1	96.4	88.4	87.3	92.5	94.0	90.2	88.8	93.4	84.9
1955	95.1	102.4	89.7	89.7	98.0	94.6	94.0	90.5	93.4	89.3
1956	99.0	104.6	94.0	94.1	104.6	97.8	97.8	95.3	97.2	94.3
1957	99.0	98.5	99.0	98.2	101.7	100.3	100.2	104.4	97.2	98.2
1958	98.9	97.0	100.5	100.6	96.7	99.6	100.0	96.3	101.0	99.8
1959	102.1	104.5	100.5	101.3	101.6	100.0	99.8	99.4	101.8	102.1
1960	100.5	99.8	100.7	101.5	103.1	98.2	96.7	91.6	101.9	103.1
1961	98.6	94.7	103.6	102.3	103.2	94.6	97.0	98.6	103.8	103.2
1962	98.3	96.5	103.8	102.4	100.1	93.2	100.6	94.8	105.0	103.5

SOURCE: *Housing Statistics—Annual Data*, Washington, D.C.: Housing and Home Finance Agency, May 1963.
* Includes materials not shown.

Table 6–12

PRIVATE NONFARM DWELLING UNITS STARTED, BY SIZE OF BUILDERS OPERATIONS, 1949

Size of Operations	*Builders*		*Houses*	
	Number	*Percent*	*Number*	*Percent*
1 unit	46,500	42%	46,500	7%
2–4 units	40,550	37	107,850	15
5–9 units	11,700	11	70,400	10
10–24 units	6,900	6	95,050	14
25–49 units	2,000	2	67,350	10
50–99 units	1,250	1	75,100	10
100 or more units	900	1	235,950	34
Total	109,800	100	698,200	100

SOURCE: U.S. Department of Labor, *Structure of the Residential Building Industry in 1949*, Bulletin No. 1170, Washington, D.C.: U.S. Government Printing Office, November 1954, p. 21.
Note: Public housing production is not included.

Table 6–13

SIZE OF HOME BUILDER OPERATIONS, SALES, AND RENTAL UNITS, 1959

Size of Operations	*Sales Homes*	*Rental Units*	*Total*	*Cumulative*
1 to 5 units	14.8%	38.3%	13.5%	13.5%
6 to 10 units	17.9	15.2	17.1	30.6
11 to 25 units	27.3	16.0	26.9	57.5
26 to 50 units	17.0	12.7	17.6	75.1
51 to 75 units	6.1	4.7	6.6	81.7
76 to 100 units	5.5	4.3	5.6	87.3
101 to 250 units	7.3	6.9	8.1	95.4
251 to 500 units	2.8	1.2	3.1	98.5
Over 500 units	1.3	0.8	1.5	100.0
Median builder		20 units		

SOURCE: "NAHB Builder Survey," *Journal of Homebuilding,* March 1960.

Table 6–14

PERCENTAGE DISTRIBUTION OF NEW PRIVATE NONFARM ONE-FAMILY HOUSES, BY TYPE OF RESIDENTIAL BUILDER, 1949 AND OCTOBER 1956

Type of Builder	*1949*	*1956*
Owner builders	34%	14%
Commercial builders	66	86
General contractors	16	24
Homebuilders	41	62
Home builders—general contractors	9	—

SOURCE: U.S. Departments of Labor and Commerce, *Construction Review,* Vol. 4, No. 8–9, August-September 1958.

Table 6–15

COSTS OF THE COMPOSITE HOUSE CLASSIFIED BY MAIN EXPENDITURES AND SIZE OF BUILDER, 1951

	Size of Builder			*Size of Builder*		
Expenditures	*Small*	*Medium* (in dollars)	*Large*	*Small*	*Medium* (percent of total)	*Large*
Direct labor	$1,485	$1,300	$1,100	16%	14%	13%
Direct materials	2,235	1,925	1,825	24	21	21
Subcontracts	3,379	3,031	2,657	35	33	30
Plumbing	889	765	640	9	8	7
Painting	626	587	537	7	6	6
Flooring	396	370	343	4	4	4
Cement and concrete	314	285	259	3	3	3
Masonry	235	205	180	2	2	2
Sheet metal and heating	225	212	175	2	2	2
Electric wiring and fixtures	220	207	180	2	2	2
Ceramic tile	180	141	130	2	2	1
Roofing	174	168	148	2	2	2
Grading	52	33	19	1	*	*
Linoleum	35	31	24	*	*	*
Shades and blinds	33	27	22	*	*	*
Incidentals	410	410	310	4	4	4
Land	1,250	1,250	1,250	13	14	14
Overhead and profit	741	1,334	1,608	8	14	18
Total cost	$9,500	$9,250	$8,750			

SOURCE: Sherman J. Maisel, *Housebuilding in Transition.* Berkeley and Los Angeles: University of California Press, 1953, p. 372.

*Less than one half of 1 percent.

Table 6–16

COMPARISON OF RESIDENTIAL CONSTRUCTION COSTS AND CONSUMER PRICES, 1945 TO 1962
(1957–1959 = 100)

Year	*Construction Costs**	*Consumer Prices*
1945	52.3	62.7
1946	57.4	68.0
1947	69.5	77.8
1948	78.2	83.8
1949	76.2	83.0
1950	80.3	83.8
1951	86.5	90.5
1952	88.8	92.5
1953	90.4	93.2
1954	89.7	93.6
1955	92.4	93.3
1956	96.5	94.7
1957	98.3	98.0
1958	99.2	100.7
1959	102.5	101.5
1960	104.2	103.1
1961	104.5	104.2
1962	106.3	105.4

SOURCE: *Housing Statistics—Annual Data,* Washington, D.C.: Housing and Home Finance Agency, May 1963.
* E. H. Boeckh Index.

Table 6–17

COST BREAKDOWN OF PREFABRICATED HOUSE, 1951

	*Mean Percentage**
House package and transportation	41.0%
Preparation of site and slab or basement	10.0
Erection and finishing	17.0
Plumbing Installation	10.0
Heating installation	4.0
Wiring installation	2.0
Completing job and rough grading	4.0
Overhead and profits	12.0

SOURCE: Glenn H. Beyer and Theodore R. Yantis, *Practices and Precepts of Marketing Prefabricated Housing.* Washington, D.C.: U.S. Government Printing Office, November 1952, p. 3.
* These percentages are based on reports of estimated cost breakdown by 72 dealers.

Table 6–18

NUMBER OF MANUFACTURED HOMES SHIPPED, AND PERCENT OF TOTAL SINGLE-FAMILY HOUSING STARTS, 1946 TO 1962

Year	*Manufactured House Shipments*	*Single-Family Housing Starts*	*Percentage Manufactured Homes*
1946	37,200	590,000	6.31%
1947	37,400	742,000	5.04
1948	30,000	766,600	3.91
1949	35,000	794,300	4.41
1950	55,000	1,154,100	4.78
1951	50,000	900,100	5.56
1952	57,000	952,500	5.98
1953	55,000	937,800	5.89
1954	77,000	1,000,000	7.70
1955	93,000	1,189,000	7.88
1956	94,790	990,000	10.00
1957	93,546	872,700	11.00
1958	110,080	977,300	11.26
1959	132,054	1,100,000	12.00
1960	126,867	965,600	13.13
1961	156,004	941,300	16.57
1962	186,152	965,000	19.29

SOURCE: Unpublished data obtained from the Home Manufacturers Association.

Table 6–19

ESTIMATED GEOGRAPHICAL DISTRIBUTION OF MANUFACTURED HOMES SOLD AND NUMBER OF COMPANIES SHIPPING INTO STATE, 1962

	Units Sold	*No. of Companies Shipping into State*		*Units Sold*	*No. of Companies Shipping into State*
Alabama	1,938	26	Nebraska	941	28
Alaska	131	19	Nevada	191	16
Arizona	2,374	17	New Hampshire	971	39
Arkansas	469	18	New Jersey	2,089	49
California	4,744	41	New Mexico	343	21
Colorado	2,989	30	New York	8,565	76
Connecticut	3,755	52	North Carolina	4,722	30
Delaware	451	36	North Dakota	386	18
D. C.	355	12	Ohio	20,955	102
Florida	2,345	33	Oklahoma	747	24
Georgia	6,416	30	Oregon	871	26
Hawaii	24	5	Pennsylvania	7,225	77
Idaho	309	22	Rhode Island	434	28
Illinois	13,647	86	South Carolina	2,121	26
Indiana	15,719	91	South Dakota	422	13
Iowa	2,083	49	Tennessee	1,862	27
Kansas	1,164	30	Texas	2,629	43
Kentucky	3,535	46	Utah	1,082	20
Louisiana	1,812	17	Vermont	402	35
Maine	763	39	Virginia	3,954	46
Maryland	5,024	58	Washington	3,284	32
Massachusetts	3,105	47	West Virginia	1,730	38
Michigan	4,817	74	Wisconsin	3,115	43
Minnesota	611	27	Wyoming	467	20
Mississippi	910	15	Overseas	631	11
Missouri	4,020	43	Canada	6,906	59
Montana	565	24			

SOURCE: Unpublished data obtained from the Home Manufacturers Association.

Table 6–20

MANUFACTURERS' SHIPMENTS OF MOBILE HOMES AND TRAVEL TRAILERS, 1958–1962

Year	*Total*	*Mobile Homes*	*Travel Trailers*	*Total Shipments as a Percentage of Private Housing Starts*
1958	133,800	n.a.*	n.a.*	11.7%
1959	162,500	120,500	42,000	10.7
1960	144,000	103,700	40,300	11.5
1961	130,700	90,200	40,500	10.0
1962	175,000	118,000	57,000	12.0

SOURCE: U.S. Department of Commerce, *Construction Review.* Figures are published currently.
* n.a.—not available.

Part 3

****

ACQUISITION AND CONSUMPTION OF HOUSING

CHAPTER 7

*

Home Ownership

Home ownership has been traditional in this country. There has never been a year, since housing construction has been recorded, that homes built for ownership have not outnumbered those built for rent. Even though some homes originally owner-occupied move into the rental category as they become older, the total percentage of owner-occupied structures has been increasing each year. In 1960 this proportion reached an all-time high of 62 percent of the total number of occupied dwellings in the country.

Although there is undoubtedly much truth in a statement made in a government publication in 1931 that "Deep in the hearts of most American families glows, however faintly, the spark of desire for home ownership,"[1] it must also be recognized that our public housing policy has, for many years, encouraged ownership. This policy has been expressed not only in legislation which, since at least 1934, has tended to encourage the building of owner-occupied homes as against rental housing, but also in the statements of at least three presidents. Calvin Coolidge said: "No greater contribution could be made to the stability of the Nation, and the advancement of its ideals, than to make it a Nation of home-owning families. All the instrumentalities which have been devised to contribute toward this end, are deserving of encouragement."[2]

Herbert Hoover said:

> Maintaining a high percentage of individual home owners is one of the searching tests that now challenge the people of the United States. The present large proportion of families that own their own homes is both the foundation of a sound economic and social system and a guarantee that our society will continue to develop rationally as changing conditions demand.[3]

Franklin D. Roosevelt said: ". . . a nation of homeowners, of people who own a real share in their own land, is unconquerable."[4]

[1] U.S. Department of Commerce, National Committee on Wood Utilization, *How to Judge a House.* Washington, D.C.: U.S. Government Printing Office, 1941, p. 1.

[2] *Building Age,* May 1925, p. 103, quoted in John P. Dean, *Home Ownership: Is it Sound?* New York: Harper & Bros., 4th ed., 1945, p. 40.

[3] J. M. Gries and J. S. Taylor, *How to Own Your Own Home.* Washington, D.C.: U.S. Government Printing Office, 1925, Foreword, quoted in Dean, *op. cit.,* p. 40.

[4] Speech before the United States Savings and Loan League, quoted in the *New York Times,* November 17, 1942, quoted in Dean, *op. cit.,* p. 41.

In 1921, when Herbert Hoover was Secretary of Commerce under President Coolidge, he created a Division of Building and Housing. One of its later chiefs said at the close of the 1920's:

> One of the principal aims of the Division is to encourage home ownership on a sound economic basis. In acquiring a home, a family usually learns habits of saving for a definite end, and develops more of a sense of civic responsibility. Home ownership also stimulates a continued demand for new dwellings, and promotes interest in sound construction.[5]

During the early days of the Federal Housing Administration, in the mid-1930's, that government agency used several techniques to get more homes built. It organized "Better Selling" meetings; it supplied free posters proclaiming such sentiments as "Own a modern livable home! Pay for it like rent!" It even conducted radio programs on the networks aimed at encouraging more families to buy their own home.

Whether as a result of this kind of encouragement or for other reasons, the proportion of families buying homes increased significantly in the 1930's, and has remained high.

However, it has been shown in earlier chapters that there has been some slowing down in the last few years, as evidenced by the increase in the proportion of rental housing built since 1958. As a result of this history, it is proper to raise some basic questions at this time: What are the characteristics of homeowners as compared with renters? What are the actual costs of home ownership? Who can afford it? What are the real reasons for home ownership?

CHARACTERISTICS OF HOMEOWNERS

It has been shown in an earlier chapter that home ownership is more prevalent outside metropolitan areas than inside them, and that inside metropolitan areas the rate is substantially higher outside central cities than in them. It also has been shown that owner-occupied housing is generally of better quality than rental housing. Owner units usually are larger than rental units, and most owned units are in single-family structures.

One of the characteristics of owners is that they are less mobile than renters. This, of course, is due in part to the fact that ownership implies a stronger legal and financial attachment to a home than renting. Another characteristic that has been indicated is that owners, when they do move, tend to upgrade their housing situation more than do renters.

In this section attention will be given to additional characteristics of owners. One of the most important is that their income is higher, on the average, than that of renters. In 1960 one out of every four renters had an income of less than $2,000, compared with only 16 percent of the owners. At the other end of the income scale, only 7 percent of the renters had

[5] James S. Taylor, in *The Better Homes Manual*, Blanche Halbert, ed. Chicago: University of Chicago Press, 1931, p. 765.

an income of $10,000 or more, compared with 17 percent of the owners. A more general comparison of the levels of income between the two groups is afforded by the median income figures for 1959: owners, $5,900; renters, $4,100 (Table 7–1, p. 275).

One of the reasons for the higher average incomes among owners is their occupational patterns. They comprise more of the higher paid occupations—professional, managerial and self-employed, and skilled. They comprise fewer of the unskilled and service occupations (Table 7–2, p. 275).

Another of the reasons is their age. In the youngest age group of heads of families, eighteen to twenty-four years, only 14 percent are owners. However, when the group forty-five to fifty-four is reached, 69 percent are owners. The proportion of owners declines somewhat after that, but this is due primarily to reasons other than an increase in renting. For example, one out of every six families over the age of fifty-five lives in housing it receives rent free as part of its compensation, or rents or shares part of another family's dwelling, or is not a clear-cut owner or renter for some other reason (Table 7–3, p. 275).

Owner households, on the average, are larger than renter families. This is due in large part to the smaller proportion of one-person households (10 percent) among owners than among renters (19 percent). However, at the other end of the size-of-household scale—those containing six persons or more the proportions are approximately the same: 11 percent of both owners and renters. Nevertheless, the median size of owner households was 3.1 persons and that of renter households, 2.7 persons, in 1959 (Table 7–4, p. 276).

There sometimes is the image of owner families as families with children in contrast to renter families without children. This is largely a myth, as data from the U. S. Census show. In 1959, 51 percent of the owners and approximately the same proportion of renters (52 percent) had *no* children. However, owners tend to have *older* children than renters: in 1959 only 9 percent of the owners, as compared with 17 percent of the renters, had children under six years of age; 25 percent of the owners and 17 percent of the renters had children between the ages of six and seventeen years (Table 7–5, p. 276). This obviously reflects the tendency of families to become homeowners as their children grow older.

Finally, there are some important differences between owners and renters with respect to household composition. Among families comprised of a male head with wife present but no relatives in the household, the proportion of renters is higher than owners for the families where the head is under forty-five years of age; the proportion of owners is higher when the head is above that age. However, among households of two or more persons having a female head, there is generally a higher proportion of renters than owners.

It has already been indicated that one-person households tend toward renting rather than owning. Sometimes this is attributed primarily to characteristics of the population aged sixty-five years and over. However, the proportion of renters in one-person households to total renters is higher under sixty-five years than over that age (Table 7–6, p. 277).

Nevertheless, tenure tends to operate in a cycle. In the early stages of the family life cycle, renting is the predominant pattern. Then, as children begin to reach school age and the family's financial position has improved, home ownership becomes predominant. Finally, in the later stages of the life cycle, especially if widowhood is reached, there again is a tendency toward renting. The only time this cycle seems to be disrupted in any major fashion is when households are headed by females earlier in life—renting then becomes the predominant pattern before the later stages of the life cycle are reached.

COSTS OF HOME OWNERSHIP

The largest single investment made by most American families is their home. Many families, despite this fact, enter into arrangements for purchasing a home without being fully aware of the extent of the total commitment in which they are becoming involved. Many may simply consider the traditional rules of thumb which they have heard about (described later) and feel that if they are within the limits of those rules they are making a well-considered and sound decision.

Those rules, however, apply generally only to the purchase price of the house or the monthly payments that must be made after the purchase arrangements are completed. Buying a house requires a considerable additional cash outlay at the outset. Some of the costs are quite apparent, but frequently they are overlooked. Furthermore, there are certain costs that are not so apparent. It is the purpose of this section to discuss the major items of cost that are generally involved.

Down Payment

The amount of down payment required, under various circumstances, was discussed in Chapter 5. It will be recalled that there was considerable variation, depending upon the kind of financing. The range generally is from 5 to 30 percent. Lowest percentage down payments are required where there are government-supported (FHA and VA) mortgages, and highest where conventional mortgages are involved. Different kinds of lending institutions also have different policies and practices.

Closing Costs

The amount of cash that may be involved in closing costs often is not recognized by the ordinary home buyer. There is a wide range in both the number and the level of such costs which must be paid by the home buyer, depending upon such factors as local practices, state laws, contractual arrangements between buyer and seller, whether a new mortgage or simply a mortgage take-over is involved, and so on. The most usual costs that must be paid by the buyer, and the approximate level of those costs, is as follows:

Buyer's attorney (title search, etc.)	1.0% of purchase price
Bank's services	0.5% of purchase price (or mortgage)
Advance real estate taxes	Up to ½ year's taxes
Advance fire insurance	Up to 3 years' insurance
Mortgage tax	0.5% of mortgage
Mortgage recording fee	$5 to $20

Sometimes there are other costs. One of these may be the cost of a survey of the property, frequently ranging from $35 to $150. (This is sometimes paid by the seller.) Another is the cost of a title insurance policy, required in some states and areas, which may range from $60 to $100. This may be paid by the seller, depending upon custom or agreement. Another may be a fee paid to a licensed engineer for checking the structure, the condition of wiring and plumbing, and so on. Few home buyers actually use such services today, and engineers may disclaim responsibility for overlooking certain defects, but the average cost of $25 to $50 for a general inspection of this type can serve as considerable protection for the prospective home buyer.

Most of the remaining costs of acquiring a home are paid by the seller. The most important of these include the real estate broker's commission (usually 5 to 6 percent of the sale price), cost of lawyer's services for transfer of title (approximately 0.5 percent of purchase price), Federal Internal Revenue tax stamps ($1.10 for $1,000 of sale price), abstract brought down to date (minimum of $10), and tax search ($3 to $10). In certain areas, lawyers, representing purchasers of existing homes, require a termite inspection (approximately $25).

The costs of "closing" to the buyer usually range between $200 and $400, but they may run over $500, depending upon the variation in the different factors listed earlier.

Debt Service

One of the most important costs of home ownership is the monthly mortgage payment. For most families this payment absorbs from 5 to 15 percent of the family's income. For some families, however, it accounts for much more; for example, in 1960 it took one fifth of the income for 14 percent of the families holding conventional mortgages (Table 7–7, p. 277).

In dollar amount, the median monthly payment for amortization and interest was $59 for all mortgage holders in 1960. There was, of course, variation based on type of financing and type of mortgage holder (Table 7–8, p. 278). (This median reflects the average payments on *all* mortgages outstanding in that year. Obviously, many of these mortgages have been in existence for several years.) Average payments on new mortgages are appreciably higher than on old ones. As an example of the trend upward in recent years, total monthly payments on mortgages for new single-family homes insured by the FHA (Section 203) increased from $46 in 1946 to $107 in 1961.[6]

Taxes

One of the important items in housing expenditure is taxes.

At least four major aspects of local real estate taxation are important: (1) the local property tax rate; (2) special assessments, including their purposes and the extent of their use; (3) the relation of assessed to actual or appraised value; and (4) local tax delinquencies, including the practices used locally to meet this problem.

The local tax rate, i.e., the amount of taxes levied annually per $1,000 valuation, is probably the most important item. It supplies a measure of the tax burden on real estate relative to that on other kinds of property. It is also important because there is almost always more than a single taxing jurisdiction in an urban area and, hence, differential rates will exist.

In most American communities real property carries a heavy, if not a disproportionate, share of the burden of supplying the revenue for the operation of the city government and the increasing number of services it supplies. Local communities typically have not developed other sources of revenue, in some instances because they lacked authority and in others because of inertia. Even if a new tax source, such as a sales tax, has been established, it is not unusual for the real estate tax rate to remain the same; the city has merely tapped a new source in order to get the additional revenue it requires.

Local tax rates may be high for other reasons. A frequent cause is the large amount of tax-exempt real estate, such as schools and charitable institutions, that may exist in a particular community. The net result of this situation, of course, is that the real estate remaining on the tax rolls contributes a steadily increasing share of the total city revenue gained from realty taxes. Another cause of heavy tax burdens in the central community may be the removal of large industries with their large assessments and heavy taxes from the center to the fringes of the urban area or to other areas. If a large factory moves, the lost revenue must be recovered by heavier levies on the remaining property. The so-called decentralization of industry, which has been taking place in many cities, thus has an important dollars-and-cents relationship to housing; it adds to the tax burden while shrinking the economic base and decreasing the available job supply.

Another peculiarity of local real estate taxation, which has special significance for housing, is its so-called "regressivity"—that is, the lack of relation between tax rate and ability to pay. Like the sales tax, it hits hardest those least able to afford it, because the tax rate typically is uniform for all kinds and qualities of real estate within any given tax jurisdiction.

[6] Housing and Home Finance Agency, *15th Annual Report 1961*. Washington, D.C.: U.S. Government Printing Office, Table III-35, p. 104.

A final consideration with respect to the tax rate is the extent to which such rates vary in different parts of an urban area, as already mentioned. In many instances taxes in suburbs are lower than in central cities. Wherever the rate is out of line, it will have the effect of discouraging investments in real property, including residential real estate.

Some states have laws permitting what is termed "homestead exemption" from real estate taxes.[7] The exemption is usually a specific dollar amount which is applied against the assessed value of the home. (In Florida this exemption is $5,000; in Wyoming it is $500.) Where the assessed valuations are low—say, 25 or even 50 percent—these dollar amounts may represent a major portion, if not all, of the tax on the home. Many states offer a substantial exemption from real estate taxes to widows, and some offer exemptions to veterans.

A second important factor (in addition to the local property tax rate) is special assessments. These assessments raise the question of whether the tax cost for housing in suburban areas, just mentioned, are actually lower than in the central city. Frequently the outlying areas are without many of the services provided inside the city. Hence, the usual method of financing them, when they are required by residents of the area, is through special assessments. These assessments thus become "hidden taxes." They are quite as much a part of the tax cost of housing as the tax rate, and they have the disadvantage of not being predictable.

A third factor is the relation of assessed to actual or appraised value. This is the aspect of local real estate taxation related to administration. The relation of assessed to actual value is especially significant in measuring the tax burden, and much depends upon the methods by which this relationship is determined and the efficiency with which the determinations are made. It should be noted, in this connection, that a high tax rate *per se* does not necessarily mean a heavy tax burden, especially if assessed values represent only a small fraction of actual or appraised value. Of course, it should be recognized that the highly difficult task of assessing all of the property in a community for tax purposes has led to many shortcuts and rule-of-thumb measures of value, which are not only unscientific but often inequitable.

Another frequent result of the typical operation of local tax machinery is the lack of assessment adjustment after value of the property changes. Such inequalities as these are especially important for housing when they represent differences in the tax burden of residential as compared with other kinds of real estate, thus increasing the local costs of housing.

Finally, there is the matter of local tax delinquency. This also is a problem of local tax administration, since it involves the matter of enforcement of tax laws. If tax delinquency is ignored or allowed to accumulate for unreasonable periods, it will tend to increase the burden on the taxpaying properties (among which residential properties always predominate). Vacant

[7] This is not to be confused with "homestead exemption" from claims of creditors, which represents another usage of the same term in some states.

lots have commonly been a conspicuous element in tax delinquency. The community as a whole frequently suffers from such laxity and from the further fact that the procedures for tax foreclosure are usually always cumbersome, slow-moving, and costly. For that reason, tax-delinquent properties, rather than being foreclosed promptly and cleared up for another user, typically stay out of circulation for a considerable period of time, often increasing blight and certainly hindering normal developments of sizable areas, particularly if the sites are unimproved.

Beyond these generalizations, it is difficult to treat the matter of local real estate taxation more specifically because the tax structures of communities vary so widely. The best that can be done is to show some broad figures reflecting some of the variations that exist. The figures in Table 7–9 (p. 278) reflect a composite of local differences based on homeowner mortgaged properties held in 1960.

The median amount of real estate tax per $1,000 value on single-family properties was found to be $14. Mutual savings banks, as can be seen from the table, tend to operate in higher taxation areas than do the other types of lending institutions. The median tax per $1,000 value was $18 on properties they had mortgaged. This is in contrast to a median of $13 on properties mortgaged by savings and loan associations, indicating that they tend to operate in lower taxation areas.

The data in the table also indicate that conventional mortgages and government-supported mortgages are often granted on properties in different taxing jurisdictions, since there was some variation in these amounts in 1960.

The cost of taxes will always be an important housing cost. There is a common misconception that the government need not pay for all of the services it renders, or that the cost of those services, for some reason or other, are not influenced by the same increases in wages and materials that influence other services. *The government must obtain the necessary revenues from somewhere if it is to be able to pay for the services it renders.*

Over the years, there have been many ideas and theories that purported to be more equitable than our present method of taxation. One of the most celebrated of these is the "single tax" theory, of which Henry George was the primary proponent. This theory takes its name from the fact that its adherents would urge this tax to the exclusion of all others. It would be based upon the economic rent that land would draw. It would be levied annually, so that equitable adjustments could be made for land value and improvements.

Groves lists a number of criticisms of the theory: (a) "It is too single"; (b) it is "an attempt to pick up spilled milk"; (c) it "flagrantly disregards the principle of ability to pay"; and (d) ". . . the distinctions drawn between land and capital can nowhere be as sharply defined as they are in theory."[8] Today this theory still has some strong adherents, though it does not attract the interest it attracted at one time.

[8] Harold M. Groves, *Financing Government*, 5th ed. New York: Holt, Rinehart, and Winston, 1958, pp. 321–322.

Housing Costs Not So Apparent

To make the analysis of the cost of home ownership complete, still other factors should be recognized. Some of these are more apparent to the homeowner than others, but data are either scarce or nonexistent for all of them.

For example, when comparisons are made between owning and renting, the cost of repairs and maintenance should be included in the costs of owning, since these costs are covered in monthly rents paid. However, data on these costs are generally unavailable.

Another item that owners frequently fail to consider, probably because it is not a cash outlay, is depreciation and obsolescence. Physical wear is not the only thing involved. Obsolescence may also be caused by neighborhood changes, changing house styles, technological improvements, or changes in ways of living that make some houses particularly out of date.

Because down payments absorb much, if not all, of the family's savings, the loss of interest on the equity that would have been earned had those funds been invested elsewhere should be considered. Finally, as houses become farther and farther from place of work, it would not be unfair to add a portion of the commutation expense to the costs of ownership.

All these factors added together original cash outlays, debt service (less the income tax deduction permitted for interest payments), taxes and insurance, depreciation and obsolescence, repairs and maintenance, loss of interest on equity, and possibly a part of commutation costs—would permit a fair estimate of the actual economic costs of home ownership.[9]

The analysis is not complete at this point, however, since the family does hold an equity in the home which may be considered savings or investment. At a future date, when the loan is repaid, the family may be expected to enjoy the results of earlier financial strain. Furthermore, many families today purchase and resell two or three houses, using the equity in the house previously owned for down payment on their new purchase.[10] When there are ample buyers in the market for used houses, home ownership does not represent the inflexible situation that prevails when existing houses cannot be readily sold.

REASONS FOR HOME OWNERSHIP

From the above discussion, it can be concluded that if home ownership is not generally more costly than renting, at least there is no clear-cut indica-

[9] Some of these factors, together with many related factors, are discussed in Dean, *op. cit.* In this book, Dean emphasized the difficulties and hardships that can be experienced through home ownership. Quite a different point of view is taken by Louis Winnick in his article, "The Burden of the Residential Mortgage Debt," *The Journal of Finance*, Vol. XI, No. 2, May 1956, pp. 166–179. Winnick concludes that: "It would be hard to demonstrate that either the current mortgage burden or total housing burden is particularly onerous."

[10] For example, a University of Michigan study conducted in 1949 and 1950 found that 43 percent of owner families interviewed had owned another house. Edward T. Paxton, *What People Want When They Buy a House.* Housing and Home Finance Agency, Washington, D.C.: U.S. Department of Commerce, 1955, p. 5.

tion that it is less costly. This, then, brings the discussion to why home ownership has played the important role it has in this country. It could hardly be argued, in the light of the facts presented above, that financial goals are paramount, although it must not be forgotten that many families undoubtedly buy a home with such goals in mind. For example, the building up of equity in a home represents a form of forced saving that many families prefer. Home ownership also is a hedge against inflation; costs of housing construction have been rising more rapidly than the other costs reflected in the Consumers Price Index. In addition, there are certain income tax benefits from owning one's home. The Federal Government and most states allow the deduction of real estate taxes and interest paid on mortgage. (No portion of the rent on a home, of course, can be deducted from taxable income, even though the rent paid includes taxes and perhaps interest on mortgages paid by the landlord.)

A sociological study undertaken in 1947 indicates that there are other important reasons for home ownership.[11] It found that certain emotional goals of families are important motivations. Listed as goals were (a) ego satisfaction (family pride in owning, and its desire for self-expression and creativity), (b) family security (a stable location and family symbol), and (c) psychic security (being one's own boss, having a sanctuary, and the romantic nostalgia attached to home ownership).

This study found that status and prestige also ranked high in importance. Following were certain living-pattern goals (domicile, facilities, neighborhood, and location). Then came financial goals and, finally, other reasons such as a family tradition or a passively accepted cultural goal.

This study, then, casts some light on why so many families want to own a home of their own. It deprecated the idea that the primary motive is the economic one, that is, that it is cheaper to own than to rent (or that rent money spent is money lost). Rather, it proposed equally important psychological factors.

Another study stated the case for home ownership, also in terms of social and economic reasons.[12] The social reasons emphasized, which overlap in part with those listed above, were (a) security and stability, (b) security in old age, (c) higher status in the community, (d) home ownership as an educational influence, (e) virtue of private property ownership, (f) better citizenship, (g) opportunity to build the kind of home you desire, (h) other amenities of home ownership, as allowing tinkering around house and garden, and (i) home as an asset to be passed on to heirs. The economic reasons emphasized were (a) home as a good investment, (b) the incentive to save,

[11] Irving Rosow, "Modern Architecture and Social Change" (unpublished thesis, Wayne University, 1948) and summary, "Home Ownership Motives," *American Sociological Review*, Vol. 13, No. 6, December 1948, p. 751. Findings were based on case studies of 33 homeowners. See also, Coleman Woodbury, *The Future of Cities and Urban Redevelopment*. Chicago: University of Chicago Press, 1953, pp. 322–329. The latter author summarizes the results of a number of studies pertinent to this subject.

[12] Henry McCulley Muller, *Urban Home Ownership—A Socio-Economic Analysis with Emphasis on Philadelphia*, Ph.D. dissertation, University of Pennsylvania, Philadelphia, 1947.

(c) improvement of credit standing in the community, and (d) home ownership as freedom from landlords.

There are, of course, arguments in favor of renting. Some of these are:

1. Renting may more readily permit taking advantage of different occupational opportunities. Closely related to this is the greater "bargaining" power if a man is not tied to a job because of the location of his house. It permits the freedom of mobility for the family, which might be desired for other than occupational reasons.
2. Renting permits changing housing in order to meet changing family needs more readily than when a family owns. This includes family disintegration as well as family growth.
3. In renting, there is not the risk of loss of savings due to a deteriorating neighborhood. Old neighborhoods easily fall into the "blighted" category over a period of years.
4. Renting does not carry with it the responsibility for upkeep of the property, for which many families lack the time and inclination. Services of a janitor and a building manager are often included in rent charges. Sometimes "furnished" apartments can be rented.
5. Renting frequently permits living in a location more convenient to work, especially in large cities.

A question that frequently develops is when to buy. Should a home be purchased early in the family life cycle, with a long-term commitment, or later, when a higher down payment can be made but the use-life of the house will be shorter? This is a matter for each family to consider.

These are all important questions. Most of them are so basic that they do not hinge upon either prosperity or depression, although the differences in national economic conditions could certainly be expected to have some influence upon them.

In conclusion, then, social and psychological factors probably play a role just as important as, if not more important than, economic factors when the individual family makes a decision concerning whether or not to buy a home. In a democracy, everyone has the right to make certain decisions for himself and this right carries over to the matter of home ownership. A family should be permitted to make any decision it likes, but preferably it should be an enlightened one. The implications of the decision should be recognized.

It is necessary to stress the need for enlightenment, because not only does our culture tend to support home ownership, but there are pressures in favor of it from business and from the government, as indicated. Naturally, those business enterprises which profit from home ownership encourage it. Building homes is the business of the home builder. Buying and selling them is the business of real estate agents. Financing them is the business of the lending institutions. The interest of the last group differs from that of the first two only insofar as it is more concerned with the financial risks involved.

The real question raised on the important problem of home ownership is:

Can a family's need be met through the proper kind of tenancy rather than through owning?

The trend toward home ownership results only in part from the demand of families who have the income and job stability which encourages them to buy. It also results from the fact that many families, at lower income levels and with less job stability, cannot find an apartment or house to rent that meets their family requirements, and who are encouraged to buy by the liberal financing terms that are available. This latter group might prefer some of the advantages of renting, but this desire must be sacrificed in favor of finding shelter that meets their requirements in the best manner possible. What is "available," that is, houses for sale, will probably continue to be a major factor in the future owning–renting ratio, especially since the rental units being built are primarily high-rent apartments. But there are some new developments. These include the building of more cooperative apartments today than ever before, and the development of the condominium. Both of these developments are discussed later in this chapter.

WHO CAN AFFORD HOME OWNERSHIP?

Even though social and psychological factors in home ownership may play as important a role or an even more important role than economic factors, there arrives the moment of truth when a family must determine whether it can afford it. The liberal financing terms that have been in effect for many years have sometimes been criticized for encouraging home purchase even among families who could not properly afford it. This has applied especially to families well down the income scale who have taken on this obligation.

There have been several traditional rules of thumb for home buyers, the most important of which are these:

1. A home buyer should pay no more than two or two and a half times his annual income.
2. One month's house expenses should not exceed one week's pay, or between 20 and 25 percent of his monthly income.
3. One week's pay should equal 1 percent of the price of the house; i.e., $60 a week for a $6,000 house; $100 a week for a $10,000 house.

Of course, any rule of thumb should be treated with reservations. Perhaps the most important variable in the case of housing is the size of the family. The number of children is important, and the stage of their financial demand (for example, a college education) must be taken into consideration.

Another important factor to consider is the stability of the household head's job and future prospects concerning his income. If he has just reached a certain income level, it may be better for him to estimate his house-paying ability on the basis of the income he has been receiving for some time.

Another factor is the amount of savings the family has accumulated. The buying of a house requires a considerable cash outlay, as already indicated.

In considering this commitment, a sufficient reserve should be maintained to meet possible family emergencies.

Still another important factor is the scale of preferences of the family. Different families prefer to allocate a different proportion of their budgeted expenditures for housing. Some give a higher priority than others to such items as food, clothing, education, and other essentials, and even vacations.[13]

Of course, ''take home'' pay should be considered in these evaluations. In the 1930's, a $50-a-week wage meant nearly $50 in net income. Today, with higher taxes, social security, group insurance, and sometimes other withholding items, net income is considerably less than gross income for any family. In fact, because of the increased cost of living, the old rule that one month's house expenses should not exceed one week's pay (or either of the other two rules cited above) no longer applies. Today, the average homeowner should be earning an annual salary of at least 60 times his monthly housing costs, rather than 52. This means that if costs, including mortgage payments, real estate taxes, property insurance, and utilities, amount to $100 per month, he should be earning no less than $6,000 a year. These costs, in other words, should not exceed 20 percent of his salary.

When real estate taxes, property insurance, and utilities are included in an estimate of housing costs, it is found that today those costs absorb approximately one fifth of the average family's income. There are, of course, differences among families whose mortgages are held by different types of mortgagees and also mortgages involving different types of financing, as shown in Table 7–10 (p. 279). These figures indicate that approximately half of all homeowners are below the upper limit of that income which should normally be paid in housing costs, *but another half are above that limit.*

The trend for total monthly housing expenses (including taxes, insurance, and utilities) has risen in a manner similar to that for mortgage payments. Taking the example of new single-family homes purchased with FHA-insured mortgages, monthly costs rose from $63 in 1946 to $132 in 1961.[14]

In discussing housing expense, it is important to take cognizance of Schwabe's Law which states, in effect, that expenditures for housing increase with increases in family income, but at a slower rate as income increases. How this ''law'' operates with regard to selling price and monthly payments can be seen in Table 7–11 (p. 279). In the income bracket of less than $3,500, the median selling price of houses (new and existing) was $10,320. This amounted to 3.5 times annual income. However, in each succeeding income class, as the median price of houses increased, the ratio of income to selling price declined. For example, in the income class of $15,000 and over, the median selling price of houses was $29,000 and the ratio of income to selling price was only 1.7.[15]

[13] The extent of some of these other preferences is described in Glenn H. Beyer, Thomas W. Mackesey, and James E. Montgomery, *Houses are for People.* Ithaca, N.Y.. Cornell University Housing Research Center, 1955, pp. 44–48.

[14] HHFA *15th Annual Report, op. cit.,* Table III-35, p. 104.

[15] A recent theoretical study attempts to refute this theory. The author suggests just the reverse, i.e., that as income increases housing expenditures tend to increase at a faster rate. However, the study is not entirely convincing in the light of facts such as

THE PROCESS OF PURCHASING A HOME

The housing market, housing finance, and housing production were discussed at some length in earlier chapters. This chapter has thus far focused on the characteristics of homeowners, the costs of ownership, who can afford it, and the real reasons for home ownership.

This section will focus on the process of purchasing a home. This process, in brief, includes the selection of the home desired, making a purchase offer, obtaining a mortgage loan, and "closing."[16]

Role of the Real Estate Broker

General considerations concerning selection—location, price range, size, structural soundness, design, and so on—are discussed elsewhere and will not be elaborated upon here. When a family has made at least tentative decisions concerning these factors, the usual practice is to contact one or more real estate brokers who serve as "middlemen" between buyers and sellers, although it must be remembered that they most frequently are hired by sellers. Real estate brokers usually have salesmen, and in most states both brokers and salesmen must be licensed. (In many states they must be bonded.) These factors protect the prospective purchaser to a degree, but do not necessarily preclude certain malpractices that still sometimes exist.[17]

Sales Agreement

When a particular home has been found that seems to meet the general requirements of the prospective buyer, the next step is making a purchase offer. If there is general agreement between buyer's offer and seller's demands, a purchase agreement, which may have any of several names—an "offer," a "binder," a "sales agreement," a "contract," a "deposit receipt," or some other name—is drawn up. This is a legally binding agreement, when signed, and requires the utmost attention on the part of the buyer if later expenses and difficulties are to be avoided. (Before signing such an agreement, buyers are well advised to seek the counsel of a good lawyer with a general practice who has had considerable experience with real estate in the particular locality.) Purchase agreements vary greatly in their nature and complexity.

Frequently the seller will require a deposit or "earnest money" with the signing of the purchase agreement, pending completion of the sales arrangements. This deposit is either paid to the seller or held in escrow by some neutral party.

---

those shown in Table 7–11. See Margaret G. Reid, *Housing and Income*. Chicago: University of Chicago Press, 1962.

[16] A more detailed discussion of what the average homeowner should know about handling home purchase arrangements wisely may be found in John H. Denton, *Buying or Selling Your Home*. New York: M. Barrows and Co., 1961.

[17] Denton, *op. cit.*, pp. 44–47.

Clear Title

When the purchase agreement is signed it is necessary to confirm, as well as possible, the clear ownership of the property; that is, evidence of a clear "title" is sought. This is done in different ways in different states and localities. Sometimes an abstract company updates the legal history of a property (makes an "abstract") at either the buyer's or seller's expense. At other times, the buyer's lawyer may examine past ownership (title search) and prepare a "title certificate." This merely represents his considered opinion concerning a clear title; it has no legal status. Sometimes "title insurance" is purchased from title companies as at least partial protection against financial loss due to possible defects in titles.

Closing

The next stage of the house purchasing process is called the "closing." This covers the remainder of the arrangements to complete the purchase. The purchase transaction is actually effected through a "deed," which is the written instrument transferring ownership. Obviously, before title is transferred through a deed, the financing arrangements for the purchase must be completed.

As indicated in Chapter 5, few families purchase a house with cash. Most use credit, and the instrument involved here is the mortgage. A mortgage may be defined as a pledge of property made to secure payment of a debt. The lending institution or other source of mortgage loan is called a mortgagee and the owner who has obtained a loan on his property is called a mortgagor.

To obtain a mortgage, the prospective buyer, of course, must apply to a lending institution (a process that involves both the selection of the type of institution and the type of financing desired, as discussed in Chapter 5 and other chapters).

If that institution is interested in granting a mortgage on the property, it will (a) make an investigation concerning the buyer's credit standing and (b) make an appraisal of the property to determine its value. If the credit report is satisfactory, the lending institution then makes a commitment (agreement) to the purchaser, usually in some written form, to make the loan. Before obtaining the actual funds from the lending institution for the purchase of a particular home, the buyer is required to sign both a formal note (covering loan) as well as the mortgage, for that institution. When this is done he receives the loan in the form of a certified or cashier's check from the lending institution. He must supplement it with the cash required from him representing down payment (equity) and, when both the amount of the loan and the down payment are paid to the seller, he receives the deed.

Husband-and-Wife Ownership

The laws with which a home buyer becomes involved when buying a home vary greatly in different states and localities. One of the most important differences relates to husband–wife ownership. It is fully as important to have a lawyer explain the rights and obligations under existing laws in a particular state regarding such ownership at this stage of the purchasing arrangements as it is to have him protect the prospective buyer when the purchase offer is drawn up and signed.

Originally, the most basic differences relating to husband–wife ownership in different states could be traced to the source of the particular state's laws. Most states derived their laws from early English law and consequently the laws of many of these states had certain things in common. Others, however, were derived from early Spanish and French laws, and those laws had certain things in common. In both instances, however, there have been many changes through the years.

One of the forms of ownership in early English law was called joint tenancy (the word "tenancy" as used here means ownership; it should not be confused with the common usage in relation to a landlord with regard to rental properties). Where the joint-tenancy form of ownership exits, the survivor, in the event of the death of one party, receives full ownership of the property. One of the difficulties that may arise under joint tenancy, however, is that either party can deed his ownership to a different party, thus destroying the joint tenancy. This form of ownership exists in Alabama, Connecticut, Kansas, Illinois, Iowa, Maine, Minnesota, Nebraska, New Hampshire, Ohio, West Virginia, and Wisconsin.

Some states, however, undoubtedly wanting to correct some of the inherent weaknesses of the joint-tenancy form of ownership, have adopted a form called "tenancy by the entirety." When title is taken in the names of both husband and wife, each in effect owns the whole property while both are living, and the survivor owns it upon the death of the other. Neither of the parties can dispose of the property or any part of it without the agreement of the other. Tenancy by the entirety does not exist, of course, if title is taken in a separate name, either the husband's or the wife's.[18]

Some of the states recognizing tenancy by the entirety are Arkansas, Delaware, Florida, Indiana, Maryland, Kentucky, Massachusetts, Michigan, Mississippi, Missouri, New Jersey, New York, North Carolina, Oregon, Pennsylvania, South Carolina, Tennessee, Vermont, and Wyoming.

Those states which derived their laws from early Spanish and French law are called community property states. In these states the property

[18] In some states with tenancy by the entirety, as well as in others not having tenancy by the entirety laws, if title is taken only in the husband's name, his widow upon his death is assured of receiving at least one third of the property. This is called "dower." In numerous states dower has been either eliminated or modified by intestacy (inheritance) laws which now govern what a widow is to receive upon the death of her husband in the absence of a will.

is "community property," that is, half interest is owned by the husband and half interest by the wife, regardless of whether title is in both of their names or in the name of only one of them (in the absence of agreement to the contrary and so long as the property was purchased with the earnings of either subsequent to their marriage). There is a lack of uniformity among the state laws with regard to survivorship. Usually, upon the death of one of the parties, half of the property is retained by the survivor and, in the absence of a will, the remainder passes to children. The problem of the survivor in some states is overcome by husband and wife making mutual wills declaring the other to be the beneficiary in the event of death. The survivor thus becomes the owner of the entire property. Some community property states have imported the joint tenancy form of ownership, but tenancy by the entirety is not recognized in any of them. The community property states include Arizona, California, Idaho, Louisiana, Nevada, New Mexico, Texas, and Washington.

There are other legal means of taking ownership to property in most states and certainly other details which, in the interest of simplicity and brevity, have not been described here. However, the forms of ownership that have been described are the most commonplace in the various states today. This discussion has assumed a harmonious relationship between husband and wife. Where such a situation does not exist, and where one party or the other seeks full, separate rights to property because of this or for some other reason, title should be taken in the form which would assure those rights. Again, legal advice undoubtedly would be required.

COOPERATIVE HOUSING

There has been increased interest in cooperative housing in the United States in recent years. This interest undoubtedly has been stimulated by urban families who want to retain the amenities of apartment living but who dislike the fact that in ordinary rental housing they must include certain profit for landlords in their rental payments without the opportunity of building up any personal equity in the property as a result of their rental payments.

What is a Cooperative Apartment?

Isaacs has said: "If a layman were asked, 'What is a cooperative apartment?', he would say, 'Why, it is a building owned by the tenants,' and there would be many quick to agree." But he goes on to point out that, in a legal sense, the building is not owned by the tenants; rather, the title to the land and building is usually held by a stock corporation and the stockholders simply hold leases on their individual apartments.[19]

[19] Lewis M. Isaacs, Jr., " 'To Buy or Not to Buy: That is the Question' . . . What is a Cooperative Apartment?" *The Record* of the Association of the Bar of the City of New York, Vol. 13, No. 4, April 1958, p. 207. Much of the content of Isaacs' article is reported in Harold N. Vogel, *The Co-op Apartment.* New York: Libra Publishers,

Isaacs points out the difficulties in defining a cooperative apartment and indicates that, in fact, no sound definition exists. To quote him further:

The absence of a precise definition as to what is a cooperative apartment arises because it is not a creature of statute but an agglomeration of legal concepts, some of which are in essence incompatible. It is a fiction which takes its existence partly from a corporation, which is another fiction. It is therefore at best an anomaly. The cooperative owner is something more than a tenant of his apartment and something less than an owner.[20]

He goes on to say: ''Those who first contemplated the creation of a cooperative apartment were aware of some of the problems which arose from the anomaly of the legal fiction, but they did not seem to be aware of the fact that they were conceiving, as it were, a new legal baby . . .''[21] Isaacs' review of many of the decisions regarding cooperative apartments from the Courts of New York State led him to conclude that there were eight elements or symptoms that might represent a summary statement concerning them from a legal point of view:

1. The plan of ownership must provide for the use of all apartments in the building for dwelling purposes by the stockholders of the owning corporation.
2. The expense of operating and maintaining common portions of the property (as well as paying taxes and mortgage charges) must be shared by all cooperative owners in an equitable fashion.
3. Control of the management, operation and maintenance of the building must lie with those who occupy apartments.
4. The determination of who shall become an owner or occupant of an apartment must be within the control of those who own and occupy the other apartments.
5. The operation of the property must be on a non-profit basis.
6. A substantial majority of the tenant owners . . . shall determine (a) when and if leases shall terminate and the property shall be sold, altered, demolished, or continued as is; (b) whether mortages shall be procured, increased, reduced or satisfied; (c) whether changes shall be made in the terms of proprietary leases; (d) provisions of the By-laws and any amendments thereto.
7. The price paid for the stock must bear a reasonable relationship to the value of the corporate equity in the real estate.
8. The plan must fulfill the requirements of Federal and State Tax Laws so as to grant to tenant-stockholders the income tax deductions available to cooperative apartment owners.[22]

Inc., 1960. It should be pointed out that while the kind of cooperative apartment discussed by Isaacs is the traditional kind in which the tenant purchases stock and is a shareholder in the entire project, there is another type known as the ''tenancy in common'' cooperative in which the purchaser merely obtains an undivided interest in the whole, as evidenced by deed, with the right to occupy a particular unit. For example, if there are ten apartments in a building, the purchaser in a ''tenancy in common'' cooperative would receive one tenth interest in the whole property—land, building, and services. This type of cooperative is less common.

[20] *Op. cit.*, p. 204.

[21] *Ibid.*, p. 209.

[22] Isaacs, *op. cit.*, pp. 211–232.

A cooperative apartment is, of course, also distinguished by other than legal characteristics. These may be most concisely defined as being personal and economic in character. Vogel has pointed out that residents in cooperative housing must be willing to accommodate themselves to the neighbors in their small community ". . . more than in a rented apartment or a private house."[23] The matter of economics is important simply because most families interested in cooperative housing probably have that interest stimulated to a large degree by the hope of effecting some savings in their ordinary cost of housing.

Historical Development in the United States

The cooperative housing idea, as we think of it today, was translated into brick and mortar in the United States much later than in Europe. (See Chapter 16.) Also, since the first projects were built, this type of housing has found slower acceptance here than in the Northern European countries. Nevertheless, more and more projects of this type are being built in this country every year. Perhaps one of the reasons is that it is hoped to be one of the answers to the housing problems of the middle- and lower-middle-income groups (although cooperative housing is not necessarily limited to those groups).

It will be helpful to note some details of the historical development of cooperative housing in this country in order to understand better the present-day status of such housing. What might be considered to have been one of the first cooperative associations was the Barrington Apartment Association, formed in 1882 in New York City. The stated purpose of this corporation was:

> Purchasing, acquiring and improving real estate for residences, homesteads and apartment houses, to be leased and conducted by the corporation so formed and occupied by the stockholders thereof and others, and apportioning and distributing the same among the stockholders and members of the company.[24]

The word "cooperative" was not used at that time; it did not appear in relation to apartments until the early 1900's. About that time several other projects were built or planned, but they generally tended to be no more than ordinary joint ownership ventures built primarily for high-income families.[25]

Cooperative housing for middle- and lower-middle-income families did not arrive on the American scene until 1926, when some members of the Amalgamated Clothing Workers' Union formed the Amalgamated Housing Corporation to build a cooperative project in New York City. According to Voorhis: "The Amalgamated project turned out to be a brilliant success."[26] He supports this conclusion by indicating (a) that 75 percent

[23] *Op. cit.*, p. 4.
[24] Isaacs, *op. cit.*, p. 209.
[25] Vogel, *op. cit.*, p. 2.
[26] Jerry Voorhis, *American Cooperatives*. New York: Harper & Bros., 1961, p. 45.

of the families resident in the first apartment building built are either the same families or direct descendants of the families who lived there when the building was opened, (b) that the sponsoring corporation has added a number of buildings to the original group, and (c) that the corporation has never failed to pay interest and principal in full on time. (This project could not be considered low-cost housing, however, since the cost of building averaged about $1,500 per room and a member had to make a down payment of $500 per room.)[27] Between 1926 and 1951, thirteen structures were built under the sponsorship of this union, all in New York City.

A few other cooperative housing corporations were established in the late 1920's, but some of them did not weather the Depression years. Not until after World War II did the tempo again pick up. Since then, other unions have entered the field. They usually had two primary purposes: (a) to increase the supply of moderate cost housing for their members and (b) to serve as a source for investment of a part of their rapidly growing union welfare and pension funds.[28]

In the postwar, as in the prewar, period, the leading cooperative housing developments have occurred in New York City. This probably has been due in large part to the favorable tax laws in the State of New York, any kind of nonprofit housing there being able to qualify for tax abatement for twenty-five years. However, it is also probably due in part to the fact that New York City has more immigrant families or first-generation American families than most other cities, and such families might well tend to be more familiar with and amenable to the cooperative-housing type of living. (It will be seen in Chapter 16 that such housing has existed in various European countries for many years.) Some of the credit for the spread of the movement in this city should also be given to a strong leader—Abraham E. Kazon, who was the first manager of the clothing workers' housing projects and who later became President of the United Housing Foundation, one of the first and strongest organizations established after World War II to encourage the construction of cooperative housing in New York City.

However, there have been developments in other cities. Tenants in some housing projects built for war workers, such as in Dayton, Ohio, South Bend, Indiana, and Dallas, Texas, organized cooperative associations and "bought" the home they had been renting from the government. Also, an organization similar to the United Housing Foundation, but with interests across the nation, was formed. It was known as the Foundation for Cooperative Housing (Winslow Carlton was the key personality behind this organization). Through this organization, a number of existing projects

[27] *Nonprofit Housing Projects in the United States.* Bulletin 896, U.S. Department of Labor, Bureau of Labor Statistics, Washington, D.C.: U.S. Government Printing Office, 1947, p. 6.

[28] Jean A. Flexner, "Cooperative Housing in the United States," *Construction Review*, Vol. 4, No. 6, June 1958, U.S. Departments of Commerce and Labor, p. 8.

were converted to cooperative associations—in Bridgeport, Connecticut, Greenbelt, Maryland, Kansas City, Missouri, and other places.[29]

Governmental Financial Assistance

Cooperative housing has been growing more rapidly in the early 1960's than during any earlier period. This growth undoubtedly has resulted from favorable Federal and state laws that have provided financial assistance to groups interested in building and living in such housing.

There are various sources of governmental financial assistance for cooperative housing. The most important source is Section 213 of the National Housing Act administered by the Federal Housing Administration. The program under this law was enacted to aid cooperative housing exclusively. The other sources deal with cooperative housing as one of the various types covered by the particular legislation. They include the Section 221(d)(3) program, also administered by the FHA, and the so-called Mitchell-Lama Act program in New York State.

Under Section 213 authorized in the National Housing Act of 1950, mortgages could be insured on two types of housing projects: (a) "management type," which approximates a form of rental housing with occupancy limited to cooperative members; and (b) "sales type," which permits release of the dwellings when a project is completed. (Since the dwellings become owner-occupied, in the conventional manner, after they are built and sold, "sales type" units built under Section 213 should not be considered cooperative housing. It is generally agreed that Section 213 was simply used as a device for obtaining more favorable financing terms for certain sales housing for a time. This part of the program is being curtailed by the FHA. Therefore, there is no further discussion of such housing in this section.) The 1950 legislation also authorized Federal Government advice and assistance to groups and individuals with regard to organization and legal matters, technical advice concerning land planning and architectural matters, and assistance in matters of management including their administrative, fiscal, and maintenance activities. The Act of 1959 liberalized the loan-to-replacement cost ratios for management type of projects to 97 percent for both veterans' and nonveterans' projects. The Housing Act of 1961 reduced the minimium number of dwelling units required in a cooperative project from eight to five.

By the end of 1962, the amount of mortgage insurance for management type projects under Section 213 reached 648 million dollars. A total of 366 projects with about 51,000 living units had been approved.[30] From these figures it can be seen that the average management type of project contained approximately 140 units.

Although this is an impressive gain over the estimated 4,500 cooperative

[29] Voorhis, *op. cit.*, p. 48.

[30] Housing and Home Finance Agency, *16th Annual Report 1962.* Washington, D.C.: U.S. Government Printing Office, 1963, Table III-2, p. 51.

apartments in the nation when the Section 213 program was originated, it still represents an extremely small proportion of the total FHA housing program, not to mention the total housing program of the nation.

Section 221(d)(3) of the National Housing Act, authorized in 1961, provides special terms, primarily in the form of a subsidized interest rate, for housing located in approved urban renewal areas and sponsored by public agencies (other than local housing authorities), *cooperatives* (including those investor sponsored), other nonprofit corporations or associations, and limited-dividend corporations. (Some authors have indicated that cooperative housing is authorized under Title I of the National Housing Act of 1949, but no such housing can be financed directly under that program. The confusion may have arisen from the fact that certain cooperative housing, as that built under Section 221(d)(3), must be located in approved urban renewal areas.) With such sponsorship the interest rate can be reduced to a rate as low as the average current yield on marketable obligations of the United States Treasury (3⅛ percent in early 1963). On mortgages carrying this rate, FHA waives its mortgage insurance premium and the mortgages will be purchased by the Federal National Mortgage Association. Eligible mortgagors may obtain 100 percent mortgages, with the result that cooperative members under this program need only make down payments to cover the 1 or 2 percent working capital requirement. The cooperative member not only receives these advantages over regular rental housing, but rents also are lower because there is no profit involved for a sponsor, and cooperatives do not require allowances for vacancy and collection losses. Housing built under early authorizations of Section 221 was limited to families displaced by the urban renewal program, but this restriction has been lifted. Income limitations have been set in an effort to limit the program to families with less-than-average income. Unions and other groups have expressed interest in the program, but few projects (which can consist of five or more apartments) have been built, owing in part to the limited amount of FNMA special assistance funds available for purchasing the mortgages.

Under the Mitchell-Lama Act, permanent financing for housing projects is furnished by the State of New York (through the sale of housing bonds to the public) if the builders agree to limit the profit on their investment, thus permitting nonprofit housing cooperatives to qualify. Equity of 10 percent of the construction cost must be provided by the sponsor. Interest is subsidized to the extent that rates are limited to what is paid on the housing bonds. The largest housing cooperative built under this program—in fact, what is claimed to be the world's largest housing cooperative—is Rochdale Village in the borough of Queens, New York City.[31] This project, sponsored by the United Housing Foundation, will house 5,860 families when completed. The total cost of development is 90 million dollars

[31] This group of apartments was named in honor of twenty-eight poor weavers who founded what is claimed to be the first consumer's cooperative at Rochdale, England, in 1848.

—10 million dollars in equity and 80 million dollars in mortgages. The New York State Division of Housing is providing 23 million dollars and the New York State Teachers Retirement System and the New York State Employees Retirement Fund are each providing 28.5 million dollars of the mortgage funds. The first families occupied apartments in 1963.

Advantages and Disadvantages of Cooperative Housing

The advantages and disadvantages of cooperative housing vary somewhat, depending upon the legal form of the particular project. In summarizing these it is important to distinguish between cooperative housing and rental apartments, on the one hand, and cooperative housing and owner-occupied housing in the conventional sense, on the other.

The advantages, over renting, might be considered to be these:

1. There should be some cost saving, owing to the fact that landlord's profit has been eliminated and income tax deductions are permitted covering a proportionate share of real estate taxes and interest paid on mortgage.
2. Some equity is built up through contributions made against principal of mortgage on building.
3. Permanent occupancy is guaranteed.
4. More control exists over management of project regarding such factors as what services are to be provided in the building, what expenses are to be undertaken, and general standards of maintenance, through a vote in corporate matters.

The disadvantages, as compared with renting, include the following:

1. A substantial down payment in the form of equity in the corporation (ranging from 3 percent to 10 percent) is required before occupancy.
2. Equity could be lost if real property values decline. (This has not been found to be a serious threat in recent years.)
3. Occupant is responsible for equipment and decoration.
4. Occupant must deal with corporation rather than a single landlord on other problems.
5. Today there generally is less choice of apartments in cooperative housing than in private rental housing.

Some of the advantages, over owning, are as follows:

1. There should be some cost saving because of economies that occur through a large-scale enterprise as well as savings in such matters as closing costs, transfer of title costs (if occupant decides to leave the property), and so on.
2. The corporation carries many of the legal and other business responsibilities for the property.
3. For the urban dweller who prefers to live relatively near his work,

such projects are usually more desirable from the standpoint of location than new housing available for owner occupancy.

4. For the urban dweller who desires less responsibility for property maintenance and upkeep, this is provided in cooperative apartments.

The primary disadvantages, as against owning, seem to be:

1. The occupant is less independent. He may not sell or sublease the property without approval of the corporation; he lacks control (except to the extent that he has a single vote) over many matters of management, including such factors as what services are to be had in the building, what loans are to be secured by mortgages, and standards of maintenance; equity in corporation cannot be used as security for loans; and the occupant's share of mortgage cannot be paid off in a shorter period than that stipulated for the entire building. There also is some possibility that tax deduction could be lost if the corporation's gross income exceeds that permitted by the Internal Revenue Code or the state tax laws. Furthermore, if the corporation fails to meet its obligations, foreclosure could take place without the cause originating with the particular occupant.

2. Carrying charges may increase, based on capital improvements voted by the corporation or because of increases in operating costs.

3. Today there is generally less choice in cooperative housing than in private housing available for sale.

4. Finally, since the corporation has the right to select prospective occupants, any particular family may find itself involved in both a business enterprise and a neighborhood with neighbors not of his personal choice. (To an extent, this of course can also happen in private housing, but the legal and business relationships are not as close.)

Thus it can be seen that cooperative housing offers opportunities not available in other types of housing. In turn, certain inherent disadvantages exist with regard to this type of housing. The individual family must weigh one set of factors against the other. Any imbalance in the number of items listed above should be overlooked and attention should be focused on the nature of the items which have been described, since they obviously are not all of equal weight to any family.

CONDOMINIUMS

A recent development in home ownership in the United States is that of the condominium. A condominium may be defined as a *multifamily building* which has individual ownership of the single units and an undivided (common) ownership of the common areas and facilities serving the structure, such as halls, stairs, elevators, lobbies, driveways, and so forth.

FHA mortgage insurance was authorized for structures of this type under Section 234 of the Housing Act of 1961. Before this, however, some condominiums had been built in other countries (especially in Brazil) and in Puerto Rico. In fact, they date back to the sixth century B.C., when the Romans passed the first legislation permitting "homes of communal ownership" but specifically providing individual ownership of a given portion of the land and the structure. Although there has been a vast span of years since the fall of the Roman Empire, during which time this form of ownership was practically forgotten, the Roman law heritage in certain countries has undoubtedly been responsible for the legal concept existing in some of their present-day legal systems.

Although the condominium is in a sense a cooperative venture involving a multifamily structure, it differs significantly from both the traditional type of cooperative apartment where the occupant is a shareholder in a corporation and the "tenancy in common" type of cooperative, where the purchaser by deed obtains merely an undivided interest in the whole. The FHA has differentiated between condominiums and cooperative housing as follows:

1. In condominiums, individuals take title to their units; in cooperatives, individuals (usually) have a stock ownership in the cooperative and the right of occupancy to a specific unit. (In condominiums, as in cooperative housing, the individual must be an occupant but, different from in a cooperative, he may own as many as three units in the building in addition to the one he occupies.)[32]
2. In condominiums, individuals vote on a proportionate basis; in cooperatives, each individual has one vote regardless of the size of his unit.
3. In condominums, individuals are taxed separately on their units; in cooperatives, individuals pay their share of taxes on the project in their monthly carrying charges.
4. In condominiums, individuals are responsible only for mortgage indebtedness and taxes involving their own property and their proportionate share of the expenses of operating the common property and have no mortgage indebtedness, tax, or other liability for the other properties; in cooperatives, each individual is dependent upon the solvency of the entire project.[33]

Under the Section 234 program, the mortgage amount in 1962 on a single unit was limited to not more than (1) $25,000; (2) 97 percent of $13,500 of value, plus 90 percent of the next $4,500, and 70 percent of value above $18,000; (3) $2,500 per room, or $9,000 per unit if the number of rooms in the building was less than four per unit. The maximum loan maturity was thirty years.

In many states, enabling legislation is necessary before the Section 234 program can become workable, because the program can only operate in jurisdictions that recognize the division of ownership on a condominium basis, that provide for taxes to be levied against the individual unit together with its undivided interest in the common elements in the condominium, and so on.

Much interest has been evident in this form of home ownership since the new Federal legislation was enacted in 1961.

[32] HHFA *15th Annual Report 1961, op. cit.*, p. 46.

[33] *Fact Sheet.* "FHA Mortgage Insurance on Condominiums." FHA No. 491, Rev. November 1962, p. 3.

READING LIST

HOME OWNERSHIP

Dean, John P. *Home Ownership: Is It Sound?* 4th ed. New York: Harper & Bros., 1945.

Gries, John M., and James Ford (eds.) *Home Ownership, Income and Types of Dwellings.* Vol. IV, The President's Conference on Home Building and Home Ownership, Washington, D.C., 1932.

Ratcliff, Richard U. *Real Estate Analysis.* New York: McGraw-Hill Book Co., 1961, Chapter VIII.

Reid, Margaret G. *Housing and Income.* Chicago: The University of Chicago Press, 1962.

Winnick, Louis. "The Burden of the Residential Mortgage Debt." *The Journal of Finance,* Vol. XI, No. 2, May 1956, pp. 166–179.

Woodbury, Coleman (ed.) *The Future of Cities and Urban Redevelopment.* Chicago: The University of Chicago Press, 1953, pp. 322–329.

TAXES

Groves, Harold M. *Financing Government,* 5th ed. New York: Holt, Rinehart, and Winston, 1958, Chapter 15.

Morton, Walter A. *Housing Taxation.* Madison: University of Wisconsin Press, 1955.

PURCHASING A HOME

Denton, John H. *Buying or Selling Your Home.* New York: M. Barrows and Co., 1961.

Kratovil, Robert. *Real Estate Law,* 3d ed. Englewood Cliffs, N.J.: Prentice-Hall, 4th printing, 1961.

COOPERATIVE HOUSING

Vogel, Harold N. *The Co-Op Apartment.* New York: Libra Publishers, Inc., 1960.

CONDOMINIUMS

"Condominiums—A Symposium," Series of three articles. Carl D. Schlitt, "History of Condominiums"; William J. Lippman, "Legal Problems of Condominiums"; and Raymond T. O'Keefe, "Financial Aspects of Condominiums," *The Appraisal Journal,* Vol. XXX, No. 4, October 1962, pp. 453–469.

Leonard, William T. (ed.) *Condominium Abecedarium.* Compiled by Associated Home Builders of the Greater Eastbay, Inc., Berkeley, California (undated) (loose-leaf 3-ring binder).

Table 7–1

PERCENTAGE DISTRIBUTION OF 1959 INCOME OF PRIMARY FAMILIES AND INDIVIDUALS, BY TENURE

Income	*Owner*	*Renter*
Total families (number in thousands)	32,797	20,227
Less than $2,000	15.7%	24.4%
$2,000 to $2,999	7.2	11.7
$3,000 to $3,999	7.8	12.5
$4,000 to $4,999	9.4	12.6
$5,000 to $5,999	11.4	11.4
$6,000 to $6,999	10.5	8.2
$7,000 to $7,999	8.7	5.8
$8,000 to $9,999	12.1	6.8
$10,000 to $14,999	11.7	5.0
$15,000 or more	5.5	1.6
Median	$5,900	$4,100

SOURCE: Derived from U.S. Bureau of the Census, *Census of Housing 1960.* Metropolitan Housing, HC(2), No. 1, United States, p. 1–9.

Table 7–2

PERCENTAGE DISTRIBUTION OF OCCUPATION OF FAMILY HEAD, 1960

Occupation	*Owner*	*Renter*	*Other**
Professional	58%	37%	5%
Managerial and self-employed	75	22	3
Clerical and sales	59	37	4
Skilled	64	32	4
Semiskilled	58	40	2
Unskilled and service	39	46	15
Retired	65	28	7

SOURCE: *Survey Research Center, 1960 Survey of Consumer Finances.* Ann Arbor, Mich.: University of Michigan, 1961, p. 60.

* Families that rent or share part of another family's dwelling, receive housing as part of compensation, live temporarily in houses they have sold, etc.

Table 7–3

PERCENTAGE DISTRIBUTION OF AGE OF HEAD OF FAMILIES, 1960

Age of Head	*Owner*	*Renter*	*Other**
18 to 24 years	14%	70%	16%
25 to 34 years	44	50	6
35 to 44 years	64	33	3
45 to 54 years	69	27	4
55 to 64 years	62	29	9
65 years and over	65	27	8

SOURCE: Survey Research Center, *1960 Survey of Consumer Finances.* Ann Arbor, Mich.: University of Michigan, 1961, p. 60.

* Families that rent or share part of another family's dwelling, receive housing as part of compensation, live temporarily in houses they have sold, etc.

Table 7–4

PERCENTAGE DISTRIBUTION OF NUMBER OF PERSONS IN HOUSEHOLDS, BY TENURE, 1959

Persons	*Owner*	*Renter*
Total households (number in thousands)	32,966	19,990
One person	9.5%	18.5%
Two persons	29.1	27.7
Three persons	18.6	17.7
Four persons	19.5	15.8
Five persons	12.3	9.1
Six persons or more	10.9	11.3
Median	3.1	2.7

SOURCE: U.S. Bureau of the Census, *Census of Housing 1960.* Components of Inventory Change, HC(4), Part 1A-1, 1950–1959 Components, United States and Regions, p. 28.

Table 7–5

PERCENTAGE DISTRIBUTION OF NUMBER OF OWN CHILDREN IN DIFFERENT AGE GROUPS IN HOUSEHOLDS, BY TENURE, 1959

Number and Age Groups of Children	*Owner*		*Renter*	
Total households (number in thousands)	32,966		19,990	
No children	50.5%		52.2%	
Under six years only	8.9		17.1	
One child		3.7		8.3
Two children or more		5.3		8.9
Six to seventeen years only	25.4		16.6	
One child		11.2		6.9
Two children		9.2		5.8
Three children or more		5.1		3.8
Both age groups	15.1		14.1	
Two children		4.0		3.2
Three children		5.1		3.8
Four children or more		6.0		7.1

SOURCE: U.S. Bureau of the Census, *Census of Housing 1960.* Components of Inventory Change, HC(4), Part 1A-1, 1950–1959 Components, United States and Regions, p. 32.

Table 7–6

PERCENTAGE DISTRIBUTION OF HOUSEHOLD COMPOSITION, BY TENURE

Household Composition	*Owner*	*Renter*
Total households (number in thousands)	32,797	20,227
Two-or-more-person households	91.2%	79.3%
Male head, wife present, no relatives	79.2	63.4
Under 45 years	*36.6*	*40.6*
45 to 64 years	*31.7*	*17.7*
65 years and over	*10.9*	*5.1*
Other male head	4.5	4.6
Under 65 years	*3.2*	*3.9*
65 years and over	*1.3*	*0.7*
Female head	7.5	11.3
Under 65 years	*4.9*	*9.6*
65 years and over	*2.6*	*1.7*
One-person households	8.8	20.7
Under 65 years	4.2	13.9
65 years and over	4.6	6.8

SOURCE: Derived from U.S. Bureau of the Census, *Census of Housing 1960*. Metropolitan Housing, HC(2), No. 1, United States, pp. 1–9.

Table 7–7

PAYMENT ON FIRST MORTGAGE AS PERCENT OF INCOME FOR ONE DWELLING-UNIT HOMEOWNER PROPERTIES, BY TYPE OF FINANCING, 1960

Payment as Percent of Income	*FHA*	*VA*	*Conventional*
Less than 5 percent	6.8%	3.2%	7.3%
5 to 9 percent	41.2	43.6	32.0
10 to 14 percent	37.1	39.2	32.6
15 to 19 percent	9.4	9.1	13.8
20 or more percent	5.5	4.9	14.3
Median percent	10.0%	10.0%	12.0%

SOURCE: U.S. Bureau of the Census, *Census of Housing 1960*. Vol. V, Residential Finance, Part 1, Homeowner Properties, p. xxvi.

Table 7–8

MEDIAN AMOUNT OF REGULAR PAYMENTS OF INTEREST AND/OR PRINCIPAL ON FIRST MORTGAGE ON ONE DWELLING-UNIT HOMEOWNER MORTGAGE PROPERTIES, BY TYPE OF HOLDER OF FIRST MORTGAGE AND TYPE OF FINANCING, 1960

	Median			
Holder of Mortgage	*Total*	*FHA*	*VA*	*Conventional*
Savings and loan associations	$60	$55	$57	$62
Commercial banks	59	56	59	60
Mutual savings banks	58	59	58	56
Life insurance companies	63	57	61	73
Individuals	56	—	—	56
All groups*	59	57	58	61

SOURCE: U.S. Bureau of the Census, *Census of Housing 1960*. Vol. V, Residential Finance, Part 1, Homeowner Properties, pp. 15, 19, 23, 27.

* Includes first mortgages held by a few other groups not listed because proportions held were appreciably smaller than those listed. These other groups include mortgage companies, real estate and construction companies, the Federal Government (principally FNMA), state governments, nonprofit organizations, and a few other groups.

Table 7–9

MEDIAN AMOUNT OF REAL ESTATE TAX PER $1,000 VALUE ON ONE-UNIT HOMEOWNER MORTGAGED PROPERTIES, BY TYPE OF HOLDER OF MORTGAGE AND TYPE OF FINANCING, 1960

	Median			
Holder of Mortgage	*Total*	*FHA*	*VA*	*Conventional*
Savings and loan associations	$13.00	$12.00	$15.00	$13.00
Commercial banks	14.00	15.00	15.00	12.00
Mutual savings banks	18.00	18.00	18.00	20.00
Life insurance companies	13.00	12.00	13.00	14.00
Individuals	12.00	—	—	12.00
All groups*	14.00	14.00	15.00	13.00

SOURCE: U.S. Bureau of the Census, *Census of Housing 1960*. Vol. V, Residential Finance, Part 1, Homeowner Properties, pp. 16, 20, 24, 28.

* Includes first mortgages held by a few other groups not listed because proportions held were appreciably smaller than those listed. These other groups include mortgage companies, real estate and construction companies, the Federal Government (principally FNMA), state governments, nonprofit organizations, and a few other groups.

Table 7–10

MEDIAN ANNUAL HOUSING COSTS* AS PERCENT OF INCOME FOR ONE DWELLING-UNIT HOMEOWNER MORTGAGED PROPERTIES, BY TYPE OF HOLDER OF FIRST MORTGAGE AND TYPE OF FINANCING, 1960

	Median			
Holder of Mortgage	*Total*	*FHA*	*VA*	*Conventional*
Savings and loan associations	20%	17%	19%	20%
Commercial banks	19	18	19	19
Mutual savings banks	20	20	20	20
Life insurance companies	18	18	18	18
Individuals	21	—	—	21
All groups†	19	18	19	20

SOURCE: U.S. Bureau of the Census, *Census of Housing 1960.* Vol. V, Residential Finance, Part 1, Homeowner Properties, pp. 16, 20, 24, 28.

* This item includes payment on principal and interest (and other items included in mortgage payment), real estate taxes, property insurance, and utilities.

† Includes first mortgages held by a few other groups not listed because proportions held were appreciably smaller than those listed. These other groups include mortgage companies, real estate and construction, the Federal Government (principally FNMA), state governments, nonprofit organizations, and a few other groups.

Table 7–11

MEDIAN SELLING PRICE, RATIO OF INCOME TO SELLING PRICE, MONTHLY PAYMENT, AND PAYMENT AS PERCENT OF INCOME, BY INCOME CLASS, FOR HOUSES PURCHASED IN SELECTED COMMUNITIES IN UPSTATE NEW YORK, 1957–1962 TOTAL

	Median			
Income Class	*Selling Price*	*Ratio of Income to Selling Price*	*Monthly Payment*	*Payment as Percent of Income*
Less than $3,500	$10,320	3.5	$57	22%
$3,500 to $4,999	11,615	2.6	67	18
$5,000 to $7,499	13,875	2.3	89	18
$7,500 to $9,999	17,535	2.1	111	16
$10,000 to $12,499	20,800	1.9	130	14
$12,500 to $14,999	24,770	1.8	150	13
$15,000 and over	29,000	1.7	151	10

SOURCE: Unpublished data from Cornell Home Buying Study, 1957–1962.

CHAPTER 8

*

Housing Design

Everything that is not used in the form in which it was developed by nature is, in effect, designed. This means that all housing is designed. It does not imply, however, that all houses are of *good* design.

To be of good design a house should be so planned and built that it will accommodate in the best manner possible all of the activities that go on in it; this is what is meant by "functional design." Beyond that, the house should give the appearance not only to its occupants, but also to others, of being simple, comfortable, and interesting rather than ornate or disruptive.

No formula for a house will meet all requirements. Families differ from each other in what they can afford and where they live. Also, families within themselves are constantly changing and with those changes develop different housing design requirements. Different families do different things, and within the same family there is tremendous variation in activity not only at one time, but from time to time. Also, such factors as color, light, noise, odor, texture, space, and mass operate to make the home environment one that can be either pleasant and satisfying or irritating and frustrating.

Finally, our lives at home are not confined to the interior of the house. The trend today is toward more outdoor living. Thus, more and more importance is being given to the house site, including the nature and the layout of the lot and the orientation of the house.

Winston Churchill once said that we shape our buildings and then they shape us. There is no doubt about the truth of this statement in housing. Once a family occupies a house or apartment, it has to adjust itself to the plan and conveniences (or lack of conveniences) provided. For this reason, probably more than for any other, it is important to learn more about families, because design operates from the *inside* out. One does not start with the shell; the shell is merely used to cover the space required for family living.

Most of the discussion in this chapter will focus on livability requirements. However, certain other matters that are highly important in housing design will be mentioned briefly. These include the structural quality of the house; the suitability of storage and mechanical equipment; the visual appeal of the house; and, finally, the nature of the site, site utilization, and orientation.[1]

LIVABILITY OF A HOUSE

The degree of livability that a house design provides depends upon how well the architectural features of that house meet the needs of those who carry on the activities within it.

Before discussing either kinds of families or specific activities, however, it is desirable to point out, in general terms, some architectural problems that to some extent involve planning and design for all families. The most important of these are space utilization, room characteristics, room orientation, circulation, privacy, and light and ventilation.

General Architectural Problems

One of the most important features of a well-designed house is the distribution of the space in that house so that it may be economically, efficiently, and practically used and so that it may afford the maximum of living comfort and convenience. Halls and passages should not have excessive space. Jogs and other irregularities of plan, which reduce the useful space in rooms and closets, should be avoided.

The sizes of the living room, dining space, and kitchen, and the number of bedrooms, should be proportioned to the needs of the family. The shapes of the various rooms have an important bearing on livability. They should readily accommodate suitable furniture properly grouped to provide comfort and convenience without interfering with circulation. Although low ceilings tend to produce a more intimate and homelike effect, they may prevent adequate circulation of air.

Rooms should be so placed and their openings so arranged as to take full advantage of prevailing breezes, protection against cold winds, and sunshine or shade in the principal rooms. Room orientation should take cognizance of the different climatic conditions of the different regions.

Living convenience is enhanced by a circulation pattern which facilitates direct passage from room to room and throughout the house. The attainment of direct circulation depends upon the arrangement of rooms in proper sequence, and upon the placing of doorways so that the most direct route may be followed without interference from furniture suitably placed. Doorways that are too narrow and doors that swing in the wrong direction, interfere with each other, or are so placed that they cannot be opened for their full width usually impede direct circulation. Doors

[1] Some of the dicussion of these matters is drawn from the architectural "feature analysis" in *FHA Underwriting Handbook—Home Mortgages.* Washington, D.C.: U.S. Government Printing Office, currently revised September 1959.

placed too close to the top or bottom of stairways are hazardous. Stairways that are overly steep, have single risers, are designed so that the moving of furniture is difficult or precluded, and that lack convenient handrails also offer hazards to the occupants of the house.

A high degree of privacy, from without as well as from within the dwelling, enhances livability. For example, it should not be possible to view the bathroom from the living portion of the house. It generally is undesirable to have a bathroom opening into two adjoining rooms. Bathrooms should not be so located that it is necessary to get to them by passing through the living room, dining room, or kitchen from a bedroom. Windows should not be placed so that they permit a view of the interior of any rooms by passersby. Outdoor living facilities should be arranged to give privacy from the neighbors.

Finally, light and ventilation have an important bearing on the desirability, livability, and healthfulness of a house. During recent years there seems to have been an increased desire for large expanses of glass, when properly oriented and protected from extreme summer heat. An abundance of daylight within all parts of a room enhances the effect of spaciousness. A comparatively large area of glass, commanding an unobstructed view of a yard, garden, or landscape, has the effect of opening a room to the out-of-doors. Equal in importance to the glass area provided is the uniform distribution of daylight throughout a room. This can be achieved by careful window placement.

It has been mentioned that rooms should be placed so that they may take full advantage of prevailing breezes. Natural ventilation can be accomplished only when the exterior and interior openings are of adequate size and so arranged that the natural flow of fresh air is not impeded or does not leave a major portion of the room unventilated. Most satisfactory ventilation is achieved when ample exterior openings are located in the opposing walls of a house. Somewhat less effective ventilation is achieved where the openings occur in walls that meet at a corner, so that the natural flow of air crosses the room in a diagonal direction. The least desirable method of natural ventilation is by single exposure or one-sided ventilation which occurs when all exterior openings are located on one exterior wall.

These general recommendations cover only briefly some of the most important problems relating to the design of housing, regardless of the kind of family living in the dwelling. We will now look at some of the differences in families which, of course, dictate specific differences in housing design.

Different Kinds of Families

A number of things about families are important from the standpoint of housing design. Some of these, such as the region in which they live, the personal values they hold, or even their income, do not change drastically or frequently for many families. Others, such as the family size, the stage in the family life cycle, or even the type of household, may change drastically and frequently.

The discussion in this chapter is confined primarily to the single-family house, though in many instances the comments are equally appropriate to apartments. The nature of the house a family buys or builds is determined by family income probably as much as by any other single factor. Forgetting for the time being the neighborhood (see Chapter 9), there is probably a direct correlation between income and size of house and its furnishings. The new houses that most lower-middle-income families have purchased since World War II have less than 1,400 square feet of floor area. This has meant that in part the plan of their house has been dictated to them; that is, there has been a small kitchen, a living room with a dining alcove in it (no dining room), probably an inadequate utility room if there was no basement, and three moderate-sized bedrooms (one of these frequently being very small). On the other hand, for higher-income families all of these rooms would be larger. There would be more automatic equipment and the equipment would be more expensive.

None of this is to say, however, that the *basic needs* of these families are greatly different. On the contrary, those needs are generally the same for both high- and low-income families.

Because houses are generally inflexible, many families during the postwar period of prosperity have changed houses. When a middle-income family has moved into the upper-middle, or upper, income bracket, it has been more practical to buy another house than to increase the space available in the one previously occupied.

Another basic factor in housing design is the family size—not only the size at present, but the size to be planned for. For a two-person family, a one-bedroom apartment or a two-bedroom house generally has been satisfactory. However, as extra members are added, the housing requirements become more complex. At this point, in fact, the factors of the stage in the family life cycle and the type of household become more important than the simple number in the family.

One housing study delineated four stages of the family life cycle important to housing design. These four stages may be identified as follows:

1. *Young couple*—the family type in which the woman is under thirty-five years of age and there are no children.
2. *Founding family*—the family type having some children, all under the age of eight.
3. *Expanding family*—the family type having some children between the ages of eight and eighteen (there may be some children below eight or some over eighteen).
4. *Contracting family*—the family type in which the woman is thirty-five years old or older and there are no children under the age of eighteen.[2]

[2] Glenn H. Beyer, *Farm Housing in the Northeast*. Ithaca, N.Y.: Cornell University Press, 1949, pp. 10–11.

These different groups have very different housing requirements. As indicated above, sometimes the different requirements are met by changing to a different apartment or house. At other times, the adjustments take place within the same house.

One of the first housing needs when children arrive is an extra bedroom. The lack of an adequate number of bedrooms becomes more intolerable as the children grow older and as their numbers increase (especially if they are of opposite sexes). Below the age of eight (or, perhaps, six as some studies have recommended), children do not assert their independence and demand separate bedroom facilities. Such facilities may be desirable, especially in times of illness or when there are guests, but economics probably is the important factor.

With the approach of adolescence, however, not only do children want more privacy from their parents and their brothers and sisters, but for opposite sexes privacy is generally recognized as a requisite. Teen-age children have their own friends, their own activities, and their own possessions. Their housing requirements continue until they leave for college or leave their family to join the labor force or to get married.

There is a stage, during the first phase of the "contracting" period, when grown children may make heavy demands during trips home for weekends or trips back to see the parents after the children have become married. Elderly couples, on the other hand, may have infrequent demand for greater space. At this stage in the life cycle more attention needs to be given to such matters as compactness and single-story planning, privacy, noise, ease of maintenance, and safety. Greater consideration should also be given to heating and lighting, and quite often, in the case of very compact houses, it may be desirable to provide large window areas to create a sense of greater spaciousness. A pleasant view also becomes very important, particularly to those persons who may be infirm and are shut-in (see Chapter 13).

One other factor in family composition that is important to housing design is the presence of adults other than the head and wife. These "other adults" may or may not be elderly persons living with their children. They may be lodgers or boarders. In any event, space demands in the home are accentuated.

Household Activities and Areas

A knowledge of the household activities that take place in the home determines the patterns of space requirements of that home. In this discussion design requirements are considered from the point of view of these activities because, although most houses represent a collection of rooms, what goes on in specific rooms varies greatly among different families.[3]

[3] There have been many studies of individual activities carried on in the home. They have been summarized in *Farmhouse Planning Guides—Household Activity Data and*

The activities can best be discussed individually. However, it should be understood that activities are not actually carried on individually in the home. There is constant overlapping among them, and it is this, in fact, that makes the problem of housing design so difficult. For example, were a designer to plan a kitchen merely for the purpose of having dinner prepared there, his task would be simple. What makes it complex is that people want to eat in the same room, the mother has to care for and supervise her small children while she is cooking, and, probably the dog will have to be fed at the same time.[4]

The activities that are carried on in the house also vary greatly among themselves. By their very nature, some do not suggest general isolation (the example of the mother supervising the child while she is cooking). On the other hand, some activities suggest a need for the highest degree of privacy. These factors are important to the designer when the individual activities of a family are being analyzed.

Meal Preparation and Eating

Attention is given first to meal preparation and related activities, since the woman, who spends more time in the home than any other member, normally devotes more time to this activity (frequently up to a third) than to any other duties she performs during the day.

The kitchen, which houses this activity, has a number of requisites for the process of food preparation. These include storage space, counter space, and such facilities as water, heat, light, and power.

In planning for this activity, several of the variables concerning different kinds of families immediately come into play. For example, a low- or lower-middle-income family is not likely to have the advantage of an automatic dishwasher, a garbage disposer, or even such minor equipment as an electric mixer. At the other extreme, a high-income family may have built-in range and refrigeration, and perhaps even a micro-wave oven.

The type of family becomes an important factor because of activities related to food preparation that are likely to be carried on in the kitchen. If there are small children in the family, they are likely to be under foot. If the family prefers to eat most of its regular meals in the kitchen, as many families do, the size of the family will have an important bearing on the amount of space needed.

Some research has shown that a well-planned kitchen is very likely

---

Space Needs Related to Design. A Northeastern Regional Research Publication. Ithaca, N.Y.: Cornell University Agricultural Experiment Station, 1959, pp. 7–50. Another good over-all reference, though some of the contents are now out of date, is American Public Health Association, *Planning the Home for Occupancy.* Chicago: Public Administration Service, 1950.

[4] One recent study focused on the nature of activities carried on simultaneously. Although the study covered farm households, many of the results would seem to also reflect urban household activity patterns. See *Farmhouse Planning Guides—Household Activity Data and Space Needs Related to Design, ibid.*, pp. 51–124.

to follow what has been called the "work center" concept. A kitchen under this concept is planned in terms of its major centers of activity.[5]

Different researchers have suggested different "work centers." The Cornell study suggested: sink, mix, range, and serve, with auxiliary oven and refrigerator units. These centers are sometimes designed into "kitchen units." This has the advantage of providing storage *at the point of first use,* one of the important principles to be followed in home planning in general.[6]

Another highly important factor in kitchen planning is the layout of the kitchen. Most plans reflect variations of the "U," "L," or corridor plan. The major deviations are the open-sided "U" and the open-sided "L," or one of these plans with an island in the center.

It is generally recognized that the sink is the area of most frequent use.[7] Undoubtedly this is because water is required in connection with so many food preparation tasks. It is desirable, therefore, to plan the sink area so that adequate storage space, counter space, and other facilities are provided at or adjacent to this area. The range has been found to rank second in use. The mix center ranks third. These were followed by the refrigerator and serving china center.

Regardless of the plan used, close proximity is desirable between the range and the sink. Also, the mixing center should be nearby.

One of the general deficiencies in kitchen planning has been the inadequacy of lighting. Because the woman spends so much time in this area, and is frequently working at tasks that require careful attention, good lighting, without shadows covering her work, is essential.

Another deficiency has been the lack of adequate space for eating. As already indicated, many families prefer to eat many of their regular meals in the kitchen. Few prefer to eat regular meals in a dining room, although many families, several studies have shown, want a dining room for Sunday meals or formal occasions.

It is a common misconception that the kitchen is only a "work" room.[8]

[5] See Glenn H. Beyer, ed., assisted by Frank Weise, *The Cornell Kitchen—Product Design Through Research.* Ithaca, N.Y.: Cornell University, Agricultural Experiment Station, 3d printing 1955, pp. 58–63. This booklet summarizes extensive research in kitchen design undertaken recently at Cornell University, and summarizes the history of the American kitchen, sociological aspects of kitchen design, technical aspects of design, kitchen standards, and describes the product resulting from the Cornell research.

[6] The detailed amounts of storage space required and other preferred dimensions in kitchen planning are not given here; they are available in a number of kitchen research publications, including the one cited above.

[7] Mary Koll Heiner and Rose E. Steidl, *Guides for Arrangement of Urban Family Kitchens.* Bulletin 878, Ithaca, N.Y.: Cornell University Agricultural Experiment Station, October 1951. In this study, the oven was a part of the range.

[8] This must have been the conception when the minimum space standards for kitchens were established by the FHA. For one- and two-bedroom houses, only 60 square feet of floor area is required. If a house has three bedrooms, the minimum requirement is increased to 70 square feet, and for four-bedroom houses, to 80 square feet. If dining space is included in the kitchen, the minimum areas are 100 square feet for one- and two-bedroom houses, 110 square feet for three-bedroom houses, and 120 square feet for

Considerable social activity is carried on there, not only among family members but between the housewife and her neighbors and friends. The kitchen is becoming a "living room."

In summary, it may be said that in some respects the kitchen is one of the most important parts of a house. In its planning, each family should ask itself what it intends to do there *in addition to* preparing meals. The answers may point to the inclusion of some provision for such diverse things as the following:

1. *Views,* which should be both attractive and supervisory of the yard, driveway, front door, and so on.
2. *Supervision* within the house.
3. *Infant care,* with provision for washing, storage.
4. *Child play,* which should be nearby but not underfoot, and with its own toy storage space.
5. *Eating facilities,* whether for regular meals or infrequent snacks.
6. *TV,* whether an extra set is desired and where it may be located for optimum use.
7. *Accessibility* to the telephone, front and back doors, laundry, and so on.
8. *Grooming,* if not readily accessible to a bath, whether some provisions may be desired for "sprucing up."
9. *Living area,* with provision for an easy chair or divan.

In addition, one of the most important planning considerations, not only for the kitchen but highly important there, is provision for safety and protection against accidents. In 1962 there were approximately 4,300,000 disabling injuries and 28,500 accidental deaths in the home. The deaths represented 29 percent of the total national accident fatality toll in that year. Falls caused 45 percent of the deaths; burns, over one fifth; all other types, one third. Nearly half of those killed were persons sixty-five years old and older. About a fourth were children under fifteen years.[9]

Child Care

The American family is becoming more and more child conscious. Perhaps this is the operation of the *equality* value, mentioned in Chapter 2. There is evidence of this from the preferences of home buyers today for features in new homes that are especially planned for children.

For families in the "founding" stage of the family cycle, child care is an important factor to be considered in house design. Certain child psychologists have recommended that families take what they term a "permissive"

---

four-bedroom houses. See Federal Housing Administration, *Minimum Property Standards for One and Two Living Units.* Washington, D.C.: U.S. Government Printing Office, November 1958, p. 32. One of the problems concerning these requirements is that, once they are established, *minimum requirements tend to become maximum building standards,* i.e., most builders build houses to conform to the standards, rather than utilizing those standards merely as a base below which construction cannot take place.

[9] *Accident Facts.* Chicago: National Safety Council, 1963.

FIGURE 12. *Most kitchen plans are variations of the "U," "L" and corridor arrangements. The object generally is to plan shorter distances between closely related work "stations" but not forget possible relationships with other areas. (Photographs courtesy of Youngstown Kitchens.)*

attitude toward their children. This means that children's play needs, for example, should be considered in terms of the house as a whole and not limited to a corner of a room, a child's own bedroom, or, in summer, the sand pile. Children should "have permission" to use the house as adults use it, because their play is extremely important in their growth and development.

Admittedly, the requirements of small children are temporary. Sometimes the period is as short as five or six years, where only one child is involved; in other instances, where there may be three or four children, their physical requirements may carry over for a period of ten to twelve years or more.

The requirements of small children are varied; more important, these requirements occur at a time when the mother is frequently engaged in some other task. Therefore, dressing and undressing, or even bathing, helping at the toilet, or supervising play activities is likely to be carried on simultaneously with cooking, setting the table, cleaning up, or washing dishes.

The mother also needs to help the infant with other tasks, some normally carried on in the bathroom (probably during the period of bathroom congestion in the morning) and others almost anywhere else in the house. Washing, combing and brushing hair, swabbing of sore throats, reading to the child, helping with lessons, or merely comforting, have implications for the plan of the house. A sick child, or any other sick members of the household, frequently must be isolated. Furthermore, small children are notorious for requiring that their play equipment, including wagons and tricycles, be used where their performances can be observed. Several problems are created—play area, circulation, and storage.

Leisure and Entertainment

These terms include a wide variety of functions in the home. There is considerable divergency among these functions, and various implications for house planning. For example, reading, listening to radio and records or just resting, suggest privacy or, at least, quiet. Watching television also suggests quiet, but frequently involves groups as well as individuals.

On the other hand, visiting by adults, children's and teen-agers' parties, and dating are activities involving two or more people. These activities generally are not confined to one room of the house as cooking is to the kitchen, personal hygiene to the bathroom, and sleeping to the bedroom. True, a living room is commonly available for these functions, but they might also be carried on in a playroom, a music room, a study, or even one of the other rooms mentioned above.

The particular needs of the family are likely to be dictated by the stage of the family in the life cycle. Teen-agers are usually active participants in home group activities. In contrast, young couples with their first infant are not likely to make comparable demands on the living room. If there is a grandparent, special leisure or recreation facilities may be required; for example, a bedroom planned to make reading comfortable.

Television has become one of the most prominent leisure activities of both young and old. One recent study has shown that approximately seven out of ten elderly people watch television, and the median number of hours per day is three.[10] No data are available concerning younger groups, but the percentage must be equally high, if not higher. Although this activity has frequently been criticized, in view of the nature of many of the TV programs, it must be recognized that television can be given credit for restoring, at least to some degree, part of the function of leisure to the home.

Planning for television presents a special problem for the family because of the need for adequate seating arrangement, somewhat theater style. Also, some members of the family may prefer privacy and quiet while programs are being seen.

Telephoning is another important home activity. Both privacy and quiet are important. The needs of the mother, who is likely to be interrupted while working in the kitchen by the telephone ringing, and those of the teen-ager, who may require the phone for considerable periods of time, are one of the difficult planning problems to work out, especially where only a single telephone installation is provided.

The FHA minimum space standards require only 160 square feet of floor area for the living room in one- and two-bedroom houses, 170 square feet in three-bedroom houses, and 180 square feet in four-bedroom houses. Where the dining space is included in the living room, the areas must be a minimum of 180 square feet, 200 square feet, and 220 square feet, respectively. These, it should be repeated, represent *minimum* areas that would be approved.

Sleeping

Planning for sleeping is not the least of the planning problems of the home. Because space costs money, the recent practice has been to keep bedrooms small. In many instances, they have in fact been too small to accommodate the bed, permit cleaning under the beds, and provide for the necessary storage and closet facilities. Too often, space in the bedroom is overlooked for certain small items commonly used there: clocks, radio, medicine, writing and reading equipment, sewing supplies (if sewing is done there), and a container for rubbish.

Another problem in bedroom planning has been the location of the bedroom. One study pointed out that parents did not prefer having younger children's, and especially teen-agers', bedrooms near theirs. The bedroom ranks with the bath as an area where privacy is a requirement.[11]

[10] Glenn H. Beyer and Margaret E. Woods, *Living and Activity Patterns of the Aged.* Research Report No. 6. Ithaca, N.Y.: Cornell University Center for Housing and Environmental Studies, 1963.

[11] Glenn H. Beyer, Thomas W. Mackesey, and James E. Montgomery, *Houses Are for*

An important factor in bedroom planning is the requirement dictated by elderly persons, if such are present in the household. Also, all families have illness at times, the effects of which (both physical and psychological) would be less serious if some provision were made in the house for such contingencies. Statistics indicate that families attend to illnesses as often during a year as they entertain guests. For example, one medical authority has found that, on the average, each person, whether adult or child, has a disabling illness seven days a year.[12] A family of four would thus have illness in the household twenty-eight days a year; it would entertain guests twenty-four days a year.[13]

One of the possible solutions in house planning is to provide a bedroom for the patient near the kitchen, where the homemaker spends so much of her time. If it is the homemaker who is ill, she can assist in making decisions about running the household if she is near the kitchen. These are only some of the considerations that apply to the problems of the aged and the infirm. Others will be discussed in Chapter 13.

The FHA minimum standards require only 200 square feet of bedroom space in a two-bedroom house, 280 square feet in a three-bedroom house, and 380 square feet in a four-bedroom house. One of the bedrooms may have only 80 square feet of floor area. These dimensions, again, obviously are *minimum*.

Personal Hygiene

Americans are known to place a high emphasis on cleanliness. In planning the bathroom, the problems of congestion and privacy probably should be considered above all others.[14] It is quite common today, even in moderately priced houses, to install at least an extra half bath (i.e., lavatory and toilet). This not only alleviates congestion during peak periods of use, as in the morning, but also permits the use of other than the regular bath by guests.

The bathroom, next in rank to the kitchen, has the most equipment built into it. Normally, the room is small, frequently only 5 feet by 7 feet or 5 feet by 8 feet. In planning the bathroom, it is important to study the

---

People. Research Publication No. 3. Ithaca, N.Y.: Cornell University Housing Research Center, 1955, p. 26.

[12] Louis I. Dublin, *The Facts of Life from Birth to Death*. New York: The Macmillan Co., 1951, pp. 81–85.

[13] An average from several Cornell studies.

[14] An extensive study of personal hygiene activities related to bathroom planning was undertaken in the Center for Housing and Environmental Studies at Cornell University between 1958 and 1964. This study had two major phases: (a) a field survey to determine attitudes and practices and (b) laboratory experimentation aimed at establishing criteria for the design of bathroom fixtures and facilities. Two publications describing the research results are anticipated: one authored by Marilyn Langford, tentatively entitled *Personal Hygiene Attitudes and Practices in 1,000 Middle Class Households*, and another by Alexander Kira as yet untitled. Publishers have not been announced. The history of the bathroom is described in Lawrence Wright, *Clean and Decent*. London: Routledge & Kegan Paul, 1960.

equipment, plumbing, and the wall covering. (Bathroom planning has been made more difficult in houses that do not have a basement, because of the plumbing problems created.)

Sometimes some of the activities that take place in the bathroom are overlooked. In addition to the toilet, bathing, washing, and grooming activities, the bathroom is also used for shaving and make-up, which require equal distribution of light and minimization of shadows. An auxiliary light is sometimes desired for reading. A strip window (or large window) satisfies daytime lighting requirements and also aesthetic needs. Today, mechanical ventilation usually supplements natural ventilation obtained through the use of the windows. Toilets today also are made so that noise from the flush valve is greatly reduced.

Most men prefer showers to taking baths in tubs, and the percentage of women preferring showers is increasing. During the period when babies must be cared for, a convenient counter for bathing them needs to be provided at the lavatory (though it is not an uncommon practice to undertake this function at the kitchen sink).

Because both the space and equipment for bathrooms are costly, there is considerable variance in what can be provided among families. For the lowest-income groups who can afford houses, the compact 5 foot by 7 foot bath is probably typical. At the other extreme, high-income families may provide a separate bath with each bedroom, the master bath being compartmentalized and having dressing areas.

Laundering

The term "laundering" includes a host of tasks in addition to washing, drying, and ironing clothes. It also includes collecting, transporting, sorting, dampening (before ironing), and, finally, folding and putting clothes away.

In addition to the standard equipment of a washing machine and either a hand iron or electric mangle, this activity requires a deep sink, sorting table or counter, preferably a nearby heating surface, and storage facilities for soiled clothes, washing supplies, and baskets. Of course, clothes can either be dried outdoors or with an indoor dryer.

The room in which the clothes are washed should be dry and heated. If a "laundry room" is planned, it should be well lighted, have enough electrical outlets, and have them properly located. Adequate ventilation to remove steam and moisture is a requirement. The room should be easily accessible to outdoor summer-drying areas. If modern equipment is used—and it greatly reduces the amount of fatigue—it should be arranged in a sort of assembly-line layout.

If space can be made available on the first floor, that area is generally the preferred location for the laundry center. It is difficult to carry heavy containers of clothes up and down stairs and any considerable distance. Furthermore, it is desirable to have the laundering area near (but probably not in) the cooking area, so that work in both areas can be carried on simultaneously. It is often more economical to plan a warm, dry, and well-lighted room on the first floor than in the basement.

The manner in which this activity is planned for in the home is likely to vary considerably among families in different income groups. Desirably, a laundry center (perhaps also accommodating some other activity, such as sewing) would be provided. This center would include modern equipment and meet the requirements of counter space, sink, and other desirable features listed above. However, both the modern equipment and the separate space are too expensive for many families. In such instances, this activity is carried on with nonautomatic equipment and with nature providing the warmth and dryness outdoors for drying the clothes.

With automatic equipment, many families wash clothes three or four days a week. Some do it daily, depending upon the size of family, especially the number of children. With nonautomatic equipment, Monday probably remains the traditional washday, although in families with infants washing is done on other days as well. The frequency of the activity is important in space planning.

Other Activities

Some families need to pay special attention, in planning their home, to sewing. Since sewing and mending are often necessary before clothes are washed or after they are ironed, that equipment should be easily accessible to the washing and drying equipment. Women usually do not want to move their sewing when it is time to eat or go to bed, or their table and chairs when they have to sort or iron clothes. Therefore, if this is an important activity in the household, it is desirable to make special plans for it.

For some families, hobbies are important. A number of the hobbies demand special space; for example, the dark room for photography.

Most families have pets. Their care can be more easily provided for if it is planned.

Of course, housekeeping is one of the important activities of the woman. This generally includes maintaining the inside of the house and keeping it clean. Probably the most important planning problem here is storage for cleaning equipment. This factor is discussed in more detail later in this chapter.

Special Planning Factors: Physical–Emotional Relationships

Houses, from an objective point of view, are composed of certain physical elements: light, color, texture, lines, and so on. These should be combined and organized in such a way as to provide the greatest possible satisfaction to family members engaged in various activities. The optimal satisfactions are found at some point on each of the emotional continuums indicated below:

Physical Variables		*Emotional Continuums*	
Light		Interest	Boredom
Color	Family Members	Unity	Disunity
Texture		Spaciousness	Crowding
Lines		Intimacy	Distance
Surfaces		Security	Insecurity
Mass	*THE HUMAN SENSES*	Privacy	Sociability
Temperature and humidity		Pleasantness	Irritation
Sound	Visual	Satisfaction	Frustration
Odor	Auditory	Stimulating	Sedative
Space	Olfactory	Peaceful	Disruptive
	Tactile	Tense	Relaxed
	Gustatory	Ordered	Disordered
		Simple	Ornate
		Beautiful	Ugly
		Comfortable	Uncomfortable
		Formal	Informal[15]

Much more research is required before we can adequately understand these physical–emotional relationships. However, it is possible to show their probable importance by citing one area to which considerable attention has been given—that of lighting in the home. Some of the requirements of this "physical variable" are described below.[16]

The most obvious and basic requirement of lighting in the home is that it permit vision so that we may perform the many activities that take place there—remembering that the home is a place to relax and to entertain friends, as well as a place to rear children and to carry on necessary household "work" and other activities.

However, in addition to these direct and presumed requirements, there are a number of other more complex, but still fundamental, requirements that should be satisfied. Lighting should provide certain emotional and aesthetic satisfactions. It should make a positive contribution to our physical and mental health, to our physical comfort, and to our safety—all in relation to the activities that take place in the home. Obviously, there is a relationship among the asserted requirements themselves.

On the operational level, lighting must take into account such matters as atmosphere, display, privacy, prestige, and mood, as a part of the general social and emotional context in which an activity occurs, as well as the simple visual task requirement (Figure 13).

For example, if we consider formal dining as the activity, most of the

[15] Beyer and Weise, *op. cit.*, p. 18.

[16] Much of this discussion is based on Alexander Kira, "The Requirements of Lighting in the Home: A Definition of the Problems," Ithaca, N.Y.: Cornell University Housing Research Center, March 1958, mimeo.

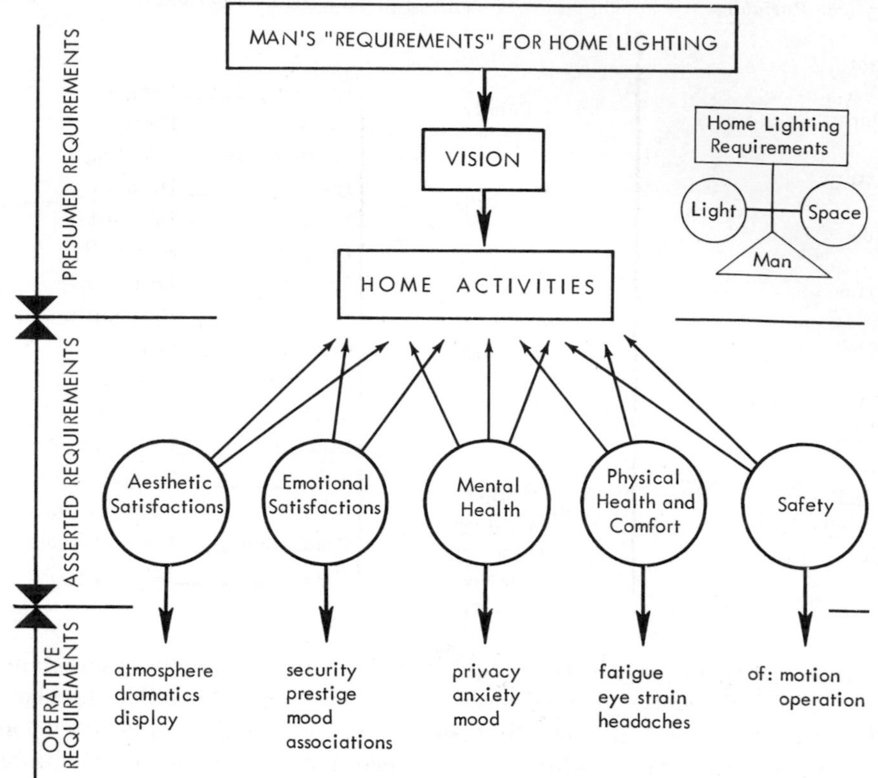

FIGURE 13. *Physical-emotional relationships involved in home lighting. (Source: Alexander Kira, "The Requirements of Lighting in the Home: A Definition of the Problems," Ithaca, N.Y.: Cornell University Housing Research Center, March 1958, mimeo.)*

requirements of lighting are extra-visual. We must consider whether the dining space looks attractive, whether the food appears appetizing, whether the crystal and china are shown to best advantage, whether the light is flattering to people, whether the proper atmosphere has been created for the particular circumstances of the occasion, and finally, of course, whether there is enough light to permit one to see what he is eating.

Different household activities require different types of lighting. Being able to change lighting for some activities is desirable, just as it is desirable to be able to change furniture arrangements from time to time. For example, for festive occasions, when large or small groups are being entertained or informal gatherings are held, the lighting should provide bright, gay feelings, probably emphasizing colors, contrasts, and forms. Or, let us take the other extreme. An individual by himself can hardly be very romantic. But when there is a group of two and the mood is one of romance, an intimate, enchanting, poetic, or even mysterious atmosphere may be desired. This is not accomplished by glowing lights and high over-all illumination. It can probably be best encouraged by low-level illumination commonly achieved by weak isolated point sources: lamps turned low, candlelight, or even firelight.

Light also is one of the most important decorating elements we have, for it can effect a wide variety of changes in the appearance of a room and its furnishings—their colors, textures, and forms. Light can make a room seem large or small, bright or dismal, restful or exciting. Light can create different moods or atmospheres. The importance of this aspect of light must not be overlooked, because light exerts its influence upon our perceptions and emotions, whether or not we use it consciously and creatively.

Kira, in his exploratory study, described some possible home activities, together with the rooms in which the activities were likely to be concentrated, common mood and "atmosphere" associations, and the generalized characteristics of the lighting techniques by which the situations might be implemented. Four "situations" adapted from his study are described below.

Activity Situation 1: Almost all household work: food preparation and clean-up, washing, ironing, machine sewing, working at hobbies, studying, personal hygiene, infant care.

Rooms:

Kitchen, bathroom, children's bedrooms, library, study, workshop, sewing room, laundry.

Mood or atmosphere:

Clean, immaculate, hygienic, fresh, revealing.

Working, quiet, functional, businesslike, studious, efficient, well ordered.

In practice, it most closely approximates the "productive," whereas in theory it takes on some of the qualities of "gay and cheerful" as these are representative of freshness and cleanliness.

Lighting:

High over-all illumination.

Supplementary sources of "working" light for particular critical tasks.

Emphasis on easy visibility and comfort.

There should be a considered balance of brightnesses and a freedom from glare and distraction.

Absence of shadows and dark areas is particularly important.

Specular reflections are particularly important because of the highly polished surfaces generally in use in such areas, i.e., floors, walls, counter tops, etc. These surfaces may be tile, glossy paint, plastic laminates, or polished metals.

Activity Situation 2: General entertaining (large and small groups, adults and children, or informal gatherings and formal parties).

Rooms:

Generally public areas where one can be comfortable.

Specifically, social spaces such as living and dining areas, foyers, front entrances, gardens.

Mood or atmosphere:

Bright, gay, happy, sunny, lively, merry, jolly, joyful, radiant, glowing, sparkling, brilliant, glittering, blazing, exciting, colorful.

Lighting:

Generally high illumination, to give "bright, gay" feeling, to emphasize colors, contrasts and forms—and thereby heighten the liveliness and busyness.

Brilliance for emphasis and highlights, to assist in creating the illusion only—for sparkle, glitter.

Activity Situation 3: Generally passive, requiring little if any physical activity.

Specifically, napping, relaxing, resting, reading, conversing, informal entertaining of small groups, listening to or playing music, watching TV.

Generally person is sitting or reclining in a fixed position.

Emphasis is on relaxation, both mental and physical.

Some mild activity may also take place, such as reading, hand sewing, doing puzzles—in the case of bedrooms, getting ready for bed, dressing, grooming—activities which derive their "quiet" connotation from the general association with sleep.

Rooms:

Bedrooms, living room, den, library or study, porch.

Mood or atmosphere:

Quiet, relaxing, cozy, tranquil, calm, friendly, harmonious, warm or cool, soothing, relieving, comfortable.

Lighting:

General low over-all illumination, a minimum of contrast, freedom from glare.

Some supplementary sources for reading, or other activities.

Activity Situation 4: Vision for night-time movements, accident prevention, convenience, protection against prowlers, reassurance.

Room:

Porch, garage, driveway, hallway, entrances, stairs, nursery, bedrooms, closets.

Mood or atmosphere:

Necessary, purposeful, convenient, safeguard, desirable, useful.

Lighting:

Specific manner of application important.

Indoors: low, widespread, diffused illumination, avoidance of too great a contrast and exposed sources.

Outdoors: strong floodlighting.[17]

These groupings must be considered "tentative," and they are admittedly incomplete. However, they serve to illustrate the nature and complexity of the interrelationships that exist between the various activity groups and man's visual and extra-visual requirements.

The importance of light to physical health has long been recognized.[18] Only recently have we come to appreciate its importance to mental health as well. Improper and/or inadequate light can, in addition to causing such symptoms as fatigue, irritability, and nervousness, result in frustrations and conflicts between family members. In the matter of social density, light can play a major role, for it permits the segregation of various activities by creating areas of relative visual privacy.

Most of the other physical variables are not as complex as lighting, and solutions may be simpler, but they should not be overlooked. One of these is sound. Although family members may become accustomed to noises that occur in the home, the meager evidence available suggests that their not

[17] Kira, *op. cit.*, pp. 7–13.

[18] Of course, the matter of natural light also is highly important. See Publication 478, *Windows and Glass in the Exterior of Buildings.* Washington, D.C.: Building Research Institute, National Academy of Sciences—National Research Council, 1957.

being consciously aware of it is no indication that it does not affect them. Sound-deadening materials in the walls and on the ceiling and floor help to reduce many noises.[19]

Another important factor is odor. Ventilating fans in bathrooms are commonplace today. Similarly, considerable attention is being given to the removal of kitchen odors.

Another is temperature and humidity. Air conditioning is becoming prominent not only in the South, but also in the North. In the early 1960's, the "unit" air conditioner, which can be installed after occupancy, has been more popular than over-all built-in air conditioning. Temperature of rooms in winter is an especially important factor for older people, since they usually require rooms to be 5 to 8 degrees warmer than do young people.

Materials used in the construction of cabinets and other fixtures and furniture in the house are of emotional and social significance to the homemaker and other family members. Wood, metal, glass, and plastic all have a certain social importance, varying with background, locale, and other characteristics of family members. Wood is preferred by many individuals because it is traditional, durable, and can be worked with. Metal is felt to be strong, permanent, easy to clean, and modern. Custom and convention have slowed the acceptance of plastics; customers must usually be educated in the use of new materials before acceptance is widespread, unless market conditions are unusual.

All of these physical variables cause certain personal reactions that can be located somewhere on the emotional continuums indicated at the outset of this discussion. The points on the continuum at which they fall are extremely important.

Personal Values and Design

The concept of personal values was discussed in Chapter 2, and a number of values that can be related to housing were described. There is still a need for exploration of what value orientations such as these can actually mean in terms of house design, as will be mentioned in Chapter 15. Some of the answers, however, are obvious. For example, an orientation toward economy would certainly speak for a simple, compact house—one that is economical to construct and maintain. An orientation toward family centrism would encourage planning a "family room" in which all members could commonly be together to enjoy each other's work and pleasures. The physical health value would call for the provision of ample daylight and fresh air, and probably would emphasize safety features at the cost of certain other

[19] Three reports explore this problem. Homer J. Smith, ed., *Noise Control in Building Design*. Washington, D.C.: Building Research Advisory Board, National Academy of Sciences—National Research Council, 1959; *Noise Control in Buildings*. Publication 706, Washington, D.C.: Building Research Institute, National Academy of Sciences—National Research Council, 1959; *Impact Noise Control in Multifamily Dwellings*. FHA No. 750. Washington, D.C.: Federal Housing Administration, January 1963.

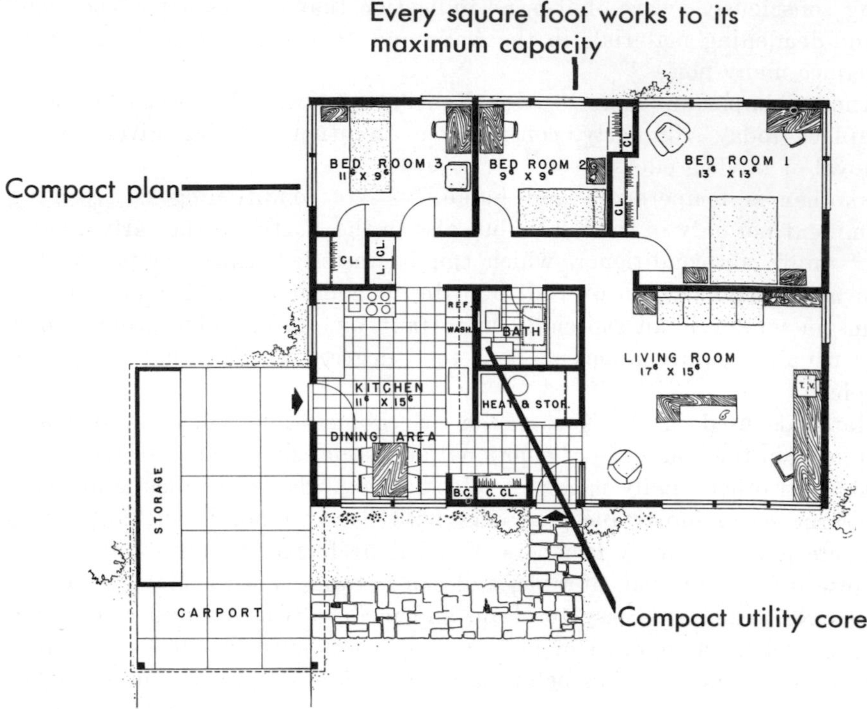

FIGURE 14. *This type of plan has merit for families dominantly oriented toward economics. (Source: Glenn H. Beyer, Thomas W. Mackesey, and James E. Montgomery,* Houses are for People. *Ithaca, N.Y.: Cornell University Housing Research Center, 1955.)*

things. Where there is emphasis on aesthetics, greatest satisfaction probably would be found in contemporary design and furnishings, use of natural materials, continuous lines, and simplicity of design which is often obtained through greater open planning.

Where there is an orientation toward leisure, the design probably would provide privacy areas for reading or listening to music (including adequate storage for records, books, and recreational equipment). In a house plan recognizing an orientation toward equality, the relationships of husband-wife, parent-child, children-children, and in-law families might be accommodated through a den, play room, separate bedrooms where desirable, and the like. An orientation toward freedom would speak for planning against interference in certain activities within the family, and against interference from the neighbors. One example of satisfying the orientation toward mental health would be to plan the home so that the mother has peace of mind regarding the activities of her small children (the "in sight but not under foot" concept, for example). The social prestige value probably would call for more formal planning than in most other types—a terrace, a fireplace (to serve the purpose of a symbol), and display space for special items.

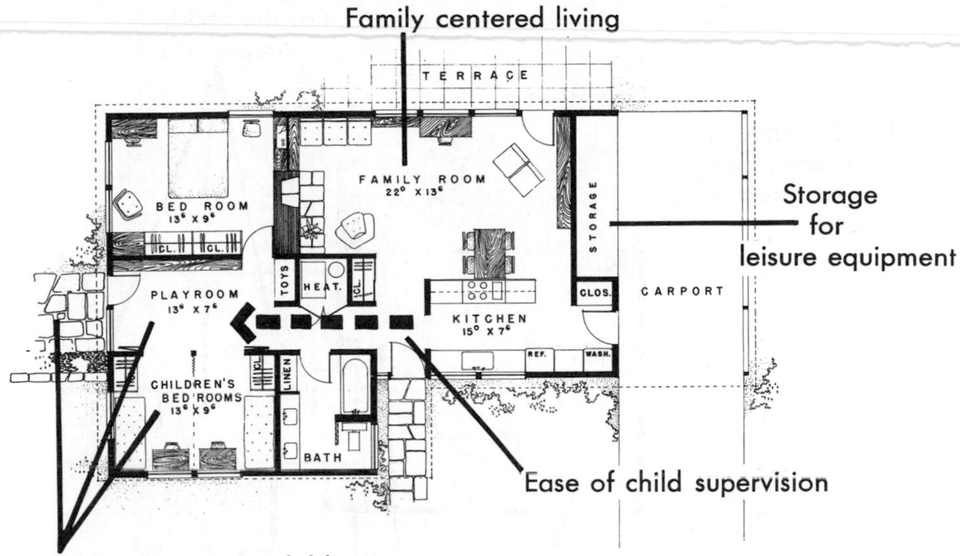

FIGURE 15. *This type of plan has merit for families dominantly oriented toward family-centered living. (Source: Glenn H. Beyer, Thomas W. Mackesey, and James E. Montgomery,* Houses are for People. *Ithaca, N.Y.: Cornell University Housing Research Center, 1955.)*

These are only a few examples, listed in order to provide a better understanding of the values concept and its great potential application to housing design. In studying values, however, two additional facts should be kept in mind: (1) Cornell researchers found that the different orientations overlap in individuals; in other words, certain individuals may rank high on aesthetics, leisure, and equality while others may be oriented more toward family centrism, physical health, and mental health. (The tendency with which certain values may cluster together has not yet been adequately explored.) (2) The same feature in a home may be a source of satisfaction for widely different value orientations in different individuals. The fireplace example may be used again. For the family oriented toward family centrism, it may serve as the locale for family get-togethers; for the prestige-oriented family, as a symbol.

The particular house a family may select *at a given time* will, of course, be selected on the basis of many factors, of which personal values are only one. The stage of the family life cycle is important in determining the amount of physical space required. The income of the family, at the time, is important in determining the price of the house that can be acquired. Basically, however, given the facts on the two above-listed items, the degree of satisfaction that will be derived ultimately from the house will be a determinant of the family's value orientation.

With respect to changed needs over a period of time, the greatest changes

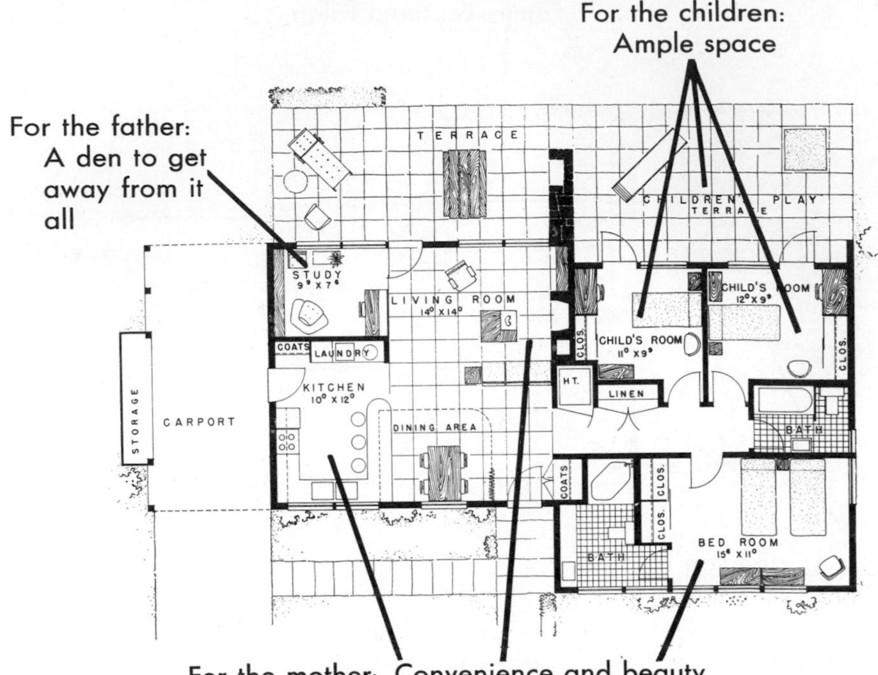

FIGURE 16. *This type of plan has merit for families dominantly oriented toward leisure and aesthetics. (Source: Glenn H. Beyer, Thomas W. Mackesey, and James E. Montgomery,* Houses are for People. *Ithaca, N.Y.: Cornell University Housing Research Center, 1955.)*

probably will result from changes in the stage in the life cycle, with further changes due to possible changes in income. The *values* a family holds *tend to endure* through time, and, therefore, although they may change to a degree, would be less likely to cause different requirements than the other factors discussed.

STRUCTURAL QUALITY

Up to this point we have been concerned with the livability of a house. Matters such as space utilization, room characteristics, circulation, privacy, and light and ventilation can usually be quite soundly evaluated by a family in relation to its needs.

It is more difficult for most people to evaluate the structural quality of a house. Yet, this is an extremely important matter. It is not possible here, nor would it be desirable because of the difficulty of interpretation, to provide a detailed list of sound engineering criteria.[20] It need only be said that structural design, suitability of construction materials, and quality of workmanship are all important. There should be no deficiencies in the

[20] A general reference is American Public Health Association, *Construction and Equipment of the Home.* Chicago: Public Administration Service, 1951.

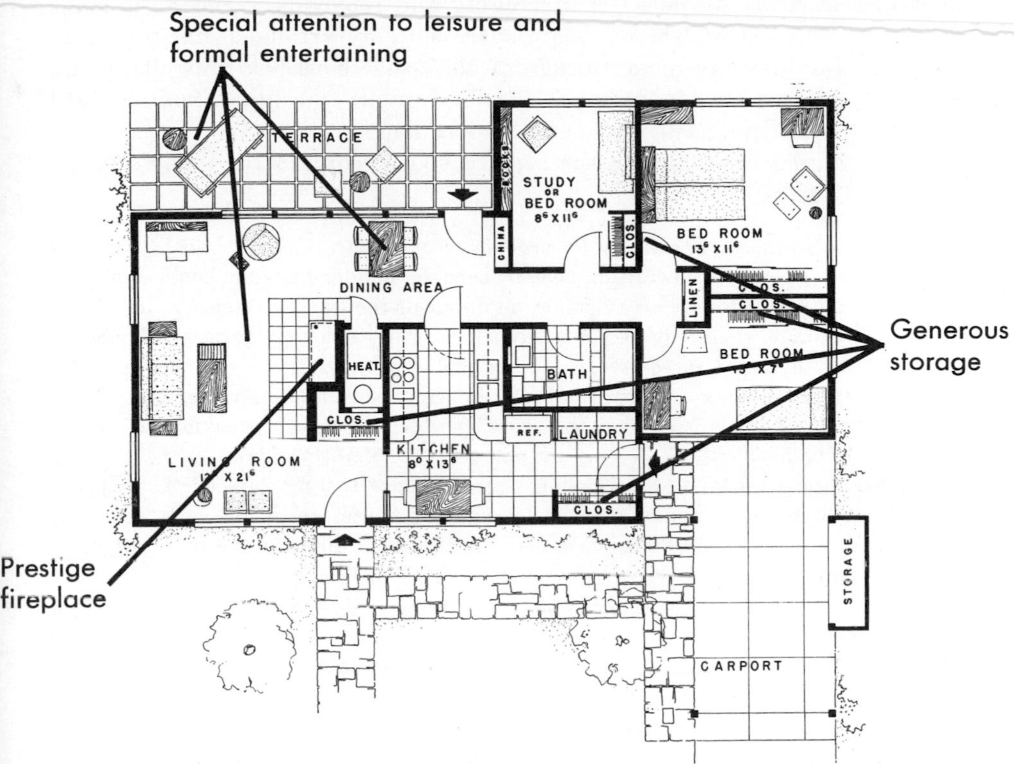

FIGURE 17. *This type of plan has merit for families dominantly oriented toward status and prestige. (Source: Glenn H. Beyer, Thomas W. Mackesey, and James E. Montgomery,* Houses are for People. *Ithaca, N.Y.: Cornell University Housing Research Center, 1955.)*

foundation, in wall construction, partitions, or in the construction of floors, ceilings, or roof. Materials should not only be adequate structurally, but they should resist the damaging effects of weather, decay and corrosion, fire, insects and other pests, as well as the deterioration likely to result from wear due to occupancy. Structural deficiencies may cause accelerated depreciation and costly repairs. The FHA minimum standards are explicit concerning both construction and materials.

SUITABILITY OF STORAGE SPACE AND MECHANICAL EQUIPMENT

Adequacy of storage spaces is one of the most important elements in the design of a house. One of the serious deficiencies in many of today's small houses (and even in many large ones) is inadequate storage space. Each kitchen should have adequate and accessible storage space for food and utensils, and space for performing the necessary functions. Closet space should be ample and convenient and should not contain such objectionable features as doors so placed that hanging and removing garments is made difficult. There should be adequate space suitably arranged and placed to provide for the convenient storage of the usual household miscellany, including brooms, mops, vacuum cleaner, sewing machine, folding card tables, sports equipment, toys, and similar items.

Some guides for planning the type of space required for today's living are listed below.

1. *Active storage space should be provided in the place where it will be used* (as against being permitted to fall in rooms where the builder finds the cubic footage); seasonal and dead storage areas should be in out-of-the-way locations.
2. All storage spaces (whether shelving, closets, attic, or garage) should be thoughtfully designed for *greater visibility* and *easy accessibility* of items in order to reduce outstanding hazards and unnecessary consumption of energy. Dark corners, deep and narrow spaces, and shelving which encourages stacking and layering should be avoided.
3. *Flexibility* should be provided in storage space to take care of the growing family. A high percentage of families buying new houses are in the early stages of the family life cycle and their space needs are likely to increase the first few years they are in the house.
4. *Built-in* storage walls have many merits. Not only do they save the construction of a partition and replace the need for conventional storage furniture, but they give a psychological feeling of greater spaciousness to the room.[21]

Some studies have shown that families in the lower- and middle-income brackets store just as great a quantity of certain household items as families in the upper-income groups. Equivalent space, therefore, is needed for such important items as groceries and clothing. For certain other items such as dishes, silverware, linen, and bedding the number of bedrooms in the home may be considered broadly as criteria for the amount of storage space needed.[22]

Also important to the livability of a house is the mechanical equipment. This includes plumbing, heating, and electrical systems. The equipment should provide for comfort, convenience, and operating economy. Again, it is not desirable to list specifications here. They are available elsewhere; for example, in the FHA minimum property standards. It will only be mentioned here that attention is frequently given to the major items, such as heating equipment and plumbing, while some minor items may be overlooked. For example, electrical outlets should be not only adequate in number, but should also be arranged for effective illumination in rooms, work areas, and passages, and should provide flexibility in the placing of lamps to suit a variety of furniture arrangements in each room.

[21] Condensed from Glenn H. Beyer, "Storage Space Tips from Housing Research," *NAHB Correlator*, February 1952, pp. 128–130.

[22] For a detailed discussion of types and specific dimensional requirements of household storage facilities, see Helen E. McCullough, *Space Design for Household Storage*. Bulletin 557. Urbana, Ill.: University of Illinois Agricultural Experiment Station, August 1952.

VISUAL APPEAL OF THE PROPERTY

Visual appeal of a property involves three things: the exterior design of the structure, the setting, and the interior design. The Federal Housing Administration suggests that each of these features be considered in relation to the three qualities of ''simplicity,'' ''harmony,'' and ''refinement,'' which are defined as follows:

(a) Simplicity is freedom from complexity, intricacy and elaborateness. It does not mean mere bareness, but rather the avoidance of excessive embellishment, of features and motifs which compete for attention, of the meaningless use of ornament, of immoderate variation and inappropriateness in the use of materials as well as of architectural features, and of exaggerated effects.

(b) Harmony results when there is a pleasing arrangement of well-proportioned elements, and when there is such accord between the various parts of the composition that the effect of unity is produced. Consideration of harmony in studying the elements of this feature also requires that all parts of the composition be in scale.

(c) Refinement, sometimes termed "good taste," is characterized by freedom from ostentation, and by restraint in design.[23]

The exterior of the dwelling should be attractively and effectively related to the size, shape, and topography of the lot. It should not be so similar to other structures, if it is in a group, as to produce the effect of monotony. The setting should be studied in relation to the surroundings on the plot, including any accessory buildings (such as garage), walks, driveway, grading, lawn, planting, and other lot improvements, as well as any natural features of the terrain. The ideal setting results from a unified composition of the house and its surroundings, appropriately related to the characteristics of a suitable site. It augments the architecture of the dwelling and utilizes most effectively the advantages of the topography. The house should not be so close to one side or to the front or rear of the plot, or so high above or far below the street level that it is not presented to its best advantage. The interior design should give the effect of spaciousness. Attention should be given to the design of the trim and cabinet work and the character of hardware, electric and plumbing fixtures, and the extent to which these features either enhance or impair the appeal of the interior.

SITE UTILIZATION AND ORIENTATION

Two other factors regarding the house that are extremely important are site utilization and house orientation.

By ''orientation'' is meant placing the house on the lot so that it enjoys the advantages of direction. For example, it should seek the most pleasant view possible.

Different orientations are frequently dictated by different climates. For example, the Gulf breezes in certain sections of the South are essential to

[23] *FHA Underwriting Handbook—Home Mortgages, op. cit.,* 70718.4.

sleeping comfort, and therefore houses should be planned to take advantage of these breezes in the bedrooms. In the Northern Hemisphere a house on a sloping lot, facing south, will enjoy the advantage of the winter sun, whereas one facing north tends to have cold winds penetrating its living areas.

Rarely does one site lend itself to taking advantage of all the important factors in orientation. It then becomes the task of the builder to make the wisest choice possible, in order to provide for the family those amenities that will be most satisfying.

The lot on which a house is located must meet certain requirements beyond those already mentioned if it is to prove desirable. Some of these requirements concern its physical characteristics; others concern the availability of sanitary and protective services, freedom from local hazards and nuisances, and access to utilities and essential community facilities.[24]

The FHA minimum property standards require that a single-family house not cover more than 30 percent of the lot. It is important that the unoccupied space be distributed and developed so as to afford not only adequate service areas and freedom from obstructions to light, air, and outlook, but also ample space, suitably arranged, for the enjoyment of outdoor living and recreation. The FHA requires a minimum distance from front or rear building line to property line, at any point, of 15 feet (except for garage or carport, which have minimums of 10 feet to front property line and 3 feet to rear property line).

HOUSING STYLES

A description of the early styles of housing in the United States was given in Chapter 1. Over the years, as families migrated, many carried with them the house style from their region to wherever they happened to be going. Thus today, examples of many of these styles may be found almost anywhere in the country. Furthermore, where builders (and families) have not had the benefit of professional advice, imitations of these styles still appear, although the styles were generally developed a century ago. One of the best examples is the so-called "ranch house." This title has been bestowed quite indiscriminately on almost every long one-story house built in the last ten years. The end product frequently bears little resemblance to a real ranch house.

Another instance of the misuse of a concept and a name is illustrated by the "split-level" house, originally developed as a means of taking the fullest advantage of a steeply sloping site, but now used indiscriminately even on flat sites.

The prevalence of these practices brings up two important points: first, the small number of instances in which professional architectural advice has been sought; second, the tenacity with which the average person hangs on to traditional concepts in housing.

[24] American Public Health Association, *Planning the Neighborhood*. Chicago: Public Administration Service, 1948, pp. 4–23.

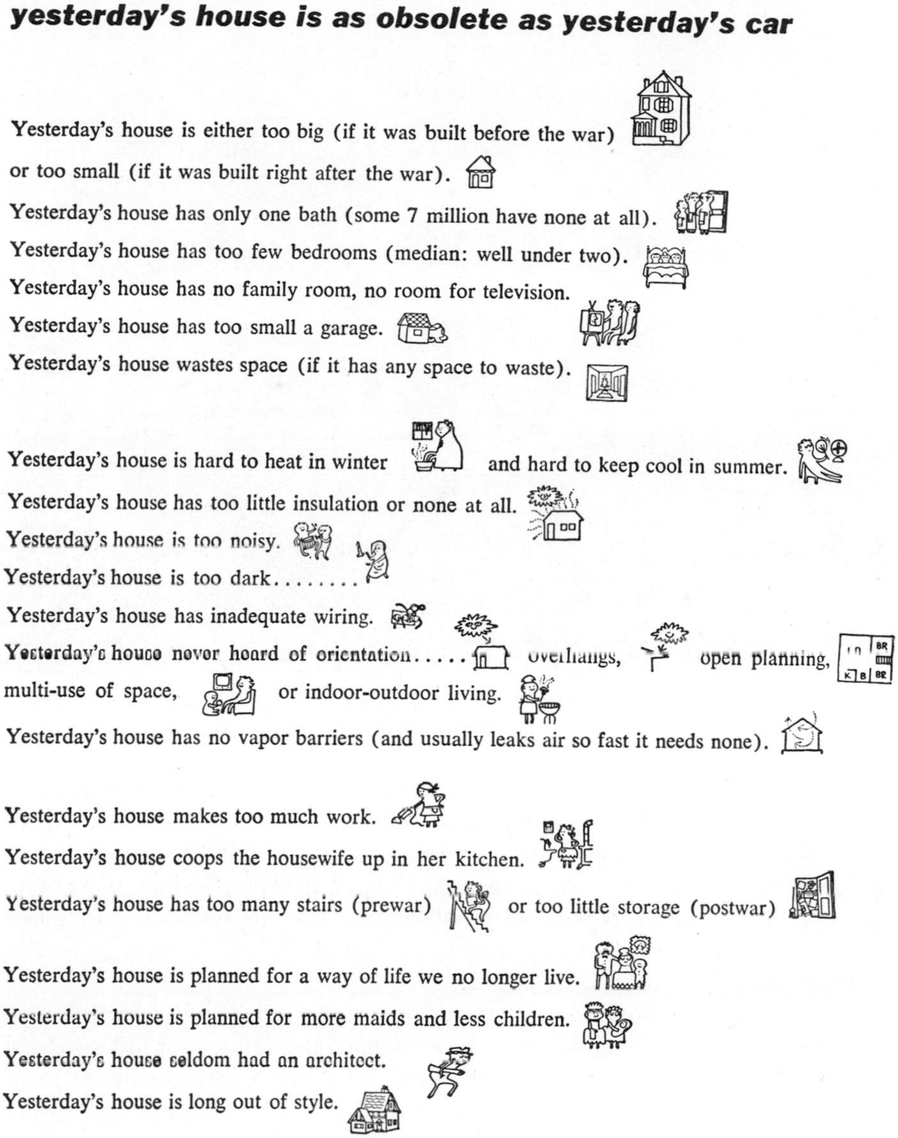

yesterday's house is as obsolete as yesterday's car

Yesterday's house is either too big (if it was built before the war)

or too small (if it was built right after the war).

Yesterday's house has only one bath (some 7 million have none at all).

Yesterday's house has too few bedrooms (median: well under two).

Yesterday's house has no family room, no room for television.

Yesterday's house has too small a garage.

Yesterday's house wastes space (if it has any space to waste).

Yesterday's house is hard to heat in winter and hard to keep cool in summer.

Yesterday's house has too little insulation or none at all.

Yesterday's house is too noisy.

Yesterday's house is too dark........

Yesterday's house has inadequate wiring.

Yesterday's house never heard of orientation..... overhangs, open planning, multi-use of space, or indoor-outdoor living.

Yesterday's house has no vapor barriers (and usually leaks air so fast it needs none).

Yesterday's house makes too much work.

Yesterday's house coops the housewife up in her kitchen.

Yesterday's house has too many stairs (prewar) or too little storage (postwar)

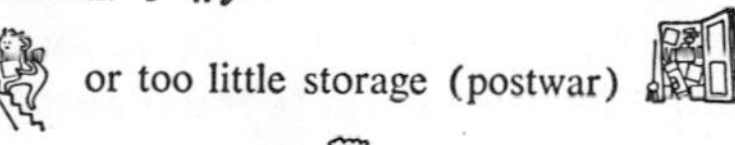

Yesterday's house is planned for a way of life we no longer live.

Yesterday's house is planned for more maids and less children.

Yesterday's house seldom had an architect.

Yesterday's house is long out of style.

FIGURE 18. *(Courtesy House and Home Magazine.)*

FIGURE 19. *Savoye House, Poissy-sur-Seine, 1929–1930. LeCorbusier and Jeanneret, architects. (Photograph used with permission Charles Edward LeCorbusier.)*

In almost no other sphere of human activity has there been such resistance to change as in housing, the one area that probably affects us most immediately and directly. We content ourselves with, or even insist upon, plans and construction methods that predate central heating, indoor plumbing, and improved new materials and techniques, not to mention the social changes that have occurred—the absence of servants, the changes in family attitudes, and the advent of TV.

The logic of this argument is usually recognized when it is applied to automobiles, electrical appliances, and industrial plants, but disregarded in the purchase of a house, the average person's single greatest investment. The combination of these two factors goes a long way toward explaining the general absence of good design and planning.

To effect change, however, is always more difficult than to continue with what has been tested and accepted. Yet, if a certain diet does not provide a person with the proper calories or, more seriously, if an allergy develops, the diet is changed.

On the positive side, the consumer can look to two sources: first, the shelter magazines, which are doing an educational job by frequently exposing the lay reader to new materials, good space planning, and good design; and second, the custom-built, architect-designed houses.

FIGURE 20. *Tugendhat House, Brno, Czechoslavakia, 1930. Mies van der Rohe, architect. (Photograph used with permission Ludwig Mies van der Rohe.)*

Much of the pioneer work in contemporary architecture has been done in the design of houses and is still being done. Many of the features and techniques that we have come to accept unhesitatingly in our building today had their start in the homes of adventurous clients. Frank Lloyd Wright, despite the pyrotechnics of his later years, is perhaps still best known for his early houses, as are most of the great names of this generation: LeCorbusier, for his Savoye House; Mies van der Rohe and the Tugendhat House; Marcel Breuer, Richard Neutra, Harwell Harris, Carl Koch (and his Techbuilt house), and, of course, Philip Johnson and his own world-famous "glass house."

That these early houses have had wide influence in our building is an undisputed fact and an understandable one, since most of the significant building today is being done by the same men or students of theirs. That this influence has filtered down in much-diluted and/or distorted form to the mass housing market is also true. More important, however, is that the home building industry is beginning to become aware of certain economic facts that many other durable goods industries have recognized for years, namely, that good planning and design need cost no more, and in fact, are a competitive advantage.

When the general public becomes as aware of its housing as it is of the

FIGURE 21. *Robie House, Chicago, 1908–1909. Frank Lloyd Wright, architect. (Photograph used with permission Frank Lloyd Wright.)*

automobiles and appliances it buys, then the builders will find that they must move boldly forward. This day may not be far off.

There are exceptions today, to be sure. More and more builders are turning to architects for professional advice. This includes some of the leading prefabricators as well as some of the largest conventional builders, many of whom are the leaders in their field.

THE ROLE OF THE ARCHITECT

The role of the architect, who is a professional man, is to act in an objective and impartial capacity with regard to his client—the family. He must assure the family of getting a home that meets its particular needs and that is the best building within its budget.

In this capacity he acts as consultant and technical adviser to and agent for the client in dealing with the thousands of technical, financial, legal, and labor problems associated with any building project. Unfortunately, in the popular conception, this vital service which the architect is prepared to perform is too often overlooked.

The business world recognizes the value of the architect much as it recognizes the value of its legal adviser. The average person, however, has a

FIGURE 22. *Kaufman House ("Falling Waters"), Bear Run, Pennsylvania, 1936. Frank Lloyd Wright, architect. (Photograph by Hedrich-Blessing.)*

proportionately greater need to obtain such expert advice and assistance since, as was pointed out earlier, the purchase of a house represents the average person's greatest single investment.

Unfortunately, the average person does not usually seek out an architect. When he does—perhaps even more unfortunately—the economics of design often does not permit the architect to accept a job for a house because he cannot perform his full service and ask the necessary commission. The fact is that a house, being made up of many diverse requirements and elements, is a very complex and time-consuming design problem. It is easily as complex as any number of larger building types, but the fee, being based on total building costs rather than degree of complexity, is disproportionately small for the average house. For example, it would probably cost as much to design an efficient and attractive low-cost house as it would to build it.

This illustration points out the economic dilemma facing the architect and the average potential home buyer. The only easily discernible answer for houses of good design, below the upper price brackets, is large-scale production. The builder, who is responsible for fulfilling the demands of the middle-priced housing market, should make increased use of architectural services if the product is to be improved. The builder, unlike the individual, can spread this cost over a large number of identical units and still obtain good design.

READING LIST

FAMILY PREFERENCES

Foote, Nelson N., Janet Abu-Lughod, Mary Mix Foley, and Louis Winnick. *Housing Choices and Housing Constraints.* New York: McGraw-Hill Book Co., Inc., 1960.

GENERAL DESIGN

American Public Health Association. *Planning the Home for Occupancy.* Chicago: Public Administration Service, 1950.

Beyer, Glenn H., Thomas W. Mackesey, and James E. Montgomery. *Houses Are for People.* Research Publication No. 3. Ithaca, N.Y.: Cornell University Housing Research Center, 1955.

Faulkner, Ray. *Inside Today's Home.* New York: Holt, Rinehart and Winston, rev. ed., 1960.

Kennedy, Robert Woods. *The House and the Art of Its Design.* New York: Reinhold Publishing Corp., 1953.

Klaber, Eugene Henry. *Housing Design.* New York: Reinhold Publishing Corp., 1954.

Rogers, Kate Ellen. *The Modern House, U.S.A.* New York: Harper & Bros., 1962.

Wright, Mary, and Russel Wright. *Guide to Easier Living.* New York: Simon and Schuster, rev. 1954.

SPECIFIC PLANNING

Beyer, Glenn H. (ed.), assisted by Frank Weise. *The Cornell Kitchen—Product Design through Research.* Ithaca, N.Y.: Cornell University Agricultural Experiment Station, 3d printing, 1955.

Farmhouse Planning Guides—Household Activity Data and Space Needs Related to Design. A Northeast Regional Research Publication. Ithaca, N.Y.: Cornell University Agricultural Experiment Station, 1959. Summary of Existing Space Requirements Studies, pp. 7-50.

McCullough, Helen E. *Space Design for Household Storage.* Bulletin 557. Urbana, Ill.: Illinois Agricultural Experiment Station, August 1952.

Minimum Property Standards for One and Two Living Units. Federal Housing Administration, Washington, D.C.: U.S. Government Printing Office. Currently revised, December 1960.

Small Homes Council. *Circular Series.* Urbana, Ill.: University of Illinois. Published periodically on various housing design and construction subjects.

HOUSEHOLD EQUIPMENT

Agan, Tessie. *The House: Its Plan and Use.* Rev. ed. Chicago: J. B. Lippincott Co., 1956.

American Public Health Association. *Construction and Equipment of the Home.* Chicago: Public Administration Service, 1951.

CHAPTER 9

*

The Neighborhood

The desirability of having our homes planned to provide the greatest degree of comfort and convenience is so obvious that this matter need not be emphasized further. However, the most satisfactorily designed house or apartment can become an unsatisfactory place to live if it is not in a desirable location. In fact, if a choice is required between a house that lacks certain design qualities but which is situated in a desirable location and one that is well designed but situated in an undesirable location, most families probably would choose the former. Some evidence of this phenomenon is found in the housing market. A house of poorer qualities located in a group having high qualities will have a higher value than if it were located in the midst of units similar to itself; conversely, a house of good quality located in a group that is generally of poorer quality will have its value pulled down by the surrounding units.

What is meant by "location"? Different areas have been identified as "neighborhoods." The origin and development of neighborhoods has run parallel with the growths of cities themselves.

FACTORS DETERMINING NEIGHBORHOODS

Traditionally, three groups of factors have contributed primarily to the formation of neighborhoods: (a) social, (b) physical, and (c) institutional or organizational. Each of these will be discussed briefly.

Social Factors

Historically, it would seem that the most important aspect in the development of neighborhoods has been the social factor. The existence in neighborhoods of certain homogeneous qualities has been considered by many to be of crucial importance in social group formation. This was noted in the discussion in Chapter 3 of the historical development of our cities, and it will become even more evident in the discussion in Chapters 10 and 11, concerned with current problems of our central cities and the development of suburbia. Early in our history, as immigrants came to America they frequently grouped together with those having the same ethnic background —who spoke the same language, had the same religious beliefs, and were of the same racial background. As some of their numbers gained greater wealth, they tended to move outward from the densely populated central city and formed exclusive neighborhoods founded on differences in social and economic status. As Gallion has indicated: "Different environmental standards were established and people who desired and could afford them gathered there to secure these amenities."[1]

What is behind the desire of individuals to cluster among their own kind? This undoubtedly is a human trait. A major social problem frequently can be created by the bringing together of large groups of people; the term for it is "anomie." Tannenbaum characterizes an anomic society as one comprised of weak group integration and a lack of cohesion between members of the collectivity. She then goes on to say: "Group support is the strongest factor making for security in the individual." This suggests that if we must have large groups, comprised of many kinds of individuals, thrown together in our cities, the manner in which individual security can best be achieved is through the formation of subgroups which have a certain cohesion among members within those large groups. Tannenbaum concludes, ". . . the neighborhood theory still has much to commend it in terms of solving or improving the problem of anomie."[2]

How does neighborliness develop? It has already been mentioned that people tend to seek out an area where people like themselves live. In addition to some of the similar characteristics that have already been mentioned, there is the matter of economics. Families select a home they can afford in a neighborhood where they can afford to live. Once they arrive on the scene, the neighboring process frequently originates with young children becoming acquainted with their neighbors. School children living near each other frequently become close friends. Housewives usually get to know other housewives through such simple processes as the emergency need for borrowing a loaf of bread or a quart of milk, or the need for telephoning other nearby parents of children with whom their own have made an acquaintance or formed a close friendship. Some young mothers are likely to meet other young mothers while pushing the baby carriage along the walk or in a nearby park. It is through activities such as these that many friendships are formed. And, it has been argued, the greater the similarity of the individuals, the more quickly will social adjustment take place.

Physical Factors

Frequently, it is impossible to determine the physical boundaries of a neighborhood. On the other hand, certain physical factors sometimes provide delineations. These factors may be of different types.

[1] Arthur B. Gallion, *The Urban Pattern*. Princeton, N.J.: D. Van Nostrand Co., Inc., 1950, p. 277.

[2] Judith Tannenbaum, "The Neighborhood: A Socio-Psychological Analysis," in *Land Economics,* Vol. XXIV, No. 4, November 1948, pp. 358–369. Weber, writing in 1899, touched on this same point. He said: "Every man of the world knows that isolation and

The first general type consists of natural and man-made barriers and topography. We have often heard of the family that lives "on the other side of the tracks." There are also those who live "on South Hill," "in the Hyde Park section," or "near the Lake."

In addition, there are the areas that have developed as a result of particular patterns of city growth. Here we frequently find certain clearly delineated slum areas, blighted areas, or areas near the central city which still contain well-built and well-maintained old homes. (See Chapter 10.)

Perhaps the most important factor in the development of new neighborhoods has been the availability of large areas of land, less expensive than that in our central cities, on the fringes of our cities. With the general development of our modern highway and primary road systems, and the common availability of not just one, but frequently two cars to the family, this land can be developed for use by our expanding city populations. When large tracts of land are developed, large numbers of dwellings are built in groups and new "neighborhoods" are automatically created.

Institutional or Organizational Factors

Although it is known that the neighborhood concept was taken into account 2,000 years ago,[3] the "neighborhood unit" principle was not clearly formulated for planning purposes until Perry undertook his studies for the New York Regional Plan Association in the mid-1920's. He suggested that if planners would follow six principles, ". . . there will result a neighborhood community in which the fundamental needs of family life will be met more completely . . ." The six principles were:

1. *Size.* A residential unit development should provide housing for that population for which one elementary school is ordinarily required, its actual area depending upon its population density.
2. *Boundaries.* The unit should be bounded on all sides by arterial streets, sufficiently wide to facilitate its by-passing, instead of penetration, by through traffic.
3. *Open Spaces.* A system of small parks and recreation spaces, planned to meet the needs of the particular neighborhood, should be provided.
4. *Institution Sites.* Sites for the school and other institutions having service spheres coinciding with the limits of the unit should be suitably grouped about a central point, or common.
5. *Local Shops.* One or more shopping districts, adequate for the population to be served, should be laid out in the circumference of the unit, preferably at traffic junctions and adjacent to similar districts of adjoining neighborhoods.
6. *Internal Street System.* The unit should be provided with a special street system, each highway being proportioned to its probable traffic load, and the street net

---

solitude are found in a much higher degree in the crowded city than in a country village, where one individual's concerns are the concern of all." Adna Ferrin Weber, *The Growth of Cities in the Nineteenth Century.* Originally published New York: The Macmillan Co., 1899. Republished Ithaca, N.Y.: Cornell University Press, 1963. Quotation from p. 432.

[3] C. Z. Chen, "Some Ancient Chinese Concepts of Town and Country," in *The Town Planning Review* (Liverpool), Vol. XIX, Nos. 3 and 4, Summer 1947, pp. 160–163.

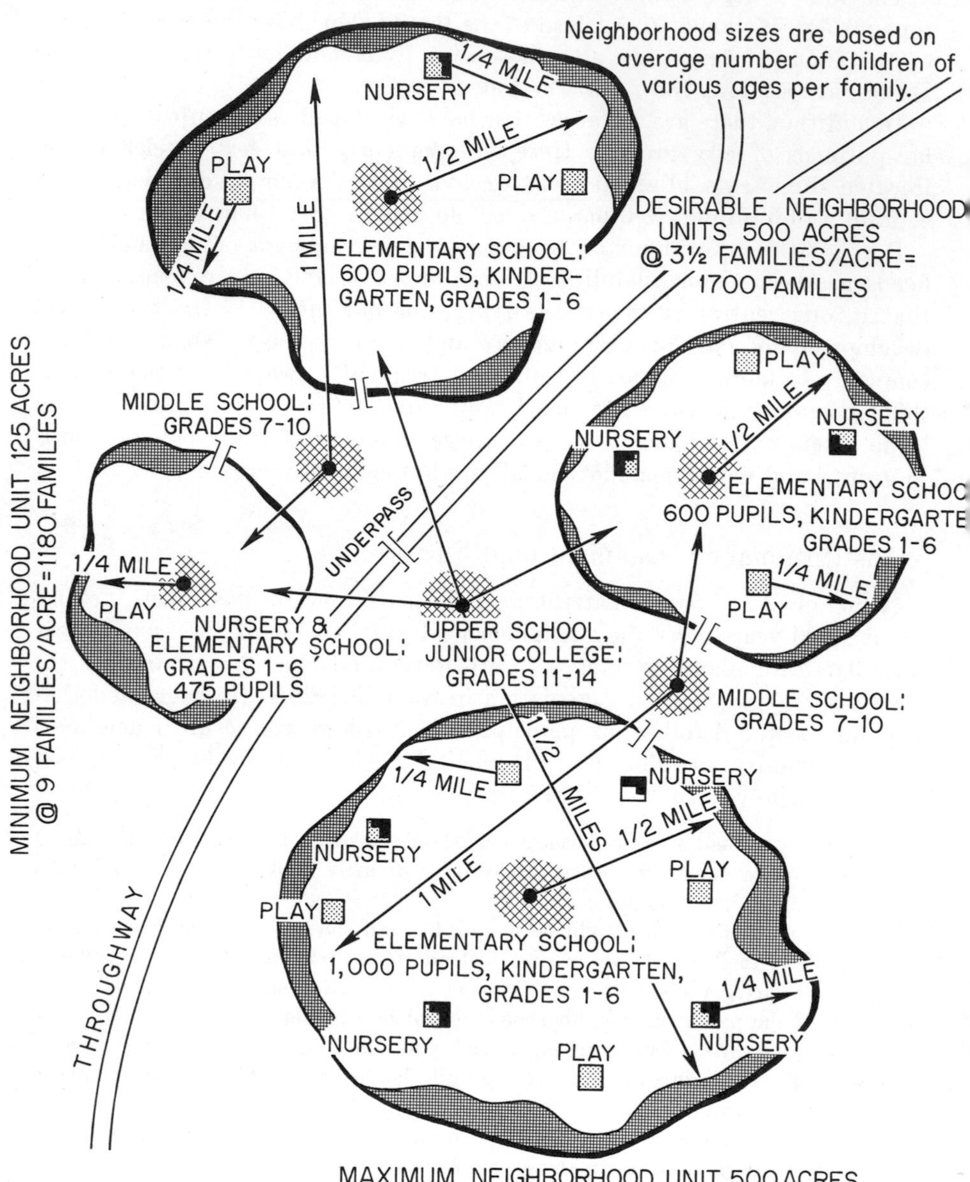

FIGURE 23. *School and neighborhood planning. (Used with permission The Architectural Forum and N. L. Engelhardt.)*

as a whole being designed to facilitate circulation within the unit and to discourage its use by through traffic.[4]

The focal point of neighborhood planning, according to Perry, was the elementary school. He suggested a maximum of a half-mile walk to the school from the farthest dwelling. Based on the size recommended for a normal school district, he suggested that a neighborhood should contain between 5,000 and 10,000 persons.

Although it was not directly evident from his six principles, other writings of Perry suggest that one of the purposes he had in mind for his neighborhood unit was to recreate rural-type neighborhoods in metropolitan areas. In fact, much of the literature, including the writings of Adna Weber, suggested that this should be one of the purposes of neighborhood planning.

CRITICISM OF THE NEIGHBORHOOD UNIT PLANNING CONCEPT

The neighborhood unit concept went unchallenged as a basic planning concept for many years. In fact, in a report in 1948 the American Public Health Association said: "The neighborhood concept has been generally accepted by planners as a sound basis for the development of residential areas."[5] From about that date on, however, there has been criticism of the concept, ranging from moderate to extreme.

Basic criticism has been of four types. First, the concept suggests a unit of planning which is too inflexible. It is generally not possible to develop new and completely self-contained residential areas having the statistical, architectural, and social dimensions suggested. For example, some old and new neighborhoods are smaller in size than the minimum suggested and have fewer facilities. Small neighborhoods are required for genuine "neighboring," but large ones are necessary if there is to be variety in function and facilities. Second, the nature of our large metropolitan communities makes the creation of rural-type neighborhoods an impossibility. (As one writer has indicated, we can't have the New England village in the center of Manhattan or the "home-town" in Chicago!) The discussion in Chapters 11 and 12 will point out some of the basic differences between suburban and village forms of living. Third, planning on the neighborhood basis has sometimes been substituted for over-all city planning. This criticism may not be as valid for the redevelopment of our central city areas today as it was a few years ago because of requirements for over-all planning under the urban renewal program. However, over-all planning still exists more in theory than in practice in many communities. (Of course, it might also be added that the same holds true to a considerable extent for neighborhood planning.) Finally, the most serious criticism is aimed at the concept on

[4] Clarence Arthur Perry, *Housing for the Machine Age.* New York: Russell Sage Foundation, 1939, pp. 51–52.

[5] American Public Health Association, *Planning the Neighborhood.* Chicago: Public Administration Service, 1948, p. 2.

the basis that it suggested segregation of racial, ethnic, religious, and economic groups, thus resulting in "undemocratic ends."[6]

FUTURE PLANNING OF NEIGHBORHOODS

How sound is this criticism? If it is sound, what concept of planning residential areas should be substituted? Is planning needed at all? The answers might be provided by more careful consideration of the physical, social, and economic factors and the personal values involved.

Physical Factors

General

It can hardly be agreed that "that planning is best that plans least." As will be shown in Chapter 11, this philosophy has already prevailed too long with regard to the growth of our cities. In planning for the expansion of our metropolitan communities, it will probably remain necessary to break down the master maps into reasonable, manageable subsections unless we want to return to the monotonous and wasteful gridiron pattern of city development prevalent in the nineteenth century, with no planned boundaries, perhaps few open spaces, and with schools and shops falling wherever they may. The critics of the neighborhood unit plan do not seem to have suggested any sound alternative, although a game of semantics has sometimes been played by suggesting the use of different terms, such as "residential area" or "planning district."[7] It has been indicated that the new "areas" or "districts" should be planned more flexibly, possibly treating each case as an individual problem.

Probably no more needs to be said about the merits of planning neighborhoods or "residential areas" as against not planning them. However, there is more to the matter of physical planning than deciding whether a city should be planned on the basis of manageable subsections, and what they should be called. Zoning, which applies to all land in the city and not merely that devoted to residential use, is important. In the development of new areas, subdivision controls become important. There also are other city planning controls. Finally, since they have not yet completely disappeared from our private property, there must be recognition of the existence of certain restrictive covenants. Each of these matters is discussed briefly below before the discussion moves on to the social factors involved in the future planning of neighborhoods.

[6] One of the first to express this criticism was Catherine Bauer, in her article, "Good Neighborhoods," *The Annals of the American Academy of Political and Social Science*, Vol. 242, November 1945, pp. 104–115. A few years later Isaacs wrote an article, voicing more extreme criticism. See Reginald R. Isaacs, "The 'Neighborhood Unit' is an Instrument for Segregation," in *Journal of Housing*, August 1948, pp. 215–219. The same author also wrote on "Are Urban Neighborhoods Possible?" in the July 1948 issue of that *Journal*.

[7] See "'Neighborhood' Concept is Submitted to Questioning," *Journal of Housing*, December 1948, pp. 299–304.

Zoning Ordinances

Zoning ordinances are one of the most important local controls affecting housing in a community. Although their impact and influence are not limited to neighborhoods *per se*, they do regulate the types of use for both land and buildings in specific areas of the community. Their purpose is to protect the character of a given district by stopping incompatible uses of property, to lessen congestion in the streets and avoid undue concentration of population, to insure adequate light and air, and to promote health and the general welfare. This purpose is achieved by detailed regulations regarding the types of use permitted in specific areas, the height and bulk of buildings, and the density of land use, including the proportion of the lot that may be built upon.

The net effect of such controls, when they are properly designed and reasonably administered, is to minimize risk to the stability of real estate values from the way in which individual properties are used. To the extent that this objective is achieved, zoning is not only justified economically, but becomes an asset to individual property owners in the form of preservation of the amenities of urban living, as well as to the community itself in the form of a more stable tax base.

Too often, however, zoning ordinances have not been very effective in producing the desired results. One of the chief weaknesses of many ordinances, like building codes mentioned in Chapter 6, is that after they were initially drafted twenty or thirty years ago they were never revised and brought up to date to take cognizance of changes in the city's development. Many of them were also written without the benefit of any master plan to guide the direction of development. This is particularly important, because zoning is a device for implementing planned future growth as well as for maintaining status quo and stabilizing property values. All of these factors, coupled with what might be termed a community's "hopeful ego," have produced an unrealistic situation in which almost every community has been hopelessly overzoned for commercial and business uses and, quite often, for multifamily residences. The results of this static overzoning have been quite serious. Properties have stood idle for years, yielding no income, often becoming tax delinquent; they have been dumps for all sorts of refuse and become eyesores; they have stood in the path of natural growth that may have been taking place.

In the last few years, the renewed interest in planning and the seriousness of these ills have resulted in a widespread updating as well as upgrading of ordinances. Proper planning studies are now being undertaken beforehand in many localities.

As has just been pointed out, zoning is not simply a legal device for preventing the auto body shop from moving into the residential neighborhood; it is also a means for actively encouraging and furthering the community's plans for its development. It is a fact of life that communities will grow and develop inexorably and in spite of the best-laid plans or lack of them. All planning, and the regulations passed in its name, must recognize this and be dynamic and flexible enough to adjust to whatever comes. This concept has not always been appreciated and, in fact, the general public still does not appreciate it. (Witness the number of cases brought to court by people who considered their zoning classification to be immutable and sacred.) In recognition of this, many of the new ordinances have express provisions calling for an annual or bi-annual review by the planning board.

Another long-standing source of difficulty has been "spot zoning," the granting of unwarranted exceptions by the local Boards of Zoning Appeals. These boards are set up to hear appeals from the zoning ordinances and are authorized to grant exceptions and variances in the event of demonstrable unique hardship. A well-recognized and long-standing body of legal precedent governs the conditions that must be met before an appeal can be considered as proving a unique hardship. However, in practice it has been rare to find a board which was cognizant of its responsibilities or, if cognizant, chose to exercise them. It has been estimated that fully half of the variances granted have been done so illegally. It has been noted recently that the Board of Appeals device originated as a "safety valve" but has ended up as a big "leak."

There are a number of reasons for this state of affairs. One of the most important is political expediency. In the early days, zoning was looked upon by many as just another invasion or abridgement of private rights. In many communities it was felt that unless there was extreme leniency in enforcing the regulations, public opinion would force the abandonment of the whole idea, as well as voting the incumbents responsible out of office. Since that time, public acceptance has grown faster than proper enforcement. It has also been true that, because the necessary legal precedents were not clearly established at the time, many of the old ordinances did not spell out exactly the conditions to be met. New ordinances are careful to specify the proper procedure.[8]

Subdivision Controls

An essential supplement to the zoning ordinance, in a comprehensive plan of control over urban development, is the subdivision control ordinance which applies to the creation of new neighborhoods in the urban area. The need for such control is obvious in the light of the general character of suburban growth and the resulting subdividing activity today. The episodic character of subdividing requires its control in the interests of economic and orderly development of any urban area.

[8] The reader interested in an introduction to the principles and purposes of zoning is referred to Martin J. Rody and Herbert H. Smith, *Zoning Primer*. West Trenton, N.J.: Chandler-Davis Publishing Co., 1960. See also Richard B. Andrews, *Urban Growth and Development*. New York: Simmons-Boardman Publishing Corp., 1962, Chapter 9. For more detail concerning the technical aspects of zoning, including an illustrative zoning ordinance, see *Zoning in New York State: A Guide to the Preparation of Zoning Ordinances*. Albany, N.Y.: State Department of Commerce, Rev. 1958. (A number of other

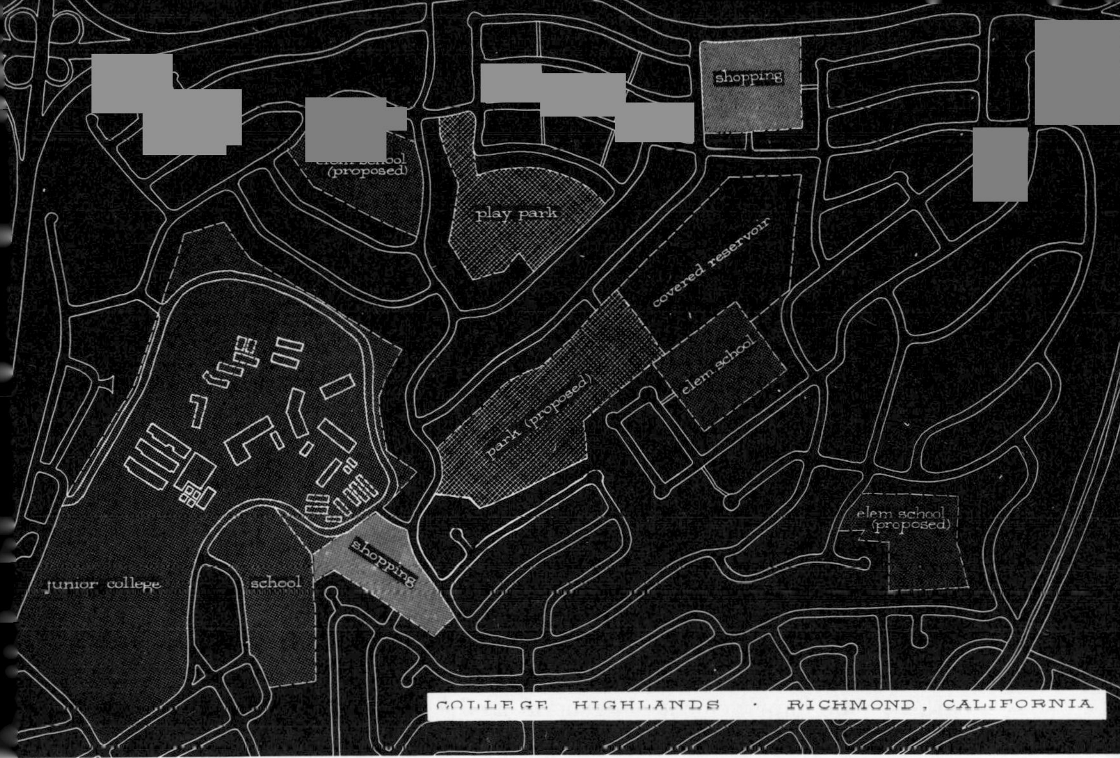

FIGURE 24. *A well planned large-scale development also distinguishes between residential streets and major traffic arteries, and makes provision for adequate community facilities. (Used with permission House and Home Magazine and Barrett Construction Company, Richmond, California.)*

Until very recently, whatever subdivision controls existed were confined typically to controls over the physical layout of new areas—the size of the lots, the width of the streets, building lines, street contours and their intersection with existing streets, and so on. All of this is useful, if the regulations are reasonable and appropriate in terms of local conditions and other controls established in the area. But such ordinances affect only the quality of the new building sites; they do nothing about their quantity, which, as has been shown, is one of the basic economic problems of a city, having an intimate relation to housing patterns and housing costs.

An increasingly frequent requirement is that subdividers include utilities and other basic improvements necessary, such as certain specified amounts of open space (for parks, playgrounds, etc.), in their plans. They must designate and lay out adequate shopping centers in terms of the master plan for the area if such exists, sometimes including parking areas, school sites, and sites for community facilities. Such requirements increase the amenities of the new area and, by increasing the financial responsibilities of the developer, curb excessive provision of lots as well as easing the burden on the community. Few communities exercise any control over site selection or amounts of land to be developed.

---

states have published similar guides; for example, New Jersey, Pennsylvania, and Wisconsin.)

All of these factors have become extremely important today, not only in the development of the numerous new suburban communities, but also in lesser housing developments. The types of facilities described are required where any substantial clusters of population are being formed.

The effectiveness of subdivision control—aside from its specific provisions described in broad outline above—depends in large degree upon the extent of the jurisdiction of the central city in such matters. In some cases that jurisdiction extends for a specified distance beyond the corporate limits of the community. In others, it is not sufficient to control the areas likely to be subdivided for urban use by that community in the forseeable future. In some instances small adjoining communities have strict ordinances.[9]

City-Planning Controls

Local city-planning ordinances are the remaining major type of urban real estate controls to be considered. From the point of view of housing the important thing is that the new neighborhood be treated as an integral part of the community, to be planned to the same extent that highways, parks, public improvements in general, and commercial and industrial uses are planned for. A healthy sign is the growing awareness of this fact by city-planning commissions. Instead of their former, almost exclusive, preoccupation with the planning of public improvements, many commissions are today engaged in housing studies that will supply the facts upon which housing and residential land uses generally can be integrated into the master plan. (The subject of city planning, generally, was discussed in Chapter 2.)

Restrictive Covenants

One other control device should be mentioned, namely, restrictive covenants in deeds. Although these are private rather than public measures, they are included in this discussion because the controls they embody resemble in many respects those contained in zoning and city-planning ordinances.

Although their use has been waning since the Supreme Court decision of May 1948 against them, they are still a factor to be reckoned with in many areas. The restrictions embodied in these deed covenants range all the way from racial and religious discrimination to architectural styles and house costs. Originally, many of these restrictions were formulated in lieu of then nonexistent public controls and served a useful purpose. In time, however, they have tended to become an extremely restrictive and negative nuisance, chiefly because of their permanent nature—once written into a deed they cannot be removed except by court order and the expenditure of much time and trouble. The result has often been the freezing of such prop-

[9] For the reader interested in more information on subdivision controls, including the form and content of subdivision regulations, reference should be made to *Control of Land Subdivision*. Albany, N.Y.: State Department of Commerce, 1963.

erty into incompatible uses and, occasionally, even to uselessness. Racial and religious restrictions have been held to be unenforceable by the courts.

Social Factors

In considering social factors related to the future planning of neighborhoods, it would seem that two primary factors need to be taken into consideration. The first is the positive contribution that the neighborhood concept can make to planning; the second is the misuse of what seems to be an otherwise sound concept.

Let us look first at the positive contributions made by this concept. Many sociologists feel that neighborliness is basically a good thing, because it satisfies certain individual and family desires, and that neighborliness is best achieved in groups that have more similarities than differences. According to Abu-Lughod and Foley:

> When the housing consumer evaluates his neighborhood satisfaction, his central concern is neither geographic site nor physical characteristics. Among consumers satisfied with their location (nearly two-thirds to three-fourths of all consumers), the chief reason for satisfaction seems to be the social characteristics of the neighbors. Among consumers dissatisfied with their neighborhood location (one-fourth to one-third of all consumers), the basic cause seems to be, again, the social characteristics of their neighbors.
>
> In general, the higher the socio-economic status of the individual, the more likely he is to be content with his neighbors (indicating that to live among neighbors of comparable status may be more easily achieved in higher-income areas). Good or desirable neighbors are characterized as friendly, kind, or neighborly. Undesirable neighbors are characterized as belonging to a low or uneducated class, as being noisy, or as having "undesirable," i.e., different racial, ethnic, or religious characteristics.[10]

The fact that neighborhoods are likely to continue to be more homogeneous than heterogeneous from the standpoint of the social characteristics of the residents is indicated by Foote:

> Thus neighborhood differentiation of styles of life will probably occur along with differentiation of family styles of life. Through clustering of families who seek to be near friends, neighborhoods will become more homogeneous within and more different from other neighborhoods.[11]

Handlin supports this point of view even more explicitly. He says, in reference to the anticipated future in-migration of nonwhites into New York City:

> . . . there is no reason to suppose that the Negroes will be thoroughly dispersed throughout the region, any more than other ethnic groups are. Rather it is to be expected that common interests will lead to the development of Negro communities

[10] From *Housing Choices and Housing Constraints,* by Nelson N. Foote, Janet Abu-Lughod, Mary Mix Foley, and Louis Winnick. Copyright 1960. McGraw-Hill Book Company, Inc. Quotation from pp. 183–184, used by permission.

[11] *Ibid.,* p. 325.

which are as coherent as those of the Irish, Jews, or Italians and which offer a variety of types of accommodations without the stigma of inferiority.[12]

Although the subject was not brought up in the immediate discussion of these writers, it is doubtful that any of them, or most other sociologists who hold similar views, are in favor of forced segregation. Rather, they are stating what they undoubtedly believe to be a general social phenomenon, namely, that the neighborhood idea is the result of a deep-seated human instinct. President Kennedy's Executive Order on "Equal Opportunity in Housing" (discussed in Chapter 11) should be a major step in the direction of forbidding forced segregation.

Economic Factors

One of the primary considerations in planning neighborhoods in the past has been the economic one. This factor enters into the picture because some individuals and groups have felt that the physical characteristics of the houses being built and the social characteristics of the occupants have a direct bearing on property values. Wehrly has commented on this as follows:

> FHA, city planners and developers of residential property are bound . . . to recognize and take account of a public demand which reflects itself directly in the investment of the individual property holder as well as that of the developer, mortgage holder, the financial institution which is investing other people's money, and the city tax base, among other things. The jealous protection of property rights and values is deeply rooted in American tradition and public policy. These rights and values are inseparable from other rights of the individual.[13]

Colean, writing twenty years ago, gave this opinion:

> There seems no sound reason why a neighborhood should contain exclusively one type of housing, one level of density, or one narrowly restricted group of residents. The tendency toward what FHA refers to as "homogeneity" may be overplayed, whether it be in types of houses or the incomes of their occupants, to the disadvantage of neighborhood stability and a democratic way of life. . . .
>
> Diversity, of course, can—like uniformity—be carried too far. We have to recognize again that we are dealing with people who have preferences and prejudices as to the people around them. To the extent that such attitudes exist, they are facts that must be taken into account by the planner. The difficulty is in knowing positively to what extent they are facts, rather than something the planner himself takes for granted, and to what extent and through what means they might be successfully overcome should he have good cause for doing so. Here we need more enlightenment and perhaps greater willingness to experiment.[14]

[12] Oscar Handlin, *The Newcomers.* Cambridge, Mass.: Harvard University Press, 1959, p. 92. There is an elaboration of this quotation in Chapter 11.

[13] Max S. Wehrly, "Comment on the Neighborhood Theory," *Journal of the American Institute of Planners,* Vol. XIV, No. 4, Fall 1948, p. 33.

[14] "Fundamentals of Land Planning," *The Architectural Forum,* Vol. 79, No. 4, October 1943, p. 67. In regard to the reference to the FHA, it should be pointed out that official policy has been revised considerably from that practiced by that agency in the 1930's and 1940's.

There have not been many ''studied'' experiments, but one recent research effort followed up Colean's suggestion. A broad-scale study made by the Commission on Race and Housing provided evidence that the entry of nonwhite residents into previously all-white neighborhoods need not cause a decline in property values. The study indicated that, on the contrary, real estate values are apt to rise.[15]

While Laurenti contended strongly that ''race should gradually lose its significance as a consideration in the real estate market,'' he presented some possible exceptions to his findings that may leave the door open far enough for real estate groups, certain planners, and other individuals and groups who have their own strong opinions on this matter. He indicated that some of the rises in property values he found may have merely reflected stiffer local conditions that nonwhites had to meet and that smaller down payments may have inflated some selling prices. Nevertheless, he found the number of integrated neighborhoods to be growing.

Personal Values

Finally, conflicting opinions concerning the planning of neighborhoods should be placed in the context of the concept of personal values, described in Chapter 2. Although the discussion of personal values in that chapter was primarily in the context of individuals as family members, the ''values'' concept may also be related to individuals as businessmen, public officials, and citizens in general. Some individuals may adopt a different personality, different attitudes, and the like away from home, but normally it is to be expected that the values one holds exert their influence anywhere, whether at home or away from it. For this reason, it is entirely proper to consider them in the context of attitudes toward neighborhood planning.

It has been seen, throughout much of the discussion in this chapter, that there are some basic philosophical differences between those who agree with and those who oppose the neighborhood unit theory for planning. On the one hand are individuals who support the concept on the basis that it protects the rights of individuals to a private life. Basically they are saying, ''No man has a 'right' to another man's association.'' They would thus preclude ''undesirables'' from invading a neighborhood on two primary counts: first, a neighborhood is intended for neighborliness and they suggest that neighborliness is not fostered by putting together people of basically different occupational patterns (plumbers and doctors and lawyers), different income levels (those who cannot afford to pay a high rent and those who can afford all of the luxuries of life, including residential privacy), different races (white and colored), and so on. They emphasize the *freedom* of the individuals living there to select their own neighbors (but not the freedom of outsiders to enter the neighborhoods). Behind some of this feeling is the attitude that, because they feel the conditions described would make

[15] Luigi Laurenti, *Property Values and Race.* Berkeley: University of California Press, 1961.

the neighborhood unattractive to people who have the means of choosing where they want to live, they would pass up such neighborhoods for others, and the result would be deflated property values.

On the other hand, those opposed to the concept have more of the characteristics related to the value of *equality*. They are more group-minded than individualistic. They feel that it is undemocratic to segregate the different kinds of families indicated. They feel that, given time, the various kinds of families will find themselves to be compatible to the benefit of all. They either are willing to overlook the economic problem or evade the issue by indicating that this alleged economic problem is only a myth.

There is considerable similarity in the alignment of the different groups with reference to how neighborhoods should be planned in other matters related to housing. This is treated in more detail in the discussion of housing laws and pressure groups in Chapter 14.

Several observations may be made, however, in conclusion. First, while there are still some people who hold extreme positions, most individuals are perhaps more objective and would fall somewhere between the two extremes in their attitude. As a case in point, Laurenti has indicated the rightness of the principle that individuals, regardless of race, creed, or color, should be able to live where they desire, but he indicated that this can best be accomplished by not trying to change all new neighborhoods overnight:

> The major threat to prices seems to be a too sudden and large addition to the neighborhood supply of housing available to nonwhites. Time, therefore, has a major influence on how racial change will affect (economic) values. Racial transition that is accomplished gradually is likely to have very different effects on house prices than a sudden shift.[16]

Second, it must be recognized that there are still important unanswered questions that arise in the present-day process of building our housing and developing our communities. Bauer has raised some of the most pertinent ones: "... what is the relation between homogeneity and heterogeneity and the quality of neighborly social life?" "Should the families at this intimate grouping be fairly similar, perhaps self-selected, or would this merely result in isolated cliques? What is the influence of family income, age levels, cultural background, and other factors?"[17] These questions go to the heart of the discussion in this chapter.

When we have sound, objective answers to questions like these, we will be able to discuss sound principles for neighborhood planning, rather than merely pointing up the problems and the different points of view that currently exist.

Some of the problems that have been discussed in this chapter will inevitably arise in chapters that follow, especially those concerning the problems of the central city and suburbia.

[16] *Ibid.*, p. 56.

[17] Catherine Bauer, "Social Questions in Housing and Community Planning," *Journal of Social Issues*, Vol. VII, Nos. 1 and 2, 1951, pp. 25, 29.

READING LIST

SOCIAL ASPECTS OF NEIGHBORING

Foote, Nelson N., Janet Abu-Lughod, Mary Mix Foley, and Louis Winnick. *Housing Choices and Housing Constraints.* New York: McGraw-Hill Book Co., Inc., 1960.

Handlin, Oscar. *The Newcomers.* Cambridge, Mass.: Harvard University Press, 1959.

Tannenbaum, Judith. "The Neighborhood: A Socio-Psychological Analysis," *Land Economics,* Vol. XXIV, No. 4, November 1948.

NEIGHBORHOOD PLANNING

American Public Health Association. *Planning the Neighborhood.* Chicago: Public Administration Service, 1948.

Bauer, Catherine. "Good Neighborhoods," *The Annals of the American Academy of Political and Social Science,* Vol. 242, November 1945.

———, "Social Questions in Housing and Community Planning," *The Journal of Social Issues,* Vol. VII, Nos. 1 and 2, 1951.

Dahir, James. *The Neighborhood Unit Plan—Its Spread and Acceptance.* New York: Russell Sage Foundation, 1947.

Dewey, Richard. "The Neighborhood, Urban Ecology, and City Planners," in Paul K. Hatt and Albert J. Reiss, Jr., eds., *Cities and Society.* New York: The Free Press of Glencoe, Inc., 3d printing, August 1961.

Isaacs, Reginald R. "Are Urban Neighborhoods Possible?" *Journal of Housing,* July 1948, and "The 'Neighborhood Unit' is an Instrument for Segregation," *loc. cit.,* August 1948. The essence of these arguments is published in "The Neighborhood Theory," *Journal of the American Institute of Planners,* Vol. XIV, No. 2, Spring 1948. Comments on the Isaacs articles appear in *Journal of Housing,* December 1948, and *Journal of the American Institute of Planners,* Vol. XIV, No. 3, Summer 1948. See also Max S. Wehrly's answer to Mr. Isaacs' position in *Journal of the American Institute of Planners,* Vol. XIV, No. 4, Fall 1948.

Perry, Clarence Arthur. *Housing for the Machine Age.* New York: Russell Sage Foundation, 1939.

ZONING

Andrews, Richard B. *Urban Growth and Development.* New York: Simmons-Boardman Publishing Co., 1962.

Rody, Martin J. and Herbert H. Smith. *Zoning Primer.* West Trenton, N.J.: Chandler-Davis Publishing Co., 1960.

SUBDIVISION CONTROLS

Control of Land Subdivisions. Albany, N.Y.: State Department of Commerce, 1963.

Martin, Preston. *Real Estate Principles and Practices.* New York: The Macmillan Co., 1959, Chapter 3.

Wissink, G. A. *American Cities in Perspective.* Assen, The Netherlands: Royal Van Gorcum, Ltd., 1962, pp. 266-283.

Part 4

****

HOUSING PROBLEMS AND PROGRESS

CHAPTER 10

*

Housing Problems of Our Central Cities

It is generally recognized that the greatest proportion of poor-quality housing in the United States is in the central cities of our metropolitan areas. This has resulted from the fact that throughout our history many of the families who have lacked adequate means to afford a decent standard of living have congregated there. Workers in many of these families have always held low-paying factory jobs and have wanted to be near their places of work.

The present housing problems of our central cities, then, had their origin during the periods of early growth of those cities. Although the general nature of the problem has remained unchanged over the years, the composition of the population has changed. A century ago most of the families crowding into cities were immigrants from other countries—Italians, Irish, Germans, Bohemians, Russians, French, Spanish, Scandinavian, Chinese, and others. With the curtailment of immigration in the 1920's and economic expansion in the 1940's, several groups have moved in to take the jobs no longer being filled by immigrants.[1] One of these is the Southern Negroes, whose migration since Emancipation had been checked by white, foreign in-migration before 1920. Another includes the Southern whites. Still another group is the Puerto Ricans, who, as American citizens, have been free to move without restraint and who have done so. For example, the 1960 Census indicated that the number of persons of Puerto Rican birth in the United States had reached 617,000—most of whom have sought greater opportunities in New York City and a few other cities than they were offered on their farms in Puerto Rico. Finally, many Mexicans have moved to the West and Southwest after either being solicited by the United States to cross the border or having crossed it illegally. Many Mexicans, of course, are employed on farms rather than in large cities.

The effect this movement has had can be seen from location of residence and place of work data that are available. In 1960, for example, 80 percent of the nonwhite workers in large metropolitan areas lived in the central cities, compared with only 50 percent of the white workers (Table 10–1, p. 351). A high proportion of that 80 percent undoubtedly live in the same

[1] Charles Abrams, "Public Housing Myths," *The New Leader*, Vol. XXXVIII, No. 30, July 25, 1955, pp. 4–5. See also Raymond W. Mack, "The Changing Ethnic Fabric of the Metropolis," in B. J. Chandler, *et al.*, eds., *Education in Urban Society*. New York: Dodd, Mead & Co., 1962, pp. 54–69.

neighborhoods where earlier immigrants lived. In fact, it is possible in most large cities to reach areas in which many of them live by a short ten or twelve block walk from the City Hall or the main shopping area of the cities.

PERIOD OF IMMIGRATION

Although similar problems of urban congestion developed in many European cities as a result of the Industrial Revolution and the emergence of hundreds of new factories in cities, the problem had an added dimension in America—the rapidly growing city populations were made up in large part of immigrants from other countries.

To understand the impact of this immigration, we can look at the period from 1830 to the end of that century. There was great heterogeneity among the immigrants, as already indicated. Most of them from 1830 until the Civil War were Irish, British, and German. After that war, the proportion of Irish steadily decreased each decade, while the proportion of Germans —37 percent of all immigration in the decade 1851 to 1860—remained large through the last decade of the century. Immigrants from Italy, Austria-Hungary, Russia, and Poland began appearing in noticeable numbers between 1871 and 1880, when they made up 7 percent of all immigration. From 1881 to 1890, they represented 18 percent—nearly one fifth—of all arrivals, and between 1890 and 1900, they comprised almost half (46 percent). During that decade, Irish, British, Germans, and Scandinavians together made up 45 percent (Table 10–2, p. 351).

The immigrants from the different countries were sometimes made up of different ethnic groups. For example, both Jews and Slavs came from Russia and Poland; and Slavs, Germans, Magyars, and Jews came from Austria and Hungary.

Most of the immigrants came through the port of New York, and many from every nation tended to remain there, giving that city the most heterogeneous population of any in the United States. Within the city the different groups tended to cluster among their own kind. Some of the groups, however, went in large numbers to other cities; for example, the Poles to Detroit and Chicago, and the Germans and Scandinavians to certain Midwest cities.

Many of the immigrants had one characteristic in common—they arrived on these shores with few, if any, resources. This meant that they could afford housing of only the most minimum standards. The literature of the period is filled with descriptions of substandard housing, a common characteristic being that it was frequently seriously overcrowded. For example, Dr. John H. Griscom, the City Inspector of the New York Board of Health, in his Annual Report to the Board of Aldermen in 1842, drew attention to the crowded conditions, with insufficient ventilation, of a great number of dwellings in that city. He said:

This subject is properly to be regarded in a twofold aspect. First as respects the direct physical influence of the impurity of the atmosphere arising from the abundant animal and vegetable exhalations. Second, with regard to the depraved effects which such modes of life exert upon the moral feelings and habits, with the tendency of that depravity to increase or modify the severity and forms of disease.

The influences of a confined atmosphere are nowhere more marked than among the residents of those houses which are occupied by one or two and sometimes even more families in each room. It is truly surprising how small a space some families can reside in, and how densely they are willing to crowd themselves.[2]

The housing they occupied tended to be of two types. First, old, one-family dwellings were used as tenements, which was mainly responsible for the growth of the great "cellar" population—those living in the highly unsanitary cellars and basements of the buildings. Second, tenement buildings or "barracks" built in every possible unoccupied space in the poorer neighborhoods—in sets or rows, one behind the other or side by side, along narrow courts or alleys, or in the back yards of old buildings—provided equally poor quarters. Frequently there were outdoor privies, and many of the buildings had pigs and other animals roaming in the yards.

Some description of the situation in other cities was provided in Chapter 1, and it is important to recall the descriptions of that period in order to understand how the present housing situation in our central cities originated.

POPULATION CHARACTERISTICS IN CENTRAL CITIES TODAY

One of the major characteristics of our central cities has already been mentioned: the migrants drawn to them frequently are members of racial minorities. While the number of nonwhite households represented only 10 percent of all households in the nation in 1960, in central cities the proportions increased to 15 percent.[3] In many cities, of course, the percentages are higher. In Washington, D. C., for example, nonwhites represent 55 percent of the population; in New Orleans, 37 percent; in Baltimore, 35 percent; in Detroit, St. Louis, and Cleveland, 29 percent; in Philadelphia, 27 percent and Chicago, 24 percent. The proportions of nonwhites in our twenty largest central cities are shown in Table 10–3 (p. 352).

Regardless of the exact proportions in any single city, the special characteristics of the nonwhite population make it important to separate this group out in any general discussion of these areas. For this reason, when particular characteristics of both population and housing are discussed below, the nonwhite group will be identified separately.

One of the characteristics of families living in cities is that they are some-

[2] Quoted in Robert W. DeForest and Lawrence Veiller, eds. *The Tenement House Problem*, Vol. I. New York: The Macmillan Co., 1903, p. 72.

[3] Derived from U. S. Bureau of the Census, *Census of Housing 1960*. Components of Inventory Change, HC(4), Part 1A-1, 1950–1959. Components, United States and Regions.

what smaller than those living elsewhere. Nonwhite families living in central cities, in particular, tend to be smaller than those not living in central cities. For example, in 1960 the average size of all white families in the nation was 3.58 persons, but among those living in urban areas the average size was 3.51. For all nonwhites in the nation the average family size was 4.31 persons, but for nonwhites living in urban places it was 4.07. The difference between the median size of white and nonwhite families is caused primarily by the significant proportion of large nonwhite families. For example, in 1960 a total of 14 percent of those families living in urban areas had seven or more persons. Only 4 percent of the white families were that large (Table 10–4, p. 352).[4]

Income levels of families living in cities, on the other hand, usually are higher than those of families living elsewhere. For example, in 1959 the median income of all white families in the United States was $5,893, but among those living in urban places it was $6,433. The figures for the nation as a whole are weighted down, of course, by the generally low incomes of rural families. For all nonwhites in the nation it was $3,161 but among those living in urban places it was $3,711. Although the figure for incomes in urban places is significantly higher than the national figure, it still is low when compared with that for white families and generally represents the income level of a high proportion of our families living in urban areas.

Although poverty is not exclusively an urban phenomenon, as we will see from the discussion in the chapter on rural housing, the city is, as some authors have indicated, ". . . the home of the most drastic inequalities in wealth and income."[5] For example, in 1959 only one third of the urban nonwhite families had an income of $5,000 or over, compared with over two thirds of the urban white families. Of course, the fact that 5 percent of the nonwhite families had incomes of $10,000 and over indicates that not all nonwhites have low incomes. However, many of them do—40 percent were below the $3,000 level in 1959 (Table 10–5, p. 353).

Many studies have shown that there is a well-established association between income, occupation, and educational attainment, and this close association can be seen regarding different groups in our cities.

Let us look, then, at the distribution of occupations of heads of urban families. A total of 13 percent of the heads of white urban families were professional or technical workers and 14 percent were managers, officials, or proprietors in 1960. The comparative figures for heads of urban nonwhite families were 5 percent and 3 percent. At the other end of the occupational ladder, 17 percent of the urban nonwhite heads of families were unskilled laborers, compared with 4 percent of the urban white heads of families. Or, one may observe the picture with reference to service workers. Here the

[4] For some characteristics such as this, Census data are not available for central cities only. In such cases, data for "urban" places are used in this discussion. The coverage of particular data is always clear from the terminology used.

[5] "The Problems of Urban America," reprinted in Paul K. Hatt and Albert J. Reiss, Jr., eds., *Cities and Society*. New York: The Free Press of Glencoe, 3d printing, 1961, p. 743.

differences are accentuated even more: 23 percent of the nonwhite heads of families were engaged in service occupations, compared with only 6 percent of the white heads of families (Table 10–6, p. 353).

What accounts for these differences? Undoubtedly there are several important factors leading to the generally poor occupational position of the nonwhite head of family, some of which cannot be measured. One that can be measured, however, is the level of educational attainment.

At the time the last decennial census was taken, 41 percent of the heads of nonwhite families had not been educated beyond the seventh-grade level. This would mean, of course, that they often were capable of performing only the service or common labor types of occupations that have been mentioned. Some white family heads, of course, also had not passed this level of educational attainment, but the proportion was much smaller—16 percent. At the other extreme of educational attainment, only 9 percent of the nonwhite family heads had attended college (4 percent of those heads having been graduated), compared with 23 percent of the white family heads (12 percent of them graduates). (Table 10–7, p. 354). Although the general levels of education for nonwhites still are low, it was pointed out in Chapter 2 that striking gains are being made, and if the progress of the last two decades is maintained or improved upon, we should soon see the eradication of a major part of the illiteracy and semi-illiteracy which can still be found among this minority group today.

HOUSING CHARACTERISTICS

In discussing housing characteristics in central cities, it must first be recognized that a significantly higher proportion of the units are rented than in other types of areas. This can be seen from the following Census data for 1960:

	Percentage Distribution		
	Owned	*Rented*	*Vacant*
United States total	56.4	34.2	9.4
In SMSA's			
In central cities	46.8	48.0	5.2
Outside central cities	66.7	26.3	7.1
Outside SMSA's	56.9	28.7	14.4

Furthermore, the proportion of renters (to total) is much higher among nonwhites in our central cities than among whites. To show this, data must be limited to structures that are occupied. Among such structures occupied by white families, 48 percent were rented and 52 percent owned. However, among those occupied by nonwhites, 67 percent were rented and 33 percent owned.

With this as background concerning tenure, the detailed characteristics of housing in central cities can be discussed. These characteristics include the value and rent levels of the dwelling units, their quality, their age, their size, and their density of occupancy. In this chapter, the discussion will be limited to the total supply of such housing, special attention being given to that portion of the central city housing occupied by nonwhite households. No comparisons will be made with housing outside of central cities. (That comparison will be made in Chapter 11.)

The median value of owner-occupied housing in central cities was $12,300 in 1960. This average for all housing in those areas is well above the median for housing occupied by nonwhites only, which was $9,000. The difference in these medians is attributable in large part to the heavy proportion of nonwhite housing valued at less than $10,000. This included 58 percent of the housing occupied by nonwhite households, but only one third of the housing occupied by white households. Furthermore, one out of every seven nonwhite families owned dwellings valued at less than $5,000 (Table 10–8, p. 354).

The trend is the same for rental housing. The median gross rent of all rental housing in central cities was $72 in 1960. For dwelling units occupied by nonwhites, the median was only $65. One out of every four nonwhite households lived in units having a gross rent of less than $50 per month (Table 10–9, p. 355).

Low property values and low rents, of course, do not in themselves reflect an unsatisfactory housing situation. In fact, from the family's point of view, the situation is quite the reverse. However, the difficulty is that they reflect poor quality of housing.

As discussed in Chapter 4, data are limited concerning the quality of housing. It is necessary to rely on Census figures indicating condition of structure and availability of plumbing facilities.

When these figures are reviewed, it immediately becomes apparent that owner-occupied dwelling units are generally of better quality than renter-occupied dwellings. For example, 91 percent of all of the owner units in central cities, compared with only 72 percent of the renter units, were found to be in sound condition, with all plumbing facilities. Also, while only 1 percent of the owner units were found to be dilapidated, 5 percent of the renter units were found to be in that condition.

The Census figures also show clearly the poorer condition of units occupied by nonwhite households. Three out of every four of the dwellings owned by nonwhite households were in sound condition and had all of the plumbing facilities. Among the renter-occupied units, slightly over half were in that category. Furthermore, 5 percent of the units owned by nonwhite households and 12 percent of those rented were found to be dilapidated (Table 10–10, p. 355).

Obviously one of the causes of poor quality is the age of the structures, related undoubtedly to lack of adequate maintenance. Data on age are available from the Census. These data indicate that 58 percent of the owner-occupied units in central cities and 76 percent of the rented units were built before 1940. Owner-occupied dwellings occupied by nonwhite households were appreciably older, on the average, than those occupied by white households—72 percent were built before 1940. There was no great difference, however, between the ages of rental units occupied by the total population in central cities and those occupied by nonwhite households. Although we have experienced a heavy volume of new construction in the nation as a whole during the last decade, it is obvious that a smaller percentage of this construction has taken place in central cities than outside them. (See discussion in Chapter 11.) It is also obvious that even in central cities the rate of new construction of housing occupied by nonwhite households has not kept pace with that occupied by white households (Table 10–11, p. 356).

In one characteristic of housing there is practically no difference between dwellings occupied by white and nonwhite households. That characteristic is the size of dwelling units. The median owner-occupied unit had 5.5 rooms for the total of all units in central cities in 1960 and for those occupied by nonwhite households only. The median figure for rental units was 3.7 for both groups. There was little difference, as well, in the percentage distributions of the number of rooms for the two groups (Table 10–12, p. 356).

However, nonwhite households frequently are larger than white households, and therefore they frequently are more crowded in their dwelling units. The extent of this can be seen in persons-per-room data. Of the dwellings owned by all households, 49 percent had an occupancy rate of 0.50 or less. The comparable figure for nonwhite households only was 43 percent. The difference among rental units was sharper. For all households the proportion was 36 percent and for nonwhite households, it was only 27 percent. Those figures also indicate the greater density of occupancy of rental units than owner-occupied units (Table 10–13, p. 357). This results in large part from the fact that rental dwellings are smaller than owner-occupied dwellings, rather than the fact that families who rent are larger than those who own. (In fact, it has been shown earlier that although there is some difference in size of families between owners and renters, that difference is not as great as the difference in the size of dwelling units.)

SUBCLASSIFICATIONS OF CENTRAL CITIES

Thus far we have discussed central cities as a whole. Although it has been pointed out that those cities are made up of populations of different socioeconomic classes, there has been no attempt to relate the specific groups to particular areas of the city. In practice, however, the various groups are clearly related to specific kinds of areas, because different areas usually have different value and rent levels for housing.

These different value and rent levels are usually the result of the economic and physical desirability of the different areas. This has a direct bearing on the housing located in them. *Housing, almost more than any other commodity, is a product of its environment.* The value of a house depends as much upon the character of the immediate environment and neighborhood as it does upon the character or suitability of the house itself. A house is wedded to the land and remains there, for better or for worse.

If a neighborhood becomes undesirable in a shorter period of time than a well-planned house within that neighborhood, the loss is reflected in the decreased value of the house. Few people care to build new houses in declining neighborhoods, and few care to pay high prices for a sound house in a declining neighborhood. All the factors of depreciation and obsolescence that occur within a neighborhood—whether they affect the houses, schools, streets, sewers, playgrounds, or any of the community facilities—have an "averaging" effect upon any individual house in the area.

Neighborhood facilities, therefore, add to or detract from the value of a dwelling unit, depending upon the degree of adequacy and deterioration of these facilities. The manner in which the houses of a neighborhood are maintained also adds to or detracts from this value. Undesirable developments may enter a neighborhood, such as an odor-producing industry or a noisy commercial establishment, hazardous heavy traffic, or the conversion of existing structures to other types of uses which detract from the original character of the area.

The degree of deterioration and obsolescence classifies an area according to one of three remedial and preventive planning processes: (1) redevelopment, for slum areas which are economically or physically beyond repair and which must be cleared, replanned, and redeveloped; (2) rehabilitation, for declining areas where houses and neighborhood facilities can be restored by degrees of modernization (repairs and modifications) which would enable the neighborhood to come up to good health and safety standards; and (3) conservation, for areas which are generally stable but which may have need for minor changes and protective measures.[6]

Slums and Redevelopment Areas

When a housing area reaches the point of deterioriation and obsolescence, where the dwelling units have passed any possible stage of rehabilitation in order to provide decent living quarters, that area constitutes a slum.

The housing in such an area is a detriment to physical well-being. Usually such areas lack sunlight and fresh air, adequate water supplies, and sewage control, and often there are fire and accident hazards, as well as severe overcrowding.

A large proportion of older people with inadequate means of livelihood are frequently found in these areas. The occupants of slum areas normally have less education and a higher rate of illiteracy than those

[6] Protection against the encroachment of undesirable commercial and industrial uses, prevention of violations of existing zoning laws, or a need for rezoning, encouragement of a continuous modernization process, or the expansion of existing facilities (schools, playgrounds, utility services, and other neighborhood facilities that add to the desirability and stability of the neighborhood).

of other urban areas. The areas also are frequently occupied by groups who because of minority status or physical and mental abnormalities find it difficult to make a decent living within the society. Despair and its effects are evident—alcoholism, vice, venereal and other communicable diseases are prevalent.[7] The neighborhood facilities are inadequate or completely nonexistent; children attend overcrowded schools and play in the streets.

Generally, most of the dwellings in such areas are rented rather than owner-occupied. Although the rents here are lower than in other areas, slum dwellings yield a much higher return to the landlords than most other types of real estate investment, primarily because the costs of maintenance are usually nil and assessments and the resultant taxes are low. The rents, relatively speaking, are nevertheless high, considering the conditions slum dwellers must endure. Most of the housing consists of dilapidated structures that have outlived their usefulness and are unfit for human habitation, but which have sufficient economic value, because of the tight housing market, to produce a high rate of return.

How and why have the slums developed? The best summary discussion of this question is provided by Ford:

> Although no single cause of slums can be specified, and no group of clear-cut causes of measurable influence and intensity, there is value in outlining the imponderable, precipitating, and causative factors, since they unquestionably suggest possible points of attack upon the contemporary problem and devices for prevention. For convenience these may be listed under the following headings: physical factors, population factors, economic factors, architectural and engineering factors, political factors, and social factors. Inevitably and invariably they interpenetrate and operate together and . . . the slum becomes an outgrowth of the development of a dynamic total situation in which relations of elements are as important as the elements themselves, rather than the resultant of a single cause or group of causes. . . .
>
> The physical factors comprise topography, land configuration, climate, and natural resources, no one of which in itself is a cause of slums. If, however, man makes unwise use of physical features, slums may originate. . . . Many cities show slums on the edges of swamps, in hollows, adjacent to railroad tracks, or, as in Pittsburgh, on hillsides where street systems and housing were not conformed to topography. Similarly, slums may grow up on the borders of rivers and harbors, if man pollutes them by dumping his refuse or emptying his sewers there. . . .

[7] Much has been written concerning the mal-influences of slum conditions on family life and health. General observation tells us that slum conditions reflect unhealthy conditions. However, this seems to be a kind of subject that evades statistical documentation. In fact, a comprehensive recent study failed to reveal any really major differences between a group of subjects living in new public housing and another group living under slum conditions. The study was undertaken in Baltimore between 1955 and 1960 and covered 1,000 Negro families—600 of whom were living in slum housing and 400 of whom had moved into new housing projects. Some differences were reported in favor of the new housing: there was less illness, more neighboring, and the children did somewhat better in school. However, the differences between the two groups with regard to these factors were not large. See Daniel M. Wilner, Rosabelle Price Walkley, Thomas C. Pinkerton, and Matthew Tayback, *The Housing Environment and Family Life.* Baltimore: The Johns Hopkins Press, 1962.

FIGURE 25. *Houses such as these can still be found in almost all of our cities. (Photographs courtesy the New York State Division of Housing.)*

The population factors comprise the movement and pressure of population, immigration, and rapidity of growth. . . .

. . . to population growth may be ascribed three major categories of slums. First, there are the shanty towns and squatter colonies on the periphery at each stage of growth, and usually, though not invariably, in unfavorable locations near swamps, dumps, railroads, or other regions of ugliness and neglect. . . . Next there are the abandoned dwellings of the well-to-do, suffering from impromptu conversion and use by persons of lower standards. . . . Third, there is the type more generally visualized . . . in which many-storied dwellings of high land coverage were erected under earlier and inferior legislation, for rental chiefly to European immigrants.

The economic factors are represented in the change of location of commercial and industrial establishments and the pressure of new shops and factories upon neighboring residential areas, as well as the rise in land values consequent upon population growth and commercial or industrial pressure. . . .

Low wages to the industrial population . . . meant low rent-paying capacity which made it necessary for workers to hire miserable quarters or take in lodgers, and for owners to pack as many families as possible on the land. . . .

The engineering and architectural factors in slum causation cover all errors in the planning and designing of cities, of their street systems and public utilities, of residences and their internal equipment, of transit and transportation facilities, and of municipal sanitation. . . .

The causes of slums that are inherent in our political structure and administration have already largely been suggested. Survivals of old principles of land ownership and control are at the bottom of our difficulties. . . .

Legislative controls through statute law are at every point far short of perfection. At best, building, housing, and zoning legislation provide only minimum standards, and fail to incorporate well conceived norms for human welfare. . . .

A separate category for discussion of the social factors that produce slums seems hardly necessary in view of the fact that in one sense or another all of the factors so far considered have grown out of our social structure and organization, or the social process. The ignorance of landlord, tenant, or public official; the lack of perspective in each; speculation, greed, corruption, apathy, fashion, and imitation; the rise of standards which create obsolescence—all originate in our social system. . . .

Other attitudes play a role in the creation of slums. The reputation of a district, if bad, may keep self-respecting citizens out, even though that reputation is undeserved. . . .

Another such attitude is the general assumption on the part of many of the well-to-do that the poor are inured to poverty and hardship and are incapable of making proper use of better housing. . . .

All of the above causes, whether listed as originating in physical conditions, population growth, economies, engineering, architecture, or social organization and human attitudes, continue to operate either because of ignorance on the part of some individual or group, or because of private or public neglect. It is to these that slums must be chiefly ascribed.[8]

A few years before Ford's book was published, Hoyt conducted a study in Chicago which also threw some early light on the causes of slums. He

[8] Reprinted by permission of the publishers from James Ford, *Slums and Housing*, Vol. I. Cambridge, Mass.: Harvard University Press, Copyright, 1936, by the President and Fellows of Harvard College, pp. 443–454.

pinpointed his findings, suggesting that racial and national movements, bringing in people of low economic status and low standards of living, caused physical deterioration of properties. He went so far as to list in priority form the different nationalities and racial groups exerting the most detrimental effect on property values and neighborhoods generally.[9] Hoyt's thesis, however, has recently been challenged. As mentioned earlier, Laurenti, basing his report on a five-year examination of "property values and race" in six cities, concluded that the entry of colored residents into previously all-white neighborhoods need not cause a decline in property values. On the contrary, real estate values are apt to rise.[10] Race, in itself, then, may not be the important factor many have considered it to be. Other studies will undoubtedly be made in the future to further test these hypotheses.

Rehabilitation Areas

Rehabilitation areas are, as the name implies, those areas which are potential slums but which can, by appropriate action, be saved. Generally speaking, these are the fringe areas surrounding a slum. Some of the dwellings in these areas are fit only for demolition, but most are simply in a poor state of repair. Generally, the basic structures are sound and capable of being salvaged without disproportionate expense. The salvage of rehabilitation areas constitutes one of the most pressing—and rewarding—tasks facing communities today. If appropriate steps are taken, these areas can be made to serve the community for at least another generation.

Rehabilitation is not a process which can be brought about by the *individual* action of tenants or homeowners; it is not an economically sound policy to invest in areas that are showing signs of decay and are gradually losing their investment value. Undesirable uses have begun to appear; neighborhood facilities such as schools, playgrounds, streets, and sewer systems are showing evidence of deterioration and obsolescence. It is extremely difficult to persuade individual homeowners and landlords to make improvements under these conditions. In addition, there are such problems as laxity of local health, safety, building and zoning regulations, improper planning practices, and, in many cases, a complete absence of such regulatory safeguards.

Perhaps a more basic problem in these areas is not so much reluctance to invest, but rather, inability to invest. In most instances, these areas accommodate low-income groups of one sort or another: unskilled workers, old people, and widows struggling along on pensions. These groups are in a poor position to do much about their environment, even if they wanted to.

Recognition of these circumstances and an appreciation of the public responsibility inherent therein have resulted in the legislative machinery

[9] Homer Hoyt, *One Hundred Years of Land Values in Chicago*. Chicago: University of Chicago Press, 1933, pp. 314–316.

[10] Luigi Laurenti, *Property Values and Race*. Berkeley: University of California Press, 1961, pp. 47–65.

necessary to attack these problems. The basic approach is many-sided: private cooperative action, citizen participation, eased financing terms by institutions, Federal aid, and vigorous local government action along all fronts.

Conservation Areas

The last of the three major types of areas found in central cities are the conservation areas. These are areas in which housing and neighborhood facilities are generally good, with a few exceptions. They are not necessarily new areas; many areas manage to retain their desirability as residential neighborhoods for years. Low income is not necessarily a significant factor, since these areas seldom provide accommodation for other than middle- and upper-income groups. The basic problem here is one of maintaining local regulations (zoning, building, health, and safety) and neighborhood facilities by local governments.

Conservation is primarily a governmental responsibility. Even though neighborhoods have maintained their stability with little or no exercise of the governmental function, the fact that neighborhood facilities are the responsibility of local government means that neighborhood stability can seldom be effectively maintained without the assumption and exercise of such functions by the local government.

THE FILTERING CONCEPT

The so-called "filtering concept" is a theory by which housing is said to pass down the ladder, over a period of time, to families of lower incomes. Ultimately, better housing should be made available to families at the lowest income levels.

Several reasons are advanced for this moving-down of houses. One, of course, is the deterioration that might be expected to set in with age. Another is changing styles, causing some houses to become out of date. Still another is the declining character of some neighborhoods. Whatever the reason, the housing is expected to become less desirable for families at the income levels it has been serving, and as new and presumably better housing comes on the market the used housing must give way and find its market among the next lower income group of families. For those families, it is expected to represent better housing than they have previously had, and therefore finds a ready market. This process, in turn, causes other housing that has been occupied by these families to become vacant and available, and it too has to move down in the price scale to find a market.

On the surface, this theory would seem to have some validity. However, its various elements and requirements (or the assumptions behind it) should be examined more carefully.

First, it will be noted that the process necessarily takes a long period of time, because houses, being as permanent as they are, do not change readily. During this period, many developments can interfere with the process. For example, the theory assumes that incomes would remain fairly constant while house prices are declining. This income–price relationship is a requisite. Should incomes decline consistently with house prices, as they did during the Depression, or should they increase as house prices increase (as during the postwar years), it is highly questionable whether the filtering process could operate.

But the greatest fallacy of the theory develops out of the requisite that there be surpluses of housing at the different price levels in order to force some units down the price ladder. These surpluses normally do not exist, at least for the necessary period of time. In the ordinary housing market builders usually stop building in a price class as soon as they see a surplus being created. This is only natural.

In conclusion, it can be admitted that as some houses become older, their prices may decline and they may become available to a lower-income group. Generally speaking, however, these developments are spotty and never operate in any systematic sense. Some families may receive better housing, but seldom does decent housing filter down to low-income families. Usually when units do, through what might be considered the filtration process, they are already substandard housing and do not meet the needs of low-income families.

Unfortunately, research concerning the filtration process involves such complications, e.g., the following of the same units through long periods of both income and price change, that it is difficult to determine whether the theory operates in any degree.[11]

HOUSING STANDARDS

"Standards" should be the housing *goals* toward which a nation strives. The Housing Act of 1949 set our nation's standards in broad, general terms when it established the goal of "a decent home and a suitable living environment for every American family. . . ." This statement from the Act's preamble also had one other significant aspect—it emphasized both *homes* and *environment*.

Despite the many social and technological advances that have been made in this country, no definitions of "a decent home" or "a suitable living environment" have yet been established or accepted by the people as a whole. One reason for this may be that the public has been too absorbed in some of the housing controversies (e.g., public vs. private housing) to unite on a set of standards. Another, of course, is the sheer complexity of standards. It is not difficult to arrive at a desirable level of housing based on construction standards, but it is more difficult to take proper cognizance of such factors as new materials, site and environmental characteristics and, most important of all, the human requirements of housing.

[11] One excellent study of this process, however, is reported in Leo Grebler, *Housing Market Behavior in a Declining Area.* New York: Columbia University Press, 1952.

It is difficult to develop a generally acceptable, over-all housing standard because different population groups have different goals. For example, the goals are somewhat different between urban and farm families. Goals are also likely to be different among different ethnic groups and groups having different customs and habits.

Furthermore, families are dynamic. As has been indicated in several instances earlier, family living patterns change. New materials and new methods of construction also are developed. Therefore, if housing standards are defined as "what housing ought to be," then standards would of necessity always be ahead of current building practices.

Confirmation of the argument that insufficient attention has been given to the establishment of real housing standards is evident from many sources. For example, the U. S. Census (the source of broadest housing statistics) does not even approach the subject; it merely limits its statistics to structural condition (sound, deteriorating, and dilapidated), facilities (e.g., running water and electricity), and equipment (e.g., private toilet and bath). The Census Bureau has never defined "standard" or "substandard" housing.

Unfortunately, most so-called housing standards today reflect *minimum* situations; that is, they reflect the level below which housing is considered to be unsafe or unsanitary. However, a house that is safe and sanitary does not necessarily represent an adequate or a desirable home.

Housing Codes

A number of cities have attempted to upgrade their old housing by establishing a housing code. These codes generally cover three subjects: (a) minimum facilities and equipment, (b) maintenance of the dwelling unit and of facilities and equipment, and (c) conditions of occupancy.

Under "minimum facilities and equipment" are included such items as general lighting and ventilation, garbage and waste disposal, heating, water supply, toilet, and egress. "Maintenance" covers such items as general sanitary conditions, chimneys and flues and other fire hazards such as wiring, pest infestation, internal and external structural repair, and dampness. "Conditions of occupancy" includes general room crowding (persons per room or persons per sleeping room) and area crowding (e.g., sleeping and nonsleeping areas).

The nature and scope of these codes vary greatly among the different cities. In many of them, only general words and phrases are used to indicate the requirements—phrases such as "good repair" or "safe condition." These terms are, of course, subject to different interpretations by different people. Therefore, although many of the codes of different cities carry the same stipulations, there may be a difference in actual enforcement among them. They are usually enforced by the health authorities or are under the local police power.

American Public Health Association Standards

The Committee on the Hygiene of Housing of the American Public Health Association developed an "Appraisal Method for Measuring the Quality of Housing" in 1940. The primary purposes of this effort were

to provide a reliable measure of compliance with the full range of modern standards [as expressed in the same Committee's *Basic Principles of Healthful Housing*]; to measure this compliance in a manner that will meet the needs of various agencies concerned with housing; and by this means to foster a joint attack rather than separate attacks on related problems of housing, redevelopment, and city planning.[12]

The principles of healthful housing, including physical as well as emotional needs, are defined in four categories:

1. Fundamental physiological needs.
2. Fundamental psychological needs.
3. Protection against contagion.
4. Protection against accidents.[13]

Under "fundamental physiological needs" eight specific items are included, among them the maintenance of a thermal environment which will avoid undue heat loss from the body and provision of adequate space for exercise and for the play of children. Under "psychological needs" such items are included as the provision of adequate privacy for the individual, the provision of opportunities for normal family and community life, and the provision of possibilities for aesthetics in the home and its surroundings. Under "protection from contagion" such items as these are included: provision of a water supply of safe, sanitary quality and avoidance of unsanitary conditions in the vicinity of the dwelling and exclusion from the dwelling of vermin which may play a part in the transmission of disease. Under "protection against accidents" are included protection against gas poisoning and the danger of electric shocks and burns, protection against falls and other mechanical injuries in the home, and protection of the neighborhood against the hazards of automobile traffic.

The "yardstick" developed to measure, in specific terms, these basic qualities of the house takes into consideration the facilities, maintenance, and occupancy of the house through consideration of some thirty items, each of which has a weighted penalty point score, depending on its significance to the health of the individual in the particular community.[14]

The APHA method also recognizes the role of housing *environment* and categorizes different environmental factors into six groups: (1) land crowd-

[12] Allan A. Twichell, "Measuring the Quality of Housing in Planning for Urban Redevelopment." Part I in Coleman Woodbury, ed., *Urban Redevelopment: Problems and Practices*. Chicago: University of Chicago Press, 1953, p. 25.

[13] *Basic Principles of Healthful Housing*, American Public Health Association, Committee on the Hygiene of Housing, 2d ed. New York: The Association, 1946.

[14] *An Appraisal Method for Measuring the Quality of Housing: A Yardstick for Health Officers, Housing Officials and Planners*. Part I: "Nature and Uses of the Method." New York: American Public Health Association, 1945, p. 66.

ing, (2) nonresidential land uses, (3) hazards and nuisances from the transportation system, (4) hazards and nuisances from natural causes, (5) inadequate utilities and sanitation, and (6) inadequate basic community facilities.

The APHA method has been used by a number of cities to determine the quality of their housing supply. It provides a method of determining which housing falls below acceptable standards for a city, and is therefore used in connection with old houses. Although cities find it more expensive to conduct surveys using methods such as this, the results they obtain are considerably more refined than those based on the U. S. Census enumeration.

THE OLD CONFLICT

Colean has said:

> Amid the increasing diversity of governmental powers many old conflicts have persisted and new ones have appeared. Conflicts, of course, are inevitable as long as interests differ; and the making of working compromises between interests is the basis of all law. The conflicts, however, do not arise merely from differences among the interests in an otherwise private transaction but also in different sets of governmental jurisdictions, among contrary attitudes of the function of government, and among the very objectives that government undertakes to achieve. No resolution of these conflicts has yet been accomplished.[15]

It is obvious from the discussion earlier in this chapter that any sound program to improve housing in our central cities must entail both slum clearance and rehabilitation. This suggests bringing together interests that have tended to be incompatible in housing ever since there was an awakening to our social responsibilities.

The methods by which the two aspects of this program are to be accomplished must of necessity be different. Private enterprise should assume much of the responsibility for stopping the *spread* of blight by an aggressive rehabilitation program. Real estate and other groups in some communities have already taken the lead in getting such programs under way, the most notable successes being in Baltimore and Philadelphia. However, rehabilitation on any broad scale requires large-scale private investment, and this has not generally been forthcoming. It usually is expensive to remodel the kinds of properties that need rehabilitation, and real estate investors often can obtain a better return on their capital in other ways. Landlords have no incentives toward improvement—in fact, they usually profit by keeping the dwellings in their present condition. In general, private enterprise is not very charitable in matters such as these.

Some Federal funds are now available for rehabilitation, and, as will be mentioned in Chapter 14, greater emphasis is constantly being placed on this kind of activity.

[15]Miles L. Colean, *The Impact of Government on Real Estate Finance in the United States*. New York: National Bureau of Economic Research, 1950, pp. 157–158.

Even the most aggressive rehabilitation program, however, will not clear the slum areas, where redevelopment is the only answer. The plight of these areas is something a community cannot afford to neglect. *A slum is like a cancerous growth; if unchecked, it will continue to spread and kill.* As with cancer, the treatment must be swift, drastic, and surgical.

The means for remedying the situation lies in the urban renewal program, discussed in Chapter 14. This program has been only partially successful to date, despite its growth in the last few years. Yet private and public groups in more and more cities are discovering that they must join forces if their city is not to fall into a state of complete decay.

READING LIST

SLUMS

Abrams, Charles. *The Future of Housing.* New York: Harper & Bros., 1946, Chapter 3.

Colean, Miles L. *Renewing Our Cities.* New York: The Twentieth Century Fund, 1953.

DeForest, Robert W., and Lawrence Veiller (eds.) *The Tenement House Problem.* Vols. I and II. New York: The Macmillan Co., 1903.

Ford, James. *Slums and Housing.* Vols. I and II. Cambridge, Mass: Harvard University Press, 1936.

Gries, John M., and James Ford (eds.) *Slums, Large-Scale Housing and Decentralization.* Vol. III. The President's Conference on Home Building and Home Ownership, Washington, D.C., 1932.

Monson, Astrid. "Slums, Semi-Slums, and Super-Slums," *Marriage and Family Living,* Vol. XVII, No. 2, May 1955, pp. 118-122.

Rummey, Jay. "The Social Cost of Slums," *The Journal of Social Issues,* Vol. VII, Nos. 1 and 2, 1951, pp. 69-85.

Schorr, Alvin L. *Slums and Social Insecurity.* Research Report No. 1, Division of Research and Statistics, Social Security Administration, U.S. Department of Health, Education, and Welfare, Washington, D.C.: U.S. Government Printing Office, 1963.

Stokes, Charles J. "A Theory of Slums," *Land Economics,* Vol. XXXVIII, No. 3, August 1962, pp. 187-197.

Wilner, Daniel M., Rosabelle P. Walkley, Thomas C. Pinkerton, and Matthew Tayback. *The Housing Environment and Family Life.* Baltimore: The Johns Hopkins Press, 1962.

Woodbury, Coleman (ed.) *The Future of Cities and Urban Redevelopment.* Chicago: University of Chicago Press, 1953.

HOUSING OF MINORITY GROUPS

Abrams, Charles. *Forbidden Neighbors.* New York: Harper & Bros., 1955.

Commission on Race and Housing. *Where Shall We Live?* Berkeley: University of California Press, 1958.

Deutsch, Morton, and Mary Evans Collins. *Interracial Housing—A Psychological Evaluation of a Social Experiment.* Minneapolis: University of Minnesota Press, 1951.

Glazer, Nathan, and Davis McEntire (eds.) *Studies in Housing and Minority Groups.* Berkeley: University of California Press, 1960.

Grier, Eunice, and George Grier. *Privately Developed Interracial Housing.* Berkeley: University of California Press, 1960.

Handlin, Oscar. *The Newcomers.* Cambridge, Mass.: Harvard University Press, 1959.

Kessler, Matthew A. "Economic Status of Nonwhite Workers, 1955-62," *Monthly Labor Review,* Vol. 86, No. 7, July 1963, pp. 780-788.

Laurenti, Luigi. *Property Values and Race.* Berkeley: University of California Press, 1961.

Nesbitt, George B. "Relocating Negroes from Urban Slum Clearance Sites," *Land Economics,* Vol. XXV, No. 3, August 1949, pp. 275-288.

Weaver, Robert C. *The Urban Complex—Human Problems in Urban Life.* Garden City, N.Y.: Doubleday & Company, Inc., 1964, Chapter VI.

Wilner, Daniel M., Rosabelle P. Walkley, and Stuart W. Cook. *Human Relations in Interrracial Housing.* Minneapolis: University of Minnesota Press, 1955.

REHABILITATION

Meyerson, Martin, Barbara Terrett, and William L. C. Wheaton. *Housing, People, and Cities.* New York: McGraw-Hill Book Co., 1962, Chapter 11.

Nash, William W. *Residential Rehabilitation: Private Profits and Public Purposes.* New York: McGraw-Hill Book Co., 1959.

THE "FILTERING" CONCEPT

Fisher, Ernest M., and Louis Winnick. "A Reformulation of the 'Filtering' Concept," *The Journal of Social Issues,* Vol. VII, Nos. 1 and 2, 1951, pp. 47-58.

Grebler, Leo. *Housing Market Behavior in a Declining Area.* New York: Columbia University Press, 1952.

Ratcliff, Richard U. *Urban Land Economics.* New York: McGraw-Hill Book Co., 1949, pp. 321-334.

HOUSING STANDARDS

Basic Principles of Healthful Housing, 2d ed. American Public Health Association, Committee on the Hygiene of Housing. New York: The Association, 1946.

"Housing Needs and Standards," Panel Discussion of the Symposium on Frontiers of Housing Research, *Land Economics,* Vol. XXV, No. 1, February 1949 (Supplement), pp. 116-131.

Table 10–1

PLACE OF WORK, WORKERS LIVING IN SMSA'S OF 100,000 OR MORE, WHITE AND NONWHITE, 1960

Place of Residence and of Work	*White*	*Nonwhite*
Total workers in SMSA (number in thousands)	37,255	4,522
Living in central city	49.7%	79.6%
Working in central city	41.3	64.3
Working in SMSA ring	4.6	6.6
Working outside SMSA of residence	1.3	1.2
Place of work not reported	2.5	7.5
Living in SMSA ring	50.3	20.4
Working in central city	16.8	5.2
Working in SMSA ring	28.8	13.1
Working outside SMSA of residence	2.8	0.7
Place of work not reported	1.9	1.4

SOURCE: Derived from U.S. Bureau of the Census, *Census of Population 1960*, Detailed Characteristics, PC(1), 1D, U.S. Summary, p. 1–576.

Table 10–2

PERCENTAGE OF IMMIGRATION OF CERTAIN NATIONALITIES TO TOTAL IMMIGRATION FOR SUCCESSIVE PERIODS, 1831 TO 1899

	1831 to 1840	*1841 to 1850*	*1851 to 1860*	*1861 to 1870*	*1871 to 1880*	*1881 to 1890*	*1891 to 1899*
Irish	35%	46%	35%	19%	16%	13%	10%
British	13	15	17	26	19	15	10
German	25	25	37	34	26	28	16
French	8	—	—	—	—	—	—
Scandinavian	—	—	—	5	8	11	9
Russian and Polish	—	—	—	—	—	5	15
Hungarian	—	—	—	—	—	7	15
Italian	—	—	—	—	—	6	16

SOURCE: Robert W. DeForest and Lawrence Veiller, eds., *The Tenement House Problem*, Vol. II. New York: The Macmillan Company, 1903, p. 80.

Table 10–3

PERCENTAGE DISTRIBUTION OF NONWHITE POPULATION IN TWENTY LARGEST URBAN PLACES, 1960

Urban Place	*Total Population*	*Nonwhite*
New York	7,781,984	14.7%
Chicago	3,550,404	23.6
Los Angeles	2,479,015	16.8
Philadelphia	2,002,512	26.7
Detroit	1,670,144	29.2
Baltimore	939,024	35.0
Houston	938,219	23.2
Cleveland	876,050	28.9
Washington	763,956	54.8
St. Louis	750,026	28.8
Milwaukee	741,324	8.9
San Francisco	740,316	18.4
Boston	697,197	9.8
Dallas	679,684	19.3
New Orleans	627,525	37.4
Pittsburgh	604,332	16.8
San Antonio	587,718	7.4
San Diego	573,224	7.8
Seattle	557,087	8.4
Buffalo	532,759	13.8

SOURCE: U.S. Bureau of the Census, *Census of Population 1960.* General Population Characteristics, PC(1), 1B, U.S. Summary, pp. 1–181 to 1–185.

Table 10–4

PERCENTAGE DISTRIBUTION OF FAMILY SIZE, URBAN FAMILIES, WHITE AND NONWHITE, 1960

Number of Family Members	*White*	*Nonwhite*
Total families (number in thousands)	28,711	3,229
Two persons	33.9%	30.3%
Three	22.4	20.2
Four	20.8	15.8
Five	12.6	11.8
Six	6.0	8.4
Seven or more	4.3	13.5
Average No. persons per family	3.51	4.07

SOURCE: U.S. Bureau of the Census, *Census of Population 1960.* Detailed Characteristics, PC(1), 1D, U.S. Summary, pp. 1–466, 1–467.

Table 10–5

PERCENTAGE DISTRIBUTION OF INCOME, URBAN FAMILIES, WHITE AND NONWHITE, 1959

Income	*White*	*Nonwhite*
Total families (number in thousands)	28,711	3,229
Under $1,000	3.0%	10.4%
$1,000 to $1,999	4.7	14.0
$2,000 to $2,999	6.0	15.2
$3,000 to $3,999	7.8	14.7
$4,000 to $4,999	10.3	13.0
$5,000 to $5,999	12.9	10.2
$6,000 to $6,999	12.0	6.9
$7,000 to $9,999	24.0	10.5
$10,000 to $14,999	13.2	4.1
$15,000 and over	6.1	1.0
Median income	$6,433	$3,711

SOURCE: Derived from U.S. Bureau of the Census, *Census of Population 1960*. Detailed Characteristics, PC(1), 1D, U.S. Summary, p. 1–597.

Table 10–6

PERCENTAGE DISTRIBUTION OF OCCUPATIONS, HEADS OF URBAN FAMILIES, WHITE AND NONWHITE, 1960

Occupation	*White*	*Nonwhite*
Total heads of families (number in thousands)	23,410	2,401
Professional, technical, and kindred workers	13.3%	4.9%
Managers, officials, and proprietors, except farm	14.3	2.9
Clerical, sales, and kindred workers	17.4	8.0
Craftsmen, foremen, and kindred workers	21.9	11.1
Operatives and kindred workers	19.0	25.4
Service workers, including private household	6.1	22.7
Laborers, except farm and mine	3.9	16.8
Farmers and farm managers	0.4	0.5
Farm laborers and farm foremen	0.3	0.9
Occupation not reported	3.4	6.9

SOURCE: U.S. Bureau of the Census, *Census of Population 1960*. Detailed Characteristics, PC(1), 1D, U.S. Summary, pp. 1–476, 1–477.

Table 10–7

PERCENTAGE DISTRIBUTION OF EDUCATION ATTAINMENT, HEADS OF URBAN FAMILIES, WHITE AND NONWHITE, 1960

Years of School Completed by Head	*White*	*Nonwhite*
Total heads of families (number in thousands)	28,711	3,229
Elementary school:		
Zero to seven years	16.4%	40.7%
Eight years	16.0	13.6
High school:		
One to three years	20.4	21.7
Four years	24.7	15.2
College:		
One to three years	10.7	5.0
Four years or more	11.8	3.7

SOURCE: U.S. Bureau of the Census, *Census of Population 1960.* Detailed Characteristics, PC(1), 1D, U.S. Summary, pp. 1–471, 1–472.

Table 10–8

PERCENTAGE DISTRIBUTION OF VALUE OF OWNER-OCCUPIED HOUSING UNITS, IN CENTRAL CITIES, BY TOTAL AND NONWHITE, 1960

Value	*Total*	*Nonwhite*
Total owner-occupied units (number in thousands)	7,384	754
Less than $5,000	5.9%	15.2%
$5,000 to $7,400	11.3	22.0
$7,500 to $9,900	15.8	20.6
$10,000 to $12,400	18.1	16.0
$12,500 to $14,900	15.4	10.4
$15,000 to $17,400	11.5	6.6
$17,500 to $19,900	7.5	3.5
$20,000 to $24,900	7.1	3.0
$25,000 to $34,900	4.4	1.7
$35,000 or more	3.0	1.0
Median value, dollars	$12,300	$9,000

SOURCE: Derived from U.S. Bureau of the Census, *Census of Housing 1960.* States and Small Areas, HC(1), No. 1, U.S. Summary, pp. 1–45, 1–227.

Table 10–9

PERCENTAGE DISTRIBUTION OF MONTHLY GROSS RENT OF RENTER-OCCUPIED HOUSING UNITS, IN CENTRAL CITIES, BY TOTAL AND NONWHITE, 1960

Gross Rent	*Total*	*Nonwhite*
Total renter-occupied units (number in thousands)	9,729	1,952
Less than $30	3.0%	4.9%
$30 to $39	5.6	8.5
$40 to $49	9.1	12.9
$50 to $59	12.6	15.0
$60 to $69	15.0	15.9
$70 to $79	13.6	13.1
$80 to $99	20.0	16.6
$100 to $119	9.6	7.0
$120 or more	8.7	3.8
No cash rent	2.8	2.3
Median rent, dollars	$72	$65

SOURCE: Derived from U.S. Bureau of the Census, *Census of Housing 1960*. States and Small Areas, HC(1), No. 1, U.S. Summary, pp. 1–45, 1–227.

Table 10–10

PERCENTAGE DISTRIBUTION OF CONDITION AND PLUMBING FACILITIES IN CENTRAL CITIES, BY TENURE, TOTAL AND NONWHITE, 1960

Condition and Presence of Plumbing Facilities	*Owner-Occupied*		*Renter-Occupied*	
	Total	*Nonwhite*	*Total*	*Nonwhite*
Total housing units (number in thousands)	8,777	892	9,729	1,952
Sound	91.8%	78.0%	79.0%	60.7%
With all plumbing facilities	90.5	74.6	71.9	52.2
Lacking some or all facilities	1.3	3.4	7.1	8.5
Deteriorating	6.9	17.3	16.4	27.8
With all plumbing facilities	6.0	13.6	11.5	17.2
Lacking some or all facilities	0.9	3.7	4.9	10.6
Dilapidated	1.3	4.7	4.6	11.5

SOURCE: Derived from U.S. Bureau of the Census, *Census of Housing 1960*. States and Small Areas, HC(1), No. 1, U.S. Summary, pp. 1–40, 1–225.

Table 10–11

PERCENTAGE DISTRIBUTION OF YEAR STRUCTURE BUILT, IN CENTRAL CITIES, BY TENURE, TOTAL AND NONWHITE, 1960

Year Structure Built	Owner-Occupied		Renter-Occupied	
	Total	Nonwhite	Total	Nonwhite
Total housing units (number in thousands)	8,777	892	10,840	1,952
1955 to March 1960	13.1%	7.0%	6.6%	4.8%
1950 to 1954	14.3	8.3	7.2	7.2
1940 to 1949	15.0	12.9	10.0	9.8
1939 or earlier	57.6	71.8	76.2	78.2

SOURCE: Derived from U.S. Bureau of the Census, *Census of Housing 1960*. States and Small Areas, HC(1), No. 1, U.S. Summary, pp. 1–42, 1–226. Renter-occupied data for U.S. total are not reported by the Census, but were derived by subtracting number of owner-occupied units from total, which obviously includes some error because all persons did not report on year structure built. The percentage distribution shown for renter-occupied units, however, should generally approximate actual figures.

Table 10–12

PERCENTAGE DISTRIBUTION OF NUMBER OF ROOMS, IN CENTRAL CITIES, BY TENURE, TOTAL AND NONWHITE, 1960

Number of Rooms	Owner-Occupied		Renter-Occupied	
	Total	Nonwhite	Total	Nonwhite
Total housing units (number in thousands)	8,777	892	9,729	1,952
One	0.1%	0.2%	7.8%	7.9%
Two	0.7	0.8	10.8	11.0
Three	3.5	4.8	26.3	27.0
Four	15.2	16.2	27.0	27.1
Five	30.5	27.9	16.8	15.8
Six	28.7	27.3	8.1	7.8
Seven	12.1	11.8	2.1	2.2
Eight or more	9.2	11.0	1.1	1.2
Median No. of rooms	5.5	5.5	3.7	3.7

SOURCE: Derived from U.S. Bureau of the Census, *Census of Housing 1960*. States and Small Areas, HC(1), No. 1, U.S. Summary, pp. 1–41, 1–226.

Table 10–13

PERCENTAGE DISTRIBUTION OF PERSONS PER ROOM, OCCUPIED HOUSING UNITS IN CENTRAL CITIES, BY TENURE, TOTAL AND NONWHITE, 1960

	Owner-Occupied		*Renter-Occupied*	
Persons Per Room	*Total*	*Nonwhite*	*Total*	*Nonwhite*
Total housing units (number in thousands)	8,777	892	9,729	1,952
0.50 or less	49.3%	42.6%	35.7%	26.7%
0.51 to 0.75	23.6	21.9	23.4	19.5
0.76 to 1.00	20.1	20.4	26.8	26.4
1.01 to 1.50	5.7	10.5	9.0	15.0
1.51 or more	1.3	4.6	5.1	12.4

SOURCE: Derived from U.S. Bureau of the Census, *Census of Housing 1960.* States and Small Areas, HC(1), No. 1, U.S. Summary, pp. 1–43, 1–226.

CHAPTER 11

*

Suburbia

Suburbia has been a popular subject in recent literature. Books have been written on the subject by a wide range of specialists—sociologists, psychologists and psychiatrists, political scientists, and many others (including some free-lance writers whose particular background qualifications remain unknown).

It is only natural, with such a heterogeneous group of authors that the subject has become both complicated and controversial. It is the purpose of this chapter to attempt to cut through the maze of differing opinions by defining the term itself and then describing how and why suburbia developed. Later in the chapter there will be an analysis, based on the most pertinent data currently available, of the people who live in suburbia and how they are housed.

DEFINITION OF A SUBURB

There are many definitions of a suburb. Here are a few examples that at least have a common thread running through them, with reference to the location of suburbia:[1]

An outlying part of a city or town: a smaller place adjacent to or sometimes within commuting distance of a city.[2]

Suburbs are roughly defined as communities immediately surrounding a central city. They are characterized by less density of population than is found in the inner city but greater density than is characteristic of rural areas. They differ from independent towns of equal size because the city performs many functions for them.[3]

Suburbs are primarily residential areas (communities), usually lying outside the limits of the central city. They remain to a degree dependent upon the city as

[1] Sometimes other terms are used with reference to residential communities outside, but related to, central cities. One example is the term ''exurbia'' used by Spectorsky. According to this author, exurbia begins where suburbia stops. It is less densely settled and usually caters to people in the arts, professions, and so on. See A. C. Spectorsky, *The Exurbanites.* Philadelphia: J. B. Lippincott Co., 1955.

[2] *Webster's Third New International Dictionary,* Unabridged. Springfield, Mass.: G. and C. Merriam Co., 1961.

[3] From *The American City,* by Stuart A. Queen and David B. Carpenter. Copyright 1953, McGraw-Hill Book Co., Inc. Quotation from p. 119 used by permission.

a source of necessary goods and services and many of their employed persons work outside of the community.[4]

Suburbs . . . are simply forms of land use and development, together with the concomitant political, economic and social forms and attitudes, that take place relatively near to but outside of sizable cities and that are influenced materially by the economy and ways of life of these central cities.[5]

Martin has given further elaboration of these definitions by indicating that suburbs generally do not fall at either of the two extremes of size and density. Oakland, for example, is not generally termed a suburb of San Francisco, and certain low-density, small, unincorporated areas are ". . . more appropriately labelled fringe areas rather than suburbs."[6]

In addition to the "residential" suburb, to which the above definitions relate, some writers have suggested a second type, i.e., the "industrial" suburb. However, since by definition the industrial suburb ". . . tends to attract more workers to its confines every day than the number of working people who sleep there every night,"[7] it is of quite different nature from the residential suburb, and is outside the scope of the discussion in this chapter. Sometimes satellite cities are considered suburbs, but because they are similar to the industrial suburb, they likewise will not be considered here.

Suburbs may develop anywhere around a city, given suitable factors of land, feasibility of development, and transportation facilities; they do not follow any uniform pattern of development. Larger cities usually have several suburban developments, not only in different outlying sections, but sometimes extending one beyond another in the same direction. (Since land is the first requisite for suburban development, and since much of the land available is some distance out, many new suburbs are at some distance from the city.) They may be quite close together or separated by open or rural areas, villages, or other newly developing suburbs. In many instances, the residential expansion is accompanied by commercial and shopping facilities to serve the expanding neighborhoods.

Obviously, the suburb, though situated in the country, is not rural in

[4] G. A. Wissink, *American Cities in Perspective.* Assen, The Netherlands: Royal Van Gorcum, Ltd., 1962, p. 176.

[5] Coleman Woodbury, "Suburbanization and Suburbia," in *American Journal of Public Health,* Vol. 45, No. 1, January 1955, p. 2. Copyright 1955, by the American Public Health Association, Inc.

[6] Walter T. Martin, "The Structuring of Social Relationships Engendered by Suburban Residence," in William M. Dobriner, ed. *The Suburban Community.* New York: G. P. Putnam's Sons, 1958, p. 100; originally published in *The American Sociological Review,* Vol. 21, No. 4, August 1956, pp. 446–453. It should be noted that the term "fringe" as used by Martin does not have the same definition as that used by the U. S. Census. Martin's concept is far less inclusive and reflects the more general usage of the term. Burnham Kelly defines the "metropolitan fringe" as "the 'cutting edge' of suburban growth biting into rural areas" (*Problems of America's Expanding Metropolitan Fringe Areas,* report of Conference held at Cornell University June 15–16, 1961, sponsored by the Cornell University Center for Housing and Environmental Studies and College of Architecture. Mimeo., p. 2).

[7] Leo F. Schnore, "The Growth of Metropolitan Suburbs," in William M. Dobriner, *op. cit.,* p. 30; originally published in *The American Sociological Review,* Vol. 22, No. 2, April 1957, pp. 165–173.

nature. Its economy is not that of the farm. It has the same dependence on the agricultural centers for its food supply that the city has; in short, it is not agriculturally productive. It is further different from a rural area in that a majority of its population depends on urban sources for employment. In addition, the residents of suburbia tend to bring with them a way of living to which they grew accustomed in the city. They do not, as a rule, seek out for permanent affiliation many existing rural community activities, though they may, of course, enjoy whatever recreational and other facilities such areas offer. Even in the scattered housing developments on the edge of the city, residents tend to retain their individual alliances with urban facilities.

From its situation in an outlying area, the suburb might seem at first glance to be only another small village. This comparison might especially be drawn if the size of the suburb is comparable with that of a small village. Suburbs, however, develop from the city. Villages, on the other hand, have developed from a surrounding rural area; their interests are identified with those of the rural area rather than with those of a city. Furthermore, villages are relatively complete political, economic, and social entities, whereas suburbs are not. Other important characteristics of suburbs will be described as the discussion in this chapter proceeds.

HOW AND WHY SUBURBIA DEVELOPED

Suburban growth, frequently cited as a twentieth-century phenomenon, actually has paralleled the growth of our cities. In the eighteenth century, for example, residents of Philadelphia, New York, Boston, and probably other cities were moving to the suburbs for much the same reasons as those given by today's suburbanites—quiet, better air, comfort, and more room. With the growth of industrialization in the nineteenth century, cities became centers of manufacturing, commerce, and transportation. Employment opportunities attracted large numbers of people from both rural areas and foreign countries. The city expanded, moved upward and outward, taking in more territory for its activities, and city dwellers who could afford to escaped to the suburbs. From 1805 to 1895, the suburbs of New York and Boston were growing more rapidly than the metropolitan areas themselves. According to the Massachusetts state census, between 1885 and 1895 the population in one Boston suburb (Everett) increased 219 percent, while in Boston itself the increase was only 28 percent.[8]

Between 1910 and 1920 the United States had changed from a rural to an urban nation, in that more of its people lived in cities than in rural areas. During that decade, suburban growth around 62 of its largest cities had outdistanced population growth within them.[9]

Residence in the early suburbs was limited to those who could afford to

[8] Adna Ferrin Weber, *The Growth of Cities in the Nineteenth Century*. New York: The Macmillan Co., 1899; republished Ithaca, N.Y.: Cornell University Press, 1963, p. 38.

[9] Robert C. Wood, *Suburbia—Its People and Their Politics*. Boston: Houghton Mifflin Co., 1958, p. 60.

live away from the city and were financially able to maintain some means of transportation between the city and their homes. As railroads or trolleys came to be provided, wealthy citizens built estates within driving or walking distance of them. In the twentieth century, however, several factors combined to bring suburban living within the means of an ever-increasing proportion of the population.

Chief among these, as might be expected, was improvement in economic welfare. National wealth increased tremendously in the 1920's. Though it was not widely distributed, prosperity created an attitude of anticipation, and people expected to have more money. Suburbs, once limited to the wealthy, now were opened to the middle class, many of whom sold their homes in the city and bought new ones in the residential areas farther out. Credit was available to supplement resources. Developers laid out sites for homes and sometimes installed sewers and built streets, but the buyer provided his own house.

The gateway to suburbia was opened wider in the 1930's with the provision of the FHA-mortgage system. Long-term mortgages and low down payments made home ownership possible for a larger number of people than heretofore. Home-builder organizations began building more houses for sale. Following World War II, the provisions of VA-guaranteed mortgages, with lower down payments and interest rates and longer amortization periods than FHA loans, increased the possibility of home ownership, especially for young families of veterans. Conventional loans also were offered on a more liberal basis.

Important as the matter of credit was, it was not the only factor. Numerous groups were in a favorable economic position after World War II. The general level of prosperity in the United States was high and income levels rose. With prosperity came a lower age at marriage, either because young people could afford to marry earlier or because parents were in a position to help finance such marriages.[10] Another result of prosperity was larger families. New homes and more space were needed by the newer families.

At the same time, the middle class was favored by the income tax provisions that encouraged home ownership. The upper class, on the other hand, with unfavorable tax provisions found it difficult to hold on to idle land. Consequently more land gradually became available for development.[11]

Technological advances, as well as economic ones, entered into the situation. The septic tank provided a better means of sewage disposal for small residential communities than the old-time cesspool. Improvements in the design and construction of cesspools removed many of their objectionable features. New methods of house construction kept the cost of new houses within reach, and they could be put up fairly rapidly. Sometimes entire suburbs might be built at one time to provide for the influx of homeowners from nearby cities. More automatic equipment was invented. This not only

10 Ernest R. Mowrer, "The Family in Suburbia," in William M. Dobriner, *op. cit.*, p. 151.

11 William N. Leonard, "Economic Aspects of Suburbanization," in William M. Dobriner, *op. cit.*, pp. 184–185.

made housework easier, but it also enhanced the appeal of the new house over older houses. The automobile was, very likely, the one technological improvement that made living in suburbs feasible for large numbers of people. With most people able to provide their own transportation, suburbs could be situated almost any place where land, water, and other resources were available, rather than only near public transportation facilities. (There is generally considered to be a point beyond which travel to and from the city is impractical, in terms of the time and effort required. To date, however, this point has not been determined.)

Home ownership meant, for most families, ownership of a single-family home. Given the congestion in cities and the limitations on expansion within their borders, this, in turn, indicated suburban living. Some authorities, however, have pointed out that the move to suburbia for many people may have been less from choice than from necessity:

> There is considerable debate as to whether suburban location is a specific and valid preference or merely a by-product of other preferences. Some persons believe improvements in transportation and communication merely made it possible for people to do what they had always wanted: to live in an environment with green space and air and sunshine, but to keep their chances of making a living in the great metropolitan labor market.
>
> Others are less convinced of the validity of this position and see in the modern suburban movement a pincers action: people who want to escape some aspects of their present location and housing can find what they consider to be more desirable conditions only if they sacrifice locational convenience, time, and effort.[12]

To some authorities characterization of the move to suburbia as a flight from the city or a social revolution seems too severe. Political considerations enter in. Wissink points out that there was no alternative to draining people from the central city, given the condition that the boundaries of the city could not be extended once they had been adjoined by incorporated suburban municipalities. The cities had little choice.[13]

However, some changes on the urban scene may have served to enhance the desirability of suburban living. Whether or not cities were congested, there were other disadvantages, such as deterioration of public transportation, obsolescence in housing, high land costs, and, in some, encroachment of manufacturing or service industries in some residential areas.

Changes in working conditions may also have served to enhance the desirability of suburban living. The period of time spent at work, both daily and weekly, was shorter, thus giving more time for family life, the cultivation of friendships and hobbies, and participation in group activities.[14]

Some other clues concerning the growth of the suburbs may be found in reasons given for moving there. Chief among these reasons is the feeling that

[12] From *Housing, People, and Cities*, by Martin Meyerson, Barbara Terrett, and William L. C. Wheaton. Copyright 1962, McGraw-Hill Book Co., Inc. Quotation from p. 87 used by permission.

[13] *Op. cit.*, p. 229.

[14] Mowrer, *op. cit.*, pp. 153–154.

suburban areas offered a desirable place in which to bring up children by providing space to play, playgrounds, and safety from traffic. Other reasons for a move to suburbia were to be near family or friends or the "right sort of people."[15] Economic reasons, such as lower cost of living in suburbia, were cited less rarely, mainly by those with lower incomes. Achieving higher social status may have been a factor in some cases.[16]

In general, authorities incline to the theory that a basic reason for the move to suburbia is the desire to combine the advantages of living in a rural setting with those of working in a city. Mumford discusses nineteenth-century suburbs from this point of view:

> Further, suburban living encouraged a complete segregation of consumption from production: there was no visible connecting link, except the iron rails that led to the city, between the barbarous industries that manufactured the goods and the romantic suburban homes, remote from the grime and the sweat, where these things were consumed.
>
> In short, the romantic suburb was a collective attempt to live a private life: an effort to make the apparatus of Coketown tolerable to the possessing classes by enabling them to profit by its goods and avoid its evils, to have the best of both worlds.[17]

Woodbury, also, states: "My own estimate, from the very inadequate evidence at hand, is that the essentially simple conditions of decent family living are the most powerful magnet."[18]

With this background concerning why and how our suburbs have developed, it is desirable to see how significant the suburban trend is today.

Between 1950 and 1960, the rural population of the nation showed a net loss for the first time in history. The location within urban areas in which the greatest increases occurred was the suburb, as can be seen from the following data:

	Percent
Total U. S. population increase, 1950-1960	18.5
Urban increase	29.3
Urbanized areas	38.4
Central cities	19.8
Urban fringe	81.5
Other urban	6.6
Rural decrease	−0.8[19]

When the population change during the same period (1950 to 1960) is viewed for metropolitan areas only, a similar trend is observed. For

[15] Glenn H. Beyer, Thomas W. Mackesey, and James E. Montgomery, *Houses Are for People*. Research Publication No. 3. Ithaca, N. Y.: Cornell University Housing Research Center, 1955, pp. 31–32.

[16] Wood, *op. cit.*, p. 64.

[17] Lewis Mumford, *The Culture of Cities*. New York: Harcourt, Brace, and World, 1938, p. 215.

[18] *Op. cit.*, p. 6.

[19] U.S. Bureau of the Census, *Census of Population 1960*. General Population Characteristics, PC(1), 1B, United States Summary.

example, for all metropolitan areas combined there was an increase in population within the *1950 central city limit areas* of less than 2 percent, while outside those areas the increase amounted to 62 percent. For areas having a population of three million or more, there was practically no increase in population in the areas comprising the city limits in 1950, but an increase of 72 percent outside those areas. For areas having a population of one million to three million, there actually was a slight decline in the areas representing the central cities during the past decade, while the population outside those areas increased by over 50 percent. The same trend existed for areas of other sizes (Table 11–1, p. 379).

Data also can be shown for a group of selected cities, covering the period between 1900 and 1960, but these data cannot be based on the same geographical areas for these two years for the particular cities. Despite the fact that many have annexed some territory over this period, the results are still interesting. The figures below indicate the proportion of population living outside the central cities in 1960 compared with twenty years and sixty years earlier:

City	*1900*	*1940*	*1960*	*City*	*1900*	*1940*	*1960*
Chicago	19	26	43	St. Louis	30	44	64
Boston	58	65	73	Baltimore	26	25	46
New York	10	14	27	Washington	26	32	62
Philadelphia	32	40	54	Atlanta	55	46	52
Pittsburgh	58	68	75	New Orleans	7	10	28
				Miami	—	36	69
Cleveland	17	31	51	Los Angeles-Long Beach	45	43	58
Detroit	33	32	56	San Francisco-Oakland	25	36	60
Minneapolis-St. Paul	20	19	46	Seattle	40	38	50[20]

These data are only a crude means of indicating the growth of suburban areas, because not all of the areas "outside central cities" as defined by the U.S. Census should be included if we adhere to the definitions of suburbia provided at the outset of this chapter. Most, if not all, metropolitan areas contain some areas outside central cities which have the same characteristics as the central cities themselves. If better lines of demarcation for suburbia could be drawn, and if data were available for such newly delineated areas, it may reasonably be assumed that even sharper rates of growth for the outlying areas would be shown. Census data, however, are the only data available for this purpose.

The movement to the suburbs today has one important and highly unfavorable characteristic in common with the movement that has been taking place earlier in our history: the progress in the physical expansion of our cities is neither orderly nor methodical. Our rural political units have not established the controls needed for proper planning that exist in most of our urban areas, and many builders (but certainly not all) have tended to

[20] U.S. Bureau of the Census, *Census of Population 1960*. Standard Metropolitan Statistical Areas, PC(3), 1D.

take advantage of this lack of controls. There will be more discussion of this problem later in the chapter.

WHO LIVES IN SUBURBIA?

Undoubtedly, all types of people can be found in suburbia, if one takes the time to search for them. Much of the literature, for many years, has tended to give the image of a single type of family—young, white, middle class, white collared, well educated, and upwardly mobile. This stereotype generally fits Whyte's "Organization Man," Vance Packard's "status seeker," Seeley's Crestwood Heights family, and many others. It came as a surprise to many when Berger, in his book, *Working-Class Suburb,* reported that automobile workers, who did not seem to fit this stereotype, made up the population of one suburb near San José, California.

Of course, the reason for the stereotype is that there is some basis for it. Although not all suburbanites fit the precise description, many undoubtedly do, as will be seen from the analysis that follows.

Let us look first at the population distributions. The most appropriate tool at hand for a factual analysis, again, is Census data; and the most appropriate data from that source are the figures for *central* cities of our metropolitan areas compared with those for areas *outside those cities.* The limitation of such data has already been indicated, but it will serve the purpose here again by at least pointing up the trends.

Household Composition

A higher proportion of the population in the urban fringe than in central cities is married, and lower proportions are single, widowed, or divorced—but the differences are not sharp. For example, among women in central cities in 1960, 61 percent were married, as compared with 69 percent in the urban fringe (Table 11–2, p. 379). The proportions were similar for men. A total of 21 percent of the women in central cities, compared with 18 percent in the urban fringe, were single (fourteen years old and over). A total of 14 percent of the women in central cities, compared with 10 percent in the urban fringe, were widowed. (In this instance, and others, many may be living in the inner parts of the Census definition of "urban fringe," not considered to be suburbia, since it is generally established that few widowed individuals live in suburbia.)

Looked at in another manner, from the standpoint of household relationships, 59 percent of the population living in the urban fringe compared with only 51 percent in central cities is comprised of wives of heads of households and children under the age of eighteen (Table 11–3, p. 380). The higher proportion of young children in the urban fringe can also be seen from a distribution of the age of population: 33 percent of the population there was comprised of children under fourteen years of age, compared with 28 percent in central cities. On the other hand, only 26 percent of the population in the urban fringe, compared with 32 percent in central cities, was comprised of individuals forty-five years old and over (Table 11–4, p. 380). It is clear from these data that families in suburbia do tend to be younger than those in central cities. Because of the number of children, suburban families also tend to be slightly larger.

Although this generalization undoubtedly is valid, there are exceptions in some suburbs. One author, for example, has indicated that upper class suburbs "have fewer children, more older people, and more women than the national average."[21]

The presence of a somewhat higher proportion of young married families with young children is not, however, the only characteristic of our suburbs.

Income Levels

One difference between suburb and central city is income level—families living in suburbia tend to have higher incomes than others. This can be seen from the fact that among families having an income below $3,000 in 1959, 60 percent lived in central cities; the remaining 40 percent lived outside those cities. At the other extreme, of those having an income of $10,000 and over, 45 percent lived in central cities, compared with 55 percent who lived outside them (Table 11–5, p. 381).

Occupations

Some pronounced differences are also seen with reference to occupations. Interestingly, 1960 Census figures show no differences in the distribution of individuals in professional, technical, and kindred occupations between central cities and areas outside those cities; however, among individuals engaged in clerical work, 58 percent lived in central cities, compared with 42 percent in outlying areas. There also was a difference, though not as great, with regard to sales personnel (Table 11–5, p. 381). It is generally recognized that one of the greatest differences exists with reference to manual occupations, most manual workers living in the central cities, but comparable data from the 1960 Census are not available.

Educational Levels

Education is frequently discussed when attention is being given to the suburbs. This matter is important from two points of view: the educational level attained by the parents and the kind of education parents desire to have provided for their children.

Parents living in suburbia have a somewhat higher level of educational attainment than their counterparts in the central city, but the differences are not strikingly sharp. In 1960, for example, among persons twenty-

[21] Egon E. Bergel, *Urban Sociology*. New York: McGraw-Hill Book Co., 1955, pp. 161–162.

five years and over who had not gone beyond the elementary grades, 58 percent lived in central cities; 42 percent lived in the outlying areas. Of college graduates, 48 percent lived in the central cities and 52 percent outside those cities (Table 11–5, p. 381).

The more important difference between central cities and suburbia, with regard to education, seems to rest in the advantages that suburban schools have. These are summarized by one author as follows:

> They are able to attract better teachers, since they pay higher salaries and give other teacher satisfactions.
>
> Buildings are newer, classrooms modern and up to date. Almost every suburb is engaged in a huge building program.
>
> More attention is paid to the individual child because of smaller classes.
>
> Standards are kept higher in the suburbs because as a rule there is a more homogeneous population. . . .
>
> The economic level in the suburbs is usually higher. The suburbs spend more money on their public schools.
>
> Parents, through their Parent-Teachers Association and citizens' committees, take more active part in the day-to-day operation of the schools.
>
> New teaching practices and methods are introduced and evaluated. Suburban schools, being smaller, experiment more than do the city schools. Sometimes this proves to be a boomerang. On occasion the parents will kick up their heels at "progressive" methods, and force school programs to return to a more traditional pattern.[22]

Though a superior educational system is a major objective in almost all suburbs, there are some difficulties in achieving it or sustaining a high level of performance throughout the curriculum. Suburbs share with other areas the problems of the cost of maintaining school facilities, the shortage of qualified teachers, and population growth. In some suburbs, school population has outgrown the facilities and some of the problems of cities—overcrowded classrooms, inadequate facilities, and large classes, for example—are being encountered. Some suburbs have additional complications, in the form of local conflicts over the school curriculum, control of the school board, or objections by older residents to the costs of education.

The increasing cost of providing educational facilities, in the face of rapidly increasing populations of school-age children, is a major concern. Meyerson states:

> Most suburbanites regard good schools as the most essential local government service. But a superior school system costs $400 to $500 per child per year. Thus the new suburban family with two or three children may cost the locality $800 to $1,500 per year, when it expects to pay no more than $200 or $300 per year in local taxes. Indeed, many new suburbanites in rapidly growing areas do pay such low taxes at first. But a single elementary school is not a school system; as the population increases, taxes will be doubled and often doubled again. The

[22] Benjamin Fine, "Educational Problems in the Suburbs," in William M. Dobriner, *op. cit.*, pp. 318–319; originally published in the *New York Times* January 30, 1957. © 1957 by The New York Times Company. Reprinted by permission.

tax rate of some suburbs is higher than the tax rate of the central cities they adjoin.[23]

In one respect, at least, the suburban school curriculum is not as adequate as those of schools in other areas—in the provision of vocational and technical training. Some parents now moving to suburbia find that their children, who may not be going on to college, have little or no opportunity to obtain specialized job training. Industries in the locality cannot turn to the local suburb for their labor supply, but must import trained workers from other areas.

Consolidation or centralization of the local suburban schools would serve to lessen the financial burden on the locality, in most instances, and, in some, would provide educational facilities geared to the needs of the community through grammar and high school. This, however, would mean that each local community would have considerably less influence on the over-all school system. In suburbia, there is a strong tendency to retain control of the educational system in local hands, even though the alternative is higher taxes.

One measure of the success of the schools in inculcating and maintaining at a high level interest in careers is the high percentage of suburban high school graduates who go on to college. The proportion who go on to college seems to be well over half of the high school graduates of suburbia, and in many suburbs, it is considerably higher.

Nonwhites in Suburbia

Another characteristic of our suburbs is that the communities are composed largely of white people. In 1960, for example, when 34 million occupied housing units existed in our metropolitan areas, it was found that 2.8 million were occupied by nonwhites in central cities—approximately 8 percent of the total—but that only 643,000 (2 percent) were occupied by nonwhites in areas outside the central cities. (In comparison, 46 percent of the total number of occupied units in metropolitan areas were occupied by whites in central cities and the remaining 44 percent, by whites outside central cities.)[24]

Over the years there has been some increase in the proportion of nonwhites living outside central cities, but the rate of change from central cities has not kept pace with that of whites. For example, in 1900 the white population living in metropolitan areas was distributed as follows: in central cities, 63 percent; outside central cities, 37 percent. At that time the distribution for the nonwhite population was as follows: in central cities, 54 percent; outside central cities, 46 percent. Until 1930, the proportion of whites in central cities increased but it has declined consistently since that

[23] *Op. cit.*, p. 322.

[24] Derived from U.S. Bureau of the Census, *Census of Housing 1960.* States and Small Areas, HC(1), No. 1, U. S. Summary.

time. In contrast to the recent trend concerning whites, the proportion of nonwhites in central cities has continued to increase each decade. In 1960, only 20 percent of the nonwhite population was living outside central cities —a significant decline from the 46 percent in 1900. (Table 11–6, p. 381).

The lag in the nonwhite population moving out of central cities has been due, of course, to several factors, one of the most important being the prejudice that has deprived Negroes of free choice of residence. An attempt was made in November 1962 to provide greater freedom of choice for this group when President Kennedy issued an Executive Order forbidding racial discrimination in public housing and dwellings financed with Federal Housing Administration mortgage insurance and Veterans Administration loans or guarantees.[25]

It is not to be anticipated, however, that the signing of an Executive Order will automatically mean heavy nonwhite migration to the suburbs. Several factors will perhaps preclude this. First, attitudes cannot always be changed by laws. (Laws can, however, effect changes in behavior; also, laws are sometimes educational.) Second, it is not known what proportion of the nonwhite population desires to be integrated with the white population. It was pointed out in Chapter 9 that many individuals prefer to live "among their own kind." Handlin confirms this belief and applies it to the present housing situation of nonwhites:

> If the barriers created by prejudice are relaxed and individuals become free to find the quality of housing they wish where they like, it is altogether possible that a gradual shift of Negro families into previously white neighborhoods will ease existing apprehensions and improve relations between the old and the new groups. Under those conditions, there is no reason to suppose that the Negroes will be thoroughly dispersed throughout the region, any more than other ethnic groups are. Rather it is to be expected that common interests will lead to the development of Negro communities which are as coherent as those of the Irish, Jews, or Italians and which offer a variety of types of accommodations without the stigma of inferiority. In the study of the motives for Negro movement, not one respondent suggested that an integrated neighborhood was in itself an attraction and relatively few gave that factor any weight at all.[26]

Suburbia and Mobility

Finally, in considering who lives in suburbia, it should be noted that not all of the families come from the central city of which the particular suburb may be a part. Census data show that half of the individuals living in central cities in 1960 were living in a different house from the ones they had occupied in 1955. Of the proportion that had moved, nearly two thirds had stayed in the same county, but the remaining third had moved from a

[25] Executive Order, "Equal Opportunity in Housing," signed by President John F. Kennedy, The White House, November 20, 1962.

[26] Oscar Handlin, *The Newcomers*. Cambridge, Mass.: Harvard University Press, 1959, p. 92.

different county. Many of these individuals moved to a location outside a central city. For example, of all of the movers who moved from one county to another, 42 percent had moved into the central city and 58 percent had moved to a location outside a central city (Table 11–7, p. 382). Whyte comments on the movers as follows:

> Always, they will be moving on. For most of its renters Park Forest is a sort of way station, a phase of life, and beyond a certain point continued residence can carry overtones of failure. Very few "flunk out" of Park Forest because they are not making the grade; far more leave precisely because they *have* made the grade.[27]

Berger cites several reports of the transient nature of suburban residents. The suburb he studied, however, did not fit this description. Rather, most of the auto workers felt that they were at the top of their ladder and were pleased with themselves for having progressed as far as they had.[28]

HOW ARE SUBURBANITES HOUSED?

We now have at least a brief description of who lives in suburbia. The next important question is *how* suburbanites live—how are they housed?

It might first be said that suburbanites are inclined to describe their communities as "classless," or, perhaps more realistically, as being composed of one class. The degree of homogeneity of suburban population, already described, lends fair credence to this claim. The cost range of suburban life in itself precludes it for people below a certain income level (another reason why our suburbs are not likely to attract as high a proportion of the nonwhite as white population in the immediate future). This type of selectivity may be reinforced in some suburbs by definite restrictions.

Wood says: "The most fashionable definition of suburbia today is that it is a looking glass in which the character, behavior, and culture of middle class America is displayed. . . . Suburbia, according to this interpretation, reflects with fidelity modern man, his way of living, his institutions and beliefs, his family and his social associations."[29]

Housing, its nature and location, is an important factor in class structure and social stratification. It is important, therefore, that we have a description of housing found in the suburbs, noting especially how it differs from that in central cities.

Tenure

One of the most striking features of suburban housing is the high proportion of home ownership. For example, of all of the housing units

[27] William H. Whyte, Jr., *The Organization Man.* Garden City, N.Y.: Doubleday & Co., 1956, p. 319. ("Making the grade," of course, refers to moving to a more exclusive suburb, not returning to the city.)

[28] Bennett M. Berger, *Working-Class Suburb.* Berkeley: University of California Press, 1960, Chapter II.

[29] *Op. cit.*, p. 4.

in metropolitan areas in 1960, 26 percent were owner-occupied units in central cities and 29 percent were renter-occupied units. However, 33 percent of the units were owner-occupied units outside central cities (and the remaining 12 percent were renter-occupied units outside those cities).[30] The picture can be described from another point of view. A total of 53 percent of all of the housing in central cities, as compared with only 27 percent of all of the housing not in central cities, was renter-occupied (Table 11–8, p. 382).

House Value and Rent

Another striking feature of suburbs is the higher value of housing units. In comparing the total inventory of owner-occupied housing outside central cities in 1960 and the total inventory of owner-occupied units inside those cities, houses outside central cities had a median value of approximately $2,000 more in that year—$14,400 as compared with $12,300 (Table 11–9, p. 383). These figures, however, tell only a part of the story and actually conceal important recent trends. Of the new units built between 1950 and 1959, the median value for those built outside central cities was $16,100. The median value of those built inside those cities was $15,600—but a most important fact to remember is that during that nine-year period a total of 71 percent of all of the new housing built in metropolitan areas was built outside the central cities.[31] If this trend continues, and it is expected to, there will be an increasing difference in the value of houses inside central cities and those outside them.

Quite a different picture is seen with reference to rental units. First, it should be indicated that there also was a difference in median gross rent levels in 1960—$81 per month outside central cities, as compared with $72 inside those areas (Table 11–10, p. 383). However, in contrast to the trend for owner-occupied housing, 45 percent of all of the new rental units built in metropolitan areas between 1950 and 1960 was built outside of central cities, and there was only a small difference in median gross monthly rents for the new units—$97 per month for those built outside of central cities compared with $93 inside those areas. If these trends continue there is not likely to be a striking increase in the difference with regard to rentals for the two areas.

Quality of Housing

From the standpoint of condition and availability of plumbing facilities, there is surprisingly little difference between either owned or rented housing in the two areas (Table 11–11, p. 384). Nine out of every ten owner-occupied units in both the central cities and outside them were

[30] Derived from U.S. Bureau of the Census, *Census of Housing 1960*. States and Small Areas, HC(1), No. 1, U. S. Summary.

[31] U.S. Bureau of the Census, *Census of Housing 1960*. Components of Inventory Change, HC(4), Part 1A-1, 1950–1959 Components, United States and Regions.

found to be sound and to have all plumbing facilities in 1960. Seven out of every ten renter-occupied units were found to be in this good condition in both areas.

Age of Houses

This comparably good condition existed despite the fact that both owned and rented units in central cities were generally older than those outside those cities. For example, one out of every four owner-occupied units built outside central cities had been built between 1955 and 1960, compared with only 13 percent of the units inside those cities. At the other extreme, only 36 percent of the units outside central cities had been built before 1940, compared with 58 percent of those inside central cities. The trends were similar for renter-occupied housing, but such housing was generally appreciably older than owner-occupied units (Table 11–12, p. 385).

House Size

Interestingly, houses in suburbia are generally the same size as those in the central cities. The highest proportion of owner-occupied units had either five or six rooms—a median of 5.5 in 1960 for units both in central cities and outside those cities (Table 11–3, p. 385). The median size of houses built between 1950 and 1959 is slightly smaller—5.2 rooms for houses in central cities and 5.3 rooms for those built outside central cities. In 1960, renter units in central cities had a median of 3.7 rooms; outside central cities, 4.1 rooms. The median size of renter units built between 1950 and 1959, for both areas, remained about the same as the median indicated for 1960.

Persons-per-Room Ratio

It was indicated earlier in this chapter that families living in suburbia tend to be slightly larger than those living in central cities. Since the size of houses in both areas was approximately the same, it could be anticipated that suburban families are somewhat more crowded for space than others. This is confirmed by Census data on persons per room. In 1960, 32 percent of the owners living outside central cities, compared with 27 percent of those living within central cities, had a persons-per-room occupancy ratio of 0.76 or more. This difference, however, is hardly significant. Among renters the difference was negligible (Table 11–14, p. 386).

The data that have been presented above provide the best available empirical evidence of the differences between suburban and central city housing. The limitations of the data with reference to depicting the particular subject under consideration, i.e., the character of strictly suburban housing, should be kept in mind. Although these limitations exist, the trends seem to be quite clear-cut and give us the over-all perspective needed.

However, there is much the data do not show, and at least a few words should be directed to that. Most important, satisfactions in living are not simply attained from a "decent, safe, and sanitary" house. Other features of the house, especially the setting of that house in a neighborhood, are equally or more important. Burchard touches on this:

FIGURE 26. *"Yoo hoo, Harry! Over here!" (Copyright by The New York Times. Reprinted by permission.)*

In terms of superior safety, health, convenience, democratic standards, indeed in terms of most social standards which are currently accepted, they [the suburbs] represent a considerable step forward and not only in comparison to the slum. But something is still missing from this new suburban aesthetic: Something of beauty, something of humor, something of informality, something of surprise, something in short of nature.[32]

Riesman is more specific. In his criticism of life in suburbia in general, and housing in particular, he says:

What is true of the planning, or lack of it, of our road-centered culture as a whole is also true of domestic architecture. Efficiency here is less stark—and consequently often less attractive—since it must compete with traditional definitions of a suburban free-standing home. But, as many architects have pointed out, the interiors are highly modern in the sense of mechanization. Indeed, one reason why husbands have been willing to become domesticated is that they have been promoted from dishwashers to operators of dishwashers. Similarly, they use power

[32] John Ely Burchard, "The Urban Aesthetic," in *The Annals of the American Academy of Political and Social Science,* Vol. 314, November 1957, p. 117.

mowers to give crew cuts to handkerchief-sized lawns and pierce their wives' and neighbors' ears with the screams of high-fidelity music.[33]

He also remarks: ". . . writers point to the uniformity of the ranch style, the ever-present television antennae, the lamp, if not the crack, in the picture window—which usually provides a view of the nearly treeless street, the cars, and someone else's picture window."[34]

The planning (or lack of it) of our new suburban communities has, in fact, been one of the primary criticisms of the nature of growth of our cities. It has been a serious problem in the development of our suburbs to date; it could be an even more serious problem in the future, because most population authorities agree that our population, by the end of the present decade, will double. This will mean that twice as many houses as we have today will be needed before the end of the next four decades. Some of the implications of the problem will be discussed in the remainder of this chapter.

THE FUTURE OF SUBURBIA

The nature of our suburbs in the future will depend in large part on whether we follow our practice of the past and just let them grow, or whether we begin taking them seriously, make an attempt to determine certain sound planning criteria, and establish whatever controls are necessary for adhering to those criteria.

When the HHFA Administrator submitted his proposals for the Housing Act of 1964 to Congress, he included a suggestion that the Federal Government assist developers in planning "New Towns," as has been done in England. This is not a revolutionary idea for this nation; we flirted with it in the New Deal days of Roosevelt by building some "greenbelt" towns and some new towns in the TVA region. Furthermore, some private developers, without special Federal legislation, have built and others are today building communities which are planned entities. Yet, even if some future Federal legislation should look favorably upon the New Town idea and give it support, we should not expect this approach to solve our suburban growth problem. That problem will still be with us, though perhaps to a somewhat lesser degree. Let us look, therefore, at what we ought to do—and, more important, what we should know before doing it—if we accept the fact that (1) our cities will continue to grow, perhaps even at a stepped-up pace; and (2) that growth is likely to continue in a form in the future similar to that of the past, that is, ever outward.

It would seem that in any analysis of the "problems and prospects" of our future suburban growth, three basic questions should be asked: (1) what criteria should be considered in the selection of land for development; (2) what criteria should be established for proper planning, including

[33] David Riesman, "The Suburban Dislocation," in *Annals of the American Academy of Political and Social Science,* Vol. 314, November 1957, p. 140.

[34] *Ibid.,* p. 142.

necessary controls; (3) what sociological, psychological, and perhaps even political consequences should be anticipated?

Criteria for Selection of Land

In this summary analysis, it is well to begin by recalling that the primary factor that makes our ever-new and ever-growing suburbs possible is a rather extensive supply of relatively inexpensive land made available because of the automobile and our modern freeways and other primary roads. In selecting particular parcels of land for development in the past, the primary requisite has been that the land be cheap. Perhaps an important secondary requisite has been that the developer have few controls imposed upon him.

Leopold has said: "The outstanding scientific discovery of the twentieth century is not television, or radio, but rather the complexity of the land organism."[35] Hamilton comments on the utilization of our land, with special reference to its constant absorption for our new suburban residential developments:

> There are portions of the natural environment which have a unique and valuable natural resource complement. Such areas often fall before the onslaught of unplanned residential use, because they are beyond the ken of subdividers, real estate speculators, lot purchasers, public officials or others with an urban orientation. Thus it may occur that valuable gravel deposits become lost to use if residences physically occupy the site, or even locate nearby and then pass ordinances against gravel exploitation. Similarly with unique recreational sites, important waterfowl areas, key areas for future water storage, etc. Such areas can be readily identified in advance by natural resource specialists, and urban developments guided onto other areas, if available.
>
> Similarly, areas of highly productive soils, uniquely adapted to agricultural production (especially for specialty crops), can be identified and saved until absolutely needed for building sites, airports, highways and parks. Too frequently our prime agricultural soils are taken over by urban uses while there are still many alternative sites which are equally or better adapted for these uses. Currently agriculture is annually losing to such uses over one million acres of our very best farmland. In 1958 Agricultural Economist Hugh Johnson predicted that if these withdrawals continued at the present rate for another 15 years, a total of about 100 million acres of our flattest and most fertile farmlands will have been converted. The few areas of specialty cropland coincide alarmingly with the expanding metropolitan fringe. While some of this conversion is necessary and inevitable, consideration should be given to minimizing "urban erosion" until absolutely necessary.[36]

These remarks summarize well the manner in which much of the land has been selected for new development purposes in the past, and suggest some important considerations if we are to do a better job in the future.

[35] Aldo Leopold, *Round River*. New York: Oxford University Press, 1953, p. 146.

[36] Lawrence S. Hamilton, "An Ecological Perspective on the Metropolitan Fringe," in *Problems of America's Expanding Metropolitan Fringe Areas*, *op. cit.* (pp. 4–5, last article in report).

Need for Proper Planning

It has been suggested that criteria be established for the better planning of our suburbs in the future. In many European countries, the entire nation is divided into "municipalities" similar to our counties. These municipalities exercise extensive control over any land development within their boundaries. This is not true of our counties. In fact, many county governments are not equipped to exercise control over more than the most elementary requirements for health and, as a result, the developer of a building site has had extremely loose rein over any subdivision he was building. (Subdivision controls were discussed in Chapter 9. It was pointed out in that chapter, however, that many rural areas likely to be subdivided do not exercise these controls.)

Until this situation is altered, we cannot expect to have new residential developments, which are being built in our rural areas, conform to the standards required in urban areas. So long as unrestricted areas are available, they will be found and acquired by large suburban builders. We are likely to continue to have a chaos of clutter. Not only should new suburban developments be required to adhere to modern subdivision regulations, zoning ordinances, and building codes, but because of the unique character of our suburbs—owing to their location—we need to give special attention to transportation, the problems of journey to work, and the like.

Social and Political Aspects

Finally, there is the problem of the sociological, psychological, and even political consequences of the development of our new suburban communities. On this subject, unfortunately, more fiction than fact exists today.[37] We need to know much more than we do about the emerging communities and their structure—stratification, leadership, and so on. Most suburbs are areas of rapid growth and development, and it is generally recognized that these factors result in extreme discontinuity in social relationships. One of the questions that remains unanswered is whether selectivity in migration to the suburbs on the basis of economics, and certain factors relating to the new environment being sought, have carried with them selectivity on the basis of other values, attitudes, and personalities. It is sometimes asserted that many families move from the central city in search of a new and better sense of "community." Is this sense being satisfied? Thompson has said:

> America's expanding metropolitan fringe areas provide rich fare for sociologists. The very fact of metropolitan expansion, of course, is of central concern to the demographer. For those of an ecological bent, urban fringe development is a major challenge of prediction and thus a principal testing ground for theoretical formulations. For those interested in major social institutions, the urban fringe provides

[37] An excellent study of the politics of suburbia exists, however, in Robert C. Wood, *op. cit.*

> an arena within which institutional change, development and interrelationships are sharply focussed. Finally, for the sociologist interested in community structure . . . the urban fringe presents a three-fold problem for research: the dissolution and reintegration of existing communities; the emergence of community structure within the fringe area as such; and the integration of these areas into the larger urban community of which they are a part.[38]

These are some of the sociological areas in which our knowledge is lacking. Some authorities also believe that the characteristics of modern suburbia also have an influence on psychological characteristics and the emotional well-being of the residents of these new communities.[39]

It can be seen that the many problems concerning the rapid growth of the outlying fringes of our cities involve a wide variety of specialists and disciplines. The problems are not likely to diminish as our cities continue to grow. What is sorely needed is more knowledge in order to cope with that growth more intelligently, on the one hand, and a better application of the knowledge we already have, on the other.

The fact remains, of course, that not all suburban growth has been faulty, nor has it all reflected the serious problems alluded to in the foregoing discussion. Some suburban communities have been carefully planned with well-designed homes, ample yard space (and the desired botanical embellishments), ample swimming pools, ball fields and other playgrounds, "village greens," and essential shopping and recreational centers. The density of population has been kept low. Such new communities represent an incredible improvement in living conditions over the conditions in most of the tenement houses of Manhattan or the older, single-family row or apartment buildings in almost any of our other cities. Yet new communities having these amenities are likely to be the exception rather than the rule, and some of them perhaps could have made a wiser selection of location and provided even more appropriate amenities if the real needs had been better known.

In any event, observing the development of suburbia in the last two decades, as a whole, America can do better in the future than it has in the past.

READING LIST

Andrews, Richard B. *Urban Growth and Development.* New York: Simmons-Boardman Publishing Corp., 1962, Chapter 5.

Berger, Bennett M. *Working-Class Suburb.* Berkeley: University of California Press, 1960.

Dobriner, William M. *Class in Suburbia.* Englewood Cliffs, N. J.: Prentice-Hall, Inc., 1963.

[38] Wayne E. Thompson, "The Urban Fringe: First Thoughts on Sociological Perspectives," in *Problems of America's Expanding Metropolitan Fringe Areas, op. cit.* (unpaged).

[39] A pertinent study is reported in Richard E. Gordon, Katherine K. Gordon, and Max Gunther, *The Split-Level Trap.* New York: Bernard Geis Associates and Random House, 1960.

Dobriner, William M. (ed.) *The Suburban Community.* New York: G. P. Putnam's Sons, 1958. (A series of 24 articles on suburbia).

Douglass, Harlan Paul. *The Suburban Trend.* New York: The Century Co., 1925.

Gordon, Albert I. *Jews in Suburbia.* Boston: Beacon Press, 1959.

"The President's Executive Order on Equal Opportunities in Housing." Packet of Documentary papers prepared by the Housing and Home Finance Agency (generally dated November 1962).

Greeley, Andrew M. *The Church and the Suburbs.* New York: Sheed & Ward, 1959.

Higbee, Edward. *The Squeeze—Cities Without Space.* New York: William Morrow & Co., 1960. Reprinted, New York: Apollo Editions, 1962.

Keats, John. *The Crack in the Picture Window.* Boston: Houghton Mifflin Co., 1956, 3d printing 1957.

Seeley, John R., R. Alexander Sim, and Elizabeth W. Loosley. *Crestwood Heights—A Study of the Culture of Suburban Life.* New York: Basic Books, 1956, 2d printing 1958.

Spectorsky, A. C. *The Exurbanites.* Philadelphia: J. B. Lippincott Co., 1955.

Stein, Maurice R. *The Eclipse of Community.* Princeton: Princeton University Press, 1960, Chapter 9.

Tyler, Poyntz (ed.) *City and Suburban Housing.* New York: The H. W. Wilson Co., 1957.

Warner, Sam B., Jr. *Streetcar Suburbs: The Process of Growth in Boston, 1870–1900.* Cambridge, Mass.: Harvard University Press, 1962.

Whyte, William H., Jr. *The Organization Man.* Garden City, N.Y.: Doubleday & Co., 1956. (Paperback.)

Wissink, G. A. *American Cities in Perspective—With Special Reference to the Development of Their Fringe Areas.* Assen, The Netherlands: Royal Van Gorcum, Ltd., 1962.

Wood, Robert C. *Suburbia—Its People and Their Politics.* Boston: Houghton Mifflin Co., 1958.

Table 11–1

PERCENT OF CHANGE IN STANDARD METROPOLITAN STATISTICAL AREAS, BY SIZE OF AREA, 1950 TO 1960, BASED ON 1950 LIMITS OF CENTRAL CITIES

Size and Component Parts of SMSA	*Percent of Change, 1950 to 1960*
All SMSA's	26.4%
Central cities	1.5
Outside central cities	61.7
3,000,000 or more	23.2
Central cities	0.6
Outside central cities	72.2
1,000,000 to 3,000,000	25.0
Central cities	–2.2
Outside central cities	52.7
500,000 to 1,000,000	36.0
Central cities	4.8
Outside central cities	81.1
250,000 to 500,000	25.6
Central cities	2.2
Outside central cities	51.9
100,000 to 250,000	25.8
Central cities	4.6
Outside central cities	54.5
Under 100,000	[illegible]1.1
Central cities	8.6
Outside central cities	69.9

SOURCE: U.S. Bureau of the Census, *Census of Population 1960.* Vol. I, Characteristics of the Population, Part A, Number of Inhabitants, p. xxvi.

Table 11–2

PERCENTAGE DISTRIBUTION BY MARITAL STATUS AND SEX, IN CENTRAL CITIES AND URBAN FRINGE, 1960

	Male		*Female*	
Marital Status	*Central Cities*	*Urban Fringe*	*Central Cities*	*Urban Fringe*
Total urban population 14 years old and over (number in thousands)	20,076	12,536	22,369	13,491
Single	25.8%	21.6%	20.7%	17.8%
Married	67.3	73.9	61.4	69.3
Separated	2.2	1.0	3.1	1.4
Widowed	4.1	2.8	13.9	10.3
Divorced	2.8	1.7	4.0	2.6

SOURCE: U.S. Bureau of the Census, *Census of Population 1960.* General Population Characteristics, PC(1), 1B, U.S. Summary, p. 1–156.

Table 11–3

PERCENTAGE DISTRIBUTION OF HOUSEHOLD RELATIONSHIPS, IN CENTRAL CITIES AND FRINGE, 1960

Household Relationships	*Central Cities*	*Urban Fringe*
Total persons (number in thousands)	57,975	37,873
In households	97.2%	98.1%
Head of household	31.9	28.7
Wife of head	21.1	23.1
Child under 18 of head	29.7	35.5
Other relative of head	12.2	9.4
Nonrelative of head	2.4	1.4
In group quarters	2.8	1.9

SOURCE: U.S. Bureau of the Census, *Census of Population 1960.* General Population Characteristics, PC(1), 1B, U.S .Summary, p. 1–157.

Table 11–4

PERCENTAGE DISTRIBUTION OF AGE OF POPULATION, IN CENTRAL CITIES AND URBAN FRINGE, 1960

Age of Population	*Central Cities*	*Urban Fringe*
Total Persons (number in thousands)	57,975	37,873
Under 14 years	28.1%	32.7%
15 to 29 years	19.7	18.2
30 to 44 years	20.2	22.8
45 to 64 years	22.0	19.1
65 years and over	10.0	7.2

SOURCE: U.S. Bureau of the Census, *Census of Population 1960.* General Population Characteristics, PC(1), 1B, U.S. Summary, pp. 1–148, 1–149.

Table 11–5

PERCENTAGE DISTRIBUTION OF 1959 FAMILY INCOME, SELECTED OCCUPATIONS, AND EDUCATIONAL ATTAINMENT, INSIDE STANDARD METROPOLITAN STATISTICAL AREAS, 1960

	Total Number (in Thousands)	*In Central Cities*	*Not in Central Cities*
Family Income in 1959			
Under $3,000	4,336	59.9%	40.1%
$3,000 to $9,999	18,899	51.4	48.6
$10,000 and over	5,385	45.3	54.7
Selected Occupations—Employed Persons			
Profess'l, tech., kindred	5,205	50.0	50.0
Clerical and kindred	7,148	57.7	42.3
Sales	3,288	52.1	47.9
Years of School Completed (Persons 25 Years Old and Over)			
Elementary—0 to 8 years	22,734	57.9	42.1
High school 1 to 4 years	20,313	51.1	48.9
College —1 to 3 years	6,108	50.1	49.9
4 years or more	5,632	48.2	51.8

SOURCE: U.S. Bureau of the Census, *Census of Population 1960.* Standard Metropolitan Statistical Areas, PC(3), 1D, pp. 329, 539, 679.

Table 11–6

PERCENTAGE DISTRIBUTION OF PROPORTION OF POPULATION INSIDE STANDARD METROPOLITAN STATISTICAL AREAS, BY RACE, 1900–1960

	White		*Negro*	
Year	*In Central Cities*	*Not in Central Cities*	*In Central Cities*	*Not in Central Cities*
1900	62.8%	37.2%	54.5%	45.5%
1910	64.9	35.1	60.4	39.6
1920	65.9	34.1	67.2	32.8
1930	63.9	36.1	72.8	27.2
1940	61.6	38.4	74.6	25.4
1950	56.6	43.4	77.2	22.8
1960	47.8	52.2	79.6	20.4

SOURCE: U.S. Bureau of the Census, *Census of Population 1960.* Standard Metropolitan Statistical Areas, PC(3), 1D, p. 1.

Table 11–7

PERCENTAGE DISTRIBUTION OF MOBILITY OF POPULATION FIVE YEARS OLD AND OVER, BASED ON RESIDENCE IN 1955, INSIDE STANDARD METROPOLITAN STATISTICAL AREAS, 1960

Mobility Status	*Total Number (in thousands)*	*In Central Cities*	*Not in Central Cities*
Total reporting	100,064	51.7%	48.3%
Same house 1960 as 1955	48,028	52.3	47.7
Different house in U.S.	48,591	50.5	49.5
Same county	31,212	55.6	44.4
Different county	17,379	41.5	58.5
Same state	7,814	37.5	62.5
Different state	9,566	44.7	55.3

SOURCE: U.S. Bureau of the Census, *Census of Population 1960.* Standard Metropolitan Statistical Areas, PC(3), 1D, p. 399.

Table 11–8

PERCENTAGE DISTRIBUTION OF TENURE AND COLOR OF OCCUPANCY, OCCUPIED HOUSING UNITS, INSIDE STANDARD METROPOLITAN STATISTICAL AREAS, 1960

Tenure and Color	*In Central Cities*	*Not in Central Cities*
Total occupied units (number in thousands)	18,506	15,494
Owner-occupied	47.4%	72.7%
White	42.6	70.5
Nonwhite	4.8	2.2
Renter-occupied	52.6	27.3
White	42.0	25.3
Nonwhite	10.6	2.0

SOURCE: Derived from U.S. Bureau of the Census, *Census of Housing 1960.* States and Small Areas, HC(1), No. 1, U.S. Summary, p. xxvii.

Table 11–9

PERCENTAGE DISTRIBUTION OF VALUE OF OWNER-OCCUPIED HOUSING UNITS, INSIDE STANDARD METROPOLITAN STATISTICAL AREAS, 1960

Value	*In Central Cities*	*Not in Central Cities*
Total Owner-occupied Units (number in thousands)	7,384	9,883
Less than $5,000	5.9%	5.4%
$5,000 to $7,400	11.3	7.3
$7,500 to $9,900	15.8	10.2
$10,000 to $12,400	18.1	15.0
$12,500 to $14,900	15.4	15.9
$15,000 to $17,400	11.5	14.0
$17,500 to $19,900	7.5	10.1
$20,000 to $24,900	7.1	10.6
$25,000 to $34,900	4.4	7.2
$35,000 or more	3.0	4.3
Median value, dollars	$12,300	$14,400

SOURCE: Derived from U.S. Bureau of the Census, *Census of Housing 1960*. States and Small Areas, IIC(1), No. 1, U.S. Summary, p 1–45.

Table 11–10

PERCENTAGE DISTRIBUTION OF GROSS RENT OF RENTER-OCCUPIED HOUSING UNITS, INSIDE STANDARD METROPOLITAN STATISTICAL AREAS, 1960

Rent	*In Central Cities*	*Not in Central Cities*
Total renter-occupied units (number in thousands)	9,729	4,131
Less than $30	3.0%	2.8%
$30 to $39	5.6	3.8
$40 to $10	9.1	6.3
$50 to $59	12.6	8.9
$60 to $69	15.0	11.2
$70 to $79	13.6	12.2
$80 to $99	20.0	22.1
$100 to $119	9.6	12.5
$120 or more	8.7	12.8
No cash rent	2.8	7.4
Median rent, dollars	$72	$81

SOURCE: Derived from U.S. Bureau of the Census, *Census of Housing 1960*. States and Small Areas, HC(1), No. 1, U.S. Summary, p. 1–45.

Table 11–11

PERCENTAGE DISTRIBUTION OF CONDITION AND PRESENCE OF PLUMBING FACILITIES, INSIDE STANDARD METROPOLITAN STATISTICAL AREAS, BY TENURE, 1960

Condition and Presence of Plumbing Facilities	*Owner-Occupied*		*Renter-Occupied*	
	In Central Cities	*Not in Central Cities*	*In Central Cities*	*Not in Central Cities*
Total housing units (number in thousands)	8,777	11,259	9,729	4,235
Sound	91.8%	92.8%	79.0%	79.6%
With all plumbing facilities	90.5	90.5	71.9	74.2
Lacking some or all facilities	1.3	2.3	7.1	5.4
Deteriorating	6.9	5.6	16.4	14.7
With all plumbing facilities	6.0	4.0	11.5	10.0
Lacking some or all facilities	0.9	1.6	4.9	4.7
Dilapidated	1.3	1.6	4.6	5.7

SOURCE: Derived from U.S. Bureau of the Census, *Census of Housing 1960.* States and Small Areas, HC(1), No. 1, U.S. Summary, p. 1–40.

Table 11–12

PERCENTAGE DISTRIBUTION OF YEAR STRUCTURE BUILT, INSIDE STANDARD METROPOLITAN STATISTICAL AREAS, BY TENURE, 1960

	Owner-Occupied		*Renter-Occupied*	
Year Structure Built	*In Central Cities*	*Not in Central Cities*	*In Central Cities*	*Not in Central Cities*
Total housing units (number in thousands)	8,777	11,259	10,840	5,502
1955 to March 1960	13.1%	26.2%	6.6%	16.5%
1950 to 1954	14.3	21.2	7.2	12.9
1940 to 1949	15.0	17.0	10.0	17.5
1939 or earlier	57.0	35.6	76.2	53.1

SOURCE: Derived from U.S. Bureau of the Census, *Census of Housing 1960.* States and Small Areas, HC(1), No. 1, U.S. Summary, p. 1–42. Only total U.S. and owner-occupied data are reported by the Census. The renter-occupied data shown are derived by subtracting the latter from the former, which obviously includes some error because all persons did not report on year structure built. The percentage distribution shown for renter-occupied units, however, should generally approximate actual figures.

Table 11–13

PERCENTAGE DISTRIBUTION OF NUMBER OF ROOMS, INSIDE STANDARD METROPOLITAN STATISTICAL AREAS, BY TENURE, 1960

	Owner-Occupied		*Renter-Occupied*	
Number of Rooms	*In Central Cities*	*Not in Central Cities*	*In Central Cities*	*Not in Central Cities*
Total housing units (number in thousands)	8,777	11,259	9,729	4,235
One	0.1%	0.2%	7.8%	3.4%
Two	0.7	0.9	10.8	6.8
Three	3.5	3.3	26.3	22.5
Four	15.2	14.8	27.0	30.1
Five	30.5	30.8	16.8	20.7
Six	28.7	27.7	8.1	10.4
Seven	12.1	12.8	2.1	3.5
Eight or more	9.2	9.5	1.1	2.6
Median No. of rooms	5.5	5.5	3.7	4.1

SOURCE: Derived from U.S. Bureau of the Census, *Census of Housing 1960.* States and Small Areas, HC(1), No. 1, U.S. Summary, p. 1–41.

Table 11–14

PERCENTAGE DISTRIBUTION OF PERSONS PER ROOM, INSIDE STANDARD METROPOLITAN STATISTICAL AREAS, BY TENURE, 1960

	In Central Cities		*Not in Central Cities*	
Persons Per Room	*Owner*	*Renter*	*Owner*	*Renter*
Total housing units (number in thousands)	8,777	9,729	11,259	4,235
0.50 or less	49.3%	35.7%	41.9%	33.4%
0.51 to 0.75	23.6	23.4	25.8	25.9
0.76 to 1.00	20.1	26.8	24.1	26.3
1.01 to 1.50	5.7	9.0	6.7	9.8
1.51 or more	1.3	5.1	1.5	4.6

SOURCE: Derived from U.S. Bureau of the Census, *Census of Housing 1960*. States and Small Areas, HC(1), No. 1, U.S. Summary, p. 1–43.

CHAPTER 12

*

Rural Housing

The two preceding chapters have discussed the central city and suburbia. Continuing the "areal" approach, this chapter will focus on the rural territory. This area is, in a way, more difficult to describe, because it encompasses families vastly different in their basic characteristics.

DEFINITION OF RURAL HOUSING

The U.S. Census has long followed a rather simple differentiation between the two primary groups living in rural areas: it has defined one of the groups on the basis of occupation, i.e., farmers, and then defined the remaining groups not engaged in that occupation as "nonfarmers." The two common terms that result are "farm" and "nonfarm" housing. To be more specific, and to distinguish such housing from that in urban areas, the following summary definition may be given:

> Urban housing comprises all housing units in urbanized areas and in places of 2500 inhabitants or more and a few areas classified as urban under special rules. Housing not classified as urban constitutes rural housing. In rural territory, occupied housing units are subdivided into rural-farm and rural nonfarm units on the basis of number of acres in the place and total sales of farm products in 1959; i.e., occupied housing situated on places of 10 or more acres from which sales of farm products amounted to $50 or more or on places of less than 10 acres from which sales of farm products amounted to $250 or more are classified as farm units. The remaining occupied units and all vacant units in rural territory are classified as nonfarm units.[1]

EVOLUTION OF RURAL SOCIETY IN THE UNITED STATES

It was indicated in Chapter 1 that some understanding of the history of the United States is necessary if we are to understand our society today. This is especially true with reference to understanding our rural society.

[1] Summarized from U.S. Bureau of the Census, *Census of Housing 1960*. Vol. VI, Rural Housing, p. xv. Because of a change in the definition of farm residence, 1960 and 1950 Census data are not comparable. A detailed explanation of urban-rural residence in past censuses is given in U.S. Bureau of the Census, *Census of Housing 1960*. States and Small Areas, HC(1), No. 1, U.S. Summary.

Taylor has succinctly described some of the historical differences between this country and others:

The rural life of most other countries developed out of feudal systems, and in many cases the farmers are still peasants. In fact, there are millions of farmers in the world today who are farming with oxen or with no animals or motive power whatever, but agriculture in the United States was relatively mechanized even in its earliest days. Furthermore, farming in this country has always been relatively commercialized, and farmers have been comparatively free from the domination of a

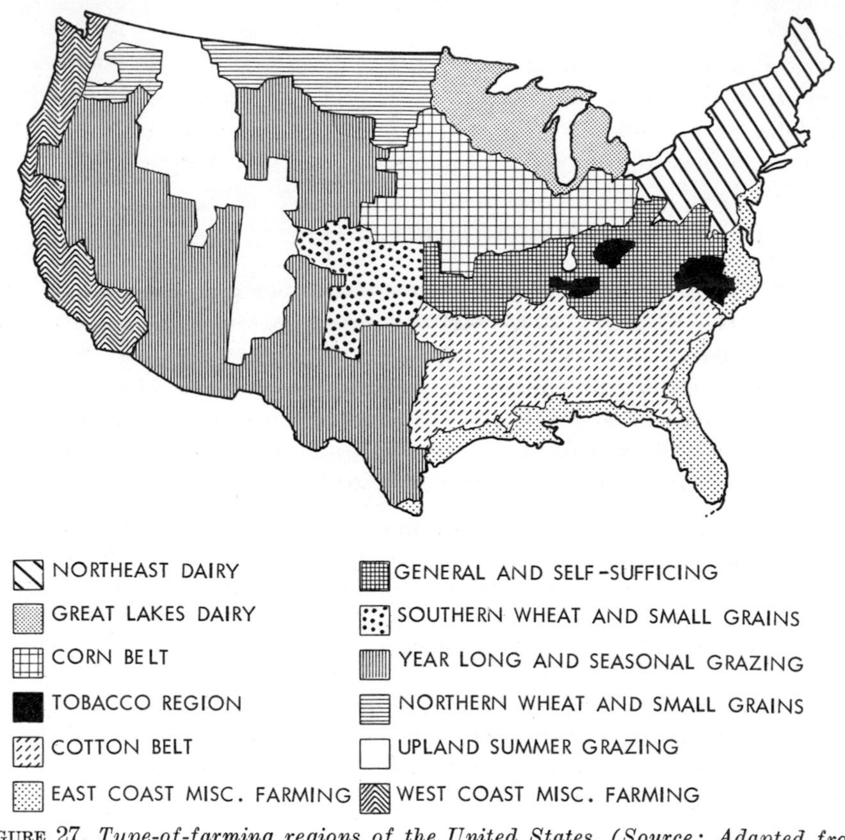

FIGURE 27. *Type-of-farming regions of the United States. (Source: Adapted from Glenn H. Beyer and J. Hugh Rose,* Farm Housing. *New York: John Wiley & Sons, Inc., 1957, Fig. 1, p. 6. Used with permission of the publisher.)*

rich, absentee, urban-dwelling landlord class such as exists in many European and South American countries. In short, rural society in the United States is composed chiefly of operators of small or medium-sized farms who are either owners or tenants, and who live on individual farmsteads and in neighborhoods and communities in which they are not only the dominant occupational group but also the dominant social group. They are not peasants, and they would resent an inference that they occupy a social status inferior to that of any other group of citizens.[2]

[2] "Rural Life and Rural Sociology," in Carl C. Taylor, *et al., Rural Life in the United States.* New York: Alfred A. Knopf, 1949, p. 11.

It will be recalled that some regions were settled by cohesive religious and national groups, whereas others were settled by various and diverse groups, some of whom were "dissenters" and others simply adventurers. Much of the land was developed in small farms from the start, with no planned settlement pattern; other land was laid out in large farms. Some farms were established around village settlements, whereas many others were isolated for years in wilderness. In the South some farms developed as plantations and even "feudal estates." Most of these had Negro laborers, about the only people who did not have an opportunity to move freely into the frontier and avail themselves of cheap, or sometimes free, land of their own.

From the earliest times, agriculture in this country has been diversified, except in the tobacco and cotton regions where cash-crop farming was established at the start. Tobacco was the first American cash crop, followed by cotton, which was given tremendous impetus by the invention of the cotton gin. The first commercial crop in the North was wheat. As time passed, farmers gradually shifted to the most feasible and profitable types of production. Today, most of the nation can be divided into identifiable type-of-farming regions, including, in addition to those regions already mentioned, the Northeast and Great Lakes dairy belts, the grazing regions of the Mountain states, and the miscellaneous farming areas on the East and West coasts. "General" and "self-sufficing" areas remain in the mountainous territory from the Piedmont Plateau in Virginia and North Carolina to the Ozark Mountains in Arkansas and Missouri (Figure 27).[3]

Historically, there have been some significant differences between our urban and rural societies, differences that were especially striking when most farm families were relatively isolated from their urban counterparts. Farming has usually been a family enterprise, and, as a result, farm families generally have been more cohesive units than urban families. Even today the vast majority of our farms are "family farms."

RECENT TRENDS IN RURAL POPULATION

In 1960, the distribution of the population of the nation was as follows:

	Number	*Percent*
Total U.S. population	179,325,657	100.0
Urban	125,283,765	69.9
Rural nonfarm	40,567,121	22.6
Farm	13,474,771	7.5

[3] Larson, however, has pointed out: "While farms have increasingly specialized in what they produce, there have been some changes in area of specialization as well. Production areas have shifted; more diversity has been introduced within areas; and there have been small areas of increased specialization, usually with a new enterprise. To generalize broadly—cotton has moved from the old Cotton Belt east of the Mississippi to Texas, New Mexico, Arizona and California, where it is relatively less dominant; soybeans have been added to the Corn Belt; the Corn Belt has moved outward; and the Cotton Belt has diversified and shifted more to livestock." (Olaf F. Larson, "Rural Society in Transition in the American Setting," paper presented at the annual meeting of the Rural Sociological Society at Iowa State University, Ames, Iowa, August 27–29, 1961 (mimeo.), pp. 20–22.)

It can be seen from these data that the rural population—rural nonfarm and farm combined—represented 30 percent of the total population of the nation in 1960. About one sixth of the rural population lives in villages; those remaining live outside of villages, generally in the open country. In the open country, it is interesting to note that nonfarmers outnumber farmers about two to one. The trend since 1910 is shown in Table 12–1 (p. 404). It can be seen from the data in that table that most of the decrease in percentage of the total U. S. population has taken place outside of villages.

There has been a constant trend of population away from farms since the mid-1930's. In 1935, the farm population of the nation numbered approximately 32,161,000 persons. This number represented one fourth of the population of the nation. By 1950, the farm population was reduced to approximately 23,332,000 persons, 15 percent of the total population. It can be seen, from the 1960 figures given in Table 12–2 (p. 405), how drastic the decline was between 1950 and 1960.

In the meantime, the number of farms also has been declining. From a total of approximately 6,812,000 in 1935, the number declined to about 4,782,000 farms in 1950 and further to 3,710,000 in 1959. The number of persons per farm has varied over the years, the peak average number having been 5.01 in 1940. By 1960, the average had declined to 3.62 (Table 12–2). There were, in 1960, only 3,566,321 farm households. (This figure is not directly comparable with the 1950 and 1940 Census figures, because of a change in definition of farm residence. This change resulted in a substantial reduction in the number of housing units reported in the farm housing inventory.)

It is common knowledge that while the number of farms is declining, their average size is increasing. In 1950, for the nation as a whole, the average farm had 215 acres. By 1954 it had increased to 242 acres and by 1959, to 302. This trend has been common to all regions (Table 12–3, p. 406). The greatest decrease in the number of farms has taken place in the South Atlantic states (Delaware, Maryland, Virginia, West Virginia, North Carolina, South Carolina, Georgia, Florida) and New England (Maine, New Hampshire, Vermont, Massachusetts, Rhode Island, and Connecticut) —over a 30 percent decline between 1954 and 1959. There has also been a sharp decline in the East South Central states (Kentucky, Tennessee, Alabama, and Mississippi) where the smallest farms are found. The largest farms, of course, are found in the Mountain states (Montana, Idaho, Wyoming, Colorado, New Mexico, Arizona, Utah, and Nevada).

FARMING AND FARM LIVING TODAY

Two primary factors have contributed to the decline in farm population. First is the attraction of urban life for farm youths. Second are the rapid technological advances that have taken place in farming, permitting increased production with less manpower.

The technological improvements in farming have been the increased use of mechanical power and modern farm machinery, the increased use of fertilizers and the wide adoption of artificial insemination and hybrid seed. In the seventeen-year period 1945 to 1962, for example, the number of farm tractors in use doubled, from 2,354,000 to 4,690,000. The number of grain combines increased from 375,000 to over 1,000,000. Mechanical cornpickers increased almost five times, from 168,000 to 815,000. The amount of principal plant nutrients used increased from 2,692,000 tons to 8,400,000 tons.[4] An additional illustration of improved technology is the use of airplanes in farm production. In 1959, planes were flown 879,750 hours in covering 50,891,000 acres for insect, disease, and weed control, fertilizing, seeding, and other purposes.[5]

What has been the result? It has been said that it takes only 48 minutes to plow an acre of land with a tractor compared with over 2½ hours with horses; only 48 minutes to combine and store an acre of wheat, compared with 5 hours without a combine; and less than 2 hours to harvest and crib an acre of corn, compared with 7 hours without a cornpicker. The relative contribution of the farm labor force, therefore, has greatly increased. In 1910, one farm worker supported 7.1 other persons; by 1950, this average had increased to 15.5; and by 1960, to 26.0. According to one authority: "Without advance in farm productivity since 1910, nearly 20 million more workers [than the 7.1 million employed] would have been needed in farming to meet domestic food needs and exports at 1959 levels."[6]

Problems have accompanied this increase in productivity. One of these is the surplus of agricultural products that has developed (a problem beyond the scope of this book and, therefore, not discussed further). Another is the increase in assets required to conduct farming on a competitive and profitable basis. Heady and Ackerman have shown that the productive assets per farm worker amounted to only $3,370 in 1910, compared with $13,630 in 1950 and $18,470 in 1955.[7] Profitable commercial farming, therefore, is not a poor man's occupation today.

What are the implications of these sharp changes from the standpoint of farm living patterns? Ogburn has suggested ". . . social trends seldom change their direction quickly or sharply."[8] This statement is borne out only in part with relation to farmers. Details of their families and their housing will be provided later. At this point some general observations will be made.

[4] *Changes in Farm Production and Efficiency,* U.S. Department of Agriculture Statistical Bulletin No. 233, Revised July 1963, Tables 8 and 13, pp. 22, 30.

[5] *FAA Statistical Handbook of Aviation,* 1961 edition, Federal Aviation Agency, Washington, D.C.: U.S. Government Printing Office, p. 58.

[6] Earl O. Heady, "Nature of the Farm Problem," in Mervin G. Smith and Carlton F. Christian, eds., *Adjustments in Agriculture—A National Basebook.* Ames, Iowa: Iowa State University Press, 1961, pp. 72–73.

[7] Earl O. Heady and Joseph Ackerman, "Farm Adjustment Problems: Their Cause and Nature and Their Importance to Sociologists," in *Rural Sociology in a Changing Economy.* Published by Department of Agricultural Economics, University of Illinois College of Agriculture, Urbana, Illinois, November 13, 1958 (mimeo.), p. 6.

[8] William Fielding Ogburn, "Technology and Cities: The Dilemma of the Modern Metropolis," in *The Sociological Quarterly,* Vol. 1, No. 3, July 1960, p. 150.

Farm families have made important gains in their levels of living in the past twenty-five years. The telephone, electricity, running water, and the automobile have brought many changes to life on the farm. Great strides have been made in medical care.

In the meantime, the roles and status of family members have been changing, especially those of women and children. Women are becoming more active outside the home in paid work, including professional careers, and in social activities. There is less contribution to farm operation on the part of children. In short, the patriarchal type of family is decreasing and more and more family groups are characterized by patterns of equality among family members. The average work-week for the gainfully employed is becoming shorter. A generation ago many farmers put in 16- to 18-hour days, compared with 10-hour days in winter months and 12-hour days in summer months today.[9]

Wilkening has pointed out that with the increased size and specialization of farms, the institutions of farm and of family are becoming more distinct. "The farm no longer functions to provide for family needs and interests, but for those of the market. 'Making money' as a goal of the farm replaces that of 'making a living for the family.' " He also points out the serious problems created by the heavy capital investment needed today in land and farm equipment. A third problem, which he mentions, relates to "the process of socialization, occupational choice, and migration of farm youth." He points out the crucial choices concerning their future careers that must be made by farm boys and girls during and immediately after their high school years.[10]

All of these factors have an important bearing on farm living patterns and, similarly, on the farm housing situation.

RURAL NONFARM AREAS

Earlier in the history of this country the rural nonfarm population grew, because the small villages serviced and were the market places of the heavy farm population. This growth has generally stopped, as indicated by Census data concerning the proportion of the population in villages between 1910 and 1960 (see Table 12–1, 404).

Precise information concerning the reasons for this change is lacking, but some facts are generally known. It is known, for example, that with the advent of automobiles and especially the development of modern highways, many farm people travel to larger communities to do much of their shopping. Farm marketing also frequently takes place in larger places: cotton, livestock, and grain can be trucked to larger centers; food processing is being centralized in fewer plants in larger cities; and there is bulk tank

[9] "Keeping Abreast of Change in the Rural Community," Agriculture Information Bulletin No. 215, Federal Extension Service, U.S. Department of Agriculture, Washington, D.C., October 1959.

[10] E. A. Wilkening, "Trends in the Farm Family," in *Rural Sociology in a Changing Economy, loc. cit.*, pp. 37–38.

pickup of fluid milk which is taken to cities. Frequently, farm families travel to several larger centers for services, not merely a single one. In some instances, rural communities favored by their location on a primary highway have had a precipitous drop in business when a parallel throughway has been built only a few miles distant. Changing patterns in the use of time and demands with regard to leisure require recreational services that have not existed, and therefore individuals and families have transferred their attention to larger places for such services. Finally, with a smaller farm population, fewer people have been needed in rural villages to service their needs.

Some rural villages have been industrial. Where this has resulted from decentralization of industry, the communities have remained stable or even increased in size. In other instances, however, where the village has served a population working in an area blighted by the depletion of its natural resource base (as, for example, in some coal mining areas), there has been a decline in the need for community services and a resulting loss in village population.

The segment of the population that has remained in the rural nonfarm areas has been primarily one attached to the community and able to continue to maintain a livelihood in the face of the changes that have been taking place. Many of our small villages will undoubtedly continue to serve a useful function, although competition between the small village and the larger marketplace is not likely to diminish in the future.

Some villages have, of course, been attracting urban population—workers who have found less expensive houses there and have been willing to pay the cost in both time and money to commute to their work in the larger city. (In some instances, for example, where commuting has been to urban areas having populations from 10,000 to 50,000, these costs have not been large.) With our expanding urban population, and with space in our cities becoming ever more crowded, more villages are likely to find new residents of this type. If this becomes an important trend (if, indeed, it is not one already), our villages are likely to find themselves housing individuals and families with attitudes, value patterns, and ideas concerning community structure and community needs different from those of their traditional residents. There is likely to be an increased effort to improve educational and religious facilities, medical services, provisions for security and welfare, recreational services, and the like.[11]

RURAL POPULATION CHARACTERISTICS

It is now important to obtain a more precise understanding of rural nonfarm and farm families, especially as their characteristics may be compared with those of urban families. In this discussion, since the nonwhite segment of the population has distinctive characteristics, special attention will be directed to those families.

[11] For elaboration, see Olaf F. Larson and E. A. Lutz, "Adjustments in Community Facilities Taking Place and Needed," in Mervin G. Smith and Carlton F. Christian, eds., *op. cit.*, pp. 285–336.

Occupations

It should be pointed out, first, that not all heads of families classified as farmers by the U. S. Census definition have farming as their primary occupation. In fact, among white families who fit the Census definition, only 69 percent of the heads either managed or worked on a farm as their major occupation in 1960 (63 percent as farmers or farm managers and 6 percent as farm laborers or foremen). The remaining 31 percent were distributed fairly evenly in other types of occupations. Among nonwhite families counted in the Census definition of farmers, 78 percent of the heads listed farming as their primary occupation (50 percent as farmers and farm managers and 28 percent as farm laborers or foremen). Of the remaining 22 percent, the largest proportion were operatives and common laborers.

The highest proportion of white rural nonfarm workers were craftsmen and operatives (approximately half of the nonfarm workers). Important proportions, however, were engaged as managers, officials, and proprietors (12 percent) and in clerical and sales operations (10 percent). Three out of four rural nonfarm nonwhite workers were engaged as operatives (24 percent), common laborers (22 percent), farm laborers (15 percent), and service workers (14 percent). (See Table 12–4, p. 407).

Family Size

One of the common characteristics of rural families is that traditionally they have been larger than urban families. This was confirmed in the 1960 U. S. Census. For example, 17 percent of the white farm families contained six or more persons. This compared with 14 percent of the white nonfarm families and only 10 percent of the white urban families. The medians also reflect the difference: urban, 3.51 persons; rural nonfarm, 3.73 persons; farm, 3.80 persons.

Nonwhite families were significantly larger than white families. In 1960, 22 percent of these families, living in urban areas, contained six or more persons. In rural nonfarm areas, the proportion increased to 34 percent and on farms, to 45 percent—nearly half of all of the nonwhite families (Table 12–5, p. 408).

Age Structure

A comparison of the age structure of the farm population with that of other groups indicates that it is undergoing an interesting change. In 1960, the median age of the farm population was 29.6 years, compared with a median of 26.7 years for the rural nonfarm group and 30.3 years for the urban group. Despite the higher fertility of farm women (averaging 3.33 children, as compared with 2.88 for rural nonfarm women and 2.26 for urban women), there is evidence that in a couple of decades the farm population will become older than either the urban or rural nonfarm segments. In observing the proportion of children in the three lowest five-year age classes, it can be seen that for the urban population a higher proportion are aged under five than between five to nine, and a higher proportion are aged five to nine than ten to fourteen. A similar trend, but not as accentuated, occurs among the rural nonfarm population. However, the reverse is true with regard to the farm population. The figures are as follows:

	Percentage of Total Urban, Rural Nonfarm, and Farm Population		
Age Class	*Urban*	*Rural Nonfarm*	*Farm*
Under five years	11.2	12.1	9.9
Five to nine years	10.0	11.3	11.0
Ten to fourteen years	7.0	10.3	11.6[12]

The trend of the farm population is undoubtedly a result of the steady out-migration of young adults which has brought about a steady reduction of the number of births on farms over the past fifteen years, rather than from low fertility of farm married couples or from high mortality.

Income Levels

Another important characteristic of rural families, and especially of farm families, is their lower income than that of urban families. Before citing specific income figures, it is well to point out that the farming industry is not a homogeneous one. Broadly speaking, farmers may be divided into two groups: (1) commercial farmers who have mechanized their farms and have achieved a high rate of agricultural production in other ways, and (2) chronically low-income farmers who own so few production resources that their incomes will remain meager at any level of farm prices. The latter group of farmers is concentrated in the South, although some are located in all regions.

Incomes of farmers have been lower than incomes of urban families for two basic reasons. With regard to the second group of farmers mentioned above, the reason is evident—they are primarily subsistence farmers. For the first group—commercial farmers—the heavy capital investment required today in a typical operation has already been mentioned. Unfortunately, that investment continues to absorb an increasing proportion of gross farm income. (From 1950 to 1959 alone, this proportion rose, on the average, from 60 percent to 70 percent.) Thus, while farmers must use every means at hand to increase production if they desire to reach higher income levels, the net income they receive does not rise in direct proportion to their investment.

In 1959, the median income of white farm families was only $3,472, compared with $4,981 for white rural nonfarm families and $6,433 for white urban families. A total of 57 percent of the farm families had incomes under $4,000, compared with 37 percent of the rural nonfarm and 22 percent of the urban white families.

[12] Derived from U.S. Bureau of the Census, *Census of Population 1960*. Detailed Characteristics, PC(1), 1D, U. S. Summary.

Incomes of most nonwhite families were significantly lower, especially those of farmers. In 1959, the median income of nonwhite farm families was only $1,263. For rural nonfarm nonwhite families it was $1,917, and for nonwhite urban families, $3,711. Nine out of ten nonwhite farm families had incomes below $4,000, compared with four out of five nonwhite nonfarm families and approximately half of the urban nonwhite families (Table 12–6, p. 408).

Although it is possible for many farm families to offset their low income through home consumption of some of the farm products they raise, such as vegetables, poultry, and livestock, the importance of this practice in the farm family budget seems to be steadily declining. The practice undoubtedly exists more for the lowest-income families than for those of higher income. However, as more farmers specialize in certain types of farming, they tend to buy more of the food they need in the market.

Educational Attainment

Another distinctive characteristic of rural families is the lower level of educational attainment of heads of families. In 1960, 57 percent of the heads of white farm families had not gone beyond elementary school. The proportion for rural nonfarm families was 45 percent, and for urban families it was appreciably lower—only 32 percent. At the other end of the educational ladder, only 8 percent of the white farmers had attended college, compared with 14 percent of the white nonfarm heads of families and 23 percent of the white urban heads of families.

The picture is much less favorable with regard to nonwhite families. Among nonwhite farmers, nine out of every ten had not gone beyond elementary school, and most of them had not reached the eighth grade. Eight out of every ten of the nonwhite rural nonfarm heads of families also had not passed the eighth grade, and most of them had not reached that grade. A total of 54 percent of the urban nonwhite heads had completed elementary school, however, and another 37 percent had entered high school (though less than half of that number were graduated). (See Table 12–7, p. 409).

Today the proportion of children of elementary and high school age from farm families who are enrolled in school has reached urban standards, but some of these children, especially in the South, are below their normal grade.

This, then, is a brief résumé of some of the characteristics that distinguish our urban from our rural population today.

HOUSING CHARACTERISTICS OF THE RURAL POPULATION

In analyzing the housing characteristics of the rural population, two factors, tenure and race, must always be kept in mind because they are so influential in determining the level of the different characteristics.

Tenure and Race

Ownership of farms has tended to be even more traditional in this country than ownership of urban homes. In 1960, approximately three out of every four farmers owned their farm. The rate of home ownership in nonfarm areas also is high—70 percent of the occupied dwellings in 1960, compared with 58 percent of those in urban areas (Table 12–8, p. 409).

More nonwhite farmers, however, are tenants than owners (Table 12–8). This fact undoubtedly results from their generally low income, which has been described. A comparison of median incomes for 1959 supports this conclusion:

	Owners	*Renters*
White		
Nonfarm	$4,800	$3,500
Farm	$3,400	$2,400
Nonwhite (total)	$1,800	$1,400

The median figures for farm and nonfarm nonwhite owners and renters are not available, but percentage distributions shown in Table 12–9 (p. 410) show the differences. Nearly four fifths of the nonwhite farm families who were renters had 1959 incomes of less than $2,000. Among those who owned their farms, 63 percent fell in this low-income class. The proportions for white families living on farms were 35 percent and 30 percent, respectively.

Nonwhite families living in nonfarm areas fare somewhat better than those living on farms, but still appreciably worse than white families living either on farms or in nonfarm areas. In 1959, 62 percent of the nonwhite renter families living in nonfarm areas had incomes below $2,000, compared with one fourth of the white renter families living in those areas. Slightly over half of the nonwhite owner families living in nonfarm areas had incomes this low, compared with one fifth of the white owner families. (Table 12–9.) From these figures the strong influence of income on housing characteristics can be seen.

Value and Rent

Value and rent data for farmers are not reported here, since those data would cover the entire farm plant and land, rather than only the house on the farm. Thus, the figures would not be comparable with figures for housing in rural nonfarm or urban areas.

Rural nonfarm housing generally is significantly lower in value than urban housing. The general differences are reflected in the median for 1960 —for all rural nonfarm housing the median value was $8,300 and for urban housing, $12,900. Nonwhite urban housing had a median value of $7,800 and the median for nonwhite nonfarm housing was below $5,000 (the actual figure is not available). Nearly three fourths of the nonwhite dwelling units located in nonfarm areas had a value of less than $5,000 (Table 12–10, p. 410).

Median values varied appreciably among different regions and states. Highest valued housing units were found in Hawaii, Connecticut, New Jersey, New York, Nevada, California, and the District of Columbia. Lowest values were found in Arkansas, North Carolina, Oklahoma, Mississippi, West Virginia, and South Carolina.

Gross monthly rents show a similar picture. The median rent for all rural nonfarm housing was $55 per month in 1960, compared with $73 for all urban housing. Nonwhite rents were significantly lower—$61 for urban housing and only $27 for housing in nonfarm areas (Table 12–11, p. 411).

Approximately 1.4 million nonfarm renter-occupied units were occupied in 1960 on a "no cash rent" basis (nearly one fourth of the total). Among these were dwelling units provided by relatives not living in the unit and occupied without rental payment, and units provided in exchange for services rendered. Nearly half of the no-cash-rent units were in the South.

There was a considerable difference in rent levels among different regions and states. Highest rents were found in Alaska, Nevada, Illinois, New Jersey, and the District of Columbia. Lowest were found in Mississippi, South Carolina, Arkansas, and Alabama.

Quality of Housing

The standards of rural nonfarm and farm housing are also well below those in urban areas. Since farms have traditionally lacked municipal water and sewage systems, frequently even prosperous farm families have lived without running water and plumbing facilities for decades after these amenities were commonplace in urban housing. Although there has been real progress toward improvement since World War II, many nonfarm and, especially, farm homes still remain without these facilities.

Only 57 percent of all of the owner-occupied farm dwellings and 70 percent of those located in nonfarm areas, as compared with 90 percent of the owner-occupied urban dwellings, were reported in sound condition and as having all plumbing facilities—piped hot water, private flush toilet, and bathtub or shower in 1960. Another 7 percent of the farm and nonfarm dwellings, as compared with 5 percent of the urban dwellings, had all plumbing facilities but were in deteriorating condition, i.e., they were not dilapidated but needed more repair than would be provided in the course of regular maintenance. The remaining units were dilapidated or lacked one or more plumbing facilities.

Renter-occupied dwelling units were in significantly poorer condition than owner-occupied units. Only one third of all of the renter-occupied farm dwellings were reported in sound condition and as having all plumbing facilities, compared with 45 percent of the nonfarm dwellings and 72 percent of those located in urban areas. Another 8 percent of the renter-occupied farm dwellings, 10 percent of the nonfarm dwellings, and 12 percent of the urban dwellings had all plumbing facilities but were in deteriorating condition.

The farm and rural nonfarm housing occupied by nonwhite families is generally of the poorest quality found in the nation. Only 13 percent of the owner-occupied housing occupied by nonwhites living on farms and 18 percent of such housing units in nonfarm areas was found to be in sound condition with all plumbing facilities in 1960. The comparable percentage for urban nonwhite families was 66 percent, which shows how much more poorly rural families are housed than urban nonwhite families.

The situation with regard to rural nonwhite families who rent is even more serious. Almost no nonwhite farm families (only 2 percent) live in housing units that are sound and have all plumbing facilities. Among nonwhite rural nonfarm families, the proportion is less than one out of ten. (The comparable figure for nonwhite renters living in urban areas is 47 percent.) The problem encompasses both poor structural condition and lack of plumbing. For example, among nonwhite renters living on farms, 42 percent lived in housing which was in a deteriorating condition and which lacked some plumbing and another 36 percent lived in dilapidated dwelling units—the combination of these two characteristics representing nearly four out of every five dwellings on farms occupied by nonwhite families in 1960. The nonfarm picture is only slightly brighter (Table 12–12, p. 411).

Age of Housing

One—but, of course, only one—of the factors contributing to the poor quality of farm housing is the matter of the age of the housing. With reference to age, however, rural nonfarm housing more closely parallels urban than farm housing.

Almost two fifths of the total 1960 stock of owner-occupied urban and rural nonfarm housing had been built since 1950. However, only 14 percent of the farm houses in existence in 1960 had been built that recently, and many of these units were in the West and North. Fewer new renter than owner-occupied units were built, but, interestingly, the highest proportion of new renter units was in rural nonfarm areas. Nearly one fourth of all such dwelling units in existence in nonfarm areas in 1960 had been built since 1950. (This proportion compares with 18 percent in urban areas and only 8 percent on farms.) The precise reason for this relatively high percentage is not known. Many of them probably are located in small villages that represent a type of "suburbia" around urban areas having a population of less than 50,000 (which, therefore, would be classed as nonfarm by the U.S. Census). Others may house families living outside metropolitan areas, whose heads commute to work in those areas. Some may have been built to house new residents brought to villages as a result of decentralization of some industries. It is most likely that few have been built to house the regular population of these villages—the craftsmen, operatives, managers, and sales and clerical people who actually work there. The primary incentives to build in these places have probably been lower land costs and lower taxes than in the larger urban areas.

Approximately one out of every five of the dwelling units occupied by nonwhite owners in urban areas and on farms was built between 1950 and 1960. The majority of the units, however, were built before 1940. The proportions of owner-occupied units occupied by nonwhites that were that old, however, was not as large as the proportions of renter-occupied units. Approximately three out of every four units occupied by nonwhite renters were built before 1940 (Table 12–13, p. 412).

House Sizes

A remaining important characteristic of housing is the size of the dwelling. Farm houses—both those owned and those rented—tend to be larger than others, but the differences are not as great concerning owner-occupied as renter-occupied units. The median sizes for owner-occupied units in 1960 were as follows: farm, 5.9 rooms; rural nonfarm, 5.2 rooms; urban, 5.5 rooms. For renters, the medians were: farm, 5.1 rooms; nonfarm, 4.3 rooms; urban, 3.8 rooms. The rented units probably are larger on farms because they are single-family houses rather than apartments.

Dwelling units occupied by nonwhite families tended to be somewhat smaller than the total. The median size of owner-occupied units in 1960 was as follows: farm, 5.1 rooms; rural nonfarm, 4.6 rooms; urban, 5.3 rooms. For renters the medians were: farm, 4.1 rooms; rural nonfarm, 3.8 rooms; urban, 3.6 rooms. It is especially important to note the proportion of small units rented by nonwhite families. On farms, 28 percent lived in homes with three rooms or less. The comparable figure for nonfarm areas was 41 percent and for urban areas, 46 percent (Table 12–14, p. 413). The implications of these figures, when related to the sizes of families, is made clear below.

Persons-per-Room Ratio

The importance of the persons-per-room ratio as an instrument for describing one aspect of housing conditions has been mentioned in an earlier chapter. For the population of the country as a whole, it has been shown that overcrowding is not among our most serious housing problems. However, the picture is different for at least one segment of the rural population.

Nearly one out of every five (17.2 percent) nonwhite owners living on farms had an occupancy rate over 1.50 persons per room. This compared with only 3 percent for the total owner-occupied farm population. Among nonwhite renters living on farms, 37 percent had this rate of occupancy, compared with 13 percent for all farm renters in the total population (Table 12–15, p. 414).

When these crowded conditions are observed, one may wonder if the single factor of space does not have a definite bearing on the public welfare. This seems to be the point made by the American Public Health Association when it cited a report issued in 1949 by the Ministry of Reconstruction and Housing of The Netherlands. Included in that report was this information:

Around the turn of the century ". . . each inhabitant of the country disposed of only half a room on the average and the consumption of gin was 7½ liters a year per head. In 1938 each Dutchman had more than one room to live in and on the average drank only 1½ liters of alcohol a year."[13]

The report continues by indicating that, of course, it would be much too simple to consider the one purely the result of the other—both trends must be observed together as a manifestation of the social development that occurred in that country during that period. Nevertheless, the point is an interesting one.

Nearly one out of every five of the rural nonfarm, nonwhite owners (as distinguished from the farmers mentioned above) also had an occupancy rate of over 1.50 persons per room. For renters, the proportion increased to 28 percent. In both instances, the percentage figures for the total nonfarm population were significantly lower. (Table 12-15 also shows comparative data for urban housing.)

Thus it can be seen that not only is the rural (farm and nonfarm) nonwhite population generally living in housing of poor structural quality and lacking plumbing facilities, but many of the dwellings are overcrowded as well.

THE FUTURE OF RURAL HOUSING

Any discussion of the future of rural housing, like discussions of its past and present, must recognize that this term includes both farm and rural nonfarm housing. Furthermore, each of these groups may be divided into two subgroups. Rural nonfarm housing is generally occupied by two types of families: those who live and work in the villages (or who live in the villages but work on the farms) and those who live in the villages or open country but work in urban areas. Farm housing is generally occupied by these two types of families: those who operate commercial farms and those who are barely able to maintain a level of subsistence on small-scale, marginal farms. About the only factor that is common to the four groups is the fact that there is likely to be little change in the existing housing supply of any of the groups in the foreseeable future.

Let us look first at the rural nonfarm picture. The first group mentioned, i.e., those who live and work in the villages, is likely to remain quite stable. If there is any change in the size of the group, it will probably be downward rather than upward. On the other hand, there may be some increase in the number of urban workers living in rural areas. Some of these workers will be taking over the better-quality housing vacated by farm and village families. Others will probably be occupying new housing built in these areas.

[13] American Public Health Association, *Planning the Home for Occupancy.* Chicago: Public Administration Service, 1950, p. 1 footnote.

It should be remembered that cities under 50,000 population, as well as those over that size, are growing, and the "suburbs" of those cities are often represented by nearby villages, defined as rural by the U.S. Census.

In attempting to make any predictions about the future of farm housing, one must begin with the assumption that the number of farm households will continue to decline for some years in the future. The U.S. Bureau of the Census has projected this decline for the period 1960 to 1970 on the basis of the percentage decline that has been occurring since 1940. Their Series A and Series C projections are as follows:

Year	*Series A*	*Series C*
1960	5,400,000	5,316,000
1970	4,594,000	4,357,000
Decline	806,000	959,000[14]

On the basis of these projections, it can be seen that the number of farm households is likely to decline substantially in the present decade—by between 800,000 and 960,000 households.

In analyzing the farm housing situation, it is important, as already indicated, to distinguish between two general types of farmers—commercial and small-scale, subsistence farmers.

Many commercial farmers are caught in the bind of desiring to increase their income and their level of living, but finding that much of their increased income must be added to their already great capital investment in farm machinery and used for fertilizers, hybrid seeds, artificial insemination, and other costs of increased production. Housing improvement is likely to lag behind those investments. Nevertheless, modern communications and other contact with urban living patterns are strong influences for housing improvement—at least for certain amenities considered essential by urban families, such as running water, indoor plumbing facilities, and perhaps modern household equipment. Housing on commercial farms is likely to show continued improvement in these facilities.

Migration among this group of farmers will be limited in general to growing children. This will mean that some of the farms will not have operators

[14] "Study of Mortgage Credit," Hearings before a Subcommittee of the Committee on Banking and Currency, United States Senate, Eighty-sixth Congress, First Session. Washington, D.C.: U.S. Government Printing Office, 1959, p. 55. The Series A projection made by the Bureau of the Census for the total population is based on the following method: the average annual change from 1950 to 1957 in the proportion of persons in each age group who were household heads was assumed to continue to 1965. One half of this average annual change was assumed for the period 1965 to 1970. The Series C projection was based on this method: one quarter of the average annual change from 1950 to 1957 was assumed for the period 1957 to 1965. It was assumed that no change would occur thereafter. The Bureau of the Census also provides Series B and Series D projections. Series B is not shown, since it represents an intermediary projection between Series A and C. Series D is not shown, because it has not reflected actual experience, in recent years, as well as the other series have. It should be remembered, in referring to the farm household projections given above, that they reflect numbers based on the definition of a farm residence used in 1950 rather than 1960. The change in definition, as indicated earlier in this chapter, resulted in reporting a substantial reduction of housing units in the farm housing inventory. In fact, rather than 5,400,000 farm households projected in Series A, there were only 3,566,321, in actuality, under the new definition in 1960.

when the parents retire. Where this occurs, the land is likely to be combined with that of other farms. The houses may be taken over by nonfarm families, and thus become residential farms.

The real problem concerns the farmer living on a small, inefficient, marginal farm. It has been pointed out that the houses occupied by such farmers, especially the large group of nonwhite tenant farmers in the South, represent the worst housing in the nation. Such housing represents rural slums in the clearest sense of the term.

The problem is a multifaceted one. First, it has been shown that most of the houses have reached such a state of deterioration that it is not economical to attempt rehabilitation. Many of the units are not only in poor structural condition and lack plumbing facilities, but they are also overcrowded according to our general standards. Any one of these deficiencies would represent a serious situation where it exists on so broad a scale, but when all three are combined, the picture becomes so grave that it cannot be overlooked for long. Second, the families themselves live in poverty, and because of their low cultural attainment, it becomes difficult for them to meet society's standards for entrance into other job opportunities.[15]

In summary, insofar as the farm housing problem is concerned, it will be alleviated to some extent during the next decade as the result of continued rural-to-urban migration (thus moving a part of the problem to the city). The question remains as to what can be done about the housing not so vacated. The answer goes beyond that of "housing reform" (in the Riis and Veillers sense) in our rural areas; it must be related to the much broader problem of lifting certain members of our society out of the low caste in which they are still living.

READING LIST

Bertrand, Alvin L. *Rural Sociology.* New York: McGraw-Hill Book Co., 1958.

Beyer, Glenn H., and J. Hugh Rose. *Farm Housing.* A Volume in the Census Monograph Series. New York: John Wiley & Sons, 1957.

Duncan, Otis D., and Albert J. Reiss, Jr. *Social Characteristics of Urban and Rural Communities 1950.* A Volume in the Census Monograph Series. New York: John Wiley & Sons, 1956.

Kolb, John H., and Edmund deS. Brunner. *A Study of Rural Society,* 4th ed. Boston: Houghton Mifflin Co., 1952.

Nelson, Lowry. *Rural Sociology,* 2d ed. New York: American Book Co., 1955.

Rogers, Everett M. *Social Change in Rural Society.* New York: Appleton-Century-Crofts, 1960.

Smith, T. Lynn. *The Sociology of Rural Life,* 3d ed. New York: Harper & Bros., 1953.

Smith, Mervin G., and Carlton F. Christian. *Adjustments in Agriculture—A National Basebook.* Ames, Iowa: Iowa State University Press, 1961.

Taylor, Carl C. *et al. Rural Life in the United States.* New York: Alfred A. Knopf, 1949.

[15] Stokes has an excellent analysis of this same problem related to our urban slums; it is equally appropriate in reference to this discussion. See Charles J. Stokes, "A Theory of Slums," *Land Economics.* Vol. XXXVIII, No. 3, August 1962, pp. 187–197.

Table 12–1

URBAN AND RURAL POPULATION, BY SIZE OF RURAL PLACES, 1910 TO 1960

	1910	*1920*	*1930*	*1940*	*1950*	*1960*
			Population in Thousands			
Urban	41,999	54,158	68,955	74,424	96,468	124,699
Rural	49,973	51,553	53,820	57,246	54,230	53,765
Places of 1,000 to 2,500	4,234	4,712	4,821	5,027	6,473	6,440
Places under 1,000	3,930	4,255	4,363	4,316	4,031	3,888
Other rural	41,809	42,586	44,637	47,903	43,725	43,437
United States, total	91,972	105,711	122,775	131,669	150,697	178,464
			Total Population			
Urban	45.7%	51.2%	56.2%	56.5%	64.0%	69.9%
Rural	54.3	48.8	43.8	43.5	36.0	30.1
Places of 1,000 to 2,500	4.6	4.5	3.9	3.8	4.3	3.6
Places under 1,000	4.3	4.0	3.6	3.3	2.7	2.2
Other rural	45.5	40.3	36.4	36.4	29.0	24.3

SOURCE: U.S. Bureau of the Census, *Census of Population 1960*. Vol. I, Characteristics of the Population. Part A, Number of Inhabitants, p. 1–14.

Table 12–2

FARM POPULATION, PERCENTAGE OF TOTAL POPULATION AND AVERAGE NUMBER OF PERSONS PER FARM, 1935 TO 1960

Year	*Population (in thousands)*	*Total Population*	*Farms (in thousands)*	*Average No. Persons Per Farm*
1935	32,161	25.3%	6,812	4.72
1940	30,547	23.1	6,102	5.01
1945	25,295	18.1	5,859	4.32
1950	23,332	15.4	5,388	4.34
1954	21,890	13.5	4,782	4.58
1960	13,445	7.5	3,710 (1959)	3.62

SOURCE: U.S. Bureau of the Census, *Census of Agriculture 1959*. General Report, Vol. II, Statistics by Subjects, p. 13.

Table 12–3

NUMBER AND SIZE OF FARMS, 1959, 1954, AND 1950, UNITED STATES AND DIVISIONS

Division	*Number Farms (in thousands)*			*Decrease*	*Acreage Per Farm*		
	1959	*1954*	*1950*	*1954–1959*	*1959*	*1954*	*1950*
United States	3,704	4,782	5,382	−22.6%	302.4	242.2	215.3
New England	57	82	103	−30.5	163.8	135.8	121.5
Middle Atlantic	198	257	297	−23.1	135.1	116.2	107.4
East North Central	666	799	885	−16.6	155.2	136.0	126.6
West North Central	795	905	983	−12.2	354.9	314.7	289.3
South Atlantic	592	859	959	−31.1	140.7	114.4	106.5
East South Central	563	790	913	−28.7	121.4	97.8	87.2
West South Central	491	668	780	−26.5	419.0	315.6	271.0
Mountain	149	180	195	−17.2	1773.7	1449.5	1284.1
Pacific	193	243	267	−20.3	397.3	315.1	278.5

SOURCE: U.S. Bureau of the Census, *Census of Agriculture 1959*. General Report, Vol. II, Statistics by Subjects, p. 34.
Note: Alaska and Hawaii not included.

Table 12–4

PERCENTAGE DISTRIBUTION OF OCCUPATIONS OF EMPLOYED HEADS OF FAMILIES, URBAN, RURAL NONFARM, AND RURAL FARM, WHITE AND NONWHITE, 1960

	White			*Nonwhite*		
Occupation	*Urban*	*Rural Nonfarm*	*Rural Farm*	*Urban*	*Rural Nonfarm*	*Rural Farm*
Total heads of families (number in thousands)	23,410	6,980	2,581	2,401	485	219
Professional, technical, and kindred workers	13.3%	8.9%	2.0%	4.9%	2.9%	0.7%
Managers, officials, and proprietors, except farm	14.3	11.6	3.4	2.9	1.6	0.4
Clerical, sales, and kindred workers	17.4	10.4	3.2	8.0	1.9	0.5
Craftsmen, foremen, and kindred workers	21.9	24.8	7.6	11.1	9.0	2.4
Operatives and kindred workers	19.0	24.7	9.1	25.4	23.9	7.7
Service workers, including private household	6.1	4.5	1.3	22.7	13.8	3.1
Laborers, except farm and mine	3.9	0.0	2.7	10.8	22.1	0.1
Farmers and farm managers	0.4	3.3	63.2	0.5	6.7	50.0
Farm laborers and farm foremen	0.3	2.4	6.1	0.9	15.2	27.9
Occupation not reported	3.1	2.8	1.3	6.0	2.8	1.0

SOURCE: U.S. Bureau of the Census, *Census of Population 1960*. Detailed Characteristics, PC(1), 1D, U.S. Summary, pp. 1–476, 1–477, 1–478, 1–479.

Table 12–5

PERCENTAGE DISTRIBUTION OF SIZE OF FAMILIES, URBAN, RURAL NONFARM, AND RURAL FARM, WHITE AND NONWHITE, 1960

	White			*Nonwhite*		
Number of Family Members	*Urban*	*Rural Nonfarm*	*Rural Farm*	*Urban*	*Rural Nonfarm*	*Rural Farm*
Total families (number in thousands)	28,711	9,109	3,053	3,229	747	279
Two	33.9%	31.0%	31.8%	30.3%	24.7%	19.2%
Three	22.4	20.8	20.2	20.2	16.5	13.7
Four	20.8	20.2	18.1	15.8	13.2	11.8
Five	12.6	13.6	13.1	11.8	11.4	10.6
Six	6.0	7.5	8.1	8.4	9.8	10.2
Seven or more	4.3	6.8	8.6	13.5	24.4	34.6
Median No. of family members	3.51	3.73	3.80	4.07	4.83	5.60

SOURCE: U.S. Bureau of the Census, *Census of Population 1960*. Detailed Characteristics, PC(1), 1D, U.S. Summary, pp. 1–466, 1–467, 1–468.

Table 12–6

PERCENTAGE DISTRIBUTION OF FAMILY INCOMES, URBAN, RURAL NONFARM, AND RURAL FARM, WHITE AND NONWHITE, 1960

	White			*Nonwhite*		
Income	*Urban*	*Rural Nonfarm*	*Rural Farm*	*Urban*	*Rural Nonfarm*	*Rural Farm*
Total families (number in thousands)	28,711	9,109	3,053	3,229	747	279
Under $2,000	7.7%	15.6%	28.6%	24.4%	52.1%	71.2%
$2,000–$2,999	6.1	9.9	15.2	15.2	18.0	12.6
$3,000–$3,999	7.8	11.6	13.3	14.7	11.2	6.2
$4,000–$4,999	10.3	13.1	11.0	13.0	7.3	3.7
$5,000–$9,999	48.9	40.1	24.7	27.5	10.0	5.3
$10,000 and over	19.2	9.7	7.2	5.2	1.4	1.0
Median income, dollars	$6,433	$4,981	$3,472	$3,711	$1,917	$1,263

SOURCE: U.S. Bureau of the Census, *Census of Population 1960*. Detailed Characteristics, PC(1), 1D, U.S. Summary, pp. 1–597, 1–598, 1–599, 1–600.

Table 12–7

PERCENTAGE DISTRIBUTION OF YEARS OF SCHOOL COMPLETED BY HEADS OF FAMILIES, URBAN, RURAL NONFARM, AND RURAL FARM, WHITE AND NONWHITE, 1960

Years of School Completed by Head	*White*			*Nonwhite*		
	Urban	*Rural Nonfarm*	*Rural Farm*	*Urban*	*Rural Nonfarm*	*Rural Farm*
Total families (number in thousands)	28,711	9,109	3,053	3,229	747	279
Elementary school:						
Zero to seven years	16.4%	24.7%	28.6%	40.7%	70.0%	80.5%
Eight years	16.0	19.9	28.5	13.6	0.6	8.3
High school:						
One to three years	20.4	19.3	15.6	21.7	11.1	6.9
Four years	24.7	22.4	19.7	15.2	6.1	3.0
College:						
One to three years	10.7	6.8	4.9	5.0	1.6	0.8
Four years or more	11.8	6.8	2.8	3.7	1.7	0.6

SOURCE: U.S. Bureau of the Census, *Census of Population 1960*. Detailed Characteristics, PC(1), 1D, U.S. Summary, pp. 1–471, 1–472, 1–473, 1–474.

Table 12–8

PERCENTAGE DISTRIBUTION OF TENURE AND COLOR OF OCCUPANCY, OCCUPIED HOUSING UNITS IN URBAN AND RURAL AREAS, 1960

Tenure and Color	*Urban*	*Nonfarm*	*Occupied Farm*
Total occupied units (number in thousands)	38,320	11,137	3,566
Owner-occupied	58.3%	70.3%	73.8%
White	54.5	66.5	70.7
Nonwhite	3.8	3.8	3.1
Renter-occupied	41.7	29.7	26.2
White	35.1	25.7	20.9
Nonwhite	6.6	4.0	5.3

SOURCE: Derived from U.S. Bureau of the Census, *Census of Housing 1960*. States and Small Areas, HC(1), No. 1, U.S. Summary, p. 1–40.

Table 12–9

COMPARISON OF INCOME, RURAL NONFARM, AND RURAL FARM FAMILIES, OWNER- AND RENTER-OCCUPIED HOUSES, WHITE AND NONWHITE, 1959

	Rural Nonfarm		*Rural Farm*	
Income	*White*	*Nonwhite*	*White*	*Nonwhite*
Owner-Occupied Units:				
Less than $2,000	19.7%	51.9%	30.1%	62.8%
$2,000 to $2,999	8.9	16.1	13.9	13.4
$3,000 to $3,999	9.9	11.0	12.3	7.9
$4,000 to $4,999	11.6	7.8	10.6	5.4
$5,000 to $5,999	12.5	4.8	8.9	3.4
$6,000 or more	37.4	8.4	24.2	7.1
Renter-Occupied Units:				
Less than $2,000	25.6	62.0	34.7	78.7
$2,000 to $2,999	12.6	16.6	18.2	11.3
$3,000 to $3,999	14.3	9.1	14.8	4.6
$4,000 to $4,999	14.0	5.2	10.5	2.3
$5,000 to $5,999	11.7	2.9	7.2	1.3
$6,000 or more	21.8	4.2	14.6	1.8

SOURCE: Derived from U.S. Bureau of the Census, *Census of Housing 1960*. Vol. VI, Rural Housing, pp. 5, 7.

Table 12–10

PERCENTAGE DISTRIBUTION OF VALUE OF OWNER-OCCUPIED HOUSING UNITS, URBAN AND RURAL NONFARM, TOTAL AND NONWHITE, 1960

	Urban		*Rural Nonfarm*	
Value	*Total*	*Nonwhite*	*Total*	*Nonwhite*
Total owner-occupied units (number in thousands)	19,871	1,272	6,301	344
Less than $5,000	7.3%	26.6%	27.4%	72.0%
$5,000 to $7,400	10.3	21.1	18.2	14.4
$7,500 to $9,900	13.5	17.1	13.6	5.3
$10,000 to $12,400	16.6	13.4	12.7	3.6
$12,500 to $14,900	15.1	8.6	8.6	1.5
$15,000 to $17,400	12.2	5.5	6.7	1.2
$17,500 to $19,900	8.2	2.9	3.9	0.6
$20,000 to $24,900	8.2	2.6	4.3	0.7
$25,000 to $34,900	5.3	1.4	2.8	0.4
$35,000 or more	3.3	0.8	1.8	0.3
Median value, dollars	$12,900	$7,800	$8,300	*

SOURCE: Derived from U.S. Bureau of the Census, *Census of Housing 1960*. States and Small Areas, HC(1), No. 1, U.S. Summary, pp. 1–45, 1–227.

* Less than $5,000.

Table 12–11

PERCENTAGE DISTRIBUTION OF GROSS RENT OF RENTER-OCCUPIED HOUSING UNITS, URBAN AND RURAL NONFARM, TOTAL AND NONWHITE, 1960

Rent	*Urban*		*Rural Nonfarm*	
	Total	*Nonwhite*	*Total*	*Nonwhite*
Total renter-occupied units (number in thousands)	15,986	2,538	3,308	632
Less than $30	3.6%	8.9%	14.2%	25.3%
$30 to $39	5.8	10.5	9.1	6.6
$40 to $49	8.9	13.2	9.8	4.2
$50 to $59	12.0	14.1	9.8	2.7
$60 to $69	14.1	14.3	9.0	1.8
$70 to $79	13.1	11.6	7.9	1.5
$80 to $99	19.8	14.7	10.0	1.7
$100 to $119	9.8	6.1	4.0	0.5
$120 or more	9.0	3.4	3.2	0.3
No cash rent	3.9	3.2	23.0	55.1
Median rent, dollars	$73	$61	$55	$27

SOURCE: Derived from U.S. Bureau of the Census, *Census of Housing 1960.* States and Small Areas, HC(1), No. 1, U.S. Summary, pp. 1–45, 1–227.

Table 12–12

PERCENTAGE DISTRIBUTION OF CONDITION AND PRESENCE OF PLUMBING FACILITIES, BY TENURE, URBAN, RURAL NONFARM, AND RURAL OCCUPIED-FARM, TOTAL AND NONWHITE, 1960

Condition and Presence of Plumbing Facilities	*Total*			*Nonwhite*		
	Urban	*Rural Nonfarm*	*Rural Farm*	*Urban*	*Rural Nonfarm*	*Rural Farm*
Owner-occupied units (number in thousands)	22,335	7,829	2,633	1,440	422	111
Sound	91.9%	81.1%	75.5%	71.9%	44.3%	42.7%
With all plumbing facilities	90.3	70.3	57.2	65.8	18.1	12.9
Lacking some or all facilities	1.6	10.8	18.3	6.1	26.2	29.8
Deteriorating	6.6	14.2	19.7	20.2	32.5	36.3
With all plumbing facilities	5.3	6.5	7.4	13.0	4.3	2.9
Lacking some or all facilities	1.3	7.7	12.3	7.2	28.2	33.4
Dilapidated	1.5	4.7	4.8	7.9	23.2	21.0
Renter-occupied units (number in thousands)	15,986	3,308	933	2,538	445	188
Sound	78.2%	58.8%	53.3%	56.0%	24.6%	20.5%
With all plumbing facilities	71.6	45.3	33.0	46.7	8.6	2.1
Lacking some or all facilities	6.6	13.5	20.3	9.3	16.0	18.4
Deteriorating	16.6	27.1	32.0	28.8	36.0	43.2
With all plumbing facilities	11.5	9.9	7.5	15.5	2.7	1.0
Lacking some or all facilities	5.1	17.2	24.5	13.3	33.3	42.2
Dilapidated	5.2	14.1	14.7	15.2	39.4	36.3

SOURCE: Derived from U.S. Bureau of the Census, *Census of Housing 1960.* States and Small Areas, HC(1), No. 1, U.S. Summary, pp. 1–40, 1–225.

Table 12–13

PERCENTAGE DISTRIBUTION OF YEAR STRUCTURE BUILT, BY TENURE, URBAN, RURAL NONFARM, AND RURAL OCCUPIED-FARM, TOTAL AND NONWHITE, 1960

	Total			*Nonwhite*		
Year Structure Built	*Urban*	*Rural Nonfarm*	*Rural Farm*	*Urban*	*Rural Nonfarm*	*Rural Farm*
Owner-occupied units (number in thousands)	22,335	7,829	2,633	1,440	422	111
1955 to March 1960	18.6%	22.1%	6.7%	9.1%	15.9%	9.7%
1950 to 1954	17.4	14.7	6.9	10.3	13.6	10.9
1940 to 1949	16.0	16.4	12.2	15.9	23.2	22.1
1939 or earlier	48.0	46.8	74.2	64.7	47.3	57.3
Renter-occupied units (number in thousands)	18,422	6,166	933	2,538	445	188
1955 to March 1960	8.8%	12.7%	3.4%	5.2%	6.7%	3.4%
1950 to 1954	8.8	10.9	4.9	8.0	8.0	4.9
1940 to 1949	12.5	17.1	10.7	11.9	17.3	13.4
1939 or earlier	69.9	59.3	81.0	74.9	68.0	78.3

SOURCE: Derived from U.S. Bureau of the Census, *Census of Housing 1960*. States and Small Areas, HC(1), No. 1, U.S. Summary, pp. 1–42, 1–226. Renter-occupied data for U.S. total are not reported by the Census but were derived by subtracting number of owner-occupied units from total units, which obviously includes some error because all persons did not report on year structure built. The percentage distribution shown for renter-occupied units, however, should generally approximate actual figures.

Table 12–14

PERCENTAGE DISTRIBUTION OF NUMBER OF ROOMS, BY TENURE, URBAN, RURAL NONFARM, AND RURAL OCCUPIED-FARM, TOTAL AND NONWHITE, 1960

	Total			*Nonwhite*		
Number of Rooms	*Urban*	*Rural Nonfarm*	*Rural Farm*	*Urban*	*Rural Nonfarm*	*Rural Farm*
Owner-occupied units (number in thousands)	22,335	7,829	2,633	1,440	422	111
One or two	1.0%	2.9%	1.2%	1.4%	8.5%	5.8%
Three	3.4	6.3	3.2	6.0	11.4	7.8
Four	15.5	21.1	13.6	19.4	28.5	22.9
Five	30.8	27.4	21.3	28.7	23.1	23.3
Six	27.7	22.4	24.0	25.3	19.2	25.4
Seven	12.4	11.0	16.5	10.3	5.9	9.1
Eight or more	9.2	8.9	20.2	8.9	3.4	5.7
Median No. of rooms	5.5	5.2	5.9	5.3	4.6	5.1
Renter-occupied units (number in thousands)	15,986	3,308	933	2,538	445	188
One or two	15.9%	9.3%	4.3%	18.5%	16.0%	7.6%
Three	25.4	15.8	9.3	27.9	25.0	20.6
Four	27.9	30.5	23.7	27.6	34.0	38.2
Five	18.0	21.4	20.0	15.3	14.8	18.7
Six	8.8	12.9	17.7	7.5	7.3	10.8
Seven	2.5	5.5	11.1	2.0	1.8	2.6
Eight or more	1.5	4.6	13.9	1.2	1.1	1.5
Median No. of rooms	3.8	4.3	5.1	3.6	3.8	4.1

SOURCE: Derived from U.S. Bureau of the Census, *Census of Housing 1960*. States and Small Areas. HC(1), No. 1, U.S. Summary, pp. 1–41 and 1–225.

Table 12–15

PERCENTAGE DISTRIBUTION OF PERSONS PER ROOM, OCCUPIED-HOUSING UNITS, BY TENURE, URBAN, RURAL NONFARM, AND RURAL OCCUPIED-FARM, TOTAL AND NONWHITE, 1960

	Total			*Nonwhite*		
Persons Per Room	*Urban*	*Rural Nonfarm*	*Rural Farm*	*Urban*	*Rural Nonfarm*	*Rural Farm*
Owner-occupied units (number in thousands)	22,335	7,829	2,633	1,440	422	111
0.50 or less	46.7%	44.6%	52.0%	42.0%	34.6%	31.6%
0.51 to 0.75	24.3	22.0	21.2	21.0	16.5	16.8
0.76 to 1.00	21.6	21.4	16.9	20.0	17.5	18.7
1.01 to 1.50	6.0	8.4	7.1	11.2	14.2	15.7
1.51 or more	1.4	3.6	2.8	5.8	17.2	17.2
Renter-occupied units (number in thousands)	15,986	3,308	933	2,538	445	188
0.50 or less	35.3%	29.5%	29.2%	26.4%	22.3%	14.8%
0.51 to 0.75	24.1	21.2	21.5	19.0	13.8	12.4
0.76 to 1.00	26.6	25.9	22.4	25.6	18.9	16.4
1.01 to 1.50	9.1	13.6	13.7	15.2	16.6	19.1
1.51 or more	4.9	9.8	13.2	13.8	28.4	37.3

SOURCE: Derived from U.S. Bureau of the Census, *Census of Housing 1960*. States and Small Areas, HC(1), No. 1, U.S. Summary, pp. 1–43, 1–226.

CHAPTER 13

*

Housing of the Aged

The discussions of housing problems in the three chapters preceding has been on an areal basis, because the problems discussed lend themselves to discussion in that form. For example, it has been shown that there are some basic economic and social differences among the populations living in our central cities, our suburban and fringe areas, and our rural areas. Special groups have been the focus of discussion in each of these areas—nonwhites in the central cities; young, white middle-income families in the suburbs; and farmers (and nonwhites in the South) in rural areas. Although other groups, to be sure, live in each of these areas, the particular groups mentioned represent heavier than usual concentrations.

Still another group in our population represents a special housing problem, but discussion of that group cannot be adequately pigeonholed into any one area. This is the group representing our aging population. Although the largest number of this group live in central cities (nearly 5,750,000), a large number live in places having a population of less than 1,000 or on farms (nearly 4,250,000). They have their highest proportions of the total population in places having a population of 1,000 to 2,500 (12.2 percent compared with 9.2 percent for the nation as a whole) and places 2,500 to 10,000 (11.0 percent) (Table 13–1, p. 441).

THE AGED: A SPECIAL GROUP

Several factors make it desirable to treat the aging as a special group in any discussion of our nation's housing problems. The first of these concerns their large and increasing numbers. The second is the size and nature of their households. The third concerns their economic status. The fourth concerns the physical changes that take place in an individual when he reaches an advanced age. The fifth concerns certain special social and emotional factors that are often associated with this group. The last concerns their housing situation. Each of these factors will be discussed in some detail.

Population Trends of the Aging

One out of every eleven persons in the United States is aged sixty-five or over, and the number of aged persons is growing at the rate of over 1,000 a day. The aged portion of the population is increasing both numerically and as a proportion of the total population. Since the beginning of the century the number of persons aged sixty-five and over has increased 438 percent, from 3,100,000 to 16,600,000, while the total population has increased only 136 percent. Older people represented only 4.1 percent of the population in 1900; today they make up 9.2 percent (Table 13–2, p. 442).

In the 10 years between 1950 and 1960, the aged population increased by nearly 35 percent, a rate of growth exceeded only in the case of children aged five to fourteen years. In contrast, the total population increased by only 18.5 percent. Furthermore, even within the age group sixty-five and over, the oldest age classes are increasing faster than the younger ones, which gives evidence of the definite increase in average life expectancy. For example, during the period 1950 to 1960 there was an increase of only 25 percent in the age group sixty-five to sixty-nine years, compared with 61 percent for the group eighty-five years and over (Table 13–3, p. 442). Further evidence of the trend toward greater life expectancy can be observed when the increase between 1920 and 1960 is noted. During this period, the age group sixty-five and over increased by 236 percent. If only the group aged seventy-five and over is considered, the increase is 279 percent, and if the observation is limited to the group aged eighty-five and over, an increase of 920 percent is noted. The average *life expectancy at birth* has risen from 49.2 years in 1900 to an estimated 70.2 years in 1961.

The *proportion* of older people is expected to increase only slightly during the 1960 to 1970 decade; nevertheless, by 1970 there will be 20,000,000 persons aged sixty-five and over, and by 1980, the number will reach nearly 24,500,000 (Table 13-2). Projections made by the Department of Health, Education, and Welfare indicate that in the forty years between 1960 and 2000, the aged population will more than double in number, bringing the total to more than 30,000,000 people.[1]

One of the other important characteristics of the aging is that women outlive men. It is interesting to note that while under five years of age in 1960 there were 103.6 males for every 100 females, the trend reversed beginning with age group twenty to twenty-four years. When the age group sixty-five to sixty-nine was reached, there were only 87.3 males per 100 females. At seventy-five years and over, there were only 74.4 males for every 100 females (Table 13–4, p. 443). In 1960, there were nearly 1.6 million more women than men aged sixty-five years and over. Stated another way, of all persons aged sixty-five years and over, 55 percent were women. Women made up 61 percent of the population aged eighty-five years and older (Table 13–5, p. 443).

[1] "New Population Facts on Older Americans, 1960." A Staff Report to the Special Committee on Aging, U.S. Senate, Eighty-Seventh Congress, First Session, with a Statistical Supplement Prepared by the Department of Health, Education, and Welfare's Special Staff on Aging. Washington, D.C.: U.S. Government Printing Office, 1961.

Size and Nature of Households

The ramifications of the larger proportion of women in the aged population are far greater than a mere observation of the statistics might suggest. For example, in 1960 nearly half of all the aged in the United States were widowed, single, or divorced—and this represented 35 percent of the aged women and 13 percent of the aged men. Since children had usually left home by this stage, this has meant a large proportion of small households. Census data indicate, in fact, that one out of every five aged households contained only one person and another 54 percent contained only two. The average aged household, therefore, is significantly smaller than the average for the total population (Table 13–6, p. 443).

Most older people continue to live in their own households. For the total group of men aged sixty-five years and over in 1960, 83 percent still maintained their own households; 13 percent lived in the households of others, usually their children's, and the remaining 4 percent lived in group quarters, usually some kind of an institution. For the total group of women aged sixty-five years and over, the percentage living in their own households was smaller—70 percent. One fourth of the elderly women lived in the households of others, usually their children's, and 5 percent lived in group quarters.

From the preceding discussion of the proportion of men and women in the aged population and their marital status, it is obvious that there are some basic differences in other household and family characteristics. For example, of the aged men living in their own households, two thirds were married and living with spouse, while the comparable proportion for women was only one third. There is an appreciable change in these proportions as the aged become older, as shown in Table 13–7 (p. 444).

Other data, covering elderly people not living in institutions, provide more detail concerning living arrangements and household composition.[2]

	Percent
Living in own household, total	*81*
Alone	24
With spouse only	34
With children (This category includes married couples and widowed, single men and women who have children living with them)	13

[2] Glenn H. Beyer and Margaret E. Woods, *Living and Activity Patterns of the Aged.* Research Report No. 6, Ithaca, N.Y.: Cornell University Center for Housing and Environmental Studies, 1963. The Cornell Research program on housing for the aged included interviews with 5,202 persons (none of whom was living in an institution) in four statistical samples (a fifteen-county area in central New York, Cook County, Illinois, the St. Louis metropolitan area, and Los Angeles County, California) drawn by the Bureau of Old-Age and Survivors Insurance.

With others (This category includes married couples and widowed, single men and women who have relatives other than children and/or nonrelatives living with them)	10
Not living in own household, total	*18*
With children (This category includes some married couples but is comprised primarily of widowed, single men and women who live in their children's households)	11
With others (This category includes married couples and widowed, single men and women who live in the households of relatives other than children or in the households of nonrelatives)	7
Living in group quarters	*1*

Only a few years ago we were bemoaning the plight of the aged parent or grandparent that resulted from the tendency of the young in our generation to leave home at an early age. We attributed this breaking up of the two- and three-generation household to the change from a rural to an urban economy. The inference usually made was that with this change, the position of the elderly changed from that of being an economic asset to an economic liability, and as the children left, it was assumed that the elderly became isolated in their large old homes, with few social or economic relationships with the younger generation.

Several studies have shown that the picture in actuality is not nearly this bleak. A study by the National Opinion Research Center of the University of Chicago, for example, based on a nation-wide sample of aged persons living outside of institutions, indicated that four of every five aged reported they had living children. It also reported that 36 percent of all persons with children still lived in a household with at least one child. An additional 24 percent, while they lived apart from their children, had at least one child who lived in the same block as they did or within walking distance. Six of every ten older persons with children, then, lived with at least one child, or within walking distance of at least one child. An additional 25 percent of the older population with children reported that their nearest child was a short ride away. In only 15 percent of all cases was the nearest child of older people, who had living children, as far from them as a day's travel or more. These data, then, indicate that although the three-generation household, all living under the same roof, may now be less prominent than it was in our earlier history, most older people are not physically isolated from their children. United three-generation families, therefore, are not necessarily limited to residence under a common roof.[3]

[3] Ethel Shanas, "Living Arrangements of Older People in the United States," in Clark Tibbitts and Wilma Donahue, eds., *Social and Psychological Aspects of Aging.* New York: Columbia University Press, 1962, pp. 462–463.

Economic Status of the Aging

Let us look now at how economic status sets this group apart from younger age groups. Most aged are retired (some data show that about a third in the age group sixty-five to seventy are still in the labor force, many as part-time workers, but that this proportion drops appreciably with an advance in age beyond that point). This means, of course, that they no longer have income from wages or salaries. Since they generally receive only Social Security payments (or other retirement benefits), their income declines drastically. Census data for 1959, in fact, show that while the median income for all families was $5,660, it declined to $3,050 for husband–wife families where the head was sixty-five years old or over. For aged individuals no longer living with spouse, it was even lower—for males living alone or with unrelated individuals the median was only $1,342 and for women, only $916 (Table 13–8, p. 445). Women in the most advanced age groups are generally in the most unfavorable position, economically, because many of them have not been wage earners and they frequently receive low benefits, if any, under the Social Security program.

There are certain other important factors which should, of course, be acknowledged when consideration is given to the economic status of the aging. In 1960, 69 percent of those aged sixty years and over owned their own homes (Table 13–9, p. 445). Equity in a home enables homeowners to have lower housing expenses than renters, despite the burden of taxes and repairs. But because the average cash value of homes owned by older people is not high, most of these homeowners would be unable to obtain comparable rental housing if they sold their homes and invested the equity. The 1960 Census data show that some 53 percent of the nonfarm homes owned by persons aged sixty-five and over were valued at less than $10,000. The median value of owner-occupied homes was $9,900 for those in the age group sixty-five to seventy-four and $8,600 in the age group seventy-five and over. Persons with higher incomes had higher equity in their homes.

Citing figures for broad categories such as these tends to cover up some important differences based on living arrangements, marital status, sex, household composition, and the occupancy status of the aging. The Cornell research found that elderly people living with their spouse had higher incomes than unattached men, and unattached men had higher incomes than unattached women. Also, in each of those categories, persons living in their own households had higher incomes than those living in the households of others; owners had higher incomes than renters; and elderly people living with other than children had higher incomes than those living with their children. It can be seen, therefore, that the category of older people having the highest median income was comprised of couples living in their own households and who owned their homes. The category having the lowest median income was comprised of widowed, single women living with their children (Table 13–10, p. 446). These data confirm the fact, especially emphasized in the findings of the Cornell research, that *if the resources of either the elderly person or of the children permit independent living on the part of the aged person, they tend to live in that manner, the only exception being certain elderly people who experience some health problems. On the other hand, most elderly people who are living with their children seem to be doing so because of economic reasons.* Much the same situation prevails with respect to the people who live with their children as among those who live in institutions. Frequently the solution is born of necessity and, like most such solutions, it represents an attempt to make the best of a poor situation.

Equity in the homes that are owned represents most of the savings of the aged. Their liquid assets usually are small. The 1960 Survey of Consumer Finances, for example, indicated that 30 percent of the spending units (roughly equivalent to "households") having a head aged sixty-five and over, had *no* liquid asset holdings; 6 percent had some, but less than $200; and 30 percent had some, but less than $2,000.[4] In other words, only four out of ten elderly had $2,000 or more. Although liquid assets are not required at this age to meet some kinds of expenditures required earlier in life—paying for children's education, meeting home mortgage payments, paying premiums on life insurance, and generally supporting larger families—the drastic decline in income, based on present Social Security and other sources, hardly suffices to meet the costs of a standard of living to which most of these individuals have become accustomed. Furthermore, medical expenses may be higher than in early years, and there is an increasing need to hire help for certain duties and responsibilities.

Yet, our society has been fortunate in being able to abandon the "poor farm" of yesteryear. This has been accomplished because of two major developments of the last three decades. The first is the growth of the Social Security program. In 1960 approximately two thirds of the nation's elderly population had become Old-Age and Survivors Insurance beneficiaries—68 percent of the men and 61 percent of the women. Another 9 percent in that year were eligible but were not yet receiving benefits. Only 27 percent, about 4,500,000 persons, were not eligible. This group divided roughly into thirds: about one third received benefits under other social insurance programs or programs for veterans; one third were dependent on public assistance; and the remaining third were without income from employment or public programs. Some of this last group were supported by children or other relatives, some were in public institutions, and some were living on private investment income. Approximately two thirds of *all* those not eligible for Old-Age and Survivors Insurance benefits were women.[5]

The second development has been the constant increase in the proportion of families owning their own homes; it was mentioned earlier that more than two out of every three fall in this category today. Admittedly, many of these homes have inadequacies. However, an important factor concerning

[4] "1960 Survey of Consumer Finances," Institute for Social Research, Survey Research Center, The University of Michigan, Ann Arbor, 1961, p. 80.

[5] Letter received from the Social Security Administration, Washington, D.C., dated July 27, 1961.

them is the fact that mortgages are usually paid, leaving only operating costs, property maintenance, and taxes as the primary costs to be met.

There is still another development, quite different from the two just mentioned, which undoubtedly has been an aid to the elderly in maintaining their own households and thereby permitting them to live independently. This concerns the continuing family relations between the elderly and their children. Although research is limited regarding the economic implications of the proximity of family members, there are some indications that because of it, financial crises for the elderly that might otherwise occur are frequently avoided.[6]

Physical Changes with Age

In addition to the economic status of the elderly, which sets many individuals apart from those in the younger segments of our population, there also is the factor of health.

On the matter of health there have been some important changes in public attitude over the years. A century ago it was often considered that an old person must be a sick person. Today, aging is looked upon as a process rather than a state of being. There is no single point in time when individuals achieve a state of "oldness." Changes are always in progress, and adaptation to them is always ongoing. Each person is different from all others and each should be dealt with as an individual. These facts make it dangerous to generalize with regard to the health status of the aging as a group.

On the other hand, it is known that both the incidence and the prevalence of chronic disease and impairment increase with age. Dr. Wilma Donahue of the University of Michigan, has indicated that *prevalence* rates for chronic disease and impairment "for 50 year olds is 58 per 100 persons, for 60 year olds it has stepped up to 79, and by age 75 it amounts to 156 per 1000." The *incidence* rates follow a similar trend with age. "One third of the persons who have escaped chronic illness and impairment up to age 65 will develop some problem requiring medical treatment during the next 5 years. Of the group still in good health at age 75, approximately 50 percent will experience the onset of a major disease or major impairment during the next 5 years, and by age 90, there are 9 chances out of 10 that people in this age group will be chronically ill or disabled."[7]

The Department of Health, Education, and Welfare has indicated that older persons are twice as likely as those under sixty-five to have one or

[6] A more detailed discussion of the economic status of the aging, in relation to housing, is provided in Glenn H. Beyer, *Economic Aspects of Housing for the Aged.* Research Report No. 4. Ithaca, N.Y.: Cornell University Center for Housing and Environmental Studies, 1961.

[7] Wilma Donahue, "Physical and Psychological Changes with Age and Their Relation to Management of Housing for the Elderly." Paper delivered at the Seminar for the Development of a Training Program for the Management of Public Housing for the Elderly, Center for Continuing Education, University of Chicago, February 14, 1963 (mimeo.), p. 17.

more chronic conditions. While some of these are relatively minor afflictions such as sinusitis, hay fever, or bronchitis, others, such as high blood pressure, heart disease, or diabetes, are more serious. On the basis of data collected in the National Health Survey covering the period July 1957 to June 1959, the Department reported that 149 per 1,000 persons aged sixty-five and over had a heart condition, 129 per 1,000 had high blood pressure, and 266 per 1,000 had arthritis or rheumatism.[8]

What are the implications of this picture for independent, as opposed to institutional, living? The Cornell research found that 67 percent of the 5,200 elderly interviewed needed no help with their day-to-day activities. This proportion increased to 92 percent when the categories of doing "everything without help" and doing "most things without help" were combined. This response led to examination of a question asking whether they had given up any of a selected group of activities *because of their health,* such as working at their regular jobs, taking long trips, doing heavy work around the house, or simply going up and down stairs. A total of 37 percent of all respondents had given up their jobs for health reasons, 48 percent had given up certain heavy work, but the proportions that had given up other activities were negligible.[9]

Although it is clear that physical changes are always in progress, *adaptation* to those changes is an individual matter. Even an older person can adapt to many infirmities. This does not mean, however, that the infirmities should be overlooked. It should be remembered, for example, that older people frequently have a diminishing field of vision, a decline in the sense of smell, and an increased sensitivity to heat and cold. These factors should be compensated for when new housing is designed for them.

Social and Emotional Characteristics

Other major distinguishing characteristics of the aging can be characterized as social and emotional in nature. Social and emotional problems are much more difficult to measure than economic and health problems, but they are just as real.

Two primary social roles, those of work and parenthood, are taken away from individuals who have reached an advanced age. Since social roles are important to everyone, the loss—especially of two so important—presents serious problems of readjustment. Serious gaps have been left that must be filled by other social roles if satisfying emotional conditions are to be maintained. This is true despite the fact that physical capabilities and mental acuity may have declined with advanced age.

The fact that many elderly people and their older children may still be in close contact is a positive factor in this regard. Yet, some aging people do not have this physical proximity to their children, and if they do, it does not offset many of their problems.

[8] "The Older Population," *Indicators,* U.S. Department of Health, Education, and Welfare, November 1962.

[9] Beyer and Woods, *op. cit.,* pp. 2–4.

Unfortunately, there is no good indication of the extent of social and/or mental problems, much less an indication of the degree of seriousness of those problems, among our aging population. Donahue has estimated that less than 1 percent of the elderly are in the hospitalized, psychotic group. This is a low percentage, but it still represents one in every four admissions to mental hospitals. Also, while the group aged sixty-five and over constitutes only a little more than 9 percent of the general population, it makes up more than 25 percent of the population of mental hospitals.[10]

The problem of loneliness, so prevalent among older people, is often different from that of isolation. The elderly may not be isolated, but they may not have the warm, friendly contacts so sorely needed at this stage in life—in fact, at all stages.

Advanced age also frequently brings with it many related problems. Because of the situations in which many of these individuals find themselves, they lose their sense of belonging to the community. After active lives, many now find themselves literally cast out from society. As a result, they tend to lose their self-esteem, a quality that engenders happiness and satisfaction with oneself.

Perhaps one of the most serious emotional problems concerning the aging is the loss of a feeling of security. Many, as already pointed out, are in a precarious economic position, but they also have other fears. Not the least of these is where they will be living and who will be caring for them. Study after study has shown that the elderly want to remain where they are rather than to move to another location. The reason behind this often-stated preference is the fact that they know about their present arrangements, and they tend to feel secure (even when somewhat uncomfortable) in them. They have not been sufficiently informed about possible new accommodations to feel equally secure about them (or, if the future possibly holds dreary institutional accommodations for them, they have heard enough about *those* to prefer to remain where they are, despite the difficulties and hardships involved).

Adjustment to New Patterns of Living

Few data available indicate how the elderly have made the adjustment from active lives, including the roles of employment and parenthood, to retirement and separation from their children. The Cornell research attempted to gain some insight into this matter by inquiring into the daily patterns of activities of the individuals studied.

The three leisure activities in which a large proportion of respondents reported participation were watching television, visiting, and reading. In addition, a relatively high proportion was found to have spent some time in idleness (relaxing or doing such things as "sitting and looking out the window") and napping.

A total of 85 percent of the respondents owned television sets and 70

[10] Donahue, *op. cit.*, pp. 20–22.

percent had watched television on the day before the interviews. More time was consumed by this activity than by any other. Half of the elderly who watched television spent two to three hours in this manner, and nearly 40 percent spent four or more hours. The median time was three hours.

Approximately the same percentage that had watched television had visited with someone on the preceding day (68 percent). Half of those who visited had done so from two to three hours during the day, and almost a third from one to one and one-half hours. The median time spent in visiting was two hours. It was found that a somewhat lower proportion of widowed, single individuals living *alone,* especially men, had visited with someone on the previous day than had married couples or widowed, single individuals who had someone living with them. This reflects both the fact that there was no one in the household with whom to visit and also the fact that those living alone had fewer people stop by.

Most of the regular social contacts of the elderly were with relatives, children being the primary source of contact. Two thirds of the respondents who lived in their own households and who had living children had children come to see them at least once a week. Even among those elderly people living in the households of others, half had children stop to see them weekly or more often.

Reading also was a rather widespread leisure activity among the elderly people covered by this study, approximately 60 percent having done some reading on the previous day. The time spent on reading varied greatly, but about half of the respondents had spent an hour on this activity.

Over half of the 5,200 elderly individuals interviewed reported that there was some time during the previous day when they were not actively doing something. This time was spent in sitting or standing, or perhaps looking out the window watching people, cars, birds, and the like. Some napping also took place. It was not possible to determine what portion of this time may have been spent in essential activities (such as needed rest) or in enjoyable activities, and what portion was spent merely in idle time.

While there were no significant differences based on age classes for most of the activities mentioned, there was a marked increase with advanced age in the proportion who reported time spent in napping and idleness, from half of the age group sixty-five to sixty-nine years to three fourths of those aged eighty years and over. Furthermore, there was a difference in the median amount of time spent—with one and one half hours for the age group sixty-five to sixty-nine years and two hours for the age groups above that.[11]

An attempt was made in the analysis to establish the patterns of activities for different periods of the day. It was found, broadly speaking, that mornings were occupied with obligated time activities, which included meal preparation and eating, housecleaning, laundering, personal care, and shopping; afternoons were spent primarily in a variety of forms of leisure and idleness; evenings were devoted primarily to a single form of leisure—

[11] Beyer and Woods, *op. cit.,* pp. 13–14.

watching television. No single activity was as outstanding for the afternoon as was work around the house in the morning and watching television in the evening. Except for the time spent in idleness in the afternoon, a wide range of activities was performed. Some, such as shopping, may have been quite necessary. Others may have been performed either because they were enjoyed or because they merely filled up time. However, it should not be assumed that, because many activities were performed, these activities absorbed a significant amount of time; it should be remembered that most of the afternoon was taken up in idleness and visiting.

Information was not obtained in the study concerning the degree to which *each* activity was enjoyed; however, when respondents were asked what they did yesterday that was enjoyed most, visiting stood out as that activity. It was selected by about half of those who had visited the previous day. This outstanding response, especially when compared with the size of the response for other activities indicated as enjoyed most, confirms the importance that should be attached to providing more opportunities for visiting for elderly people living in existing housing as well as in new housing accommodations.

Following visiting, the activity enjoyed most was watching television. Although seven out of ten respondents watched television on the previous day and spent substantial time doing it, only one out of seven enjoyed it more than anything else. The remaining group may have enjoyed watching television, but they did not rank their enjoyment of it above everything else. They may have watched television merely for the purpose of filling a period of time. Reading was enjoyed most by nearly as high a percentage of the respondents as was watching television—10 percent of those who had read on the previous day.[12]

From a review of much of the current literature, it might easily be assumed that few older people achieve *adequate* adjustment in their lives, despite these apparently busy days, and that many of them live in a state of loneliness, frustration, despair, and increasing senility.

Although adequate medical attention can do much to alleviate health problems, and adequate pensions and other assistance grants or subsidies can do much to alleviate economic problems, there are no such simply defined solutions to social and emotional problems. This is an area to which much more attention must still be given before we find the best solutions—not to mention the problem of finding means of *applying* those solutions.

HOUSING SITUATION OF THE AGING

The last of the major distinguishing characteristics of the aging is the nature of the housing they occupy.

It has been mentioned that 69 percent of those aged sixty years and over owned their own homes in 1960. About nine out of ten owner households lived in single-family housing units, and the remainder (with the exception of

[12] *Ibid.*, pp. 17–18.

1 percent who lived in trailers or mobile homes) lived in structures with two or more units. Among renter households, 42 percent lived in single-family units, 24 percent in two- to four-family structures, and the remaining one third, in buildings with five or more units.

Age of Dwellings

Generally, their housing is older than that occupied by younger families. In 1960, three fourths of the elderly lived in structures built before 1939, compared with 58 percent of the population of the nation as a whole. Only 6 percent lived in dwellings built since 1955, compared with 15 percent of the population as a whole (Table 13–11, p. 447).

Quality of Housing

Age in itself is not a bad feature of housing, but frequently with age go features that *do* make for undesirable housing—poor structural condition, poor planning (especially when the occupant is at a stage in life when good planning is all the more essential), inadequate facilities (such as the lack of a complete bathroom and running water), large size (at a time when the occupant finds it difficult to do housecleaning even in a smaller unit), and location in run-down neighborhoods.

As mentioned in Chapter 4, it is not feasible to measure all of these factors in a large-scale enumeration such as that carried out by the U.S. Bureau of the Census, and we do not, therefore, have data showing how deficient the housing occupied by the elderly may be. It is known, however, that older people are more likely than younger people to have poor housing. In 1960 one out of every five housing units occupied by families having a head sixty years old or over was dilapidated or lacked some plumbing facilities. The comparable proportion for the population as a whole was 16 percent (Table 13–12, p. 447). This is not an appreciable difference, but there is evidence that the homes of the aging had many other deficiencies. The Cornell research found, for example, that among the various deficiencies studied, the most prevalent one was access to bathroom only through some other room (one fourth of the dwelling units). It was followed by missing handrail on some stairs used regularly (18 percent of all dwelling units). Both of these deficiencies were most common in dwelling units that were rented or occupied rent-free. Other deficiencies found in more than 10 percent of the dwelling units were lack of direct source of heat in the bathroom or aged person's bedroom, no clothes closet in bedroom, damage to small area of foundation, deep wear on steps and doorsills, shaky porch, rotted or loose window frames, and rusted or missing gutters and downspouts.

An appreciably greater proportion of deficiencies was found in dwelling units occupied by families having an income under $1,000 per year than among those occupied by families in the higher income brackets. A total of

22 percent of those families lacked hot running water in their dwelling units and 29 percent lacked a complete bath. Also, 26 percent had no direct source of heat in the bathroom and an equal proportion lacked direct heat in the bedroom. A total of 43 percent had access to the bathroom only through other rooms. These percentages declined somewhat when the income group $1,000 to $2,000 was considered, and decreased more for the income group $2,000 to $3,000. Practically no major, and relatively few minor, deficiencies were found in dwelling units occupied by individuals having incomes of $3,000 or more.

Among units occupied by the aged living in their own households, those occupied by widowed or single men contained more deficiencies than those occupied by widowed or single women, and those occupied by widowed or single women had appreciably more deficiencies than those occupied by married couples. Among units occupied by widowed or single men, one fourth lacked a complete bath and 35 percent had access to the bathroom only through some other room. More than one out of every five had no clothes closet in the respondent's bedroom, had missing handrail on some stairs, had holes or cracks over a small area of the foundation and inside walls, and had deep wear on doorsills.

The principal deficiencies among units occupied by widowed or single women were similar, although only 11 percent lacked a complete bath. The most common deficiency among units occupied by couples was access to the bathroom only through some other room (one fourth of the dwelling units). It was followed by missing handrail on some stairs (19 percent of the dwelling units). Also lacking in a significant number of instances was direct source of heat in the bathroom and the respondent's bedroom and clothes closet in the respondent's bedroom.[13]

Size of Dwellings and Persons-per-Room Ratio

It is often stated that the elderly generally live in large houses. However, the term "large" is a relative term. From the standpoint of the number of rooms, there is little difference between the size of housing occupied by the elderly and the total housing occupied by younger families. What is different, however, is the fact that the families of the aging usually are smaller in size than younger families, and therefore aged families have more space "per person." Census data confirm this, showing that less than 3 percent of the families having a head sixty years old or older have an average occupancy ratio of 1.01 persons per room or more, compared with 12 percent for all families.

MOBILITY

It is generally recognized that elderly households are less mobile than younger ones. Census data show that only one fourth of the households

[13] Beyer, *op. cit.*, p. 30.

with a head aged sixty-five years or over, compared with one half of all households in the nation, moved at least once during the period 1955 to 1959. Homeowners are less mobile than renters. Among elderly households, 45 percent of those who owned their homes had lived in the same place for more than twenty years, compared with only 16 percent among those who were renters.

ATTITUDES TOWARD VARIOUS LIVING ARRANGEMENTS

It has been shown that many older persons live under housing conditions that ought to be improved. Some live in dilapidated housing or housing lacking plumbing facilities. This group, however, is a minority. More live in houses that are structurally sound and have the requisite plumbing facilities, but their homes are not suited to them for other reasons. For example, many elderly do not need as much space as they have in their present places, and they often are not able to care for that space. Others live in houses that, in addition to being too large, are poorly planned, primarily because they are old houses. The old age of many of their houses also means that the houses are likely to need major repairs in the near future and, if these cannot be afforded, the houses are likely to become run-down. The fact that the number of our aging is increasing so rapidly makes these problems necessary of attention.

Despite these problems, most elderly people do not want to move. Some of the reasons for this have already been discussed. Yet, it is a fact of modern-day life that many of them will move sometime during the remainder of their lifetime, and this fact makes it important to know something about their attitudes toward various living arrangements.

In order to obtain information concerning the attitudes of the elderly toward different kinds of living arrangements, the Cornell research asked them what kind of arrangements they thought were best for people over sixty-five. The question asked what arrangement they thought best for elderly "who can take care of themselves," and what arrangement they considered best for those "no longer able to take care of themselves."[14]

The persons studied were given a choice of three situations for elderly who can take care of themselves. These situations, and the proportion of the total group responding to each, were as follows: (a) to live by themselves but *near* relatives, 52 percent; (b) to live by themselves *away* from their relatives, 31 percent; (c) to live *with* their families, 17 percent.

The results of the survey followed closely the arrangements in which the respondents were living—81 percent were living in their own households and 18 percent were not living in their own households. However, despite the comparability of the above figures, many elderly people actually suggested an arrangement different from their own. For example, approximately half of those not living in their own households recommended living

[14] Beyer and Woods, *op. cit.*, pp. 19–25.

by themselves, and this was offset by about an equal number who were living by themselves but who felt it would be better to live with their families. There were two primary reasons for the latter preference—either advanced age or poor health.

An interesting sidelight is the fact that the choices of widowed, single men were quite different from those of couples and widowed, single women. For example, a higher proportion of those men who lived alone (52 percent) than couples (37 percent) or widowed, single women (35 percent) thought that the best arrangement was for the aged to live by themselves *away* from relatives.

Age had some influence on the stated choices of living arrangements, but perhaps this factor was not as important as might have been expected. Among respondents who presently were living with their children (or had children living with them), three fifths of those eighty years and over, compared with two fifths of those under age seventy, thought that living with their families was the best arrangement for the elderly. As the preference for living with relatives increased with age, there was a corresponding decrease in the percentage who thought elderly should live by themselves but near relatives. (The choice for living by themselves, away from relatives, remained about the same.) The influence of health also was more limited than might have been expected. For example, among those who lived in their own households, 21 percent of the respondents in the poorest health favored living with their families, compared with 7 percent of those in good health who favored this arrangement.

The persons studied also were given four choices concerning the kind of living arrangement they thought was best for the person over sixty-five who could *no longer* take care of himself. These choices included (a) living in his own home with nursing care, (b) living with his family, (c) living with his relatives, and (d) living in a nursing home. The question did not specify the type of nursing care proposed or the amount of time it would be available. It is probable that most respondents were considering care by a practical nurse or personal care bordering on practical nursing. It is doubtful that many were considering care by skilled nurses, because this would entail heavy costs. It should be remembered that only a small proportion of the elderly interviewed were actually in the physical condition suggested by the question.

When all respondents were considered as a group, it was found that 38 percent thought that the elderly, when they were unable to care for themselves, should live in nursing homes; 39 percent said they should live in their own homes with nursing care; and the remaining 23 percent believed they should live with their families.

Some differences were found in the choices of living arrangements of older persons who could not take care of themselves, with regard to marital status and sex: 44 percent of the couples, compared with 35 percent of the widowed, single women and only 28 percent of the widowed, single men suggested that elderly people in this physical condition should live in their own homes with nursing care. On the other hand, only 35 percent of the couples, compared with 40 percent of the widowed, single women and 44 percent of the widowed, single men, felt they should live in nursing homes.

Less favorable attitudes toward living in nursing homes were found with advance in age. For the total group of respondents, the proportion declined from 41 percent of the age group sixty-five to sixty-nine to 32 percent of the age group eighty years and over. *This would indicate that the closer the aged were to the possibility of dependent living, the less favorably inclined they were to the idea of moving into a nursing home.* This is possibly explained by a combination of two closely related factors which may set in with senility. On the one hand, there is likely to be an increase in the bias against "institutional" accommodations that exists on the part of many people at all ages and, on the other hand, there is likely to be a stronger emotional attachment to family members.

TYPES OF NEW ACCOMMODATIONS FOR THE AGING

Many groups have become involved in providing better shelter for the aging. These groups have ranged from the government at different levels, through private profit-motivated groups and nonprofit groups (church groups, labor unions, and the like) to educational institutions, whose primary interest has been in research.[15]

In the meantime, a new semantics has developed—we have moved beyond the simple terms of houses and apartments, "homes for the aged," nursing homes, and mental institutions to such new terms as "dispersed residences" (meaning homes scattered among other homes in the neighborhood or community), "proximate residences" (meaning housing accommodations for the elderly in groups, not scattered), "congregate living" (meaning a group of elderly people living under the same roof), and "protected living" (meaning the aged are in such physical condition that they have been provided with institutional care). The term "segregated" is used for clusters of housing for the aged not mixed with housing for younger people, and the term "integrated" is used if such housing is mixed with that for younger groups. One other term also appears in the literature, "geriatric complex." This refers to a combination of different types of accommodations, including houses or apartments for those elderly who can live independently, nonhousekeeping rooms for those who are not chronically ill but can live only moderately independently because of some physical limitations, and rooms for the chronically ill. The latter may be of the nursing home type and/or the type contained in geriatric units in hospitals for those experiencing acute conditions, with a chance of becoming fully or partially recovered.

[15] The reader may be interested in a set of papers from two conferences on the subject of types of accommodations, as well as related subjects, published as *Building for Older People*. New York: The National Council on the Aging, 1961 (mimeo).

Governmental Programs

The new accommodations being built for the aging in the United States can best be described on the basis on which they are being financed.

The largest program is the public housing program. Public housing is subsidized by the Federal Government through its assumption of the deficits incurred by local housing authorities. These subsidies make up that part of the annual interest and principal not covered by rental income. In the case of special public housing for the elderly, both the annual subsidy (up to $120 per unit) and the cost of construction per unit (by as much as $1,000 per room) may be higher than for conventional public housing. In 1961, the average monthly rents (including utilities and maintenance) of specially designed, public housing units for the elderly was $28 for units occupied by single persons and $34 for those occupied by couples. A total of 42,000 specially designed units for the elderly had been built or committed through 1962 under this program. (It was estimated that 120,000 persons aged sixty-two and over were living in public housing units—specially designed and regular—this number being approximately a fifth of the total number of all public housing units that have been built.)

Public housing projects often include activity centers for the aging of the community. These centers, often the first of their kind in a community, embrace recreation, education, preventive health, and other facilities. Their operation often involves many local and state organizations.

The next largest Federal program is the mortgage insurance program under the Federal Housing Administration's Section 231. Housing for the elderly can be built under this program on both a profit-motivated and a private nonprofit basis (the financing terms being more liberal for nonprofit sponsors). In 1961 the average monthly rents for the profit-motivated housing built under this program were as follows: efficiency apartments, $112; one-bedroom units, $120; two-bedroom units, $132. For the nonprofit housing, the average rents were: efficiency apartments, $72; one-bedroom units, $98; and two-bedroom units, $132. Sponsors of these projects may also establish admission or "founder's" fees as a prerequisite to occupancy. (In many instances, these fees amount to $5,000 or more.) Through 1962, 25,000 specially designed dwelling units had been built or committed under this mortgage insurance program.

Typical of this housing is housing in the new "retirement communities" being built for older people, especially in such warm-climate locations as Southern California, Arizona, and Florida. These are generally large subdivisions of single-family, detached dwellings having only one or two bedrooms. Sometimes the subdivisions depend upon the neighboring community for services; in other instances, they are practically self-contained. Since the dwellings must be purchased, these developments naturally cater to those elderly persons who have sufficient savings or income to move to the southern climates and establish residence there for their remaining days.

The third major program of the Federal Government is known as the

Victoria Plaza Apartments, San Antonio, Texas. Noonan and Thompson and Krocker and Marmon and Mok, architects. A fine example of public housing especially planned for the aged. (Photograph by R. J. Leydon, courtesy the Housing Authority of San Antonio.)

Peninsula Volunteer Retirement Apartments, Menlo Park, California. Skidmore, Owings & Merrill, architects. A fine example of nonprofit housing for the aged. (Photograph by Morley Baer, courtesy Skidmore, Owings & Merrill.)

FIGURE 28. *New housing for the aged.*

.Sun City, Arizona. An outstanding example of a new privately developed community for the aged. (Photographs courtesy Del E. Webb Corporation.)

"direct loan program." This is the newest of the three programs. Under it the Housing and Home Finance Agency is authorized to make loans to private nonprofit corporations, consumer cooperatives, and public bodies, excluding local housing authorities. The loans are on a more liberal basis than under the mortgage insurance program. In 1961, the average monthly rents for units built under this program were as follows: efficiency apartments, $62; one-bedroom units, $78; and two-bedroom units, $85. Through 1962, 8,800 specially designed dwelling units were built or committed under this program.

There is considerable variation concerning the nature of services included in these projects—meals, special diets, medical care, surgical insurance, nursing care, infirmary facilities, drugs, physical therapy, psychiatric care, services of a social worker, maid service, linen supply, laundry, furniture, recreation, hobby shops, barber shop, beauty parlor, telephone service, library, transportation, and so on.

Under the three programs, therefore, nearly 76,000 specially designed dwelling units totaling $950,000,000 in cost were built or committed through 1962.

Several state governments also have passed legislation which has encouraged the provision of better housing for older people. By 1962 the states of New York, Massachusetts, Connecticut, Pennsylvania, New Jersey, and California had such legislation. Generally, however, only small numbers of units have been involved.

The philosophy behind both Federal and state legislation has been one of encouraging independent living for those elderly who are still able to care for themselves. Most of the dwelling units that have been built would be characterized as "proximate residences," since they have provided for groups of elderly living together, rather than in scattered locations.

There has been no governmental program to finance "homes for the aged," that is, institutional accommodations for those who are not chronically ill but still in need of considerable care.[16] However, there are two Federal programs which assist in the financing of nursing homes, one under the Federal Housing Administration which provides assistance to profit-motivated or "proprietary" nursing homes and another under the Public Health Service (Hill-Burton Act) which provides assistance for such homes built by public and nonprofit groups.

Planning and Design Criteria

In view of the many special characteristics that the aging have, when compared with those of younger families, it would seem that there should also be special criteria for the planning and design of the housing accommodations built for them.[17]

The Federal Government has developed a number of broad principles relating to its housing programs for this group. The most important are as follows:

1. Such housing should be designed and located to promote and sustain the dignity and maximum independence of the older individual.
2. Such housing should be in accordance with the municipality's over-all plan of development and growth.
3. Such housing should promote and take advantage of modern concepts of health maintenance through preventive medicine and community health services.

[16] For the reader interested in institutional housing for the aging, three references are provided: Geneva Mathiasen and Edward H. Noakes, eds., *Planning Homes for the Aged.* New York: F. W. Dodge Corp., 1959; Robert E. Rutherford and Arthur J. Holst, eds., *Architectural Designs—Homes for the Aged—The European Approach.* Peoria, Ill.: Howard Co., 1963; and F. H. J. Nierstrasz, ed., *Building for the Aged.* Amsterdam and New York: Elsevier Publishing Co., 1961.

[17] Noverre Musson and Helen Heusinkveld, *Buildings for the Elderly.* New York: Reinhold Publishing Corp., 1963.

4. Such housing should be convenient to and part of essential, social, cultural, and commercial facilities and services.[18]

These principles become important at several stages of the decision-making process with regard to planning and designing new accommodations for older people. First, it must be determined whether dispersed or proximate living will be provided. Next, there must be a decision with regard to type and size of structure and the kinds of auxiliary facilities to be provided if the decision is in favor of proximate living. Then, consideration must be given to site factors. Finally, special attention must be given to the design of the individual living units.

Dispersed or Proximate Housing Accommodations

There has been considerable controversy, both in the United States and in several foreign countries, concerning whether or not housing accommodations for the elderly should be dispersed among housing accommodations built for younger families.

Some sociologists and psychologists have developed and tested a theory, called the "theory of disengagement," that has a bearing on this problem. The theory states, in effect, that ". . . aging includes an intrinsic process of withdrawal or disengagement from social interaction and that the individual tends to become disengaged with little or no loss of satisfaction."[19] Applied to housing, the theory would tend to support "proximate housing" as against "dispersed housing" since it suggests that aging individuals withdraw more markedly from classes of people different from themselves (e.g., young people, especially those not related to them) and remain relatively close to others (e.g., other people their own age and kind). Older people obviously do not want to be completely isolated. However, it would appear that when they do want social contact, they would prefer contact with their age peers, rather than with persons who have dissimilar social characteristics.[20]

Considerable practical experience tends to support the research hypotheses advanced above. The major large-scale experiment has been in Sweden where, a few years ago, it was decided that all new government-supported housing for older persons should be mixed with that for younger families. That

[18] Excerpts from 1962 draft of a statement of over-all policy relating to the programs under the jurisdiction of the Housing and Home Finance Agency. Used with permission.

[19] R. J. Havighurst, B. Neugarten, and S. Tobin, "Disengagement, Personality and Life Satisfaction in the Later Years." From abstract of paper delivered at the Sixth International Congress of Gerontology, Copenhagen, Denmark, August 14, 1963. This paper reported on some of the findings of one of the most comprehensive studies on this subject, the Kansas City Study of Adult Life. See Robert J. Havighurst, "Successful Aging," *The Gerontologist*, Vol. I, No. 1, March 1961, pp. 8–13, for a more complete description of this theory. Another report on the findings of the Kansas City study is Elaine Cumming and William E. Henry, *Growing Old*. New York: Basic Books, 1961.

[20] This is the major hypothesis being investigated in research being undertaken at Western Reserve University; see Irving Rosow, "Local Concentration and Social Contacts of Older People." Paper delivered at the Sixth International Congress of Gerontology, Copenhagen, Denmark, August 14, 1963.

policy is now under review, with the possible result that proximate housing will again be made available to older persons.[21]

Type and Size of Structure and Auxiliary Facilities

Where a cluster of older persons or families are to be housed together, the first question that tends to arise is "How many?" Here there is considerable experience to draw upon, especially in Europe. It is generally agreed that the number should be limited. In some European countries, the figure is set at 100 apartments in a building as a maximum. In the United States the matter of economics and problems of managing small apartment buildings has caused the number to frequently go as high as 250 or 300.

There also has been much experience with various types of structures for housing older persons—single-family detached cottages, row housing, and multistory housing up to high-rise apartments. The first types mentioned have usually been considered satisfactory, but for some time there was a general attitude that high-rise structures would be unacceptable because of a possible fear of living on upper floors of such structures (including the fear of using an elevator to reach those floors on the part of older persons). To the surprise of many, however, where older people have been housed in tall structures, those structures have proved to be highly acceptable for the majority, primarily because of one outstanding amenity which had been overlooked—the view provided from the upper floors. High-rise structures are now quite universally considered satisfactory.

There is also the question concerning auxiliary facilities to be provided. Many facilities seem to be desired and needed at certain times—central dining room, other communal rooms, infirmary, and the like. Facilities such as these, however, are expensive to provide and operate, and their provision is usually determined on an economic rather than a "need" basis. One facility usually incorporated in new apartment building for the aging, which does not present the same economic problems since the development of the automatic coin machines, is laundering facilities. Certain recreation facilities, at least a communal sitting room, also are usually provided.

Site Factors

It is generally agreed that most older people want to stay in surroundings with which they are familiar; few, for example, want to move to the suburbs (which is the direction of movement for many younger families). They want to retain as much proximity as possible to friends, to shopping facilities, and to community services. They should not be far from hospitals or other medical facilities where they can obtain medical care and services. These desires usually speak in favor of a "downtown" location. Yet, the site for a project for elderly people should be away from major traffic hazards. It should be sheltered to avoid sources of annoyance such as children's play-

21 Glenn H. Beyer and F. H. J. Nierstrasz, *Aging and Independent Living.* Amsterdam and New York: Elsevier Publishing Co. (to be published 1965).

grounds, which cause not only undue noise but also fears of damage to windows and gardens.

The approach to a site should not be steep, and access to a block of dwellings should be so planned that few steps need to be climbed.

Orientation is a highly important factor, because so many older people spend much of their time sitting and looking. Therefore, an interesting and pleasant view is highly desirable.

Standards of Design

Because of the physical and emotional characteristics already described, certain special design standards are recommended for housing for the elderly. One government report summarizes them as follows:

To be suited for the elderly, the house *must* incorporate the following features:

1. It must be possible to have complete dwelling facilities, including a bathroom, on one floor with that floor reached by few, if any, steps.
2. All thresholds and other tripping hazards must be absent or eliminated.
3. Nonslip surfaces must be installed in hallways, bathrooms, and kitchens to minimize the dangers of falling.
4. Handrails must be installed by all steps and inclines.
5. There must be adequate handgrips, capable of supporting a heavy person, by all bathtubs and toilets.
6. All steps and other potentially hazardous areas must be adequately illuminated.
7. Where central heat is required, the installation must be fully automatic.

Other features which *should* be present are:

1. Availability of at least one bedroom and avoidance of any layout which contemplates continued use of the living room for sleeping purposes.
2. Installation of windows that can be easily operated and cleaned.
3. Presence of doors wide enough to facilitate moving about the dwelling in a wheel chair.
4. A bathroom large enough and suitably designed to permit its use by a wheel-chair patient.[22]

Desirable, although not always practical to obtain, is:

1. Provision of bells with buttons in bathroom and bedroom, sounding either in an adjacent dwelling unit or at some point where someone is on duty most of the time.
2. Orientation of floor plan and design of windows to permit good penetration of sunlight into living room, especially during winter months.

[22] E. Everett Ashley, III, "A Happy Home for the Later Years," in *A Guide for Selecting Retirement Housing.* Housing and Home Finance Agency, Washington, D. C., 1957. More detailed standards have been developed by George E. Kassabaum, "Housing for the Elderly—Technical Standards of Design," *Journal of the American Institute of Architects,* September 1962, pp. 61–65.

Obviously, many of these design criteria are also important for younger families, but they become especially important for the aging.

DOMICILIARY CARE AND COMMUNITY SERVICES

A discussion of housing for the aging would not be complete without considering a most important and closely related factor, domiciliary care and community services. Such care and services can be an important influence in maintaining independent living for the elderly, for many additional years. They can be especially important in permitting the elderly to live in their own homes longer.

There are many different types of care and services, and they will be described only briefly.[23] The most important types include health services, meals, home help, and visiting.

Perhaps the best known of these services in the United States are the visiting nursing services. In many cities, these are available to the elderly at all income levels. Those who can afford it pay the full cost of the service, but where incomes are extremely low, the city's Department of Welfare may pay the costs. (Generally, these services are available to all age groups, but older persons frequently account for half or more of the visits.)

Another service that has been growing in importance is the meals distribution program. Sometimes older people are not able to prepare meals themselves because of illness or disability; at other times they cannot afford adequate meals or simply do not take the trouble to prepare them. Such services are usually operated by voluntary organizations, and a single meal a day, usually on certain days a week, is delivered to the home of the older person. (The "meals on wheels" program is more prominent in England than in any other country.)

In some instances the elderly need temporary or periodic assistance with housekeeping, as well as with washing clothes, cooking meals, purchasing food, and sometimes with dressing and personal hygiene. In the United States these services have been provided primarily by voluntary organizations and have been concentrated in cities in New York, Pennsylvania, Massachusetts, Ohio, and Illinois. Sometimes the workers are on a full-time basis; at other times, they are on call.

One of the newer services provided, considered important to offset the problem of loneliness on the part of older people, is the visiting service. The first service of this type in the United States was established by the Public Assistance Division of the Cook County (Chicago) Department of Welfare. Other small programs have been established in Philadelphia, San Francisco, Washington, Boston, and a few other cities. Under these programs volunteers usually visit housebound older persons one or more days a week. While they usually just visit with them, or read the newspaper or other

[23] For more detailed discussion, including discussion of the care and services offered to older people in some European countries, see Beyer and Nierstrasz, *op. cit.*, Section III.

material to them, sometimes the ''visitors'' perform other functions such as assisting in certain household tasks or advising on community services available.

All of these services permit older persons to live more satisfying lives in their own homes, and some of them lessen greatly the demand for hospital beds by providing the necessary care for minor illnesses at home.

The services described above are usually directed at the housebound. For older persons who are able to get out, many communities provide activity centers and social clubs. These may be provided in connection with a housing development for the aging, or they may be independent. The primary purpose is to provide a location where elderly people can go several days of the week to socialize with others of their same age. They may engage in various forms of recreation, work on hobbies, or simply use the library.

In conclusion, then, it is evident that the aging segment of the population will need—and probably will be attracting—more special attention in the future than it has, even in the recent past. Communities will be challenged to gain a better understanding of the many and complex problems surrounding this segment of our population and to make decisions concerning what they want to do and the extent of the action they will want to take in solving those problems. They will need to decide whether or not they want to regiment the forces at hand in order to permit the elderly to remain in their own homes as long as possible. They will need to decide whether or not they want to urge the provision of an ample supply of new housing accommodations for those elderly who are not infirm but who cannot continue to remain in their present homes. They will need to decide how adequate cultural, recreational, and social programs can be arranged so that the noninfirm elderly may continue to live meaningful lives in their community. Finally, they will need to decide how to provide adequate care and facilities for the chronically ill—for the rehabilitation of those patients capable of regaining independent living and for the care of those for whom there is no alternative but institutional care.

READING LIST

GENERAL

Beyer, Glenn H., and F. H. J. Nierstrasz. *Aging and Independent Living.* Amsterdam and New York: Elsevier Publishing Co. (to be published 1965).

Beyer, Glenn H., and Margaret E. Woods. *Living and Activity Patterns of the Aged.* Research Report No. 6. Ithaca, N.Y.: Cornell University Center for Housing and Environmental Studies, 1963.

Building for Older People. New York: The National Council on the Aging, 1961, (mimeo).

Burgess, Ernest W. *Aging in Western Societies.* Chicago: The University of Chicago Press, 1960. (See especially article "Housing and Community Services," by Wilma Donahue.)

Kutner, Bernard, *et al. Five Hundred over Sixty.* New York: Russell Sage Foundation, 1956.

Langford, Marilyn. *Community Aspects of Housing for the Aged.* Research Report No. 5. Ithaca, N.Y.: Cornell University Center for Housing and Environmental Studies, 1962.

Tibbitts, Clark (ed.) *Handbook of Social Gerontology.* Chicago: The University of Chicago Press, 1960. (See especially article "Housing and Community Settings for Older People," by Walter K. Vivrett, pp. 549-623.)

See also various reports and publications of the government, especially of the Housing and Home Finance Agency, the Department of Health, Education, and Welfare, and the U.S. Senate special committees on problems of the aging.

ECONOMIC ASPECTS

Beyer, Glenn H. *Economic Aspects of Housing for the Aged.* Research Report No. 4. Ithaca, N.Y.: Cornell University Center for Housing and Enviromental Studies, 1961.

Corson, John J., and John W. McConnell. *Economic Needs of Older People.* New York: The Twentieth Century Fund, 1956.

Steiner, Peter O., and Robert Dorfman. *The Economic Status of the Aged.* Berkeley: University of California Press, 1957.

ARCHITECTURAL ASPECTS

Kassabaum, George E. "Housing for the Elderly," *Journal of the American Institute of Architects.* (1) Site Selection, August 1962; (2) Technical Standards of Design, September 1962; (3) Functional Program, October 1962, Vol. XXXVIII, Nos. 2–4.

Musson, Noverre, and Helen Heusinkveld. *Buildings for the Elderly.* New York: Reinhold Publishing Corp., 1963.

INSTITUTIONAL ACCOMMODATIONS—DESIGN

Mathiasen, Geneva, and Edward H. Noakes (eds.) *Planning Homes for the Aged.* New York: F. W. Dodge Corp., 1959.

Nierstrasz, F. H. J. (ed.) *Building for the Aged.* Amsterdam: Elsevier Publishing Co., 1961.

Rutherford, Robert B., and Arthur J. Holst. *Architectural Designs—Homes for the Aged—The European Approach.* Peoria, Ill.: Howard Co., 1963.

Table 13–1

LOCATION AND SIZE OF PLACE, BY TOTAL U. S. POPULATION AND POPULATION AGE SIXTY-FIVE YEARS AND OVER, 1960

	Total U.S. Population	*Population 65 Years and Over*	*Percent of Total*	*Population 65 Years and Over*
Urbanized areas	95,848,487	8,476,729	8.8%	51.2%
Central cities	57,975,132	5,738,131	9.9	34.7
Urban fringe	37,873,355	2,738,598	7.2	16.5
Other urban	29,420,263	3,049,463	10.4	18.4
Places of 10,000 or more	16,172,839	1,590,742	9.8	9.6
Places of 2,500 to 10,000	13,247,424	1,458,721	11.0	8.8
Urban, total	125,268,750	11,526,192	9.2	69.6
Rural areas (places of 1,000 to 2,500)	6,496,788	794,717	12.2	4.8
Other rural	47,557,637	4,238,671	8.9	25.6
Rural, total	54,054,425	5,033,388	9.3	30.4
Total, all areas	179,323,175	16,559,580	9.2%	100.0%

SOURCE: U.S. Bureau of the Census, *Census of Population 1960*. General Population Characteristics, PC(1), 1B, U.S. Summary, p. 1–148.

Table 13–2

TOTAL POPULATION AND POPULATION AGED SIXTY-FIVE AND OVER, IN THE UNITED STATES, 1900 TO 1960 WITH PROJECTIONS FOR 1970 AND 1980

	Total Population		*Population Aged Sixty-five and Over*		
Year	*Number*	*Percent Increase since 1900*	*Number*	*Percent Increase since 1900*	*As Percent of Total Population*
1900	75,995,000	—	3,080,000	—	4.1
1910	91,972,000	21	3,950,000	28	4.3
1920	105,711,000	39	4,933,000	60	4.7
1930	122,775,000	62	6,634,000	115	5.4
1940	131,669,000	73	9,019,000	193	6.8
1950	151,326,000	101	12,295,000	299	8.1
1960	179,323,000	136	16,560,000	438	9.2
Projections*					
1970					
Series II	214,222,000	182	20,035,000	550	9.4
Series III	208,931,000	162	20,035,000	550	9.6
1980					
Series II	259,584,000	242	24,458,000	694	9.4
Series III	245,736,000	223	24,458,000	694	10.0

SOURCES: Data for 1900–1940 from U.S. Bureau of the Census, *1950 Census of Population*. Vol. II. Characteristics of the Population, Part 1, U.S. Summary, pp. 1–5. Data for 1950 and 1960 (except percentage of increase since 1900) from U.S. Census data as reported in "New Population Facts on Older Americans, 1960." A Staff Report to the Special Committee on Aging, U.S. Senate, with Statistical Supplement prepared by the Department of Health, Education, and Welfare's Special Staff on Aging. Washington, D.C.: U.S. Government Printing Office, May 24, 1961. Projections for 1970 and 1980 (except percentage of increase since 1900) from U.S. Bureau of the Census, *Current Population Reports,* Population Estimates, "Interim Revised Projections of the Population of the United States, by Age and Sex: 1975 and 1980," Series p–25, No. 251, July 6, 1962.

* Projections are based on 1960 Census statistics adjusted to include Armed Forces abroad. The two series are based on these assumptions:

Series II Fertility remains constant at the 1955–1957 level (about the same as the 1958–1960 level) throughout the projection period to 1980.

Series III Fertility declines from the 1955–1957 level to the 1949–1951 level by 1965–1970 and then remains at that level to 1980.

These assumptions do not exhaust the possible range of reasonable variation as to fertility.

Table 13–3

POPULATION AGED SIXTY-FIVE AND OVER, 1950 AND 1960

Age	*1950*	*1960*	*Increase, 1950 to 1960*
65 to 69 years	5,013,490	6,257,910	24.8%
70 to 74 years	3,419,208	4,738,932	38.6
75 to 84 years	3,284,061	4,633,486	41.1
85 years and over	577,939	929,252	60.8
Total	12,294,698	16,559,580	34.7

SOURCE: "New Population Facts on Older Americans, 1960." A Staff Report to the Special Com. mittee on Aging, U.S. Senate, with a Statistical Supplement prepared by the Department of Health, Education, and Welfare's Special Staff on Aging. Washington, D.C.: U.S. Government Printing Office, May 24, 1961, p. 2.

Table 13–4

PERCENTAGE DISTRIBUTION OF NUMBER OF MALES PER 100 FEMALES, UNITED STATES, 1960

Age	*Males per 100 Females*	*Age*	*Males per 100 Females*
Under 5 years	103.6	40 to 44 years	95.5
5 to 9 years	103.5	45 to 49 years	96.8
10 to 14 years	103.7	50 to 54 years	96.6
15 to 19 years	101.7	55 to 59 years	94.9
20 to 24 years	95.7	60 to 64 years	90.8
25 to 29 years	96.3	65 to 69 years	87.3
30 to 34 years	95.6	70 to 74 years	84.8
35 to 39 years	94.9	75 years and over	74.4

SOURCE: U.S. Bureau of the Census, *Census of Population 1960*. General Social and Economic Characteristics, PC(1), 1C, U.S. Summary, p. 1 200.

Table 13–5

MEN AND WOMEN AGED SIXTY-FIVE AND OVER, 1960

Age	*Men*	*Women*	*Women as a Percent of Total*
Total 65 years and over	7,503,100	9,056,500	54.7%
65 to 69 years	2,931,100	3,326,800	53.2
70 to 74 years	2,185,200	2,553,700	53.9
75 to 79 years	1,359,400	1,694,100	55.5
80 to 84 years	665,100	914,800	57.9
85 years and over	362,300	567,000	61.0

SOURCE: "New Population Facts on Older Americans, 1960." A Staff Report to the Special Committee on Aging, U.S. Senate, with a Statistical Supplement Prepared by the Department of Health, Education, and Welfare's Special Staff on Aging. Washington, D.C.: U.S. Government Printing Office, May 24, 1961, p. 5.

Table 13–6

PERCENTAGE DISTRIBUTION OF SIZE OF HOUSEHOLD, OF OCCUPIED HOUSING UNITS, U. S. TOTAL AND HEAD 60 YEARS OLD OR OVER, 1960

Size of Household	*Total U.S.*	*Head 60 Years Old or Over*
Total households (number in thousands)	53,024	19,305
One person	13.3%	19.5%
Two persons	28.0	53.5
Three persons	18.9	16.2
Four or more persons	39.8	10.8

SOURCES: U.S. Bureau of the Census, *Census of Housing 1960*. States and Small Areas, HC(1), No. 1, U.S. Summary, p. xxix, and U.S. Bureau of the Census, *Census of Housing 1960*. Housing of Senior Citizens, Vol. VII, United States, States, Selected Metropolitan Areas, p. xii.

Table 13–7

PERCENTAGE DISTRIBUTION OF LIVING ARRANGEMENTS OF MALE AND FEMALE PERSONS AGED SIXTY-FIVE AND OVER, BY AGE GROUPS, 1960

Living Arrangements	*Total 60 Years and Over*	*60 to 64 Years*	*Total 65 Years and Over*	*65 to 69 Years*	*70 to 74 Years*	*75 Years and Over*
Males, total (number in thousands)	10,665	3,375	7,291	2,877	2,133	2,281
In households, total	96.1%	97.1%	95.6%	97.0%	96.4%	93.0%
In own households, total	85.2	89.9	83.0	88.6	85.3	73.8
Married, wife present	*69.4*	*78.3*	*65.4*	*74.5*	*67.8*	*51.6*
Alone or with others	*15.8*	*11.6*	*17.6*	*14.1*	*17.5*	*22.2*
Not in own households, total	10.9	7.2	12.6	8.4	11.1	19.2
Parent of head or wife	*5.0*	*1.6*	*6.5*	*2.9*	*5.3*	*12.2*
Other relative of head	*3.4*	*3.3*	*3.4*	*3.1*	*3.2*	*4.0*
Living with nonrelatives	*2.5*	*2.3*	*2.7*	*2.4*	*2.6*	*3.0*
In group quarters, total	3.9	2.9	4.4	3.0	3.6	7.0
Inmate in institution	2.9	1.9	3.4	2.1	2.7	5.7
Other	1.0	1.0	1.0	0.9	0.9	1.3
Females, total (number in thousands)	12,602	3,719	8,883	3,297	2,518	3,068
In households, total	95.7%	97.9%	94.9%	97.5%	96.4%	90.7%
In own households, total	74.2	84.2	70.1	80.4	73.5	56.1
Wife of head	*40.6*	*57.2*	*33.7*	*47.5*	*35.3*	*17.6*
Alone or with others	*33.6*	*27.0*	*36.4*	*32.9*	*38.2*	*38.5*
Not in own households, total	21.5	13.7	24.8	17.1	22.9	34.6
Parent of head	*13.1*	*6.5*	*15.9*	*9.6*	*14.4*	*24.1*
Other relative of head	*6.1*	*5.1*	*6.5*	*5.4*	*6.2*	*7.7*
Living with nonrelatives	*2.3*	*2.1*	*2.4*	*2.1*	*2.3*	*2.8*
In group quarters, total	4.3	2.1	5.1	2.5	3.6	9.3
Inmate in institution	3.4	1.2	4.1	1.6	2.7	8.0
Other	0.9	0.9	1.0	0.9	0.9	1.3

SOURCE: Derived from U.S. Bureau of the Census, *Census of Population 1960*. Detailed Characteristics, PC(1), 1D, U.S. Summary, p. 1–457.

Table 13–8

PERCENTAGE DISTRIBUTION OF INCOME IN 1959 OF ALL FAMILIES AND HUSBAND–WIFE FAMILIES AND UNRELATED INDIVIDUALS WITH HEAD SIXTY-FIVE YEARS AND OVER

		Head 65 Years and Over		
			Unrelated Individuals	
Family Income	*All Families*	*Husband-Wife Families*	*Male*	*Female*
Total (number in thousands)	45,129	4,778	1,194	2,565
Under $1,000	5.6%	10.6%	39.3%	54.6%
$1,000 to $1,999	7.5	21.5	31.4	25.5
$2,000 to $2,999	8.3	17.3	11.9	8.6
$3,000 to $3,999	9.5	11.6	5.7	4.2
$4,000 to $4,999	11.0	8.6	3.7	2.4
$5,000 to $5,999	12.3	6.9	2.6	1.5
$6,000 to $6,999	10.7	5.2	1.5	0.9
$7,000 to $9,999	20.0	9.1	1.9	1.1
$10,000 to $14,999	10.5	5.6	1.0	0.6
$15,000 and over	4.6	3.6	1.0	0.6
Median income, dollars	$5,660	$3,050	$1,342	$916

SOURCE: Derived from U.S. Bureau of the Census, *Census of Population 1960.* Detailed Characteristics, PC(1), 1D, U.S. Summary, pp. 1–594, 1–595.

Table 13–9

PERCENTAGE DISTRIBUTION OF TENURE OF OCCUPIED HOUSING UNITS, U.S. TOTAL AND HEAD SIXTY YEARS OLD OR OVER, 1960

Tenure	*U.S. Total*	*Head 60 Years Old or Over*
Total occupied units (number in thousands)	53,024	13,271
Owner	61.9%	68.8%
Renter	38.1	31.2

SOURCES: U.S. Bureau of the Census, *Census of Housing 1960.* States and Small Areas, HC(1), No. 1, U.S. Summary, p. 1–40, and U.S. Bureau of the Census, *Census of Housing 1960.* Housing of Senior Citizens, Vol. VII, United States, States, Selected Metropolitan Areas, p. xiv.

Table 13–10

MEDIAN AND PERCENTAGE DISTRIBUTION OF INCOME OF AGED COUPLES, UNATTACHED WOMEN AND UNATTACHED MEN, BY LIVING ARRANGEMENTS AND TENURE (NUMBER REPORTING, 4,611)

Marital Status	*Median Income*	*Percentage Distribution of Income*
Couples:		
Living in own household		
Owners	$2,335	35%
Renters	2,325	9
Not living in own household		
With other than children	1,750	*
With children	1,595	1
Widowed, single men:		
Living in own household		
Owners	1,735	6
Renters	1,490	4
Not living in own household		
With other than children	1,355	2
With children	1,220	3
Widowed, single women:		
Living in own household		
Owners	1,425	16
Renters	1,385	11
Not living in own household		
With other than children	1,115	5
With children	840	8
Median income, dollars	$1,730	

SOURCE: Glenn H. Beyer, *Economic Aspects of Housing for the Aged.* Research Report No. 4, Ithaca, N.Y.: Cornell University Center for Housing and Environmental Studies, 1961, p. 18.
*Less than 0.5 percent.

Table 13–11

PERCENTAGE DISTRIBUTION OF YEAR STRUCTURE BUILT, U.S. TOTAL AND HOUSING UNITS OCCUPIED BY FAMILIES WITH HEAD SIXTY YEARS OR OVER, 1960

Year Structure Built	*U.S. Total*	*Head 60 Years Old or Over*
Total housing units (number in thousands)	58,318	13,271
1955 to March 1960	14.6%	5.5%
1940 to 1954	27.8	18.9
1939 or earlier	57.6	75.6

SOURCES: Derived from U.S. Bureau of the Census, *Census of Housing 1960*. States and Small Areas, HC(1), No. 1, U.S. Summary, p. 1–42, and U.S. Bureau of the Census, *Census of Housing 1960*. Housing of Senior Citizens, Vol. VII, United States, States, Selected Metropolitan Areas, p. xv.

Table 13–12

PERCENTAGE DISTRIBUTION OF CONDITION AND PRESENCE OF PLUMBING FACILITIES OF OCCUPIED HOUSING UNITS, U.S. TOTAL AND HEAD SIXTY YEARS OLD OR OVER, 1960

Condition and Presence of Plumbing Facilities	*U.S. Total*	*Head 60 Years Old or Over*
Total occupied units (number in thousands)	53,024	13,271
Sound or deteriorating, with all facilities	84.0%	79.6%
Dilapidated or lacking facilities	16.0	20.4

SOURCES: Derived from U.S. Bureau of the Census, *Census of Housing 1960*. States and Small Areas, HC(1), No. 1, U.S. Summary, p. 1–40, and U.S. Bureau of the Census, *Census of Housing 1960*. Housing of Senior Citizens. Vol. VII, United States, States, Selected Metropolitan Areas, p. xv.

CHAPTER 14

*

History of the Government's Role in Housing

When a problem develops that affects the public welfare, it is the responsibility of the government, at some level, to do something about it.

However, since there must first be a problem, any government legislation or regulations attempting to alleviate it must come afterward. Sometimes the legislation comes promptly, as during war or other crises, but usually it comes slowly, because of the normal character of the democratic process.

ORIGIN AND EARLY HISTORY OF GOVERNMENT HOUSING POLICIES

The first public policies concerning housing in this country were established at the local level, and date back to the period of the colonies. Many houses of the early settlers had wooden chimneys and thatch roofs, which were the cause of frequent fires. As a result, several of the colonies passed local ordinances outlawing them. One of the first was in the Plymouth Colony in 1626. The law stipulated that new houses should not be thatched, but roofed "with either board or pale and the like." In 1648, wooden or plastered chimneys were prohibited on new houses in certain areas of New Amsterdam, and chimneys on existing houses were decreed to be inspected regularly. After a disastrous fire in Charleston, in 1740, the General Assembly passed an act that ". . . all building should be of brick or stone, that all 'tall' wooden houses must be pulled down by 1745, and that the use of wood was to be confined to window frames, shutters and to interior work."[1] This law must have been found to be unenforceable, however, because we learn from an article in *The London Magazine* of 1762 that some Charleston houses were of brick, "but more of timber."

Social control over housing was exerted in other ways. One of these required the improvement of certain primitive dwellings in which some families were still living. Shurtleff says of the early Pennsylvania settlement, "Most of the first settlers literally dug into the banks of the Delaware for their temporary shelters, much as the pioneers of Concord and of Hartford had done almost half a century before. Some of these were still being used for dwellings in 1687, when the Provincial Council ordered their denizens to 'provide for themselves other habitations, in order to have the

[1] Thomas J. Wertenbaker, *The Old South: The Founding of American Civilization.* New York: Charles Scribner's Sons, 1942, p. 276.

said Caves or houses destroy'd.' "[2] In some New England communities, forty years later, standards were being raised considerably higher by local ordinance. For example: "In East Greenwich it had been the custom to build houses fourteen feet square, with posts nine feet high; in 1727 the town votes that houses shall be built eighteen feet square, with posts fifteen feet high, with chimneys of stone or brick as before."[3]

Sanitary regulations of different types were enacted by different communities during this early time. Outdoor privies were, of course, general. The principal problems seemed to be having them on flat ground, too near the street, or having their contents accessible to hogs and goats, which were general public scavengers in most places. Boston in 1652 prohibited the building of privies within 12 feet of the street or the house, and many other communities established similar regulations. In 1648, a public law in New Amsterdam required hogs and goats, in certain areas of the community, to be kept within fences. A new type of sanitary legislation also was enacted in New Amsterdam in 1657; it prohibited ". . . the throwing of rubbish and filth into the streets or canal, and requiring the householders to keep the streets clean and orderly."[4]

Apparently the first attempt to enact a "use zoning" ordinance, as we know such ordinances today, was in New Amsterdam in 1664, but it was unsuccessful:

> Willem Abrahamzen van der Borden and Daniel Verveelen appearing represent, that a tannery is established between their houses and lots and as they fear their water shall be thereby spoiled and they shall also have to endure great stench from the tanning of skins, they request, that such be forbidden, especially the digging of a pit, in which the skins are soaked and washed. Burgomasters and Schepens decree as others have been allowed to make a tannery behind their house and lot, such cannot be forbidden.[5]

Thus we see the variety of the early housing ordinances and regulations, and their varying degrees of success. Those prohibiting thatched roofs as a fire prevention measure were more successful than most of the others, because both violation and possible resulting disaster were so obvious. The sanitary regulations were generally less successful, because violations could be more easily concealed and the resulting damage was less obvious.

ORIGIN OF SLUMS AND THE REFORM MOVEMENTS

Next we come to the era when our cities were experiencing growth of populations which exceeded growth in number of adequate housing units.

[2] Harold R. Shurtleff, *The Log Cabin Myth.* Cambridge, Mass.: Harvard University Press, 1939, p. 124.

[3] William B. Weeden, *Economic and Social History of New England, 1620–1789.* Boston: Houghton, Mifflin and Company, 1891, p. 528.

[4] Reprinted by permission of the publishers from James Ford, *Slums and Housing,* Vol. I. Cambridge, Mass.: Harvard University Press, Copyright, 1936, by the President and Fellows of Harvard College, p. 30.

[5] *Ibid.*, p. 33.

It was not only a question of not enough housing; many of the families, as pointed out in Chapter 1, could not afford ordinary rents and therefore either had to crowd in with other families or occupy cellar quarters or other accommodations that demanded only cheap rents.

We have the most information about New York City, because the situation there is generally recognized to have been the worst of any city in the country. This was due in large part, as indicated in Chapter 10, to the fact that this city became the melting pot of the world. It was the port through which most of the immigrants entered the country, and many of them remained there. To aggravate the housing problem, many of the vast numbers that arrived were penniless on arrival.

As suggested in Chapter 1, the serious housing problems began in New York around 1840 when the first tenements were built. They provided such substandard housing and such unhealthy, crowded living conditions that it was only natural that a social reform movement should get under way, poor housing being one of its primary targets.

As indicated at the outset of this chapter, laws and regulations are frequently slow to follow the development of a problem. This was the case in New York City. During the early part of the nineteenth century, the only housing control was that vested in the fire wardens, whose sole object it was to prevent fires, and health wardens, who were charged with the duties of general sanitation. (The first health law was not enacted until 1866.) The first New York City law concerned directly with substandard housing was the Tenement House Act of 1867. This law represented the first comprehensive legislation of its kind in this country. The principal features of this Act are summarized by Ford:

> It required for every room occupied for sleeping in a tenement or lodging housing, if it did not communicate directly with the external air, a ventilating or transom window to the neighboring room or hall; a proper fire-escape on every tenement or lodging house; the roof to be kept in repair and the stairs to have bannisters; water-closets or privies—at least one to every twenty occupants for all such houses; after July 1, 1867, permits for occupancy of every cellar not previously occupied as a dwelling; cleansing of every lodging house to the satisfaction of the Board of Health, which was to have access at any time; reporting of all cases of infectious disease to the Board by the owner or his agent; inspection and, if necessary, disinfection, of such houses; and vacation of buildings found to be out of repair. There were regulations also governing distances between buildings, rear dwellings, heights of rooms, and dimensions of windows. The terms "tenement house," "lodging house," and "cellar" were defined.[6]

Although this act had some beneficial influences on overcrowding, sewage, and light and ventilation, it did not correct the evils of crowding on lots and providing for adequate light and ventilation for inside rooms.

The second tenement house act, in 1879, amended the Act of 1867 to the extent that the amount of lot coverage was limited and every room was required to have a window with an opening of at least 12 square feet. The

[6] *Ibid.*, pp. 154–155.

enforcement of both of these provisions, however, was left to the discretion of the Board of Health, and this resulted in only partial fulfillment of the intent of the law.

In 1882 there was another act that mainly assembled the provisions of previous regulations and laws. This act was amended in 1887 as a result of the findings of the Tenement House Commission of 1884. It limited the number of families who could occupy a dwelling unit—a provision found to be unenforceable. Still another act in 1895 attempted to make the earlier acts more enforceable.

Although these numerous acts remedied the serious problems of the tenements of the city only slightly, they are mentioned to show the city's acknowledgment of the necessity for something to be done. This public acknowledgment, however, was not often shared by the private interests which owned the tenements, nor was it shared in some instances by the courts. The most famous example was that of the Trinity Church case in 1892. In this case, the City of New York accused Trinity Church, then one of the largest owners of tenements in New York City, of violating certain provisions of the Act of 1882 as amended in 1887. The specific count was that the landlord had failed to provide running water on every floor of the building, as required by the law of 1887. The District Court levied a fine of $200 against the Church, after which the Church appealed to the Court of Common Pleas to have the law set aside as unconstitutional. In an unanimous opinion, the Court upheld the landlord's position:

> There is no evidence, nor can the court judicially know, that the presence and distribution of water on the several floors will conduce to the health of the occupants. . . . There is no necessity for legislative compulsion on a landlord to distribute water through the stories of his building; since, if tenants require it, self-interest and the rivalry of competition are sufficient to secure it. . . . Now, if it be competent for the legislature to impose an expense on a landlord in order that tenants may be furnished with water in their rooms instead of in the yard or basement, at what point must this police power pause? . . . A conclusion contrary to the present decision would involve the essential principle of that species of socialism under the regime of which the individual disappears, and is absorbed by a collective being called the "state,"—a principle utterly repugnant to the spirit of our political system, and necessarily fatal to our form of liberty.[7]

Three years later the city Health Department was granted an appeal from the court's order, and eventually the constitutionality of the law was upheld in the Court of Appeals. Nonetheless, the strong wording of the opinion of the Court of Common Pleas suggests the prevailing laissez-faire social philosophy of the time.

The twentieth century opened with a wave of social reform. Laws were being enacted not only to improve conditions for the laboring man and to reduce disease and public corruption, but also to correct some of the existing

[7] *Health Department of City of New York v. Rector, etc., of Trinity Church in the City of New York:* 17 N.Y. Supp. 510, at 515. Quoted in Nathan Straus, *The Seven Myths of Housing.* New York: Alfred A. Knopf, 1944, pp. 200–201.

housing conditions. Jacob A. Riis, through his book *How the Other Half Lives,* Lawrence Veiller, and others, had done much to bring to the attention of those living on a higher plane the problems of the tenements.

The Tenement House Act of 1901 has been termed ". . . the most signficant regulatory act in America's history of housing. . . ."[8] The Act was extremely comprehensive for its time. It began with clear-cut definitions of certain terms that were to become important in court actions—"court," "shaft," "public halls," and the like. It contained a new provision for protection from fire, requiring that every tenement house erected thereafter and exceeding 60 feet in height should be fireproof. There was specific provision with regard to fire escapes for both new and existing houses. More light and greater ventilation were guaranteed by a provision permitting not over 70 percent coverage for interior lots and 90 percent for corner lots. There was special provision concerning the rear yard, inner courts, and buildings on the same lot with a tenement house. At least one window of specified dimensions was required for every room, including the bathroom. Minimum sizes of rooms were specified, as were certain characteristics of public halls. There were certain provisions concerning planning of the individual apartments in order to insure privacy.

One of the most important sections of the 1901 Act covered sanitary requirements. There was a provision requiring running water and water closets in each apartment in new tenement houses erected. Special attention was given to basements and cellars, requiring that they be damp proof, and also requiring that permits be obtained before occupancy in order to insure relative healthfulness. The Act contained a novel section that prohibited any part of the building to be used for the purpose of a house of prostitution. (This section proved most difficult to enforce.)

The Act contained many additional, detailed provisions. Most important, it also included a series of powers granted to the Tenement House Department, which it established to carry out the purposes of the Act, as well as a series of penalties for a series of violations.

The principles and methods established in the Tenement House Act of 1901 still underlie much of the housing legislation of New York City today. Furthermore, it served as a pattern for regulatory legislation in many other cities.

It was mentioned in Chapter 1 that Boston faced the same kind of tenement house problems faced by New York City, but even there the problem was not of the same proportions. However, although Boston enacted several early housing laws, in 1892, 1895, and 1897, those laws were not as satisfactory as the New York City law of 1901.

Philadelphia is recognized by many authorities as having had more foresight in the control of its housing than almost any other large American city, although the city may be compared with New York from the standpoint of age. It had an early, rapid growth in population. After 1909 its housing

[8] Ford, *op. cit.*, p. 205.

was subject to continual inspection and improvement by the Philadelphia Housing Association.

Chicago, although two centuries younger than New York, was enacting housing legislation as early as 1889, and health legislation as early as 1881. Certain regulations relating to ventilation, light, drainage, and plumbing of buildings were put into effect in 1896. Because housing for wage earners was largely built of wood, dilapidation and the risk of conflagration were among the city's most serious problems.

Most other cities had similar legislation, with varying degrees of vigorous enforcement. By 1910, over one fourth of the states had passed laws more or less patterned after the 1901 New York City Act. Many of these granted power to state authorities to take action where municipalities failed.[9]

About the same time some laws directly called "housing laws" were passed in some cities. These were different from the tenement house laws inasmuch as they had wider application, covering one- and two-family houses, hotels, and all other types of dwellings. The earliest law of this type was the Columbus, Ohio, ordinance of 1911. Housing laws were passed in a number of cities and in some states between 1913 and 1919.[10]

The Federal Government entered the picture in 1892. In that year, the Congress passed a resolution authorizing an investigation of slums in cities containing 200,000 inhabitants and over. The cities included in this resolution were Baltimore, Boston, Brooklyn, Buffalo, Chicago, Cincinnati, Cleveland, Detroit, Milwaukee, New Orleans, New York, Philadelphia, Pittsburgh, St. Louis, San Francisco, and Washington, a total of sixteen.[11]

There was much controversy concerning this resolution when it was introduced in the Senate. Various objections were raised based upon the Federal Government's intervention in the matter of private housing. Before it could pass, it had to be amended and the Commissioner of Labor was required to write an extensive legal opinion justifying the constitutionality of such an expenditure. Only $20,000 was authorized to cover expenses. This amount was determined by the Department of Labor to be "altogether inadequate for the collection of the facts called for," and an estimate for additional appropriation was made, but the funds were not provided. Therefore, the actual investigation was limited to Baltimore, Chicago, New York, and Philadelphia, and to only certain districts of those cities.

Facts obtained in this investigation were only general, being concerned with such matters as the number of saloons per number of inhabitants, number of arrests, the distribution of males and females, the proportion of inhabitants foreign born, the degree of illiteracy, the number of voters, the kinds of occupations of the residents, their earnings, and the condition of their health.

[9] Miles L. Colean, *Renewing Our Cities*. New York: The Twentieth Century Fund, 1953, p. 44.

[10] Edith Elmer Wood, *Recent Trends in American Housing*. New York: The Macmillan Company, 1931, pp. 10–11.

[11] U. S. Bureau of Labor, *The Slums of Baltimore, Chicago, New York and Philadelphia*. Washington, D.C.: U.S. Government Printing Office, 1894, p. 11.

This resolution, then, resulted in only a slight contribution, if any, to existing knowledge of our slums. Its primary importance lay in the fact that it was the first occasion upon which the Federal Government intervened in the nation's housing situation.

There was little new regulatory legislation in most states and cities during the first three decades of the twentieth century. One exception was the Multiple Dwelling Law enacted by the New York State Legislature in 1929. This law continued the Tenement House Department in New York City but replaced many of the provisions of the 1901 law with provisions *less strict* in character.

In the meantime, it was also recognized that while regulatory legislation could do much to improve bad housing, such legislation did not necessarily encourage the provision of new, good housing. Limited-dividend housing companies attempted to satisfy a part of this need.

These companies were predominantly philanthropic or civic in their underlying motive. An example was the City and Suburban Homes Company, organized in New York City in 1896. This company had among its shareholders a large number of the wealthiest men in the city, but it also invited others by establishing the denomination of the shares at $10. The original 4 percent return on invested capital was raised to 6 percent after World War I. Its object was to supply to wage earners in New York improved, sanitary housing at current rents. (The company also built some suburban homes, which could be purchased by the tenants and paid for in monthly installments over periods of ten, fifteen, or twenty years.) City and Suburban Homes was to become America's largest undertaking in the field of limited-dividend housing. (It was landlord to 3,000 families in 1917.)

Other examples of limited-dividend housing in the United States included the Boston Cooperative Building Company (1871), the Alfred T. White model tenements of Brooklyn (1878–1890), the Sanitary Improvement Company (1897), and the Sanitary Housing Company (1904) of Washington. Some authorities have indicated that the best results with regard to both rentals and standards were achieved by the Model Homes Company of Cincinnati (1911). Very few of the limited-dividend companies were active after World War I. Most of them were discouraged by the high cost of building.

Just as the Multiple Dwelling Law of New York lessened the restrictions on building there, other cities tended to be less strict in their enforcement of building laws during the period of rapid, confident growth of the 1920's. Colean states: "This relaxation contributed much to the deplorable state in which cities found themselves when interest in the housing problem was renewed in the early 1930's."[12]

PERIOD OF FEDERAL DOMINATION

It has been mentioned that the Federal Government's first important action in relation to housing was taken in 1892 when Congress passed a

[12] *Op. cit.*, p. 44.

resolution to provide $20,000 for an investigation of slums in cities of 200,000 people or more. The next major activity of the Federal Government occurred during World War I. There was an extreme shortage of housing for war workers, with the result that there was a high turnover of labor in war industries. Individual employers were unable to alleviate the situation under wartime conditions, and Congress was compelled to act. There was considerable debate, during which Senator Warren G. Harding proposed as an amendment to the bill that the rents to be charged would provide a profit of 6 percent on the government's investment. In May and June of 1918 Congress appropriated $50,000,000 (later increased to $75,000,000) to be used by the U. S. Shipping Board (Emergency Fleet Corporation) for housing for workers in shipyards, and $60,000,000 (later increased to $100,000,000) to be used by the U. S. Housing Corporation for housing for workers in munitions factories and related industries.

These funds, however, were not entirely used because the housing was not all built before the Armistice. A major controversy then began over the future of the two corporations. It was during this period that the first major battle occurred between those individuals who felt that the Federal Government *should* engage in housing activities which were needed and which private enterprise could not perform, and those individuals who felt that the Government *should not* engage in any aspects of the housing business. It was finally decided that the Federal Government should sell all of the properties that were not turned over to other government agencies. This battle did not flare up again until the Depression days of the early 1930's.

Before continuing this discussion on a chronological basis, let us jump ahead for a moment to 1949 when one of the major housing acts of recent years was passed. The reason for this leap is that the Act summarized so well the different facets of the housing problem in recent years. In the declaration of National Housing Policy set forth in that Act, we read:

> The Congress hereby declares that the *general welfare* and security of the nation and the health and living standards of its people *require* housing production . . . sufficient to remedy the serious housing shortage, the elimination of substandard and other inadequate housing through the clearance of slums and blighted areas, and the realization as soon as feasible of the goal of a decent home in a suitable living environment for *every* American family . . . [italics by author].

However, the Act then says:

> The policy to be followed in attaining the national housing objective . . . shall be: (1) *private enterprise* shall be encouraged to serve as large a part of the total need as it can; (2) governmental assistance shall be utilized where feasible to *enable private enterprise* to serve more of the total need; (3) appropriate *local public* bodies shall be encouraged and assisted to undertake positive programs . . . ; (4) *governmental assistance* to eliminate substandard and other inadequate housing through the clearance of slums and blighted areas, . . . shall be extended to those localities which estimate their own needs and demonstrate that these needs are not being met through reliance solely upon private enterprise, and without such aid; and (5) *governmental assistance* for decent, safe, and sanitary farm dwellings

and related facilities shall be extended where the farm owner demonstrates that he lacks sufficient resources to provide such housing on his own account and is unable to secure necessary credit for such housing from other sources on terms and conditions which he could reasonably be expected to fulfill. The Housing and Home Finance Agency and its constituent agencies, and any other departments or agencies of the Federal Government having powers, functions, or duties with respect to housing, shall exercise their powers, functions, and duties under this or any other law . . . [italics by author].

Three broad conclusions can be drawn from this statement of policy: (1) there can be little doubt that we currently consider that a housing problem exists, (2) that it is a problem for which we feel social responsibility, and (3) that it is currently considered the proper function of government to concern itself with the problem.

In other words, emphasis is placed on the role of private enterprise, in implementing this policy. Yet, private enterprise is to be given governmental assistance and encouragement, as the first opportunity, and should private enterprise fail, the alternative is clearly spelled out.

Although this policy was clearly spelled out in the Act of 1949, it was the same policy that had been more or less followed in legislation beginning in the 1930's.

The discussion that follows is organized on the basis of the priorities suggested in our national policy. Aids to private housing will be discussed first, to be followed by the discussions of public housing and urban renewal, both programs being heavily subsidized by the Federal Government.

Aids to Private Housing

The Depression of the 1930's, more than any other factor, brought the Federal Government into the housing picture on a broad, national scale. In 1931, President Hoover called the "President's Conference on Homebuilding and Home Ownership." This was followed, in July 1932, by the passage of the Federal Home Loan Bank Act (during the Hoover administration). Under this Act, this Board had authority to make advances to all types of lending institutions over the country. These advances were secured by first mortgages. It was the hope at the time that by providing these local lending institutions with a means of raising money there would be less necessity for foreclosures.

This effort, however, was not successful and, in 1933, nonfarm homes were being foreclosed at a rate of 1,000 a day. To meet the crisis, Congress passed the Home Owners' Loan Act of 1933.

Home Owners' Loan Corporation

The specific purpose of the Home Owners' Loan Act was to relieve the distress of homeowners faced with foreclosure, and to aid lending institutions. This was accomplished by the HOLC accepting poor-risk mortgages held by private financial institutions in exchange for HOLC bonds. The delinquent mortgages were, in effect, refinanced through the issuance to home owners of new mortgages at a lower interest rate (originally 5 percent, later 4½ percent) and with longer repayment periods. All obligations on the property, including unpaid taxes, were satisfied through the refinancing arrangements, permitting homeowners to start anew on their home-buying arrangements.

The HOLC remained in existence until 1951, although its refinancing operations ceased in 1937. During this period it made approximately one million loans, amounting to approximately 3 billion dollars. Of the total, only one fifth needed to be foreclosed and these properties were eventually resold. The HOLC operation was liquidated at a slight profit.[13]

Federal Housing Administration

One of the most important acts of Congress relating to housing was the National Housing Act passed in 1934. One of the purposes of this Act was to create a sounder mortgage system through the provision of a permanent system of government insurance for residential mortgages made on a long-term, amortized basis. Another purpose was that of "pump-priming," needed during this period when the rate of new construction was extremely low. The Federal Housing Administration was created to carry out these objectives of the Act.

The FHA does not itself lend money. However, it encourages lending institutions to loan money on both new and old residential properties by *insuring* their loans. This establishes the character of the agency, making it similar to a private insurance company. Accordingly, it requires "economic soundness" in any market where it operates. (This requirement was removed for housing for war workers, under wartime amendments to the Act. Recognition was given to the fact that the government should be more liberal at a time when housing needed to be provided in order that war production might not be impeded.)

The FHA operates through district and state "insuring" offices located in all states and territories. These offices process the mortgage loan applications received from approved lending institutions. Detailed plans and specifications for the house under consideration must be filed with the application. It is through a review of these plans that the agency determines whether the property meets the minimum requirements described in Chapter 8. Each dwelling unit is appraised by an FHA staff appraiser in order to determine its reasonable value, upon which the amount of the mortgage is ultimately based. For new construction, inspectors visit the site during the building operation in order to check conformance with plans and approve the quality of workmanship.

The agency insures mortgages on both sales and rental units, but over the years the sales program has been by far the largest from the standpoint of number of loans insured. In fact, from the inception of the FHA program

[13] For more detailed discussion, see C. Lowell Harriss, *History and Policies of the Home Owners' Loan Corporation.* New York: National Bureau of Economic Research, 1951.

through 1961, 85 percent of the mortgages insured have been for sales housing; in 1961, the proportion was 81 percent.[14]

There have been different programs over the years under which both sales and rental unit mortgages could be insured. The most prominent is known as the Section 203 program. It applies to homes for sale. In 1961, it represented 97 percent of all mortgages insured by FHA on sales housing and 79 percent of *all* the units insured under FHA programs in that year. The most prominent rental housing program is known as the Section 207 program. In 1961 this program included 58 percent of the rental units on which mortgages were insured, but only 10 percent of all units insured by the FHA.

Another important FHA program in recent years has been the Section 213 program. This program permits insurance on cooperative housing, discussed in Chapter 7. It began late in 1950, and has varied in volume considerably over the years since that date. Other FHA programs, including the program for mortgage insurance of urban renewal projects under Section 220 and the program of housing for the elderly under Section 231, are small in comparison to those described.

In recent years, the FHA has insured approximately one fifth of the mortgages on new nonfarm dwellings, which represented approximately 15 percent of the total home mortgage lending, as indicated in Chapter 5. Yet, as pointed out earlier, its impact has been much greater than that percentage would tend to indicate. It has influenced the programs of lending institutions and the national mortgage market. The standards it has established were discussed in Chapter 8. These have forced at least sound minimum design and better site planning. However, the FHA has not considered its role primarily one of requiring better housing *per se;* rather, the standards it has established have been required more because they represented sound mortgage lending practices.

The FHA has also contributed to improved appraisal standards, as against the "windshield" variety that was so common before the FHA came into existence.

Another important function of the Agency has been to insure qualified lending institutions against losses on loans made to finance the alteration, repair, improvement, or conversion of old homes. These are known as Title I loans.

Title I loans assist homeowners, but also are popular with lending institutions and materials suppliers. The maximum charge to the borrower is $5 per $100, or an effective interest rate of approximately 9.7 percent. There is little red tape in arranging such a loan between the homeowner and the lending institution. The ordinary FHA "insurance premium," charged on mortgages, is not required. Building material and equipment dealers have found these loans to be a useful means of developing a large volume of business. The maximum limit of these loans was placed at $3,500 and the

[14] This heavy concentration on sales housing has been criticized by some. See especially Charles Abrams, *The Future of Housing*. New York: Harper & Bros., 1946, pp. 224–225.

repayment period at five years (on single-family structures) under the Housing Act of 1956.

In 1961, approximately 855,600 such loans were made. This represented a decline from the one million annually during the years 1955 to 1960. The average amount of loan has been increasing slightly each year since the program began in 1934. During the period 1934–1939, loans averaged $353. By 1950 the amount increased to $479. In 1960, the average loan was $1,000.

By 1961, loans of larger amounts, with longer maturities, were considered needed to supplement Title I. As a result, the Housing Act of that year authorized the FHA to insure loans in amounts up to $10,000 per unit, payable up to terms of twenty years, at an interest rate not to exceed 6 percent.

Today, the original objective of the FHA has, by and large, been accomplished. A sound mortgage system has become established, with a policy of monthly amortization payments, longer repayment periods, and low interest rates on loans.

This is not to say that this phase of the government's operations will or should be abandoned. FHA mortgages are more commonly concentrated among families having lower incomes than those served by conventional mortgages. The FHA program tends to assure housing for the middle-income group. Furthermore, it is doubted that it will ever be *politically expedient* to abandon a program that has achieved such widespread acceptance, without any cost to the government (the FHA is one of the few government agencies that actually operates at a profit).

Veterans Administration

Another Federal agency playing an important role in postwar residential financing is the Veterans Administration.

In 1944 Congress passed the Servicemen's Readjustment Act, or as it became known, the "GI Bill of Rights." Its purpose was to assist returning veterans to purchase housing on a liberal basis. The primary requirement needed to qualify was evidence of income that would indicate good repayment possibilities.

Under this Act, the Veterans Administration can "guarantee" a part of a loan made by a lending institution—in 1963, the maximum guarantee was $7,500 or 60 percent of the loan. There was no provision regulating loan-to-value ratios, as required by the FHA.

From 1944 until 1950, the Act permitted combination VA–FHA loans. Under this arrangement veterans could purchase houses with a 100 percent loan, i.e., no down payment. For example, the FHA would insure the first 80 percent and the VA would guarantee the balance of 20 percent. After 1950, however, a family could no longer use both sources on a single loan.

There have been a number of other differences between the FHA and VA programs. The VA relies on local appraisers for determining valuation, and on lending institutions for determining quality of construction. The VA program is a temporary one, with an expiration date set by law. As indicated earlier, the interest rate is 5¼ percent on VA-guaranteed and 5¼ on FHA-insured loans, but on FHA-insured mortgages an additional ½ percent insurance premium is charged, bringing the total charge to an equivalent of 5¾ percent.

The VA program has declined significantly since 1957. In the last few years only 6 percent of the mortgages on new homes have been VA-guaranteed, compared with 30 percent at the peak of the program in 1955.

Home Loan Bank Board

Other governmental aids to private housing have been mentioned elsewhere, but their influence generally has not been as significant as that of the FHA and the VA. The Home Loan Bank Board, which had been a constituent unit of the Housing and Home Finance Agency until Congress made it independent in 1956, supervises the Federal Home Loan Banks, charters and supervises Federal Savings and Loan Associations, and operates the Federal Savings and Loan Insurance Corporation which insures the *accounts* of savings and loan associations and similar institutions. The HLBB does not insure mortgages or have the other direct relationships with the public that the FHA and VA have.

Federal National Mortgage Association

The operations of the Federal National Mortgage Association were described in Chapter 5, under the discussion of the secondary mortgage market. FNMA had several predecessors before it assumed its present form.[15] The Federal Government, under Title III of the Housing Act of 1934, made an effort to promote the creation of an adequate secondary market for mortgages on residential housing. At that time, many financial institutions had reached the limit for home mortgages in their portfolios and therefore needed a market for their mortgages so that they would have liquid funds to finance additional new construction. In addition, lender confidence in the new FHA-insured mortgages was found lacking.

This Act provided for the establishment of national mortgage associations which were to be private organizations, operating under the supervision of the FHA and authorized to borrow money needed for their programs through the public sale of notes, bonds, debentures, and so on.

In 1935 the Reconstruction Finance Corporation created the RFC Mortgage Company "to assist in the re-establishment of a normal mortgage market." In 1938, the Federal National Mortgage Association, as we know it, was established, largely because no private mortgage associations were formed under the authorization of the 1934 Act. The RFC Mortgage Company continued to purchase certain FHA-insured mortgages which were not eligible under the new Association. It also purchased VA-guaranteed mortgages until 1947. In 1948, the FNMA program was extended to include these mortgages.

[15] "Background and History of the Federal National Mortgage Association," Washington, D.C.: Federal National Mortgage Association, April 30, 1955 (mimeo).

FNMA remained a subsidiary of the RFC until September 1950, when it was transferred to the Housing and Home Finance Agency. Under the Housing Act of 1954 its borrowing authority was substantially modified. The Association now conducts the major part of the government's secondary market operations for residential housing mortgages.

The operations of FNMA have been especially important in recent years because of the scarcity of investors who are interested in acquiring residential mortgages. The large-scale production of urgently needed housing has been materially facilitated, and often made possible, through the availability of FNMA's financial assistance.

Community Facilities Administration

This constituent agency of the Housing and Home Finance Agency is included here as one of the agencies providing aids to private housing because of its program of housing for the elderly, known as the Section 202 program (mentioned earlier in Chapter 13). Under this program, which was created under the Housing Act of 1959, the Community Facilities Administration may make loans directly to nonprofit groups. The program provides low-interest, long-term loans to finance housing for persons sixty-two years of age and older. Loans may be repaid over periods up to fifty years. The maximum interest rate is one fourth of 1 percent above the average annual interest rate of all interest-bearing obligations of the United States Government. (This rate was 3⅜ percent in 1961.)

The Community Facilities Administration also administers a college housing program, a program of advances for public works planning, a public facility loan program, and a school construction program (as agent of the U.S. Office of Education).

The organization of all these agencies has changed from time to time. Prior to 1942 they were generally independent. In an Executive Order that year, however, the President established the National Housing Agency and placed, as constituent units under it, the Federal Housing Administration, the Federal Home Loan Bank Administration, and the Federal Public Housing Authority. In 1946 the Office of Housing Expediter was formally created under the Veteran's Emergency Housing Act as another agency. In 1947 the Housing and Home Finance Agency was created, succeeding the NHA (see Figure 29 for organization).

Federal Reserve Board and the Treasury Department

It was pointed out in Chapter 5 that the number of new housing units built in the nation during any given period can be regulated, in large part, by the Federal Government through the mediums of money, interest rates, and terms. Directly or indirectly, the amount of money in the secondary mortgage market can be controlled in large part by the policies of the Federal National Mortgage Association; and the interest rates and terms can be controlled, also in large part, by the policies of the Federal Housing

Administration and the Veterans Administration. However, the policies of these agencies are, in turn, governed by two other agencies, the Federal Reserve Board and the Treasury Department, which control our national fiscal policy and are responsible for the delicate balance of our economy. Because of the significance placed upon the level of residential construction in our economy, these two agencies, as of any particular moment, have an extremely significant influence on the housing situation of the nation.

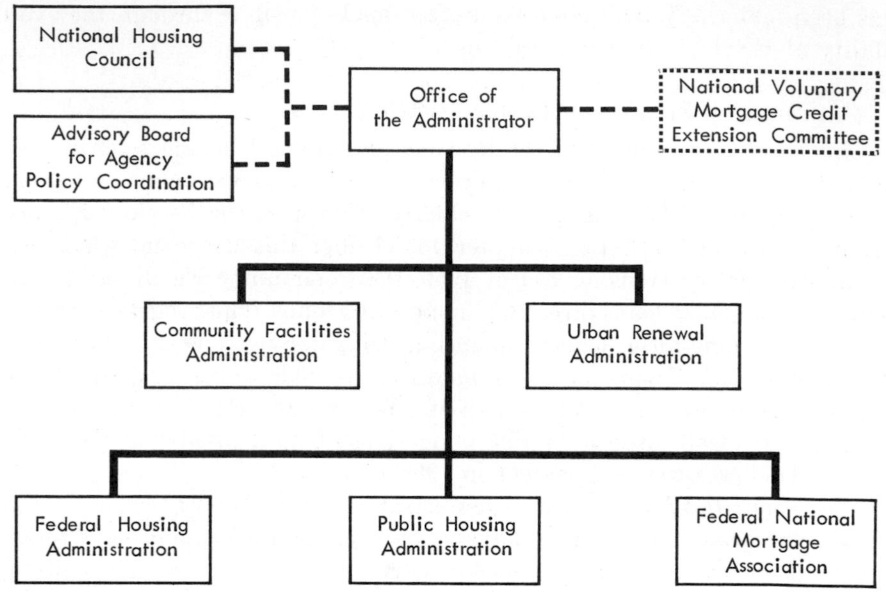

FIGURE 29. *Organization chart of the Housing and Home Finance Agency.*

Public Housing

It was mentioned earlier in this chapter that the role of the Federal Government in the field of housing has been controversial from the start. This controversy has not so much involved the aids provided to private housing, because those aids were admittedly designed to assist "private enterprise." However, the controversy has been strong concerning the public housing and slum clearance programs.

Even though our cities faced some of their most serious problems in the need to provide housing for low-income families and the need for slum clearance in the 1930's, and although there was considerable public recognition that something should be done about these problems, the philosophy of *laissez faire* was still strong. The writings of Adam Smith, Herbert Spencer, and William Graham Sumner were widely quoted and their tenets widely held during that period. It is not necessary to present more than a couple of quotations from Sumner's writings to illustrate his general philosophy. One of these is: "Before the tribunal of nature, a man has no more right to life than a rattlesnake; he has no more right to liberty than any wild beast . . .'' Another: ''Let every man be sober, industrious, prudent, and wise, and bring up his children to be so likewise, and poverty will be abolished in a few generations.''[16] These are strong statements, and they are included here only to give the reader an idea of the strong feelings of some of the prominent people of the time.

It is well to bear in mind the philosophy supported by these statements, because that philosophy has been continually in the foreground whenever housing subsidized directly by the Federal Government has been under discussion in the Congress of the United States.

Public housing, as we know it today, had its beginning in the United States under the Emergency Relief and Construction Act of 1932, which authorized the Reconstruction Finance Corporation to make loans to corporations formed to provide housing for families of low income. Only two loans were made under this law, one to finance Knickerbocker Village in New York City and the other to finance some rural homes in Ford County, Kansas. Undoubtedly, one of the reasons for such limited success was lack of sufficient inducement, in the form of adequate return on investment, to interest capital. The housing built also was above the reach of the families for whom it was intended.

Public Works Administration

The following year, Congress passed the National Industrial Recovery Act to stimulate employment during the Depression. This Act authorized the use of Federal funds to finance low-cost housing, slum clearance, and subsistence homesteads. Under this Act, the Public Works Administration, engaging in direct housing construction, built some fifty low-rent public housing projects in thirty-seven cities. These projects accommodated approximately 21,600 families. In addition, this Act provided for 15,000 units in resettlement projects in the three Greenbelt towns (Greenbelt, Maryland; Greendale, Wisconsin; and Greenhills, Ohio). Loans were also made to a number of limited-dividend projects. *The need for creating jobs, rather than the need for adequate housing,* per se, *was the principal reason for this housing construction.*

One of the major problems the PWA faced was acquiring land. A number of adverse court decisions limited the power of the Federal Government to condemn land for housing or other purposes, indicating that the power of eminent domain was a power to be exercised by the states.[17] These decisions were responsible for the establishment of the local housing authorities we have today, under state-enabling legislation, in order that the problem of land acquisition might be surmounted. Still, the program ran into many

[16] These two quotations are from Sumner's articles ''The Boon of Nature'' and ''The Abolition of Poverty,'' in Albert G. Keller and Maurice R. Davie, eds., *Essays.* New Haven: Yale University Press, 1934, pp. 385 and 109. Source: Lewis Lattin Bower, ''An Examination of the Emergence, Development, and Current State of Urban Land Use Theory.'' Unpublished D.S.S. dissertation, Syracuse University, 1964.

[17] *U.S. v. Certain Lands in City of Louisville,* 78 F. (2d) 684, 1935; *U.S. v. Certain Lands in City of Detroit,* 12 Fed. Supp. 345, 1935; *In the Matter of the Acquisition of All Privately Owned Land, Etc.,* 63 Wash. Law Rep. 822, 1935.

problems and its principal contribution was in the important pioneering task it undertook.

In 1935 and 1936, there was a considerable increase in home building throughout the nation, but most of the new construction was limited to houses built for owner occupancy. The building of rental units lagged. Also, the units being built for owner occupancy did not meet the needs of low-income families and did not assist in clearing slums.

Public Housing Administration

This demand brought about the United States Housing Act of 1937, under which the United States Housing Authority was created. Under the USHA, the concept of building housing for low-income families changed rather drastically from the PWA projects. The USHA, succeeded in 1942 by the Federal Public Housing Authority and in 1947 by the Public Housing Administration, provided loans and annual contributions to local public housing agencies for low-rent housing and slum-clearance projects. Since aid could only be provided to public bodies, local housing authorities were established under state-enabling legislation for the purpose of building and operating these projects.

The 1937 law prescribed certain conditions for eligibility and specific preferences in the selection of tenants by local housing authorities. They remained in force until 1961, when they were eliminated and local housing authorities were given the responsibility of determining policies for admission of tenants. As stated in the Senate Committee report commenting on the Housing Act of 1961:

> Local housing authorities have had many years of experience under these Federal regulations and should be relied upon to be competent and fair; and there is no question that they are in a much better position than the Federal Government to ascertain the myriad factors which may be involved in a particular situation and to determine their proper weight.

At the same time, the 1961 Act stipulated that the housing authorities were to give full consideration to:

> . . . its responsibility for the rehousing of those displaced by urban renewal or other governmental action, to the applicant's status as a serviceman or veteran or relationship to a serviceman or veteran, or to a disabled serviceman or veteran, and to the applicant's age or disability, housing conditions, urgency of housing need, and source of income.

Each local authority decides how to meet this responsibility, whether by setting up conditions for eligibility, by preferences, or by using both methods.

A basic requirement of Federal law is that only families of low income may be housed in public housing projects. By statute, the term "families" is defined to mean "families and certain categories of single persons (elderly, disabled, or the remaining member of a tenant family)." However, the local housing authority has the power to determine what constitutes low income (subject to PHA approval). The income limits are determined on basis of the number of persons in a family and the annual family income after exemptions. (Payments of the United States Government for disability or death in connection with military service are exemptions most frequently permitted by the local authorities. Other exemptions permitted by various local authorities are usually incomes or benefits not considered as fully available to the head of the family, such as part of the income of children and of adult secondary wage earners. Allowances, usually $100, may be made for a dependent family member.)

The median income limit for admission to public housing was, at the end of 1961, $3,200 for a family of average size; i.e., husband, wife, and two children.

In addition to establishing income limits as a means of determining eligibility, the local authority has the option of making other stipulations. Among these are the requirement of a minimum period of residence in the locality, a limitation on assets, or similar restrictions.[18]

There are construction cost restrictions for these projects. The 1937 law also contained an ''equivalent elimination'' provision, that is, for the public housing units built, a substantially equal number of unsafe or unsanitary units in the community must be eliminated, repaired, or closed.

Public housing has been opposed, largely by real estate groups and builders, because it has been interpreted as a move toward socialization of housing in this country and, they allege, it competes with private housing despite the 20 percent noncompetition gap required between new public and standard private housing. The contention by some is that much of the need of the low-income families can be met through the ''filtration'' process (discussed in Chapter 10), and through remodeling and rehabilitation of old houses (which would be discouraged by construction of new, subsidized housing). They also question whether families of low income should be provided with better housing than families at the income level immediately above them. They allege that in practice, the needs of the lowest-income groups have not been met by the public housing that has been built, since local project managers prefer to accept tenants whose rent-paying ability is assured. (This practice in effect prevents occupancy by welfare families and possibly others who do not have stable occupations—groups perhaps most seriously in need of such housing.) They claim that the tax exemption granted government projects works an additional hardship on owners of properties, since they are required to pay property taxes. This whole controversy is discussed in more detail later in this chapter.

The question of exact need is a difficult one and there remain many problems regarding the public housing program which deserve extensive research and considerably more attention than they have been given. However, the program has provided decent shelter for many families who could not otherwise have afforded it.

The Housing Act of 1949 amended the United States Housing Act of 1937

[18] The source of the above is *15th Annual Report,* Housing and Home Finance Agency, *op. cit.,* p. 211.

and authorized a broader public housing program. Under this Act, Federal contributions and loans were authorized for a maximum of 810,000 low-rent public housing units over a six-year period. This authorized number of units has not been built, however, since Congress did not subsequently appropriate the funds needed for the construction. As of December 31, 1962, there were 646,600 units of Federally-aided public housing under management, or in preconstruction or construction stages. Of this number, 525,679 were built and being managed (318,931 units built under Public Law 171, the Housing Act of 1949; 114,185 under PL 412; 46,735 under PL 671; 21,067 under PL 11, 67 (PWA); 24,178 under PL 475; and 583 in farm labor camps). Another 42,507 were under construction and 78,414 were in a preconstruction stage.[19] Some state programs, notably in New York State, have provided similar assistance.

The question arises: If public housing is not provided, what are the alternatives? One of the alternatives that has been suggested from time to time is public assistance in the nature of rent certificates. Advocates of this plan would have local welfare agencies issue a grant (in the form of a "rent certificate") to bridge the gap between what the family can afford to pay and the rent charged for suitable private housing. This aid would be given only to needy families, for the period of their actual need, and the funds would be restricted so that they could be used only for rental payments. There would be some control over rents charged, so that profits to the owner would be kept at a reasonable level.

Although there has been no experience with this type of plan for low-income families in the United States, the principal drawback would seem to be that it probably would not bring up the standard of poor housing appreciably. It would be difficult to administer such a program, and the costs are unknown. This type of subsidy also tends to run counter to some commonly accepted public welfare principles.

Another alternative has been the encouragement of housing cooperatives. Some efforts have been made to stimulate this type of housing in the United States, as already mentioned. It is highly questionable, however, whether large groups of low-income families could ever be thus accommodated. Still other alternatives are family income subsidies (which would have drawbacks similar to those described for the rent certificate plan) and the use of capital grants (used by the PWA). Several European countries have had experience with most of these plans (see Chapter 16).

Public housing, after years as a social reform movement in the United States, has neither taken hold nor died off—the usual alternatives for such programs. In Catherine Bauer's words: "But public housing, after more than two decades, still drags along in a kind of limbo, continuously controversial, not dead but never more than half alive."[20] In her critical reassessment of the program to date, she concludes, among other things ". . . public

[19] Figures from HHFA-PHA Program Planning Division, Statistics Branch, released January 16, 1963.

[20] Catherine Bauer, "The Dreary Deadlock of Public Housing," *Architectural Forum*, Vol. 106, No. 5, May 1957, p. 140.

landlordship might have been given up and in any case it should have been possible to subsidize various forms of private housing enterprise, including suburban tracts for individual ownership, in order to meet a wider range of need and popular desire (and, incidentally, to bring some private building interests over to advocacy of public housing).''[21] Her recent arguments have been supported by Abrams, who is also intimately acquainted with the United States housing problem and who also has been a most influential proponent of public housing over the years.[22]

It seems inevitable that public housing policy will be re-examined, from a comprehensive point of view. Not only will the matter of financing and sponsorship some day be re-examined, but attention will undoubtedly also be focused on such matters as physical design and management—all problems under the present program.

Slum Clearance and Urban Renewal

Early History of Slum Clearance

Although the Congress gave some evidence of its concern regarding our slums as early as 1892, little attention was directed to this problem until the President's Conference on Home Building and Home Ownership, held in December 1931, during the Hoover administration.

Although the matter of slums did not appear to justify inclusion in the title of that Conference, nevertheless one of the committees, Committee No. 8, devoted its attention to this subject. This Committee studied: ''(1) the causes which have produced blighted areas, particularly those that contain slums; (2) how these areas can be converted into desirable neighborhoods; and (3) how the growth of blighted areas and slums can be prevented in the future.''[23]

However, the laissez-faire philosophy so prevalent at the time seems to have been an extremely important factor in influencing the legislative suggestions developed by this Committee. We read, ''This committee lists many projects that require legislation but, because of their controversial character, withholds recommendations.''[24] Abrams summarized the accomplishments of the conference: ''They produced a twelve-volume report instead of a two-page appropriation bill which might have accomplished something constructive.''[25]

There was no direct Federal action until the United States Housing Act

[21] *Ibid.*, pp. 219, 221.

[22] See, for example, his suggestion for a re-examination of the original theories of public housing in ''Public Housing Myths,'' *The New Leader*, Vol. XXXVIII, No. 30, July 25, 1955, pp. 3–6.

[23] John M. Gries and James Ford, eds., *Slums, Large-Scale Housing and Decentralization*, Vol. III, The President's Conference on Home Building and Home Ownership, Washington, D.C., 1932, p. 1.

[24] John M. Gries and James Ford, eds., *Housing Objectives and Programs*, Vol. XI, The President's Conference on Home Building and Home Ownership, Washington, D.C., 1932, p. 107.

[25] Charles Abrams, *The Future of Housing*, *op. cit.*, p. 211.

of 1937 which, through its requirement of eliminating one slum dwelling for every new unit built under the USHA program, pointed toward the removal of some slum housing. Some states followed (Illinois' Neighborhood Redevelopment Corporation law and New York's Urban Redevelopment Corporation law, both enacted in 1941), but it was not until the Housing Act of 1949 that Federal slum clearance legislation, in any comprehensive form, was passed. Title I of this Act recognized slums as a national problem.

Under this Act, loans and grants were made to a local public agency, such as the local housing authority, a special redevelopment agency, or a department of the city. That local agency was authorized (under the redevelopment laws of its state) to carry out a slum-clearance program. In order to prevent the recurrence of slums as well as to eliminate them, the community was required to have a general plan for the development of the community as a whole. This was to include the modernization of building codes and other city controls, including health and safety codes and land-use regulations. The community also was required to make provision for the rehousing of displaced families.

The Federal Government could meet up to two thirds of the cost incurred in buying, clearing, and preparing slum lands and disposing of them for redevelopment. The city would need to make up the balance, either through payment in cash or by contributing land, services, or improvements for the project.

One of the difficulties with the program under this Act, however, was that no clear consensus existed as to its primary goals or, for that matter, the means of achieving them. Catherine Bauer wrote at the time:

> One reason Title I and the state enabling acts had so little opposition is the fact that different groups of people, like the blind men feeling the elephant, made entirely different assumptions as to the essential nature and purpose of this legislation.
>
> To the housers and social welfare groups it simply extended our power to get rid of bad living conditions and provide everyone with a decent home in a decent neighborhood. To most of those who started the "urban redevelopment" movement, however, . . . the goals were quite different, namely, to bolster up waning property values in central areas and to devise a substitute for the Housing Act of 1937 that would facilitate slum clearance, but *without* public housing. . . .
>
> The leaders of the city planning profession had still a different idea. They saw redevelopment as the means toward more rational and efficient organization of central areas, by removing wasteful or inappropriate land uses and facilitating new development in conformance with some kind of plan for the area. . . .
>
> All in all, quite an array of purposes for a single piece of legislation to fulfil! Seldom has such a variegated crew of would-be angels tried to sit on the same pin at the same time. As it turned out, the legislative framework reflects mainly a kind of shotgun marriage between the housers and the planners. . . .[26]

In the Housing Act of 1954, the financial aids described above were con-

[26] Catherine Bauer, "Redevelopment: A Misfit in the Fifties," in Coleman Woodbury, ed., *The Future of Cities and Urban Redevelopment*. Chicago: University of Chicago Press, 1953, p. 9.

tinued and additional emphasis was placed on prevention of the spread of blight into good areas of the community. This was to be accomplished through strict enforcement of housing and neighborhood standards and the rehabilitation of salvable areas by replanning, removing congestion, providing parks and playgrounds. This program is discussed below.

Urban Renewal

Urban renewal is the Federal Government's most recent attempt, based upon the experience and philosophy developed during the past quarter of a century, to cope with the problem of urban America's housing needs. This program came into official existence as part of the Housing Act of 1954, which amended the previous legislation of 1949. Just as the 1949 law recognized that slums were a national problem, the Act of 1954 recognized the causes of slum formation, and the interwoven role of Federal, state, and local governments and institutions within the broad program of slum prevention and clearance.

This program includes the individual efforts of the owner-occupant, of the tenant and landlord, of private enterprise, of the local and Federal governments and their agencies. It involves the upgrading of local laws and regulations, strict enforcement of existing and new laws, citizen participation, encouragement and inducement of lending institutions and other private businesses to participate, the establishment of local Urban Renewal administrative offices, and the encouragement of better community planning. The law also establishes machinery for granting financial aid to communities that are willing to consider seriously and act on their problems of urban decay.

The urban renewal concept had been taking shape in the thinking of city planners and housing officials for many years and finally found expression in the Housing Act of 1954. Urban renewal procedures require a great deal of government action, such as the acquisition of land, the establishment and enforcement of laws and regulations, the planning of all physical developments, and so on. Private enterprise has seldom been motivated to undertake such projects. Therefore, urban renewal has been based on public interest and welfare rather than private enterprise. The new Federal program deals with the specific problems of residential areas: the slum, which is to be cleared and redeveloped; the generally run-down area found near the slums, which is to be prevented from becoming a future slum by upgrading and rehabilitation; the stable area, which is to be maintained and prevented from developing problems of urban decay by the enforcement of the necessary laws and the encouragement of the proper neighborhood spirit; and the incorporation of good planning methods in order to eliminate slum-producing factors in new and existing residential developments.

In order to take part in this program, and become eligible for the various Federal aids and benefits, the local community must take the initiative and establish a "workable program"[27] for itself. The Federal program outlines

[27] Housing and Home Finance Agency, *How Localities Can Develop a Workable Program for Urban Renewal.* Washington, D.C.: U.S. Government Printing Office, 1955, rev. 1956.

the basic principles of a proper development and renewal scheme, and makes adherence to the principles a primary requisite for receiving financial and administrative assistance. The seven basic principles outlined were as follows:

1. THE PROVISION FOR ADEQUATE LOCAL LEGISLATION AND ENFORCEMENT. The community must establish adequate minimum standards of health, sanitation, and safety, for dwellings which are to be lawfully occupied, since the vigorous enforcement of proper standards will of itself do much to aid in the long-run prevention of slum formation and spread. These laws are to include *minimum housing standards,* which prescribe the minimum conditions under which dwellings are to be occupied, such as minimum space requirements for each occupant, basic sanitation, light and ventilation, structural requirements, heating requirements, and the safe and sanitary maintenance of the building and its facilities.

Where building standards do not exist, they are to be established, and where they do exist, they are to be enforced. It must be remembered that in many instances the problem is not lack of regulations, but rather, lack of proper enforcement. This aspect of the program brings into play the local governmental role in inspection and enforcement, and makes these standards the responsibility of the local community.

2. ESTABLISHMENT OF A PROPER PLAN FOR COMMUNITY DEVELOPMENT. The formulation of an official community plan is basic to the whole program of urban renewal. In those communities where planning is either inadequate or nonexistent, appropriate agencies must be set up and a comprehensive community plan developed to guide the future physical growth.

3. A STUDY OF THE COMMUNITY'S NEIGHBORHOODS. This includes an inventory of the residential areas in order to determine the type of action to be taken—conservation, rehabilitation, or redevelopment—as well as an examination of the neighborhood facilities. The study involves analysis of type of occupancy, and environmental conditions, such as traffic and street arrangements, extent of undesirable encroachments, zoning, and other elements affecting the neighborhood.

4. ADMINISTRATION OF THE "WORKABLE PROGRAM." In order that this program may be activated, it is necessary to establish the administrative agencies to make the required inspection and surveys that are to be the basis for enforcement of the regulatory laws, primarily the minimum housing standards. It is necessary, for full effectiveness, that all aspects of the program be coordinated and that clear-cut lines of authority be established.

5. THE FINANCING OF THE PROGRAM. The community must take into consideration the costs involved in undertaking such a program, and must work out a means of financing it, so that all the conditions of the formulated program can be met. This includes not only the cost of inspections, surveys, enforcement of codes, and the establishment of a community plan with an agency to carry out the necessary planning work, but consideration of slum clearance and rehabilitation costs from the standpoint of providing and

improving community facilities, the acquisition of land, and various other elements of the program.

6. The problem of displacing families. In implementing the program, many displaced families will need to be relocated. This applies especially in cases of redevelopment and less so in rehabilitation. It is, therefore, necessary to consider the housing resources of the community as a whole, and devise a program before relocation becomes necessary in order that proper housing will be available to those families which are to be displaced. This may necessitate a piecemeal approach to the basic program if communities find their existing supply of housing inadequate.

7. Citizen participation. Because the program is to be a community effort, and in order to maintain the long-term enthusiasm necessary for successful urban renewal, it is extremely important that effective citizen participation be secured. Widespread participation of community and neighborhood groups is a "must" at the outset of the program and should be so organized as to permit it to continue indefinitely. The establishment of a citizen's advisory committee and the organization and incorporation of neighborhood groups is essential to the complete understanding by the community of the goals of its urban renewal program.

Once a community is prepared to carry out an urban renewal program it can obtain Federal financial assistance and technical aids to supplement local resources. The five principal types of financial aids are as follows:[28]

1. Grants to pay up to two thirds of the cost of preparing community renewal programs, as authorized by the Housing Act of 1959. These programs identify and measure the slums and blighted areas in an entire community, evaluate the financial and other resources needed to improve such areas, and schedule the types of activity—both with and without Federal assistance—that appear to be required.

2. Planning advances to finance surveys and plans for specific urban renewal areas and projects, surveys to determine whether urban renewal projects will be feasible, and the preparation of general neighborhood renewal plans. This involves initial survey and analysis of areas of existing slum or blight. From these analyses, the boundaries of proposed projects are delineated, and decisions are made for new land uses in the area, including the degree to which rehabilitation of existing structures is feasible and the extent to which clearance and redevelopment will be necessary. After a determination that the project is eligible for assistance, that it is feasible, and that the relocation and other statutory requirements can be met, the local public agency prepares detailed plans for land acquisition, site improvements, relocation of families, land disposition, and estimates of project cost and financing.

[28] Much of the following summary is from "Progress Report on Federal Housing Programs." Hearing before a Subcommittee of the Committee on Banking and Currency, United States Senate, Eighty-Seventh Congress, Second Session. Washington, D.C.: U.S. Government Printing Office, August 29, 1962, pp. 106-108.

Advances are repayable with interest from funds becoming available for the execution of urban renewal projects.

3. TEMPORARY LOANS AND FEDERAL GUARANTEES OF PRIVATE LOANS TO PROVIDE WORKING CAPITAL FOR CARRYING OUT URBAN RENEWAL PROJECTS. Commitments for temporary loans are made to assist local public agencies by providing for the interim financing necessary to carry out an urban renewal project. Such loans are repaid with interest from funds derived from borrowings from private sources, or from funds received as proceeds of the sale or lease of project land, Federal capital grants, or local cash grants-in-aid.

Borrowings from non-Federal sources for project expenditures are made where loans can be obtained from private sources at interest rates lower than specified in the contract for direct Federal borrowings. The Federal loan commitment is pledged by the local public agency as security for such a private loan. Most communities arrange to utilize this method of financing after the initial months of project operations, since the lower interest costs of non-Federal borrowings reduce project costs.

4. GRANTS TO COVER THE COST OF RELOCATING FAMILIES, INDIVIDUALS, BUSINESS CONCERNS, AND NONPROFIT ORGANIZATIONS DISPLACED FROM URBAN RENEWAL AREAS. One of the basic objectives of the urban renewal program is the proper rehousing of families displaced from urban renewal projects. Of particular concern is the need to assure the availability of decent, safe, and sanitary housing to such families. The Housing Act of 1956, as amended, authorized Federal grants to reimburse local public agencies for relocation payments to displaced individuals, families, business concerns, and nonprofit organizations for reasonable and necessary moving expenses and any actual direct losses of property with the exception of good will and profit. Such payments are currently limited to $200 for individuals or families and to $3,000 (or, if greater, the total certified actual moving expenses) in the case of business concerns or nonprofit organizations.

In general, statistics would indicate that relocation efforts have evidenced a respectable record, almost 80 percent of all families relocated being placed in standard housing. In some areas, however, unforeseen difficulties have resulted in many families' finding it necessary to move into inadequate or substandard housing.

5. GRANTS TO COVER FROM TWO THIRDS UP TO THREE FOURTHS OF THE NET COST OF CARRYING OUT URBAN RENEWAL PROJECTS. In the main, these costs reflect the writedown of slum property values to a level permitting redevelopment of the project area by private enterprise for the new uses specified by the urban renewal plan. For any municipality having a population of 50,000 or less (or 150,000 or less for a municipality in a redevelopment area designated as such under Section 5(a) of the Area Redevelopment Act of 1961), the Federal contribution is three fourths of net project cost. For any other municipality, the Federal contribution is two thirds of net project costs. In these latter communities, however, the Federal share may be increased to three fourths if the locality elects to exclude from project cost all local administrative, legal, survey, and planning expenses.

Local grants-in-aid for the remaining portion of new project costs may consist of cash, donations at cash value of land or other real property, demolition and removal work, installation of necessary site improvements, or the provision of public buildings (or other public facilities) necessary to accomplish the approved urban renewal plan for the area. In addition, certain expenditures made by colleges, universities, or hospitals for acquisition of land in or near an urban renewal project, demolition or rehabilitation of the buildings, and relocation of the occupants, are eligible as local grants-in-aid.

Where it is feasible to carry out an urban renewal project without direct Federal financial assistance, special mortgage insurance may still be provided by FHA under Section 220 of the National Housing Act. One of the requirements for such insurance is that the project area be covered by a locally developed urban renewal plan which has been approved by the Administrator.

In the last few years, new and important emphasis has been placed upon the maximum use of conservation and rehabilitation techniques in carrying out programs of urban renewal and revitalization. In urban renewal projects where existing structures are hopelessly deteriorated or land uses are incompatible with the community's over-all plans, the entire area may be acquired, cleared, and sold for redevelopment. Where existing structures are basically sound but have deteriorated to the point where they are a blighting influence on the neighborhood, they may be salvaged through a program of rehabilitation and reconditioning. Special FHA mortgage insurance is available to aid in financing structural rehabilitation. In addition, the locality may with Federal assistance upgrade the project area by the provision of community facilities (such as schools, parks, playgrounds, streets, and sewers) to make it a better place in which to live and work as well as to raise and stabilize property values.

The Housing Act of 1961 authorized rehabilitation demonstration projects in order to provide one effective way of minimizing renewal costs, and also as a way of treating evidences of deterioration and blight in time to prevent the further spread of slum areas. One of the features of the rehabilitation and conservation approach, though perhaps a minor one from the standpoint of the number of dwellings involved, is the preservation of historic sites and areas. This is a tool through which historic structures can be retained and preserved. Examples of its use are Philadelphia's Washington Square East project, Wooster Square in New Haven, Providence's Lippett Hill area, and Portsmouth, New Hampshire's "Strawberry Banke."

Funds for the payment of urban renewal grants are provided by appropriations. The original Title I authorization provided for an aggregate grant contract amount of $500,000,000. The authorization had been increased under amendatory statutes to a cumulative total of 4 billion dollars by 1962.

Progress made under the Federal urban renewal program has been slow, but a total of 520 cities were participating in it in one degree or another by the end of 1961. More than 60 percent were cities under 50,000 population, and about 20 percent had fewer than 10,000 inhabitants. A total of 944 Title I projects had been approved in these cities, involving Federal grants estimated at $2,295,000,000. Of these 944 projects, 518 were in execution and 361 were in various stages of planning. The remaining 65 projects were either completed or well under way.

Other Federal Government Activities

The other roles of the Federal Government probably are not as important today as the three mentioned above, but each has had its significance.

Defense and War Housing

The "defense" period of 1940–1942 brought with it special housing needs. Many new workers needed to be brought into localities having defense industries and stepped-up military activity. The families had to be housed, and the Federal Government became the largest landlord and housing manager in history.

Apparently the public and the lobbying groups usually opposing direct government intervention in housing matters recognized the exigencies of war, since the government program did not run into the same obstacles and controversy that had been experienced under similar circumstances in 1917 and 1918. More than 1,900,000 dwelling units were produced for war workers and their families under the government's vast defense and war housing program. More than half of this total was financed and built by private builders. The balance was publicly aided.

The most prominent legislation during this period was the Lanham Act, passed in 1940. Under this Act and related statutes, both permanent and temporary public housing were authorized for essential war workers. Nearly all of the permanent public war housing was built before Pearl Harbor. Temporary housing (that is, housing that was unsuited for long-term use) was built near military establishments and war industries where there was a great influx of personnel and labor. This housing was put up quickly, at minimum cost, and frequently utilized inferior materials since a permanent need was not expected. It included family units, dormitories, and trailers.

The law required that the temporary war housing be removed as promptly as possible when it was no longer needed. Removal was mandatory not later than two years after the end of the emergency, unless the government, in consultation with the local community, found it was needed for a longer period of time.

Because of the extreme housing shortage after World War II, the disposition of this housing moved slowly, and a few projects are still occupied today. In some instances, localities determined that the housing was satisfactory for long-term use (which was permitted under a later revision of the law), and acquired the projects.

The Lanham Act permitted the conveyance of *permanent* projects to local housing authorities for low-rent use for low-income families. A need for the housing had to be demonstrated in the community. Most of these projects were made up of multifamily structures. Some, however, consisted of individual houses, two-family houses, or group houses. In selling these units, the Public Housing Administration encouraged individual home ownership, especially by veterans.

The public war-housing program also included 35,000 trailers, which were first used as temporary emergency housing for veterans and servicemen, and then disposed of by the War Assets Administration. It also included approximately 49,000 apartment units which were converted from existing structures (to save money and building materials), and which were returned ultimately to their original owners under terms of the leases.

All war housing, after 1942, was "programed" for communities; i.e., the need, type of ownership, proportion for rent or sale, price range, number of units, and location were determined by the National Housing Agency. First priority was given to private construction (which produced over a million units under the liberalized credit terms of Title VI of the National Housing Act), and the balance of the units were earmarked for public construction. During this period, all building materials were allocated by the War Production Board. Price controls, including rent controls, were determined by the Office of Price Administration.

Naturally, the war situation—and the war *housing* situation—had an impact on all communities. This problem has been discussed in detail in other volumes, and is not considered to be within the scope of this discussion.[29]

Veterans Emergency Housing

Because of the heavy demands for housing in urban areas during the war, and the low volume of new construction resulting from the scarcity of building materials, there was an extreme housing shortage in the nation at the war's end when millions of veterans returned home and sought a place to live.

The 1944 "GI Bill of Rights" has already been described. In 1946 Congress enacted the Veteran's Emergency Housing Act, in order to encourage the construction of more housing for returning veterans. An Office of the Housing Expediter was formally created by Congress, and the Expediter was given broad powers to establish selling prices and rents for new houses and to allocate priorities for the delivery of materials or facilities for constructing those houses. The Reconstruction Finance Corporation was authorized to make premium payments to producers of building materials, in order to step up the production of certain types of house construction materials. The RFC was also authorized to guarantee the market for new types of building materials and for prefabricated houses. Veterans were granted preference for the new housing built.

The Veteran's Emergency Housing Program was a zealous one, planning for 2,700,000 new homes during 1946 and 1947—which would have been the

[29] One study of a war area that underwent extreme change is Lowell J. Carr and James E. Stermer, *Willow Run*. New York: Harper & Bros., 1952.

highest home-building rate in the nation's history up to that time. The program was to depend primarily on private enterprise. It had three major objectives: (1) to stimulate the production of building materials, (2) to see that adequate quantities of such materials were directed into housing, and (3) to insure that veterans received the first benefits and that such housing was within their financial reach.[30]

The target for 1946 was 1,200,000 homes started, of which 700,000 were to be conventional units, 250,000 permanent prefabricated houses, or houses assembled from prefabricated parts, and 250,000 temporary units. A total of 1,500,000 starts were planned for 1947: 900,000 conventional houses and 600,000 prefabricated houses.

A number of unprecedented devices were employed in an effort to meet these goals. For example, premium payments were promised industry for increased building material production, their markets for the materials were to be guaranteed by the Federal Government, priorities and allocations were established for equipment and materials, wage–price adjustments were to be made where necessary, war plants were to be made available for production, and so on. The markets for prefabricated houses also were to be guaranteed, as mentioned above, and loans were to be made by the Reconstruction Finance Corporation for both materials and prefabricated house construction.

One of the objectives of the program was low-cost housing. It was hoped that most of the homes would sell for not more than $6,000, and the apartments would rent for not more than $50 per month.

The program, however, was operative for only about five and one-half months—from the date of passage of the Veteran's Emergency Housing Act in the middle of May 1946 until price decontrol in November of the same year. Many of the controls were removed during the next seven months. In June 1947, Congress passed the Housing and Rent Control Act of 1947 which limited the Housing Expediter's responsibilities, concerning this program, to completion of government commitments with respect to existing guaranteed market contracts and certain premium payment contracts.

During 1946, 83 percent of the total number of units planned were actually started, but the proportion of various types of housing did not follow the pattern programed. The 700,000 conventional units were started (although this included 66,000 conversions), as were the 250,000 temporary units (including 47,100 trailers). However, only 37,200 of the planned 250,000 prefabricated houses were begun. The year 1947 saw a continuance of this high rate of construction. Output of the most critical building materials had increased from 50 percent to 100 percent during 1946.

From these data it can be seen that an outstanding stimulus had been provided to the home-building industry during this period. The program may have started the unprecedented climb to new all-time highs in volume construction. (This is necessarily a matter of conjecture, since it is not known how many units would have been started *without* the program.) The low-

[30] Nat Rogg, "A History of the Veteran's Emergency Housing Program," Office of the Housing Expediter, Washington, D.C., n.d. (mimeo).

cost objectives of the program definitely were not met. Most of the units built sold for well over the $6,000 limit. And the "factory-made" house aspects of the program were a bitter failure.[31]

The Veteran's Emergency Housing Program was ended prematurely because of changing postwar conditions. Probably the largest single factor in the abandonment of the program earlier than expected was the unfavorable public attitude toward the housing controls, which were more extensive than those during the war period. The role played by the RFC, with the liberal loan program it was asked to carry out (e.g., the Lustron case) was broadly criticized. At any rate, the only controls that were to continue were those on rents, and they remained highly controversial until 1952, when they were abandoned.

Farm Housing

Another important but seldom-emphasized role of the Federal Government has been assistance to farm housing.

In 1917 a system of Federal Land Banks was established to provide farmers with long-term mortgages at low interest rates. In 1933 these banks were placed under the supervision of the Farm Credit Administration (later made a division of the U. S. Department of Agriculture). Land bank loans could be made in amounts from $100 to $50,000, but not in excess of 65 percent of the appraised normal value of the farm, which served as security on the mortgage. These loans could be used to build or remodel farm buildings, including houses. Actually, only a small volume of loans was made for housing.

In the 1930's a host of other agencies were established which were authorized to make loans to farmers. The Production Credit Association (established under the FCA) was created in 1933 and could finance short-term loans for minor repairs and alterations of farm homes. The Division of Subsistence Homesteads was established as a unit of the Department of

[31] The best-known example of prefabricated homes started under this program was the Lustron home, made of steel. This house was conceived as more than prefabrication; it was to be an all-out attempt at mass production of an industrial house costing approximately $6,500 (without land), produced in a factory that could turn out 450 houses a day. It was financed by RFC loans exceeding $37,000,000. The design had a high degree of acceptability despite the fact that an unconventional material (steel) was used. However, problems of working out the technical difficulties of the house's design, tooling up the factory, establishing a vast marketing organization, and convincing lending institutions of the soundness and marketability of this new product, were so great that only 2,600 units had been produced and sold when the Federal Government refused additional financing needed to continue production in 1951. The operation had not yet reached the profit-making stage. The heavy government investment in this project, together with the small amount of capital invested by the single individual who was largely responsible for it and who became the President of the Lustron Corporation, was the source of many popular magazine articles at the time. (For example, one entitled "Lustron—The House that Lots of Jack Built" appeared in *Collier's* for November 5, 1949.) Many of these articles were critical of the financing details involved in setting up this massive operation, and they tended to give a poor image to the public of the entire venture. Few, if any, took equal cognizance of the attractiveness and livability of the house in relation to its cost (which averaged $10,000 rather than the $6,500 anticipated) and the possible impact of this experiment in mass production on the technology of housing if the venture had been allowed to continue over a longer period of time.

Interior, also in 1933. Under this program, communities of new homes were built, each with a small tract of land, ranging from ½ to 5 acres in size. (Although the houses were "rural," most of the families had urban employment.) The State Rural Rehabilitation Corporation, operating under the Federal Emergency Relief Administration in 1934 and 1935, attempted economic rehabilitation of rural families at their place of residence.

The Rural Electrification Administration, established in 1935, was permitted to make loans for modernization of farm buildings, including houses, and for certain items of household equipment. This agency has played a highly important role up to the present, by bringing electricity to most of the farms of the nation.

In 1937 the Farm Security Agency was established under the Department of Agriculture. It replaced the Resettlement Administration, under which the three Greenbelt communities had been built, and continued the making of grants and loans for farm family rehabilitation. The FSA also provided permanent and mobile camps for migratory farm laborers.

The Bankhead–Jones Farm Tenant Act of 1937 (administered by the FSA) authorized the Secretary of Agriculture to make liberal (forty-year amortization, 3 percent interest) loans to farm tenants, laborers, and sharecroppers in order to finance the purchase of farms and make farm repairs and improvements, including those on housing. Funds under this Act, and several subsequent acts, have also permitted research aimed at improving farmhouses. This research is administered through many state Agricultural Experiment Stations.

Both the United States Housing Act of 1937 and the National Housing Act (as amended in 1938) carried provisions for rural housing. Neither was very active, although some public rural housing projects were built in the South.

The most recent action of the Federal Government in the farm housing picture was the Farmers' Home Administration Act of 1940. This Act abolished the Farm Security Administration and required the Farmers Home Administration (also referred to as FHA, and not to be confused with the Federal Housing Administration) to operate some parts, and liquidate others, of that program.

Rural housing loans are made by the Farmers Home Administration to eligible farm owners and owners of nonfarm tracts in rural areas and small rural communities with populations of not more than 2,500. Loans are made for the construction and repair of needed homes and essential farm buildings.

Each loan is scheduled for repayment in accordance with the borrower's ability to repay, over a period not exceeding thirty-three years. The interest rate is 4 percent.

Loans average around $9,000 but vary considerably in amount, depending upon the needs of the applicants. Funds may be used only to finance dwellings and farm service buildings that are adequate but modest in size and design.

Insured loans may be made to individual farmers, groups of farmers, and public or private nonprofit organizations to finance housing facilities for domestic farm labor.

Housing loans may be made to elderly people, sixty-two years of age and over, who live in rural areas to buy previously occupied housing as well as to build or improve their homes. Elderly people can use a housing loan to finance the cost of a building site as well as the dwelling. When they do not have enough ability to repay they may use co-signers to assume responsibility for loan payments.

Insured loans may be made in rural areas to individuals, corporations, and partnerships to provide rental housing for elderly rural people. The maximum amount of a loan is $100,000. The interest rate is 5¾ percent.

The Farmers Home Administration also makes loans to rural groups for other purposes, including operating loans, farm ownership loans, water development and soil conservation loans, and loans for other purposes.

HOUSING LAWS AND PRESSURE GROUPS

It has been seen, from some of the discussion in this chapter, that the role of the Federal Government in the field of housing has been controversial since the first attempt to enact Federal housing legislation. This is not surprising if it is recognized that any broad programs in this field must necessarily impinge upon two opposing concepts—that which emphasizes the freedom of the individual and is generally expressed throughout our private enterprise system, and another, which emphasizes society in general and is frequently identified with the need for government intervention (which private enterprise often considers present or potential competition). These two concepts might be related, to a degree, to two of the values defined in Chapter 7—*freedom* and *equality*.

These two values undoubtedly have been the basis for an apparent conflict that has existed since the inception of our national government. The statement in the Declaration of Independence that "all men are created equal" marked the furthest limit that the majority of our Founding Fathers wished equality to be extended. However, while they believed the Creator might "equally" create, they apparently did not feel that it was the function of government to assume the role of Creator in assuring equality thereafter. For example, they indicated that government functions should be generally limited to defense and to assuring a maximum of *individual freedom* so that the natural social and economic forces resulting might operate at peak efficiency for the benefit of all.

The Constitution and the Bill of Rights, as well as the Declaration of Independence, also contained elements of compromise between these two conflicting values. It is interesting to note that the Bill of Rights, last drawn in point of time, was written with the express purpose of assuring certain liberties for all posterity.

Although emphasis in the direction of *freedom* may be detected in those historical documents, significant changes in emphasis appear to have taken place in our concept of the proper role of government since the early days of our nation. The government's role in advancing "the general welfare" is considered by many a *fait accompli.* However, this is not to say that the conflict has been resolved; in fact, it seems to be revealed almost daily in the press in reports of differences between the so-called "private housers" and "public housers."[32]

The basic concepts held by the different groups—those opposed to government intervention in the housing situation and those who feel it has been necessary—have already been indicated. In brief, the first group has felt that housing was a "business" and should be left in the hands of private enterprise for the solution of its problems, whereas the second group has maintained that private enterprise has not been able to solve all of the problems and it is therefore the government's responsibility, in the interest of the public welfare, to step in.

Until World War I, there was little *organized* pressure against the laissez-faire concept. Most of the pressure for governmental action resulted from the influence of a small group of social reformers, exerted on receptive government officials in high places. In 1917 and 1918, however, some groups, as groups, officially pressured for better housing through governmental action. One of the leaders was the American Federation of Labor, interested in low-rent housing for workers. Other groups active in opposing such a role for the government included the National Association of Real Estate Boards (NAREB) and building and loan groups, both groups interested in promoting home ownership.

McDonnell describes the activity and public attitude after World War I:

> In the years following World War I the battle for some kind of a permanent housing program administered by the state and federal governments was hard fought, and the real-estate association defeated early attempts to enact housing legislation. Soon after the war, certainly by 1924, a certain apathy seized the people who formerly were so interested in housing. . . . But despite this apathy on the part of the general public certain definite changes had taken place in the thinking of the people concerning the housing problem. The Federal government was now considered to have a definite part to play in any kind of program that eventually would be worked out."[33]

McDonnell's study had as its primary purpose description in detail of the nature and practices of the powerful lobby groups who represented various interests while the Housing Act of 1937 (which established the public housing program) was being considered. He describes the four existing "and well-organized lobbies" that opposed the bill: the National Association of

[32] This conflict is not, of course, limited to housing. For the reader interested in exploring the different basic philosophies and the pressure groups supporting each, in more detail, the following references are recommended: Sidney Fine, Laissez Faire *and the General-Welfare State—A Study of Conflict in American Thought, 1865–1901.* Ann Arbor, Mich.: University of Michigan Press, 1956; V. O. Key, Jr., *Politics, Parties, and Pressure Groups,* 4th ed. New York: Thomas Y. Crowell Company, 1958.

[33] Timothy L. McDonnell, *The Wagner Housing Act—A Case Study of the Legislative Process.* Chicago: Loyola University Press, 1957, p. 22.

Real Estate Boards (through the office of their Executive Vice-President, Herbert U. Nelson); the United States Building and Loan League (represented in Washington by Morton Bodfish, Executive Vice-President of that League); the National Retail Lumber Dealers Association (represented by their Washington representative, Frank Carnahan); and the United States Chamber of Commerce (represented by E. Stuart Fitzpatrick, Washington representative for the Construction and Civic Development Department of that organization). Concerning their activities, McDonnell says:

> These men did not coordinate their efforts during the early part of the campaign, but they were all agreed in this: public housing was a dangerous socialistic experiment which threatened free enterprise and the traditional American principles of government; public housing also threatened the continued prosperity of the enterprise that each of them represented. . . . They demanded that the government get out of the housing business and stay out.[34]

On the other side, a group of socially conscious and civic-minded individuals began to organize their efforts in favor of this kind of legislation as early as 1931. The first organization formed was called the National Public Housing Conference—Mary Simkhovitch, Helen Alfred, Ira Robbins, and Louis Pink being prominent among the organizers. The first two were social workers and the latter two were lawyers. This group gave strong support to Secretary of the Interior Harold L. Ickes and his program to promote slum clearance and to build low-rent housing. The second group was the National Association of Housing Officials, formed in 1933. One of the persons most responsible for the organization of this group was Ernest J. Bohn of Cleveland. The group's first Executive Director was Charles Ascher, followed by Coleman Woodbury. The primary purpose of this group was to assist local, state, and national housing officials in developing adequate programs of low-cost housing and slum clearance, rather than serving as a housing lobby. The third major group interested in the public housing program was the Labor Housing Conference, which had the active support of several labor unions. Catherine Bauer was the first Director of that group.

Both sides brought extreme pressure to bear upon Federal legislators—pressure which, according to McDonnell, ". . . was within the bounds of the democratic legislative process."[35]

After the Housing Act of 1937 was passed, there continued to be some activity on the part of these groups, but it did not again become intense until 1944 when three senators, Wagner of New York, Ellender of Louisiana, and Taft of Ohio, drafted another major piece of housing legislation that was to become the Housing Act of 1949. The alignment remained the same, some new groups joining in. By this time the National Association of Home Builders had become organized, first as a unit under the National Association of Real Estate Boards, but later independent. This organization (together

[34] *Ibid.*, p. 62.

[35] *Ibid.*, p. 63. McDonnell, in his case study of the Housing Act of 1937, cites extensive detail concerning how the pressure groups operated for and against this piece of legislation.

with a smaller group, the Prefabricated Home Manufacturers Association) joined ranks with NAREB. Also aligning themselves with this group were such organizations as the American Bankers Association, the Mortgage Bankers Association of America, the Building Products Institute (comprised largely of producers of household equipment and building materials), and the Associated General Contractors. Supporting the bill were such additional groups as the five leading veterans' organizations, organizations representing the three major religious denominations, the U.S. Conference of Mayors, the National Association for the Advancement of Colored People, and many related groups.

There has been no omnibus housing bill since that year as broad as the 1949 Act, but these groups have sometimes made an appearance when certain pieces of legislation were being considered, especially legislation including provisions for additional public housing. The entire Federal housing program was reviewed at the request of the Housing and Home Finance Administrator in 1959,[36] but no action was taken to implement the recommendations.

Although many of the pressure groups have remained the same over the years, the character of their activities has changed in some respects. There is still the

> . . . torrent of letters, wires and phone calls . . . plus a few personal visits. . . . But the modern lobbyist is more likely to be a polished, businesslike technician, who deals largely with facts and, as a rule, works out in the open. [The lobbying groups today cater] . . . to the legislator's judgment and his re-election hopes, rather than to his purse as pressure groups of yesteryear did.[37]

In order to bring their work still more "out in the open," a 1946 law requires registration of lobbyists and a listing of their expenses involved in direct efforts to influence legislation.

Although the activities of these pressure groups are sometimes looked upon in a negative manner, they may serve highly useful purposes. In a field such as housing, specific legislation proposed can oftentimes become so highly complex that it becomes difficult for many legislators to understand its intricacies. It is the practice of many lobbying groups not only to explain these intricacies, but some are staffed to actually draw up new legislation to be introduced by the legislators. Many of the groups also maintain handbooks of activity in Washington, distributed for the purpose of keeping

[36] Ernest M. Fisher, *A Study of Housing Programs and Policies.* Prepared for U.S. Housing Administrator Norman P. Mason, Housing and Home Finance Agency, January 1960. Dr. Fisher's major recommendations included (1) the combining of Federal housing agencies into a single, over-all agency and the establishment of a single public agency in each community to handle housing problems, (2) giving local public agencies the widest possible latitude in the use of funds provided by the HHFA, (3) the matching *in cash* by local agencies of funds provided by the Federal Government, at a single ratio to be fixed by Congress, (4) building up and maintaining a balanced inventory of graded public housing facilities by acquisition and management of existing houses in urban renewal areas, and (5) the establishment of a broad-scale Federally financed housing research program.

[37] "The Housing Lobby," *The Wall Street Journal,* Vol. CLIII, No. 65, April 3, 1959.

their members abreast of activity of interest to them. All in all, this represents the democratic process in operation.

READING LIST

HISTORY OF THE GOVERNMENT'S ROLE IN HOUSING

Colean, Miles L. *American Housing—Problems and Prospects.* New York: The Twentieth Century Fund, 1947, Chapter 10.

Gries, John M., and James Ford (eds.) *Housing Objectives and Programs.* Vol. XI. The President's Conference on Home Building and Home Ownership, Washington, D.C., 1932.

Harriss, C. Lowell. *History and Policies of the Home Owners' Loan Corporation.* New York: National Bureau of Economic Research, 1951.

Meyerson, Martin, Barbara Terrett, and William L. C. Wheaton. *Housing, People, and Cities.* New York: McGraw-Hill Book Co., 1962, Chapter 13.

Rogg, Nat. "A History of the Veterans Emergency Housing Program," Washington, D.C.: Office of the Housing Expediter (undated, mimeo, with hard cover).

"A Study of Housing Programs and Policies," by Ernest M. Fisher. Washington, D.C.: Housing and Home Finance Agency, January 1960.

Subcommittee on Housing of the Committee on Banking and Currency, U.S. Senate, Eighty-Seventh Congress, Second Session, *Progress Report on Federal Housing Programs.* Washington, D.C.: U.S. Government Printing Office, August 29, 1962.

Veiller, Lawrence. *Housing Reform.* New York: The Russell Sage Foundation, 1910.

"Your Congress and American Housing," The Actions of Congress on Housing from 1892 to 1951, by Jack Levin, Legislative Reference Service, Library of Congress. House Document No. 532. Eighty-Second Congress, Second Session. Washington, D.C.: U.S. Government Printing Office, 1952.

AIDS TO PRIVATE HOUSING

Colean, Miles L. *The Impact of Government on Real Estate Finance in the United States.* New York: National Bureau of Economic Research, 1950.

Grebler, Leo. *The Role of Federal Credit Aids in Residential Construction.* Occasional Paper 39. New York: National Bureau of Economic Research, 1953.

Haar, Charles M. *Federal Credit and Private Housing.* New York: McGraw-Hill Book Co., 1960.

Wendt, Paul F. *The Role of the Federal Government in Housing.* No. 460 in the series "National Economic Problems." Washington, D.C.: American Enterprise Association, 1956.

PUBLIC HOUSING

Abrams, Charles. *The Future of Housing.* New York: Harper & Bros., 1946.

Bauer, Catherine. "The Dreary Deadlock of Public Housing," *Architectural Forum,* Vol. 106, No. 5, May 1957, pp. 141-142.

Fisher, Robert Moore. *Twenty Years of Public Housing.* New York: Harper & Bros., 1959.

Straus, Nathan. *The Seven Myths of Housing.* New York: Alfred A. Knopf, 1944.

———. *Two-Thirds of a Nation: A Housing Program.* New York: Alfred A. Knopf, 1952.

Wood, Elizabeth. *The Small Hard Core—The Housing of Problem Families in New York City.* New York: Citizen's Housing and Planning Council of New York, 1957.

URBAN RENEWAL

Colean, Miles L. *Renewing Our Cities.* New York: The Twentieth Century Fund, 1953.

Duggar, George S. (ed.) *The New Renewal.* Proceedings of a Civic Seminar: The Next Big Tasks in Urban Renewal. Berkeley: Bureau of Public Administration, University of California, 1961.

Johnson, Thomas F., James R. Morris, and Joseph G. Butts. *Renewing America's Cities.* Washington, D.C.: The Institute for Social Science Research, 1962.

Rapkin, Chester, and William G. Grigsby. *Residential Renewal in the Urban Core.* Philadelphia: University of Pennsylvania Press, 1960.

Rossi, Peter H., and Robert A. Dentler. *The Politics of Urban Renewal.* New York: The Free Press of Glencoe, Inc., 1961.

Van Huyck, Alfred P., and Jack Hornung. *The Citizen's Guide to Urban Renewal.* West Trenton, N.J.: Chandler-Davis Publishing Co., October 1962, paperback.

Weaver, Robert C. *The Urban Complex—Human Values in Urban Life.* Garden City, N.Y.: Doubleday & Company, Inc., 1964.

Woodbury, Coleman. *The Future of Cities and Urban Redevelopment.* Chicago: University of Chicago Press, 1953.

———. *Urban Redevelopment: Problems and Practices.* Chicago: University of Chicago Press, 1953.

POLITICS AND PRESSURE GROUPS

Fine, Sidney. Laissez Faire *and the General-Welfare State.* Ann Arbor, Mich.: University of Michigan Press, 1956.

Key, V. O., Jr. *Politics, Parties and Pressure Groups.* New York: Thomas Y. Crowell Co., 4th ed., 2d printing, 1958.

McDonnell, Timothy L. *The Wagner Housing Act—A Case Study of the Legislative Process.* Chicago: Loyola University Press, 1957.

Meyerson, Martin, Barbara Terrett, and William L. C. Wheaton. *Housing, People, and Cities.* New York: McGraw-Hill Book Co., 1962, Chapter 15.

GENERAL

Housing and Home Finance Agency, *Annual Reports.* Washington, D.C.: U.S. Government Printing Office.

CHAPTER 15

*

Future Need and Housing Research

What does the future hold for housing in this nation? To many—builders, lending institutions, public officials, citizens groups, and families themselves—the answer to this question may be more important than discussions of our past or our present housing situation.

Yet the future is related directly to the past and the present. At mid-century the United States has an inheritance of much new housing that has been built by a more progressive householding industry than the nation has heretofore seen. Forward strides have been made in the realm of home financing, and we have learned a great deal about design and planning requirements.

But we also have an inheritance of slums, still existing in almost all of our cities, regardless of size. The low-income family still faces the dilemma of obtaining decent shelter. One of the real problems today is that of reducing costs. In addition, even the new houses being built today are designed more to satisfy the way people lived yesterday than the way they live today and will live tomorrow. The industry has, in fact, been encouraged to retain its traditional approach to a considerable extent by the Federal Government which ". . . has leaned toward the use of established, old time housing practices rather than leading the industry into the use of innovations."[1]

In attempts to evaluate the future, two questions must be asked: (1) what is likely to be the quantitative need? and (2) how might the houses built more closely meet both our economic and social requirements? The answer to this second question would seem to lie largely in research.

DEMAND, NEED, AND ATTAINABLE NEED

First of all, the terms "demand" and "need" should be understood. They are frequently used interchangeably, but the technical difference between the two terms should be recognized. Briefly stated, housing demand is generally considered to be *market* demand. For example, how many houses are likely to be sold, based on what families are willing and able to pay, in any given period?

[1] *Better Housing for the Future.* A Report to the Panel on Civilian Technology, Office of Science and Technology, Executive Office of the President, from its Sub-Panel on Housing. Washington, D.C.: U.S. Government Printing Office, April 1963, p. 11.

Housing need, on the other hand, is represented by the total housing requirements of individuals and families based on standards of minimum social acceptability, whether or not they can afford what is available. Of course, there is overlapping between the two terms, and this is in part the cause of the confusion. For example, most new families formed by marriage not only create a need but they often also constitute a market demand. Furthermore, families living in substandard housing, who have had a rise in family income, can create a "demand" for better housing if they can then afford what is being built.

Neither of these terms, however, can be used to reflect the volume of new construction that is likely to be built during any immediate future period. A "demand" estimate would be too narrow, because it would not include subsidized public housing units for low-income families; and any sound estimate of total "need" would be too broad, because it would have to assume the replacement of *all* substandard units—a goal which cannot realistically be achieved in the next ten-year period. What can be expected, however, is that the effective demand will be met and that a high proportion of the substandard units occupied by low-income families will be replaced by standard units built for those families. The term selected to represent this combination of demand and partial need is "attainable need."

ATTAINABLE HOUSING NEED, 1965–1975

The size of the housing job between 1965 and 1975 should surpass that of any previous ten-year period. The new housing construction activity required for this period is projected at between 15,800,000 and 21,000,000 housing units. This would suggest an average annual rate of between 1,580,000 and 2,100,000 units a year to be built during that decade (Table 15–1, p. 507).

Many factors must be taken into consideration in such a projection of future housing need. The basic one is anticipated new household formation. It, however, represents only a part of the attainable need. For example, although the number of households increased about 8,000,000 between 1950 and 1959, the number of new housing units built was about 15,000,000.[2] Other factors that must be considered are the needs of migrants who move into areas of short housing supply, the number of conversions or mergers of housing units in existing structures, the demolition of units because of natural causes (floods, fire, etc.) and for purposes of slum clearance, and, finally, the need for a certain proportion of vacant units in order to facilitate mobility and to enable households to exercise some appropriate (though limited) choices in the selection of suitable housing accommodations.

The basis for the need projected here for the period 1965–1975 is described below. An underlying assumption in these estimates is, of course, that there will be no war or other major catastrophe, and that our national economic

[2] U.S. Bureau of the Census, *Census of Housing 1960*. Components of Inventory Change. HC(4), Part 1A-1, 1950–1959 Components, United States and Regions, p. 20.

situation will not become depressed, but will continue to support high employment levels during this period.

Household Formation

Projections of the estimated number of households in the United States are provided by the U.S. Census for a period to 1980. These estimates are based on extensions of changes in marital and household status since 1950 and on a projected growth in population. The Census makes four projections, labeled Series A, B, C and D. The two used here for high and low estimates are Series A and C. The Series A projection indicates a possible 58,637,000 households in 1965 and 70,036,000 households in 1975, or an increase of 11,399,000. The Series C projection indicates a possible 55,311,000 households in 1965 and 64,906,000 households in 1975, or an increase of 9,595,000.[3]

Rural to Urban Migration

It was indicated in Chapter 12 that the U.S. Census projections would indicate a decline in farm households for the period 1960 to 1970 similar to the decline experienced in the two preceding decades. The Series A projection indicated a possible decline of 806,000 rural households and the Series C projection, a possible decline of 959,000 households, over the ten-year period.[4] Because there has been neither a sharp increase or decrease in the rate of farm migration for many years, these figures are used here for the projection for the period 1965–1975.

Conversions and Mergers

During the period 1950–1959, there was a gain of approximately 800,000 dwelling units through structures being converted into a larger number of units, and an offsetting loss of approximately the same number of units through mergers in structures that resulted in a smaller number of units. Beyond that, however, there also was a gain of approximately 1,000,000 units created from nonresidential space and units created from nondwelling unit quarters or quasi-units.[5] This experience is expected to continue, and it may be expected that between 750,000 and 1,000,000 of the dwelling units needed between 1965 and 1975 will become available in this manner.

[3] The methods and assumptions used to prepare these projections are described in detail in U.S. Bureau of the Census, *Current Population Reports,* Population Characteristics, "Illustrative Projections of the Number of Households and Families: 1960 to 1980," Series P-20, No. 90, December 29, 1958. The projections for Series A are in *Current Population Reports,* Population Characteristics, "Interim Revised Projections of the Number of Households and Families: 1965 to 1980," Series P-20, No. 123, April 11, 1963.

[4] "Study of Mortgage Credit," Hearings before a Subcommittee of the Committee on Banking and Currency, United States Senate, Eighty-Sixth Congress, First Session. Washington, D.C.: U.S. Government Printing Office, 1959, p. 55.

[5] U.S. Bureau of the Census, HC(4), Part 1A-1, 1950–1959 Components, *op. cit.,* pp. 20–21.

Units Lost Through Demolition or Becoming Vacant and Uninhabitable

This represents the most difficult estimate to make because there probably cannot be great reliance on past experience. However, some basic facts are known. A total of 2,900,000 dilapidated dwelling units and 3,156,000 dwelling units in deteriorating condition which lacked some or all plumbing facilities, existed in 1960. Some of these may be demolished and others restored between 1960 and 1965. However, it is likely that other units will fall into these categories in the meantime. Many of these substandard dwelling units will be torn down under our urban renewal programs. Still others, perhaps including many in better structural condition, will be demolished to make way for new modern highways and throughways, parking needs, and other public and private construction. Some not demolished but of a low standard are likely to become vacant and await replacement. It is perhaps optimistic, but not to be unhoped for, that as many as 6,750,000 substandard units will be taken out of the housing supply through demolition (including a high proportion of the dilapidated units) during the 1965–1975 period. A conservative estimate is 4,000,000 units. Even the most optimistic of these figures would not rid the nation of all of its slums, because the spread of blight will not have been stopped, and other units that in 1960 were found to be in fair condition will have reached the substandard level.

Units Lost Through Other Means

Approximately 1,900,000 to 2,000,000 units may be expected to be lost through other means, including units destroyed by natural causes, units changed to nonresidential use, units moved from site, and units changed to nondwelling unit quarters or quasi-units. Between 1950 and 1959, 1,783,000 units were lost through these causes.[6]

Vacancy Allowance

As already indicated, a certain proportion of vacant units is needed in order to facilitate mobility and to enable households to exercise some appropriate, though limited, choices in the selection of suitable housing. The vacancy allowance is usually higher for rental units than for units for sale —6 percent and 2 percent being reasonable estimates for this purpose. Since it may be anticipated that approximately three fourths of the new units would be sold and the remaining one fourth rented, an over-all 3 percent vacancy ratio is in order for estimating purposes.

Through the sort of analysis indicated above it may be estimated that the "attainable need" for the period 1965 to 1975 will constitute between

[6] *Ibid.*, p. 21.

15,800,000 and 21,000,000 new dwelling units. The construction of these units is not likely to be uniform during this period, because the growth in number of households and other factors will not be uniform. The household projections, for example, indicate substantially greater average annual growth between the years 1970–1975 than from 1965–1970. However, generally speaking, it may be expected that the lower figure will be met at the beginning of the period in the mid-1960's and that the higher figure should be reached near the end of the period. The midpoint in the estimate, an average of approximately 1,840,000 units a year, probably will be reached sometime after the midpoint of the decade. It can be seen from these projections that the new construction in the years around 1965 and 1966 is not expected to be much higher than in some recent years.

There will continue to be regional differences. A continued, accentuated growth will be found in the West and South, because of the attractiveness of the climates of these regions, and related factors. Urban renewal needs will be greater in large cities for the simple reason that there are more people there and, accordingly, more new units will be needed there than in smaller places to replace slum dwellings.

One of the most important factors in determining how close we may come to the high projection indicated will be the progress made in the housing industry itself. If a breakthrough occurs in the construction cost problem, a vast new market could be opened in the lower-middle income bracket. This matter, together with the need for research in housing generally, is discussed in more detail in the remainder of this chapter.

HOUSING RESEARCH

Housing touches every individual at all periods of his life span. It may be theorized that, despite man's adaptability, housing may be a determining factor in his attitudes and his way of life. On the other hand, it must be admitted that much of what we think we know about housing is based upon intuition or our subjective evaluation of what we think man desires. There has been all too little objective and patient study of what shelter should do to improve living conditions. Today there is no science of housing, there are only opinions, convictions, and prejudices about it.[7] It is remarkable that the construction industry, which represents such an important proportion of the gross national product (nearly 24 billion dollars annually) has not developed a scientific and technological tradition.

It is recognized that few of the complex problems of housing fall neatly into the traditional scientific classifications. Many of them are interdisciplinary, overlapping different fields of knowledge. They require both technical and socioeconomic research.

However, to reflect the nature of the problems, it is useful to identify

[7] Ernest M. Fisher, ''The Role of the University in Housing Research,'' an address at the Conference of the Housing Committee of the Social Science Research Council held at the University of Michigan, Ann Arbor, Michigan, January 27–29, 1949.

them separately in some frame of reference. For purposes of systematizing the discussion, a parallel might be drawn to Newton's spectrum—a solar ray of light being separated by a prism into seven principal colors. As the single ray of building knowledge is passed through a prism representing the requirements of building, and subjected to dispersion, the series of resulting fields of knowledge brought to a focus on building construction and use might be labeled as follows: (1) the natural and physical sciences, (2) engineering and technical knowledge, (3) economics, (4) laws and regulations, (5) humanities and behavioral sciences, (6) design and planning, and (7) manufacturing and construction. Using even briefer descriptions, we might say Nature, Technology, Money, Law, Man, Design, and Construction.

Natural and Physical Sciences

Knowledge in the natural and physical sciences is basic to building technology. The research referred to in this category is of a pure, or basic, rather than applied, nature. It includes knowledge of chemistry, physics, climatology, geology, entomology, public health, and so on.

Technical Knowledge

Much of the research in the area of building technology would represent an application of the knowledge already existing or being developed in the natural and physical sciences. As an example, knowledge of chemistry and physics usually must be applied for the invention of new building materials. Knowledge of soils, their characteristics and behavior in relation to structure, sanitary disposal, landscaping, and planting, also is needed. The importance of fungi and natural phenomena causing deterioration needs to be recognized. Weather, including temperature and humidity, wind, rainfall, snowfall, and the like, plays its role. Closely related are matters of acoustics, illumination, and even fire prevention, about which we still know too little. The various applications would be directly related to the development of materials, structure, and mechanical equipment.

The whole matter of building technology is most importantly related to the matter of building costs, and it is, therefore, discussed somewhat further in the following section on Economics.

Economics

One of the most serious housing problems is the constantly rising cost of construction. Two indexes may be cited as an example of the increase in construction costs during a recent period: the E. H. Boeckh construction cost index for single-family residences rose from 107.7 in 1950 to 139.7 in 1960 (1947–1949 = 100) and the Consumer Price Index for Housing rose from 106.1 to 131.5 during the same period.[8]

[8] These indexes are published currently by the U.S. Department of Commerce and the U.S. Bureau of Labor Statistics, respectively.

The rapid increase in the cost of housing is not necessarily typical of all industries. The Consumer Price Index for food increased from 101.2 to only 119.6; the Consumer Price Index for apparel, from 98.1 to only 109.3; and the Bureau of Public Roads highway construction index, from 95.6 to 111.5, during the same period (Figure 31).

Some interesting questions may be asked at this point. In view of the marked difference in the price trends cited, are our houses *that much* better than our food, apparel, or our highways? Has the quality of what we buy for our housing dollar increased so much more than the quality of what we buy with our food, clothing, or highway dollars? This may be doubted.[9]

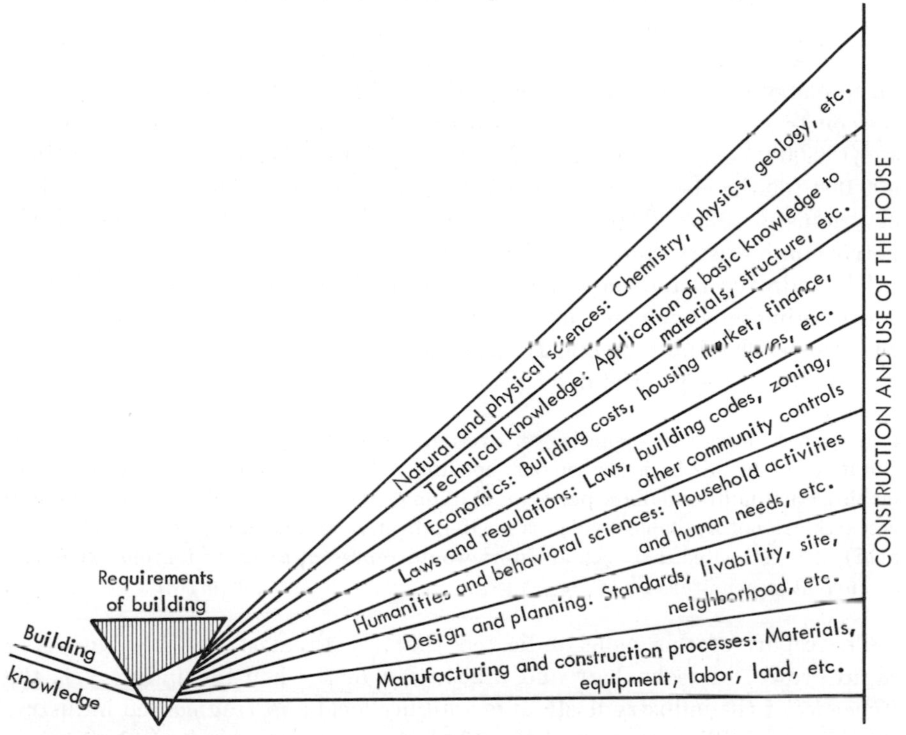

FIGURE 30. *Spectrum of knowledge concerning housing.*

Undoubtedly, one of the reasons for the disproportionate increase in costs in the housebuilding industry has been the lag in research and development in construction processes. There are no separate data for housebuilding, but there are some figures for the over-all construction industry of which it is a part.

[9] Some defenders of the high cost of housing have argued that the increase in per capita income has kept pace with building costs and that, therefore, building costs are within our ability to pay. This would seem to be a weak argument for accepting high housing costs. It would seem, rather, that the nation is making an inordinate investment in housing at the expense of other portions of the economy, and that high housing costs might be viewed as an unwarranted drain on the national economy.

Let us now see how that industry stands, in research and development, in relation to certain other industries. One of the measures of the amount of research and development activity in an industry is the number of research engineers and other scientists employed by that industry. Despite the tremendous dollar volume of new building annually taking place (in 1962, 61 billion dollars, including 25.8 billion dollars for new housing), the construction industry is at the bottom of the ladder in number of research personnel. In 1960, it had only 2,000 persons—1,600 engineers and 400 other specialists—employed in research and development. This figure may be compared with 64,600 in the aircraft industry, 62,600 in the electrical equipment industry, 36,600 in chemicals, 28,200 in machinery, and so on.[10] The comparisons are shown in Figure 32.

Another measure of the amount of research and development activity in an industry is the amount of funds allocated for such purposes. Here again the construction industry is at the bottom of the ladder. In 1956, it spent only $24,100,000, compared with $517,700,000 for the chemical industry, $461,000,000 for the electrical equipment industry, $390,300,000 for the machinery industry, $269,900,000 for the aircraft industry, $203,400,000 for the petroleum industry, and so on.[11] (Figure 33.)

The industry's traditional position toward financing research and toward encouraging government funds for this purpose has been discussed in Chapter 6. The Sub-Panel on Housing of the Panel on Civilian Technology has confirmed the general description provided, in these words:

> . . . growth industries spend on an average roughly 1½ percent of sales income for R & D. On this basis the current housing industry should conceivably spend as much as 360 million dollars per year. Although data on expenditures for building research are not available (which is itself indicative of the status of research in the field), it is estimated that such an effort would represent a six- to tenfold expansion of current expenditures.[12]

The report of this panel indicated that the greatest obstacle hindering rapid growth of technology and innovation in the housing industry is the structure of the industry itself. It is a highly local and fragmented industry. Of the 1.28 million units built in 1960, for example, no single builder or home manufacturer accounted for more than 5,000 units, and most erected fewer than 20. This fragmentation makes promotion of innovations difficult and expensive. Furthermore, most of the money paid by the house purchaser flows into the hands of people and companies having little opportunity to improve their profits by spending money for research and development, and

[10] National Science Foundation, *Scientific and Technical Personnel in Industry, 1960.* N.S.F. Report 61–75, Washington, D.C.: U.S. Government Printing Office, p. 28.

[11] National Science Foundation, *Science and Engineering in American Industry,* N.S.F. Report 59–50, Washington, D.C.: U.S. Government Printing Office, p. 48. The figures for the construction industry are based on a sample of about 150 building contractors and do not, therefore, include the amounts that building material manufacturers and similar groups put into product development.

[12] *Better Housing for the Future, op. cit.,* p. 5.

this tends to preserve the *status quo.* Nevertheless, until we have a revolutionary change in this situation, housing consumers are likely to have to continue to pay increasing costs for this commodity, rather than lower costs resulting from some technological advances in the industry that could be brought forth only through an aggressive research program.

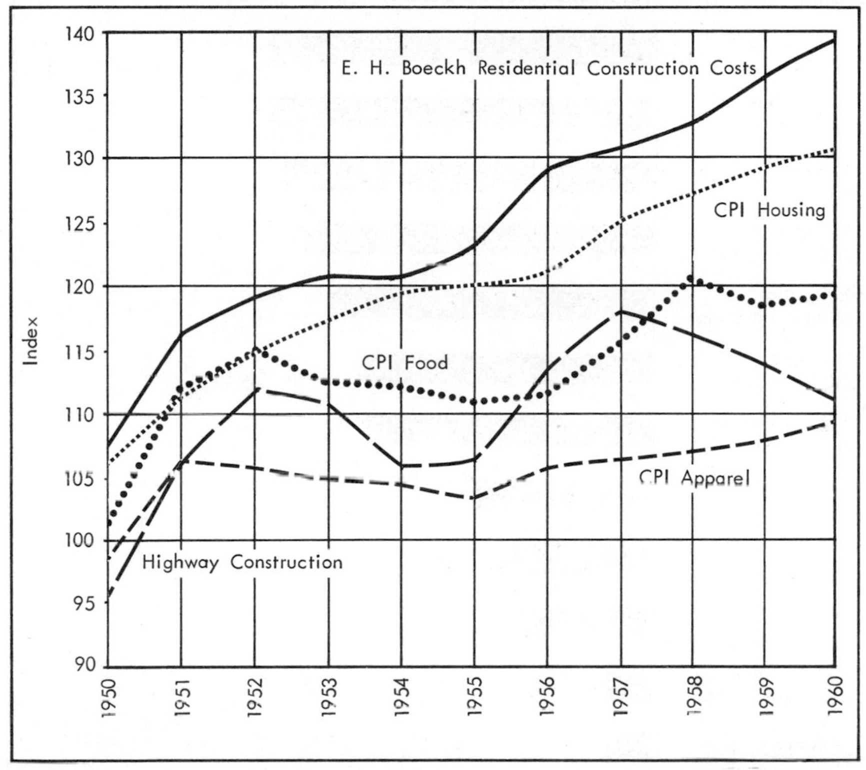

Note: 1947–1949 = 100.

FIGURE 31. *Housing cost indexes compared with cost indexes for selected other items, 1950 to 1960. (Sources of data: Consumer price indexes—U.S. Bureau of Labor Statistics; E. H. Boeckh residential construction costs—U.S. Department of Commerce; and highway construction—U.S. Bureau of Public Roads.)*

But housing costs represent only one of the areas that suggest additional research. The area of economics covers many subjects, including the housing market, housing finance, slums and public housing, taxes, and family expenditure patterns.

Formal studies of local housing markets were begun in the Federal Housing Administration in the mid-1930's. The traditional studies matched, in a broad manner, demand factors against supply factors in the local market. Out of this were developed some general conclusions regarding type, size, price, and location of additional units that might represent sound mortgage investments (see Chapter 4).

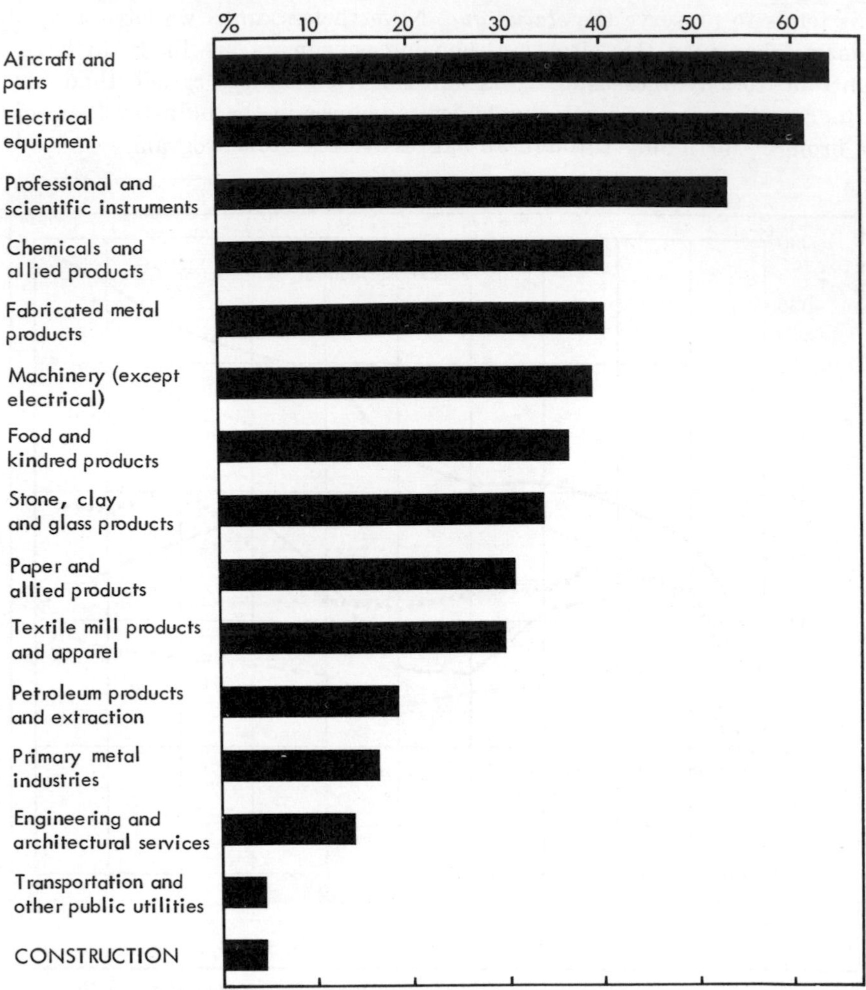

FIGURE 32. *Scientists and engineers primarily engaged in research and development as percent of scientists and engineers in all activities, by industry, January 1960. (Source of data: National Science Foundation,* Scientific and Technical Personnel in Industry 1960. *NSF 61–75. Washington, D.C.: U.S. Government Printing Office, 1961, Table A-9, p. 27.)*

A refined technique for market analysis is required. For example, at any given time the relationship of demand to supply is reflected in price and vacancy. There is a possibility that if simple, practical measures of these factors could be developed, better short-term market predictions could be made.

More attention also needs to be given to the filtering concept. Present evidence would tend to justify discarding this theory. Yet this should not be done until further attempts have been made to obtain more empirical evidence.

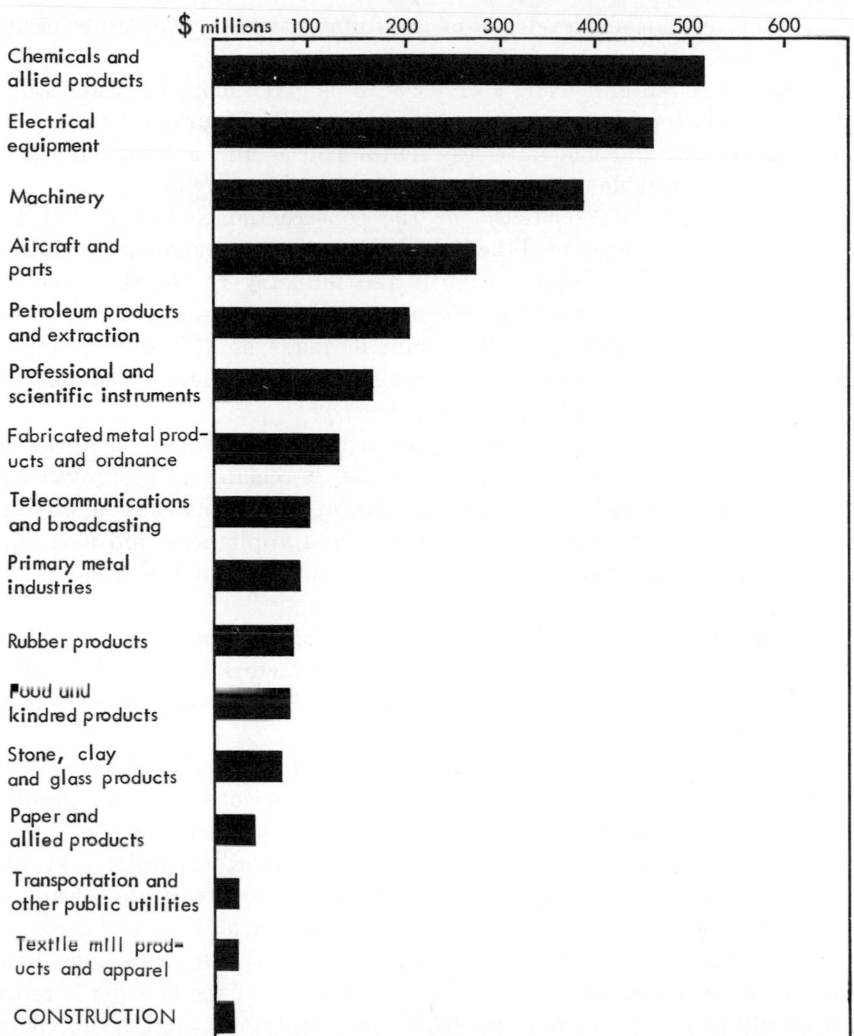

FIGURE 33. *Expenditures by private industry for research and development conducted within and outside company, by industry, 1956. (Source of data: National Science Foundation,* Science and Engineering in American Industry. *NSF 59050. Washington, D.C.: U.S. Government Printing Office, 1959, Table A-4, p. 48.)*

Closely related to market research is research concerned with housing finance. There are only singular studies of the mortgage market, yet today mortgage indebtedness is at an all-time peak. Data that would permit the study of both short- and long-term trends are needed. There is no adequate broad-scale current information regarding the trend of values, mortgage-to-value ratios, debt service-to-family income ratios, and the like, even in the simplest form (not to mention the desirability of having the same information for different income levels, all of the different types of lending institutions, different cities, and so forth).

The matter of rental housing also needs to be given more intensive study. Until a formula for financing is developed that will encourage the construction of more low- and moderate-cost rental houses and apartments, many families will not be able to obtain the type of housing they desire.

There has been much criticism of the construction industry. Yet few studies have actually examined the industry's various economic aspects. Does monopolization exist in some parts of the industry to the detriment of housing? Are the existing channels of distribution unduly costly? Are shorter channels feasible? (Studies could be made of a selected group of building materials, following them through each distribution channel and establishing costs and mark-ups at each level.)

In addition to materials and distribution costs, and despite the growing acceptance of prefabricated parts and houses, it remains to be proved how much cost saving there is, if any, in this type of home construction. Savings through standardization of materials, parts, and appliances, and modularization, need to be studied further from the standpoint of the economics of building.

Another question is: Why has cooperative housing not been more successful in this country? A careful analysis of all factors concerned, together with an examination of successful experience with this type of housing in Europe, would be useful.

The few studies that have been made of slums and public housing have usually had a social focus. Yet, slums represent a serious economic problem as well. An objective, systematic analysis should be made of the cost of slums to our cities. This type of research would have, as its corollary, studies of such factors as the economic effect of nuisance industries, the economics of neighborhood changes, and neighborhood conservation.

The economics of the public housing program raises many questions. First of all, the financial investment and the consequences of the housing it represents should be of concern to every citizen who contributes to the support of the public housing program by means of taxation. More directly, what economic effect has the program had on those owning property or living in districts adjacent to or near public housing developments? Also, what are the costs involved in relocating families from cleared sites?

What is the answer to the "no man's land in housing," that is, the price range above the upper limits of public housing and the bottom limits of new private housing? Limited-dividend corporations have attempted to make some inroads, but in numbers of units provided, they have been extremely limited. Are such corporations a possible answer, and if so, what problems must be overcome to obtain a greater volume of units of this type? A study of their experience is required. What other solutions can be advanced to take care of this important segment of our population not now being provided for by either private enterprise or public housing?

Taxes, both outright and hidden, should also be better understood, especially during this period of suburban sprawl.

Finally, it has been pointed out that the policies of the government's housing agencies are controlled by our national fiscal policy. It would be well to review those policies to determine what is necessary for a continuing prosperous housebuilding industry for the nation as a whole.

Laws and Regulations

Pursuing the rays and beams on the spectrum further, we must recognize that certain laws and regulations control, in part, the way we live. Included at the local level are building codes, housing codes, zoning ordinances, subdivision controls, and other city planning controls. At the national level, we have minimum property standards of the government housing agencies that control design and construction—from the kinds of materials and products that go into a house to structural design, to mechanical equipment, and water supply and sewage disposal requirements.

The major problems with regard to building codes may be summarized as follows: (1) because there are 5,000 or more different local codes, it is impossible for a builder to design a house that will be acceptable in many localities, thus precluding the development of a "national" housing industry; (2) many codes are still on a "specification" rather than "performance" basis, which frequently adds excessive cost to housing; (3) better and additional performance criteria need to be developed before intelligent decisions can be made concerning some elements in the building structure; and (4) local code groups have neither adequate staffs nor funds to investigate innovations in materials and concepts with sufficient vigor and competence to be able to keep codes up to date. The several "model" codes in existence have been helpful, but much more work needs to be done on the building code problem in general if codes are not to continue to be one of the major factors in keeping the cost of housing excessively high.

Much more attention needs to be given to standards for houses and apartments. Existing standards vary over a wide range—the FHA standards are definitely minimum, owing in part to the pressures exerted by builders for minimum space allowances in order to keep building costs down; the standards for public housing are, in general, somewhat higher, despite the fact that such housing is for families who cannot pay an economic rent; and standards recommended by the American Public Health Association in the early 1950's and those recommended in many College of Home Economics studies are significantly higher. What should the standards be for the more than one million new homes being built each year? We really don't know.

Humanities and Behavioral Sciences

Basic scientific knowledge in the humanities and behavioral sciences is inadequate, and much fundamental study of human behavior and institutions must be made before practical applications to many types of housing problems can be developed. On the other hand, sociologists and psychologists have developed considerable knowledge about people and families that has not been brought to bear on housing.

Such simple facts as family composition and size, stage in the life cycle, income, educational attainment, and age have important influences on changing housing demand and housing need. In many studies some of these factors have been considered. For example, studies of low-rent housing needs and market analyses for private housing have both utilized this type of information as a basis for those studies. Yet, a great deal more could be learned about each of these factors, which, supplemented by such data as trends in the rate of marriages and other vital statistics, could be of great assistance.

A whole series of studies is needed regarding the social needs of low-income families. There is ample evidence that substandard housing and other slum conditions are a menace to the health, safety, and welfare of the people. There is, however, no dependable evidence to show that the new housing being provided through public housing agencies will *in itself* assure the maximum desirable and necessary social benefits to the families affected and to others in nearby areas.[13] What other social conditions are required? How many low-income families actually want to own their own homes?

The rules of tenant selection for public housing have been established by legislative and administrative authorities primarily concerned with the construction and management of large-scale housing. Their decisions have been based on little or no research.

For public housing projects that are also slum-clearance projects, the demolition and clearance of large areas of our cities is required. When this is done, it forces the removal of the families living on the site to be redeveloped. Local housing authorities are responsible for the families dispossessed; but it is known that some of the displaced families move to other substandard sections of the city where the rents are within their means. If it is true in any degree that "people make slums," it appears that slum conditions develop or are aggravated as a result of the forced moving of the families, which is contrary to the intent of the program. What can be done about this important weakness of the program?

There are certain social-political aspects of public housing. How often might public housing *per se* be properly or improperly charged with the conflicts within groups or in the community at large because of tenant or other policies required of it as a public institution, e.g., its policy of racial intermixture? What features of public housing programs, or images of them and their product, are acquired by the various groups in a local community? By what means are these perceptions disseminated?

What happens to the "graduates" of public housing projects, who have had to move out because of too high income or for other reasons? How do the social standards of tenants of public housing projects compare with the standards of people in the community at large? This calls for additional

[13] A study pertinent here is Daniel M. Wilner, *et al.*, *The Housing Environment and Family Life*, discussed in Chapter 10 (see p. 339).

comparative statistical studies, to show the incidence of social problems (crime, juvenile delinquency, etc.) among families housed in public housing projects, compared with those housed in other areas of the city with whom comparison may be fairly made.

There also is evidence that the planning of houses in any subdivision or development has important socio-psychological implications. One study of a few years ago provided a clue indicating that friendships are formed on the basis of front-door and sidewalk arrangements.[14] There is even a question of what community facilities should be provided for a neighborhood, under a given set of conditions. These include schools, shops, and transportation services.

It was mentioned in Chapter 11 that we need to know much more about our rapidly growing suburbs—their structure, leadership, social stratification, and so on. Also, are there "subconscious" home buying motives for buying a home that we do not know about?[15] This takes us back to the matters of personal values, discussed in several preceding chapters. Different authorities on this subject have listed different values; generally the studies are focused around such items as economics, health, beauty, and safety. Some studies also have included comfort, convenience, and location,[16] while others have emphasized social prestige, freedom, equality, leisure, mental health, and family centrism.[17]

Although the existence of these values in different individuals is recognized, and the dominant values individuals hold can probably be identified and even translated into housing design, there have been no tests of the personal-values concept related to design "in the field." For example, would individuals holding one set of values adjust more easily and quickly to a house designed by architects to satisfy those values than to one that architects did not feel would satisfy them? Similarly, would individuals holding the same set of values adjust more slowly and with more difficulty (or refuse to adjust at all) to a house that did not meet the design criteria considered appropriate for that set of values? We can hypothesize concerning the answers to these questions, but human behavior is sometimes difficult to predict and before we assume the answers, the hypotheses should be put to field testing.

There are many other areas in which research related to human needs should be undertaken, but the above discussion has touched on some of the most important. Certain other areas have been mentioned in other chapters.

[14] Leon Festinger, Stanley Schachter, and Kurt Back, *Social Pressures in Informal Groups.* New York: Harper & Bros., 1950.

[15] One attempt at such a study, with an extremely small sample, is reported in Ralph Bodek, *How and Why People Buy Houses.* Philadelphia: Municipal Publications, Inc., 1958.

[16] Virginia F. Cutler, *Personal and Family Values in the Choice of a Home.* Ithaca, N.Y.: Cornell University Agricultural Experiment Station Bulletin 840, November 1947.

[17] Glenn H. Beyer, Thomas W. Mackesey, James E. Montgomery, *Houses are for People.* Ithaca, N.Y.: Cornell University Housing Research Center, Research Publication No. 3, 1955.

Design and Planning

We move now to the matter of design and planning. Obviously, since architecture represents a coordinating function, all of the subjects discussed in this chapter are pertinent here. This discussion will, therefore, focus on more direct application to design.

The basic question again is: How might houses be designed in order to make them more "livable"? True, more surveys have attempted to develop answers to this question than to any other in this field. Most of these studies have used, as the method, surveys of family preferences on such items as number of stories, and number and type of rooms. Another approach has been to analyze household activities—that is, what goes on in the house—and then bring in architectural collaboration in planning houses around the facts obtained.

The weakness of the studies that ask about dining rooms, kitchens, bedrooms, and basements is that families must answer within the practical limitations of their experience, necessarily disregarding planning possibilities beyond the scope of their experience. For example, a family that has not lived in a house with an open kitchen is not in a position to answer a question regarding the desirability of this type of plan. The "activity" approach is sounder, because there is a greater similarity among the types of activities families perform than, for example, the spaces in which they perform them. This approach also deemphasizes the influence of existing house arrangements on the research results.

Some space needs are strictly physical. For example, how much space is actually needed for families of different sizes if they want to eat their regular meals in the kitchen? How much space is needed for entertaining a number of guests in the living room? How much space is needed when the bathroom is shared?

The socio-psychological implications of these design questions are also important. For example, how much do people mind having younger children around when they are entertaining? If they mind very much, how might the younger children be accommodated with other space? Should younger children's bedrooms be near those of the parents? How annoying are kitchen noises and cooking odors in the rest of the house? How annoying is it to carry groceries in through the living room? This whole area of satisfactions and irritations concerning activities carried on in the house is one that needs more study. A number of studies of factors of this type have been carried on outside the home (for example, in factories) and their techniques could be adapted here. The answers are important to good design.

Another important design problem is the need for flexibility. It is generally conceded that not only are families different from each other, but in themselves they are constantly changing. Some of these are major changes and cannot be accommodated in today's inflexible houses. Merely following the stages of the family cycle from the young married couple through the founding stage to the stage when the children are older, and finally when the children leave, creates serious planning problems. Not many families can satisfy their requirements by leaving one house and moving to another. Therefore, what normally occurs is that they must adjust their living patterns to the plan of their house. Yet the few attempts that have been made to design and build a truly flexible house—one in which the walls could actually be moved without great difficulty as family needs changed—have failed. Why?

It is also known that such physical variables in house design as color, light, texture, line, and space have emotional effects. These effects may be of satisfaction or frustration, pleasantness or irritation, tenseness or relaxation, interest or boredom (Chapter 8). There also are the beautiful as against the ugly, comfortable as against uncomfortable, and orderly as against disorderly. No major studies have applied existing psychological knowledge and research methods in the field of housing. (Industry has studied them in factories.) Nonetheless, families have different psychological reactions to any house they see or live in.

Families adjust to man-made physical environment, but these adjustments may not always be willingly made or necessarily desirable. After the adjustments are made, however, it is difficult to determine the cause of existing reactions. Studies of the ease of adjustment of different kinds of families to different kinds of houses would be useful.

Houses designed today are basically similar to those of several decades ago. Yet there have been vast changes in our patterns of living. The builder probably has assumed that since he can sell his houses, they are acceptable. This asumption is erroneous, but he needs to have made available to him new design criteria, based on research, in order to bring existing design up to date. In brief, research is needed on design standards, first to determine what those standards should be and, second, how they can be applied.

Finally, it would be desirable to relate all of this information about design to costs. The matter of housing costs should not necessarily be a limitation placed on the research in the first place, because frequently the cost problems can be solved once a desirable physical or social solution has been achieved. However, the matter of cost must not be forgotten, and research on certain matters, such as modular coordination, may well result in cost savings.

The foregoing discussion has focused on design of the house. There remains the area of planning. It was mentioned in Chapter 9 that the location of a house is generally considered just as important, if not more so, than its design. One of the largest and most important issues we must face is the nature and general purpose of neighborhood planning. More attention must be given to the problems of physical planning of neighborhoods—subdivision regulations, zoning, and the like—but perhaps even more important are the economic and social aspects. Are property values and neighborhood "stability" better maintained in homogeneous neighborhoods? How do homogeneity and heterogeneity affect the quality of

neighborhood social life? We have had few objective studies of the influence of such factors as racial and ethnic composition, cultural background, family income, age levels, and similar factors on either the economic or social aspects of neighborhood planning.

Another major area in which more research needs to be undertaken relates to the vital question of the *journey to work*. We know that the average distance traveled, and the costs and amount of energy expended, have been increasing steadily as suburban communities have been established farther away from the central cities. However, empirical information is lacking, and we have no sound criteria for determining how much farther people will commute. This problem will become even more important in the future than it is today.

Finally, we need more understanding of how new knowledge developed on such matters as climatology may be put to use in building our housing, not only in general, but in different regions. We need to know how we can conserve on our natural resources and how we can plan for the more efficient use of our land, which may still be relatively abundant in some regions but which is rapidly approaching depletion in others. Problems such as these must be acknowledged today rather than a decade or two from now if we are to meet the expanding needs of our future population.

Manufacturing and Construction Processes

Differentiation must be made between technical knowledge and manufacturing and construction processes. The former encompasses the basic knowledge important to the components of a building; the latter encompasses the process of manufacturing those components (i.e., product development) and creating the building on the site.

Most of the research and development funds spent in the home building industry have been spent in the area of product development. As a result, our industry has come up with many new household conveniences and labor-saving devices—ranging from modern systems of home heating and ventilating to such new items of household equipment as the automatic clothes washer, the clothes dryer, dishwasher, garbage disposer, and even the micro-wave oven. These new conveniences have undoubtedly resulted in large part from the competitive character of our private enterprise system. It is to be expected that as individual manufacturing firms continue to desire to maintain or improve their own business position, they will continue to spend considerable funds on the development of these and related items, such as better building materials, better paints, better lighting, better wall coverings, and better floor coverings. This development must be encouraged.

The difficulty with this approach by itself is, however, that no attention is given to the "total" house. There is no coordination among the various facets of industry which might result in whole new concepts of construction, design, and facilities. This kind of research is not likely to be supported by individual firms or groups with vested interests because the results, though they may be in the interest of progress, are likely to be damaging to one or more segments of industry. As just one example, it is not likely that the structural clay products (brick) industry will support research that would encourage the use of substitute wall panels made of plastic, nor is the glass industry likely to support new designs using fewer windows in the interest of better thermal control.

It is not entirely out of the realm of possibility that our entire house-building industry, as it exists today, would be found to be outmoded and in need of replacement by a few large industrial firms. Many times in our nation's history a great many small manufacturing firms producing a certain commodity have had to give way to a few large industrial firms, with the advent of true mass production and other technical advances. In some instances, a new type of product replaced the old one—for example, the automobile replacing the horse and buggy (which put many village blacksmiths out of work but added many new jobs in the automobile factory). In other instances, large-scale production simply replaced small-scale production. One may wonder if we did not come close to seeing such a revolutionary change in the experiment with the Lustron house (Chapter 14). Few would deny that this particular experiment was doomed to failure because of certain conditions that surrounded it from the outset. For example, the experiment came into being in the first place only because of the "political climate" concerning the extreme need for housing for veterans that existed at the time. (It was for this reason only that the Federal Government promised to loan 50 million dollars to a private individual, with a demand for only $1,000 equity.) In the manufacture of the first of these homes, many engineering problems were faced, simply because this was the first large-scale operation of this kind in housing anywhere. Also, marketing and especially financing became problems, because financial institutions generally prefer to go along with something that has been tested and proved in the past. They are encouraged in this by the Federal Government, as evidenced by this stipulation: "It may be assumed that a property will continue to be attractive to the market for an extended period *only when it exhibits qualities and characteristics which experience has proven to be of lasting appeal. . . .*"[18] (Italics provided.)

Most of Lustron's problems, except the major one of heavy government subsidization, were being worked out when the company was required to stop manufacturing. There remained engineering problems, largely due to the use of small panels and excessive site erection costs, and there were problems of marketing and financing. However, most of these problems were not beyond being solved within a relatively short period of time. The

[18] *FHA Underwriting Handbook—Home Mortgages.* Washington, D.C.: U.S. Government Printing Office, currently revised September 1959, 70716.3. Many families who have owned Lustron homes for the past fifteen years probably take serious exception to this philosophy. As indicated in Chapter 14, the house seems to have proved to have a high degree of livability, and has been much less expensive to maintain than conventional houses.

problem of building codes also remained, but progress on this problem was being made in many areas.

The pertinence of this example in this discussion is the fact that it was anticipated that 450 houses could be produced in the Lustron factory in a single day, or approximately 120,000 houses a year. It would have required only ten such factories to turn out the entire supply of single-family houses built in the entire nation each year during the past few years. With the American genius for achieving production efficiency and lower costs through mass production and general technological improvements, it is entirely likely that housing costs could have been reduced significantly; a $17,000 house today might cost only $12,000 or less if as much as $5 per square foot could have been saved—an estimate not considered unreasonable.

But ten factories of the kind described may cost a half billion dollars. Such an investment is not likely until we have more facts and more assurance than we have today concerning the advantages of a truly mass-production approach and other technological advances. It has been made clear that industry in general will not provide either the financial or the moral support for such research. It probably remains for the Federal Government, in the interest of the public's welfare, to provide both.

Conclusion

It was indicated at the outset of this chapter that the size of the housing job in the next decade should surpass that of any previous decade. The new housing construction activity required for the ten-year period 1965 to 1975 is projected at between 17 million and 22 million housing units.

The key as to whether and how well this need is to be met lies in part in research. Research in housing has lagged behind that of other areas of comparable or lesser importance from the standpoint of the individual's daily comfort and well-being. The housebuilding industry itself has not been willing to use its influence or resources to support a broad research program.

Yet the future seems to hold greater possibilities. During the early 1960's there seemed to be a broader understanding of the need for research. This understanding may be attributed in part to a careful and comprehensive study undertaken by an *ad hoc* committee of the Building Research Advisory Board of the National Academy of Sciences–National Research Council. The committee clearly stated its views "concerning the pressing needs and stimulating opportunities for research in building in the United States."

It recommended that government financial support "at the two-million dollar level for the first year" and an annual direct appropriation "increased at a rate to achieve at least a ten-million dollar level at the end of five years" be made available.

The program recommended was as broad as that outlined earlier in this chapter. It included these examples of areas in which studies should be undertaken:

1. *Human requirements:* Studies of the needs of man to be fulfilled by his physical environment. Such studies would bring together highly-qualified persons, including those in the biological, physical and social sciences, economics, and the design professions. The concern would be continuously with the broadest problems of our physical environment, especially in terms of America's urban civilization, in the present and the foreseeable future. This work would produce the definitions of need and of research objectives which are fundamental requirements for any research program.

2. *Internal environment:* The various aspects of physical environment—temperature, humidity, ventilation, sanitation, light color, sound control; size, shape and proportion of spaces; the various types of functional use of space such as housing . . . .

3. *External environment:* The relationship of buildings and planned groups of buildings to each other and to the plan of the community—with special attention to the effects of climate on materials and structures, and to the physical problems of urban areas.

4. *Economics of building:* The broad problems of finance and economics which affect the cost of building and the ability to build, maintain, and operate buildings—such as factors affecting land cost (density of use, taxation, zoning) and economic life of buildings.

5. *Building technology:*

a. Service systems of buildings—Exploration of the potentials for service systems which produce man-made interior environmental conditions.

b. Engineering of structures—Basic principles of structural behavior of buildings and their components in relation to stability, safety, economy, and compatibility with forces of nature.

c. Behavior of building materials—Fundamental problems of the properties and performance of materials as used and combined in building products.[19]

In its report, the Sub-Panel on Housing of the Panel on Civilian Technology, referred to earlier, acknowledged the impressive gains that have been made in the provision of housing for our growing population during the past fifteen years. It indicated that our national housing shortage had been generally overcome, and the housing industry, in the meantime, has undergone a fundamental change in character, from an ill-defined handicraft activity to a local well-organized industry. It indicated, however, that this change in the structure of the industry, dramatic as it has been, is but the first in what will be a process of continuing change for many years to come. It went on to say: "Only through full exploitation of our scientific and technological capability can we produce enough housing of the right kind to lead, ultimately, to a general improvement in the living environment of the individual—a step so necessary for continued social progress."[20]

[19] *A Program for Building Research in the United States.* A Report prepared for the National Bureau of Standards by the Building Research Advisory Board. Publication 994, Washington, D.C.: National Academy of Sciences–National Research Council, May 1962, pp. 12–13.

[20] *Better Housing for the Future, op. cit.,* p. 5.

If a broad research program can be undertaken, America should find itself with the improved housing situation which it is fully capable of creating. Such a program, however, is faced with considerable barriers and obstacles, including those discussed in the section concerning Housing Laws and Pressure Groups in the previous chapter, as well as some mentioned immediately above.

READING LIST

Better Housing for the Future. A Report to the Panel on Civilian Technology. Office of Science and Technology, Executive Office of the President, from its Sub-Panel on Housing. Washington, D.C.: U.S. Government Printing Office, April 1963.

Fields of Research in Building Science. Washington, D.C.: Building Research Institute, 1963.

Fisher, Ernest M. *A Study of Housing Programs and Policies.* Prepared for the U.S. Housing Administrator Norman P. Mason. Washington, D.C.: Housing and Home Finance Agency, January 1960.

Magenau, Eugene F. (ed.) *Research for Architecture.* Proceedings of an AIA Conference held at Ann Arbor, Michigan, Mar. 10-12, 1959. Washington, D.C.: The American Institute of Architects, November 1959.

Perloff, Harvey S. *A National Program of Research in Housing and Urban Development.* Washington, D.C.: Resources for the Future, Inc., September 1961.

A Program for Building Research in the United States. Report prepared for the National Bureau of Standards by the Building Research Advisory Board. Publication 994. Washington, D.C.: National Academy of Sciences–National Research Council, May 1962.

"Social Policy and Social Research in Housing." Entire issue of *The Journal of Social Issues,* Vol. VII, Nos. 1 and 2, 1951.

Woodbury, Coleman. *A Framework for Urban Studies.* Highway Research Board Special Report 52, Publication 722. Washington, D.C.: National Academy of Sciences–National Research Council, October 1959.

Table 15–1

ESTIMATE OF ATTAINABLE HOUSING NEED, 1965–1975

	Low	*High*
1. Household formation	9,595,000	11,399,000
2. Rural-urban migration (net)	806,000	959,000
3. Subtotal	10,401,000	12,358,000
4. Less conversions (net)	1,000,000	750,000
5. Balance	9,401,000	11,608,000
6. Units lost through demolition or becoming vacant and uninhabitable	4,000,000	6,750,000
7. Units lost through other means	1,900,000	2,000,000
8. Total need less vacancy allowance	15,301,000	20,358,000
9. Vacancy allowance (3 percent)	459,030	610,740
10. Total need	15,760,030	20,968,740
11. Average per year (rounded)	1,600,000	2,100,000

Part 5

****

INTERNATIONAL HOUSING

CHAPTER 16

*

Housing in Western Europe and the United Kingdom

It is the purpose of this chapter to review briefly the housing trends and policies in a group of selected Western European countries and the United Kingdom. These are interesting because of the wide variation found, not only with respect to the United States but also among the various European countries themselves.[1]

WAR AND POSTWAR HOUSING POLICIES

All of the countries to be discussed have certain things in common. Like the United States, they all faced a serious housing shortage after World War II. The most immediate cause was the war itself. In some countries, much of the housing in existence at the beginning of the war was destroyed, and much of that not destroyed was badly damaged. Housebuilding during the war either stopped altogether or declined, so that production was insufficient to meet even the normal housing requirements of the particular countries, much less any new requirements. Many of the dwellings that were not destroyed or damaged became obsolescent because they were not adequately maintained. Also, many of the countries had had a housing shortage when they entered the war.

At the same time, most of the countries experienced a large increase in population during the war, and this was generally accompanied by a sharp rise in new family formation (marriages). Incomes rose, accompanied by a rise in the standard of living. This, in turn, led to undoubling of some families who could now afford it, and a demand for different, better houses, by others. In most countries, the concentration of war industries in cities caused a stepping up of rural-to-urban migration. In some, especially West Germany but also The Netherlands and some other countries, large numbers of refugees entered the countries. (It is said 12 million refugees have entered West Germany from Eastern countries.)

The United Kingdom, of course, was one of those countries most affected by the war. Over 225,000 houses were entirely destroyed (approximately 7 percent of the total), 550,000 were severely damaged, and many others

[1] Much of the information contained in this chapter, and many of the general conclusions, are based on a ten-month field study of Western European countries undertaken by the author in 1961–1962.

were damaged to a lesser extent. Although that nation faced no serious housing shortage when the war began, over half of the existing units were more than fifty years old. While there were well over 2,000,000 marriages during the war, the number of houses built did not exceed 200,000.[2]

The situation in West Germany was the most serious. More than one fifth of the dwelling units which had existed in 1939 were destroyed (about 2,300,000 homes) and an even higher proportion was badly damaged.[3] This country also experienced a high rate of family formation. These two problems—heavy war damage and an increased rate of marriage—were superimposed on the problem of a serious housing shortage which had existed before the war began. France and The Netherlands each lost approximately 8 percent of their dwelling units.[4] In The Netherlands this amounted to approximately 100,000 dwellings, and more than 550,000 additional were seriously damaged.[5] Belgium lost approximately 6 percent and Norway 4 percent of their total habitable housing supply.[6] Although Sweden, Denmark, and Switzerland lost no homes through the ravages of the war, the direct effects of the war were sorely felt through the lack of labor and materials for any significant volume of new housing construction, on the one hand, and through the increase in family formation and rise in personal income creating heavy new housing demand, on the other. (Sweden, however, did begin a program of housing subsidies during the middle of the war, with the result that housing production rose during the period 1942 to 1945 sufficiently to meet most of the increasing needs in urban areas.)[7]

During the period from the end of World War II until the time when most of the countries again became more stabilized (for our purposes here, a period varying from seven to ten years after the war), housing policies and housing actions varied greatly among the different countries, depending upon the extent of war damage, the availability of reconstruction resources, and the character and policies of existing governments. In the United Kingdom, a Labor Government took over in 1945. The key elements of this government's program were rent control and government assistance to local housing authorities.[8] The Conservative party was victorious in

[2] Abner D. Silverman, *Selected Aspects of Administration of Publicly-Owned Housing: Great Britain, Netherlands, and Sweden.* Public Housing Administration, Housing and Home Finance Agency, Washington, D.C.: U.S. Government Printing Office, January 1, 1961, p. 35.

[3] *Housing and Urban Development in the Federal Republic of Germany.* Published by The Federal Ministry of Housing, Bonn, 1961, p. 4.

[4] Heinz Umrath and P. Lamartine Yates, "Housing," Chapter 9 in J. Frederic Dewhurst, John O. Coppock, P. Lamartine Yates, and Associates, *Europe's Needs and Resources.* New York: Twentieth Century Fund, 1961, p. 214.

[5] *Building in The Netherlands, 1949–1959.* Compiled by Bouwcentrum, with the collaboration of the Ministry of Housing and Building. Rotterdam: Bouwcentrum, 1959, p. 9.

[6] Umrath and Yates, *op. cit.*, p. 214.

[7] Leonard Silk, *Sweden Plans for Better Housing.* Durham, N.C.: Duke University Press, 1948, p. 57.

[8] Paul F. Wendt, *Housing Policy—The Search for Solutions.* Berkeley: University of California Press, 1963, pp. 24–25.

1951. Although a new housing act was passed the following year, it took nearly four years before a reorientation of general policy was effected. In 1956, a policy of progressive abolition of rent control was adopted, and subsidies were limited to special types of housing for slum clearance, New Towns, agricultural dwellings, and so on.[9]

It has already been indicated that actual war damage was greatest in West Germany. Furthermore, there was the problem of no continuing government, which delayed an immediate attack on the serious housing problems that existed. To meet the emergency housing situation created by World War II, people were at first housed in air-raid shelters and in undamaged buildings. Emphasis in the early postwar years was on repairing damaged buildings rather than on new construction. The major problem was to restore the economy of West Germany and reorganize the government. As part of the plan of economic development, housing for coal miners in the Ruhr, who were practically homeless in 1945, received early attention. (This housing was financed by a tax on coal rather than from government funds.) Postwar conditions prevented a direct attack on housing problems until the currency had been stabilized and the food supply increased. Currency reform was effected in 1948, and in 1949 the Federal Republic of Germany was formed. One of its major objectives was to end the housing crisis.[10] Several measures were directed toward this end in the Housing Acts of 1950 and 1956. Both of these Acts divided housing projects into three categories: (1) social housing projects carried out with government subsidy, (2) housing projects aided by tax preferences, (3) privately financed projects. The social housing projects were primarily for the broad masses of families with limited means. They were financed either by public loans at a low interest, interest subsidies on loan capital from private sources, assistance with rentals, or some form of equalization of the burden. Nearly one third of the total expenditure on building during the period 1950–1960 was provided by governmental bodies and from the "Lastenausgleich" (Equalization of Burdens). This tax has been levied on real estate which was not affected by the war and its consequences, and the resulting income has been used for the good of those who suffered war damages or lost their homes and possessions and had to start life anew as a result of the war. Projects built under preferential conditions of taxation were exempt for a certain period (ten years). Both social housing projects and housing built under preferential conditions of taxation were subject to limitations on size.[11] The privately financed housing was built without government financial assistance and was not subject to restrictions of any kind. During the early years only a small proportion of the houses built fell in this category, but, as will be seen later, the proportion increased rapidly in recent years.

[9] Silverman, *op. cit.*, pp. 39–40.

[10] Wendt, *op. cit.*, pp. 120–123.

[11] *Germany Reports: Building.* Published by the Press and Information Office of the Federal Government. An extract from the book, Professor H. Arntz, gen. ed., *Germany Reports.* 3d ed., 1961 (no publisher listed), pp. 430–433.

In The Netherlands, at the end of the war the government took over control of the national reconstruction program. Building programs were drawn up for every year, in which the available volume of investment was subdivided among the various types of building—houses, factories, schools, and so on. In 1950, the initiation of building programs was shifted to municipal authorities under the Reconstruction Act. Because of the massive scale of the reconstruction required, and the resulting shortage of labor, the volume of new housing constructed was severely limited there.

It has already been mentioned that Sweden began devoting special attention to its housing problems before the war was ended. After the war, the national government continued its program as part of a general plan of economic development. Because of the scarcity of labor, permission was necessary before any kind of building could be undertaken, even in the early postwar years. During the years 1947–1951 housing production was held down in order that production in other industries could proceed more rapidly. Housing production sank to its lowest level in 1951, but thereafter increased year by year.[12] As will be described later, the basic form of financial assistance was the guaranteeing of the interest rate on first and second mortgages, which were obtained from private sources, and a subsidy which, in most instances, constituted a third mortgage, provided directly by the government.

Although there were some differences between the housing policies of Denmark and Sweden, basically the assistance provided by the Danish government was similar to that provided by the state in Sweden.[13] A similar policy was also followed in Norway. However, the policy in that country was carried out through a National Housing Bank, which was established in 1946. This bank served as a financing organ, both for reconstruction and for housing in general, for the entire country. Slightly more emphasis appears to have been placed on home ownership in Norway than in the other Scandinavian countries.[14]

The programs described above show the variation in methods adopted by several European countries to solve their housing problems immediately after the end of World War II. It can be seen that the three Scandinavian countries took a more or less common approach, but each of the other countries tended to have its own approach and solution.

NATURE OF THE BUILDING INDUSTRY

As in the United States, adequate and up-to-date statistics concerning the nature of the building industry are not available for any of the countries. The statistics that are available frequently cover a year in the early 1950's, or before that. They generally indicate that most of the

[12] *Housing in the Northern Countries.* Copenhagen: (no publisher listed), 1960, pp. 121–132.

[13] *Ibid.*, pp. 28–36.

[14] *Ibid.*, pp. 90–100.

building firms were extremely small. For example, firms having five or fewer employees represented 79 percent of the building firms in Sweden in 1951, 86 percent of those in Denmark in 1948, 75 percent of those in The Netherlands in 1950, 86 percent of those in France in 1954, and 65 percent of those in Switzerland in 1955. Firms having four or fewer employees represented 66 percent of the building firms in West Germany in 1950 and 87 percent of those in Belgium in 1947.[15] We know, of course, that the average size of firm in the United States during that period was also extremely small but that there has been a significant increase in average size since that date.

There is some reason to believe that a similar trend has taken place in most of the European countries, although perhaps not to the same extent. For example, it will be shown later that a considerable share of the housing in Sweden is accounted for by cooperative and nonprofit firms, and this housing is often built by large contractors.[16] A similar situation exists in Denmark. Although a considerable number of large apartment buildings also are being built in at least the largest cities in The Netherlands, Switzerland, Belgium, and the United Kingdom, there has been a considerable amount of speculative building of single-family homes in these countries.[17] Many of these homes have been built by small building firms. In some countries (Sweden, Denmark, France, and Germany) many rural houses are being built, frequently on a self-help basis.

In Sweden and Denmark (and, to some extent, in West Germany and France), prefabrication has made considerable strides. Prefabricated panels have been used most widely in the construction of apartment buildings, but in some instances (for example, in Sweden), some small homes are completely prefabricated and assembled at the site. (These are generally found only in smaller communities.) Also in Sweden, some of the major building material manufacturers play a leading role in the planning and financing of some of the large-scale housing projects. In some instances, they prepare the building plans, estimate costs, finance land acquisition and construction, and furnish almost all of the material required for a particular project.[18]

Even in those countries where an important proportion of the new housing is built by the state or municipalities, the contractors themselves are usually private firms. Some local authorities in the United Kingdom conduct their own building operations, but the proportion in relation to the total volume of housing built is small. In most countries, general contractors usually subcontract much of the work to the various trades (plumb-

[15] Dewhurst, *et al.*, *op. cit.*, Table C, Appendix 7–1, p. 983.

[16] Holm has said: "The term 'entrepreneur' is peculiarly applicable to them: not only do they direct construction activity, but they also organize the planning and designing of new houses and manage their administration after they are completed. In most cases the actual work of construction is carried out by *private* contractors." Per Holm, *Swedish Housing*, 2d ed., Stockholm: The Swedish Institute, 1959, p. 36.

[17] United Nations Economic Commission for Europe, *European Housing Trends and Policies in 1960*. Geneva: United Nations, p. 15.

[18] Wendt, *op. cit.*, p. 88.

ing, electrical, etc.), although, as in the United States, some of the largest contractors employ their own specialists.

The character of most of the construction firms—their smallness and their generally inefficient operations—has caused them to be criticized as representing a "backward industry"—criticism not unlike that in the United States. Wendt has pointed out that there has been a great deal of such criticism of the industry during the postwar period in the United Kingdom.[19]

VOLUME OF HOUSING CONSTRUCTION

Although a shortage of housing still exists in almost every country, new housing construction has progressed at an impressive rate in each of the countries since the mid-1950's. Production of housing has found its place in the economy of every nation.

Among Western countries, the highest level of production has taken place in the country that experienced the most serious war damage—West Germany. As Wertheimer has indicated: "The magnitude and speed of housing construction in West Germany since the war has been outstanding."[20] A total of approximately 561,000 dwellings was completed in 1956, representing 11 new dwellings for every 1,000 inhabitants. In 1960, 551,000 dwellings, representing 10.5 new dwellings per 1,000 inhabitants were built (Table 16–1, p. 537).

The next highest rates of new construction by 1956 were found in Norway, Sweden, and Switzerland, each nation building approximately 8.0 new dwellings per 1,000 inhabitants. The rate in Norway had declined slightly by 1960, but it increased for both Switzerland and Sweden.

The rate per 1,000 inhabitants in France increased from 5.5 to 7.0 between 1956 and 1960 (where, despite heavy need, private construction has probably been impeded over many years by the continuation of controls on rents); in Denmark, from 4.5 to 6.1; in The Netherlands, from 6.4 to 7.4; and in Belgium, from 4.8 to 5.7. In The Netherlands, the amount of housing built each year is "programed" by the national government through the Ministry of Housing in The Hague, because of the continued labor shortage. The figure has remained quite uniform in the United Kingdom, with 307,300 new dwelling units built in 1956 and 307,200 in 1960, representing approximately 6.0 new dwellings per 1,000 inhabitants in both years.

FINANCING METHODS AND SPONSORING GROUPS

Although there are appreciable differences between the United States and the various Western European countries with respect to size and nature

[19] *Ibid.*, p. 45.

[20] Robert G. Wertheimer, "The Miracle of German Housing in the Postwar Period," *Land Economics*, Vol. XXXIV, No. 4, November 1958, p. 338.

of dwelling units built, the entrepreneurial systems in home building, and similar factors, perhaps the most basic differences concern the methods of financing and sponsoring groups. The kind of sponsoring group, in fact, usually determines the nature and volume of construction and the types and price (rental) of dwellings built.[21]

United Kingdom

In the United Kingdom, most housing is provided either by the local authorities directly or by private individuals without government assistance. It can be seen from the data in Table 16–2 (p. 537) that in 1957 approximately 55 percent of the dwelling units completed were built by the local authorities and 42 percent by private individuals, whereas in 1960 these percentages were reversed. This reflects a trend which began in 1954 following the withdrawal of governmental restrictions on private home building.

The local authorities in England differ from local housing authorities in the United States inasmuch as they are the councils of county boroughs, urban and rural districts, and local governing councils. Most of the housing they provide is for low-income and elderly population groups (although eligibility for council housing is not based exclusively on income), but they also engage in slum clearance and rebuilding, in the improvement of existing housing, and the development of New Towns to relieve the congestion in urban areas. A proportion of their capital is derived from the national budget through loans granted by the Public Works Loan Board. They are, however, encouraged to borrow, wherever possible, from private sources. Most local authorities operate housing of several types. The rents charged vary according to age, size, and cost of construction. Families whose incomes increase beyond certain levels are usually allowed to remain, but must pay a surcharge. Approximately one out of every five households

[21] Housing in Eastern European countries, not discussed in this book, reflects even sharper differences. In the USSR and other Eastern European countries, the state house-building sector is dominant; in fact, in the USSR the public housing sector, particularly in urban areas, continues to expand. In 1960, four fifths of the housing completed was built for the urban population and the remaining one fifth was built for collective farmers. Much of this rural housing is built in urban-type settlements to facilitate the provision of greater amenities and community facilities. All apartments built by the state are available free of charge for permanent occupancy. The USSR has experienced one of the heaviest building rates of any country—14.0 dwellings per 1,000 inhabitants in 1960. However, from the standpoint of space and equipment per apartment, new dwellings are more modest in their standards than those in Western countries. All land in the USSR is public property and its allocation for housing as well as other uses is the obligation and responsibility of state organizations. Cooperative housing shows signs of playing a growingly more important role in Czechoslavakia, Hungary, Poland, and Yugoslavia. For additional information concerning housing in the Eastern European countries, see these references: United Nations Economic Commission for Europe, *European Housing Trends and Policies in 1960, op. cit.;* United Nations, Department of Economic and Social Affairs, *Report of the* Ad Hoc *Group of Experts on Housing and Urban Development.* New York: 1962, pp. 67–72 for discussion of the USSR and pp. 74–76 for discussion of Yugoslavia; United Nations Economic Commission for Europe, *Financing of Housing in Europe.* Geneva: United Nations, 1958.

in the United Kingdom lives in local authority rental units—most of the units being of the one-family type built in rows ("terraced" housing).

England also has some 650 "housing associations" which build nonprofit housing for special groups. Private sources of funds are frequently supplemented by public funds from local councils, loans from the Public Works Loan Board, and public subsidies where applicable (e.g., for the aged, disabled, etc.).

A unique development in the United Kingdom has been the planning and construction of entirely new communities by the New Town Development Corporation. The purpose of these New Towns, as indicated above, is to relieve the congestion in urban areas. The corporations are authorized to acquire the necessary land for industrial and commercial building, and residential housing as well as any other facilities and services needed for the development and operation of the New Town. After construction is completed, the development corporation is dissolved and its assets and liabilities are turned over to the Commission for New Towns, which manages the properties. Housing can be sold to local workers, including those in industrial and commercial enterprises. That which is not sold is retained by the Commission and operated as rental property for all income groups.

The major sources of financing in the private sector of the housing market are building societies (although some private mortgage credit is available through insurance companies, banks, and other agencies). These societies—the first of which originated over 150 years ago—are private savings banks specializing in housing loans. Although the terms of loans, proportion of loan to value, period of years for amortization, and so on, vary for different types of borrowers, the most common type of loan available is a 75 percent, twenty-year loan repayable by annuity payments. Interest rates may be altered on existing loans by giving three or six months' notice to borrowers.[22]

Approximately four out of every ten houses in the United Kingdom are owner occupied. The majority are one-family housing units of the row-house or semidetached type.

Sweden

One of the most widely discussed housing programs in the world is that of Sweden. Frequently attention is focused on the cooperative housing built in that country, although such housing usually represents less than one third of the nation's housing construction. About the same proportion (as cooperative housing) of the total housing built each year in recent years has been built by state and local authorities, and a somewhat higher proportion by private enterprise—although only slightly over half of the private enterprise housing has been built for owner occupancy.

The largest housing cooperative is the national association of Tenants'

[22] Wendt, *op. cit.*, p. 42.

Savings and Building Societies, abbreviated "HSB." This cooperative is the country's biggest landlord. It was formed in 1923, although cooperative housing in Sweden goes back to the 1870's. The major objective of the national society is to arrange the building of projects which, after completion, are controlled and administered by the members of *local* housing societies. The actual work of planning a project generally takes place at HSB's Stockholm headquarters, which houses the largest office of architects in Sweden. Completed units are made available to society members, who enjoy the right of permanent occupancy at rents computed on a cost basis. The projects built are financed by members' savings, prospective members investing 5 percent of the cost of an individual home. The Svenska Riksbyggen (Swedish National Building Society), made up of building trade unions, production firms, local organizations, and building societies, is another large Swedish building cooperative. It was founded in 1941. One of the differences between the two cooperatives is that the HSB contracts for the construction of projects, whereas the SR sometimes engages in building as a means of providing more employment opportunities for member construction workers. Cooperative projects are financed through a combination of private and public loans. First and second mortgages are obtained in the open market and third mortgage loans are made by the government. The loan-to-value ratio is 95 percent when first, second, and third mortgages are combined. The government also guarantees the interest rate on the first and second mortgages, preventing it from going beyond a certain level.

Municipally sponsored housing enterprises, sometimes referred to as "public utility companies," are built with direct subsidies and loans from the government. Occupancy requires no equity by the tenants, since only rental housing is built. Occupancy is permitted to all economic classes—thus the housing built for middle-income groups is competing for the same market as that served by cooperatives. Because of the housing shortage, however, this has not deterred the building of cooperative projects.[23]

Although nearly 40 percent of the dwelling units completed in Sweden in 1960 were provided by private enterprise, it was indicated above that only slightly over half of that proportion was built for owner occupancy. This proportion—about 22 percent—representing *owner-occupied* housing (excluding the "permanent occupancy" cooperative units) represents approximately the proportion of *rental* housing built in the United States. For owner-occupied housing, first and second mortgage loans must be obtained in the private market for about 50 percent of the total cost of the dwelling unit. Public loans, which constitute a form of secondary financing (third mortgage), can be obtained up to 40 percent of the total cost. The remaining 10 percent must be supplied by the homeowner, either in cash or in labor.

[23] United Nations, Department of Economic and Social Affairs, *Housing through Non-Profit Organizations.* New York: United Nations, September 1956, pp. 94–95.

Denmark

Whereas there has been little change in the methods of financing and the importance of the various sponsoring groups with regard to new housing construction in Sweden in recent years, this is not the case for Denmark. Housing built directly with state and municipal funds has remained minimal, that built through unaided private enterprise has shown a significant increase, and that built through housing associations and aided private enterprise has declined. A fundamental change in Danish housing policy took place in 1959 when the government reduced the amount of public loan capital available and placed greater emphasis on the private mortgage market. At the present time the highest proportion of housing is built through the use of a system of mortgage credit based on cooperative societies (known as Credit and Mortgage Associations), which are made up of property owners who have mortgaged their properties. These credit institutions are not supported by public funds or guarantees; rather, they obtain their funds by selling fixed interest bonds on the stock market. First and second mortgages are obtained from the usual mortgage institutions, which are under public control and which are entitled to grant fifty-year loans (which in part accounts for the fact that two thirds of all new housing in Denmark is of the low-rent type) covering up to 75 percent of the value of the property. With state guarantees, the total loan limit is increased to 94 percent for nonprofit housing, 90 percent for owner-occupied, one-family houses for low-income groups, and 85 percent for other private enterprise housing.[24]

Dwelling units built by housing associations (nonprofit organizations, including cooperatives) are available only on a rental basis, the occupier having none of the rights of an owner. He is a member of the association, but if he wants to move only the association can dispose of the vacant dwelling and his initial deposit (but no part of any increase in the value of the dwelling that may have occurred) is returned to him.

Norway

The sponsoring groups and methods of housing finance in Norway are quite similar to those in Denmark, but the administrative organization is significantly different. Almost all housing is financed through the National Housing Bank of Norway, as mentioned earlier (although much of the housing in rural areas is financed through the Smallholding Bank, which operates in close conjunction with it). Much of the so-called private housing is built through cooperatives, which operate on the municipal level (in contrast to those in Sweden, which operate at the national level), but are coordinated through a national body called the Norwegian Housing and

[24] *Housing in the Northern Countries, op. cit.*, pp. 30–31.

Building Association. The cooperatives consist of "parent" or "mother" societies whose members pay a small membership fee (approximately $3.75 in 1961). The parent society in a particular city plans new groups of apartments, engages private architects and consultants, and contracts for the building with private contracting firms. They administer the erection of buildings and also manage them after occupancy on the basis of agreements with "subsidiary" or "daughter" societies, of which each parent society may have several in a particular municipality. (Each project or block of dwellings built by a parent society is usually organized into a daughter society.) Prospective owners must pay an initial small payment to become members of the subsidiary societies. In addition they must make a down payment (the amount varying according to the building costs of the project and the size of the apartment) before taking occupancy. The down payment has increased appreciably in recent years (the average amount reached $1,450 in 1961). Since most individuals are not capable of meeting that payment from their own resources, they arrange a loan from the employee fund where they work, from their insurance fund, from a private bank, from a pension society, or from some other source covering the whole or part of it. The municipality guarantees the down payment. One of the best-known cooperatives is OBOS (Oslo Housing and Savings Society), in Oslo. It was the first cooperative housing society in Norway, founded in 1929.

While the Housing Bank's loan regulations are particularly favorable, it is a condition of the loan that there be no vested interests beyond those of the tenants. This does not preclude admitting municipalities and other groups as members with the right to subscribe an unlimited number of shares, but the sole functions of these groups are to support the society financially. They have no claim upon the use of the properties built. The individual "tenants" are in reality neither tenants nor owners, in the strict sense of those terms. The daughter societies are the real owners of the housing, and if an occupant wants to sell his apartment (or, more precisely, his stock), this can be done only through the board of directors of the daughter society in order to prevent it from being sold for any profit.

Technically, the Housing Bank Act permits 100 percent-of-valuation loans but, in practice, they are usually limited to 90 percent of valuation. Valuation as used here differs from the concept in the United States, inasmuch as it is based on a "socially acceptable" rent, not on what the rental would be on an open market. On this basis, the customary loan amounts to about 75 percent of the cost of construction. The national government also takes recognition of increased building costs by subsidizing occupants who have incomes below a certain level. This subsidy must be repaid if there is a turnover of occupancy to a tenant having an income over the stipulated amount. Mortgages are for a one-hundred-year period and are, therefore, transferred rather than paid off.

The Netherlands

In The Netherlands most of the housing has been built by three groups: private persons or groups, municipalities, and housing societies. In the private sector, which constitutes approximately half of the new housing built in recent years, subsidies are provided by the government, which frequently reduce the economic rent by about one third. These subsidies include both a lump-sum payment to the builder when the project is under construction and annual contributions which depend on the rent charged. (Many of the privately built units are built for rent.) The formula for the amount of subsidy varies by size of town, type of building, and size of dwelling unit. The upper limits of dwelling size are controlled by the government. For owner-occupied dwellings, municipalities guarantee up to a maximum of 90 percent of the net costs of construction (30 percent of the dwellings in The Netherlands are owner occupied).

The cooperative movement has not been as strong in The Netherlands as in the Scandinavian countries. There is no large organization such as the HSB or SR in Sweden or OBOS in Oslo, Norway. There are, however, a number of nonprofit organizations which build housing, and some of these are of the cooperative nature (but in some others the association members may not themselves rent the houses). The housing associations are financed almost entirely by and work in close association with the municipalities, which, in turn, secure their funds from the national government. They build primarily for the working class. The national government makes a fixed annual contribution to cover the operating deficits resulting from rent subsidies. The size of this contribution depends on such factors as the number of occupants for whom the dwellings have been designed and, to a certain extent, on the cost of land and construction. The contribution may be granted for fifty years—the usual write-off period for so-called Housing Act houses—but this period can be reduced, depending upon circumstances. As a condition for financial aid, the government maintains strict control over the type of housing to be built.

Although the Dutch government prefers construction through housing associations to direct municipally controlled operations, because it wants tenant-members to participate in the management of the projects and share responsibility for their success, almost an equal proportion of municipal housing has been found to be necessary for the lowest-income groups and for families living in the worst slums. The boundaries between association housing and municipal housing are not always sharply defined.

West Germany

Most of the housing (approximately 70 percent) built in West Germany since the mid-1950's has been provided by private enterprise, and the largest portion of it has been built by private individuals. The government has assisted through (a) special tax concessions given to prospective home buyers when they make savings contracts with private financial institutions for the purpose of buying a home and (b) forcing the institutional sources of credit to direct a fixed proportion of their funds to residential construction at a maximum interest rate (6 percent). A multiple system of mortgage loans, somewhat similar to that in some of the other countries discussed, is used. First mortgages are provided by private financial institutions. (The growth of building societies similar to those in England in recent years has been remarkable.) Second mortgages are obtained through loans and advances by commercial banks, employers, and tenants, and from other private sources. Some capital is provided by the builder's own resources. The remainder required (in diminishing amounts in recent years) is provided by the government (Federal government, provincial government and communes, and by the Office of Equalization of Burdens),[25] in 1960, only 20 percent of the total housing construction was financed directly from public sources and the other 80 percent, from private sources.

Interest subsidies on loan capital from private sources are given to nonprofit housing groups (housing associations and cooperatives) for low-cost housing in place of direct financial aid whenever possible, in order to facilitate use of private credit sources and to restrict the use of public funds. Labor unions have played a significant part in the provision of postwar housing in West Germany. Their activities are coordinated by an Association for Union Owned Housing Enterprises.

France

In France, the proportion of housing built by private enterprise in recent years has been only slightly lower than that in West Germany, but, whereas housing built by individuals for owner occupancy has been on the increase in West Germany, it has been declining in France as a result of government encouragement of rental housing, particularly in overcrowded urban areas. However, in 1960 three fourths of the private construction was still owner occupied. Some of this construction represented cooperative housing built with low-interest public loans which supplemented the pooled resources of the members of the cooperatives. In some instances, additional private housing is provided by housing associations formed by private firms on behalf of their employees; this housing is also eligible for some public assistance. Some of the housing provided in these manners is available for low-income families. A very small proportion of the private construction is unaided by the government in some form or other.

The majority of the public assistance for housing in France is extended to the 900 or more public, private, or mixed nonprofit rental housing organizations. Over two thirds of these institutions are known as "habitations a loyers moderes" or "HLM." The public HLM's are established by the government

[25] Wendt, *op. cit.*, p. 127.

on a departmental or municipal level. Loans may be granted up to 90 percent of the cost if guaranteed by the local government. They carry interest rates of only 2 percent or 2½ percent and the term of loans varies from forty-five to sixty years.

Belgium

Belgium is in some respects unique, because it did not experience a housing shortage as serious as that in other Western European countries during and after the war and, therefore, did not have the same reasons to encourage a heavy volume of housing construction. The density of dwelling-unit occupancy there is among the lowest in Europe. In recent years, over four fifths of the housing has been built privately, and in 1960 nearly two thirds was built by individuals without public assistance. Included was a considerable amount of speculatively built housing resulting in part from a generally favorable credit market and liberalized rent policy (discussed below). Cooperative housing has not developed on any substantial scale, perhaps because national housing policy has been directed at promoting home ownership by as many low-income families as possible.

Switzerland

As in Belgium, over four fifths of the housing in Switzerland has been built by private enterprise in recent years. The electorate, in a referendum, voted against further Federal housing subsidies in 1950, but a Federal order in 1958 again initiated a limited public housing program which provides financial assistance to the cantons for no more than four years for the construction of dwellings for low-income families. Less than 3 percent of the new housing completed in 1960 was built by public bodies. No government mortgage guarantees or insurance systems are available for any housing in Switzerland. Federal aid is, however, extended in the form of interest subsidies that reduce the market rate of interest on private loans. Private builders obtain capital for home building from mortgage banks or the cantonal banks. When private capital for housing is unavailable, the Federal authorities provide the necessary capital indirectly by borrowing from private credit institutions at market rates rather than granting public loans at a lower rate of interest. Nearly two fifths of the housing built is unaided private rental housing.

Although cooperative housing accounted for only one eighth of the new construction in 1960, there has been a cooperative movement in Switzerland for many years. (Nearly half of all families in Switzerland are members of cooperative stores.) Cooperative housing societies usually obtain first mortgage loans up to 60 or 65 percent of costs from the Cooperative Central Bank, formed by cooperative stores and the unions, or from the cantonal banks. The interest is below market rates and there is no set term for the loans. Second mortgage loans up to 90 or 95 percent are either made or guaranteed by the communities. Interest rates vary, but they are usually below market rates. Maturity ranges from twenty-five to fifty years. The final 5 to 10 percent of the cost of the projects is usually raised through tenants' equities or down payments. Cooperative housing is not tax free in Switzerland.

CHARACTER OF NEW HOUSING

Dwelling units in most European countries are appreciably more modest from the standpoint of space than those built in the United States. The Netherlands most closely approximates our situation—in 1960 over 80 percent of the dwelling units completed had five or more rooms. This compares with 40 percent for the United Kingdom, 44 percent for Denmark, and 43 percent for Switzerland. On the other hand, 48 percent of the dwellings completed in France in that year had three rooms or fewer. The comparable figure for Sweden was 44 percent and for West Germany, 31 percent. No dwelling units having more than five rooms were recorded as having been built in France and West Germany in that year (Table 16–3, p. 539).

One interesting aspect of these figures is that there is no correlation between them and per capita real income. In fact, in Sweden, where there is a large proportion of small dwellings, per capita income is higher than in The Netherlands, but the dwellings are appreciably smaller. It is possible to rationalize the large dwellings in The Netherlands with the traditionally large families in that country. In Sweden, however, it can only be reasoned that there is a consumer preference for small dwellings.

Dwelling units in these countries frequently lack many of the facilities that most of newly built homes in the United States have. Although current data are not available, it is generally observed that new homes and apartments in Sweden have more modern equipment than other European countries, owing undoubtedly to the relatively high per capita income in that country. For example, in 1955 almost 90 percent of all dwellings in Sweden had running water, approximately 65 percent had central heating, 60 percent had toilets, and 40 percent had bathrooms. Refrigerators were found in 40 percent of all dwellings. These percentages, which cover rural as well as urban housing, have undoubtedly increased appreciably since 1955. Standards also are quite high in Denmark. Data for the nation as a whole are not available, but approximately 50 percent of the urban dwellings had baths and central heating, and 92 percent had indoor toilets, in the mid-1950's. (In rural districts, the situation was appreciably poorer.) The United Kingdom has high standards with regard to piped running water, baths, and indoor toilets, but central heating is still provided only in some of the new apartment blocks. An example of the improvement in standards in recent years may be cited with reference to the installation of central heating in West Germany. In 1953, only 6 percent of all homes were equipped with this facility, compared with 21 percent in 1959 and an estimated 25 percent in 1960. Today, almost no homes are built without a bath. Standards in other countries would appear to be lower, but, especially with regard to new construction, the provision of basic items of equipment is increasing rapidly.

RENT CONTROL

When there is an extreme shortage of housing, rents generally rise in a free market because of the excessive demand against the limited supply of units available. This market situation existed in all countries during and immediately after World War II.

In order to avoid the resulting undue hardship on families, and to give them security of tenure, governments of the various countries adopted policies of rent control; i.e., they stipulated the maximum amounts of rents that could be charged for rental dwellings of different sizes and types. Such policies were necessary and helpful to consumers, but because they were often objected to by owners and builders they frequently tended to reduce the amount of rental housing in the total supply. They also tended to permit the quality of existing rental housing to deteriorate, because owners often would not put any of their limited rental return into maintenance and repairs—thus aggravating, rather than improving, the over-all rental housing situation.

Rent controls were abandoned in the United States in 1952 (except in New York State, where they have been retained in New York City). However, it was felt necessary to keep them in the various European countries much longer.

In the last few years there have been two trends with regard to rents in Western European countries: (1) most countries have established the goal of eventual abolition of rent control, and (2) there has been a continuing liberalization of rent policy, resulting in rent increases where controls were retained. Also, some countries have provided occupants of new houses with certain additional subsidies in order to reduce their ratio of rent paid to income received. Examples of the trend in recent policies will be cited for several leading countries.[26]

In the United Kingdom, there was a marked reduction in rent controls and a relaxation in respect to those dwellings that remained under control, through the Rent Act of 1957.[27] In Sweden, controls were abolished for public and cooperative housing in 1958 and for all housing in sixty communes in 1959. In Denmark, substantial increases in rents were allowed, the amounts varying with the age of the dwellings, under the Landlord and Tenant Act of December 1958. In Norway, rents in new, postwar houses

[26] Most of the information in this section has been obtained from the various annual reports entitled *European Housing Trends and Policies,* issued by the United Nations Economic Commission for Europe, United Nations, Geneva.

[27] For an analysis of the effect of rent control in one particular city, see J. B. Cullingworth, *Housing in Transition.* A Case Study in the City of Lancaster 1958–1962. London: Heinemann Educational Books, Ltd., 1963.

have been based on construction and other costs and on subsidies available, but housing built before the war has had rent levels maintained at prewar levels (with some increases permitted because of increased costs of maintenance and management).

A new rent act became effective in the Federal Republic of Germany in July 1960 which provides for a progressive decontrol of rents until 1966, at which time controls will be completely abolished. Certain categories of old dwellings (for example, in some locations where no serious housing shortage existed) were immediately freed from control. Private dwellings built since 1948 without state aid have not been under rent control.

Rent control still exists in The Netherlands and in France. In The Netherlands an appreciable increase in rents (up to 20 percent) was permitted for certain categories of dwellings (i.e., prewar dwellings and many dwellings built since the war with government support) under the Rent Act of April 1960. Similar increases have been allowed in France, on a graded basis over the last several years. (France has had rent controls for about forty years.) In contrast, rent control was abolished in Belgium in 1957, and gradual abolition, over the next few years, has been scheduled in Switzerland. The housing shortage was less serious in these countries than in others.

HOUSING FOR SPECIAL GROUPS

It was recognized early in some Western European countries that a number of low-income groups, notably large families, aged persons, and farm workers, encountered particular difficulties in obtaining improved housing. Even the rents charged for housing built with government support were too high for many individuals or families in these groups. The answer did not lie solely in the additional financial support the various governments provided to cover the maintenance costs of children, to aged persons, and others; there was not an ample supply of housing available to satisfy the special needs of these groups.

Large Families

The earliest remedial steps were taken in the Scandinavian countries. Beginning about 1935, Sweden and Denmark introduced legislation, since then repeatedly amended and extended, which authorized cheap government loans for the building of approved housing projects for large families, as well as rent subsidies to individual families. Soon, however, it was decided that it was undesirable for a project to be occupied exclusively by large families, and the governments changed their policies to permit some of the units to be occupied by small families. In 1948, Sweden completely discontinued the practice of building special projects for large families and substituted a policy of providing rent subsidies which would permit such families to take up residence as ordinary families in any category of housing projects.[28]

A few special projects have also been built for other groups: bachelor girls (required in some countries, especially Germany and Austria, as a result of the heavy war loss among the male population), husbandless or widowed mothers, and invalids. The outstanding example of the last named is the Collective House for Invalids in Copenhagen.

The Aging[29]

Perhaps the most attention, however, has been given to the aging. The reasons are generally the same as the reasons given for this special attention in the United States (Chapter 13). This group has many special characteristics—the population trends (including the size and nature of aged households), their generally poor economic status, the physical changes that take place with the aging process, their social and emotional characteristics, and the nature of their present housing accommodations.

In many European countries the aging represent even a higher proportion of the total population than in the United States. These proportions during one recent year and proportions estimated for a future year are as follows:

	Recent Years		*Future Years*	
	Year	*Percent*	*Year*	*Percent*
United Kingdom	1955	11	1979	15
Sweden	1955	11	1980	17
Denmark	1955	10	1980	14
Norway	1955	10	1975	14
West Germany	1955	10	1975	14
The Netherlands	1955	8	1980	13
France	1960	12	1981	13
Belgium	1955	12	1977	15
Switzerland	1954	10	1970	12

Historical Background

Europe has had a long history of providing independent living quarters (as against so-called institutional Homes for the Aged) for the elderly. Probably the oldest special apartment project built for this age group, which is still in existence, is Die Fuggerei built in Augsburg, Germany, and chartered in 1521. This group of apartments was provided by the Fugger brothers, wealthy merchants of the German Renaissance. Family

[28] George R. Nelson, ed., *Freedom and Welfare—Social Patterns in the Northern Countries of Europe.* Sponsored by the Ministries of Social Affairs of Denmark, Finland, Iceland, Norway, Sweden, 1953 (no publisher listed), p. 299.

[29] Much of the information in this section is summarized from Glenn H. Beyer and F. H. J. Nierstrasz, *Aging and Independent Living.* Amsterdam: Elsevier Publishing Co. (to be published 1965).

heads had to be at least fifty-five years old to qualify for one of the apartments, and there was an income limit for admission. Single persons were not admitted, but there were some small apartments for widows.

The almshouses of England, which had their origin in the Middle Ages, were built for those aged who were without resources or friends. The endowments of those "houses" provided for the shelter and care of the occupants, who were required to do what work they could on adjoining agricultural land. One of the distinctive features of many almshouses, especially those built up to the eighteenth century, was their architectural beauty. Many were designed by such architects as Sir Christopher Wren and included furniture and paintings by famous designers and artists. During the eighteenth century they tended to become more institutional and less picturesque, but the accommodations they provided often were improved.

The first apartment projects specially built for the aging in The Netherlands, known as "Hofje," were built in the seventeenth century. They were generally built by wealthy Dutch merchants for their retired workers and servants. They usually consisted of two-story apartments built in a solid rectangle. The backs of the units formed a wall around the project. Inside the buildings was a pleasant court.

Denmark probably was the pioneer in moving beyond the public-assistance concept of providing only institutional homes for the aged in modern times. An act of 1891 separated "housing" for older people from institutional accommodations. Several other countries, especially Sweden, followed this pattern of building, although no single projects this large were built anywhere else.

Types of Housing Today

These types of projects have received considerable criticism in recent years, because it is claimed that such blocks of apartments solely for the elderly isolated them from the normal life of the population and impaired their opportunities of finding occasional sources of income through babysitting, mending of clothes, and so on. Still, the concept has continued to have support in certain countries (including the United States, as indicated in an earlier chapter).

Many different kinds of projects of "pensioners' dwellings," as they are known in many countries, are being built today in different European countries. In some countries a rather uniform type is being built, but in others a variety of types can be found.

Perhaps the country looked to for experience, more than any other, is Sweden. This country has been constantly reviewing and altering its policies concerning the aging over recent years. For a time, blocks of apartments were built. Then, in the light of the criticism mentioned above, a concept of "scattered flats" was adopted which provided an elderly person with an equal right to any new state-supported (which includes 90 percent of all housing construction in Sweden) apartments. This was implemented through the use of rent subsidies. Today, Sweden has a policy stressing variation, and some blocks of housing are still being built for old people. Some municipalities prefer them, in part because no multifamily structures in which "scattered flats" could be incorporated either exist or can be built in the area because of lack of demand for such multifamily structures. All apartments for older people, whether in blocks or scattered, receive the same special subsidy.

In Denmark, especially in the larger cities, it is the policy to provide apartments for the elderly in large apartment buildings also housing younger families. However, rather than scattering the apartments throughout the structure, they are provided on the ground floor. This, the Danes believe, has three advantages: (1) there are young people, including children, nearby; (2) small clusters of elderly are housed together, thus permitting greater sociability "with their own kind"; (3) elderly who have a fear of living on upper floors and of using an elevator have these fears alleviated.

Norway, in contrast, is providing ten- to twelve-story apartment buildings exclusively for the elderly, at least in Oslo. (Smaller blocks of housing exclusively for the elderly are built in the smaller and more rural municipalities.) It has been found in Oslo that most elderly actually prefer the upper floors of apartment buildings, usually because of the view that can be obtained but also because such locations are less noisy than those on lower floors.

In each of these Scandinavian countries it is the *responsibility* of municipalities to provide adequate housing for their aging. Special subsidies are provided so that no aged person need be deprived of good housing because of low income. However, no country has as yet been able to build enough new housing to meet the total need.

In the United Kingdom, "old people's bungalows" have been built for many years, and since World War II a number of grouped "warden" schemes have been provided. Under this concept, small, one-story bungalows are built in a group, frequently row ("terraced") housing built in a rectangle, each group having a so-called "warden", i.e., a single or married woman with a warm personality who can provide certain care in the event of minor illnesses and can assist the somewhat infirm in minor housekeeping tasks. The tenants live independently and may come and go as they please. In the last few years the government has promoted a "flatlet" scheme. This scheme, usually limited to between twelve and thirty dwellings in a group, provides each person with a complete, small apartment and, in addition, provides for a common-room. Plans vary, although usually the buildings are two stories high and planned around open courts. There frequently are shops nearby. Also, there is usually a "warden." One of the most recently built flatlet schemes is in the New Town of Stevenage.

What we call "geriatric complexes" in the United States are found in The Netherlands (where they are called "combined projects"), in West

Germany (where they are called "three-step projects"), and in Belgium.[30] As indicated in Chapter 13, these terms are derived from the fact that projects of this type meet the needs of the elderly during three different stages of physical ability from (1) the completely well who can live with little or no personal care, to (2) the infirm who need general care (such as provided by homes for the aged), to (3) the chronically ill who need constant nursing attention (as provided in nursing homes). All three types of accommodations are built on the same site. The number of such projects is still limited largely to one project in each of the largest cities in the countries mentioned. In The Netherlands, many communities also are building blocks of special apartments for the aging, not of the combined-project type. The latter type, which was mentioned as being prominent in Norway, is also being built in Switzerland. "Apartment colonies" have recently been built in Zurich, Basel, and Geneva. These have work and recreational facilities where the young cooperate with the old.

France also has built a number of blocks of special apartments for the elderly. However, the government is currently endorsing a scheme whereby three functions are provided in the same building: (1) "foyer," which includes housekeeping apartments for the elderly only; (2) restaurant, open to any elderly in the community who are indigent; and (3) dispensary, designed to meet the health needs of the indigent of all ages in the community. Two such projects have been built, one in Lyons and one in Robinson, a suburb of Paris.

The different kinds of housing projects in the different countries are built by different kinds of sponsoring groups. The most common sponsor is the municipality (urban and rural). However, many are built by religious groups. Some are built by labor unions and other groups. Municipal housing is, of course, supported financially by the municipalities, although frequently aid in the form of rent subsidies and special allowances is provided by the national government. The housing built by religious and other groups is often government assisted, but not always. The subsidy and allowance plans vary greatly from country to country and are often complex.[31]

In addition to providing new housing, some countries, especially Sweden, Denmark, and the United Kingdom, also provide special assistance to the elderly to maintain and improve the housing in which they live. In Sweden, for example, an elderly person may obtain an interest-free, no-amortization-

[30] The "geriatric complex" is not to be confused with geriatric units in or related to hospitals. The latter are far more specialized, having as their purposes provision of diagnostic facilities for the full investigation of illnesses of old people, treatment of severe illnesses that cannot be treated in nursing homes or elsewhere, and rehabilitation—primarily physical but sometimes also occupational—especially where this involves the work of a team of specialists. One of the outstanding geriatric units in Europe is the one attached to Ulleval Hospital in Oslo, Norway.

[31] Pension plans (but not special housing subsidies or rent allowances) are summarized in U.S. Department of Health, Education, and Welfare, Social Security Administration, *Social Security Programs Throughout the World 1961.* Washington, D.C.: U.S. Government Printing Office, 1961.

payments loan. (If the house is sold or changes occupancy, the loan must be repaid.) Also, some countries have special programs for the conversion of large old houses into small apartments for the elderly, with special government subsidies. In general, the conversion programs in foreign countries have encountered the same difficulties as such programs in the United States.

Most European countries, especially the Northern countries, also provide extensive domiciliary care and community service programs designed to permit the elderly to remain in their own homes as long as possible. These programs are usually carried out on a community rather than a national basis, although there sometimes is national guidance and financial assistance. They are operated by either the municipalities or voluntary organizations, or both.

Many different types of services are provided. The most important include health services, meals, home help, and visiting. In several European countries "home nurses" are available to visit the sick at home. (Although these services are not limited to the elderly, in most programs over half of the nurse's time is devoted to that age group.) The home nurse gives injections, applies dressings, bathes the patient, and advises relatives on simple nursing methods. Several different kinds of meal services are provided in different countries. One is the delivery of the meal to the homes of the housebound, such as the "meals-on-wheels" program in England; another is making the meal available at a central location where it can be picked up and taken home, as in the Health and Welfare Centers in Oslo; and a third is providing lunches at lunch clubs where the elderly may go to eat, as in Lyons and Robinson, France. Sweden and England have the broadest programs of "home help" services, through which the elderly are provided with periodic housekeeping assistance, including housecleaning, assistance with clothes washing, meal preparation, purchase of food, and sometimes with dressing and personal hygiene. Visiting in the home is one of the newest services to be provided, and the benefits accruing from such a service are so widely recognized that several countries are embarking on broad programs of this type. Miscellaneous home-care services include laundry service and chiropody.

The elderly in many European cities are also assisted in using their leisure hours positively through the establishment of activity centers, clubs, and the like. The variation in programs of these types is almost as great as the number that have been established.

URBAN RENEWAL IN WESTERN EUROPE

Urban renewal, as the concept has evolved in the United States, is still in its early stages in most Western European countries. That is not to say that those countries have not been involved in one or another aspect of it.

Actually, many European cities have engaged in slum clearance programs for many years. Also, many have undertaken rebuilding schemes, especially in parts of cities that suffered heavily from war damage. (Rotterdam is one of the outstanding examples.) Some have undertaken rebuilding projects associated with traffic improvement.

However, only the United Kingdom and France have, to date, adopted broad programs of general redevelopment, i.e., of mixed (residential, commercial, etc.) areas. In the United Kingdom, the costs to the local authorities of acquisition, clearance, and preparation of a site can be included in the calculations for a general grant to local authorities. In France, assistance is of two types: (a) grants to local renewal agencies (local authority, public or semipublic society, low-cost housing societies, or private societies) toward costs of acquisition and demolition to permit the agency to resell land at below cost price and (b) short-term, low-interest loans to meet operating or other costs until returns are available from sale (or lease) of the land or buildings.[32] In contrast to the lump-sum capital grants provided under the United States program, the grants under the United Kingdom program are in the form of annual subsidies to the local authorities. In France, cities are not compelled to furnish matching funds or contributions of any kind. Although the United Kingdom program has been in operation for some years, it is not progressing rapidly. The program in France was authorized only in 1958–1959 and the amount of government grants has been relatively small.[33]

There are, however, significant slum clearance programs in several countries. Grebler suggests the program in Denmark "... comes close to initiating an urban renewal program although its effectiveness remains to be seen." Under a new slum clearance act adopted in 1959, condemnation of sound as well as unfit dwellings is permitted, projects may combine complete redevelopment of some areas with the conservation and rehabilitation of others, and special subsidies may be granted for the preservation of historic areas and buildings.[34]

Slum clearance programs in other countries relate almost exclusively to housing. The programs in three countries will be mentioned here. In The Netherlands grants are made to municipalities to cover 50 percent of any difference between costs of acquisition plus demolition, and resale value of the land. (This proportion is similar to the government loan and subsidy program in Denmark.) In The Netherlands, as in the United States, national government assistance is conditional upon the preparation of a general plan for physical development of the city. In Norway, low-interest loans are made to municipalities for the acquisition of land and buildings in slum clearance areas. There are three financial aspects to the Belgium program: (a) grants to local authorities and low-cost housing societies covering the

[32] United Nations Economic Commission for Europe, *Report on the Urban Renewal Symposium Organized by the Housing Committee of the United Nations Economic Commission for Europe and Held in Geneva in June 1961.* Geneva: United Nations, 1962, pp. 48–49.

[33] Leo Grebler, "National Programs for Urban Renewal in Western Europe," *Land Economics,* Vol. XXXVIII, No. 4, November 1962, pp. 293–304.

[34] *Ibid.,* pp. 295–296.

cost of interest and amortization of the difference between the cost of acquisition plus demolition, and the final value of the land cleared as a building site; (b) grants to private individuals, with certain limits on the size of these grants, depending upon the municipality in which the slum clearance is to take place; and (c) low-interest loans repayable over sixty-six years to low-cost housing societies.[35]

Generally the same problems that are plaguing the programs in the United States are being faced in the Western European countries, except the fact that social housing has much wider acceptance there. One of the most serious problems (as in the United States) is the rehousing of families uprooted from their homes because of the clearance of a site. In all countries there is a legal or social obligation to relocate such families either in the area itself after rebuilding, or elsewhere in the city, or it is necessary to pay compensation. In Denmark, Norway, Belgium, The Netherlands, and France, rehousing is carried out largely by semipublic housing societies. Different financial schemes are followed. In the Scandinavian countries, municipal authorities subsidize rents of low-income families from clearance areas. (This also is one of the policies in the United Kingdom.) In Belgium the central government makes its loans to the two national low-cost housing societies conditional upon their giving priority to homes for former slum occupants (generally 30 percent of the loans must be earmarked for this purpose), the rents to vary according to size of family. In The Netherlands, rehoused tenants receive rent subsidies (which decrease 20 percent annually) for five years. In France, 100 percent loans are available to low-cost societies when no other possibility of rehousing exists.[36]

There are no national programs of urban renewal or slum clearance, *per se,* in West Germany or Sweden, but in both countries consideration is being given to the formulation of such programs. There also seems to be a trend toward urban renewal, as against the "merely negative objective of eliminating slums" in practically all other Western European countries.

FUTURE HOUSING NEEDS

It is not possible to discuss the future housing needs in Western European countries in the same detail provided for the United States. Fairly sound data are available regarding anticipated population growth and household formation for many countries, but statistics are scarce concerning anticipated rural-to-urban migration, the number of substandard units that should be replaced, proper vacancy allowances, and similar factors. In some countries the housing shortage growing out of the war has not yet been completely overcome.

In the mid-1950's, the countries which had come closest to satisfying their normal housing demand, not including slum clearance and the need for "social housing" for low-income families, were Belgium, Switzerland,

[35] *Report on Urban Renewal Symposium, op. cit.,* p. 37.
[36] *Ibid.,* pp. 54–57.

Denmark, The Netherlands, and the United Kingdom. The countries where the greatest need remained, even for middle-income families, were West Germany, Norway, Sweden, and France, but these countries also have made impressive strides in the last few years.

Continued population increases are anticipated in all countries, with the greatest increases expected in The Netherlands, Norway, Denmark, Switzerland, France, and West Germany. The percentage increases are expected to be lower in Belgium, the United Kingdom, and Sweden. Rural-to-urban migration is expected to continue, with highest rates in the most industrial countries; for example, Sweden, West Germany, the United Kingdom.

Those are factors reflecting housing need. However, it is important to recognize certain other factors that have an important bearing on how much residential building is actually likely to occur. Most Western European countries have, in most recent years, found it necessary to introduce restraining monetary, budgetary, and physical controls designed to alleviate the strains that have developed in their internal economies as a result of their rapid rates of growth in the postwar years. Housing was one of the consumers' goods most directly affected. In addition, countries such as Denmark, West Germany, The Netherlands, Norway, Sweden, Switzerland, and the United Kingdom still have tight labor markets, with shortages particularly in the skilled trades and supervisory staffs. Thus, while they have a rapidly increasing standard of living, the housing being demanded to fulfill that standard is not always available. Furthermore, the general policies in almost all countries to restrict or reduce the amount of government subsidies for housebuilding, and the encouragement that has been given to private enterprise, is resulting in postponement of the fulfillment of social housing needs.[37]

In analyzing future housing needs, year-to-year trends must be followed. Even short-term predictions, either specific or generalized, are hazardous for all countries. The immediate future will most certainly see a continued rise in the standard of living in all countries. Private housebuilding will no doubt continue to play a predominant role in many of them, supplemented by growing interest in and the establishment of urban renewal programs—which will, of course, include programs of slum clearance. The private programs in many countries are likely to continue to encourage the provision of moderate- to low-income housing through special aids given to cooperative and other nonprofit societies. In a few countries—especially West Germany, but also Switzerland and Belgium—the emphasis on home ownership is expected to continue.

READING LIST

GENERAL

Holm, Per. *Swedish Housing,* 2d ed. Stockholm: The Swedish Institute, 1959.

Silk, Leonard. *Sweden Plans for Better Housing.* Durham, N.C.: Duke University Press, 1948.

[37] *European Housing Trends and Policies in 1960, op. cit.,* p. 9.

Silverman, Abner D. *Selected Aspects of Administration of Publicly Owned Housing, Great Britain, Netherlands and Sweden.* Housing and Home Finance Agency, Washington, D.C.: U.S. Government Printing Office, 1961.

Umrath, Heinz, and P. Lamartine Yates, "Housing," in J. Frederic Dewhurst, *et. al., Europe's Needs and Resources.* New York: Twentieth Century Fund, 1961, Chapter 7.

United Nations Economic Commission for Europe. *European Housing Trends and Policies* (published annually). Geneva: United Nations (mimeo).

Wendt, Paul F. *Housing Policy—The Search for Solutions.* A Comparison of the United Kingdom, Sweden, West Germany, and the United States since World War II. Berkeley: University of California Press, 1963.

Wertheimer, Robert G. "The Miracle of German Housing in the Postwar Period," *Land Economics,* Vol. XXXIV, No. 4, November 1958, pp. 338-345.

HOUSING PRODUCTION

United Nations Economic Commission for Europe. *Quarterly Bulletin Housing and Building Statistics for Europe* (published quarterly). Geneva: United Nations (mimeo).

HOUSING FINANCE

United Nations Economic Commission for Europe. *Financing of Housing in Europe.* Geneva: United Nations, 1958.

COOPERATIVE AND OTHER NONPROFIT HOUSING

United Nations Department of Economic and Social Affairs. *Housing through Non-Profit Organizations.* New York: United Nations, 1956.

SPACE USE IN DWELLINGS

United Nations Economic Commission for Europe. *Utilization of Space in Dwellings.* Geneva: United Nations, 1959.

HOUSING FOR THE AGING

Beyer, Glenn H., and F. H. J. Nierstrasz. *Aging and Independent Living.* Shelter and Care of the Elderly in 13 Western Countries. Amsterdam: Elsevier Publishing Co (to be published 1965).

SLUM CLEARANCE AND URBAN RENEWAL

Grebler, Leo. "National Programs for Urban Renewal in Western Europe," *Land Economics,* Vol. XXXVIII, No. 4, November 1962, pp. 293-304.

United Nations Economic Commission for Europe. *Report on the Urban Renewal Symposium Organized by the Housing Committee of the United Nations Economic Commission for Europe and Held in Geneva in June 1961.* Geneva: United Nations, 1962.

FUTURE HOUSING NEEDS

Maddison, Angus. "Method of Projecting Housing Requirements," Appendix 7-2 in J. Frederic Dewhurst, *et al., Europe's Needs and Resources.* New York: Twentieth Century Fund, 1961, pp. 984-992.

Table 16–1

DWELLING UNITS COMPLETED AND UNITS COMPLETED PER 1,000 INHABITANTS, 1956 AND 1960, SELECTED WESTERN EUROPEAN COUNTRIES

	1956		*1960*	
	Dwellings Completed	*Per 1,000 Inhabitants*	*Dwellings Completed*	*Per 1,000 Inhabitants*
United Kingdom	307,300	6.0	307,200	5.9
Sweden	57,600	7.9	68,300	9.1
Denmark	19,800	4.5	28,000	6.1
Norway	27,300	8.0	26,800	7.5
West Germany	561,000	11.0	551,000	10.5
The Netherlands	69,200	6.4	84,600	7.4
France	240,000	5.5	316,600	7.0
Belgium	42,800	4.8	52,700	5.7
Switzerland	39,400	7.9	50,500	9.3

SOURCE: United Nations Economic Commission for Europe, *European Housing Trends and Policies in 1956*. Geneva: United Nations, July 1957. p. 2; *European Housing Trends and Policies in 1960*. Geneva: United Nations, p. 2.

Table 16–2

PERCENTAGE DISTRIBUTION OF DWELLING UNITS COMPLETED, BY TYPE OF INVESTOR, 1957-1960, SELECTED WESTERN EUROPEAN COUNTRIES

	1957	*1958*	*1959*	*1960*
United Kingdom:				
Local authorities	55.1%	51.4%	44.2%	42.2%
Other authorities	3.0	1.8	1.4	1.5
Private persons, unaided	41.9	46.8	54.4	56.3
Sweden:				
State and local authorities	30.1	30.4	27.5	31.1
Cooperatives	27.2	27.8	31.6	29.5
Private	42.7	41.8	40.9	39.4
Owner-occupiers	21.7	24.3	23.4	22.2
Others	21.0	17.5	17.5	17.2
Denmark:				
State and municipalities	7.8	4.3	3.2	4.8
Housing associations	48.7	45.1	42.2	27.5
Private persons	43.5	50.6	54.6	67.7
Aided	36.1	34.8	31.0	21.9
Unaided	7.4	15.8	23.6	45.8
Norway:				
Public authorities	3.9	3.5		
Housing associations	27.6	27.0		
Industry	1.8	3.2		
Private	66.7	66.3		

Table 16–2 (continued)

	1957	1958	1959	1960
West Germany:				
Public authorities	2.5	2.4	2.5	2.4
Housing associations and cooperatives	29.5	28.9	28.2	26.1
Private	68.0	68.7	69.3	71.5
Individuals	60.4	61.5	61.6	63.9
Housing corporations	4.4	3.8	4.4	4.1
Enterprises	3.2	3.4	3.3	3.5
The Netherlands:				
State	0.7	0.6	0.3	0.4
Municipalities	26.1	30.4	29.2	23.2
Housing associations	27.3	27.2	27.4	26.2
Private	45.9	41.8	43.1	50.2
France:				
State (reconstruction)	12.0	8.3	5.3	4.0
Public bodies (HLM-Low cost)	26.8	30.2	31.5	30.6
Private	61.2	61.5	63.2	65.4
Aided	53.2	52.7	54.4	55.1
Unaided	8.0	8.8	8.8	10.3
Belgium:				
State, local authorities	0.1	0.2	0.4	0.2
Semi-public bodies	13.9	6.5	19.2	14.1
Private	86.0	93.3	80.4	85.7
Aided	29.5	25.2	23.1	20.4
Unaided	56.5	68.1	57.3	65.3
Individuals	*54.0*	*66.1*	*54.5*	*64.3*
Enterprises	*2.0*	*2.0*	*2.8*	*1.0*
Switzerland:				
Public bodies	2.1	3.2	3.8	2.6
Cooperatives	9.7	10.6	15.3	12.6
Private	88.2	86.2	80.9	84.8
Individuals	44.2	48.9	46.2	47.1
Others	44.0	37.3	34.7	37.7

SOURCE: United Nations Economic Commission for Europe, *European Housing Trends and Policies in 1959*. Geneva: United Nations, 1960, pp. 21–24; *European Housing Trends and Policies in 1960*. Geneva: United Nations, pp. 16–19.

Table 16–3

PERCENTAGE DISTRIBUTION OF SIZE OF DWELLINGS, 1960, SELECTED WESTERN EUROPEAN COUNTRIES

	Number or Rooms				
	One or Two	*Three*	*Four*	*Five*	*Six or more*
United Kingdom	26%	34%*	—	38%†	2%‡
Sweden	20	22	29	20	9
Denmark	11	13	32	35	9
West Germany	9	22	42	27	—
The Netherlands	1	4	13	50	32
France	16	32	35	17	—
Switzerland	7	14	36	30	13

SOURCE: United Nations Economic Commission for Europe, *European Housing Trends and Policies in 1960*. Geneva: United Nations, p. 14.
* Three or four rooms.
† Five or six rooms.
‡ Seven rooms or more.

CHAPTER 17

*

Housing in the Developing Countries

The most serious housing problems in the world today are in the countries of Africa, Asia, and Latin America—countries which are experiencing the highest rates of population increase in the world.

Most of the countries on these three continents can be classified as "developing" or, to use more common terms, "undeveloped" or "underdeveloped." Generally, these terms refer to an economic situation. One author explains underdevelopment as ". . . a more polite way of saying 'backward.' " He continues:

> It is a relative term. It refers not to the cultural development of a country . . . *but to the development of its economy.* . . . What economists usually mean by the term "underdeveloped" is poor economic performance, as evidenced by a low standard of living, thus implying that the economy can be developed and the standards improved.[1]

Hoffman describes an undeveloped country as follows:

> It is a country which lacks the means to eradicate its own poverty. The roads and railroads are insufficient, the communication system is erratic, the factories and the tools for agriculture are mostly lacking. Few people have enough education and training to take part usefully in the development process. In twenty countries today, only 5 per cent of the population can read or write; in one hundred others, literacy is below the 50 per cent mark. Hospitals and other medical services are pitifully inadequate, with perhaps one doctor for every ten thousand or twenty thousand people.
>
> Whatever wealth underdeveloped countries have is often concentrated in the hands of a few people who live in comparative opulence surrounded by overwhelming poverty. An underdeveloped country's banking system is embryonic; small loans have to be obtained through money lenders who are often little better than extortionists. Not only are there scant savings from which investment could be made, but the people who have wealth usually refuse to invest it productively in their own countries.
>
> The underdeveloped nation's exports typically consist almost entirely of raw materials, ores, fruits, or some other staple product with perhaps a small admixture of handicrafts or luxury goods. Often extraction or production of these export com-

[1] Forrest D. Murden, "Underdeveloped Lands: 'Revolution of Rising Expectations,' " in D. E. Pentony, ed., *The Underdeveloped Lands: A Dilemma of the International Economy*. Headline Series, No. 119, Foreign Policy Association, Inc., pp. 3–6.

modities is wholly or partly under foreign control, with little of the profit being reinvested in the country.[2]

An underdeveloped country, however, ". . . is not simply a poverty-stricken version of a developed nation."[3] Most of the distinctive features of an advanced society are lacking. These, according to Coleman, include:

> . . . a comparatively high degree of urbanization, widespread literacy, comparatively high per capita income, extensive geographical and social mobility, a relatively high degree of commercialization and industrialization of the economy, an extensive and penetrative network of mass communication media, and, in general . . . widespread participation and involvement by members of the society in modern social and economic processes.[4]

On the contrary, most of the undeveloped countries are still made up in large part of traditional social orders which were, as Frost describes them:

> . . . oriented toward stability. For centuries or even millennia, their leaders, sages, lawgivers and priests have aimed at maintaining a particular social heritage intact. Tradition has been their guide; and the extension of tradition into the future has been the objective of their more farsighted laws, customs, and acts of policy. . . . Their members . . . are dedicated to doing what their fathers did before them, and doing it the same way. Innovations are regarded with skepticism, suspicion, and dislike. They are societies grinding along rails, laid in a straight line from past to future.[5]

Over the years, however, the traditional social order has been disrupted. The causes of this most frequently given are contact of one kind or another with advanced cultures and extensive population growth, augmented perhaps by a shifting of forces within the societies themselves as desires for improvement in status may have clashed with rigid social barriers.[6] Yet the disruption has not been sufficient to displace entirely the traditional social order nor extensive enough to lead to the creation of a modern society.

There are numerous differences among the developing countries. Again to quote Murden:

> . . . nearly all lie in the nontemperate zones or on their fringes, but vary in topography from the deserts of North Africa and the plains of Latin America to the summits of the Himalayas and the steaming Malaya jungles. Spanning four continents, these territories have primitive villages, sophisticated cities and widely diverse populations.
>
> There is among the underdeveloped peoples no common religion, culture, language or color, although they are mostly nonwhite. Some are ancient long-established nations. . . . Some of these areas are still colonial, even tribal, but nearly all aspire to self-government. Just as the advanced countries have their slums and

[2] Paul G. Hoffman, *World Without Want.* New York: Harper & Row, 1962, pp. 33–34.

[3] *Ibid.*, p. 33.

[4] James S. Coleman, "The Political Systems of the Developing Areas," in G. A. Almond and J. S. Coleman, eds., *The Politics of the Developing Areas.* Princeton, N.J.: Princeton University Press, 1960, p. 532.

[5] Raymond Frost, *The Backward Society.* New York: St. Martin's Press, 1961, p. 56.

[6] M. F. Millikan and Donald L. M. Blackmer, eds., *The Emerging Nations.* Boston: Little, Brown and Company, 1961, pp. 7–17.

sharecroppers, the backward areas have their princes, sheiks and palaces; but in neither case are these situations typical. Parts of the Orient, the Middle East and the Caribbean are experiencing acute population pressure, but Africa and Latin America have wide-open spaces reminiscent of our early Western frontier.[7]

What they have in common are their problems—poverty, disease, malnutrition, poor housing, overpopulation, and, above all, the disadvantages of living in a society in transition. Frost describes the situation:

The majority of its people live according to the old unchanging routines of their forefathers. But a minority has broken or fallen away from this traditional pattern. Their situation is less regulated by routine than it was in the old society they are leaving behind, or than it will be in the new one toward which they are striving. In production, they are experimenting with methods which are revolutionary in character compared with the old, and which require a revolution in the attitudes of those who employ them. The situation of each productive unit is subject to unpredictable shocks, emergencies, and opportunities. At any time it may be upset by shortages, power cuts, strikes, political disturbance; at another time, it may find a tremendous opportunity—some temporary monopoly, some position of absolute scarcity to exploit. . . . Nothing inside or outside the plant works exactly as it should; things often fail to work at all. Nothing can be taken for granted; every decision, every promise, must be followed up. So far as consumption is concerned, styles and fashions are changing radically; while sometimes the supply of goods is plentiful, at other times they disappear from the market. Prices fluctuate wildly under the influence of inflation, speculation, price controls, sudden changes in sales taxes and import duties. Leisure hours, like hours of work, may be irregular; and the old feasts and ceremonies have become less significant while new entertainments have not yet become established as accepted conventions. Living is altogether an *ad hoc* affair.[8]

BACKGROUND FACTORS IMPORTANT TO HOUSING SITUATIONS

The characteristics of the developing countries provide some important clues to understanding the factors underlying the housing situations in these countries. It becomes quite clear that housing is not something that can be studied by itself. Housing problems are closely interlinked with many other factors in underdeveloped countries: the effects of their history on their present living conditions, the consequences of their continually expanding populations, and the conditions that exist as a result of their economic, social, and political systems, levels of education, and even the secular influences of their religions. These elements will be discussed briefly below in order to clarify some of the important background factors before proceeding to a discussion of the housing situation and housing programs in these countries.

[7] *Op. cit.*, p. 6.
[8] *Op. cit.*, pp. 58–59.

History

As contact with the cultures of more advanced societies is generally considered a significant factor in the development of underdeveloped countries and as the most sustained contact came through colonialism, only that portion of their frequently turbulent histories will be discussed.

Most of these countries have been colonies of Western powers, and a common thread of similar effects from the colonizing process runs through the history of all of them. The most important effect, for understanding of the contemporary scene, is the extensiveness of the impact made by the colonizing forces on the early societies.

The colonizers found traditional societies at various levels of development. Some had attained elaborate social and political cultures, as in some parts of Indonesia and South Asia; most of them had reached at least the stage of settled agriculture, though a few were still nomadic in nature, as, for example, some of the Indian tribes in South America. Whether or not colonialism included political control, *its purpose was generally economic in nature.* This functional purpose meant the introduction of institutions and changes to enhance production and commerce. The extent of change varied, as did the amount of political control exercised. Pye summarizes the history of the major colonial powers as follows:

> The British tended to emphasize law and order and laissez-faire concepts of economic growth. The Dutch adopted far more paternalistic policies toward traditional Indonesian customs and through the institutions of indirect rule encouraged the development of a dual economy. In the Indo-Chinese states the French vacillated between the ideal of assimilation and that of association—that is, between drawing the Indo-Chinese into French culture and preserving the traditional culture on terms that might lead to cooperation. In the Philippines the Americans placed less stress on the administrative structure of rule than any of the other colonial powers and emphasized education and the development of political parties to a much greater extent.[9]

Some of the colonies were governed indirectly through local existing governments; others were governed directly by colonial administrators or other officials. Under either system the colonial authorities utilized, and in some cases strengthened, traditional sources of local authority in the villages to carry out their laws and regulations. As a result, a large part of the population, especially in rural areas, remained remote from the process of government and sources of change. Hence, ". . . the vast majority of the people continued to center their social lives around units no larger than the village." At the same time, under the impact of commercial expansion, trading centers were growing into cities, and cities were taking on ". . . the complex patterns of urban existence . . ." characteristic of their Western counterparts.[10]

[9] Lucian W. Pye, "The Politics of Southeast Asia," in Almond and Coleman, *op. cit.*, p. 84.

[10] *Ibid.*, pp. 81–82.

Latin America experienced colonialism earlier than the countries of Asia and Africa, under the mercantile policies of the sixteenth rather than the nineteenth century. Like many other European countries during the same period, the Spanish operated on the concept that colonies existed for the benefit of the mother country. Political control of the countries was achieved through the military, and conversion to Christianity was an integral part of colonization. In the Caribbean, so fierce was the resistance of the Indians to the Conquest that they were practically exterminated. Later, to replace them, the Spanish had to import Negro slaves from Africa. Hence, in Caribbean society, there is almost no admixture of native elements. In some other Latin American countries, the Catholic Church intervened to save the Indians from similar extermination, and, under the Laws of the Indies, Indians who accepted the Roman Catholic religion were not to be killed. This did not prevent their subjugation, however, and a feudal society developed throughout Latin America, in which the conquerors formed the elite and the Indians took their place as a lower class.[11] Following independence, the Creoles became the upper class. Though French and North American influences have been more important than Spanish ones on the subsequent development of Latin America, little change occurred in the basic social structure of most of these countries.

Though the institutional changes that accompanied colonialism in Latin America were more sweeping than in the other areas, the net result was much the same in all of them: a nonintegrated, structured society, composed of a small group, usually (but not always) found in the urban centers, who either were in control of the social forces or who had been assimilated into the new culture, and a large group, usually rural, who had no participation in any phase of the developing society. The changes that took place were not the result of improvements in familiar methods; hence, the differences within these societies were strengthened rather than lessened as the political, social, and economic changes continued after independence was achieved or became imminent.

Since the purpose of most colonialism was economic rather than social, and since the improvement of housing falls in the "social" category, this matter was given little or no consideration by the mother countries. In fact, almost no references to the housing problems of the native populations can be found in any of the literature concerning the colonial development of these countries.

Population Growth

More than two thirds of the world's three billion people in 1962 lived in Africa, Asia, and Latin America. Over half of the world's population—1,747,000,000—lived in Asia, the most heavily populated continent. Furthermore, while the average annual rate of increase of the population of the

[11] George I. Blanksten, "The Politics of Latin America," in Almond and Coleman, *op. cit.*, pp. 464–469.

world was only 1.8 percent, during the ten-year period 1950–1960, in Latin America population increased 2.5 percent and in Africa 2.0 percent, compared with 0.8 percent in Europe during the same decade. (Table 17–1, p. 575.)

The high rate of population growth in the underdeveloped countries has resulted from a decline in death rates, while at the same time a traditionally high level of birth rates has continued. Improved medical practices, which resulted in the control of malaria and similar diseases, and better health practices brought about the decline in death rates, aided also by a reduction in famines and other traditional means of lowering populations. As yet, efforts to lower the birth rate have not been equally successful.

The customary means of siphoning off the excess population are either not open to the underdeveloped countries or are not effective under present circumstances. Migrations to other countries, for example, on the scale necessary to remedy the situation, are seldom possible. In a few countries, where undeveloped land is available and suitable for cultivation, internal migrations offer some relief. The more typical situation is either that land is not available or that areas of low population reflect land not easily cultivated without improvements. Furthermore, in the absence of other changes in the economy—creation of opportunities for employment, markets for produce, transportation and educational facilities, and development of better agricultural methods—investments in developing land may fail to produce the desired effects. Not only does the newly settled area become overpopulated, but also the population removed from the established area is quickly replaced.[12]

One characteristic phenomenon in the developing countries is internal migration from rural to urban areas. The extremely low income of the rural peasant, frequently below subsistence levels, coupled with the vision of higher-paying employment and a higher standard of living in an urban area (usually the capital city) have caused an unprecedented migration from rural to urban areas in many underdeveloped countries. As these treks to the cities precede, rather than follow, industrialization, employment opportunities frequently fail to materialize and living conditions in the high-density areas are usually much worse than in the rural areas from which the migration stemmed. Increases in the ranks of the idle and restless aggravate already uneasy political situations. Yet the flow to the cities continues, always in the hope of improving living conditions.

The urban situation is described well in a publication of the United Nations:

> Despite local differences, the urban housing pattern is broadly the same. . . . Country people and immigrants seeking work or simply attracted by urban life drift to towns. They overcrowd existing buildings and squat on any land which is free. The degree of overcrowding and squatting may differ from place to place, but the problem is fundamentally the same: impure water, a lack of proper sanita-

[12] A. Pepelasis, L. Mears, and I. Adelman, *Economic Development: Analysis and Case Studies.* New York: Harper & Bros., 1961, pp. 62–64.

tion, building sites waterlogged and liable to flood, or else steeply sloped; undersized, irregularly shaped plots; no access for refuse collection, ambulance, or fire engines; and an insecurity of tenure. The buildings are unhealthy, for even when regulations require them to be reasonably well built and waterproof, they are overcrowded and poorly ventilated. Where there are no regulations, or enforcement is slack, buildings are likely to be poorly constructed and not safe in case of fire or high winds. They are rarely well maintained.[13]

In 1960 an estimated 275 million Africans, Asians, and Latin Americans were living in cities having a population of 100,000 and over. By 1975 the number will more than double. The data, together with estimates for places having a population of one million and over, are shown in Table 17–2 (p. 575).

A growth in population is generally held to be an advantage in an economy developed to the point where ". . . the expected increase in demand due to increasing population leads to additional investment and production."[14] Until that situation is attained, however, overpopulation tends to make worse every problem the developing countries face. For one thing, the number of "dependents" in the population is increased. The unskilled labor force, for whom there is already a dearth of employment opportunities, is augmented. If the excess population remains in agriculture, landholdings are further divided to provide for them, and, though the same amount of effort may be put forth, the returns are less. The demand for food and shelter increases faster than these essentials can be produced. In competition with the need for food, housing tends to occupy a lower place on a scale of wants than is customarily assigned to it when the combination of economic factors is more conducive to the attainment of a higher standard of living.

Economic Situation

The generally poor economic situation in the individual developing countries perhaps is more responsible for the present housing situation than any other single factor.

The interdependence of the four factors of production—land, labor, capital, and entrepreneurship—is particularly striking in the developing countries, where deficiencies in one sector are reinforced by deficiencies in another—a situation frequently described as a "vicious circle." The characteristics most commonly found in the underdeveloped countries include scarcity of capital, low productivity of labor, under-utilization of resources, and a dearth of managerial or skilled technical talent and experience. The distribution of these characteristics is not, of course, uniform among all

[13] G. A. Atkinson, "Aided Self-Help—Its Application to the Housing of Tropical Peoples," in *Housing and Town and Country Planning,* Bulletin 6, United Nations, Department of Social Affairs, January 1952, p. 47.

[14] Willem Brand, *The Struggle for a Higher Standard of Living.* Glencoe, Ill.: The Free Press, 1958, p. 60.

the countries, but almost all of them display certain of the characteristics designated.[15]

The basis of the economy of most underdeveloped countries is agriculture, with some variations in the form of other resource development.

Agriculture generally is held back by low efficiency and low productivity. The small landholdings typical in these countries are usually considered one of the chief reasons for this situation. Heilbroner has stated:

> What has been called "postage stamp cultivation" marks the pattern of farming throughout Asia and the Near East, and in much of South America and Africa. Not the farm, but the plot, is the standard unit of cultivation. Even when large landlord estates exist, they are typically subdivided into a crossword puzzle of minscule holdings cropped by tenants.[16]

There are many causes for this agricultural situation, including the custom of inheritance in some countries, the feudal landlord systems in many countries under which peasants cannot legally own or accumulate their own lands, and, finally, the pressure of too many people on too little arable land. As a result of these practices, in Egypt approximately 90 percent of the landholdings are less than 2½ acres. In Crete, the average size of landholdings is 0.7 acre per strip, with 13 strips per farm. In Yugoslavia, a farm of 12 acres may be divided into as many as 30 strips.[17] Obviously, it is impossible for the peasants working these small strips of land to utilize the mechanical and chemical means for achieving the higher productivity common in Western countries.

Combined with unproductive methods of land cultivation in some countries are such factors as poor soil conditions, as in some parts of Africa, or unfavorable rainfall patterns, as in some Latin American countries, which make cultivation of available land difficult or curtail the amount that can be cultivated without expensive improvements.

Neither an inauspicious climate nor a deficiency of resources, however, is considered a main reason for underdevelopment for most of these countries, although either or both may well be contributory factors. Many of these countries have considerable raw material resources; for example, petroleum reserves are plentiful in western Asia and in South America; Africa has, among other resources, impressive reserves of lead, chrome, cobalt, uranium, antimony, bauxite, tin, manganese, phosphates, and oil; and Malaya has rubber and tin. Having resources available does not, in itself, hold promise for lifting many of these countries out of poverty. Often, only limited quantities of a resource may be available, and most of the resources still await exploitation and use. Frequently, there are neither coal deposits nor hydroelectric power sources available, and lack of transportation, especially to inaccessible interior regions, often is a major handicap.

One resource of underdeveloped countries in large supply is labor, but

[15] Pepelasis, Mears, and Adelman, *op. cit.*, p. 92.
[16] Robert L. Heilbroner, *The Great Ascent*. New York: Harper & Row, 1963, p. 54.
[17] Pepelasis, Mears, and Adelman, *op. cit.*, p. 33.

this labor is usually unskilled and illiterate, many of the workers having very limited experience with the written language. Lack of training is considered a chief reason for the lack of productivity on the part of industrial workers. As a result, per capita income levels in underdeveloped countries are extremely low. Some examples of income distributions are cited by MacEoin for Latin America: "Taking the entire region, 20 percent of the people enjoy 50 percent of the income, the other 80 percent having a per capita income of approximately $130 U.S. annually. In Chile, 38 percent of the people get 76 percent of the national income. In Colombia, 2.6 percent of the people get 30 percent."[18] For Latin America, per capita income averages not more than $200 a year—and that is high compared with per capita incomes of less than $100 U.S. in some countries of Asia and Africa.

In agriculture, income is usually much lower than in other sectors of the economy. In Latin America, "The typical farm worker earns only a half or a third of his counterpart in industry, even when allowance is made for what he receives in kind or grows on his own plot of land."[19] A large proportion of the population in the rural areas of the underdeveloped countries is outside the money economy altogether.

The export of agricultural or resource products, in general, is the chief source of wealth. This wealth, however, does not return to the economy as a whole, but remains concentrated in the hands of a relatively small group.

There are several reasons for this situation, the chief of which is that the export trade has not to any large extent stimulated the development of auxiliary enterprises. For example, raw materials are the typical exports; consequently, the benefits of processing—development of products and of markets, for instance—are derived by the importing country. With so much of the population living at a bare subsistence level, national markets do not exist for many products in most of the countries. In turn, the development of markets on a national scale is hampered by such factors as lack of transportation facilities and the difficulties and expense of providing and maintaining such facilities. The uncertain political situation also plays a part in making investments within the country unattractive. The net result has been, for the most part, investments of private wealth in enterprises that yield quick returns, high profits, and from which capital invested may be obtained at short notice. Some popular forms of investment have been real estate or some form of construction, such as apartment houses, office buildings, and housing for high-income families. Even owners of small landholdings tend to buy more land rather than to invest in mechanical equipment. Thus, wealth is exchanged between members of the same class rather than invested in means of increasing productivity. As a result of this investment pattern, as well as a general lack of opportunity for productive investments, national incomes remain low and there is little

[18] Gary MacEoin, *Latin America, The Eleventh Hour*. New York: P. J. Kenedy & Sons, 1962, p. 37.
[19] *Ibid.*, p. 36.

inducement for managerial talents to develop productive enterprises with some expectation of profit.

Much of the revenue for the governments of underdeveloped countries comes from foreign trade. For a number of years export and import duties were a chief source of revenue. The newer trend is toward indirect taxes on processes associated with foreign trade as, for example, excise taxes or import duties. In Asia, for example, indirect taxes range from 61 percent to 95 percent of national revenues.[20]

Numerous potential sources of national income, such as taxes on income, inheritance, and real estate, remain largely untapped. Although the distribution of national incomes may make an income tax unfeasible as a principal source of governmental revenue, a more potent restraining force is the difficulty of enforcing tax laws or promulgating tax reforms. The high-income groups, on whom such taxes would fall, frequently have an important influence on government policy and tend to resist the introduction of a progressive tax system. In Iran, for example, a proposed income tax which reached a maximum of 80 percent for the highest income brackets was opposed by Parliament and senior public officials.[21] Where income taxes have been used, as in some countries in Latin America, their effectiveness in siphoning off wealth is limited by preferential schedules, exemptions, and the difficulty of assessing incomes except those of salaried employees.[22]

The system of land tax—another main source of revenue—prevailing in many of these countries is usually based on a single uniform rate per unit of land rather than on the productivity of the land, and the increased value of land resulting from public improvements usually remains untaxed.

Though agriculture is the basis of the economy for most undeveloped countries, the ratio of exports to national income frequently is high, in comparison with internal sources of income—on the order of 20 percent for all low-income countries taken together. In addition, much of the export trade depends quite often on only one or two products. For example, oil has accounted for 90 percent of all exports in Iran; cotton, 90 percent in Egypt; coffee, 89 percent in El Salvador; copper, 81 percent in Northern Rhodesia; rubber and tin, 75 percent in Malaya; and cocoa, 73 percent in Ghana.[23] Many additional examples could be cited.

One of the problems in the export of primary products by these countries, of course, is that the prices for those products are determined by the consumer (i.e., the world market) rather than by the producer, who thus is subject to fluctuations in price over which he has little or no control. The underdeveloped economy, therefore, reflects price changes more rapidly than does the developed economy. Furthermore, the underdeveloped economy cannot increase its income by greater production, since there is a limit to the amount of the product that can be sold on the world market, and increased production might serve only to lower the price.

[20] Brand, *op. cit.*, p. 214.

[21] *Ibid.*, p. 213.

[22] *Ibid.*, p. 218.

[23] Pepelasis, Mears, and Adelman, *op. cit.*, pp. 40–41.

Underdeveloped economies, then, with a low level of agricultural and industrial activity must depend on imports to supply many of their needs. The prices of the manufactured imports are set by the producer and do not usually change in the same direction as prices of the primary products of the underdeveloped countries. MacEoin has illustrated the impact on the underdeveloped countries by the following example:

> The concept of terms of trade is . . . the price relationship between what you have to sell and what you seek to buy with the proceeds. If, for example, you can buy a tractor with the money you get by selling twenty bags of coffee, it does not matter whether you get $80, $100 or $120 a bag for the coffee, assuming that what you want to buy is a tractor. All that concerns you is that the prices of the two items move up and down in step. However, if the price for the coffee drops from $100 to $80 per bag, while the price of the tractor rises from $2,000 to $2,400, you now must sell thirty bags of coffee in order to buy the same tractor. . . . Now you must either sell more coffee or make do with fewer tractors. And it is obvious that the additional quantity of coffee you can profitably sell at a given moment, even assuming you can produce it, is limited, because you will quickly saturate the market and break the price.[24]

Given this fluctuating basis of national revenue, it is obvious that national governments—even assuming that all their expenditures were for productive purposes—could expect to encounter difficulties in sustained investment programs. Such difficulties are all the more likely when the nature of investments expected of governments is considered. Many of these are for education, development of power sources, public utilities, irrigation works, and transportation facilities, most of which are long-range "overhead" investments that do not immediately produce higher incomes.

These factors, then—low productivity, a large supply of unskilled labor, lack of opportunity to develop profitable means of utilizing what capital is available, and the uneasy status of many of these countries with respect to their foreign trade—are responsible in large part for the extremely weak economic position of the underdeveloped countries.

Social Class

One of the most striking characteristics of societies in the underdeveloped countries is the existence, side by side, of traditional and modern social groups.[25]

Traditional society, composed chiefly of two classes, is easily delineated. In broad terms, the elite class was associated with leadership—in economic functions, as distributors of production; in military functions, as protectors of their workers or subjects; in political functions, through which they governed and administered laws. Membership in this class was determined more or less at birth and was the prerogative of wealth, high caste, or other particular mark of prestige. Usually, the roles of the elite were sanctioned

[24] *Op. cit.*, pp. 125–126.
[25] Almond and Coleman, *op. cit.*, pp. 101–103, 179–182, 283–284, 389, 462–463.

by religion and bolstered by social custom, and there was little access to this group from the bulk of the population.

Colonialism, though it tended to make few direct changes in the social order, did disturb the established pattern. The introduction of colonial authority could not help but weaken the influence of traditional leaders. Education and the use of money provided potential means of escaping the edict of birth. This, however, was the chief change—the provision of opportunity, rather than any large-scale reorganization of the social base.

Generally, any educational systems that accompanied or followed colonialism were designed for functional purposes and not intended to create a modern society, except perhaps in the Philippines. The general purpose (with variations and numerous modifications, of course) was to train native citizens to fill minor administrative or other posts, usually in the government. In the absence of emphasis on primary or secondary education, access to this source of power was confined to a relatively small group, many, if not most, of whom came from the elite of the traditional societies. The introduction of a moneyed economy changed the basis of wealth, and commercial or industrial developments made it easier to acquire wealth without regard to social status. The reasons why substantial social change did not follow differ among countries; in some, as in Indonesia, many of the new group came from foreign elements. More often, the traditional elite responded to the new opportunities to acquire wealth—the Filipinos provide one of several examples of this—and thus retained power and prestige within their own class. Such is the situation today. As stated above, both education and the acquisition of wealth in the form of money hold potential for future social change.

Some shifting to a ''modern'' social group occurred, however, under colonialism and later, in several countries, after independence. New classes composed of doctors, lawyers, teachers, businessmen, and others developed and acquired varying degrees of influence. In some of the South African countries, this group moved into the upper classes and in some instances displaced the traditional elite, though this was not a typical development. Similar groups appeared in small towns, notably in South Asia, where they provided a potential, if not actual, source of rural leadership. Technical training, in engineering and other fields, is another, more recent means of cutting across class lines.

In Latin America, although the class system is strongly entrenched and the classes well separated from each other, status in the lower orders may be improved through education, moving to a city, acquiring property, or making similar changes in circumstances. Mobility remains a slow process. In addition to the strong influence of the traditional way of life, meeting the requirements for upward mobility is difficult for large proportions of the population.

Though widespread social change did not immediately follow political and economic changes in the underdeveloped countries, a difference in attitudes can be noted. Two such new attitudes are (1) that place in society is not irrevocably fixed at birth, but can be changed by one's own efforts, and (2) that merit, expressed in some form of personal achievement, rather than inherited advantage, should be the basis of status.

Social class lines are difficult to break down, in spite of a more liberal attitude toward the requirements for social status, and relatively few individuals have access to the means of doing so. Contrasts between upper and lower classes remain sharp. In housing, most houses built on the basis of acceptable standards are built for the well-to-do and such houses are generally beyond the means of the poor groups, most of whom are forced to improvise their own homes or to crowd into the discarded quarters of others. Even among the small (but growing) middle class, there has been difficulty in obtaining adequate housing, though much of their problem is due to the lack of financial assistance and credit facilities.

Education

Education, the basic necessity for improvement of economic and social status, remains at a relatively low level. As a result, a large proportion of the population lacks the training necessary to participate in the economic and social changes occurring in their societies, and still lives at a subsistence level in which better housing is less important than acquiring sufficient food.

In most of the underdeveloped countries, opportunities to acquire education have been limited chiefly to a relatively small group, and, as already indicated, education in the modern sense follows class lines. This situation exists whether or not power remains with a traditional elite, as in Latin America, or is exercised by a new elite, for membership in which education was a prime requisite.

Partly this inaccessibility of educational opportunity results from the lack of emphasis placed on primary and secondary education in most underdeveloped countries. Partly, also, it is a result of the narrow range of opportunities for education provided by traditional and, for the most part, colonial societies. Training for the largest part of the population meant the acquisition of such skills and knowledge as would enable one to carry on successfully the functions of his particular social position. There were, of course, exceptions. Christian missionaries frequently established primary school systems. In Ceylon, as a result of this, ". . . 65.8 per cent of the population above the age of five was literate in 1953."[26] In parts of South Africa, education under the missionary school systems was available to any native who accepted Christianity, regardless of his status in traditional society.[27] The United States adapted the American educational system for use in the Philippines and placed particular emphasis

[26] Myron Weiner, "The Politics of South Asia," in Almond and Coleman, *op. cit.*, p. 177.

[27] James S. Coleman, "The Politics of Sub-Saharan Africa," in Almond and Coleman, *op. cit.*, p. 279.

on training for citizenship in a democratic society. The French used education as a means of assimilating the native populations into French culture; so, to a lesser extent, did the Portuguese. In the Belgian Congo, primary educational facilities and some form of vocational training for artisans, clerks, or skilled labor were available.

These are not, however, typical situations. By the standards of present-day education, illiteracy and lack of training to meet the requirements of contemporary society are frequently cited as serious—and sometimes, as the most serious—impediments to the development and functioning of these nations in an industrial age.

Overwhelming obstacles have prevented any measures taken from making an appreciable change in the educational status of most of the populations. Some of these obstacles include: (1) Increases in population. These offset in large measure any gains made in the growth of schools or availability of teachers. (2) Shortage of teachers. There are few training schools for teachers, and teaching is more poorly paid and less attractive than comparable positions in other fields, as, for instance, in government posts. (3) Lack of buildings. A factor in some areas is that too high standards for schools and facilities increase the costs, and the utilization of simpler designs and cheaper methods of construction might provide a larger number of adequate, even though impermanent, buildings. (4) Poor transportation facilities, with the result that children must walk to school. One basic problem is to provide schools within a reasonable walking distance of all the children in the numerous villages and hamlets throughout most of the countries. A similar problem exists in urban areas. (5) Language difficulties. There are many linguistic groups in some countries, and this creates numerous problems—the expenditure of time teaching and learning another language or languages, special training for teachers, providing books in each language, and sometimes setting up schools for different linguistic groups. (This applies especially to Asian countries.) (6) Shortage of books, materials, and teaching equipment in general.[28]

Political Situation

Governments of underdeveloped countries are frequently unstable and in no position to establish (much less implement) sound and necessary housing programs.[29]

As might be expected, there are numerous differences and variations among the underdeveloped countries in the forms and institutions of their governments, power groups, party systems, and other political structures. These arise chiefly from differences in their traditional backgrounds, their

[28] United Nations, Educational, Social and Cultural Organization, *Asia, Arab States, Africa: Education and Progress*. Paris, France: UNESCO, 1961.

[29] The political situation in these countries is the focus of the discussion in Almond and Coleman, *op. cit.*

colonial experience with Western governments, and the different levels of development so far attained.

In Africa and Asia, types of government include political democracy, with participation by most of the electorate, as in the Philippines; tutelary democracy, as in Indonesia; and oligarchies, as in Ethiopia. Latin America has three forms of ''constitutional'' government: dictatorial, semidictatorial, and representative.

How the governments carry on their legal, administrative, executive, and judicial functions is more important for understanding of the political situation in these countries than a standard classification by type of government. Almost all of the underdeveloped countries have governments modeled after or strongly influenced by those of Western Europe or North America. In other words, their governments largely are the result of adaptation rather than the development of native institutions.

The most conspicuous feature of the governmental process in most of these countries is the heavy concentration of decision-making in a central authority. A corollary of this is a lack of local autonomy and authority. Acceptance of this situation might be expected, of course, in countries where by tradition and colonial experience central authority was considered the source of all power and sometimes the leader was held to be the personification of government. Insofar as most of the electorate is concerned, the chief executives have, in general, almost complete freedom to exercise power, especially, as is customary, where they have the support of the military and of religious or other power groups. (Indeed, they frequently are able to retain office because of this support.) Opposing groups are to be found, in some countries, but they usually come from other members of the same class and represent opposing interests within the class in power rather than the interests of the citizens at large. Thus, though governments, and sometimes some of the governmental institutions, may change frequently, such change is customarily an exchange of power and not an extension of the political process to other groups, except insofar as the groups themselves are accessible to the general population. (This overview, of course, is broad and does not take into account different levels of political development which a few of the underdeveloped countries have attained.)

Whether as a result of the manner in which traditional authority is exercised (by decree, for instance), or an attitude developed through experience with paternalistic colonial governments, or because power is concentrated in the hands of a small clique, most legislatures (or parliaments) refrain from taking the initiative in proposing legislation. Rather, they tend to confine their responsibilities to sanctioning legislation proposed by others—usually the chief executive, the army, or, sometimes, a religious or other power group. One reason for this ineffectualness on the part of officials is that, even though elected, the legislators are not the means through which interests, protests, and similar articulations of their constituents are expressed.

Traditional authoritative groups of one type or another are strong in the villages and rural areas. In the new societies, these groups continue their traditional functions of interpreting legislation from the new sources of authority in much the same manner as they did from the old ones. At the same time, traditional authorities settle or arbitrate interests, protests, or differences at the local level, more or less in the traditional manner of decrees, decisions, or other forms from which appeal was not customary, possibly at times modified by legislation. Though the influence of traditional authority is less in urban centers, this authority has been replaced to some extent not by constitutional representation and legal processes but by what might be termed a single-purpose group, as, for instance, labor leaders where a labor group is strong. The interests of both rural and urban groups are essentially local in nature.

With ineffectual legislatures and noncompetitive political groupings, legislation typically reflects the wishes of either the central authority or a specific local group acting with authority. In the absence of a unified national legislative framework that includes the interests of a majority of the population, such legislation or concessions as the local groups obtain are of specific benefit to one group. They are not necessarily—though they may be—conducive to the national welfare. Most legislation is from the ruling elite and reflects their wishes for the societies they govern, whether or not those wishes are applicable to existing conditions. Not all legislation is inapplicable or nonbeneficial, of course; nevertheless, it usually fails to unify the nonparticipating public and, of necessity, the government tends to retain an authoritarian character.

Law enforcement and administration, consequently, rely more heavily on authority than is the situation where legislation is accepted by a society for its own good or can be modified or rejected through legislative channels. While there often are separate and secular judiciaries in many underdeveloped countries, most of these are quite fragile and discriminatory. Traditional means of adjudicating disputes and claims are frequently resorted to. In administration, considerable reliance is placed on decrees, and law enforcement varies from strict enforcement on some groups, sometimes supported by military means, to no enforcement on other groups who are in a better position to withstand whatever national pressure can be exerted. Dispersion of responsibility by government administrators is characteristic, as is a tendency to avoid making decisions, with the consequence that minor matters have to be decided by the highest authorities.

Stated briefly, the situation seems to be that the vast majority of the population has little or no means of acquiring familiarity with legal and constitutional processes or experience in utilizing them to achieve a better manner of living, improvement in status, or other benefits. It is further obvious that the political or national unity achieved by an integrated society working toward objectives generally understood and accepted throughout a country is a goal still to be realized.

Lack of access to an orderly political process by which a national government can exercise leadership through legislation and law enforcement that expresses the interests and needs of a majority of the population makes possible the continuation of a situation whereby certain institutional groups, such as the army, the traditional bureaucracy, or religion, are dominant in the political process. The role of the army has undoubtedly been brought about because it is generally considered responsible for the maintenance of law and order, a function recognized as necessary in the traditional societies.

Interests, or protests, expressed through riots and violence are commonplace in many of these countries. These undoubtedly result from the lack of functional groups through which interests are expressed in more stable societies, as well as from the feelings of insecurity and frustration that are universally characteristic of societies undergoing rapid change. These ''anomic movements'' frequently appear when discontent exists and normal channels are not available for its expression. These acts and movements undoubtedly help to account in part for the unpredictable character of the politics of the developing areas, and the resulting lack of stability of many institutions, which is another common characteristic of these countries. The direct relationship of this instability to housing generally, and to the feasibility of establishing broad, permanent national housing programs, specifically, is profoundly clear.

Religion

As the economic and political changes introduced into the developing countries seldom follow communal or class lines, they usually have had disruptive effects on the traditional social orders. Education, as well, is contributing to change.

The influence of religion frequently is different. Although different religions, in general, want to improve social conditions, more often than not they tend to support the traditional social order. Throughout much of the history of underdeveloped countries religion was the means of maintaining a social relationship between rulers and those ruled—it made the decrees of the rulers acceptable to their subjects and, at the same time, often forced respect for the rights of the subjects on their rulers.

In some countries there has been a close relationship—in fact, unity—between church and state. Where this situation has existed, it has meant a strong influence by religion in secular matters. Today, however, there seems to be a weakening of the traditional strength of religion as a major secular influence, especially where important social changes are taking place, such as secular education, urbanization, and general changes in patterns of living, including the declining strength of family ties. Because the goals espoused by many of the nationalistic leaders in the developing countries conflict with traditional social orders in those countries, the trend toward nationalism has frequently threatened the heretofore important influence of religious groups.

Whatever position religion may hold in governing circles, its influence, outside the sphere of religious belief lies in the acceptance of that influence by the population. However, as previously indicated, most of the people in the lowest social class still lack the economic or political means of improving their situations. Consequently, the fact that religion is still important to them as a secular force does not mean that it represents an important influence toward improving general social conditions, including the housing situation.

PRESENT HOUSING SITUATION

A high proportion of the urban and rural populations in underdeveloped countries is living in the same conditions of overcrowding and ill health that prevailed ten or twenty years ago. In fact, it would appear that the housing situation has actually deteriorated in recent years in most cities. New building has not kept pace with the natural increase in population, much less with the heavy increase caused by the flood of migrants from rural to urban areas. This situation seems to apply especially to capital cities.

Examples of the high density (occupancy) rates in dwelling units in these countries are available in data from the United Nations. As can be seen in Table 17–3 (p. 576), five persons per housing unit is the average in the underdeveloped countries cited, and these persons frequently live in dwellings having two rooms or less. The result is a high proportion of dwellings with an average of two or more persons per room. (In Panama, 46 percent of the dwellings had an average of three or more persons per room.)

A group of experts on housing and urban development reported in a 1962 United Nations publication as follows:

> In Africa, only about 50 percent of the urban population live in decent homes. The remainder still live in overcrowded dwellings, slums, improvised shelters or shack towns. In the rural areas, it appears from the available evidence that at least 50 percent of the population is badly housed, usually in huts made of mud and wattle and grass, without doors and windows. . . .
>
> It is estimated that in Asia and the Far East only 60 percent of the population in urban areas and 50 percent in the rural areas are adequately housed; the remainder are living in unsanitary and overcrowded conditions. . . .
>
> About 40 percent of the urban population in Latin America and about 50 percent of the rural population live in unhealthy crowded homes and communities. The average density of occupation of the housing stock is two or more persons per room in many Latin American countries.[30]

The typical dwelling of the working-class family in these countries is a single room without any private facilities for cooking or bathing, and with no indoor toilet. Frequently, dwellings in the slum suburbs are shacks built out of scrap material by their occupants, who often are squatters without even a rudimentary system of water supply or sewage disposal. These "shantytowns" on the outskirts of cities have different names in different

[30] United Nations, Department of Economic and Social Affairs, *Report of the* Ad Hoc *Group of Experts on Housing and Urban Development.* New York: 1962, pp. 9–10.

countries, as, for example, *favelas, mocambos,* or *alagados* in Brazil; *callampas* in Chile; *barriados* in Peru; and *ranchos* in Venezuela. All of them obviously create serious health problems.

Rural dwellings, although varying widely from region to region and from family to family, often are of similar character. A United Nations report describes some deficiencies as follows:

> Ventilation and light are inadequate; floors are dirty or muddy; roofs are low, dirty and inflammable. Facilities for preserving and preparing food are usually painfully inadequate; cooking is a dark, smoky operation; and fuel for cooking may be difficult to get or it is wasteful of valuable resources. . . . Arrangements for washing persons and utensils are at best difficult. . . . The lack of sanitation is almost always dangerous to health. The water supply is inconvenient and frequently contaminated. Rodents and insects infest the huts. . . .[31]

Sometimes there are other kinds of housing. One type is the "estate housing" built on many of the plantations. This consists of single rooms usually built in rows of varying lengths. The space is no more adequate than that described for the shacks and huts mentioned above, and there is the additional problem of a number of families being crowded together under the same roof, separated only by thin partitions. Often twenty or more families are housed in a single row of barracks.

Housing Needs

The present housing needs of underdeveloped countries are made up of three elements: (1) housing needed to remove the existing housing shortage or deficit, (2) housing needed to replace the large quantity of substandard housing now occupied, and (3) housing needed because of the additional population increase, including both the natural increase and, in urban areas, that created by migrants.

In 1962, a United Nations study attempted the difficult task of making an estimate of the needs for housing in Africa, Asia and the Far East, and Latin America. The estimates are considered conservative, because they are based on the assumption that the increased population must be housed at the average household size which exists today, despite the generally recognized fact that household sizes tend to decline with social and economic development. The estimates reported are as follows:

> It is estimated that Africa's total populations will increase in the years 1960–1975 at the average annual rate of 1.9 to 2.3 per cent with urban population increasing at roughly double that rate. To keep pace with population growth and the obsolescence of dwellings and to eliminate existing housing shortages in thirty years, it is estimated that 2.6 million to 3.2 million dwellings would be required annually. This is equivalent to about ten to eleven dwellings per 1,000 inhabitants.
>
> The population in the whole of Asia in the 1960's is growing at the average

[31] United Nations, *Low Cost Housing in South and South-East Asia.* New York: 1951, p. 16.

Interior of typical rural rancho.
Typical urban rancho constructed by migrant family.

FIGURE 34. *Typical rancho dwellings in Venezuela. (Photographs courtesy of Journal of Housing and Eric Carlson.)*

annual rate of about 2 per cent while urban populations are growing at more than double that rate. Approximately 20 million dwellings would be required annually to cope with demographic development and replacement of inadequate homes, and to liquidate existing housing shortages within thirty years. This is equivalent to building annually approximately ten dwellings per 1,000 inhabitants, or, in urban areas, more than thirteen dwellings per 1,000 inhabitants.

The population of Latin America is expected to increase at the annual average rate of 2.5 to 2.8 per cent in the period 1961–1975. Urban population is expected to grow in the same period at an annual rate of 4.1 to 4.2 per cent. To keep pace with rising population and obsolescence, and to liquidate the current housing shortage in thirty years, it is estimated that 2.6 to 3.3 million dwellings should be built annually, or about eleven to twelve dwellings per 1,000 inhabitants. In the urban areas alone, from thirteen to sixteen dwellings per 1,000 urban inhabitants are required annually.[32]

A summary of the estimated annual housing needs in Africa, Asia and Latin America for the years 1960 and 1975 is shown in Table 17–4 (p. 577). If a target of thirty years is established for meeting the housing shortage in these countries, as the United Nations recommends, and the average life of a dwelling is estimated to be about twenty-five years, then the amount of annual construction needed to meet these two requirements, as well as the requirements brought about by anticipated population growth, was approximately 22½ million units in 1960. By 1975, under the same conditions, there will be a total annual need of approximately 28 million units.

This is a heavier rate of output of dwelling units than is currently being attained in either Europe or North America. It would require, for example, annual housing programs ranging from 8 to 10.4 dwellings per 1,000 inhabitants, depending on the rate at which existing dwellings are replaced. This may be compared with the housing outputs currently being attained in Europe and North America. Only four countries have reached an

[32] *Report of the* Ad Hoc *Group of Experts on Housing and Urban Development, op. cit.,* pp. 9–10.

nual rate of eight or more dwellings per 1,000 inhabitants: Sweden (9.1), Switzerland (9.3), the Federal Republic of Germany (10.5), and the USSR (14.0). In the United States, ". . . the current rate is from 7.0 to 7.5 dwellings per 1,000 inhabitants," and several European countries ". . . currently provide from 4.0 to 6.5 dwellings annually per 1,000 inhabitants."[33]

HOUSING PROGRAMS

In the light of this great need for additional, adequate housing, it is important to observe what is being done in the developing countries to meet the housing shortage.

The first fact that becomes evident is the inadequacy of existing systems to meet either the present or the projected need. Nevertheless, it is worthwhile to review these systems briefly.

The varied approaches made by governments toward solving housing problems have depended mainly upon the specific situation encountered, the resources they could command, and the general attitude toward housing. Some governments have limited their activities to constructing housing themselves; others have encouraged private industry to build houses, through favorable legislation, such as tax exemptions or relaxation of import duties on materials, and other assistance. Some have decided that housing should be an integral part of economic development plans, while others have built new housing to meet the needs of a particular situation. Still others have assumed their housing situation would improve as general economic conditions improved.

In Puerto Rico, housing improvement has been made an integral part of national developmental planning. This, however, is not typical, in general, of attempts to solve the housing problem in developing countries. More often, the immediate problem to be solved has been responsible for determining what kind and how much housing should be built. For example, if new industries were being built, as in Africa, the provision of housing for workers near the place of employment was emphasized, in order to attract labor to the industry and help in providing a stable labor force. Calamities such as earthquakes have sometimes brought the government into the housing field and sometimes have led to the adoption of improved methods of rehousing victims of the disaster. In Ecuador, for example, following the earthquake of 1949, completely new cities were designed according to contemporary planning procedures to replace those that had been destroyed.

One development has been a growing recognition of governmental responsibility for assisting some proportion of the population to acquire housing, and for providing housing for the even larger proportion still unable to help themselves. Another result is a clarification of the place of housing as part of the larger framework of social and economic changes needed to bring about improvement of general living conditions. Almost

[33] *Ibid.*, p. 62. (Also, see Table 16–1, p. 537.)

all of the underdeveloped countries have some form of housing program. In some countries, particularly Latin America, housing programs are administered by independent agencies, usually housing banks or other institutions with responsibilities in financing and building housing. In other countries the programs are under other departments of the government. As a United Nations survey indicated:

> A housing programme cuts across so many fields that it is not surprising to find housing responsibilities associated with a variety of ministries and government functions, including agriculture, social welfare, public works, reconstruction, labour, health and local government. Housing needs are inseparable from other community needs, such as pure water supply, sanitary disposal facilities and adequate roads. Some housing projects have expanded into comprehensive community development projects, and community development programmes commonly include housing as an essential aspect.[34]

One feature common to almost all the countries is legislation requiring that housing be provided by employers in connection with industrial developments, such as large-scale petroleum developments, mining operations, or similar activities. More often than not, the housing also has to meet definite standards of livability. Whether or not these programs are effective depends upon one's point of view. They provide housing for at least a small group of the population; on the other hand, the better living conditions of this group sometimes serve to accentuate the poor living conditions of surrounding neighborhoods. This requirement, of course, is placed on rural more than on urban employers, so it leaves the problem of urban housing more or less untouched. In some of the countries, the government itself, as an employer, provides housing for its employees. These groups, however, are not usually entirely composed of those in most desperate need of housing.[35]

Housing needs are not, of course, distributed uniformly throughout the population, but are clustered in large segments. Four groups may be identified in most of the countries: a small well-to-do class that is rarely in need of assistance with housing; a somewhat larger, but still proportionately small, group who could arrange for their own housing if some means of financing were available; another group able to supplement their savings with labor or otherwise partly able to finance housebuilding; and, finally, a large group with low incomes in need of considerable material assistance and/or subsidies.

In urban areas, the second group in particular accounts for an expansion in the demand for housing. This group is made up largely of white-collar employees and better-paid artisans and workers who have been living in older parts of cities in deteriorating but expensive quarters. This group has expressed a strongly felt need for better housing and, under

[34] United Nations, Bureau of Social Affairs, *International Survey of Programmes of Social Development*. New York: 1955, p. 45.

[35] United Nations, Department of Economic and Social Affairs, *Financing of Housing and Community Improvement Programmes*. New York: 1957, p. 17.

improving economic conditions, their incomes and their standards are simultaneously rising. Among this group also there is discernible a trend away from extended family living. Families in these circumstances usually have some savings, may possibly own a little land, and, more important, are ready to invest their savings in housing. The difficulties of this group are in financing. The cost of housing is beyond their means; down payments are high, frequently as much as 50 percent of the cost; loans for mortgages (when facilities for such loans are available) are short term; and interest rates are high. For example, in Bolivia, a usual interest rate for a ten-year mortgage is 10 percent, and in Nicaragua, interest rates on private loans have cost between 1½ and 2½ percent a month.[36]

As the countries are at different levels of development, the size of this group is variable. To mention only a few examples, in Latin America it is estimated to make up about half of the urban population (using incomes of $500 a year as a base);[37] in Accra, about 37 percent of the urban population;[38] in some parts of Asia, 12 percent of the urban population, and in the Philippines and Ceylon perhaps as much as 30 percent of urban dwellers.[39] A complication in determining the composition of the group is the income base. If the income of all family members is considered, many more families might be included than if the income of only the head of the household is taken into account.[40] Potentially, this is the group that can reasonably be expected to increase as incomes and employment opportunities improve.

Efforts to improve institutional financing of houses benefit this middle-income group in particular. The crux of the problem of institutional financing is, of course, to obtain sufficient money to loan for mortgages or other purposes. Related to this is the use of the money for mortgage loans when more immediately profitable investments are at hand, such as construction of apartments for the wealthy, support of some phase of the export trade, or similar attractions. Again, governmental encouragement of savings for investment in housing has to be present in favorable legislation, controlled inflation, and, under some circumstances, through the provision of initial capital. Inflation has been an especially serious factor in hampering the development of mortgage loans, as it both discourages savings and dissipates enthusiasm for long-term investments.

There is more opportunity for institutional financing in Latin America than in countries where economic development has been more recently

[36] Charles Abrams, "Urban Land Problems and Policies," in *Housing and Town and Country Planning*, Bulletin 7, United Nations, Department of Social Affairs, 1953, p. 18.

[37] William F. Butler, "A Proposed Procedure for Private Financing of Housing in Latin America," in *Study of International Housing*, United States Senate Committee on Banking and Currency, Eighty-Eighth Congress, First Session. Washington, D.C.: U.S. Government Printing Office, 1963, p. 99.

[38] United Nations, *Financing of Housing and Community Development Programmes*, *op. cit.*, p. 8.

[39] *Ibid.*, p. 13.

[40] *Ibid.*, p. 16.

instituted.[41] Even in Latin America, however, such institutions are more likely to be found in countries where a higher level of income has been reached, such as Argentina, Venezuela, Costa Rica, Mexico, and Uruguay. Some capitalization companies, which are similar to building and loan associations, are becoming established in these countries. These companies arrange for a regular monthly savings schedule by the individual family, and mortgages are secured on a policy loan guaranteed by the government. While approximately sixty-five associations were operating in five Latin American countries by the beginning of 1964, their history is still too short to determine how successful such institutions will be.

In addition to capitalization companies, there have also been special home financing institutions in some countries, and life insurance companies have also participated in the mortgage market in varying degrees. Provident funds and social welfare institutions have been active to some extent in this program. A major benefit of some of these programs has been the low equity (down payments) required, amortization periods up to fifteen years, and moderate (compared with the going market) interest rates. Most of the more liberal financing schemes are still in their infancy and their general workability and acceptance have not yet been proved. Cooperative societies for housing purposes exist, but are not prevalent, probably because such associations require savings and also—an even greater lack—experience in this type of organized activity. The housing banks mentioned, through which some governments provide funds to finance mortgages for housing, are another recent development.

Although the direct benefits from existing institutional financing in developing countries accrue to a relatively small group, indirectly they are of benefit to lower-income groups, in encouraging savings and in reducing to some extent the pressure for housing. Another benefit, of course, is stimulation of the development of the building industry.

In rural areas, owners of small farms make up a group comparable to the medium-income group in the cities. Under prevalent systems of agriculture, many of them live in villages. Their needs are usually more for some form of village improvement, such as technical assistance in planning and the provision of sanitary facilities, street improvements, and similar public works, than for housing. Improvements in rural credit facilities, such as the agricultural banks in some of the Latin American countries, benefit this group, because they have land that can be pledged for security. As yet, these programs exist on only a limited scale and their effectiveness remains untested.

The largest groups are, of course, the urban dwellers with incomes too low to be able to afford any type of housing without substantial assistance, and the landless rural population. In urban areas, public housing has been provided, in a few instances, usually to meet some extraordinary situation, such as resettlement of war refugees, rehousing victims of natural disasters, or similar crises. A few satellite communities have been constructed which

[41] *Ibid.*, p. 34.

include housing for low-income families. Subsidies have been given to some families in this group who have a little income. Some Asian countries have made grants of up to one half or more of the cost of the house. In some African countries, some low-income householders pay rents on the basis of 12 to 15 percent of family income, and the difference between this figure and the economic rent is subsidized from governmental revenues.[42] The resources of most governments prohibit subsidies to the extent necessary, even if the housing could be made available. Financial considerations, as much as other reasons, keep public housing programs from being either continuous or provided on the scale needed.

Public housing encounters other problems than financing. Land for housing has to be acquired and in many cases improved, families selected (a difficult matter when so many need housing), sites plotted and laid out, materials assembled, supervisors and a labor force collected—to mention only a few. Once completed, the project has to be managed and maintained to prevent a recurrence of slum conditions. Even with adequate financing, the administrative and technical skills required might well be beyond the resources of most governments.

One serious defect in some of the countries in all efforts to improve urban housing has been the limited ability of municipalities to participate in housing programs. Though many municipalities have definite responsibilities in the housing field, not only in providing services and in enforcing legislation, but also in determining the most urgent local needs, in many countries most of these duties, if they are met at all, devolve on the central authorities. This, of course, reflects the centralization of authority in many of these countries, as well as a lack of citizen participation in programs. To a large extent, the development of local governmental agencies concerned with housing has been held back by " . . . the general shortage of well-trained technical and administrative personnel and the undeveloped state of municipal finance."[43]

In urban areas the acquisition of land is a special difficulty. The cost of land has spiralled in many of the countries as a result of the land speculation that usually results when ". . . population increase is accompanied by ease of land transfer."[44] This situation is typical in the undeveloped countries; sometimes the cost of land has multiplied four or more times in the last two or three decades. Eminent domain, of course, is a right of the government in all countries, but many governments, particularly those in the developing countries, tend to use this power sparingly. Governments thus tend to turn to areas outside cities where land is available. This creates problems of transportation, jurisdiction, and increased costs, where utilities and facilities have to be provided.

In some areas, this, and other practices related to land use, may aggravate

[42] *Ibid.*, p. 9.

[43] United Nations, *Report of the* Ad Hoc *Group of Experts on Housing and Urban Development*, *op. cit.*, p. 45.

[44] Abrams, *op. cit.*, p. 26.

the competition between rural and urban areas for arable land—a serious problem in some countries, especially where food is being imported to feed the urban population because of deficient agricultural supply. The housing shortage has resulted in numerous laws to control rents. These serve to protect the tenancy of some families, but have had side effects, such as increasing rental costs through the payment of "key money" and, in some places, by inhibiting new construction. In any housing development, also, there is the possibility of social stratification in the form of one-class or other homogeneous neighborhoods. (Even some of the industrial housing is stratified.) Although the need for building regulations and subdivision controls is widely accepted as essential to sound development, there has been extreme difficulty in enforcing these regulations and controls in most urban areas of the developing countries.

In rural areas, problems are perhaps more deeply rooted in living conditions. Again, legislation to inaugurate or implement large-scale land-reform programs has remained unsuccessful for the most part. Several countries have instituted measures to control rents on agricultural lands, but have found them difficult to enforce. The main obstacles to enforcement of legislation of any kind to improve the lot of tenants has been the weak economic position of the renters, their illiteracy and lack of organization, the strength of tradition, and the weakness of governmental administrative machinery. Attempts to provide crop insurance and price supports have proved to be beyond the resources of most governments, especially in view of the large proportion of the agricultural population to be covered. Though investments in agriculture are being channeled through institutions more than in the past, the traditional source of loans—the moneylender—is difficult to displace.[45] This is particularly the situation with the landless farmer, who can offer only his anticipated crop as security.

Allied to the question of housing needs, with their potential for absorbing almost all the financial resources of governments in undeveloped countries,[46] is the question of whether so much governmental revenue should go to housing, in view of the multiplicity of needs and the scarcity of resources. One argument is that housing, like education, is a long-range investment that offers little immediate monetary return. Another is that only by raising incomes can living standards—and with them housing standards—be raised. Therefore (it is argued) national resources might better be concentrated in investments in industries, small or large, in diversification of agricultural products, or in the development of export crops, rather than being spent on an investment that would, at best, alleviate the situation of a relatively small group.

On the other hand, the provision of housing in developing countries is not solely a matter of welfare, that is, of providing for the destitute and

[45] United Nations, Bureau of Social Affairs, *International Survey of Programmes of Social Development*. New York: 1959, p. 136.

[46] United Nations, *Report of the* Ad Hoc *Group of Experts on Housing and Urban Development, op. cit.*, p. 13.

homeless, though that enters into it. With such widespread need for housing, tangible contributions to the economy frequently are cited. These include stabilization of a labor force, particularly that portion which has begun to enjoy the benefits of steady income; provision of opportunity for a stable family life; acquisition or development of skills for many untrained workers; introduction to the use of money, credit, and the responsibility of financial obligations; the development of a building industry, and the stimulation to manufacturing by an increased demand for household equipment and supplies. The choice is seen to lie less between either housing development or economic development than between a selection of methods to provide housing that will meet the needs of different groups in the population and provide for full utilization of the talent and financial resources available.

AIDED SELF-HELP

In almost every developing economy, individual self-sufficiency in providing food, clothing, and shelter is a predominant characteristic. The skills acquired linger on even after specialization of functions takes place and skills are exchanged for goods and later for money. Much of the rural, and some of the urban, housing in undeveloped countries was built by the occupant, sometimes with the assistance of other family members and friends. With labor and some degree of skill in building available, aided self-help is increasingly being looked upon as the answer to the pertinent question, "What kind of house, better in quality and layout, can be built with local materials and skills at virtually no cash cost?"[47]

Aided self-help, however, is more than a gathering together of relatives and friends to help a prospective householder put up a shelter. As the name implies, it includes resources and labor provided by the individual family as well as assistance of various kinds, depending upon the particular local need, provided by others. Assistance may simply be financial; it may take the form of assisting with the provision of building material; it may provide aid in the development of building sites, with roads, water and sanitation facilities; it may represent the loan of building equipment; it may provide either technical or physical assistance for the construction of all or part of the house; it may include the preconstruction of units, such as, for instance, sanitary facilities; or it may provide any combination of these forms of assistance.

Assistance is usually provided by a governmental source—national, municipal, or village. Builders are frequently selected by a central agency such as a national housing agency, which supervises the planning and construction, and arranges for the loans, materials, and other needed facilities. In these projects, administrative and social welfare services are provided, and these continue after completion of the projects. Administrative ser-

[47] "Housing in the Tropics," in *Housing and Town and Country Planning*, Bulletin 6, United Nations, Department of Social Affairs, January 1952, p. 5.

vices are not charged to the householder, but he is expected to repay loans of money and for materials furnished, and sometimes other charges, the nature of which varies. The builder is expected to have the skill required to build the house.[48]

Some employers have also utilized this method of providing housing for workers. Ordinarily these are group projects, and willingness and ability to do the work required and to assume the financial obligations of eventual payment for the building materials, loans, and other charges are the responsibility of the builders (workers).

One of the outstanding examples of aided self-help has been the rural housing program in Puerto Rico. Plots of land have been allotted to squatters and landless families. New villages have been built and some older ones rehabilitated. Community services, including educational facilities and health centers, have been instituted. The selection of communities to be helped depends on the existence of certain well-defined characteristics, which include an interest in having better housing, an active community council, willingness to contribute labor, and some other prerequisites. Within the communities, the families selected for participation are usually from among those living in inadequate houses and having the financial ability to repay the loan in ten years. Some personal characteristics, such as good conduct, trustworthiness, and physical and mental ability to do the work, are important. Under the Puerto Rican plan, a Mutual Savings Society is established at an early stage, which collects savings and assumes the fiscal arrangements. Once this society begins to function, the government operates only in an advisory capacity.

In India, aided self-help programs have been used in village improvement schemes, particularly in villages where economic development is in progress or is planned. Payment of part of the cost is required of the builder, and this payment may be in the provision of materials or in labor. Needy families are given long-term loans, and families who cannot afford to repay loans may be granted subsidies. Similar programs are in operation in some African countries. In almost all the schemes, success depends in large measure on the effectiveness of the local organization and on the families selected to participate.[49]

The advantages of aided self-help are obvious. Both the supporting agency and the householder save the cost of labor and some of the cost of material and equipment, if sound purchasing practices have been followed. The householder acquires a better house than he might otherwise have been able to afford. The agency is able to obtain more and better-planned housing, as well as wider distribution of scarce technical assistance and finances, than would otherwise result.

In theory, this would seem to be one of the primary means of solving the poor housing condition of many families in the developing countries.

[48] United Nations, *International Survey of Programmes of Social Development*, 1959, *op. cit.*, p. 42.

[49] *Ibid.*, p. 46.

Many women have participated in the building of homes under Venezuela's rural housing program.

Construction begins on new dwelling in small rural community in Venezuela. Note rancho in background with walls of bahareque and thatched roofs which provide breeding places for disease-carrying insects.

When conditions permit, houses are built in groups, with specialized labor used to speed basic construction.

Making soil cement blocks in Venezuela. Note use of economical, easily adaptable wooden mold. Man is pushing out block from mold for drying before use in construction.

FIGURE 35. *Many dwellings are being built in developing countries on the basis of self-help. (Photographs courtesy of Eric Carlson.)*

However, although there have been sporadic efforts at getting self-help programs under way, some on a major scale, the program has to date had no significant effect on the existing housing situation of most of the countries where it has been tried. There undoubtedly have been several reasons for this.

The first reason is the difficulty of providing technical assistance when so little is available. This has not only retarded the volume of new building but has also resulted in limiting land surveying, laying out house plots, and providing community services. A second reason is that house designs have to be standard and sufficiently simple so that the houses can be built by the prospective inhabitants within the range of time, talent, and money at their disposal. Third, if a worker is regularly employed—and this is particularly pertinent in urban areas—he has little time (and perhaps less inclination) to devote his free hours to this kind of activity. His incentive may be lessened by the fact that in doing this work he has had to learn certain skills which he may perhaps never again need to use. Fourth, standard building parts and materials are not always available. Fifth, where self-help schemes have been practical and construction has been simplified, standards have frequently been relaxed to such an extent that there has been the risk of creating new slums or unsuitable living conditions rather than ideal permanent neighborhoods containing homes of fire-resistant and durable materials. Finally, in addition to technical and physical problems, administrative problems, in organizing, directing, and supervising construction and in maintaining completed projects, have been difficult to meet in many countries. With the resources available, the selection of projects to sponsor and of families to assist are particularly troublesome. With competition for housing so keen, achieving any permanent results from the necessarily limited number of projects has been difficult. For example, in urban areas, overcrowding has to be guarded against and, in order that the projects may benefit low-income families, restrictions on sale of the houses to families financially able to purchase homes have been necessary.

In rural areas, the extent to which housing can be improved unless accompanied by improvements in agricultural technology, market facilities, systems of land tenure, and rural living conditions is considered problematical. One reason sometimes cited for the poor quality of much of the present rural housing in some of the countries is that only flimsy houses are constructed on rented land, in order that they may be moved without difficulty or left without serious loss.[50] Self-help housing schemes have been made a part of programs to resettle some of the rural population on government-owned lands, as, for example, in Puerto Rico. Resettlement programs, however, are as yet relatively few and not always possible, in overpopulated countries or in countries where most of the arable land is already under cultivation.

[50] United Nations, Department of Social Affairs, *Survey of Problems of Low Cost Rural Housing in Tropical Areas.* New York: 1950, pp. 5–6.

DEVELOPMENT OF BUILDING MATERIALS INDUSTRIES

Whether or not housing is a part of developmental plans, and whether public or private or self-help construction is emphasized, most of the developing countries recognize the potential contribution to their economies of a strong construction industry. One objective in these countries is to stimulate the building industry to the point where it makes a contribution similar to that in more advanced countries. In the United States, for example, building is the second largest industry and frequently accounts for at least 4 percent of the gross national product.

Considerable attention has been given in the developing countries to the use of local materials for housebuilding. Wider use of available resources not only would reduce the cost of housing, but would also help in decreasing imports to be used for necessary but not immediately productive purposes. Of course, resources for building are more abundant in some countries than in others. For example, in Puerto Rico and Guatemala, among other countries, where favorable resources exist, cement production has expanded. In Asia and Burma, production of building materials such as cement, roof tiles, bricks, and construction blocks is increasing, and Asia also is developing forest resources. Other countries as well are exploring the possibilities of local materials.[51]

Most countries have some building materials among their natural resources. A greater drawback has been the relatively low level of technology in utilization of those resources. A United Nations report has indicated that better utilization of local resources required the development of techniques and of local industries.[52] Experiments in the use of stabilized soil construction have been carried on in some Asian and Caribbean countries, and this method of construction has been used in other countries.[53]

Another difficulty has been a neglect of native building materials (adobe, lumber, and similar resources) in favor of imported materials that are standard in other countries. Some of this seems also to be related to technology. In Latin America, for example, the prejudice against wood as a construction material may stem from the poor processing methods which frequently resulted in the use of unseasoned lumber.[54] A further drawback to the development of a local building industry has been lack of standardization in house parts and lack of standard house plans. This deficiency has

[51] United Nations, *International Survey of Programmes of Social Development*, 1955, *op. cit.*, p. 47.

[52] United Nations, *Survey of Problems of Low Cost Rural Housing in Tropical Areas*, *op. cit.*, p. 28.

[53] Leonard J. Currie, ''Role of Housing Research in Latin American Development,'' in *Housing and Town and Country Planning*, Bulletin 8, United Nations, Department of Social Affairs, November 1953, p. 92.

[54] United Nations, *International Survey of Programmes of Social Development*, 1955, *op. cit.*, p. 40.

prevented the application of mass production methods—and attendant cost reductions—to the building process.

While some of these problems are being corrected in some of the developing countries, building materials industries, and the complex components that make up such industries, are still generally lacking.

CONCLUSION

The housing situation in the developing countries and the impact of that situation may be summed up in the words of Van Ettinger:

> . . . housing has become an important public issue in most countries and the problems relating to the formulation, financing and execution of low-cost housing programmes have become more pressing from year to year. It is increasingly recognized that poor housing conditions may reduce working efficiency or lead to severe social disruptions, and that increased efforts must be made to improve housing and community facilities.[55]

Of course, it is evident from the discussion in this chapter that the housing problems of these countries cannot be treated by themselves. These problems are closely interlinked with the problems of economics, social class, politics, and education. The soundest solution to these problems would be to raise the economic level of the population to an adequate level, to overcome the problems of social class, to stabilize the political situations, and to achieve universal education. If these goals were achieved, then better housing for the majority of the population would be forthcoming. Without at least substantial progress toward these goals, a serious housing situation is likely to remain in these countries, because the only alternative for families who cannot afford to pay for decent housing is extensive government subsidies, and the present and contemplated resources of most of the governments are not adequate for this.

However, much can be done to improve the housing of at least a significant proportion of the population of these countries today. It has been indicated that four primary housing groups exist. First is the upper socioeconomic group that needs no assistance. Next is the new middle-income group—still small in size, but growing—that has sufficient income to arrange for better housing if the necessary financing and credit mechanisms are established. Third is the relatively large lower-income group that could obtain better housing if its earnings through regular wages and possible small family savings could be augmented through more financial and other assistance. Finally, there is the large group with extremely low and irregular incomes. This group, because of its size and its small economic resources, constitutes the most serious problem.

Although governments could today do much to assist the second- and third-mentioned groups, either through some of the present programs or

[55] J. Van Ettinger, *Towards a Habitable World.* Amsterdam, Holland: Elsevier Publishing Co., 1960, pp. 293–294.

through newly developed ones, it seems probable that the only sound solution for the fourth group is to attempt to reduce it appreciably in size by improving its economic position and thus permit many of these families to move up to the second or third group. The housing problems of the remaining smaller-sized group might then be alleviated to a considerable degree through both financial aid and considerable material assistance.

Two different kinds of programs, then, are needed in the developing countries. First, programs are needed to assist those families who could attain better housing conditions immediately by appropriate government aids; second, programs should be established to assist those families with the lowest incomes to improve their economic position over a long term so that they, too, can participate in the government programs. Probably, a small residual group not capable of earning enough to achieve adequate housing without substantial public assistance will always remain, but, if this group can be kept proportionately small, means of meeting its needs can be found.

One writer has indicated that many of the people living in these countries have a common awareness of their problems. It is this "common awareness" which has recently caused so much attention to be focused on their housing problems. It is also this awareness that will lead to the solution of those problems.

READING LIST

HOUSING SITUATION

Abrams, Charles. *Man's Struggle for Shelter in an Urbanizing World.* Cambridge, Mass.: Massachusetts Institute of Technology Press, 1964.

Back, Kurt W. *Slums, Projects, and People.* Durham, N.C.: Duke University Press, 1962.

Caribbean Commission, Central Secretariat. *Aspects of Housing in the Caribbean.* Port-of-Spain, Trinidad: Kent House, 1951.

Hauser, Philip M. (ed.) *Urbanization in Latin America.* A UNESCO survey. New York: International Documents Service, a Division of Columbia University Press, 1961.

Housing in Latin America. New York: The Chase Manhattan Bank, July 1962.

Subcommittee on Housing, Committee on Banking and Currency, U.S. Senate, Eighty-Eighth Congress, First Session. *Study of International Housing.* Washington, D.C.: U.S. Government Printing Office, 1963.

United Nations, Department of Economic and Social Affairs. *Financing of Housing and Community Improvement Programmes.* New York: 1957.

———, Department of Social Affairs. *Housing and Town and Country Planning.* Bulletin 6, "Housing in the Tropics." New York: 1952.

———. *Housing and Town and Country Planning.* Bulletin 7, "Urban Land Problems and Policies." New York: 1953.

———. *Low Cost Housing in South and South-East Asia: Report of a Mission of Experts.* New York: 1951.

———, Department of Economic and Social Affairs. *Report of the* Ad Hoc *Group of Experts on Housing and Urban Development.* New York: 1962.

Van Ettinger, J. *Towards a Habitable World.* Amsterdam, Holland: Elsevier Publishing Company, 1960.

Violich, Francis. *Cities of Latin America.* New York: Reinhold Publishing Corporation, 1944.

———. *Low-Cost Housing in Latin America.* Washington, D.C.: Pan American Union, 1949.

SOCIAL CONDITIONS

United Nations, Bureau of Social Affairs. *International Survey of Programmes of Social Development.* New York: 1959.

———, Department of Social Affairs. *Preliminary Report on the World Social Situation.* New York: 1952.

———. *Report on the World Social Situation.* New York: 1957.

ECONOMIC SITUATION

Brand, Willem. *The Struggle for a Higher Standard of Living.* Glencoe, Ill.: The Free Press, 1958.

Heilbroner, Robert L. *The Great Ascent: The Struggle for Economic Development in Our Time.* New York: Harper & Row, 1963.

Hoffman, Paul G. *World Without Want.* New York: Harper & Row, 1962.

MacEoin, Gary. *Latin America, The Eleventh Hour.* New York: P. J. Kenedy & Sons, 1962.

Pentony, DeVere E. (ed.) *The Underdeveloped Lands: A Dilemma of the International Economy.* San Francisco: Chandler Publishing Company, 1960.

Pepelasis, A., L. Mears, and I. Adelman. *Economic Development: Analysis and Case Studies.* New York: Harper & Bros., 1961.

United Nations, Department of Economic and Social Affairs. *World Economic Survey.* New York (published annually).

POLITICAL SITUATION

Almond, G. A., and J. S. Coleman (eds.) *The Politics of the Developing Areas.* Princeton: Princeton University Press, 1960.

EDUCATION

United Nations, Educational, Scientific and Cultural Organization. *Asia, Arab States, Africa: Education and Progress.* Paris, France: UNESCO, 1961.

Table 17–1

WORLD AND CONTINENTAL POPULATION, MID-1962 ESTIMATES

Region	*Total Population (in millions)*	*Average Annual Rate of Increase, 1950–1960*	*No. of Years to Double Population*
World	3,115	1.8%	39
Africa	267	2.0	35
Asia	1,747	1.9	36
Northern America*	206	1.8	39
Latin America	216	2.5	28
Europe	433	0.8	87
Oceania	17	2.4	29
U.S.S.R.	221	1.7	40

SOURCE: United Nations, *Demographic Yearbook*. New York 1961.
* United States and Canada.

Table 17–2

ESTIMATED AND PROJECTED URBAN POPULATION, BY SIZE GROUPS, FOR AFRICA, ASIA, AND LATIN AMERICA, 1960 AND 1975

	Population in Places 100,000 and Over (in millions)	*As Percent of Total Population*	*Population in Places 1,000,000 and Over (in millions)*	*As Percent of Total Population*
1960:				
Africa	20	8%	6	2%
Asia	204	12	102	6
Latin America	51	25	25	12
1975:				
Africa	48	16	12	4
Asia	486	22	221	10
Latin America	118	39	61	20

SOURCE: Urban Land Institute, *World Urbanization*, Technical Bulletin No. 43, April 1962.

Table 17–3

NUMBER OF PERSONS PER DWELLING AND PER ROOM IN SELECTED COUNTRIES FOR LATEST AVAILABLE YEAR

Country	Average Number of Persons per Dwelling	Percentage of Dwellings with Following Number of Rooms			Percentage of Dwellings with Following Number of Persons per Room			
		One–Two	*Three–Four*	*Five plus*	*Less than 1.5*	*1.5 and over*	*2 and over*	*3 and over*
Argentina	5–6	63%	27%	10%	19%	81%	63%	36%
Panama	5	82	14	4	27	73	66	46
Trinidad-Tobago	4–5	57	36	7	42	58	48	24
Mauritius	5	74	18	8	28	72	62	33
United States	3.5	7	34	59	97	3	—	—
Denmark	3.1	4	58	38	96	4	1	—
West Germany	4.0	17	58	26	83	17	7	1

SOURCE: United Nations, *Statistical Yearbook*, New York, 1961, excepting data for the United States, which are taken from the U.S. Census of Housing 1960.

Note: The data refer to dwellings only. A dwelling is a room or a suite of rooms and its accessories intended for private habitation, with a separate access to the street. In some countries, the data include nonpermanent structures and improvised shelters.

Table 17–4

ESTIMATED ANNUAL HOUSING NEEDS IN AFRICA, ASIA, AND LATIN AMERICA, 1960 AND 1975 (IN MILLIONS OF DWELLING UNITS)

	1960	*1975*		*1960*	*1975*
Due to population increase:			To replace stock:*		
Africa	0.84	1.50	Africa	1.03	1.03
Asia	5.30	9.40	Asia	7.10	7.10
Latin America	1.10	1.70	Latin America	0.90	0.90
To eliminate the deficit or shortage in 30 years:			Total new housing needed:		
Africa	0.73	0.73	Africa	2.60	3.26
Asia	4.80	4.80	Asia	17.20	21.30
Latin America	0.60	0.60	Latin America	2.60	3.20
			Total	22.40	27.76

SOURCE: United Nations, *World Housing Conditions and Estimated Requirements,* July 1962.

* Average life of a dwelling unit is assumed to be thirty years in urban areas and twenty years in rural areas. The 1975 figures do not take into account increments of stock between 1960 and 1975.

GLOSSARY

*

Advance commitment—conditional. A commitment by a mortgage lender to make or buy a mortgage loan for a stated amount on a specified property, existing or to be constructed, within a stated period of time to an owner-occupant home buyer whose credit will meet with the lender's approval.

Amortized mortgage. One that is repaid in specified amounts, frequently on a monthly basis, during the term of the mortgage.

Appraisal. A formal and detailed evaluation of a property resulting in an estimated price for it that a typical buyer would be justified in paying and that a seller would accept.

Blighted area. An area of declining property values caused by the deterioration and obsolescence of housing and community facilities; a slum area or one that is fast becoming "run-down."

Builder's warranty. A written statement, which the builder or seller of a new home delivers to the buyer prior to the sale of the property, that the dwelling was constructed in substantial conformity with the plans and specifications. (Usually for a one-year period.)

Building code. Local regulations that govern the types of materials used in construction, the relation of materials to design, sanitary facilities, the provision of light and air, and the like.

Building cycle theory. The concept which assumes that there is an eighteen- to twenty-year regularity in the peaks and troughs of the volume of building.

Capital grant. The Federal cash contribution of up to two thirds (under certain financing conditions up to three fourths) of the net urban renewal project costs of projects undertaken in a locality.

Channel of distribution. The course of ownership taken in the transfer of title for a product as it moves from manufacturer or producer to the final consumer.

Closing costs. Costs incidental to completing mortgage financing arrangements, e.g., title insurance, recording fees, mortgage service charge, property survey, credit reports, etc.

Commercial builder. A contract or operative home builder. Home building is his sole or principal business. (Not to be confused with a contractor building commercial properties.)

Commercial farm. Farm with a value of sales of farm products amounting to $1,200 or more annually.

Conditional commitment (FHA). A written agreement by FHA to insure a mortgage, within a stated period of time, on a specified property in the amount and under terms specified, provided a borrower is obtained whose credit is satisfactory to the FHA.

Condominium. The individual ownership of single units in a multiunit structure, with common ownership of halls, stairs, elevators, lobbies, driveways, etc.

Conservation. Protecting houses and neighborhoods against the encroachment of undesirable influences.

Construction financing. Loans required to finance the housebuilding operation.

Contract builder. A builder who builds houses under contract, that is, for a known buyer.

Contract rent. The rent contracted for by the renter, regardless of whether it includes heating fuel, cooking fuel, electricity, water, furniture, or other services sometimes provided.

Contracting family. The family type in which the woman is thirty-five years old or older and there are no children under the age of eighteen.

Conventional house. One that is constructed more or less piece by piece on the site.

Conventional mortgage. Any mortgage not insured by the FHA or guaranteed by the VA.

Cooperative housing. Type of housing in which tenant purchases stock and is a shareholder in a corporation owning and operating a multidwelling unit structure or project in which the tenant occupies one unit.

Correspondent. A bank or broker who acts as a representative of a life insurance company for handling mortgage loan arrangements.

Debt service. Payments against principal and interest on mortgage.

Delinquency. Falling behind in mortgage payments.

Demand for housing. Market demand, i.e., how many houses are likely to be sold.

Depreciation. Loss in value due to physical wear and deterioration, and deterioration due to blight and obsolescence.

Deteriorating housing. Housing units not dilapidated but needing more repair than would be provided in the course of regular maintenance.

Dilapidated house. A house that has serious deficiencies, is run-down or neglected, or is of inadequate original construction so that it does not provide adequate shelter or protection against the elements or endangers the safety of the occupants.

Dispersed residences. Homes for the aged scattered among other homes in the neighborhood or community.

Dumb-bell or *Double-decker tenements.* A type of tenement built in New York City between 1879 and 1901, situated on a 25 ft. × 100 ft. lot, usually five, six, or seven stories high, containing fourteen rooms to a floor, seven on each side. One family occupied the front four rooms and another the rear three. Front and rear apartments were connected by a hall. Term "dumb-bell" was derived from indentation at the side of the building; this shaft was to provide light and air, but became a receptable for garbage and a fire hazard.

Dwelling unit. A house, apartment, or other group of rooms or a single room when it is occupied or intended for occupancy as separate living quarters, that is, when the occupants do not live or eat with any other persons in the structure and there is either (a) direct access from the outside or through a common hall or (b) a kitchen or cooking equipment for the exclusive use of the occupants of the unit. The occupants may be a group of persons or a single person living alone.

Economic base theory. The concept that assumes that future growth of different cities or urban regions can be predicted on the basis of the economic make-up of those cities or regions.

Economic rent. The justifiable rent for a property, including profit to the owner, excluding utilities and services.

Equivalent elimination. The elimination of a substantially equal number of unsafe or unsanitary units for the number of new public housing units built in any community.

Escrow. In housing, generally "earnest money" placed in the hands of a disinterested party pending the performance of certain obligations.

Eviction. Dispossessing a family or person, through process of law, of the property occupied.

Expanding family. The family type having some children between the ages of eight to eighteen.

Family. A group of two or more persons related by blood, marriage, or adoption and residing together. (Sometimes the term "family" is used as a substitute for the term "household.")

Farm. Ten or more acres of land from which sales of farm products amounted to $50 or more or places of less than 10 acres from which sales of farm products amounted to $250 or more annually.

Feasibility survey. A survey of an urban area using Federal funds to determine if it is feasible to undertake an urban renewal project or projects within that area.

FHA-insured mortgage. Mortgage on which principal and interest are insured for the lending institution by the Federal Housing Administration.

First mortgage. A note that establishes for the lender a first claim (after taxes) against the owner's rights in the property.

Foreclosure. Transfer of ownership rights because of unpaid obligations such as delinquent mortgage or tax payments, through process of law.

Founding family. The family type having some children; children are all under the age of eight.

Functional design. House plan that accommodates the various activities that take place in it.

General plan. A comprehensive, long-range plan officially recognized as a guide for the physical growth and development of a community, together with basic regulatory and administrative controls needed to attain the physical objectives.

Geriatric complex. A combination of different types of housing accommodations for the aged, built on a single site, including houses or apartments for those who can live independently, nonhousekeeping rooms for those who can live only moderately independently because of infirmities, and nursing rooms for the chronically ill.

GI Bill of Rights. Servicemen's Readjustment Act of 1944.

Gross income. Total receipts for a given period, that is, before expenses are deducted.

Gross rent. Contract rent plus the cost of utilities.

Household. All persons who occupy a house, apartment, or group of rooms, or a room that constitutes a dwelling unit. This includes both related family members and unrelated persons.

Housing code. Locally adopted ordinance, regulation, or code, enforceable by police powers under the concept of health, safety, and welfare, which specifies the minimum features which make dwellings fit for human habitation or controls their use and occupancy.

Interest rate. The charge incurred for borrowing money.

Junior mortgage. One which gives the lender a claim against the owner which is subordinate to the rights of the holder of the first mortgage or other paramount claims.

Land use. A term referring to use of a lot or parcel of property. For example, a lot occupied by a factory is an industrial land use; that occupied by a dwelling is a residential land use.

Lease. The contract between owners and renters of properties stipulating rents to be paid, condition of the property, and other responsibilities of each party.

Lending terms. The ratio of loan-to-appraised-value of a mortgaged property, the period of the mortgage, and the interest rate.

Lien. Security for the payment of a debt obligation on property.

Local housing authority. A governmental entity or public body authorized to engage in the development or operation of public low-rent housing; usually an independent corporate body. Must be set up under state enabling legislation.

Maintenance. The act of keeping a property in proper condition for occupancy.

Market indexes. Factors that reflect the degree of imbalance between supply and demand factors in the local housing market, such as vacancy, price, and degree of overcrowding.

Master plan. A plan setting forth the relationships among the various areas and various land uses (including housing) that make up the city structure.

Maturity of mortgage. The length of the life span of the mortgage.

Mean or *"average."* When used alone without qualification, the sum total of all the figures divided by the number of figures in the distribution.

Median. That point in a distribution of figures above and below which lie fifty percent of the cases.

Megalopolism. The merging of major population centers.

Merchant builder. Term sometimes applied to medium- and large-scale commercial builders.

Metropolitan area. See Standard Metropolitan Statistical Area.

Metropolitanism. The aggregation of various politically independent communities (ranging from a few in small areas to hundreds in large areas) combined into one metropolitan whole, and the problems this brings forth.

Migration. Movement of persons or families over some distance between the beginning and the end of a specific period.

Mobility. Movement of persons or families from one house to another in the same community or county between the beginning and end of a specific period.

Mortgage. A pledge of property made to secure payment of a debt.

Mortgage liquidity. A situation of a lending institution being able to convert its mortgages into cash.

Mortgagee. The lending institution or other source of mortgage loan.

Mortgages in portfolio. The proportion of mortgages among the commercial papers and securities owned by a lending institution.

Mortgagor. The borrower who has obtained a loan on his property.

Need for housing. Total housing requirements or families based upon standards of minimum social acceptability.

Neighborhood. Clusters of homes frequently delineated by topographical barriers, natural boundaries, or major traffic arteries, with families having certain economic and/or social characteristics in common. Frequently 100 or more houses are involved.

Net income. Gross income after expenses such as maintenance, taxes, insurance, and other operating expenses have been deducted.

New law tenement. A tenement built in New York City after passage of the Tenement House Act of 1901.

Old law tenement. A tenement built in New York City prior to the year 1901.

Open-end mortgage. One that permits the mortgagor to finance further home necessities without rewriting the loan.

Operative builder. A builder who builds houses speculatively.

Option. An agreement which grants the right to buy, sell, or rent a certain property within a certain period of time for a certain price.

Orientation. Placing a house on the lot so that it enjoys the advantages of direction, such as climate, view, etc.

Originating the mortgage. Making the loan arrangements (on the part of the primary lender) with the home buyer.

Package mortgage. One that includes household equipment such as range, refrigerator, or air-conditioning unit, at the time the mortgage is arranged.

Personal values ("Social values"). The totality of a number of factors, such as an individual's ideals, motives, attitudes, and tastes, which are determined by his cultural background, education, habits, and experiences. In one sense, part of his personality traits. Little is still known about personal values related to housing design, but by their definition they are extremely important.

Prefab belt. States in which there is a concentration of prefabricated house manufacturers and, accordingly, a concentration of dealers. The core of this belt includes Illinois, Indiana, Ohio, and Pennsylvania; bordering states are Michigan, Wisconsin, Kentucky, and New York.

Prefabricated house. One having walls, partitions, floors, ceiling, and/or roof composed of sections or panels varying in size which have been fabricated in a factory prior to erection on the building foundation.

Prefabricated house package. The sections or panels and other parts of the house supplied by the prefabricated house manufacturer to the dealer or others for erection and completion at the site.

Price level. The position of prices in relation to prices as of another time (e.g., compared with 1947–49 average).

Primary family. A family that includes among its members the head of a household.

Primary lenders. Mortgage lenders who directly supply funds to borrowers, such as savings and loan associations, mutual savings banks, commercial banks, and life insurance companies.

Principal. The original amount of the loan.

Property tax. A levy by the government against the owners of property, in order to obtain income to carry out functions of the government.

Proprietary lease (cooperative housing). Lease to an apartment held by a stockholder in a corporation indicating rights and privileges of ownership of stock. No fixed rent need be stipulated; rather, each tenant-owner agrees to pay his prorata share of the annual cash requirements of the corporation.

Proximate residences. Homes for the aged built in groups, not scattered among other homes in the neighborhood or community.

Public housing. Housing provided for low-income families who cannot afford to pay an economic rent. Difference in rent paid and housing costs is made up through government subsidy.

Redevelopment. The clearing, replanning, and rebuilding of slum areas which are economically and physically beyond the stage permitting rehabilitation.

Refinancing. Changing the terms of a home mortgage.

Rehabilitation. Restoring by degrees of modernization (repairs and modifications) houses that are in poor physical condition, in order to bring them up to adequate health, safety, and good living standards.

Relocation. The process by which a local public agency fulfills the statutory requirement that decent, safe, and sanitary dwellings within their financial means be made available to families displaced from urban renewal areas or because of other governmental action.

Rent. The compensation (generally in terms of money) received by the owner of a property from the user, for its use.

Restrictive covenants. Private controls written into deeds restricting the nature of the use of a property, for example, regarding architectural style and price of house. (Racial and religious restrictions have been held by the courts to be unenforceable.)

Rural housing. Housing located in the open country (occupied either by farmers or nonfarmers) and in villages under 2,500 population not a part of an urban area.

Rural nonfarm housing. Housing located in villages under 2,500 population not a part of an urban area, and housing in the open country not occupied by farmers.

Second mortgage. See junior mortgage.

Secondary family. A family that does not include among its members the head of a household. Members of secondary families may include persons such as guests, lodgers, or resident employees and their relatives living in a household or quasi-household.

Secondary mortgage market. Financial institutions or noninstitutional individuals or groups (such as life insurance companies and the Federal National Mortgage Association) who purchase mortgages from primary-market lenders.

Sellers' market. A market in which scarcity of goods gives sellers a trading advantage over buyers.

Servicing the mortgage. Handling the monthly collection of payments and the bookkeeping on mortgages; in the event of default, handling the process of foreclosure.

Site. The location for a house or other building.

Speculative builder. A builder who builds houses in advance of their sale, anticipating a market for them.

Standard Metropolitan Statistical Area. A central city with a population of 50,000 or more in 1960 (or twin cities which have a combined population of 50,000 or more and the smaller has a population of at least 15,000), the remainder of the county in which the central city is located, and any contiguous counties that have close economic and social relationships with the central city and the populations of which are largely nonagricultural.

Straight-term mortgage. One that requires no payment on the principal during the term of the mortgage.

Subdivision controls. Local ordinances which typically have controlled the physical layout of new areas (size of lots, width of streets, building lines, street contours, etc.). Increasingly, they are also requiring the provision of utilities and other basic improvements, such as open space (parks, playgrounds), parking areas, shopping centers, school sites, and the like.

Subfamily. A married couple with or without children, or one parent with one or more children under eighteen years old, living in a household and related to, but not including, the head of the household or his wife. The most common example of a subfamily is a young married couple sharing the home of the husband's or wife's parents. Members of a subfamily are also members of a primary family.

Sublease. An agreement transferring all or part of the rights of a tenant of a house, apartment, or other building to another party.

Suburbs. Primarily residential areas relatively near to but outside of sizable cities.

They are dependent to a large degree upon the central city for sources of employment and many necessary goods and services.

Three-decker tenement. A frame building with wooden walls, used to house three or more families. Essentially a New England phenomenon.

Title I (urban renewal). That portion of the Housing Act of 1949, as amended, which contains most of the basic legislative provisions pertaining to the Federal urban renewal program.

Title I (FHA) loans. Loans made by qualified lending institutions to finance the alteration, improvement, or conversion of old homes insured by the FHA under Title I of the National Housing Act.

Traditional design. House design that has been handed down or accepted from the past.

Turnover of mortgages. Disposing of some mortgages in portfolio and taking others in their place.

Twenty percent gap. A range of noncompetition between public and standard private housing.

Urban housing. All housing in urbanized areas (see definition below) and in places of 2,500 inhabitants or more and a few areas classified by the U. S. Census as urban under special rules.

Urban renewal. The process of clearing slum areas which are economically and physically beyond repair, rehabilitating areas where houses and neighborhood facilities can be restored to come up to health, safety, and good living standards, and conserving areas which are generally stable but need protective measures in order to prevent encroachment of undesirable influences.

Urbanized area. An area that contained at least one city of 50,000 inhabitants or more in 1960 (or twin cities which have a combined population of 50,000 or more), as well as the surrounding closely settled incorporated places and unincorporated areas that meet certain U. S. Census criteria.

VA-guaranteed mortgage. Mortgage on which a portion of the principal and interest is guaranteed by the Veterans Administration.

Valuation. The process of attempting to determine the true value of a property, based on physical, economic, and social factors involved (including the neighborhood). Not to be confused with "price," which is the dollar amount the property demands.

Warehousing. Temporary bank loans used to finance the purchase or carrying of a mortgage by someone else pending its transfer to a permanent investor.

Workable program. A locality's statement of where it stands today and what it will strive to do tomorrow to remove slums and blight, to block their return, and to achieve orderly community growth.

Young-couple family. The family type in which the woman is under thirty-five years of age and there are no children.

Zoning ordinances. Local statutes that regulate the types of use for both land and buildings in specific areas of the community.

INDEX

*

Page numbers set in **boldface** type in multi-referenced items indicate basic references, usually definitions, theories or other basic information.